FOOD&WINE

ANNUAL COOKBOOK 2017

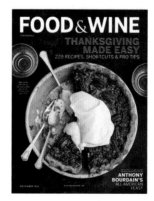

Published by Time Inc. Books
225 Liberty Street
New York, NY 10281

FOOD & WINE is a trademark of Time
Inc. Affluent Media Group, registered in
the U.S. and other countries.

ISBN 13: 978-0-8487-5223-1

ISSN: 1097-1564

Manufactured in the United States
of America

FOOD & WINE ANNUAL COOKBOOK 2017

EDITOR IN CHIEF **Nilou Motamed**

EXECUTIVE EDITOR **Kate Heddings**

EDITOR **Susan Choung**

ART DIRECTOR **James Maikowski**

DESIGNER **Alisha Petro**

COPY EDITOR **Lisa Leventer**

PRODUCTION DIRECTOR **Joseph Colucci**

PRODUCTION MANAGERS
Stephanie Thompson, John Markic

EDITORIAL ASSISTANT **Taylor Rondestvedt**

FRONT COVER

**Spaghettini with Warm Bacon-Mushroom
Vinaigrette** (recipe, p. 90)

PHOTOGRAPHER **Con Poulos**

FOOD STYLIST **Simon Andrews**

STYLE EDITOR **Suzie Myers**

BACK COVER

PHOTOGRAPHER (COCONUT CAKE)
Eva Kolenko

PHOTOGRAPHER (VEAL CHOP AND SALAD)
Con Poulos

FOOD & WINE MAGAZINE

EDITOR IN CHIEF **Nilou Motamed**

EXECUTIVE EDITOR **Dana Bowen**

DEPUTY EDITOR **Christine Quinlan**

EXECUTIVE FOOD EDITOR **Kate Heddings**

EXECUTIVE WINE EDITOR **Ray Isle**

FOOD

TEST KITCHEN SENIOR EDITOR **Justin Chapple**

TEST KITCHEN ASSOCIATE EDITOR **Anna Painter**

ASSISTANT EDITOR **Julia Heffelfinger**

TEST KITCHEN ASSISTANT **Kelsey Youngman**

FEATURES

RESTAURANT EDITOR **Jordana Rothman**

DEPUTY DIGITAL EDITOR **Lawrence Marcus**

STYLE EDITOR **Suzie Myers**

FWX EDITOR **Noah Kaufman**

RESTAURANT ASSOCIATE EDITOR **Elyse Inamine**

EDITORIAL ASSISTANTS **Morgan Goldberg,
Hannah Walhout**

AUDIENCE ENGAGEMENT EDITOR **Kristen Majewski**

ASSOCIATE DIGITAL CONTENT MANAGER
Farrah Shaikh McLaren

ART

ART DIRECTOR **James Maikowski**

ASSOCIATE ART DIRECTOR **Kelly McGuire**

DESIGNER **Mark Romero**

PHOTO

PHOTO EDITOR **Sara Parks**

PHOTO ASSISTANT **Rebecca Delman**

COPY & RESEARCH

COPY CHIEF **Elizabeth Herr**

SENIOR EDITOR **Amanda Woytus**

ASSOCIATE RESEARCH EDITOR **Erin Laverty Healy**

PRODUCTION

Joseph Colucci (Director), **John Markic,
Nestor Cervantes** (Managers)

ASSOCIATE DIGITAL PRODUCER **Elsa Säätelä**

FOOD&WINE

ANNUAL COOKBOOK 2017

AN ENTIRE YEAR
OF COOKING

FOOD&WINE
BOOKS
Time Inc. Affluent Media Group

Contents

Roman Fried
Artichokes (p. 224)
OPPOSITE Tofu
lightens up banh mi,
classic Vietnamese
sandwiches (p. 266).

Foreword

THIS YEAR HAS SEEN SOME EXCITING CHANGES AT FOOD & WINE.
First, we moved into our stunning new offices in Manhattan's Financial District—which include a state-of-the-art test kitchen and video studio. Now, not only can we develop fantastic recipes, as we've always done, but we can also create companion how-to videos on everything from crab cakes to tarte Tatin. Please visit foodandwine.com to check them out.

We also have a new editor in chief at the helm of the brand: Nilou Motamed. Born in Tehran, raised in Paris and New York, Nilou recognizes that our common language, no matter where we live, is food. A shared meal is a shared vernacular; to break bread is to break down barriers. That's why, as an inveterate traveler, Nilou's cultural peregrinations go hand in hand with culinary ones. Even her home pantry—stocked with Italian colatura, Vietnamese nuoc mam and Japanese togarashi—paints a picture of wanderlust.

In keeping with that spirit of exploration, this year's *Annual Cookbook* is our most exhaustive and adventurous ever. The recipes that follow reflect the way we eat today. We feature cooking from far-flung locales such as Liberia (Pepper Shrimp, p. 130) and Uzbekistan (Garlicky Lamb and Rice Pilaf, p. 205); ones that delve into new uses for underappreciated grains (Freekeh Fritters with Spring Pea Relish, p. 25); and vegan dishes that will wow even the most rabid carnivores (Double Drive-Thru Veggie Burgers, p. 232). That wanderlust doesn't mean we've given up the homegrown flavors you love, though. This book is packed with crowd-pleasers like our Classic BBQ Chicken Drumsticks (p. 142), Crispy Shake-and-Bake Pork (p. 172) and Mixed-Fruit Cornmeal Cobbler (p. 305).

We're beyond excited to share these flavors from the FOOD & WINE table with you, and we hope you'll use this book to broaden your cooking horizons and find your own new favorites, too.

Kate Heddings
Executive Editor
FOOD & WINE Cookbooks

STARTERS

Melon
Pâte
FRE
SARD
POC
FR

At Le Coucou in
Manhattan, chef
Daniel Rose and his
wife throw relax-the-
rules dinner parties.
OPPOSITE Chile
Oil–Marinated Goat
Cheese (p. 16).

Smoky and Chunky Guacamole

⏲ Total **35 min**; Serves **4 to 6**

Guacamole can be a divisive subject, with the mere addition of peas causing an uproar among traditionalists (we're looking at you, Barack Obama). Even die-hard purists will get behind this smoky grilled version, which involves gently charring avocado, tomato, onion and chiles, then mixing with cilantro and lime juice.

- 5 ripe Hass avocados, halved and pitted
- 2 limes, halved
- 2 plum tomatoes, halved lengthwise
- 2 serrano chiles
  Two ½-inch-thick slices of red onion
- 3 Tbsp. vegetable oil, plus more for brushing
  Kosher salt and pepper
- 3 Tbsp. chopped cilantro
- 2 garlic cloves, minced
  Tortilla chips, for serving

1. In a large bowl, gently toss the avocados with the lime halves, tomatoes, chiles, red onion slices, the 3 tablespoons of oil and a generous pinch each of salt and pepper.

2. Light a grill and oil the grate. Grill the avocados, limes, tomatoes and onion cut side down along with the whole chiles over moderate heat until charred but not falling apart, about 3 minutes for the limes, 8 minutes for the onion and 12 to 15 minutes for the avocados, tomatoes and chiles. As the items finish cooking, transfer them to a work surface and let cool. Scoop out the avocado flesh and coarsely chop; transfer to a large bowl. Remove the seeds and stems from the tomatoes and chiles, finely chop and add to the bowl. Finely dice the onion and add to the bowl along with the cilantro and garlic. Squeeze the grilled limes over the guacamole and season with salt and pepper; mix gently. Serve with tortilla chips. —*Victor Albisu*

MAKE AHEAD The guacamole can be made up to 5 hours ahead and refrigerated with a piece of plastic wrap pressed directly onto the surface.

Classic Hummus

Total **1 hr 30 min** plus overnight soaking
Makes **about 6 cups**

"The ideal party dish is one that can be made ahead, works best at room temperature and is easy to eat by hand," says food stylist extraordinaire Susan Spungen. "Hummus checks all those boxes." Here, she makes traditional chickpea hummus, plus two tasty variations.

- 2 cups dried chickpeas
- 2 tsp. baking soda
- 1 cup tahini
- ¼ cup plus 2 Tbsp. fresh lemon juice
- 3 large garlic cloves, minced
- 1 tsp. ground cumin
  Kosher salt
  Extra-virgin olive oil, sumac, pomegranate seeds, roasted chickpeas, thinly sliced radishes and fresh mint, for garnish
  Pita chips, radishes, baby fennel and carrots, for serving

1. In a medium bowl, cover the dried chickpeas with 2 inches of water and stir in 1 teaspoon of the baking soda. Refrigerate the chickpeas overnight. Drain the chickpeas, then rinse them under cold water.

2. In a medium saucepan, cover the chickpeas with 2 inches of fresh water. Add the remaining 1 teaspoon of baking soda and bring to a boil. Simmer over moderate heat for about 1 hour, until the chickpeas are very tender. Drain, reserving ¾ cup of the cooking water. Rinse under cold water.

3. In a food processor, combine the chickpeas with ½ cup of the reserved cooking water. Add the tahini, lemon juice, garlic and ground cumin; season with salt and puree until creamy (add more cooking water if necessary). Transfer to a serving bowl. Garnish with olive oil, sumac, pomegranate seeds, roasted chickpeas, thinly sliced radishes and mint. Serve with pita chips, whole radishes, fennel and carrots. —*Susan Spungen*

VARIATION Beet and Chickpea Hummus
Wrap 3 medium beets loosely in foil and set them on a baking sheet. Roast at 425° for 1 hour, or until tender. Let cool, then peel and chop. Add the beets to the other ingredients in Step 3. Garnish the hummus

with toasted almonds, crumbled feta, dukka, thinly sliced scallions and sliced watermelon radishes.

VARIATION Spinach and Herb Hummus
Blanch 6 ounces of curly spinach in boiling salted water until wilted, about 10 seconds. Drain well and cool under running water. Squeeze the spinach dry and coarsely chop. Using a blender and working in batches if necessary, add the spinach and 1½ cups mixed herbs (parsley, cilantro or dill) to the other ingredients in Step 3. Garnish with olive oil, toasted pine nuts, chopped herbs and kale chips. Serve with harissa.

Beet Hummus

Active **20 min**; Total **3 hr 20 min**
Makes **4 cups**

This stunning magenta hummus is all about the beets. Although it's made without chickpeas, it's flavored with tahini, garlic and spices, just like the classic.

- 2 lbs. red beets, scrubbed
- 2 garlic cloves, chopped
- 2 Tbsp. ground coriander
- 1 Tbsp. fresh lemon juice
- ½ cup extra-virgin olive oil
- ¾ cup tahini
  Kosher salt
  Warm pita bread, for serving

1. Preheat the oven to 425°. In a medium enameled cast-iron casserole, cover the beets with water and bring to a boil. Cover and braise in the oven for about 2 hours, until very tender. Using a slotted spoon, transfer the beets to a cutting board. When cool enough to handle, slip off the skins. Cut the beets into 1-inch pieces, spread them on a baking sheet and refrigerate until cold, about 1 hour.

2. In a food processor, combine the braised beets with the garlic, coriander and lemon juice and pulse until finely chopped. With the machine on, slowly drizzle in the olive oil until incorporated and the beet puree is smooth. Scrape into a bowl and whisk in the tahini. Season with salt and serve with pita bread. —*Eli and Max Sussman*

MAKE AHEAD The hummus can be refrigerated overnight.

Carrot Hummus

Active **15 min;** Total **1 hr;** Makes **1¾ cups**

According to Adam Coates, co-owner of The Roadhouse in Australia's Byron Bay, the restaurant's aim is to serve dishes that contain the "maximum density of nutrition" but are also delicious. One example: This tasty hummus riff made from roasted carrots tossed with coconut oil, which has a lighter flavor than olive oil. For an unexpected pop of color, try purple carrots if you can get them.

- **2½ lbs. purple or orange carrots, peeled and halved lengthwise**
- **1 Tbsp. virgin coconut oil (see Note)**
- **Fine sea salt**
- **¼ cup plus 2 Tbsp. tahini**
- **1 garlic clove, thinly sliced**
- **2 Tbsp. fresh lemon juice**
- **¼ cup extra-virgin olive oil**
- **Sweet paprika and chopped parsley, for garnish**
- **Toasted blue corn chips, for serving**

1. Preheat the oven to 350°. On a rimmed baking sheet, toss the carrots with the coconut oil and 1 teaspoon of salt. Roast for about 45 minutes, stirring once, until tender and starting to brown.

2. In a food processor, combine the warm roasted carrots with the tahini, garlic, lemon juice, olive oil and ⅓ cup of water. Process until smooth. Season with salt. Garnish with paprika and chopped parsley. Serve with blue corn chips.
—*Adam Coates*

NOTE Coconut oil is available at many supermarkets, at health food stores and at Whole Foods.

MAKE AHEAD The carrot hummus can be refrigerated for up to 3 days.

Spinach and Caramelized Onion Dip

Total **40 min;** Makes **2 cups**

This spinach dip tastes so decadent, your guests will never guess that it's made without the usual mayo and sour cream.

- **3 Tbsp. extra-virgin olive oil**
- **1 large onion, thinly sliced**
- **4 oz. curly spinach (4 packed cups), stemmed**
- **1 cup nonfat Greek yogurt**
- **¼ cup chopped chives**
- **½ tsp. freshly grated nutmeg**
- **Kosher salt and pepper**
- **Crackers, for serving**

1. In a large nonstick skillet, heat 2 tablespoons of the olive oil. Add the onion and cook over moderate heat, stirring occasionally, until deeply golden, about 15 minutes. Stir in the remaining 1 tablespoon of oil and the spinach and stir until wilted. Transfer to a medium bowl and let cool to room temperature.

2. Stir the yogurt, chives and nutmeg into the spinach and onion and season with salt and pepper. Serve the dip with crackers.
—*Kay Chun*

MAKE AHEAD The spinach and onion dip can be refrigerated overnight.

Sour Cream and Shallot Dip

Total **20 min plus 2 hr chilling**
Makes **about 2¾ cups**

In the fight against food waste, chefs are leading the charge. In 2015, Dan Barber asked Baldor, a produce wholesaler, for carrot peels and celery tops to use for his wastED pop-up dinners at New York City's Blue Hill. Inspired, Baldor has introduced SparCs (*scraps* backward), a vegetable-peel powder that can add a healthy kick to anything—like this sour cream dip.

- **1 large shallot, sliced**
- **2 Tbsp. extra-virgin olive oil**
- **2 cups sour cream**
- **½ cup mayonnaise**
- **¼ cup SparCs dehydrated vegetable powder ($6 for 8 oz.; baldorfood.com)**
- **Kosher salt**
- **Crudités or chips, for serving**

In a small skillet, cook the shallot in the olive oil over moderate heat, stirring, until softened and caramelized, about 10 minutes. Transfer the shallot to a medium bowl. Stir in the sour cream, mayonnaise and SparCs powder; season with salt. Cover and refrigerate until well chilled, about 2 hours. Serve with crudités or chips. —*Emily Tylman*

Pistachio and Yellow Lentil Dip

Total **35 min;** Makes **3 cups**

Good-for-you yellow lentils make a surprisingly luscious dip for warm pita. Plus, they cook in under 15 minutes.

- **1 cup yellow lentils (7 oz.), rinsed and picked over**
- **1²/₃ cups unsalted pistachios (8 oz.)**
- **2 garlic cloves, coarsely chopped**
- **½ cup extra-virgin olive oil**
- **¼ cup plus 2 Tbsp. fresh lemon juice**
- **2 Tbsp. ground coriander**
- **Kosher salt**
- **¼ cup chopped flat-leaf parsley**
- **Warm pita bread, for serving**

1. Cook the lentils in a medium saucepan of boiling water until tender, 12 to 15 minutes. Drain well.

2. Meanwhile, in a large skillet, toast the pistachios over moderate heat, stirring, until deep golden, 4 to 5 minutes. Let the nuts cool completely.

3. In a food processor, pulse the pistachios with the garlic until the nuts are finely chopped. With the machine on, slowly drizzle in the olive oil, then drizzle in the lemon juice and ½ cup of water and puree until smooth. Add the ground coriander and lentils and pulse until smooth. Season with salt. Scrape the dip into a bowl, stir in the parsley and serve with pita bread.
—*Eli and Max Sussman*

MAKE AHEAD The dip can be refrigerated for up to 2 days.

Spicy Thai Shrimp-and-Pork Dip

Total **45 min**; Makes **3 cups**

This rich, meaty dip is a popular snack in Thailand. It's terrific scooped up with Asian rice cakes or spooned over rice.

- 3 Tbsp. canola oil
- ½ lb. large shrimp, shelled and deveined, shells reserved, shrimp finely chopped
- 1⅓ cups unsweetened coconut milk
- 2 garlic cloves, minced
- 1 tsp. minced cilantro roots or stems plus 2 Tbsp. minced cilantro leaves
- 1 tsp. whole white peppercorns
- ½ lb. ground pork
- ¼ cup finely grated palm sugar or light brown sugar
- ¼ cup Asian fish sauce
- 1 medium shallot, thinly sliced
- ⅓ cup roasted unsalted peanuts, finely chopped
- 1 Thai chile, seeded and minced
  Kosher salt
  Crispy square Asian rice cakes (see Note) or pita chips, for serving

1. In a medium saucepan, heat 1 tablespoon of the canola oil. Add the shrimp shells and cook over moderate heat, stirring constantly, until pink and fragrant, about 3 minutes. Add the coconut milk and simmer for 15 minutes. Strain the infused coconut milk into a heatproof measuring cup; discard the shrimp shells. Wipe out the saucepan.

2. Meanwhile, in a mortar or mini food processor, pound or pulse the garlic, cilantro roots and white peppercorns to a paste.

3. In the medium saucepan, heat the remaining 2 tablespoons of canola oil. Add the cilantro paste and cook over moderate heat, stirring constantly, until fragrant, about 30 seconds. Add the ground pork, sugar, fish sauce and the infused coconut milk and cook, breaking up the pork, until no trace of pink remains, about 8 minutes. Stir in the chopped shrimp, shallot and peanuts and cook, stirring, until the shrimp is white, about 2 minutes. Remove from the heat. Stir in the cilantro leaves and minced chile and season with salt. Serve the dip warm, with rice cakes or pita chips. —*David Lebovitz*

NOTE Toasted Asian rice cakes are available in the snacks section of Asian markets.

MAKE AHEAD The dip can be refrigerated for up to 2 days. Rewarm before serving.

WINE A fruity, lively Prosecco: the NV Nino Franco Rustico.

Radishes with Seaweed-Matcha Butter

Total **10 min**; Serves **4**

- 2 Tbsp. wakame seaweed (see Note)
- ¼ tsp. matcha powder (see Note)
- 1 stick salted butter, preferably cultured (4 oz.), at room temperature
  Flaky sea salt
- 2 bunches of mixed radishes and baby turnips

In a spice grinder, grind the seaweed to a powder. Transfer to a bowl, add the matcha and butter and season with salt; mix well. Garnish with more salt and serve with the radishes and turnips.
—*Jeremiah Stone and Fabián von Hauske*

NOTE Wakame and matcha are available at Asian and natural food markets.

WINE Pét-nat (a kind of natural sparkling wine): 2014 O. Lemasson Pow Blop Wizz.

Cherry Pico de Gallo

Total **25 min**; Makes **2½ cups**

- ¾ lb. sweet cherries, pitted and coarsely chopped
- 1 pint mixed cherry tomatoes, finely chopped
- ½ cup finely chopped white onion
- 1 jalapeño—stemmed, seeded and minced
- 2 Tbsp. fresh lime juice
- 2 Tbsp. extra-virgin olive oil
  Kosher salt and pepper
- ¾ cup finely chopped cilantro
  Tortilla chips, for serving

In a medium bowl, mix the cherries with the tomatoes, onion, jalapeño, lime juice and olive oil. Season with salt and pepper. Stir in the cilantro and serve right away, with tortilla chips. —*Justin Chapple*

Herring Under a Fur Coat

Active **1 hr**; Total **2 hr**; Serves **4**

A festive traditional Russian dish, this layered pickled herring salad gets its name from the sieved eggs and grated vegetables that top it.

- 2 medium beets
- 2 medium Yukon Gold potatoes, peeled
- 2 medium carrots, peeled and halved crosswise
- 2 large hard-boiled eggs
- 1 cup finely chopped pickled herring
- ¼ cup minced sweet onion
- ¼ cup canola oil
- 2 Tbsp. chopped dill, plus sprigs for garnish
- ½ cup mayonnaise
  Kosher salt

1. Preheat the oven to 450°. Wrap the beets in foil and roast for about 1 hour, until tender. Let cool slightly, then peel.

2. Meanwhile, in a saucepan, cover the potatoes and carrots with at least 2 inches of water and boil until tender, about 15 minutes for the carrots and 20 minutes for the potatoes. Let cool to room temperature. Grate the potatoes on the medium holes of a box grater and transfer to a small bowl. Repeat with the carrots and beets, keeping the vegetables in separate bowls.

3. Halve the eggs. Push the egg whites through a fine sieve into a small bowl. Clean the sieve, then push the yolks through into another small bowl.

4. In another bowl, mix the herring with the onion, oil and chopped dill.

5. In a small bowl, mix the mayonnaise with 2 tablespoons of the grated beets.

6. Place a 4-inch round ring mold in the center of a serving plate. Using the back of a spoon, spread one-fourth of the grated potatoes inside the mold in an even layer. Season with salt. Spread one-fourth of the herring mixture on top in an even layer. Repeat the layering with one-fourth each of the carrots and beets. Season with salt. Spread 2 tablespoons of the beet mayonnaise on top. Garnish with some of the sieved egg whites, sieved egg yolks and dill sprigs. Carefully remove the ring mold and wipe it clean. Repeat to form 3 more molded salads. —*Bonnie Morales*

RADISHES WITH
SEAWEED-MATCHA
BUTTER

PICKLED SHRIMP, CRAB
DEVILED EGGS AND CRUDITÉS
WITH RANCH DRESSING

Crudités with Ranch Dressing

⟳ Total **25 min**; Makes **2½ cups dressing**

This classic ranch is the perfect dip for crisp vegetables, but it's also light enough to use on salads.

- 2 Tbsp. extra-virgin olive oil
- 1 cup finely chopped yellow onion
- ½ cup unseasoned rice vinegar
- 2 cups mayonnaise
- ½ cup sour cream
- 1 Tbsp. garlic powder
- 1 Tbsp. onion powder
- 1 Tbsp. agave nectar
  Kosher salt and pepper
  Crudités, for dipping

In a small nonstick skillet, heat the olive oil. Add the onion and cook over moderate heat, stirring occasionally, until golden brown, about 10 minutes. Scrape the onion into a blender, add the rice vinegar and puree until smooth. Transfer the puree to a medium bowl and stir in the next 5 ingredients. Season with salt and pepper and serve with crudités. —*John Besh and Chris Lusk*

Deviled Eggs with Crab and Caviar

Active **35 min**; Total **1 hr**; Makes **24**

- 1 dozen large eggs
- ¾ cup mayonnaise
- 2 Tbsp. Dijon mustard
- 2 Tbsp. minced shallot
- 2 Tbsp. thinly sliced chives, plus more for garnish
- 1 Tbsp. finely chopped parsley
- 1 Tbsp. capers, rinsed and finely chopped
- 1 tsp. finely chopped thyme
- 1 tsp. sherry vinegar
- ¼ tsp. Tabasco
  Kosher salt
- 3 oz. crabmeat, picked over
  Caviar, for garnish

1. Fill a large bowl with ice water. In a large saucepan, cover the eggs with water by 1 inch and bring to a boil. Cover the pan, remove it from the heat and let stand for 10 minutes. Drain the eggs and transfer to the ice water bath to cool completely.

2. Peel and halve the eggs lengthwise. Transfer the yolks to a medium bowl and mash with the back of a spoon. Arrange the egg whites on a platter. Add the mayonnaise, mustard, shallot, 2 tablespoons of chives, the parsley, capers, thyme, vinegar and Tabasco to the bowl with the egg yolks and whisk until smooth. Season with salt. Transfer the mixture to a piping bag and fill the egg whites (or use a small spoon). Top each deviled egg with some of the crab and garnish with caviar and chives.
—*John Besh and Chris Lusk*

Olives Escabeche

Total **40 min** plus 2 days marinating
Makes **1 quart**

Escabeche is usually a tangy, vinegar-based marinade for fish. At The Four Horsemen in Brooklyn, chef Nick Curtola turns it into a citrusy, spicy brine for Castelvetrano olives.

- 1 lb. Castelvetrano olives
- 1 star anise pod
- ½ dried New Mexico chile
- 2 tsp. fennel seeds
- 1 bay leaf
- 8 thyme sprigs
- 2 cups canola oil
- ½ cup extra-virgin olive oil
  Three 3-inch-long orange zest strips
  Two 3-inch-long lemon zest strips
- 5 garlic cloves, thinly sliced
- ¼ cup dry white wine

1. Place the olives in a heatproof container. Wrap the star anise, chile, fennel seeds, bay leaf and thyme in a piece of cheesecloth and tie with kitchen string to make a sachet.

2. In a medium saucepan, heat the canola and olive oils to 300°. Remove the pan from the heat and add the strips of orange and lemon zest and the garlic; stir constantly until the garlic softens but doesn't brown, 1 minute. Add the spice sachet and wine and let stand for 15 minutes. Pour the mixture over the olives and let cool, then refrigerate for 2 days. —*Nick Curtola*

MAKE AHEAD The olives can be refrigerated for up to 2 weeks.

Pickled Shrimp with Red Remoulade

Active **25 min**; Total **1 hr**; Serves **12**

Serve this supertangy, creamy remoulade alongside the shrimp for dipping, or toss the shrimp in the sauce and mound onto a split croissant as they do at the Pontchartrain Hotel's Bayou Bar in New Orleans.

PICKLED SHRIMP

- 1 small onion, quartered
- 1 qt. distilled white vinegar
- 1 cup sugar
- ¼ cup kosher salt
- 3 thyme sprigs
- 2 garlic cloves, crushed
- 1 Tbsp. crushed red pepper
- 2 tsp. mustard seeds
- 2 tsp. fennel seeds
- 2 whole cloves
- 24 jumbo shell-on shrimp (2¼ lbs.)

REMOULADE

- 1 celery rib, finely chopped
- 1 cup mayonnaise
- ½ cup Creole or stone-ground mustard
- ¼ cup ketchup
- 2 Tbsp. jarred horseradish
- 2 Tbsp. hot sauce
- 2 tsp. celery salt
- 1 tsp. finely grated garlic
  Kosher salt
  Lemon wedges, for serving

1. Pickle the shrimp Fill a large pot with ice water. In a large saucepan, combine all of the ingredients except the shrimp with 2 cups of water and simmer for 10 minutes. Add the shrimp, remove from the heat and let stand for 5 minutes. Transfer the shrimp and the cooking liquid to a large bowl. Set the bowl in the ice water bath and let cool completely.

2. Make the remoulade In a medium bowl, whisk all of the ingredients and season with salt.

3. Drain, peel and devein the shrimp and arrange on a platter. Serve with the remoulade and lemon wedges.
—*John Besh and Chris Lusk*

WINE Citrusy Muscadet: 2014 Domaine Michel Brégeon Sèvre-et-Maine Sur Lie.

Chile Oil–Marinated Goat Cheese

📷 PAGE 8

Total **10 min plus 3 days marinating**
Serves **6**

At the charming Les Arcades restaurant in Biot, France, servers set out a bowl of this chile-marinated goat cheese so guests can help themselves. If you like, you can add a few sprigs of herbs, such as thyme, to the oil along with the chiles.

- 9 **dried chiles de árbol**
  One 11-oz. log of semifirm goat cheese, cut into 6 pieces
- 3 **to 4 cups extra-virgin olive oil**
  Toasted sliced baguette or sourdough bread, for serving

Scatter 3 of the chiles in a small bowl at least 3 inches deep. Arrange the cheese in a single layer over the chiles; top with 3 more chiles. Pour in enough olive oil to submerge the cheese. Crumble the remaining 3 chiles into the oil. Cover and marinate in the refrigerator for at least 3 days. Bring to room temperature before serving with bread. (Once the cheese is done, strain the chile oil and use in other dishes.)
—*Adapted from Les Arcades, Biot, France*

MAKE AHEAD The cheese can be refrigerated for up to 1 week.

PAIRINGS FROM A PRO

Cheese & Wine Power Duos

At Union Larder in San Francisco, cheese sommelier Kristi Bachman offers a rotating selection of choices from around the world. Here, five of her favorite pairings.

BRABANDER California Pinot Noir

BRILLAT-SAVARIN Champagne

ÉPOISSES Rich white Burgundy

CHEDDAR Dry Provençal rosé

MANCHEGO Rioja reserva

Bread-and-Butter Pickled Eggs

Total **15 min plus 1 week pickling**; Makes **6**

Molly Yeh, the blogger behind My Name is Yeh, loves to pair these eggs with beer. She likes a creamy yolk, so she boils the eggs for just five minutes before shocking them in an ice bath and submerging them in a sweet brine. This ensures that the yolks stay soft throughout the pickling process.

- 1 **cup sugar**
- 1 **cup distilled white vinegar**
- 1 **tsp. kosher salt**
- 2 **garlic cloves, peeled**
- 6 **large eggs**
  Za'atar, flaky sea salt, black pepper and hot sauce, for serving

1. In a small saucepan, combine the sugar with the vinegar, kosher salt and 1 cup of water and bring to a boil, stirring to dissolve the sugar. Add the garlic and let the brine cool completely.

2. Meanwhile, bring a medium saucepan of water to a boil. Fill a medium bowl with ice water. Using a slotted spoon, carefully add the eggs to the boiling water and cook them for 5 minutes. Transfer the eggs to the prepared ice water bath and let cool completely. Peel the eggs and carefully transfer to a glass jar. Pour the cooled brine over the eggs; top with a small bowl or ramekin to keep the eggs and garlic submerged in the brine. Cover and refrigerate for 1 week.

3. Cut the eggs in half lengthwise and arrange on a platter. Sprinkle with za'atar, sea salt, pepper and a dash of hot sauce and serve. —*Molly Yeh*

Cracklings with Smoked Paprika

Active **20 min**; Total **4 hr**; Serves **6**

Star chef Michael Symon braises pork skin with jalapeño and coriander seeds before frying it, then sprinkles the crispy cracklings with homemade paprika salt for a smoky kick.

- 1 **lb. pork skin, cut into 4 equal pieces**
- 1 **jalapeño, halved lengthwise**
- 1 **medium yellow onion, halved**
- 1 **Tbsp. whole black peppercorns**
- 1 **Tbsp. whole coriander seeds**
- 2 **garlic cloves, crushed**
  Canola oil, for frying
- 2 **tsp. smoked paprika**
- 1 **Tbsp. kosher salt**

1. In a large saucepan, combine the pork skin, jalapeño, onion, black peppercorns, coriander seeds and garlic. Add 4 quarts of water and bring to a simmer. Cook over moderate heat until the skin is tender and pliable, about 1 hour. Transfer the pork skin to a baking sheet and let cool slightly; discard the cooking liquid. Using a sharp knife, cut off any meat and as much fat as possible from the underside of the skin.

2. Preheat the oven to 300°. Arrange the pork skin on a parchment paper–lined baking sheet and bake for about 2½ hours, turning halfway through, until deep golden and dry. Transfer the pork skin to a wire rack to cool, then break into 1-inch pieces.

3. In a large enameled cast-iron casserole, heat 3 inches of canola oil to 400°. In a small bowl, mix the smoked paprika with the salt. Working in batches, fry the cracklings, stirring, until puffed and crisp, about 30 seconds. Transfer the cracklings to paper towels and season with the paprika salt. Let cool, then serve with any remaining paprika salt. —*Michael Symon*

MAKE AHEAD The fried cracklings can be stored in an airtight container for 3 days.

CRACKLINGS WITH
SMOKED PAPRIKA

LIMA BEAN AND
RICOTTA CROSTINI

Silky Potato Fondue
⏱ Total **30 min**; Makes **3 cups**

Chef David Barzelay of Lazy Bear in San Francisco has an ingeniously simple method for making his prized master cheese sauce: He adds shredded cheddar to a blender, pours hot heavy cream on top and blends. Barzelay says you can use anything from blue cheese to Tête de Moine. In the recipe here, he transforms the sauce into a supersilky fondue that holds up at the table for far longer than most others.

- ¾ lb. Yukon Gold potatoes, peeled and cut into 1-inch pieces
- 1 garlic clove
- ¼ cup plus 2 Tbsp. dry white wine
- 1½ Tbsp. fresh lemon juice
- 1 cup heavy cream
- 2 cups shredded aged white cheddar cheese, preferably Fiscalini Bandage Wrapped Cheddar or Cabot Clothbound
- Kosher salt

1. In a medium saucepan of salted simmering water, cook the potato pieces and garlic clove over moderate heat until tender, about 12 minutes. Drain well and wipe out the saucepan.

2. In a blender, combine the potatoes and garlic with the wine and lemon juice and puree until smooth. With the blender on, gradually add the heavy cream until incorporated. Transfer the mixture to the saucepan and bring just to a simmer over moderately high heat. Return the mixture to the blender, add the cheese and puree until smooth. Scrape the fondue into the saucepan and season with salt. Serve hot. —*David Barzelay*

SERVE WITH Little Gem lettuce, haricots verts, wax beans, snap peas, snow peas, summer squash, baby zucchini, cucumbers, shishito peppers, carrots, radishes, bread or potato chips.

Marinated Piquillo Pepper and Whipped Eggplant Toasts
Total **1 hr**; Serves **4 to 6**

Compose these toasts yourself, or for a fun party idea, set out bowls of piquillos, whipped eggplant and anchovies so guests can DIY their tapas.

- 1 large eggplant
- 5 garlic cloves, thinly sliced
- 1 cup extra-virgin olive oil
- ⅓ cup red wine vinegar
- ¼ cup honey
- 1 Tbsp. minced rosemary
- 1 Tbsp. minced oregano
- 1 Tbsp. minced parsley, plus chopped parsley for garnish
- Kosher salt and pepper
- One 12-oz. jar piquillo peppers, drained well and patted dry
- 4 oz. fresh goat cheese, preferably Spanish (½ cup)
- 2 oz. cream cheese (¼ cup)
- Thick toasts and marinated white anchovies, for serving

1. Roast the eggplant directly over a gas flame, turning occasionally, until charred all over and soft, about 12 minutes. Transfer to a colander and let cool slightly, then peel and let cool completely.

2. Meanwhile, in a medium saucepan, cook the garlic in the oil over moderate heat until sizzling, about 2 minutes. Remove from the heat and whisk in the vinegar, honey, rosemary, oregano and minced parsley. Season the vinaigrette generously with salt and pepper.

3. Heat a large cast-iron skillet. In batches if necessary, add the piquillos to the skillet in an even layer. Cook over high heat, turning once, until lightly charred on both sides, about 2 minutes total. Add the piquillos to the warm vinaigrette and let cool completely.

4. In a food processor, combine the eggplant with both cheeses and puree until smooth. Scrape into a bowl and season with salt and pepper. Spread the whipped eggplant on toasts and, using a slotted spoon, spoon some of the marinated piquillos on top. Garnish with chopped parsley and serve with anchovies. —*Jose Garces*

MAKE AHEAD The piquillos and whipped eggplant can be refrigerated for up to 3 days. Serve at room temperature.

Lima Bean and Ricotta Crostini
⏱ Total **30 min**; Makes **16**

Look to the freezer section for fresh frozen lima beans so you can skip the shelling and get to snacking at your next dinner party.

- 1 cup fresh ricotta cheese
- ½ tsp. finely grated lemon zest plus 2 Tbsp. fresh lemon juice
- ¼ cup extra-virgin olive oil
- Kosher salt and pepper
- One 10-oz. package frozen lima beans
- 2 Tbsp. each finely chopped parsley and chives
- 1 Tbsp. finely chopped tarragon
- 1 dried chile de árbol, finely chopped with seeds, or ½ tsp. crushed red pepper
- Sixteen ½-inch-thick slices of baguette, toasted

1. In a medium bowl, mix the ricotta with the lemon zest, 1 tablespoon of the lemon juice and 2 tablespoons of the olive oil. Season with salt and pepper.

2. In a medium saucepan of salted boiling water, blanch the lima beans until tender, 2 to 3 minutes. Drain and cool under running water, then slip off the skins and transfer the beans to a medium bowl. Add the parsley, chives, tarragon, chile and the remaining 2 tablespoons of olive oil and 1 tablespoon of lemon juice. Season with salt and pepper.

3. Spread the ricotta mixture on the crostini, spoon the lima bean salad on top and serve. —*Justin Chapple*

Crostini with Scamorza and Peperonata

Total **1 hr**; Serves **4 to 6**

New York City chef Andrew Carmellini tops crusty grilled bread with a mildly spicy mix of peppers and scamorza, a cow's milk cheese that resembles a dry mozzarella. He swears by dried Calabrian oregano pulled right off the stem as the perfect finish to the tasty crostini.

- ½ lb. mixed baby sweet peppers, stemmed and halved if small or quartered if large
- 1 small red onion, sliced ¼ inch thick
- ¼ cup extra-virgin olive oil, plus more for brushing
- Kosher salt and pepper
- 3 garlic cloves, thinly sliced
- ¼ cup chopped pickled hot peppers, such as peperoncini and banana, plus 2 Tbsp. brine from the jar
- ¼ cup finely chopped parsley
- 1 Tbsp. finely chopped oregano
- Six 1-inch-thick slices of Italian or ciabatta bread
- 6 oz. scamorza cheese, cut into 6 slices

1. Heat a grill pan. In a medium bowl, toss the sweet peppers and sliced onion with 2 tablespoons of the olive oil and season with salt and pepper. In 2 batches, grill over moderate heat, turning occasionally, until lightly charred in spots, 8 to 10 minutes per batch. Return to the bowl. Keep the grill pan on.

2. In a small skillet, heat the remaining 2 tablespoons of olive oil. Add the garlic and cook over moderate heat, stirring, until softened but not browned, about 2 minutes. Scrape the garlic and oil into the pepper mixture. Add the pickled peppers and their brine and toss well. Stir in the parsley and oregano and season the peperonata with salt and pepper.

3. Brush the bread with olive oil and grill over moderately high heat, turning once, until lightly charred, about 2 minutes total. Transfer to a platter and top with the scamorza. Pile the peperonata on top and serve. —*Andrew Carmellini*

Mussel-and-Leek Salad Crostini

Total **50 min**; Serves **4 to 6**

Orange blossom water, a fragrant extract often used in Middle Eastern pastries, adds a subtle floral note to this light mussel, leek and tarragon salad on toast.

- ½ cup extra-virgin olive oil, plus more for drizzling
- 4 garlic cloves, crushed
- 1 Fresno chile—halved, seeded and thinly sliced
- 3 thyme sprigs
- 2 oregano sprigs
- 2 strips of lemon zest
- 1 bay leaf
- 2½ lbs. mussels, debearded
- Kosher salt and pepper
- 4 large leeks, light green and white parts only, halved lengthwise and sliced ¼ inch thick
- 2½ tsp. white wine vinegar
- ¼ tsp. orange blossom water (optional)
- ½ cup tarragon leaves
- Three 1-inch-thick slices of sourdough bread cut from a large round loaf
- 5 oz. watercress leaves and small stems (1 cup)

1. In a medium saucepan, heat ¼ cup of the olive oil. Add 3 of the garlic cloves and the chile and cook over moderately high heat, stirring frequently, until beginning to brown, 1 minute. Add the thyme, oregano, lemon zest strips and bay leaf and cook for 30 seconds.

2. Stir in the mussels and ⅓ cup of water and season with salt and pepper. Cover and cook, shaking the pan occasionally, until the mussels open, 3 to 5 minutes. Discard any that do not open. Drain the mussels in a colander set over a heatproof bowl. Remove the mussels from the shells and add to the bowl with the cooking liquid. Wipe out the saucepan.

3. Heat 3 tablespoons of the olive oil in the saucepan. Add the leeks and a generous pinch each of salt and pepper and cook over moderately high heat, stirring occasionally, until softened, 8 minutes. Add the leeks to the mussels. Stir in the vinegar, orange blossom water, if using, and tarragon and season with salt and pepper.

4. Light a grill or heat a grill pan. Brush the bread with the remaining 1 tablespoon of olive oil and grill over moderately high heat, turning once, until lightly charred, 5 minutes. Rub the grilled bread with the remaining garlic clove and cut each slice in half on the diagonal.

5. Arrange the grilled bread on a platter and top with the mussel-and-leek salad. Garnish with the watercress, drizzle with olive oil and serve immediately. —*Sarah Hymanson and Sara Kramer*

MAKE AHEAD The recipe can be prepared through Step 3 and refrigerated overnight. Serve at room temperature.

WINE A briny Muscadet: 2014 Domaine de la Pépière Les Gras Moutons.

Tuna and Apple Crostini

Total **30 min**; Makes **8**

This open-face tuna sandwich upgrade makes a fabulous impromptu starter for last-minute guests.

- Eight ¾-inch-thick baguette slices
- Extra-virgin olive oil, for brushing and drizzling
- Kosher salt
- 2 Tbsp. plus 2 tsp. mayonnaise
- 1 Granny Smith apple, cored and thinly sliced
- 8 oz. good-quality tuna packed in olive oil, drained and flaked
- Small parsley leaves, for garnish

1. Preheat the oven to 350°. Arrange the baguette slices on a baking sheet. Brush the tops with olive oil and season with salt. Toast until golden and crisp, about 8 minutes. Transfer the toasts to a platter and let them cool slightly.

2. Spread 1 teaspoon of mayonnaise on each toast, then top with a few slices of apple. Top with the tuna and garnish with parsley leaves. Drizzle with olive oil and serve. —*Justin Croxall*

WINE Bright, light-bodied sparkling rosé: 2014 Leitz Rosé Sekt.

Country Ham and Pickle Crostini

◷ Total **20 min**; Makes **8**

> **Eight ¾-inch-thick baguette slices**
> **Extra-virgin olive oil, for brushing**
> **Kosher salt**
> 8 **oz. thinly sliced country ham, preferably Edwards**
> **Sliced pickled vegetables, such as cauliflower, carrots and cucumbers, for garnish**

Preheat the oven to 350°. Arrange the baguette slices on a baking sheet. Brush with oil and season with salt. Toast until golden and crisp, about 8 minutes. Transfer to a platter and let cool slightly. Top the toasts with the ham, then garnish with pickles and serve. —*Justin Croxall*

WINE Round, fruity Chenin Blanc: 2014 François Pinon Les Trois Argiles Vouvray.

Salmon Tartare on Garlic Bread

◷ Total **30 min**; Serves **6**

> ⅓ **cup plus 2 Tbsp. extra-virgin olive oil**
> 2 **garlic cloves, crushed**
> ¼ **tsp. crushed red pepper**
> ⅓ **cup plus 1 Tbsp. chopped parsley**
> ⅓ **cup plus 1 Tbsp. chopped mint**
> **Kosher salt**
> **Twelve ½-inch-thick baguette slices**
> 12 **oz. skinless sushi-grade salmon fillet, very finely diced**
> **Mustard seed oil, for drizzling**

1. Preheat the oven to 400°. In a blender, combine ⅓ cup of the olive oil with the garlic, crushed red pepper and 1 tablespoon each of the parsley and mint; puree until smooth. Season the garlic oil generously with salt.

2. Brush the baguette slices with the garlic oil; arrange on a large rimmed baking sheet. Bake for about 10 minutes, until crisp on the outside but soft in the middle.

3. In a medium bowl, mix the salmon with the remaining 2 tablespoons of olive oil and ⅓ cup each of chopped parsley and mint. Season the tartare with salt and mound on the toasts. Transfer to a platter. Drizzle mustard oil over the tartare and serve. —*Jeremy Ford*

WINE Medium-bodied, mineral-rich Chardonnay: 2014 Lioco Sonoma County.

Rye Crisps with Tomatoes and Sardines

◷ Total **15 min**; Serves **4**

Make the most of canned sardines with these simple, no-cook canapés: Whip up a bright herb mayo to spread on rye crisps, then top them with a cherry tomato salad and good-quality sardines. The juices from the tomatoes soften the rye crisps ever so slightly.

> ½ **cup mayonnaise**
> 1 **Tbsp. finely chopped capers**
> 2 **tsp. minced hot red chile**
> ¼ **cup finely chopped parsley**
> ¼ **cup finely chopped chives**
> **Kosher salt and pepper**
> 1 **pint golden cherry or grape tomatoes, thinly sliced**
> 1 **Tbsp. extra-virgin olive oil**
> 8 **light rye crisps, such as Wasa Crispbread**
> **Two 4½-oz. cans sardines in olive oil—drained, deboned and broken into chunks (see Note)**

1. In a small bowl, mix the mayonnaise with the capers, chile and 2 tablespoons each of the parsley and chives. Season the herb mayonnaise with salt and pepper.

2. In another bowl, toss the tomatoes with the olive oil and the remaining 2 tablespoons each of parsley and chives. Season with salt and pepper.

3. Spread the herb mayonnaise on the rye crisps and top with the tomatoes and sardines. Serve right away. —*Justin Chapple*

NOTE Smoked sardines would be delicious here, too.

Crab Remick

◷ Total **30 min**; Serves **12**

In the early days of the famed Pontchartrain Hotel in New Orleans, Crab Remick was a fixture on the Caribbean Room menu. This update is brightened with lemon juice and Dijon mustard.

> 2 **slices of bacon**
> ¼ **cup mayonnaise**
> 1 **Tbsp. extra-virgin olive oil**
> 1 **Tbsp. Dijon mustard**
> 2 **tsp. fresh lemon juice**
> 1 **tsp. chili sauce**
> **Kosher salt and pepper**
> 8 **oz. jumbo lump crabmeat, picked over**
> **Snipped chives, for garnish**
> **Saltines, for serving**

1. Preheat the oven to 425°. In a nonstick skillet, cook the bacon over moderate heat until crisp, about 5 minutes. Drain, then finely chop.

2. In a medium bowl, mix the mayonnaise with the olive oil, mustard, lemon juice and chili sauce; season with salt and pepper. Fold in the crab. Spoon the mixture into 12 small ramekins and arrange on a rimmed baking sheet. Bake until lightly browned, 5 to 7 minutes. Garnish with the bacon and chives; serve with saltines. —*John Besh and Chris Lusk*

LUXE HORS D'OEUVRES

Truffled Prosciutto Grissini

To create a supersimple, ultra-indulgent party snack, Nancy Silverton of Los Angeles's Osteria Mozza spreads grissini (slim Italian breadsticks) with store-bought black-truffle butter, then wraps them in slices of prosciutto.

Red Pepper Blini with Creamed Corn and Smoked Salmon

⏱ Total **45 min**; Serves **4**

This cheeky take on blini and caviar is one of Jonathan Waxman's signature dishes at Jams in New York City. He makes tender pancakes with red pepper puree, then tops them with a sweet corn sauce, decadent smoked salmon and American caviar.

- 1 **cup corn kernels, thawed if frozen**
- ½ **cup plus 2 Tbsp. heavy cream**
- 6 **Tbsp. unsalted butter, 1 tablespoon melted**
- 1 **jarred red bell pepper, drained (2 oz.)**
- 1 **large egg, beaten**
- ⅓ **cup all-purpose flour**
- ¾ **tsp. baking powder**
- ¼ **tsp. kosher salt**
- 3 **oz. thinly sliced smoked salmon**
- **Crème fraîche, for serving**
- 1 **oz. American caviar (trout, paddlefish, salmon or whitefish)**
- **Snipped chives, for garnish**

1. In a small saucepan, combine the corn and ½ cup of the cream. Bring to a simmer and cook over moderately low heat, stirring occasionally, until the corn is tender and the cream is reduced and thickened, about 8 minutes. Remove from the heat and whisk in 3 tablespoons of the butter. Let cool to room temperature.

2. In a food processor, puree the bell pepper until smooth; scrape into a medium bowl. Add the egg, the melted butter and the remaining 2 tablespoons of cream, then add the flour, baking powder and salt. Whisk until well blended.

3. In a large nonstick skillet, melt 1 tablespoon of butter. Ladle 1 tablespoonful of batter per pancake into the skillet to make 6 pancakes. Cook over moderately low heat, turning once, until set, 3 minutes per side. Repeat with the remaining butter and batter to make 12 pancakes total.

4. Spoon the creamed corn onto plates. Arrange 3 pancakes on each plate. Top with the smoked salmon and dollop with crème fraîche. Top with the caviar, garnish with chives and serve. —*Jonathan Waxman*

WINE Lively, strawberry-inflected rosé Champagne: NV J. Lassalle Premier Cru Brut Rosé.

Tuna Poke on Nori Crackers

Total **1 hr**; Serves **8**

At Liholiho Yacht Club in San Francisco, chef Ravi Kapur serves seasoned raw tuna on battered-and-fried nori crackers. A dollop of spicy mayo is the ideal finish.

NORI CRACKERS
- **Canola oil, for frying**
- ¾ **cup cornstarch**
- **Four 8-inch-square unseasoned nori sheets, cut in half**
- **Kosher salt**

SPICY MAYO
- ¼ **cup good-quality mayonnaise**
- ¼ **tsp. tamari**
- 1 **tsp. Sriracha**

TUNA POKE
- 12 **oz. sushi-grade tuna, cut into ¼-inch dice**
- 4 **tsp. minced scallion**
- 2 **tsp. minced peeled fresh ginger**
- 2 **tsp. seeded and minced jalapeño**
- 1 **tsp. tamari**
- ½ **tsp. toasted sesame oil**
- **Kosher salt**
- **Radish matchsticks, daikon sprouts, micro red shiso and toasted sesame seeds, for garnish**

1. Make the nori crackers In a large enameled cast-iron casserole, heat 3 inches of oil to 350°. Set a rack over a baking sheet and line with paper towels.

2. In a medium bowl, whisk the cornstarch with ½ cup of water until smooth. Working in batches of 2, dredge the nori in the cornstarch mixture, letting the excess drip off. Slowly drop the nori into the hot oil and fry for 2 minutes. Flip and fry for 1 minute longer, until crisp. Transfer to the rack, season with salt and let cool completely.

3. Make the spicy mayo In a small bowl, whisk all of the ingredients together until smooth.

4. Make the tuna poke In a large bowl, fold together all of the ingredients except the garnishes; season with salt.

5. Spoon the poke onto the nori crackers and dollop with some of the spicy mayo. Garnish with radish matchsticks, daikon sprouts, micro shiso and toasted sesame seeds. Serve immediately. —*Ravi Kapur*

Cranberry-Dill Gravlax

Total **20 min plus 4 to 5 days curing** Serves **8**

Fresh cranberries give this cured salmon a beautiful scarlet tinge as well as a bit of tang. Serve the gravlax on toasts, blini or rye crackers or in bagels with cream cheese and capers.

- 2 **cups fresh cranberries (8 oz.), finely chopped**
- 2 **cups chopped dill**
- ⅓ **cup kosher salt**
- ¼ **cup packed light brown sugar**
- 2 **Tbsp. caraway seeds**
- **One 1½-lb. skin-on salmon fillet**

In a medium bowl, mix the cranberries with the dill, salt, brown sugar and caraway seeds. Place the salmon skin side down in a glass or ceramic dish lined with a large sheet of plastic wrap. Spread the cranberry mixture over the top and sides of the salmon and wrap tightly in the plastic. Top with a plate and a few heavy cans to weigh it down. Refrigerate, turning the wrapped fish once a day, until it feels firm in the center, 4 to 5 days. (If there is excess liquid, discard it as necessary and rewrap the fish and cranberry topping.) —*Kay Chun*

MAKE AHEAD The gravlax can be wrapped tightly in plastic and refrigerated for up to 1 week.

TUNA POKE ON A
NORI CRACKER

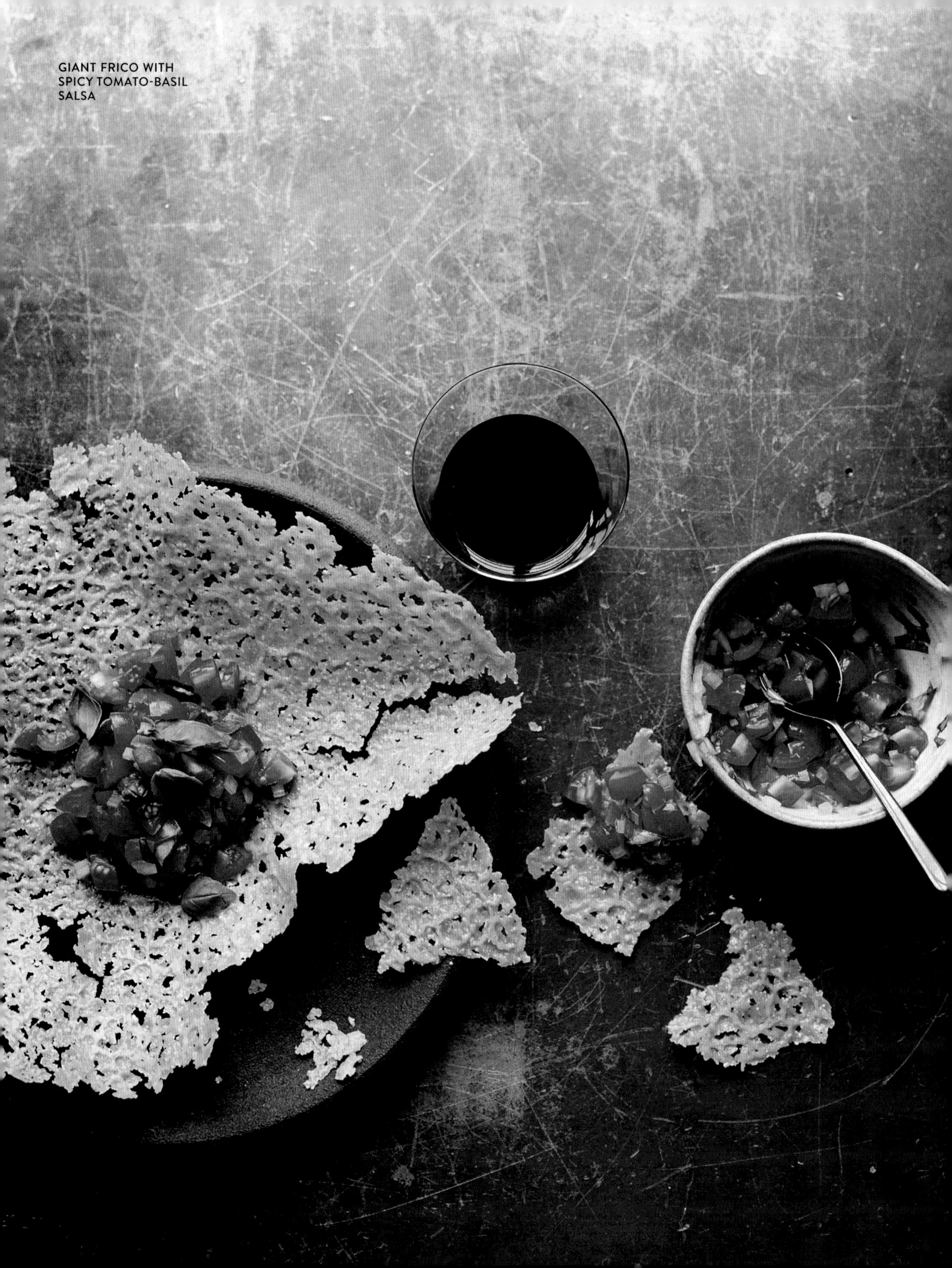

GIANT FRICO WITH SPICY TOMATO-BASIL SALSA

Freekeh Fritters with Spring Pea Relish

Total **1 hr 30 min plus 4 hr 30 min chilling**
Makes **about 2 dozen**

In this playful revamp of arancini (fried rice balls), chefs Sara Kramer and Sarah Hymanson of Kismet in Los Angeles substitute nutty-tasting freekeh (roasted green wheat) for the rice. To get the creamy-chewy texture just right, they cook the freekeh risotto-style, adding water gradually while stirring constantly.

RELISH

- ¾ cup fresh or thawed frozen peas
- 2 tsp. coriander seeds
- 5 pitted Castelvetrano olives
- 1 Tbsp. salt-packed capers, rinsed
- 1 spring garlic bulb or 2 garlic cloves, finely chopped
- ½ cup extra-virgin olive oil
- 3 Tbsp. fresh lemon juice
- ¾ cup finely chopped parsley
- 2 Tbsp. chopped tarragon
  Kosher salt and pepper

FRITTERS

- 1½ Tbsp. unsalted butter
- 1 onion, finely chopped
- 1 bay leaf
  Kosher salt and pepper
- 1 cup cracked freekeh
- 8 oz. chilled Taleggio cheese, rind removed and cheese shredded
- ¾ cup all-purpose flour
- 2 large eggs
- 1½ cups panko
  Canola oil, for frying

1. Make the relish In a small saucepan of salted boiling water, blanch the peas until just tender, 30 seconds. Drain and rinse under cold water; pat dry. In a skillet, toast the coriander until fragrant, 2 minutes. Pulse in a spice grinder until coarsely ground. In a food processor, pulse the peas with the olives, capers, spring garlic and coriander until coarsely chopped. Transfer the relish to a bowl and stir in the olive oil and lemon juice. Fold in the herbs and season with salt and pepper; refrigerate. Bring to room temperature before serving.

2. Make the fritters In a large saucepan, melt the butter. Add the onion, bay leaf and 1¼ teaspoons of salt and cook over moderately high heat, stirring occasionally, until the onion is translucent, 5 minutes. Add the freekeh and cook, stirring occasionally, until the grains are toasted, about 5 minutes.

3. Add ¾ cup of water to the freekeh and stir constantly until absorbed, about 5 minutes. Add another 3 cups of water, ¾ cup at a time and stirring constantly, until the water is absorbed between additions. The freekeh is done when it's tender and suspended in a thick sauce, about 30 minutes total. Discard the bay leaf. Reduce the heat to moderate and stir in the Taleggio. Season with salt and pepper.

4. Transfer the freekeh to an 8-by-8-inch baking dish and press a piece of plastic wrap directly onto the surface. Refrigerate for at least 4 hours.

5. Spread the flour in a shallow bowl and season with salt and pepper. In another shallow bowl, beat the eggs with 2 tablespoons of water. Spread the panko in a third bowl. Shape the freekeh into 2-tablespoon-size balls; dredge in the flour, tapping off any excess, then dip in the beaten eggs. Dredge in the panko, pressing lightly to help it adhere. Transfer the breaded freekeh to a baking dish in a single layer and refrigerate until firm, 30 minutes.

6. In a large, straight-sided skillet, heat 1½ inches of canola oil to 325°. Fry the freekeh balls in batches until golden brown, 5 minutes per batch. Drain on a paper towel–lined plate. Season with salt and serve hot with the relish.
—*Sarah Hymanson and Sara Kramer*

Giant Frico with Spicy Tomato-Basil Salsa

Total **25 min**; Serves **4**

- 1¼ cups finely grated Parmigiano-Reggiano cheese (4 oz.)
- 1 lb. tomatoes, cut into ¼-inch pieces
- 3 Tbsp. finely chopped onion
- 1 Thai chile, minced
- 1 garlic clove, finely grated
- 2 Tbsp. fresh lemon juice
- 2 Tbsp. chopped basil
  Kosher salt

1. Preheat the oven to 375°. Line a baking sheet with parchment paper. Spread the cheese in a thin layer on the paper, forming a 12-inch round. Bake for about 8 minutes, until melted and light golden. Carefully transfer the frico on the parchment to a rack and let cool completely.

2. Meanwhile, in a medium bowl, combine all of the remaining ingredients and season with salt. Mix well and serve with the frico.
—*Kay Chun*

WINE Aromatic Italian red: 2012 Cavallotto Bricco Boschis Langhe Freisa.

Gougères au Comté

Active **40 min**; Total **1 hr 15 min**
Makes **8 large gougères**

"The munchkin version of gougères is an American invention," says chef Daniel Rose. "In Burgundy, they're much larger." At Le Coucou in New York City, he serves these grapefruit-size cheese puffs for breakfast, like popovers.

- 10 Tbsp. unsalted butter, diced
- 2 tsp. kosher salt
  Pinch of white pepper
  Pinch of freshly grated nutmeg
- 2¼ cups all-purpose flour
- 8 large eggs
- 8 oz. Comté cheese, coarsely grated (2 cups)

1. Preheat the oven to 400°. Line 2 baking sheets with parchment paper.

2. In a medium saucepan, combine 2 cups of water with the butter, salt, pepper and nutmeg and bring to a boil over moderate heat. When the butter melts, add the flour all at once and beat with a wooden spoon until a tight dough forms and pulls away from the side of the pan, about 5 minutes.

3. Remove the pan from the heat and let cool for 5 minutes. Using a wooden spoon, beat in the eggs one at a time until smooth. Stir in the cheese.

4. Scoop the dough into a pastry bag fitted with a ¾-inch plain tip. Pipe 8 large mounds onto the prepared sheets, spacing them a few inches apart. Bake the gougères for 35 to 40 minutes, shifting the pans from top to bottom and front to back halfway through, until puffed and golden. Serve warm. —*Daniel Rose*

Cheesy Potato Frico

Active **45 min**; Total **1 hr 30 min**; Serves **8**

The Italian potato frico is a lot like the Spanish tortilla but with cheese standing in for the eggs. This version, from famed Friulian winemaker Giampaolo Venica, presents itself as a crusty brown disk concealing gooey Montasio, a cheese with a nutty, slightly fruity flavor.

- 1 **lb. medium baking potatoes**
- 12 **oz. Montasio or Parmesan cheese, freshly grated (4 cups)**
  Kosher salt and pepper
- 2 **Tbsp. extra-virgin olive oil**
- 1 **medium onion, minced**

1. In a saucepan, cover the potatoes with 2 inches of water and bring to a boil. Simmer until tender, about 30 minutes. Drain and let cool to lukewarm, then peel. Grate the potatoes on the large holes of a box grater set in a large bowl. Add the cheese and toss well; season with salt and pepper.

2. In a 10-inch nonstick skillet, heat the oil. Add the onion and cook, stirring, until tender, about 8 minutes. Stir in the potato mixture. Gently press down to create a large potato cake. Cook over low heat until golden on the bottom, about 15 minutes.

3. Run a spatula around and under the frico to release it from the skillet, then carefully pour off the excess oil. Gently flip the frico and continue cooking until golden and crisp on the second side, about 15 minutes longer. Slide the frico onto a large platter and blot with paper towels to remove excess oil. Season with pepper, cut into wedges and serve warm or at room temperature. —*Giampaolo Venica*

MAKE AHEAD The frico can be refrigerated overnight; reheat in a 375° oven.

Pasta-and-Pesto Croquettes

Active **1 hr**; Total **5 hr**; Makes **18 small croquettes**

At Pizzarium in Rome, chef Gabriele Bonci reimagines the classic fried risotto croquettes known as *supplì*. He swaps pasta with pesto for the usual rice and tomato sauce and fills the croquettes with creamy stracchino cheese instead of the traditional mozzarella.

- 2 **Tbsp. pine nuts**
- 1 **garlic clove**
- 1 **cup packed basil leaves**
- 1 **cup freshly grated Parmigiano-Reggiano cheese (3 oz.)**
- ⅓ **cup freshly grated Pecorino Romano cheese (1 oz.)**
- ½ **cup extra-virgin olive oil**
  Kosher salt and pepper
- ½ **lb. trofie pasta (see Note)**
- 3 **Tbsp. unsalted butter, at room temperature**
- 4 **oz. stracchino (crescenza) cheese, cut into 18 equal pieces**
  Canola oil, for frying
- 6 **large eggs**
- 2 **cups plain breadcrumbs**

1. Line a baking sheet with parchment paper. In a food processor, pulse the pine nuts with the garlic until chopped. Add the basil, Parmigiano and pecorino and pulse to combine. With the machine on, drizzle in the olive oil. Season the pesto with salt and scrape into a large bowl.

2. In a large saucepan of salted boiling water, cook the pasta until al dente; drain well. Add the pasta and butter to the pesto, season with salt and pepper and toss well. Spread the pasta on the prepared baking sheet, cover loosely with plastic wrap and refrigerate until cold, about 1 hour.

3. Using your hands, form the pasta into 18 balls. Make an indentation in each ball and fill with a piece of stracchino; shape the pasta around the cheese to enclose it. Cover the croquettes with plastic wrap and refrigerate until cold, at least 3 hours or overnight.

4. In a large enameled cast-iron casserole, heat 3 inches of canola oil to 350°. Set a rack over a baking sheet. In a medium bowl, beat the eggs. Place the

breadcrumbs in a second bowl. Season the eggs and breadcrumbs with salt. Dip each croquette in the eggs, letting the excess drip off, then roll in the breadcrumbs; repeat the dipping and rolling to make a double layer of coating. Transfer the croquettes to the rack.

5. In 2 batches, fry the croquettes, turning, until deep golden and heated through, about 5 minutes per batch. Serve hot. —*Gabriele Bonci*

NOTE Look for trofie pasta at Italian markets and specialty food shops.

MAKE AHEAD The croquettes can be prepared through Step 3 and refrigerated overnight.

Crispy Cheese Sticks

Total **45 min**; Makes **14**

F&W's Justin Chapple rolls squishy white bread superthin to wrap these hors d'oeuvres oozing with cheese.

- 1½ **cups shredded mozzarella**
- ½ **cup freshly grated Parmigiano-Reggiano cheese**
- 1 **large egg, beaten**
- 2 **Tbsp. minced parsley**
- ½ **tsp. crushed red pepper**
  Kosher salt and black pepper
- 14 **slices of white sandwich bread, crusts removed**
  Canola oil, for frying
  Warm marinara sauce, for serving

1. In a medium bowl, mix both cheeses with the egg, parsley, crushed red pepper and ½ teaspoon each of salt and black pepper; refrigerate for 15 minutes.

2. Using a rolling pin or wine bottle, flatten each slice of bread; arrange with the long sides facing you. Spoon 1 heaping tablespoon of the filling on the lower half of each slice. Brush the edges with water and roll up the bread around the filling; press the seams and open ends to seal the rolls.

3. In a large, deep skillet, heat 1 inch of oil to 350°. Fry the rolls in batches, turning occasionally, until crisp, about 2 minutes per batch. Transfer to paper towels to drain. Sprinkle with salt and serve with marinara. —*Justin Chapple*

PASTA-AND-PESTO
CROQUETTES

Crispy Oysters with Fresh Horseradish Cocktail Sauce

⏱ Total **45 min;** Serves **8**

Inspired by the nostalgic New Orleans fried oyster po'boy, Pontchartrain Hotel chef Chris Lusk prefers large, meaty Louisiana oysters for this dish. If you can't find them, Wellfleets are a good substitute.

COCKTAIL SAUCE

- 1 **jalapeño**
- 1 **cup ketchup**
- ¼ **cup finely grated peeled fresh horseradish**
- 2 **Tbsp. fresh lemon juice**
- 1 **Tbsp. Worcestershire sauce**
- 2 **tsp. Asian fish sauce**
- 1 **tsp. prepared wasabi**
- **Tabasco**
- **Kosher salt**

OYSTERS

- ½ **cup panko**
- ½ **cup masa harina (see Note)**
- ½ **cup all-purpose flour**
- 1 **Tbsp. Creole seasoning (see Note)**
- **Canola oil, for frying**
- 32 **large oysters, freshly shucked in their liquor**
- **Kosher salt**
- **Chopped chives, for garnish**
- **Lemon wedges, for serving**

1. Make the cocktail sauce Roast the jalapeño directly over a gas flame, turning, until blackened all over, about 8 minutes. Peel, seed and mince the jalapeño and transfer the crumbs to a small bowl. Whisk in the next 6 ingredients and season the sauce with Tabasco and salt.

2. Fry the oysters In a food processor, pulse the panko until finely ground; transfer the crumbs to a medium bowl. Whisk in the masa harina, all-purpose flour and Creole seasoning.

3. In a large cast-iron skillet, heat 2 inches of canola oil to 375°. Dredge each oyster in the panko mixture and transfer to a baking sheet. Line a second baking sheet with paper towels. Working in 3 batches, fry the oysters, turning, until golden brown and crispy, about 1 minute per batch. Using a slotted spoon, transfer the oysters to the paper towels to drain. Season with salt.

Garnish with chopped chives and serve immediately, with the cocktail sauce and lemon wedges. —*Chris Lusk*

NOTE Masa harina is a soft corn flour. You can find it in the ethnic food aisle of most grocery stores. Creole seasoning is sold at most grocery stores in the spice aisle.

WINE Coastal Italian white: 2015 Terenzuola Vigne Basse Colli di Luni Vermentino.

Asian Shrimp Rolls

⏱ Total **45 min;** Makes **14**

- 2 **Tbsp. canola oil, plus more for frying**
- ½ **cup minced cabbage**
- ¼ **cup minced carrot**
- 1 **Tbsp. grated fresh ginger**
- ¾ **lb. shelled and deveined shrimp, minced**
- 4 **scallions, finely chopped, plus slices for garnish**
- 2 **Tbsp. unseasoned rice vinegar**
- 2 **tsp. cornstarch**
- ½ **tsp. toasted sesame oil**
- **Kosher salt and pepper**
- 1 **large egg, beaten**
- 14 **slices of white sandwich bread, crusts removed**
- **Sambal oelek and Kewpie mayonnaise, for serving**

1. In a large skillet, heat the 2 tablespoons of oil. Add the cabbage, carrot and ginger and cook over moderate heat until softened, 3 to 5 minutes. Add the shrimp and cook until just white throughout, 3 minutes. Stir in the chopped scallions, vinegar, cornstarch and sesame oil and cook for 1 minute. Scrape into a bowl; let cool. Season with salt and pepper and mix in the egg. Refrigerate for 15 minutes.

2. Using a rolling pin or wine bottle, flatten each slice of bread; arrange with the long sides facing you. Spoon 1 heaping tablespoon of the filling on the lower half of each slice. Brush the edges with water and roll up the bread around the filling; press the seams and open ends to seal the rolls.

3. In a large, deep skillet, heat 1 inch of oil to 350°. Fry the rolls in batches, turning occasionally, until crisp, about 2 minutes per batch. Transfer to paper towels to drain. Sprinkle with scallions and serve with sambal oelek and Kewpie mayonnaise. —*Justin Chapple*

Shrimp and Pork Wontons

Total **1 hr 15 min;** Makes **3 dozen**

These wontons from Bryant Ng, the chef at Cassia in L.A., are little flavor bombs, amped up with ginger, prosciutto and scallions. To ensure juicy dumplings, it's important to use fatty ground pork.

- 5 **oz. raw shrimp—shelled, deveined and chopped**
- ¼ **lb. fatty ground pork**
- 2 **oz. napa cabbage, finely chopped (¾ cup)**
- 1 **oz. prosciutto, minced**
- 1 **oz. cod, finely chopped**
- 2 **scallions, finely chopped**
- 1 **Tbsp. minced peeled fresh ginger**
- 2 **tsp. Shaoxing wine**
- 2 **tsp. canola oil**
- 2 **tsp. cornstarch**
- 1 **tsp. kosher salt**
- 1 **tsp. Asian fish sauce**
- ¼ **tsp. ground white pepper**
- ¼ **tsp. toasted sesame oil**
- 36 **wonton wrappers**
- **Chili oil, for dipping**

1. In a large bowl, mix all of the ingredients except the wonton wrappers and chili oil.

2. Line 2 baking sheets with parchment paper. Lay out 4 wonton wrappers on a work surface; keep the rest covered. Place a rounded ½ teaspoon of filling in the center of each wrapper; dampen the edges with water and fold corner to corner to form a triangle. Press out the air and seal the edges. (Dampen the 2 points farthest from each other and pinch them together if you want to form a hat, or tortellini, shape.) Place the wontons on the prepared sheets and cover with a towel. Repeat with the remaining wrappers and filling.

3. In a large saucepan of boiling water, cook the wontons in 3 batches until just tender and the filling is cooked through, about 5 minutes. Serve hot with chili oil. —*Bryant Ng*

Pork and Shrimp Shumai

Total **45 min plus 4 hr marinating**
Makes **3 dozen**

"When I'm in the mood," says *Bizarre Foods* host Andrew Zimmern, "there's no better food than fresh shumai." This variation on the Cantonese dumpling has a simple and short ingredient list that makes the most of shrimp, pork, ginger, scallions and sesame.

DIPPING SAUCE

- ¼ cup soy sauce
- ¼ cup black vinegar
- 1 tsp. Chinese chili-garlic sauce

SHUMAI

- 12 oz. ground pork
- 6 oz. medium shrimp—shelled, deveined and finely chopped
- 4 scallions, white and light green parts only, minced
- 3 Tbsp. minced peeled fresh ginger
- 1 Tbsp. soy sauce
- 1 Tbsp. toasted sesame oil
- 1½ Tbsp. Shaoxing wine or dry sherry
- ¾ tsp. kosher salt
- All-purpose flour, for dusting
- 1 package round dumpling wrappers, thawed if frozen
- Napa cabbage leaves, for steaming
- Blanched green peas, for garnish

1. Make the dipping sauce In a small bowl, whisk the soy sauce with the black vinegar and chili-garlic sauce.

2. Make the shumai In a medium bowl, combine the pork and shrimp with the scallions, ginger, soy sauce, sesame oil, Shaoxing wine and salt. Cover with plastic wrap and refrigerate for 4 hours.

3. Lightly dust a baking sheet with flour. Hold a dumpling wrapper in your palm, keeping the rest of the wrappers covered with plastic. Place 1 tablespoon of the filling in the center of the wrapper and gather up the edges all around to form an open cup; the wrapper will adhere to the filling. Transfer the dumpling to the prepared baking sheet and cover with plastic wrap. Repeat to form the remaining dumplings.

4. Fill a wok or large skillet with ¾ inch of water and bring to a simmer. Line 2 tiers of a bamboo steamer with napa cabbage leaves, overlapping them slightly. Add the dumplings to the steamer and stack the tiers. Cover and set the steamer in the wok. Steam the shumai until firm and the filling is no longer pink, 8 to 10 minutes. Garnish each with a pea and serve hot with the dipping sauce. —*Andrew Zimmern*

WINE Rich California Riesling: 2013 Tatomer Vandenberg.

Tempura Green Beans with Old Bay and Lemon

Total **30 min**; Serves **4**

These addictive tempura green beans fried with a light, airy batter are perfect for snacking. In an unexpected twist, there's Old Bay Seasoning in the batter as well as on top as a sprinkle.

- Vegetable oil, for frying
- 1 cup all-purpose flour
- 2 Tbsp. cornstarch
- ½ tsp. baking powder
- ½ tsp. kosher salt
- 1 tsp. Old Bay Seasoning, plus more for sprinkling
- 1 cup plus 2 Tbsp. chilled club soda
- ½ lb. green beans
- Lemon wedges, for serving

1. In a large, deep skillet, heat ½ inch of oil until shimmering. In a large bowl, whisk the flour with the cornstarch, baking powder, salt and the 1 teaspoon of Old Bay. Gently whisk in the club soda until the batter just comes together; do not overmix.

2. Working in batches, dip the green beans in the batter, let the excess drip off and add them to the hot oil. Fry until light golden and crisp, 2 to 3 minutes. Using a slotted spoon, transfer to a paper towel–lined baking sheet to drain. Sprinkle with Old Bay and serve with lemon wedges. —*Justin Chapple*

Korean Seafood Pancakes

Total **1 hr 45 min**
Makes **four 8-inch pancakes**

Chef Deuki Hong, co-author of the cookbook *Koreatown*, enhances the seafood flavor in his crispy pancakes by stirring fish stock into the batter. If you don't have fish stock, you can mix bottled clam juice with some water.

PANCAKES

- 4 cups all-purpose flour
- 1¼ cups cornstarch
- 2¼ cups water
- 2¼ cups fish stock or 1 cup clam juice mixed with 1¼ cups water
- 1 large egg yolk
- 1 Tbsp. kosher salt
- 1 lb. calamari, bodies cut into ½-inch rings and tentacles halved
- 1 lb. shelled and deveined shrimp, cut into 1-inch pieces
- 2 cups scallions in 2-inch lengths
- 2 cups thinly sliced yellow onion
- 1¼ cups canola oil, for frying

DIPPING SAUCE

- 1 cup soy sauce
- ¼ cup sugar
- ¼ cup mirin
- 2 Tbsp. minced garlic
- 1 Tbsp. gochugaru (red pepper flakes)
- 1 Tbsp. toasted sesame oil

1. Make the pancakes In a large bowl, whisk the flour, cornstarch, water, fish stock, egg yolk and salt until smooth. Stir in the seafood, scallions and onion. Cover and refrigerate the batter for 15 minutes.

2. Make the dipping sauce In a medium bowl, combine all of the ingredients.

3. In a 10-inch cast-iron skillet, heat ¼ cup of the canola oil. Add one-fourth of the batter and spread in an even layer. Cook over moderate heat until deep golden on the bottom, 8 minutes. Flip the pancake, drizzle 1 tablespoon of oil around the edge and cook over moderately low heat until crisp, 8 to 10 minutes. Repeat with the remaining oil and batter. Serve hot, with the dipping sauce. —*Deuki Hong*

WINE Crisp Muscadet: 2014 Michel Delhommeau Harmonie.

VEGETABLE-CHICKEN
SUMMER ROLLS

Vegetable-Chicken Summer Rolls

Total **40 min**; Makes **8**

When the summer markets are full of great ingredients, F&W's Justin Chapple makes these gorgeous summer rolls. He slices raw beets superthin so they're tender enough to fold into the rice paper wrappers. The Asian-style dipping sauce is essential, as it's basically a dressing for all the fresh fillings.

¼ cup Asian fish sauce

¼ cup fresh lime juice

1 tsp. sugar

1 Thai chile, stemmed and very thinly sliced

Eight 8-inch round rice paper wrappers

4 baby Chioggia or golden beets, scrubbed and very thinly sliced

1 cup shredded cooked chicken (4 oz.)

2 ears of corn, kernels cut off

2 oz. sunflower sprouts (1½ cups)

1 Hass avocado—peeled, pitted and sliced

1½ cups small basil leaves

4 small red lettuce leaves, torn

1. In a small bowl, whisk the fish sauce with the lime juice, sugar, Thai chile and 2 tablespoons of water.

2. Fill a large shallow bowl with hot water. Soak 1 rice paper wrapper at a time in the water for 30 seconds, until just pliable. Spread on a work surface. Top the wrapper with some of the beets, chicken, corn, sprouts, avocado, basil and lettuce. Tightly roll up the wrapper around the filling, tucking in the sides as you roll. Repeat with the remaining wrappers and fillings. Serve the rolls with the dipping sauce.
—*Justin Chapple*

MAKE AHEAD The summer rolls can be covered in moist paper towels and refrigerated in an airtight container for 3 hours. The dipping sauce can be refrigerated overnight.

WINE Mineral-laced Italian white: 2014 Ciro Picariello Fiano di Avellino.

Mushroom Carpaccio with Chive Oil

Total **25 min**; Serves **4**

1 cup chopped chives

½ cup extra-virgin olive oil
Kosher salt

8 oz. very fresh white mushrooms, very thinly sliced on a mandoline

1 Tbsp. fresh lemon juice
Chopped roasted almonds and freshly shaved Parmigiano-Reggiano cheese, for garnish

In a blender, combine the chives and oil and puree until smooth. Strain the chive oil through a sieve and season with salt. Spread the mushrooms on a platter. Drizzle with the lemon juice and chive oil. Garnish with the chopped almonds and shaved cheese and serve. —*Kay Chun*

Green Bean and Scallion Pancake

Total **30 min**; Serves **4**

¾ cup all-purpose flour

¾ cup plus 2 Tbsp. chilled club soda

1 tsp. baking powder

½ tsp. kosher salt

½ tsp. toasted sesame oil

2 Tbsp. canola oil

12 oz. thin green beans, trimmed

6 scallions, cut into 3-inch lengths, plus sliced scallions for garnish

1 fresh hot red chile, thinly sliced
Soy sauce, for serving

1. In a medium bowl, whisk the flour with the club soda, baking powder, salt and sesame oil.

2. In a 12-inch nonstick skillet, heat the canola oil. Add the green beans and scallion pieces and stir-fry over moderately high heat until crisp-tender, about 5 minutes. Stir in the red chile and pour the batter evenly on top. Cook over moderate heat until browned on the bottom, about 5 minutes. Slide the pancake onto a plate, then invert it into the skillet and cook until browned on the second side, 3 to 5 minutes longer. Transfer to a platter and cut into wedges. Garnish with sliced scallions and serve with soy sauce. —*Justin Chapple*

Grilled Watermelon with Avocado, Cucumber and Jalapeño Salsa

PAGE 384

Total **30 min**; Serves **4**

Throwing slabs of watermelon on the grill may seem like a crazy idea, but the sweet fruit gets a smoky flavor that's outstanding with the cumin-spiked avocado salsa here. Thin slices of fresh jalapeño and lots of fresh herbs finish the dish.

1 Hass avocado, peeled and cut into ⅓-inch pieces

1 cup finely diced hothouse cucumber

3 Tbsp. fresh lime juice

1 Tbsp. minced seeded jalapeño, plus very thinly sliced jalapeño for garnish (optional)

¼ tsp. ground cumin

¼ cup extra-virgin olive oil, plus more for brushing
Kosher salt and pepper
One 4-lb. watermelon, quartered lengthwise and cut crosswise into 1-inch-thick slabs

½ cup cilantro leaves

½ cup small dill sprigs

1. Light a grill. In a medium bowl, gently mix the avocado with the cucumber, lime juice, minced jalapeño, cumin and the ¼ cup of oil. Season the salsa with salt and pepper.

2. Brush the watermelon slabs with olive oil and season with salt and pepper. Grill over high heat, turning once, until nicely charred on both sides, about 4 minutes total. Transfer to a platter. Spoon the salsa on the watermelon and top with the cilantro leaves, dill sprigs and sliced jalapeño, if using. Serve right away. —*Justin Chapple*

WINE Herb-inflected Chilean Sauvignon Blanc: 2015 Matetic Vineyards Corralillo.

Curried Squash Galette

Active **40 min**; Total **2 hr**; Serves **6 to 8**

With a superflaky crust (the secret: grated frozen butter) and a sweet-savory winter squash filling, this rustic galette makes a fabulous starter or, served with a green salad, a hearty vegetarian meal.

DOUGH

- 1¼ cups all-purpose flour
  Kosher salt and pepper
- 1 stick unsalted butter, frozen
  Ice water

FILLING

- 1 lb. butternut squash—peeled, seeded and cut into ¼-inch-thick slices
- 1 lb. kabocha squash—peeled, seeded and cut into ¼-inch-thick slices
- 1 red onion, cut through the core into ½-inch wedges
- ¼ cup extra-virgin olive oil
- 2 tsp. Madras curry powder
  Kosher salt and pepper
- ½ cup sour cream
- ½ cup shredded Manchego cheese, plus more for serving

1. Make the dough In a large bowl, whisk the flour with ¾ teaspoon each of salt and pepper. Working over the bowl, grate the frozen butter on the large holes of a box grater. Gently toss the grated butter in the flour. Stir in ⅓ cup of ice water until the dough is evenly moistened. Scrape out onto a work surface, gather up any crumbs and knead gently just until the dough comes together. Pat into a disk, wrap in plastic and refrigerate until chilled, about 1 hour.

2. Meanwhile, make the filling Preheat the oven to 425°. On a large rimmed baking sheet, toss the butternut and kabocha squash and the onion with the olive oil and curry powder. Season generously with salt and pepper. Roast for 15 to 20 minutes, until the squash is tender but not falling apart. Let cool.

3. Increase the oven temperature to 450°. On a lightly floured work surface, roll out the dough to a 14-inch round. Carefully transfer to a parchment paper–lined baking sheet. Spread the sour cream over the dough, leaving a 1½-inch border. Sprinkle ¼ cup of the cheese on top. Arrange the squash and onion over the sour cream and sprinkle the remaining ¼ cup of cheese on top. Fold the pastry edge up and over the vegetables to create a 1½-inch border.

4. Bake the squash galette for 30 to 35 minutes, until the crust is browned; let cool slightly. Sprinkle with shredded cheese, cut into wedges and serve warm.
—*Justin Chapple*

WINE Peachy Oregon Pinot Gris: 2015 Ponzi Willamette Valley.

Leeks Vinaigrette

Active **20 min**; Total **1 hr**; Serves **8**

- 8 baby leeks, white and light green parts only
- 12 medium leeks, white parts only
- ¼ cup blanched hazelnuts
- ¼ cup Champagne vinegar
- 2 Tbsp. minced shallots
- 2 Tbsp. fresh lime juice
- 2 Tbsp. honey
- ¼ cup canola oil
- 2 Tbsp. extra-virgin olive oil
  Kosher salt and pepper
  Chopped parsley, for garnish

1. Fill a large bowl with ice water. In a large saucepan of salted boiling water, blanch the leeks until tender, about 12 minutes for the baby leeks and 25 minutes for the medium leeks. Drain, then transfer to the ice bath to cool, 5 to 10 minutes. Drain well. Cut the baby leeks crosswise into 3-inch pieces and halve the medium leeks lengthwise; drain well on paper towels.

2. Meanwhile, preheat the oven to 400°. Spread the hazelnuts in a pie plate and toast for 5 minutes, until golden. Let cool, then coarsely chop.

3. In a medium bowl, combine the vinegar, shallots, lime juice and honey. Slowly whisk in both oils. Season the vinaigrette with salt and pepper.

4. Arrange the leeks on plates and season with salt and pepper. Drizzle with three-quarters of the vinaigrette and sprinkle the hazelnuts and parsley on top. Serve with the remaining vinaigrette. —*Daniel Rose*

MAKE AHEAD The vinaigrette can be refrigerated overnight.

Scallop Tartare with Green Apple–Endive Salad

Total **45 min**; Serves **8**

Daniel Rose, chef at New York City's Le Coucou, serves this elegant starter at his annual New Year's Eve party. He slices the sea scallops into sizable cubes and garnishes them with endive leaves in a curry vinaigrette.

VINAIGRETTE

- ¼ cup fresh lemon juice
- 2 Tbsp. apple cider vinegar
- 2 Tbsp. minced shallot
- 2 tsp. honey
  Pinch of curry powder
- ¼ cup hazelnut oil
- ¼ cup canola oil
  Kosher salt and white pepper

SCALLOPS AND SALAD

- 24 large sea scallops (2 lbs.), patted dry and cut into 1-inch pieces
- 1 Tbsp. hazelnut oil
  Kosher salt
- 4 endives, leaves separated, large leaves halved lengthwise
- 1 large Granny Smith apple, cut into matchsticks
  Extra-virgin olive oil, for drizzling
  Cracked black pepper and snipped chives (2-inch pieces), for garnish

1. Make the vinaigrette In a medium bowl, combine the lemon juice with the vinegar, shallot, honey and curry powder. Slowly whisk in both oils until well blended and season with salt and white pepper.

2. Prepare the scallops and salad In a medium bowl, combine the scallops with the hazelnut oil, season with salt and toss to coat. In another medium bowl, combine the endives, apple and half of the vinaigrette; season with salt and toss to coat.

3. Spoon the scallop tartare into shallow bowls and top with the salad. Drizzle with more of the vinaigrette and olive oil. Garnish with black pepper and chives and serve. —*Daniel Rose*

WINE Stony, crisp Chardonnay: 2014 Vincent Mothe Chablis.

CURRIED SQUASH
GALETTE

Scallop Carpaccio with Hand-Cut Ginger-Chive Pesto

⏲ Total **25 min**; Serves **4**

People don't think to eat scallops raw, but sliced thin and marinated, they're wonderful in ceviches, crudos and carpaccios. Flaky sea salt and crisp radish slices add layers of crunch.

- 2 Tbsp. minced peeled fresh ginger
- ¼ cup finely chopped chives
- ¼ cup extra-virgin olive oil
- 1 Tbsp. fresh lime juice, plus lime wedges for serving
  Kosher salt and pepper
- 8 oz. sea scallops, thinly sliced crosswise
  Flaky sea salt and thinly sliced radishes, for garnish

1. In a small bowl, combine the ginger, chives, olive oil and lime juice; season with kosher salt and pepper and mix well.

2. Arrange the scallops on a platter and top with the ginger-chive pesto. Season with flaky sea salt and garnish with sliced radishes. Serve with lime wedges. —*Kay Chun*

WINE Aromatic dry Riesling: 2014 Hermann J. Wiemer Finger Lakes.

PRO PARTY TIP

Go-To Finger Foods

"You can't go wrong with little fried things like mini grilled cheeses and crab cakes. You can make 4,000 variations on pigs in a blanket, and guests will eat every last one. Foods that sop up alcohol and that are really simple to eat and satisfying—and don't get stuck in your teeth—are best bets."
—*Marcy Blum, event planner and owner of Marcy Blum Associates in New York City*

Beer-Steamed Shrimp with Cocktail Sauce

⏲ Total **40 min**; Serves **4**

Suzanne Goin serves these well-spiced peel-and-eat shrimp at The Backyard at the Hollywood Bowl. The recipe comes from her husband, chef David Lentz, who's been cooking the dish for his family for years. It's easily scaled up to serve more people, which makes it ideal for parties.

- 1½ lbs. extra-large shrimp
- 3 Tbsp. extra-virgin olive oil
- 1 onion, halved and thinly sliced
- 1 head of garlic, cut in half crosswise
- 1 rosemary sprig
- 1 chile de árbol, crushed
  One 12-oz. can of beer, preferably Pabst Blue Ribbon
- 2 lemons, halved
- 2 Tbsp. Old Bay Seasoning
- ½ cup ketchup
- 1 Tbsp. drained prepared horseradish
- 2¼ tsp. fresh lemon juice
- 1½ tsp. Sriracha
- ¾ tsp. Worcestershire sauce

1. Using kitchen shears, cut along the back of each shrimp shell and remove the intestinal vein. In a large saucepan, heat the olive oil. Add the onion, garlic, rosemary and chile and cook over moderately high heat, stirring occasionally, until the onion is softened and just starting to brown, 5 to 7 minutes. Add the beer and simmer until reduced by half, about 5 minutes.

2. Add the lemon halves, Old Bay and 5 cups of water to the saucepan and bring just to a simmer. Add the shrimp and poach over low heat until just cooked through, 8 to 10 minutes. Using a slotted spoon, transfer the shrimp, onion, garlic and lemon halves to a platter to cool slightly.

3. Meanwhile, in a medium bowl, whisk the ketchup with the horseradish, lemon juice, Sriracha and Worcestershire.

4. Serve the shrimp, warm or at room temperature, with the cocktail sauce.
—*Suzanne Goin*

WINE Peppery, minerally California white: 2015 Tatomer Meeresboden Santa Barbara County Grüner Veltliner.

Glazed Korean Rice Cake Skewers with Spam

⏲ Total **45 min**; Makes **8**

For these Korean-street-food-inspired kebabs, chef Sohui Kim of Insa and The Good Fork in Brooklyn grills Korean rice cakes (which are like thick, chewy noodles) with Spam and crisp vegetables.

- ½ tsp. instant dashi (see Note)
- ¼ cup gochujang (see Note)
- 2 Tbsp. honey
- 2 Tbsp. rice vinegar
- 2 tsp. soy sauce
- 1 tsp. toasted sesame oil
- 1 lb. 3-inch-long Korean rice cakes (see Note)
- 8 oz. Spam, cut into 1-inch cubes
- 2 shallots, quartered through the root ends
- 1 zucchini, cut into 1-inch pieces
- 1 red bell pepper, cut into 1-inch pieces
- 3 Tbsp. canola oil
  Kosher salt
  Black sesame seeds, chopped cilantro and crushed peanuts, for serving

1. In a medium bowl, whisk the dashi with ¼ cup of water until dissolved. Whisk in the gochujang, honey, rice vinegar, soy sauce and sesame oil.

2. In a pot of salted boiling water, cook the rice cakes until al dente, 3 to 4 minutes. Drain well and rinse under cold water. In a large bowl, toss the rice cakes with the Spam, vegetables and canola oil and season with salt. Alternately thread the rice cakes, Spam and vegetables onto eight 14-inch-long metal skewers.

3. Light a grill. Grill the skewers over moderately high heat, turning once, until the rice cakes are lightly browned and the vegetables are softened slightly, about 8 minutes. Baste with the gochujang sauce and grill, basting frequently, until glazed and charred, about 5 minutes longer. Transfer the skewers to a work surface and brush with more gochujang sauce. Arrange on a platter and garnish with sesame seeds, cilantro and peanuts. Serve warm, passing any remaining sauce at the table.
—*Sohui Kim*

NOTE Instant dashi, gochujang and Korean rice cakes are available at Asian markets and from amazon.com.

MAKE AHEAD The gochujang sauce can be refrigerated for up to 1 week.

WINE Bright, minerally Grüner Veltliner: 2014 Forstreiter Schiefer.

Littleneck Clams Steamed in Vinho Verde

⏱ Total **40 min**; Serves **8**

At Fat Rice in Chicago, Abraham Conlon hosts after-hour parties centered around petiscos, Portugal's answer to tapas. Dishes include these littleneck clams steamed in Vinho Verde, a light and refreshing young Portuguese wine, which adds a terrific brightness to the broth.

⅓ cup extra-virgin olive oil

⅓ cup minced garlic

2 fresh long hot red chiles—stemmed, seeded and thinly sliced crosswise

64 littleneck clams, scrubbed (about 6 lbs.)

1 cup Vinho Verde or other Portuguese white wine

1 cup minced cilantro

3 Tbsp. fresh lemon juice, plus lemon wedges for serving

Kosher salt and white pepper

1. In a large pot, heat the olive oil until shimmering. Add the garlic and chiles and cook over high heat, stirring, until fragrant and the garlic is just starting to brown, 2 to 3 minutes. Add the clams and wine. Cover and steam until the clams just open, about 8 minutes. Using tongs or a slotted spoon, transfer the clams to a baking sheet; discard any that don't open.

2. Boil the cooking liquid over high heat until reduced by half, about 7 minutes. Stir in the minced cilantro and lemon juice, add the clams and season lightly with salt and white pepper; toss well. Transfer to a deep platter and serve with lemon wedges. —*Abraham Conlon*

Crab Cakes with Smoky Onion Remoulade

Active **1 hr**; Total **2 hr**; Makes **6**

One night, when he was in fourth grade, Marc Forgione put on a jacket and tie and brought an important guest to dinner at his father's restaurant: his Catholic-school teacher Sister Helen Edward. ("She used to pull my hair to keep me in line," he recalls.) Attempting to impress her with his sophistication, he ordered the crab cake. To his surprise, he loved it. Today, at his New York City steakhouse, American Cut, he serves his own pan-fried version with his dad's smoked-onion remoulade. Instead of smoked onions, the recipe here calls for charred onions seasoned with smoked salt.

REMOULADE

1 medium onion, halved and thinly sliced

1 Tbsp. canola oil

Kosher salt

¾ cup mayonnaise

1 Tbsp. white wine vinegar

1½ Tbsp. minced chives

1 Tbsp. minced shallot

½ tsp. chili powder

⅛ tsp. cayenne

Smoked sea salt, such as Maldon

CRAB CAKES

½ cup canola oil

½ cup minced fennel

¼ cup minced red onion

¼ cup minced red bell pepper

2 Tbsp. minced seeded jalapeño

2 Tbsp. brandy

1 Tbsp. Old Bay Seasoning

½ cup mayonnaise

1 Tbsp. fresh lemon juice

1 Tbsp. minced parsley

1½ tsp. minced tarragon

3 dashes of Tabasco

1 lb. jumbo lump crabmeat, picked over

3 large eggs

1¼ cups rice flour

4 cups cornflakes (4 oz.), finely crushed

1. Make the remoulade Preheat the broiler. On a large rimmed baking sheet, toss the onion with the oil and season with kosher salt. Broil 8 inches from the heat for about 8 minutes, stirring occasionally, until the onion is softened and charred in spots. Let cool, then finely chop. In a medium bowl, whisk the onion with the mayonnaise, vinegar, chives, shallot, chili powder and cayenne. Season with smoked sea salt.

2. Make the crab cakes In a large oven-proof skillet, heat 2 tablespoons of the oil. Add the fennel, onion, red pepper and jalapeño and cook over moderate heat, stirring, until softened and just starting to brown, about 7 minutes. Stir in the brandy and Old Bay and cook until the brandy has evaporated, about 1 minute. Scrape into a large bowl and let cool; wipe out the skillet.

3. Stir the mayonnaise, lemon juice, parsley, tarragon and Tabasco into the vegetables. Gently fold in the crab. Shape the mixture into 6 cakes and transfer to a wax-paper-lined plate. Refrigerate for 1 hour.

4. Preheat the oven to 350°. In a shallow bowl, beat the eggs. Spread the rice flour and crushed cornflakes in 2 separate shallow bowls. Gently but firmly pack each crab cake so it holds its shape. Dredge in the rice flour, then dip in the egg and dredge in the cornflakes, gently patting to help the crumbs adhere; transfer to the plate.

5. Heat the remaining 6 tablespoons of oil in the skillet until shimmering. Add the crab cakes and cook over moderately high heat, turning once, until golden and crusty on both sides, about 5 minutes. Transfer the skillet to the oven and bake the crab cakes until heated through, about 5 minutes. Transfer to plates and serve with the remoulade. —*Marc Forgione*

WINE Juicy, fresh sparkling rosé: NV Gruet Rosé Brut.

Grilled Chicken Lettuce Wraps with Pickled Watermelon Rind Slaw

Total **1 hr 15 min** plus **3 hr marinating**
Serves **6**

Bright, crunchy and spicy, these assemble-your-own lettuce wraps are fun for guests (and low-stress for hosts).

PICKLED WATERMELON RIND

- 1 cup unseasoned rice vinegar
- 1 cup sugar
- 1 Tbsp. kosher salt
- One 1-inch slice of crystallized ginger
- 1 star anise pod
- ¼ small watermelon, green skin and all but ¼ inch of the red flesh removed, rind sliced 1 inch thick

CHICKEN

- ½ cup fresh lime juice (from 4 to 6 limes)
- ¼ cup plus 2 Tbsp. soy sauce
- 3 Tbsp. packed light brown sugar
- 3 Tbsp. Asian fish sauce
- 2 Tbsp. Sriracha
- 2 Tbsp. minced garlic
- 1 Tbsp. minced cilantro
- 12 skin-on, boneless chicken thighs
- Kosher salt and pepper

SLAW

- 1½ cups peeled, seeded and julienned cucumber
- 1 cup julienned carrot
- ½ cup cilantro leaves
- ½ cup torn mint leaves
- ¼ cup fresh lime juice
- 3 scallions, thinly sliced
- 1 Fresno chile—halved, seeded and very thinly sliced
- Lettuce leaves, for serving

1. Pickle the watermelon rind In a medium saucepan, combine the vinegar and ½ cup of water with the sugar, salt, ginger and star anise and bring to a boil over high heat. Add the watermelon rind and boil for 1 minute, then transfer to a heatproof bowl. Let cool, then refrigerate for 3 hours. Drain well and julienne the pickled rind.

2. Meanwhile, prepare the chicken In a large bowl, whisk the lime juice with the soy sauce, brown sugar, fish sauce, Sriracha, garlic and cilantro. Add the chicken to the marinade and turn to coat. Cover and refrigerate for 3 hours.

3. Light a grill and oil the grate. Remove the chicken from the marinade and season the thighs with salt and pepper. Grill over moderate heat, turning occasionally, until the skin is crispy and the chicken is cooked through, about 15 minutes. Transfer the chicken to a cutting board and let rest for 5 minutes.

4. Make the slaw In a large bowl, toss the julienned pickled watermelon rind with all of the ingredients except the lettuce leaves. Slice the chicken and serve in the lettuce leaves, topped with the slaw. *—Ben Ford*

MAKE AHEAD The drained pickled watermelon rind can be refrigerated for up to 5 days.

WINE Citrusy white: 2014 Groth Napa Valley Sauvignon Blanc.

Chicken Curry Skewers

Total **45 min** plus **3 hr marinating**; Serves **6**

Food on a stick is always a crowd-pleaser. L.A. chef Ben Ford's chicken skewers, with curry in both the marinade and the dipping sauce, will make plenty of people happy at your next cookout.

- ¼ cup minced lemongrass, tender inner part only (2 stalks)
- 2 Tbsp. vegetable oil
- 2 Tbsp. soy sauce
- 1 Tbsp. Asian fish sauce
- 1 Tbsp. curry powder
- 1 serrano chile—stemmed, seeded and minced
- 2 garlic cloves, minced
- 2 lbs. skinless, boneless chicken thighs, cut into 1-inch-wide strips
- Long wooden skewers, soaked in water for 1 hour
- Kosher salt and pepper
- Mint and basil leaves, for garnish

1. In a large bowl, whisk the lemongrass with the oil, soy sauce, fish sauce, curry powder, chile and garlic. Add the chicken and toss to coat. Cover and refrigerate for 3 hours.

2. Light a grill. Thread the chicken pieces onto the skewers and season with salt and pepper. Grill over moderate heat, turning, until nicely charred and cooked through, about 12 minutes. Transfer the skewers to a platter and garnish with mint and basil leaves. *—Ben Ford*

SERVE WITH Curry Dipping Sauce (recipe follows) and lime wedges.

WINE Aromatic, medium-bodied white: 2014 Famille Hugel Gentil.

CURRY DIPPING SAUCE
Active **15 min**; Total **1 hr 15 min**
Makes **1¼ cups**

This tangy curry dipping sauce is equally delicious with grilled pork.

- 1 Tbsp. vegetable oil
- ½ cup finely chopped onion
- 2 Tbsp. Madras curry powder
- ½ cup yogurt
- ½ cup unsweetened coconut milk
- 2 tsp. honey
- 1½ tsp. finely grated lime zest plus 1 Tbsp. fresh lime juice
- 1 small garlic clove, minced
- ¼ tsp. cayenne
- Kosher salt

In a medium skillet, heat the oil. Add the onion and cook over moderately low heat, stirring occasionally, until softened but not browned, about 5 minutes. Add the curry powder and cook, stirring, until fragrant, about 1 minute. Scrape the mixture into a food processor. Add the yogurt, coconut milk, honey, lime zest and juice, garlic and cayenne and puree until nearly smooth. Scrape into a bowl and season with salt. Cover and refrigerate for 1 hour before serving. *—BF*

MAKE AHEAD The dipping sauce can be refrigerated for up to 5 days.

SALADS

F&W's Justin Chapple demos his Mad Genius Tip for baking taco salad bowls. OPPOSITE Little Gem Lettuce with White Anchovies (p. 40).

Little Gem Lettuce with White Anchovies

📷 PAGE 38

⏱ Total **35 min**; Serves **8**

Star chef Geoffrey Zakarian's sweet, tangy, herb-packed vinaigrette is like green goddess dressing but without the mayonnaise or sour cream. White anchovies give the salad a terrific brininess.

¼ cup Champagne vinegar

½ small shallot, chopped

1½ Tbsp. Dijon mustard

1½ Tbsp. honey

2 cups lightly packed mixed herbs, such as chives, parsley, tarragon and dill

¼ cup canola oil

¼ cup extra-virgin olive oil

Kosher salt and pepper

Six 6-oz. heads of Little Gem lettuce or hearts of romaine, dark outer leaves discarded and inner leaves separated (1½ lbs.)

8 radishes, thinly sliced

24 white anchovies (alici or boquerones)

1. In a blender, combine the vinegar with the shallot, mustard, honey and 1 cup of the herbs and puree until nearly smooth. With the machine on, gradually add both oils and puree until very smooth. Scrape the dressing into a small bowl and season with salt and pepper.

2. In a large serving bowl, gently toss the lettuce with half of the dressing and ½ cup of the herbs. Scatter the radishes, anchovies and the remaining ½ cup of herbs on top of the salad and serve, passing the remaining dressing at the table.
—Geoffrey Zakarian

MAKE AHEAD The dressing can be refrigerated for up to 3 hours.

WINE Zesty and peppery Austrian Grüner Veltliner: 2014 Leth Steinagrund.

Quick-Pickled Vegetable Salad with Harissa Vinaigrette

Active **30 min**; Total **1 hr 15 min**; Serves **4**

4 medium carrots, sliced into thin rounds

4 medium inner celery ribs, thinly sliced on the bias, plus ½ cup lightly packed celery leaves

1 cup thinly sliced white onion

¾ cup plus 2 Tbsp. distilled white vinegar

2 garlic cloves

2 Tbsp. sugar

Kosher salt and pepper

3½ Tbsp. extra-virgin olive oil

½ cup raw pepitas (hulled pumpkin seeds)

1 Tbsp. harissa

Three 6-oz. romaine hearts, dark outer leaves removed and inner leaves torn into bite-size pieces (10 cups)

1. In a heatproof medium bowl, combine the carrots, celery ribs and onion. In a medium saucepan, combine ¾ cup of the vinegar with the garlic, sugar, 1½ cups of water and 1½ tablespoons of salt and cook over moderate heat until the sugar dissolves, about 3 minutes. Pour the hot brine over the vegetables and let stand until cool, about 30 minutes. Drain the vegetables and refrigerate until just chilled, about 15 minutes; discard the garlic. Reserve the brine for another use.

2. Meanwhile, in a small skillet, heat ½ tablespoon of the olive oil. Add the pumpkin seeds and a pinch each of salt and pepper and cook over moderate heat, stirring, until lightly browned, 2 minutes. Let cool.

3. In a serving bowl, whisk the harissa with the remaining 3 tablespoons of olive oil and 2 tablespoons of white vinegar; season with salt and pepper. Add the romaine, drained pickled vegetables and celery leaves and toss well; season the salad with salt and pepper and toss again. Sprinkle the toasted pumpkin seeds on top and serve. —Justin Chapple

MAKE AHEAD The drained pickled vegetables can be refrigerated for up to 1 week.

WINE Racy, briny Greek island white: 2015 Domaine Sigalas Santorini.

Charred Broccolini and Escarole Salad

⏱ Total **40 min**; Serves **4**

By charring the vegetables, F&W's Justin Chapple turns this salad into an entrée we crave. We love the combination of smoky Broccolini with crisp escarole and garlicky sourdough croutons in a Champagne vinegar dressing.

2 lbs. Broccolini, thick stems halved lengthwise

¼ cup extra-virgin olive oil, plus more for brushing

Kosher salt and pepper

Two ¾-inch-thick slices cut from a sourdough boule

1 garlic clove, halved

¼ cup Champagne vinegar

½ cup thinly sliced red onion

8 cups torn white and light green escarole leaves

1 fresh hot red chile—stemmed, seeded and very thinly sliced

1. Light a grill or heat a grill pan. In a large bowl, toss the Broccolini with 2 tablespoons of the olive oil; season with salt and pepper. Grill over moderately high heat until lightly charred and crisp-tender, about 5 minutes. Transfer to a work surface; cut in half crosswise.

2. Brush the bread with olive oil and season with salt and pepper. Grill over moderately high heat, turning once, until lightly browned and crisp, about 3 minutes total. Transfer to a plate and rub with the cut sides of the garlic clove. Let cool slightly, then tear into bite-size pieces.

3. In a serving bowl, mix the vinegar, onion and the remaining 2 tablespoons of olive oil. Add the escarole, Broccolini, garlic bread and chile and toss well. Season with salt and pepper, toss again and serve.
—Justin Chapple

WINE Exuberant, red-fruited Sangiovese: 2013 Badia a Coltibuono Chianti Classico RS.

CHARRED BROCCOLINI AND ESCAROLE SALAD (TOP), QUICK-PICKLED VEGETABLE SALAD WITH HARISSA VINAIGRETTE

MIXED GREENS
WITH POACHED
EGGS, HAZELNUTS
AND SPICES

Mixed Greens with Poached Eggs, Hazelnuts and Spices

:) Total **30 min**; Serves **6**

No meal at Ristorante L'Arcangelo in Rome would be complete without this salad called Viaggio a Rocca Priora. The name, which translates as "a trip to Rocca Priora," is a whimsical reference to Arcangelo Dandini's hometown in the suburbs. The chef seems more interested in history than geography, however, flavoring the wild greens and poached egg with spices— cumin, licorice, fennel pollen—that evoke the ancient capital.

⅛ tsp. fennel pollen

⅛ tsp. ground cumin

⅛ tsp. licorice powder (optional)

   Pinch of ground cinnamon

1 Tbsp. distilled white vinegar

6 large eggs

½ lb. mixed salad greens, such as mizuna, wild arugula and purslane (12 cups lightly packed)

2 Tbsp. extra-virgin olive oil

   Sea salt

¼ cup chopped toasted hazelnuts

   Elderflowers or any small edible flower, for garnish

1. In a very small bowl, mix the fennel pollen, cumin, licorice powder (if using) and cinnamon.

2. Bring a large saucepan of water to a boil. Add the vinegar. One at a time, crack 3 eggs into a small bowl, then slip them into the boiling water, leaving a few inches between them in the pot. Poach over moderate heat until the whites are set and the yolks are still runny, about 3 minutes. Using a slotted spoon, carefully transfer the eggs to a paper towel–lined plate. Repeat with the remaining 3 eggs.

3. In a large bowl, toss the greens with the oil and season with salt. Mound on plates and top with the poached eggs. Sprinkle with the spice mixture, garnish with the hazelnuts and elderflowers and serve. —*Arcangelo Dandini*

WINE Floral-scented Prosecco: NV Serafini & Vidotto Bollicine.

Kale Caesar with Fried Chickpeas

:) Total **45 min**; Serves **4**

Supercrunchy pan-fried chickpeas are a fun, gluten-free alternative to croutons in this tangy kale Caesar.

   Canola oil, for frying

   One 15-oz. can chickpeas, rinsed and patted dry

   Kosher salt and pepper

½ cup mayonnaise

2 Tbsp. fresh lemon juice

2 tsp. Dijon mustard

1 garlic clove, finely grated

¼ cup shredded Parmesan, plus more for serving

1¼ lbs. curly kale, stemmed and chopped (10 cups)

1. In a large skillet, heat ¼ inch of oil until shimmering. Add the chickpeas and fry over moderately high heat, stirring occasionally, until browned and crisp, 3 to 5 minutes. Using a slotted spoon, transfer the chickpeas to paper towels to drain. Season with salt and pepper.

2. In a large bowl, whisk the mayonnaise with the lemon juice, mustard, garlic and the ¼ cup of cheese. Season with salt and pepper. Add the kale and toss to coat. Add the fried chickpeas and toss again. Top with shredded Parmesan and serve. —*Justin Chapple*

WINE Citrusy, medium-bodied Spanish white: 2015 Martínsancho Verdejo.

Winter Greens Salad with Buttermilk Dressing

:) Total **45 min**; Serves **8 to 10**

1 cup pecans, coarsely chopped

⅔ cup buttermilk

1 Tbsp. fresh lemon juice

1 Tbsp. finely chopped tarragon

1 Tbsp. finely chopped chives

1 tsp. finely grated garlic

1 cup extra-virgin olive oil

   Kosher salt and pepper

8 oz. Belgian and curly endive, chopped (4 cups)

6 cups lightly packed arugula or spinach (4 oz.)

6 cups lightly packed baby kale (5 oz.)

½ cup thinly sliced scallions

1. Preheat the oven to 350°. Spread the pecans in a pie plate and toast for about 10 minutes, until golden. Let cool.

2. In a small bowl, whisk the buttermilk with the lemon juice, tarragon, chives and garlic. While whisking constantly, slowly drizzle in the olive oil and season with salt and pepper.

3. In a large bowl, combine the endive, arugula, kale and scallions with 1 cup of the dressing. Season with salt and pepper and toss to coat. Transfer the salad to a platter, top with the pecans and serve with the remaining dressing at the table. —*Melissa Clark*

Cabbage and Kale Slaw with Toasted Yeast Dressing

:) Total **25 min**; Serves **4 to 6**

Chef Josh Lewis, an alum of Noma in Copenhagen, makes his terrific dressing with toasted nutritional yeast (a vegan umami bomb sold at health food stores). It's great on all kinds of slaws and on greens with sturdy leaves.

⅔ cup plus 1 Tbsp. nutritional yeast flakes

1 garlic clove, thinly sliced

1 Tbsp. plus ½ tsp. apple cider vinegar

2 tsp. fresh lemon juice

¼ cup grapeseed oil

¼ cup extra-virgin olive oil

   Fine sea salt

½ medium green cabbage, cored and very thinly sliced (12 cups)

1 medium bunch of Tuscan kale, stems discarded, leaves very thinly sliced (4½ cups)

1. In a skillet, toast the nutritional yeast over moderate heat, stirring frequently, until fragrant and lightly browned, about 5 minutes. Scrape the yeast into a blender. Add the garlic, cider vinegar, lemon juice and ⅓ cup of water and blend until combined. With the machine on, add the oils in a slow, steady stream. Season with salt.

2. In a large bowl, toss the cabbage and kale. Add the yeast dressing and toss. Season with salt and serve. —*Josh Lewis*

MAKE AHEAD The dressing can be refrigerated for up to 3 days.

Roasted Cauliflower Salad

Active **30 min**; Total **1 hr**; Serves **8**

- 1 **large head of cauliflower (2½ lbs.), quartered lengthwise and cored**
- ½ **cup plus 2 Tbsp. extra-virgin olive oil**
- 8 **thyme sprigs**
- 3 **garlic cloves, crushed**
- **Kosher salt and pepper**
- ½ **tsp. finely grated lemon zest plus 4 Tbsp. fresh lemon juice**
- 1 **Tbsp. white wine vinegar**
- ¼ **cup capers**
- 1 **bunch of red or green kale (8 oz.), stemmed and cut into ¾-inch-wide ribbons**
- 3 **cups baby arugula**
- 6 **radishes, trimmed and cut into ½-inch wedges**
- ½ **cup dried tart cherries, coarsely chopped**
- ¼ **cup roasted pepitas (hulled pumpkin seeds)**

1. Preheat the oven to 400°. Cut three-quarters of the cauliflower into 2-inch florets. Thinly slice the remaining cauliflower and reserve.

2. On a rimmed baking sheet, combine the cauliflower florets with 2 tablespoons of the olive oil, the thyme and garlic; season with salt and toss to coat. Spread the cauliflower in an even layer and roast for 25 to 30 minutes, stirring halfway through, until golden and tender. Discard the thyme and garlic. Sprinkle the cauliflower with the lemon zest and 1 tablespoon of the lemon juice, season with salt and toss to coat.

3. Meanwhile, in a medium bowl, whisk the remaining ½ cup of olive oil and 3 tablespoons of lemon juice with the vinegar and capers until emulsified. Season the dressing with salt and pepper.

4. In a large bowl, combine the kale with ¼ cup of the dressing and mix, gently massaging the kale to tenderize it. Add the arugula and another 2 tablespoons of the dressing and mix well.

5. Arrange the roasted cauliflower on a platter and top with the radishes, cherries, greens and the reserved raw cauliflower. Spoon on the remaining dressing, scatter the pepitas on top and serve.
—*Jessica Largey*

Spinach and Fennel Salad with Candied Bacon

Active **30 min**; Total **1 hr 15 min**
Serves **4 to 6**

- 8 **slices of thick-cut bacon**
- ⅓ **cup packed light brown sugar**
- **Kosher salt and pepper**
- ⅓ **cup plus 1 Tbsp. extra-virgin olive oil**
- 1 **medium fennel bulb—halved, cored and very thinly sliced**
- 2 **Tbsp. Dijon mustard**
- 1½ **Tbsp. fresh lemon juice**
- 1½ **Tbsp. sherry vinegar**
- 8 **oz. baby spinach (12 cups)**
- 2 **cups lightly packed basil leaves**
- 4 **oz. French feta cheese, crumbled**

1. Preheat the oven to 375°. In a large bowl, coat the bacon with the brown sugar and ½ teaspoon of pepper. Arrange the bacon in an even layer on a parchment paper–lined baking sheet. Top with another piece of parchment paper and another large baking sheet. Bake for about 25 minutes, until the bacon is lightly browned and the fat is rendered. Remove the top baking sheet and parchment paper. Bake the bacon for about 15 minutes longer, until well browned and nearly crisp. Using tongs, transfer the bacon to a rack to cool and crisp, then coarsely chop.

2. Meanwhile, in a large skillet, heat 1 tablespoon of the oil. Add the fennel and a generous pinch each of salt and pepper. Cook over moderately high heat, stirring occasionally, until just softened and lightly browned, about 4 minutes. Transfer to a plate and let cool.

3. In a large serving bowl, whisk the mustard with the lemon juice and vinegar. Gradually whisk in the remaining ⅓ cup of oil until emulsified. Season the dressing with salt and pepper. Add the fennel, spinach and basil to the bowl and toss well. Season with salt and pepper and toss again. Sprinkle the feta and candied bacon on top and serve right away. —*Alex Guarnaschelli*

WINE Minerally Chardonnay: 2012 Clos des Fous Locura 1 Cachapoal Valley from Chile.

Spinach Salad with Walnut Vinaigrette

Total **25 min**; Serves **6**

Avocado and toasted walnuts provide contrasting bites of creaminess and crunch in this ultrasimple spinach and mushroom salad.

- 1 **cup walnuts, finely chopped**
- 8 **oz. curly spinach (8 packed cups)**
- 4 **oz. white mushrooms, sliced**
- 1 **Hass avocado, sliced**
- ¼ **cup extra-virgin olive oil**
- ¼ **cup apple cider vinegar**
- **Kosher salt and pepper**

In a small skillet, toast the walnuts over low heat, stirring, until golden, 6 to 8 minutes. Transfer to a large bowl and let cool. Add the spinach, mushrooms, avocado, oil and vinegar. Season with salt and pepper, toss to coat and serve. —*Kay Chun*

Fennel and Avocado Salad with Cranberry-Nut Dressing

Total **20 min**; Serves **4**

Cranberries, often relegated to a supporting role for turkey, get their star turn in this salad dressing. The berry and grapefruit mixture invigorates avocado and fennel but could also be used on hardy greens like chicory and frisée.

- ½ **cup fresh cranberries (2 oz.), chopped**
- 1 **heaping Tbsp. honey**
- ¼ **cup chopped marcona almonds**
- 2 **Tbsp. fresh grapefruit juice**
- 2 **Tbsp. canola oil**
- **Kosher salt and pepper**
- 1 **large fennel bulb, trimmed and thinly sliced (3 cups)**
- 1 **Hass avocado—peeled, pitted and cut into thin wedges**

In a large bowl, mix the cranberries with the honey. Stir in the almonds, grapefruit juice and canola oil and season with salt and pepper. Arrange the fennel and avocado on a platter, spoon on the dressing and serve. —*Kay Chun*

FENNEL AND
AVOCADO SALAD
WITH CRANBERRY-
NUT DRESSING

Christmas Salad

⏱ Total **45 min;** Serves **10 to 12**

> **Vegetable oil, for frying**
>
> 24 **small square or round wonton wrappers**
>
> **Kosher salt and pepper**
>
> ¼ **cup plus 2 Tbsp. soy sauce**
>
> ¼ **cup plus 2 Tbsp. extra-virgin olive oil**
>
> 1 **shallot, minced**
>
> ½ **tsp. finely grated lime zest plus ¼ cup fresh lime juice**
>
> 1½ **Tbsp. toasted sesame oil**
>
> 2 **medium garlic cloves, finely grated**
>
> **Large pinch of sugar**
>
> **Three 4-oz. bunches of arugula (not baby), trimmed and very coarsely chopped**
>
> ¾ **lb. Belgian endives (4 small)—halved lengthwise, cored and thickly sliced on the bias**
>
> 2 **small fennel bulbs, halved through the core and very thinly sliced crosswise**
>
> **Two 4-oz. bunches of watercress, thick stems discarded**
>
> 1½ **cups pomegranate seeds**
>
> 1 **cup thinly sliced scallions**

1. In a large, deep skillet, heat ¼ inch of vegetable oil until shimmering. Add 2 or 3 wonton wrappers at a time to the hot oil and fry over moderately high heat, turning, until browned and crisp, 1 to 2 minutes per batch. Using tongs, transfer to paper towels to drain and season lightly with salt.

2. In a medium bowl, whisk the soy sauce with the olive oil, shallot, lime zest, lime juice, sesame oil, garlic and sugar. Season the dressing with salt and pepper.

3. In a large bowl, toss the arugula, endive, fennel, watercress, pomegranate seeds and scallions. Add the dressing and toss. Serve right away, with the crispy wontons. —*Natasha Phan*

MAKE AHEAD The salad, soy dressing and crispy wontons can all be made earlier in the day and combined just before serving.

Warm Mushroom and Charred Onion Salad

⏱ Total **30 min;** Serves **8**

For this luscious dish, Abraham Conlon, the chef at Fat Rice in Chicago, cooks a mix of meaty wild mushrooms with Madeira, garlic and lemon juice, then tosses them with charred spring onions. If you can't get spring onions, use a combination of small shallots and scallions.

> 6 **spring onions, bulbs halved lengthwise and green tops thinly sliced**
>
> 1¼ **lbs. mixed wild mushrooms, cut into 1-inch pieces**
>
> ⅓ **cup extra-virgin olive oil**
>
> 1 **Tbsp. minced garlic**
>
> **Kosher salt and pepper**
>
> ½ **cup Madeira**
>
> 2 **Tbsp. fresh lemon juice**
>
> 2 **oz. watercress, thick stems discarded, plus watercress flowers for garnish (optional)**

1. Set a very large skillet over moderately high heat until smoking. Add the onion bulbs cut side down and cook until lightly charred, about 4 minutes; transfer to a plate. Add the mushrooms and olive oil to the skillet and cook, stirring occasionally, until lightly browned, about 7 minutes.

2. Add the onion bulbs, garlic and a pinch each of salt and pepper to the skillet. Add the Madeira and cook, stirring, until the mushrooms and onions are tender, about 5 minutes. Stir in the lemon juice and onion tops. Transfer to a serving bowl. Fold in the watercress and season with salt and pepper. Top with watercress flowers, if using, and serve. —*Abraham Conlon*

Summer Vegetable and Burrata Salad

⏱ Total **45 min;** Serves **4**

Brian Clevenger of Raccolto in Seattle gives his salad irresistible lushness with burrata. This mozzarella with cream in the center is too soft to slice, so scoop it with a spoon, like they do in Italy, instead.

> 1 **lb. fresh fava beans, shelled (1 cup)**
>
> ¼ **cup extra-virgin olive oil**
>
> 3 **ears of corn (preferably white), shucked and kernels cut off the cobs (3½ cups)**
>
> **Kosher salt and pepper**
>
> 1 **Tbsp. sherry vinegar**
>
> 4 **oz. arugula (6 cups lightly packed)**
>
> 8 **oz. mixed cherry tomatoes, halved**
>
> ½ **cup coarsely chopped mint**
>
> ½ **cup coarsely chopped basil**
>
> 8 **oz. burrata cheese**

1. Fill a medium bowl with ice water. In a medium saucepan of salted boiling water, blanch the fava beans for 2 minutes. Drain and transfer to the ice bath to cool completely. Slip off and discard the skins.

2. In a large skillet, heat 2 tablespoons of the oil. Add the corn and fava beans and cook over moderately high heat, stirring occasionally, just until the corn is crisp-tender, about 3 minutes. Season with salt and pepper. Transfer to a plate and let cool to room temperature.

3. In a large bowl, whisk the vinegar with the remaining 2 tablespoons of oil. Add the arugula, tomatoes, mint, basil and the corn mixture and season with salt and pepper. Toss to coat, then spoon onto plates. Scoop the burrata into pieces and gently spoon it onto the plates. Season with pepper and serve. —*Brian Clevenger*

MAKE AHEAD The blanched and peeled fava beans can be refrigerated overnight.

WINE Delicate and floral Italian white: 2014 Monchiero Carbone Roero Arneis.

Escarole Salad with Tahini Vinaigrette

⏱ Total **30 min;** Serves **6 to 8**

"When I was a student in Rome," says Seattle chef Renee Erickson, "women at market stalls would cut up beautiful curly chicory and serve it with a super-potent dressing made with anchovies. I like those bold flavors—strong but really simple." This tahini vinaigrette, inspired by that dressing, is garlicky, earthy and delicious.

- **1 small garlic clove**
   Kosher salt and pepper
- **¼ cup tahini**
- **¼ cup apple cider vinegar**
- **¼ cup plus 2 Tbsp. extra-virgin olive oil**
- **½ cup shelled pistachios**
   One 1-lb. head of escarole, dark green leaves reserved for another use, the rest torn into bite-size pieces
- **2 Bosc pears—halved, cored and thinly sliced lengthwise**
- **1 small bunch of cilantro, sprigs cut crosswise into 3-inch lengths**
- **6 Medjool dates, pitted and cut lengthwise into ¼-inch strips**
- **½ cup mint leaves**

1. Preheat the oven to 350°. Using the flat side of a chef's knife, crush the garlic to a paste with ½ teaspoon of salt. In a small bowl, whisk the garlic paste with the tahini and vinegar, then gradually whisk in the olive oil. Season the tahini vinaigrette with salt and pepper.

2. Spread the pistachios in a pie plate and toast in the oven until lightly browned, about 10 minutes. Transfer to a work surface and let cool completely, then coarsely chop.

3. In a large bowl, toss the escarole and pears with the tahini vinaigrette. Add the cilantro, pistachios, dates and mint and season with salt and pepper. Toss the salad again and serve. —*Renee Erickson*

MAKE AHEAD The tahini vinaigrette can be refrigerated for up to 3 days. Bring the dressing to room temperature and give it a stir before serving.

WINE Bright Greek white: 2015 Domaine Skouras Moscofilero.

Chicory and Beet Salad with Pine Nut Vinaigrette

⏱ Total **45 min;** Serves **4 to 6**

To get the best pine nut flavor in the vinaigrette, chef Naomi Pomeroy insists on using the elongated, Italian variety. For more of her tips, see Chef's Kitchen Wisdom (below right).

- **1 small head of escarole, white and light green leaves only, torn**
- **½ head of radicchio, cored and torn into bite-size pieces**
- **1 Belgian endive—halved lengthwise, cored and cut into bite-size pieces**
- **3 Tbsp. pine nuts**
- **3 Tbsp. extra-virgin olive oil**
- **3 Tbsp. sherry vinegar**
- **2 small garlic cloves, finely grated**
- **1½ tsp. honey**
   Kosher salt and pepper
- **4 baby golden or Chioggia beets, scrubbed and very thinly sliced**
- **1 medium fennel bulb—halved lengthwise, cored and very thinly sliced, fennel fronds chopped**

1. Set up a large ice water bath. Add the escarole, radicchio and endive and let stand for 30 minutes.

2. Meanwhile, in a small skillet, toast the pine nuts over moderate heat until golden and fragrant, about 5 minutes. Let cool; transfer to a food processor. Add the oil, vinegar, garlic and honey, season with salt and pepper and puree until smooth.

3. Drain the greens and spin or pat dry. Transfer to a large chilled bowl, add the beets and sliced fennel and toss well. Drizzle half of the dressing around the side of the bowl, season with salt and pepper and toss. Drizzle with the remaining dressing and toss again. Top with the fennel fronds and serve right away. —*Naomi Pomeroy*

WINE Crisp Pinot Bianco: 2015 Elena Walch Alto Adige.

Warm Escarole Salad with Sausage Vinaigrette

⏱ Total **25 min;** Serves **4**

For days when cold greens won't do, this terrific warm salad is simultaneously rich and refreshing. It combines spicy sausage with zippy anchovies, lemon and capers.

- **2 Tbsp. extra-virgin olive oil**
- **6 oz. hot Italian sausage, casing removed, meat crumbled**
- **3 oil-packed anchovy fillets, drained**
- **1 Tbsp. drained capers**
- **2 Tbsp. fresh lemon juice**
- **3 radishes, thinly sliced**
- **1 head of escarole (12 oz.), leaves torn into bite-size pieces (8 cups)**
   Kosher salt and pepper
- **2 Tbsp. chopped tarragon, for garnish**

In a large skillet, heat the olive oil. Add the sausage, anchovies and capers and cook over moderate heat, stirring to break up the meat, until cooked through, about 5 minutes. Add the lemon juice, radishes and escarole and stir until the escarole is wilted; season with salt and pepper. Transfer to a platter, garnish with the tarragon and serve. —*Kay Chun*

WINE Tangy, fruit-forward Sauvignon Blanc: 2014 Emmolo Napa Valley.

CHEF'S KITCHEN WISDOM

Up Your Salad Game

SOAK BITTER GREENS Dunk radicchio and escarole in ice water before serving them in salads; the soaking eliminates some of the bitterness and makes the greens extra crisp.

TRIM YOUR ESCAROLE Pull off and discard the "furry" outer leaves.

DRESS THE BOWL For even distribution, drizzle vinaigrette down the side of your salad bowl, then toss the salad. Drizzle more dressing on the salad and toss again. —*Naomi Pomeroy, Beast, Portland, Oregon*

SUMMER SALAD WITH
MUSTARD
VINAIGRETTE

Summer Salad with Mustard Vinaigrette

Total **40 min**; Serves **4**
Makes **1¾ cups vinaigrette**

Chef Thomas Keller is a huge fan of what he calls "spontaneous salads," which change based on what he finds in the French Laundry garden. He tosses his loot with this creamy vinaigrette, which he's been making for over 30 years. If you don't want to use raw egg yolk, leave it out.

VINAIGRETTE

- 1 large egg yolk
- 2 Tbsp. Dijon mustard
- 3 Tbsp. plus 1 tsp. balsamic vinegar
- 1 large garlic clove, minced
- 1 small shallot, minced
- 1 cup canola oil
- ½ cup extra-virgin olive oil
  Kosher salt and pepper

SALAD

- 12 breakfast radishes
- 12 oz. Castelfranco or radicchio, leaves torn into large pieces
- 8 oz. small tomatoes, quartered
- 1 small red endive, leaves separated
- 5 oz. baby zucchini, halved
- 4 oz. sugar snap peas, trimmed and halved if large
- 3 oz. baby carrots, halved lengthwise
- 1 Persian cucumber, thinly sliced
- 8 thin asparagus spears, cut into 3-inch pieces
- 1 oz. baby arugula (2 cups)
  Kosher salt and pepper
  Mixed herbs, such as basil and chervil, for garnish

1. Make the vinaigrette In a food processor, combine the first 5 ingredients with 2 tablespoons of water. With the machine on, drizzle in both oils until incorporated. For a thinner vinaigrette, stir in another 1 to 2 tablespoons of water. Season with salt and pepper.

2. Make the salad In a bowl, toss all of the ingredients except the herbs. Season with salt and pepper. Toss with ¼ cup of the vinaigrette. Garnish with herbs and serve with more dressing on the side; reserve the remaining dressing for another salad. —*Thomas Keller*

Warm Escarole-and-Shiitake Salad with Crispy Beans

Total **1 hr**; Serves **4**

This substantial vegetarian salad is packed with greens, lentils and meaty mushrooms. The crunch comes, brilliantly, from oven-roasted canned kidney beans.

- One 15-oz. can kidney beans
- ½ cup plus 1 Tbsp. extra-virgin olive oil
  Kosher salt and pepper
- 2 Tbsp. Dijon mustard
- 2 Tbsp. fresh lemon juice
- 2 Tbsp. minced shallot
- 1 head of escarole (12 oz.), leaves coarsely chopped
- 1 lb. shiitake mushrooms, stemmed, caps halved
- 2 garlic cloves, thinly sliced
- 2 celery ribs, thinly sliced
- 1 cup cooked black or green lentils
- 2 Tbsp. chopped chives

1. Preheat the oven to 375°. On a baking sheet, toss the beans with 1 tablespoon of the oil and season with salt and pepper. Roast for about 30 minutes, stirring, until dry and crispy. Transfer the sheet to a rack and let the beans cool completely.

2. In a large bowl, whisk the mustard, lemon juice and shallot. Whisking constantly, slowly drizzle in 6 tablespoons of the oil; season with salt and pepper. Set the escarole on top; don't mix.

3. In a nonstick skillet, heat the remaining 2 tablespoons of oil. Add the shiitake and cook over moderately high heat, stirring, until golden and charred in spots, 3 to 4 minutes. Stir in the garlic for 1 minute. Add the hot mushrooms, celery, lentils and chives to the escarole and toss. Mound the salad on plates, top with the crispy beans and serve. —*Kay Chun*

Charred-Vegetable Salad with Halloumi

Total **1 hr**; Serves **4**

- 2½ Tbsp. apple cider vinegar
- 2 tsp. pure maple syrup
- ¼ cup plus 4 tsp. extra-virgin olive oil
  Kosher salt and pepper
- 6 fresh figs, stemmed and halved lengthwise
- 1 oregano sprig
- 1 thyme sprig
- 1 large leek, white and light green parts only, halved lengthwise through the core
- 1 medium head of radicchio, cut through the core into 8 wedges
- 4 oz. halloumi cheese, sliced ¼ inch thick
- 4 oz. arugula (6 cups packed)
  Toasted sesame seeds, for garnish

1. In a small bowl, combine the vinegar with the maple syrup. While whisking constantly, slowly drizzle in ¼ cup of the oil until incorporated. Season the dressing with salt and pepper.

2. Heat a large cast-iron skillet. In a large bowl, toss the fig halves with the oregano, thyme and 3 tablespoons of the dressing. Add to the skillet and cook over moderately high heat, turning once and basting with dressing, until the figs are golden and lightly caramelized, 2 to 3 minutes per side. Discard the oregano and thyme. Transfer the figs to a plate.

3. Rub the halved leek with 2 teaspoons of the oil and season with salt and pepper. Add to the skillet and cook over moderate heat, turning occasionally, until nicely charred and tender, 8 to 10 minutes. Transfer the leek to a cutting board. Let cool, then thinly slice crosswise. Transfer to the large bowl. Repeat with the remaining 2 teaspoons of oil and the radicchio; season with salt and pepper and add to the bowl.

4. Add the halloumi slices to the skillet and cook over moderate heat, turning once, until golden and crisp, 2 to 3 minutes per side. Add the cheese to the bowl with the leek and radicchio. Add the arugula and the remaining dressing and toss to coat. Mound the salad on plates and arrange the figs around it. Garnish with sesame seeds and serve. —*Charlotte Druckman*

Brussels Sprout Slaw with Ginger Gold Apple

Total **30 min;** Serves **4**

At Graft Wine + Cider Bar in Watkins Glen, New York, chef Christina McKeough uses local apples in everything from grilled cheese sandwiches to pies. She loves the crisp texture of a tart-sweet Ginger Gold in this slaw.

- ½ **cup walnuts, coarsely chopped**
- ½ **tsp. finely grated lemon zest plus 2 Tbsp. fresh lemon juice**
- 1 **Tbsp. minced shallot**
- 2 **tsp. Dijon mustard**
- 1 **tsp. sugar**
- ⅓ **cup extra-virgin olive oil**
  Kosher salt and pepper
- 1 **lb. brussels sprouts**
- 1 **Ginger Gold or other firm, crisp apple, julienned**
- ¼ **cup shaved Parmigiano-Reggiano cheese**
- 2 **Tbsp. snipped chives**

1. Preheat the oven to 350°. Spread the walnuts in a pie plate and toast until fragrant and browned, 8 to 10 minutes. Let cool completely.

2. In a medium bowl, mix the lemon zest and juice with the shallot, mustard and sugar. While whisking constantly, drizzle in the olive oil and whisk until emulsified. Season the dressing with salt and pepper.

3. In a food processor fitted with the slicing blade, shred the brussels sprouts; transfer to a large bowl. Add the dressing, apple, cheese and chives, season with salt and pepper and toss to coat. Garnish with the toasted walnuts and serve.
—*Christina McKeough*

Brussels Sprout Salad with Toasted Sesame Vinaigrette

Total **45 min;** Serves **4**

Chef Seamus Mullen of Tertulia and El Colmado in New York City uses white and black sesame seeds to flavor his shaved brussels sprout salad. When toasting the seeds, remove them from the pan when they become fragrant; don't worry about the color.

- ¼ **cup white sesame seeds**
- 1 **tsp. finely grated lemon zest plus ¼ cup fresh lemon juice**
- 1 **Tbsp. white wine vinegar**
- 1 **garlic clove**
- 1 **tsp. honey**
- ¼ **cup plus 2 Tbsp. extra-virgin olive oil**
  Kosher salt and pepper
- 1 **lb. brussels sprouts, very thinly sliced**
- 1 **Pink Lady apple—halved, cored and thinly sliced**
- 1 **medium shallot, halved lengthwise and very thinly sliced**
- 1 **serrano chile—stemmed, seeded and very thinly sliced**
- ½ **cup chopped mint**
  Black sesame seeds, for garnish (optional)

1. In a small skillet, toast the white sesame seeds over moderately low heat, stirring, until fragrant but not browned, about 3 minutes. Transfer to a blender and let cool. Add the lemon zest and juice, then add the vinegar, garlic and honey and puree until a chunky paste forms, about 1 minute. With the machine on, gradually add the olive oil and puree until nearly smooth, 1 to 2 minutes. Scrape the vinaigrette into a large bowl and season with salt and pepper.

2. Add the brussels sprouts, apple, shallot, chile and mint to the dressing and toss well. Season with salt and pepper and toss again. Garnish with black sesame seeds, if using, and serve right away.
—*Seamus Mullen*

MAKE AHEAD The sesame vinaigrette can be refrigerated overnight. Bring to room temperature before using.

Tomatoes with Herbs and Almond Vinaigrette

Total **45 min;** Serves **4**

New York City chef Dan Kluger makes a deeply flavorful vinaigrette with toasted almonds for summer's sweetest and juiciest heirloom tomatoes.

- ½ **cup almonds, coarsely chopped and sifted**
- ¼ **cup plus 2 Tbsp. extra-virgin olive oil**
- 1 **garlic clove, finely grated**
- ¼ **cup red wine vinegar**
- 2 **Tbsp. fresh lime juice**
- 1 **tsp. sugar**
  Kosher salt and pepper
- 2 **lbs. mixed heirloom tomatoes, some sliced, some halved**
- ⅓ **cup very thinly sliced red onion, soaked in ice water for 10 minutes**
- ½ **small jalapeño, minced**
- ¼ **cup torn mint leaves**
- ¼ **cup torn Thai basil leaves**

1. In a medium skillet, cook the almonds in the oil over moderately low heat, stirring occasionally, until well browned, about 7 minutes. Strain the oil through a fine sieve into a heatproof bowl; reserve the almonds. Immediately whisk the garlic into the warm oil and let cool slightly, then whisk in the vinegar, lime juice and sugar. Season the dressing with salt and pepper.

2. Spread the tomatoes on a large baking sheet. Season with salt and let stand for 5 minutes.

3. Drain the onion; pat dry. Scatter half of the almonds on a platter and top them with the tomatoes. Drizzle with the dressing and top with the onion, jalapeño, mint, basil and the remaining almonds. Serve.
—*Dan Kluger*

WINE Vibrant French rosé: 2015 L'Ostal Cazes Pays d'Oc.

TOMATOES WITH
HERBS AND ALMOND
VINAIGRETTE

MARINATED FETA WITH
NECTARINE AND
TOMATO FATTOUSH

Heirloom Tomatoes with Ricotta and Savory Granola

Active **40 min**; Total **1 hr 45 min**; Serves **4**

To dress up peak-season Brandywines and Green Zebras, combine them with lemony ricotta and savory granola. The toasty oats, nuts and sunflower seeds would be fantastic in any green salad.

2 **cups old-fashioned rolled oats**

¼ **cup light agave nectar**

¼ **cup plus 3 Tbsp. extra-virgin olive oil**

  Kosher salt and pepper

1 **cup shelled unsalted pistachios, coarsely chopped**

½ **cup salted roasted sunflower seeds**

1 **cup fresh ricotta**

½ **tsp. finely grated lemon zest plus 2 Tbsp. fresh lemon juice**

1 **cup sunflower sprouts**

  Two 12-oz. heirloom tomatoes, cut into wedges

1. Preheat the oven to 325° and line a large rimmed baking sheet with parchment paper. In a large bowl, toss the oats with the agave, 2 tablespoons of water, ¼ cup of olive oil and 1 teaspoon of salt until the oats are thoroughly coated. Spread the oats on the prepared baking sheet and bake for about 25 minutes, stirring twice, until the granola is light golden. Stir in the pistachios and sunflower seeds and bake for about 10 minutes longer, until golden brown and dry. Let the granola cool on the baking sheet, stirring occasionally.

2. In a medium bowl, mix the ricotta with the lemon zest, 1 tablespoon of the lemon juice and 2 tablespoons of the olive oil. Season with salt and pepper. In another medium bowl, toss the sunflower sprouts with the remaining 1 tablespoon each of olive oil and lemon juice and season with salt and pepper.

3. Arrange the tomato wedges in shallow bowls and season with salt and pepper. Spoon the ricotta around the tomatoes. Scatter the sprouts on top and sprinkle with some of the granola; save the remaining granola for another use. Serve right away. —*Justin Chapple*

MAKE AHEAD The granola can be stored in an airtight container for up to 3 weeks.

Marinated Feta with Nectarine and Tomato Fattoush

Total **45 min**; Serves **4**

In this riff on fattoush, the classic Middle Eastern pita bread salad, F&W's Justin Chapple slices feta into thin slabs to soak in coriander-spiked olive oil. He uses the amped-up feta marinade as a dressing for nectarines, tomatoes and pita chips.

  One 8-oz. block of feta cheese, cut into ½-inch-thick slabs

3 **Tbsp. red wine vinegar**

¼ **cup extra-virgin olive oil**

1 **tsp. crushed coriander seeds**

  Kosher salt and pepper

2 **nectarines—halved, pitted and cut into ½-inch wedges**

2 **medium heirloom tomatoes, cored and cut into 1-inch pieces**

1½ **cups broken pita chips**

¼ **cup finely chopped dill, plus small sprigs for garnish**

1. Arrange the feta in an even layer in a small rimmed dish. In a small bowl, whisk the vinegar with the olive oil, coriander seeds and a pinch each of salt and pepper. Pour the marinade over the feta and let stand at room temperature for 30 minutes, turning the cheese over after 15 minutes.

2. Transfer the feta to plates or a platter. In a large bowl, toss the nectarines with the tomatoes, pita chips and the feta marinade. Add the chopped dill and season with salt and pepper; toss again. Spoon the salad over the feta and garnish with dill sprigs. Serve right away. —*Justin Chapple*

MAKE AHEAD The marinated feta can be refrigerated overnight. Let stand at room temperature for 30 minutes before serving.

Tomato, Haricot Vert and Potato Salad

Total **45 min**; Serves **6**

Chef Enzo Colaiacomo serves a completely vegetarian menu at Eremito, a monastery-inspired retreat in Italy's Umbria region. This rustic Italian salad showcases perfect, in-season produce from the organic garden. Feel free to swap out the summer tomatoes and green beans for roasted root vegetables and fennel in the winter, or asparagus and shaved artichokes in the spring—the possibilities are endless.

1½ **lbs. mixed baby potatoes**

  Kosher salt and pepper

½ **lb. haricots verts, trimmed**

¼ **cup extra-virgin olive oil**

2 **Tbsp. balsamic vinegar**

1 **pint mixed cherry tomatoes, halved**

¾ **cup mixed pitted olives, halved**

½ **cup thinly sliced red onion**

2 **Tbsp. capers, drained and rinsed**

1 **cup lightly packed torn basil leaves**

½ **cup lightly packed parsley leaves**

1. In a medium saucepan, cover the potatoes with cold water and bring to a boil. Add a generous pinch of salt and simmer over moderate heat until the potatoes are tender, about 15 minutes. Drain and let cool slightly, then cut in half.

2. Bring a medium saucepan of water to a boil. Fill a large bowl with ice water. Add the haricots verts and a generous pinch of salt to the saucepan and blanch until crisp-tender, about 2 minutes. Drain and transfer to the ice bath to cool. Drain the beans again and dry thoroughly.

3. In a large bowl, whisk the olive oil with the vinegar. Add the potatoes, beans, tomatoes, olives, red onion and capers and toss gently. Fold in the basil and parsley, season with salt and pepper and serve. —*Enzo Colaiacomo*

WINE Fragrant white blend: 2015 D'Amico Noe Orvieto.

Marinated Eggplant and Tomato Salad with Buffalo Mozzarella

Active **45 min;** Total **4 hr 30 min**
Serves **4 to 6**

Scoring eggplant slices on both sides makes them extra absorbent. They completely soak up the vinegary mix of lemon, garlic and fresh basil.

- **1 lb. small or medium Italian eggplants, peeled and sliced ½ inch thick, slices scored on both sides at ¼-inch intervals**
- **Kosher salt and black pepper**
- **¼ cup extra-virgin olive oil**
- **2 Tbsp. distilled white vinegar**
- **1 Tbsp. fresh lemon juice**
- **3 garlic cloves, crushed**
- **3 basil sprigs, plus basil leaves for garnish**
- **¼ tsp. dried oregano**
- **¼ tsp. crushed red pepper**
- **2 lbs. heirloom tomatoes, coarsely chopped**
- **8 oz. buffalo mozzarella, coarsely torn or chopped**

1. In a colander set over a large bowl, toss the eggplant slices with 1½ teaspoons of salt. Let stand at room temperature for 1 hour, tossing occasionally.

2. Meanwhile, in a large bowl, whisk the olive oil with the vinegar, lemon juice, garlic, basil sprigs, oregano and crushed red pepper; season the marinade lightly with salt and black pepper.

3. Squeeze all of the water from the eggplants and pat dry. Chop into bite-size pieces. Add to the marinade and let stand for 3 hours, stirring occasionally.

4. Add the tomatoes to the eggplant mixture and toss to coat; discard the basil sprigs and garlic. Transfer to a platter and top with the mozzarella and basil leaves. —*Kay Chun*

MAKE AHEAD The recipe can be prepared through Step 3 and refrigerated overnight. Bring the marinated eggplant to room temperature before proceeding.

WINE Bright and herby Grüner Veltliner: 2014 Schloss Gobelsburg Gobelsburger.

Green Papaya Salad with Tomatoes and Basil

Total **40 min;** Serves **10 to 12**

- **½ cup macadamia nuts**
- **5 small Thai chiles**
- **2 garlic cloves**
- **1 tsp. finely grated lime zest plus ½ cup fresh lime juice**
- **¼ cup Asian fish sauce**
- **2 Tbsp. honey**
- **1 tsp. kosher salt**
- **10 cups lightly packed julienned green papaya (from a 3-lb. fruit; see Note on p. 63)**
- **1 lb. green beans, trimmed and cut into 2-inch pieces**
- **2 cups grape tomatoes, halved**
- **½ cup Thai or regular basil, sliced into ¼-inch ribbons**
- **½ cup lightly packed cilantro leaves**

1. Preheat the oven to 350°. In a pie plate, toast the nuts until golden, about 10 minutes. Let cool, then coarsely chop.

2. In a food processor, combine the chiles, garlic, lime zest and juice, fish sauce, honey and salt. Puree until smooth.

3. In a medium bowl, toss the papaya with the green beans, tomatoes, basil and cilantro. Add the vinaigrette and toss again. Fold in the nuts and serve. —*Lee Anne Wong*

Raw Asparagus, Fennel and Pecorino Salad

Total **30 min;** Serves **4**

- **½ cup extra-virgin olive oil**
- **¼ cup fresh lemon juice**
- **Kosher salt and pepper**
- **1 lb. asparagus, peeled and very thinly sliced on the diagonal**
- **1 fennel bulb—halved, cored and very thinly sliced lengthwise**
- **2 red endives—halved, cored and torn into large pieces**
- **3 oz. Berkswell or young pecorino cheese, thinly shaved**
- **2 Tbsp. capers**

In a large bowl, whisk the olive oil with the lemon juice and season with salt and pepper. Add the asparagus, fennel, endives, cheese and capers, season with salt and pepper and toss to coat. Transfer to a platter and serve. —*Margot Henderson*

Spring Vegetable and Sunflower Panzanella

Total **45 min;** Serves **4 to 6**

A classic panzanella (Tuscan bread salad) is a showcase for summer tomatoes. With fresh peas, asparagus and sunflower sprouts, this version from Los Angeles chef Jeremy Fox is an ode to spring.

- **½ lb. sunflower seed bread or other seeded bread, cut into ½-inch cubes**
- **1½ cups shelled English peas (from 1½ lbs. pods)**
- **½ cup extra-virgin olive oil**
- **¼ cup red wine vinegar**
- **2 Tbsp. chopped dill**
- **2 tsp. minced shallot**
- **Kosher salt and pepper**
- **4 Persian cucumbers (12 oz.), thinly sliced (3 cups)**
- **½ lb. pencil-thin asparagus, cut into ½-inch pieces (1½ cups)**
- **1 cup sunflower sprouts**
- **2 Tbsp. sunflower seeds**
- **Lebneh, for serving**

1. Preheat the oven to 375°. Spread the bread on a baking sheet and bake for about 10 minutes, until golden and crisp. Let the croutons cool.

2. Meanwhile, in a small pot of salted boiling water, blanch the peas until tender, 2 minutes. Drain, then transfer to a bowl of ice water to stop the cooking. Drain well and pat dry.

3. In a large bowl, whisk the olive oil, vinegar, dill and shallot and season with salt and pepper; reserve half of the dressing in a small bowl. Add the cucumbers, asparagus, peas and croutons to the large bowl and toss to coat. Mound the salad on plates and top with the sunflower sprouts and seeds. Dollop a spoonful of lebneh on each salad and serve the remaining dressing on the side. —*Jeremy Fox*

MAKE AHEAD The blanched English peas can be refrigerated overnight.

WINE Light Italian white: 2014 Matteo Correggia Roero Arneis.

SPRING VEGETABLE
AND SUNFLOWER
PANZANELLA

SUMMER BEAN SALAD
WITH ROASTED
GARLIC VINAIGRETTE

Haricot Vert Salad with Crispy Potato Chips

Active **30 min**; Total **1 hr**; Serves **8**

F&W's Justin Chapple reimagines traditional green bean casserole as a salad tossed in a punchy mustard vinaigrette. He tops it with crispy oven-baked Yukon Gold potato chips.

- ¼ cup plus 3 Tbsp. extra-virgin olive oil, plus more for greasing
- 1½ lbs. baby Yukon Gold potatoes, sliced ⅛ inch thick
- 1 tsp. finely chopped thyme
  Kosher salt and pepper
- 2 lbs. haricots verts, trimmed
- ¼ cup minced shallot
- 3 Tbsp. Champagne vinegar
- 1½ Tbsp. Dijon mustard
- 1 cup coarsely chopped parsley

1. Preheat the oven to 400° and grease 2 large rimmed baking sheets with olive oil. In a large bowl, combine the potatoes, ¼ cup of the olive oil and the thyme. Season generously with salt and pepper and toss well. Spread the potatoes in a single layer on the prepared baking sheets. Bake for about 15 minutes, until browned on the bottom. Using a thin spatula, flip the potatoes and bake for 15 minutes longer, until they are crisp. Sprinkle with salt and let cool completely.

2. Meanwhile, in a large saucepan of salted boiling water, blanch the haricots verts until crisp-tender, 2 to 3 minutes. Drain and cool under running water. Pat dry with paper towels, then cut the beans in half.

3. In a large serving bowl, whisk the shallot with the vinegar and a pinch of salt and let stand for 5 minutes. Whisk in the mustard and the remaining 3 tablespoons of olive oil. Add the haricots verts and parsley, season generously with salt and pepper and toss to coat. Scatter the crisp potatoes on top before serving. —*Justin Chapple*

MAKE AHEAD The salad can be refrigerated for up to 6 hours. Stir in the parsley before serving. The crispy potato chips can be kept at room temperature overnight.

Summer Bean Salad with Roasted Garlic Vinaigrette

Active **1 hr**; Total **2 hr**; Serves **4**

VINAIGRETTE
- 1 head of garlic, top 1 inch cut off
- ½ cup plus 1 Tbsp. canola oil
- 2 tsp. finely chopped peeled fresh ginger
- ¼ cup seasoned rice vinegar
- ½ tsp. smooth peanut butter
- ½ tsp. gochugaru (Korean red pepper flakes) or Aleppo pepper
- ¼ tsp. sambal oelek
- 1 tsp. toasted sesame oil
  Kosher salt

SALAD
- 5 Tbsp. canola oil
- 1 lb. mixed young beans, such as yellow wax beans, green and purple string beans and dragon tongue beans, trimmed
- 1 Tbsp. minced garlic
- ¼ cup torn basil leaves, plus small whole leaves for garnish
  Kosher salt

1. Make the vinaigrette Preheat the oven to 450°. Drizzle the top of the garlic head with 1 tablespoon of the canola oil and wrap tightly in foil. Roast until tender, 45 minutes to 1 hour. Let cool slightly, then squeeze the garlic cloves from their skins.

2. In a blender, puree half of the garlic cloves (reserve the remaining cloves for another use) with the ginger, rice vinegar, peanut butter, gochugaru and sambal oelek. With the machine on, drizzle in the remaining ½ cup of canola oil and the sesame oil until incorporated. Season the vinaigrette with salt.

3. Make the salad In a large skillet, heat 2 tablespoons of the oil. Add half of the beans and cook over moderately high heat, stirring occasionally, until golden and crisp-tender, about 3 minutes. Transfer to a large bowl. Repeat with another 2 tablespoons of oil and the remaining beans.

4. Wipe out the skillet. Add the remaining 1 tablespoon of oil and the garlic and cook over moderate heat, stirring, until golden, about 2 minutes. Scrape the garlic oil over the beans. Add ½ cup of the vinaigrette and the torn basil and season with salt; toss to coat. Transfer to a platter and garnish with whole basil leaves. Serve warm. —*Michael Gulotta*

WINE Floral-inflected Italian white: 2015 Matteo Correggia Roero Arneis.

Split Green Beans with Anchovy-Parmesan Dressing

Total **45 min**; Serves **4**

At The Clove Club in London, chef Isaac McHale uses a green bean slicer to both destring and halve green beans lengthwise, exposing more bean surface to the savory Caesar-like dressing. Cutting with a knife works just as well.

- 1 lb. green beans, trimmed and halved lengthwise
- 1 cup parsley leaves
- 1 cup baby spinach (1 oz.)
- 3 drained oil-packed anchovy fillets
- ½ cup freshly grated Parmigiano-Reggiano cheese
- 2 tsp. Dijon mustard
- ¼ cup extra-virgin olive oil
- ¼ cup canola oil
  Kosher salt
  Salted toasted sunflower seeds and small mint leaves, for garnish

1. In a saucepan of salted boiling water, blanch the beans until crisp-tender, about 3 minutes. Using tongs, transfer to an ice bath to cool; pat dry. Place the beans in a bowl. Blanch the parsley in the boiling water for 2 minutes. Drain and cool in the ice bath. Squeeze out all of the water.

2. In a blender, pulse the parsley with the spinach, anchovies, cheese and mustard. With the machine on, drizzle in 2 tablespoons of water and both oils and blend until combined. Season with salt.

3. Add ¾ cup of the dressing to the beans, season with salt and toss to coat. Garnish with sunflower seeds and mint; serve the remaining dressing on the side. —*Isaac McHale*

WINE Lush California Chardonnay: 2012 Dierberg Santa Maria Valley.

Raw Artichoke Salad with Mint and Pecorino

Total **40 min;** Serves **4**

½ lemon, plus 2 Tbsp. fresh lemon juice

1½ lbs. baby artichokes (about 12)

¼ cup extra-virgin olive oil

   Kosher salt and pepper

2 oz. Pecorino Romano cheese, shaved (½ cup)

   Mint leaves, for garnish

1. Squeeze the lemon half into a medium bowl of cold water, then add it to the bowl. Working with 1 artichoke at a time, pull off the tough outer leaves and trim a half inch off the top. Trim and peel the stems and halve the artichokes lengthwise. Slice very thinly lengthwise and add to the lemon water.

2. Drain the artichokes and pat dry with paper towels; clean out the bowl. Add the artichokes, olive oil and the 2 tablespoons of lemon juice, season with salt and pepper and toss to coat. Transfer the salad to 4 plates, top with the pecorino and mint and serve. —*Ravinda Weeravardana*

WINE Fruit-forward Italian white: 2015 Principe Pallavicini Roma Malvasia Puntinata.

Watermelon and Snap Pea Salad with Mint

Total **30 min;** Serves **4 to 6**

The secret weapon in this refreshing watermelon salad is the Asian dressing, which gets its umami-rich flavor from fish sauce.

3 Tbsp. unseasoned rice vinegar

2 Tbsp. minced shallot

2 Tbsp. canola oil

2 Tbsp. toasted sesame seeds

1½ Tbsp. Asian fish sauce

   One 2¾-lb. piece of seedless watermelon, peeled and cut into ¾-inch pieces (1½ lbs. of chunks)

½ lb. sugar snap peas, strings removed and peas thinly sliced on a bias

2 cups mint leaves, coarsely chopped

1 cup torn pea shoots (1 oz.)

   Kosher salt

1. In a small bowl, whisk the rice vinegar and shallot; let stand for 5 minutes. Whisk in the canola oil, sesame seeds and fish sauce.

2. In a large serving bowl, toss the watermelon with the snap peas, mint and pea shoots. Add the dressing and toss well. Season with salt and toss again. Serve right away. —*Justin Chapple*

WINE Pear-scented Pinot Gris: 2015 Montinore Estate Willamette Valley.

Kohlrabi Slaw with Harissa Dressing

Total **25 min;** Makes **about 6 cups**

Sweet, with a flavor that reminds us of broccoli stems, kohlrabi is definitely the most overlooked member of the cabbage family. Julienned and slicked with a spicy harissa dressing, it becomes an excellent make-ahead slaw for cookouts and potlucks.

4 kohlrabi (1¼ lbs.), peeled and cut into thin julienne

½ small red cabbage, finely shredded (4 cups)

2 large carrots, peeled and coarsely grated

½ small red onion, finely chopped

⅓ cup chopped cilantro leaves and stems

¼ cup chopped parsley

½ cup Kewpie mayonnaise

2 Tbsp. unseasoned rice wine vinegar

3 Tbsp. harissa

1 Tbsp. red wine vinegar

1 Tbsp. sugar

   Kosher salt

Combine all of the ingredients in a large bowl and toss to coat. Season with salt. —*Eli and Max Sussman*

MAKE AHEAD The kohlrabi slaw can be refrigerated overnight.

Kabocha Squash Salad

Active **30 min;** Total **1 hr;** Serves **6 to 8**

   One 3-lb. kabocha squash—halved, peeled, seeded and cut into ½-inch wedges

2 Tbsp. canola oil

1 tsp. ground cumin

1 tsp. ground coriander

1 tsp. ground fennel

½ tsp. ground ginger

   Fine sea salt and pepper

12 oz. dandelion or other bitter greens, stemmed

1 head of Treviso or radicchio, chopped

½ cup Toasted Pumpkin Seed and Árbol Vinaigrette (recipe follows)

1. Preheat the oven to 400°. Heat 2 large rimmed baking sheets in the oven for at least 10 minutes.

2. In a large bowl, toss the squash with the oil, cumin, coriander, fennel and ginger. Season generously with salt and pepper. Spread the squash wedges on the hot baking sheets in an even layer. Roast until tender and browned on the bottom, about 15 minutes. Let cool completely.

3. In a serving bowl, toss the greens, Treviso and squash with the dressing and season with salt and pepper. Serve right away. —*Jessica Koslow*

WINE Berry-scented Pinot Noir rosé: 2015 Meyer-Näkel.

TOASTED PUMPKIN SEED AND ÁRBOL VINAIGRETTE

Active **15 min;** Total **45 min**
Makes **1¾ cups**

A puree of toasted pumpkin seeds and chiles gives this versatile sweet-smoky dressing a bit of heft.

3 Tbsp. raw pepitas (hulled pumpkin seeds)

½ cup extra-virgin olive oil

½ cup canola oil

10 chiles de árbol, stemmed

2 garlic cloves, crushed

½ cup apple cider vinegar

3 Tbsp. piloncillo (see Note)

   Fine sea salt

1. Heat a cast-iron skillet. Add the pumpkin seeds and toast over moderate heat until golden, 3 to 5 minutes. Transfer to a small bowl. Heat both oils in the skillet until barely shimmering. Add the chiles and cook until browned in spots. Transfer the oil and chiles to a medium bowl, add the garlic and let cool.

2. In a blender, puree the toasted pumpkin seeds with the chile oil, garlic, vinegar and piloncillo until very smooth. Season the vinaigrette with salt. —JK

NOTE Piloncillo is a pure, unrefined cane sugar from Mexico that's pressed into a cone shape and grated.

English Peas with Cider Dressing, Goat Cheese and Flowers
Total **30 min**; Serves **4**

8 oz. shelled fresh English peas

1 Tbsp. chervil or parsley leaves, plus small sprigs for garnish

Kosher salt and pepper

2 Tbsp. extra-virgin olive oil

1 Tbsp. cider vinegar

1 Tbsp. apple juice

1 Tbsp. chopped mint

3 oz. semi-firm goat cheese, such as Ticklemore, thinly sliced and at room temperature

2 oz. pea shoots

Pea or nasturtium flowers, for garnish

1. In a saucepan of salted boiling water, blanch the peas for 1 minute. Drain and transfer to an ice bath to cool. Drain well and pat dry. Transfer to a small bowl.

2. On a cutting board, mince the 1 tablespoon of chervil with ¼ teaspoon of salt. In a small bowl, whisk the olive oil with the cider vinegar and apple juice and season with salt and pepper.

3. Add the mint, chervil salt and 1 tablespoon of the dressing to the peas. Season with salt and pepper and toss to coat. Spoon the peas onto plates and top with a few cheese slices.

4. In another small bowl, toss the pea shoots with 1 tablespoon of the dressing; season with salt and pepper. Spoon onto the cheese; garnish with flowers and chervil sprigs and serve. —James Lowe

Snap Peas with Green Garlic Confit and Dill Vinaigrette
Total **1 hr plus cooling**; Serves **6 to 8**

Chefs Jeremiah Stone and Fabián von Hauske of Contra and Wildair in New York City use dill and garlic-infused oil to transform sweet raw snap peas into a crazy-good summer salad.

2 stalks of green garlic, trimmed and thinly sliced crosswise

1 cup extra-virgin olive oil

¼ cup fresh lemon juice

¼ cup chopped dill

Kosher salt and pepper

1½ lbs. sugar snap peas, trimmed, some chopped and some left whole

6 white button mushrooms, thinly sliced lengthwise

¼ cup torn mint or small mint leaves

1. In a small saucepan, combine the green garlic and olive oil and bring to a simmer. Cook over low heat until the garlic is very tender, about 10 minutes. Remove the pan from the heat and let cool completely. Strain the oil into a small bowl; transfer the green garlic to a medium bowl. Add the lemon juice and dill to the green garlic and slowly whisk in the reserved oil until well blended. Season the vinaigrette with salt and pepper.

2. In a medium bowl, toss the snap peas with ¾ cup of the vinaigrette. Transfer to a platter and scatter the mushrooms on top. Garnish the salad with the mint and serve with the remaining vinaigrette. —Jeremiah Stone and Fabián von Hauske

MAKE AHEAD The green garlic–dill vinaigrette can be refrigerated for up to 2 days.

WINE Juicy sparkling wine, such as a pét-nat: 2014 Costadilà Bianco Colli Trevigiani 280slm.

Grilled Squash, Corn and Kale Salad with Sunflower Seed Vinaigrette
Total **45 min**; Serves **8**

SALAD

2 yellow squash, quartered lengthwise

2 zucchini, quartered lengthwise

4 ears of corn, shucked

¼ cup extra-virgin olive oil, plus more for brushing

Kosher salt and pepper

2 cups shredded red cabbage

1 cup alfalfa or broccoli sprouts

4 cups chopped kale

VINAIGRETTE

⅓ cup salted roasted sunflower seeds

½ shallot, chopped

1 garlic clove, crushed

2 Tbsp. fresh lemon juice

¼ cup lebneh or full-fat Greek yogurt

3 Tbsp. water

1½ Tbsp. za'atar

¼ cup extra-virgin olive oil

Kosher salt

1. **Make the salad** Light a grill. In a large bowl, coat the squash, zucchini and corn with the ¼ cup of olive oil and season with salt and pepper. Oil the grate and grill the vegetables over moderate heat, turning occasionally, until lightly charred and just tender, about 10 minutes for the squash and zucchini and 15 minutes for the corn. Cut the squash and zucchini into 2-inch pieces and return to the bowl. Cut the corn kernels off the cobs and add to the bowl; let cool to room temperature. Stir in the red cabbage, sprouts and kale.

2. **Meanwhile, make the vinaigrette** In a blender, combine all of the ingredients except the olive oil and salt and blend until slightly chunky. With the blender on, drizzle in the olive oil until the dressing is smooth. Season with salt.

3. Add half of the vinaigrette to the salad and toss to coat. Serve, passing the remaining dressing on the side. —Eli and Max Sussman

WINE Citrusy coastal Italian white: 2014 Casal de Ventozela Loureiro Vinho Verde.

Roasted Squash and Mixed Sprouts Bowl

Active **20 min**; Total **50 min**; Serves **4**

"I cook what I want to eat," says chef Jessica Koslow of L.A.'s Sqirl. "Comforting yet bright, light and delicious." Here, she spreads lebneh (Lebanese strained yogurt) in bowls to make a tangy base for her outstanding squash and sprouts salad.

- 2 **medium Delicata squash (1¼ lbs. each)—halved lengthwise, seeds removed and reserved, and squash cut into 2½-inch triangles**
- ¼ **cup plus 2½ Tbsp. extra-virgin olive oil**
- 2 **tsp. Aleppo pepper**
  Kosher salt and black pepper
- 1 **tsp. coriander seeds**
- 2 **cups lightly packed cilantro leaves**
- 1 **cup lightly packed parsley leaves**
- 1 **garlic clove, minced**
- 1 **tsp. minced serrano chile**
- 1½ **tsp. finely grated lime zest**
- ¼ **cup ice water, plus 2 large ice cubes**
- 2 **cups mixed sprouts, such as alfalfa, mung bean and lentil**
- ½ **cup pomegranate seeds**
- 1 **cup lebneh**
  Maldon salt, for sprinkling

1. Preheat the oven to 400°. On a large rimmed baking sheet, toss the squash with ¼ cup of the olive oil and the Aleppo pepper. Season generously with salt and black pepper and roast for about 30 minutes, until browned in spots and just tender.

2. Meanwhile, in a pie plate, toss the reserved squash seeds with ½ tablespoon of the olive oil and season with salt and black pepper. Spread in an even layer and bake for about 15 minutes, stirring every 5 minutes, until lightly browned and crisp. Let cool.

3. In a small skillet, toast the coriander seeds over moderate heat until fragrant, about 2 minutes. Transfer to a mortar and grind to a powder. Transfer the ground coriander to a blender; add the cilantro, parsley, garlic, chile, ½ teaspoon of the lime zest and the ice water and ice cubes. Puree until nearly smooth. Season the dressing with salt.

4. In a medium bowl, toss the sprouts and pomegranate seeds with the remaining 2 tablespoons of olive oil and 1 teaspoon of lime zest. Season with salt. Spread the lebneh in 4 shallow bowls. Mound the salad in the bowls and top with the squash. Sprinkle with the toasted squash seeds and a little Maldon salt and serve, passing the dressing at the table. —*Jessica Koslow*

WINE Rhône-style white: 2013 Qupé Marsanne from California's Central Coast.

Summer Squash with Lemon Curd and Citron Vinaigrette

Active **1 hr 30 min**; Total **4 hr**; Serves **4**

LEMON CURD

- ⅓ **cup fresh lemon juice**
- 3 **large eggs**
- 2½ **Tbsp. sugar**
- 1 **Tbsp. thinly sliced lemongrass, tender inner bulb only**
- 2 **tsp. minced peeled fresh ginger**
- 4 **Tbsp. unsalted butter, cut into tablespoons and at room temperature**
- ½ **Tbsp. extra-virgin olive oil**

ZUCCHINI-HERB PUREE

- 1 **medium yellow squash (8 oz.)—quartered lengthwise, seeded and cut into 3-inch pieces**
- 1 **small zucchini (5 oz.)—quartered lengthwise, seeded and cut into 3-inch pieces**
- ½ **cup packed basil leaves**
- ½ **cup packed parsley leaves**
- ½ **cup packed dill**
- 2 **Tbsp. extra-virgin olive oil**
  Kosher salt

VINAIGRETTE

- 2 **Tbsp. fresh lemon juice**
- 2 **tsp. white wine vinegar, preferably Chardonnay**
- 1 **Tbsp. chopped tarragon**
- ¼ **tsp. honey**
- ¼ **cup grapeseed or canola oil**
- 2 **Tbsp. extra-virgin olive oil**
  Kosher salt
- 4 **oz. marinated goat- or sheep-milk cheese, cut into chunks, for serving**
  Small tarragon, dill or watercress sprigs, thinly sliced chiles and puffed rice, for garnish

1. Make the lemon curd In a blender, blend the lemon juice, eggs, sugar, lemongrass and ginger until smooth. Strain the mixture through a fine sieve set over a heat-proof medium bowl, pressing on the solids.

2. Place the bowl over—not in—a medium saucepan of barely simmering water and cook the curd over low heat, whisking, until thickened enough to coat the back of a spoon, about 5 minutes. Remove the bowl from the heat and whisk in the butter until incorporated, then whisk in the olive oil. Press a sheet of plastic wrap directly on the surface of the curd and refrigerate until cold, about 3 hours.

3. Meanwhile, make the zucchini-herb puree In a medium saucepan of salted boiling water, blanch the squash and zucchini for 30 seconds; using a slotted spoon, transfer to an ice bath to cool completely. Blanch the herbs just until wilted, about 30 seconds. Drain and transfer to the ice bath to cool. Drain the squash, zucchini and herbs; pat the squash and zucchini dry and squeeze out all the excess water from the herbs. Reserve the squash in a small bowl. In a blender, puree the zucchini with the herbs and ½ cup of water until smooth. With the machine on, gradually blend in the oil. Season the puree with salt.

4. Make the vinaigrette In a small bowl, combine the lemon juice, vinegar, tarragon and honey. Gradually whisk in both oils until emulsified. Season with salt.

5. Spread a thin layer of the zucchini puree on each of 4 plates. Dollop a few small teaspoons of the lemon curd on the puree. Toss the squash with 2 tablespoons of the vinaigrette and season with salt (reserve the remaining vinaigrette for another use). Arrange 3 pieces of squash on each plate. Arrange the marinated cheese on the plates and garnish with herb sprigs, sliced chiles and puffed rice. —*Brad Kilgore*

MAKE AHEAD The zucchini puree can be refrigerated overnight. The lemon curd and vinaigrette can be refrigerated separately for up to 3 days.

WINE Fruit-forward sparkling wine: 2014 Bisol Crede Valdobbiadene Prosecco Superiore Brut.

ROASTED SQUASH
AND MIXED SPROUTS

BEET POKE
WITH AVOCADO-
WASABI MASH

Cathal Armstrong's Favorite Salad

Active **25 min**; Total **1 hr**; Serves **4**

Virginia chef Cathal Armstrong's favorite salad is a nutrient-packed combo of avocado, beets, eggs, pumpkin seeds and greens dressed in a mustardy vinaigrette.

- 8 **small beets (1 lb.)**
- 4 **large eggs**
- ¼ **cup raw pepitas (hulled pumpkin seeds)**
- ¼ **cup sherry vinegar**
- 2 **Tbsp. Dijon mustard**
- ½ **cup extra-virgin olive oil**
   Kosher salt and pepper
- 1 **Hass avocado, chopped**
- ½ **cup minced red onion**
- 12 **cups mixed baby lettuces (10 oz.)**
- 4 **scallions, thinly sliced**

1. Preheat the oven to 450°. Wrap the beets in foil and roast for about 45 minutes, until tender. Let cool slightly, then slip off the skins. Quarter the beets.

2. In a small saucepan, cover the eggs with 1 inch of water and bring to a boil. Let stand off the heat, covered, for 10 minutes. Drain and transfer the eggs to a bowl of ice water to cool. Peel and quarter the eggs.

3. In a small skillet, toast the pumpkin seeds over low heat, stirring, until they are golden, about 5 minutes.

4. In a small bowl, whisk the vinegar with the mustard. Whisking constantly, drizzle in the olive oil until incorporated. Season the vinaigrette with salt and pepper.

5. In a large bowl, combine the beets, avocado and onion. Add ¼ cup of the vinaigrette, season with salt and pepper and toss gently. Transfer the salad to plates. Add the eggs and drizzle with 2 tablespoons of the vinaigrette. Wipe out the bowl. Add the lettuce, scallions and the remaining vinaigrette, season with salt and pepper and toss. Mound the greens on the vegetables, garnish with the pumpkin seeds and serve. *—Cathal Armstrong*

MAKE AHEAD The cooked beets and hard-boiled eggs can be refrigerated for 2 days.

WINE Bright, pear-inflected Italian white: 2013 Zuani Collio Bianco.

Beet Poke with Avocado-Wasabi Mash

Active **45 min**; Total **2 hr 45 min**
Serves **6 to 8**

This salad is a playful take on poke, the Hawaiian dish of seasoned raw fish. The cubes of roasted beets mimic raw tuna.

- 2½ **lbs. medium beets, scrubbed**
- 1 **navel orange, halved**
   One 3-inch piece of fresh ginger, sliced and smashed
- 2 **Tbsp. extra-virgin olive oil**
   Kosher salt and pepper
- ⅓ **cup macadamia nuts**
- ½ **cup wakame seaweed (see Note)**
- ¼ **cup plus 2 Tbsp. unseasoned rice vinegar**
- 1 **Tbsp. toasted sesame oil**
- ½ **cup very thinly sliced sweet onion**
- ¼ **cup thinly sliced scallions**
- 2 **Hass avocados—peeled, pitted and cut into large chunks**
- 2 **tsp. fresh lemon juice**
- 2 **tsp. wasabi powder**
- 1 **golden beet, peeled and sliced paper-thin, for garnish (optional)**

1. Preheat the oven to 350°. Set the beets in a baking dish. Squeeze the juice from the orange halves over the beets; add the orange halves and ginger to the dish. Drizzle the beets with the oil and season with salt and pepper. Cover tightly with foil and bake for 1 hour and 15 minutes, until the beets are tender. Let cool, then peel and cut into 1-inch pieces. Leave the oven on.

2. Meanwhile, toast the nuts in a pie plate until golden, about 10 minutes. Let cool, then coarsely chop. In a bowl, cover the wakame with cold water and let stand until rehydrated, about 5 minutes; drain. Rinse under cold water, then drain again.

3. In a large bowl, toss the beets with the wakame, toasted nuts, vinegar, sesame oil, onion and scallions. Season the poke with salt and pepper. Refrigerate until slightly chilled, about 15 minutes.

4. In another bowl, mash the avocados with the lemon juice, wasabi powder and 1 tablespoon of water. Season the avocado with salt and pepper. Refrigerate until chilled, about 15 minutes.

5. To serve, mound the poke on plates and garnish with the golden beet, if using. Pass the avocado-wasabi mash at the table. *—Ed Kenney*

NOTE Wakame is dried, lightly sweet seaweed often used in salads and soups. It's available at Asian markets and from amazon.com.

MAKE AHEAD The beet poke can be refrigerated overnight. Add the nuts, then serve.

Vietnamese Green Papaya and Beet Salad

Total **30 min**; Serves **4**

- 2 **Tbsp. turbinado sugar**
- 2 **Tbsp. Asian fish sauce**
- ¼ **cup fresh lime juice**
- 1 **tsp. canola oil**
- ½ **cup salted dry-roasted peanuts**
- ¼ **tsp. ground cumin**
- 1 **head Little Gem lettuce, light green leaves only, thinly sliced**
- 2 **cups julienned green papaya (see Note)**
- 1½ **cups julienned peeled yellow or Chioggia beet (from 1 large beet)**
- ½ **cup julienned carrot**
- ¼ **cup finely diced tomatillo (from 1 large husked tomatillo)**
- ½ **cup lightly packed cilantro leaves**
- ½ **cup lightly packed mint leaves**
- 1 **Tbsp. toasted sesame seeds**

1. In a medium saucepan, combine the sugar and fish sauce and cook over moderate heat, stirring, until the sugar dissolves, about 3 minutes. Remove from the heat and whisk in the lime juice. Let cool.

2. Meanwhile, in a small skillet, heat the canola oil. Add the peanuts and cumin and cook over moderate heat, tossing, until fragrant, about 1 minute.

3. Spread the lettuce in a serving bowl. In another bowl, toss the fruit and vegetables, herbs, peanuts and sesame seeds with the dressing. Pile on top of the lettuce and serve right away. *—Angela Dimayuga*

NOTE Green (unripe) papayas are very firm, with dark green skin; if they're unavailable, you can substitute peeled daikon or unripe mango.

WINE Fruit-forward, aromatic white: 2013 Trimbach Pinot Blanc from Alsace.

Niçoise Salad with Baby Artichokes

Total **1 hr 15 min; Serves 4 to 6**

Thinly shaved baby artichokes add refreshing crunch to an otherwise classic niçoise salad. The recipe is from L'Orangerie bistro at La Bastide de Gordes, a château-turned-hotel in the south of France.

- ½ cup plus 2 Tbsp. extra-virgin olive oil
- ¼ cup balsamic vinegar
  Kosher salt and pepper
- 1 dozen quail eggs or 4 large eggs
- 8 oz. green beans, trimmed
- ½ lemon
- 4 baby artichokes
- 4 oz. mixed baby greens (8 cups)
- 4 tomatoes (1½ lbs.), cut into wedges
- 3 bell peppers, preferably a mix of colors, thinly sliced
  Two 7-oz. cans good-quality tuna in olive oil, drained and flaked
- 12 salted anchovy fillets, bones discarded, rinsed and patted dry
- 12 niçoise olives
  Chopped basil, for garnish

1. In a small bowl, gradually whisk the olive oil into the vinegar until incorporated. Season with salt and pepper.

2. In a medium saucepan, cover the quail eggs with 2 inches of water and bring to a boil. Cover the pan, remove from the heat and let stand for 5 minutes. (If using large eggs, let stand off the heat for 10 minutes.) Transfer the eggs to a bowl of ice water and let cool completely. Peel and halve them.

3. Meanwhile, in a medium saucepan of salted boiling water, blanch the beans until crisp-tender, about 3 minutes. Drain and transfer to another ice bath to cool.

4. Squeeze the lemon half into a bowl of cold water. Snap off the outer leaves of 1 artichoke. Using a sharp knife, cut off its top half and trim the base and stem. Using a melon baller or a spoon, scoop out the furry choke. Add the artichoke to the lemon water. Repeat with the remaining artichokes. Very thinly slice the artichokes and return them to the lemon water.

5. Arrange the baby greens on a platter. Drain the artichokes and pat dry with paper towels. Arrange the artichokes, tomatoes, bell peppers, tuna, anchovies, olives, eggs and green beans on the greens in rows; alternatively, gently mix the salad. Drizzle half of the dressing over the salad and garnish with basil. Serve the remaining dressing on the side. —*L'Orangerie, Gordes, France*

MAKE AHEAD The dressing can be refrigerated for up to 3 days.

WINE Minerally Côtes de Provence rosé: 2015 Château de Roquefort Corail.

Chef's Salad with Prosciutto and Tarragon Dressing

Total **40 min; Serves 4**

TARRAGON DRESSING

- 8 oz. crème fraîche
- 6 Tbsp. buttermilk
- 2 Tbsp. mayonnaise
- 1 Tbsp. fresh lemon juice
- 1 tsp. finely grated garlic
- 2 Tbsp. chopped tarragon
- 2 Tbsp. chopped chives
- 1 Tbsp. chopped parsley
  Kosher salt and pepper

SALAD

- 1 head of iceberg lettuce (1 lb.), very coarsely chopped
- 8 oz. cherry tomatoes, halved
- 8 oz. smoked turkey, cut into ½-inch cubes
- 4 oz. sharp white cheddar cheese, cubed
- 2 oz. sliced prosciutto or speck, cut into 1-inch pieces
- 2 large hard-cooked eggs, halved
  Tarragon and parsley leaves and snipped chives, for garnish

1. Make the dressing In a medium bowl, combine all of the ingredients and mix well. Season with salt and pepper.

2. Make the salad Mound the lettuce in shallow bowls. Arrange the tomatoes, turkey, cheese, prosciutto and eggs on top and garnish with tarragon, parsley and chives. Serve the tarragon dressing on the side. —*Ramon Siewert*

MAKE AHEAD The dressing can be refrigerated overnight.

WINE Full-bodied white: 2014 Lieu Dit Santa Ynez Valley Chenin Blanc.

Grilled Tofu and Heirloom Tomato Salad

Total **1 hr; Serves 4 to 6**

- ¼ cup apple cider vinegar
- 2 Tbsp. mirin
- 1½ Tbsp. toasted sesame oil
- 1 Tbsp. plus 1 tsp. soy sauce
- 1 tsp. gochugaru (Korean red pepper flakes)
- 1 garlic clove, finely grated
  Kosher salt and pepper
- 2 blocks extra-firm tofu (14 oz. each), drained
- 5 tsp. canola oil, plus more for brushing
- ¾ lb. asparagus, trimmed
- 6 small carrots, halved lengthwise
- 4 baby zucchini, thinly sliced lengthwise on a mandoline
- 1 medium summer squash, thinly sliced lengthwise on a mandoline
- 8 ears of fresh or drained canned baby corn, halved lengthwise
- 1 lb. heirloom tomatoes, sliced ¼ inch thick
- 4 large radishes, thinly sliced on a mandoline
- 2 oz. baby spinach (about 4 cups)
- 2 oz. mixed baby lettuces (about 4 cups)
  Pea shoots and black and white sesame seeds, for garnish

1. In a small bowl, whisk the cider vinegar with the mirin, sesame oil, soy sauce, gochugaru and garlic; season with salt.

2. Slice the tofu ½ inch thick and pat the slices thoroughly dry with paper towels. Cut each slice into 4 triangles and arrange on a baking sheet. Generously brush the tofu all over with canola oil and season with salt and pepper.

3. Light a grill or heat a grill pan and oil the grate. Grill the tofu in batches over moderately high heat, turning once, until lightly charred, about 5 minutes per batch. Transfer to a plate.

4. In a medium bowl, toss the asparagus and carrots with 2 teaspoons of canola oil and season with salt and pepper. Grill, turning occasionally, until the vegetables are lightly charred and crisp-tender, about 8 minutes. Transfer to a rimmed baking sheet. In the same bowl, toss the zucchini and summer squash with 2 teaspoons of canola oil and season with salt and pepper. Grill in batches over moderately high heat, turning once, until lightly charred and just tender, 1 to 2 minutes per batch. Transfer to the baking sheet with the asparagus and carrots. In the medium bowl, toss the baby corn with the remaining 1 teaspoon of canola oil and season with salt and pepper. Grill over moderately high heat until lightly charred, about 3 minutes. Transfer to the baking sheet.

5. Arrange the tomatoes, radishes, spinach and baby lettuces on a large platter. Top with the tofu and grilled vegetables and drizzle with the dressing. Garnish with pea shoots and black and white sesame seeds and serve immediately. —*Judy Joo*

MAKE AHEAD The dressing can be refrigerated for up to 1 week.

WINE Zesty Sauvignon Blanc: 2014 Kunin Wines Happy Canyon McGinley Vineyard.

Shiso Ranch Dressing
Total **10 min**; Makes **2 cups**

Fragrant shiso leaves add a zippy, almost mint-like flavor to ranch dressing. Look for the herb at Asian markets.

- ¾ cup mayonnaise
- ¾ cup sour cream
- 2 Tbsp. fresh lemon juice
- 2 Tbsp. buttermilk
- 1½ Tbsp. white balsamic vinegar
- 1 garlic clove, finely grated
- 1 tsp. Dijon mustard
- ½ cup finely chopped shiso leaves
- 2 Tbsp. finely chopped chives
- 2 Tbsp. finely chopped tarragon
- Kosher salt and pepper

In a medium bowl, whisk the mayonnaise with the sour cream, lemon juice, buttermilk, vinegar, garlic and mustard. Fold in the shiso, chives and tarragon and season with salt and pepper. —*Ravi Kapur*

SERVE WITH Grilled asparagus, mushrooms and steamed artichokes. The dressing is also great as a dip for crudités.

MAKE AHEAD The dressing can be refrigerated for up to 3 days.

Bonito Caesar Dressing
Active **20 min**; Total **2 hr 15 min**
Makes **1½ cups**

A simple dashi (made with bonito fish flakes and dried kelp) and the Japanese spice mix togarashi add depth and complexity to this fantastic Caesar dressing.

- One 5-by-3-inch piece of kombu (see Note)
- ¼ cup bonito flakes (see Note)
- 4 large egg yolks
- 1½ Tbsp. fresh lemon juice
- 1½ Tbsp. Dijon mustard
- ½ Tbsp. white balsamic vinegar
- 1 tsp. finely grated garlic
- ¼ tsp. togarashi (see Note)
- A few drops of Tabasco
- ¼ cup freshly grated Parmigiano-Reggiano cheese
- 1 cup rice bran oil or other neutral oil
- Kosher salt

1. In a large saucepan, cover the kombu with 4 cups of water and bring to a boil. Reduce the heat and simmer gently for 30 minutes. Remove the pan from the heat and stir in the bonito flakes; let stand at room temperature for 1 hour. Strain the dashi into a bowl and let cool to room temperature.

2. In a food processor, combine the egg yolks, lemon juice, Dijon mustard, vinegar, garlic, togarashi, Tabasco and cheese and pulse to combine. With the machine on, drizzle in the rice bran oil, then drizzle in ¼ cup of the dashi until incorporated (reserve the remaining dashi for another use). Season with salt. —*Ravi Kapur*

SERVE WITH Little Gem lettuce for dipping, or toss to make a salad.

NOTE Kombu is dried kelp. Bonito flakes are made from smoked bonito or tuna. Togarashi is a Japanese blend of chiles and sesame. All are available at Japanese markets and from amazon.com.

MAKE AHEAD The dressing can be refrigerated for up to 1 week.

Shrimp Taco Salad Bowls
Total **45 min**; Serves **4**

F&W's Justin Chapple has a DIY hack for making restaurant-style taco bowls without the hassle of deep-frying: He stuffs tortillas between the cups of an inverted muffin pan and bakes them. He fills the bowls with a citrusy slaw and spicy shrimp. You can also use this trick to make an edible bowl for guacamole, which Justin calls a "guacabowle."

- Four 10-inch flour tortillas
- ⅓ cup mayonnaise
- 2½ Tbsp. fresh lime juice
- ½ tsp. ground cumin
- 8 cups shredded green and red cabbage (1 lb.)
- 1 cup chopped cilantro, plus more for serving
- 3 pickled jalapeños, seeded and thinly sliced (¼ cup)
- Kosher salt and pepper
- ¾ lb. large shrimp, shelled and deveined
- ¾ tsp. chili powder
- 2 Tbsp. extra-virgin olive oil
- Sliced radishes and diced avocado, for serving

1. Preheat the oven to 400°. Invert a jumbo muffin tin on a work surface. In 2 batches, gently stuff the tortillas between the upturned muffin cups to form bowls. Bake for 15 minutes, until crisp; let cool.

2. Meanwhile, in a large bowl, whisk the mayonnaise, lime juice and cumin. Add the cabbage, 1 cup of cilantro and the jalapeños and toss. Season with salt and pepper.

3. In a large bowl, toss the shrimp and chili powder; season with salt and pepper. In a large skillet, heat the oil until shimmering. Add the shrimp and cook over moderately high heat, turning once, until just white throughout, about 3 minutes. Transfer the shrimp to a plate.

4. Fill the taco shells with the slaw and shrimp. Sprinkle with chopped cilantro, sliced radishes and diced avocado. Serve. —*Justin Chapple*

SOUPS
AND STEWS

A traditional Nordic cooking shed, where families prepare big-batch stews. OPPOSITE Celery Root Bisque and Broccoli-Spinach Soup (p. 70).

Provençal Vegetable Soup

Active **30 min**; Total **1 hr plus overnight soaking**; Serves **4 to 6**

Star chef Eric Ripert of New York City's Le Bernardin gives his vegetable-packed soup exceptional flavor with pistou, a Provençal basil puree that's similar to pesto. To make the soup vegetarian, omit the ham and substitute vegetable stock for the chicken stock.

½ cup dried navy beans, soaked overnight and drained

  One 2-inch square of ham rind or meat

2 thyme sprigs, 4 parsley sprigs and 1 bay leaf, tied together with kitchen twine

1 qt. chicken stock or low-sodium broth

1 medium tomato, cored

3 cups lightly packed basil leaves

2 large garlic cloves, finely chopped

½ cup extra-virgin olive oil

  Fine sea salt and pepper

1 medium carrot, cut into ¼-inch dice

1 medium fennel bulb—halved lengthwise, cored and cut into ¼-inch dice (1 cup)

1 small zucchini, cut into ¼-inch dice

1 small onion, cut into ¼-inch dice

6 oz. haricots verts, cut into 1-inch lengths

1. In a large saucepan, cover the navy beans, ham rind and herb bundle with the chicken stock and 2 cups of water. Bring to a boil, then reduce the heat to moderately low and simmer until the beans are tender, about 30 minutes.

2. Meanwhile, bring a medium saucepan of water to a simmer. Using a sharp paring knife, score an X on the bottom of the tomato. Add to the saucepan and blanch just until the skin starts to peel, about 30 seconds. Transfer the tomato to an ice water bath to cool. Peel and seed the tomato, then cut it into ¼-inch dice.

3. In a blender or food processor, pulse the basil with the garlic until finely chopped. With the machine on, gradually add the olive oil until incorporated. Season the pistou with salt and pepper.

4. Remove the ham and herb bundle from the beans. Add the tomato, carrot, fennel, zucchini, onion and haricots verts and season with a generous pinch of salt. Simmer over moderately low heat until the vegetables are tender, about 12 minutes. Season the soup with salt and pepper and ladle into bowls. Serve with the pistou, stirring it into the soup at the table. —*Eric Ripert*

MAKE AHEAD The soup and pistou can be refrigerated overnight. Reheat the soup; serve the pistou at room temperature.

WINE Minerally Provençal white: 2013 La Bastide Blanche Bandol Blanc.

German Chicken Soup with Dumplings

Active **50 min**; Total **3 hr**; Serves **8 to 10**

Minnesota blogger Molly Yeh loves the traditional German soup known as knoephla so much she served it at her wedding. Her take, studded with deliciously chewy dumplings, is hearty and satisfying.

DUMPLINGS

1 cup all-purpose flour

½ tsp. baking powder

½ tsp. kosher salt

  Pinch of black pepper

  Pinch of freshly grated nutmeg

SOUP

2 Tbsp. unsalted butter

1 large onion, finely chopped

2 large carrots, finely chopped

2 celery ribs, finely chopped

  Kosher salt and pepper

2 garlic cloves, minced

¼ tsp. freshly grated nutmeg

7 cups chicken or vegetable stock or low-sodium broth

2 bay leaves

1½ lbs. red potatoes, peeled and cut into ½-inch pieces

½ cup heavy cream

1. Make the dumplings In a medium bowl, whisk the flour with the baking powder, salt, pepper and nutmeg. Add 6 tablespoons of water and mix with a wooden spoon until a shaggy dough forms. Turn the dough out onto a lightly floured work surface and knead until smooth, about 5 minutes. Transfer the dough to a small bowl, cover with plastic wrap and let rest at room temperature for 1 hour.

2. Line a baking sheet with parchment paper. Roll the dough into a ½-inch-thick rope, then cut into ½-inch pieces. Transfer the dumplings to the prepared sheet and cover with a damp kitchen towel.

3. Make the soup In a large enameled cast-iron casserole, melt the butter. Add the onion, carrots and celery and season with salt and pepper. Cook over moderate heat, stirring occasionally, until softened, about 10 minutes. Add the garlic and nutmeg and cook, stirring, until fragrant, about 1 minute. Stir in the stock, bay leaves and potatoes and bring to a boil. Add the dumplings, cover and cook over moderately low heat, stirring occasionally, until the dumplings are puffed and cooked through, about 30 minutes. Stir in the cream and season with salt and pepper. Discard the bay leaves and serve. —*Molly Yeh*

WINE Bright Riesling: 2014 Leitz Eins Zwei Dry 3.

CHEF'S KITCHEN WISDOM

Essential Soup Starter

To make full-flavored chicken broth, Thomas John, the chef at Piperi Mediterranean Grill in Boston, slow-simmers chicken bones for two hours with vegetables and herbs like onions, carrots, celery and parsley as well as a knob of fresh ginger. For the most flexibility, he advises against salting the broth. "What if you decide to make a soup with something salty like chorizo?" he asks. "You can always salt later."

Creamy Spinach Soup with Dill

⟳ Total **45 min**; Serves **4**

"I tend toward soups that taste mostly of the vegetable," says Magnus Nilsson of Fäviken in Järpen, Sweden. "In fact, the ones I make are almost purees, like my spinach soup, loosened with a little stock and some cream, with a pretty garnish of hard-boiled egg."

- 1 lb. curly spinach, stemmed (20 cups)
- 2 Tbsp. unsalted butter
- 2 Tbsp. all-purpose flour
- 2 small shallots, finely chopped
- 4 cups chicken stock or low-sodium broth
- 1 cup heavy cream
- 2 Tbsp. chopped dill, plus more for garnish

  Kosher salt and white pepper

  Pinch of freshly grated nutmeg
- 2 hard-boiled eggs, halved or quartered, for garnish

1. In a pot of salted boiling water, blanch the spinach until very tender, about 3 minutes. Drain and transfer to a bowl of ice water to cool. Drain well and squeeze out any excess water. Chop the spinach.

2. In a large saucepan, melt the butter. Add the flour and cook over moderate heat, stirring, until golden, about 2 minutes. Add the shallots and cook until softened, about 2 minutes. Whisk in the chicken stock and bring to a boil. Cook for 5 minutes. Stir in the heavy cream and the 2 tablespoons of dill; cook until slightly thickened, about 5 minutes. Stir in the spinach.

3. Working in 2 batches, puree the soup in a blender until smooth; season with salt, white pepper and nutmeg. Ladle into bowls, garnish with the eggs and chopped dill and serve. —*Magnus Nilsson*

Broccoli-Spinach Soup with Crispy Broccoli Florets and Croutons

📷 PAGE 66

Active **45 min**; Total **1 hr 15 min**
Serves **8 to 10**

- ¼ cup plus 2 Tbsp. extra-virgin olive oil
- 1 medium yellow onion, finely chopped
- 2 large garlic cloves, sliced

  Kosher salt and pepper
- 2 cups chicken stock or broth

  One 8-oz. baking potato, peeled and cut into 1-inch pieces
- 2 lbs. broccoli—stems peeled and sliced, florets cut into ½-inch pieces

  One 5-oz. package baby spinach
- 4 oz. sourdough or ciabatta bread, cut into ½-inch dice
- 1 Tbsp. red wine vinegar

  Snipped chives, for garnish

1. Preheat the oven to 400°. In a large pot, heat ¼ cup of the olive oil. Add the onion and garlic and season with salt and pepper. Cook over moderate heat, stirring occasionally, until softened and just starting to brown, 6 to 8 minutes. Add 2 cups of water and the stock, potato, broccoli stems and two-thirds of the florets. Bring to a boil over high heat, then simmer over moderate heat, stirring occasionally, until the potato and broccoli are very soft, about 30 minutes. Stir in the spinach until wilted.

2. Meanwhile, on one side of a large rimmed baking sheet, toss the remaining broccoli florets with 1 tablespoon of the oil and season with salt and pepper. In a medium bowl, toss the bread with the remaining 1 tablespoon of oil and season with salt and pepper. Bake the broccoli florets for 10 minutes. Spread the bread on the other half of the baking sheet and bake for about 10 minutes, until the florets and croutons are browned and crisp.

3. Working in batches, puree the soup in a blender until very smooth, 1 to 2 minutes. Stir in the vinegar and season with salt and pepper. Ladle the soup into bowls and top with the crispy broccoli and croutons. Garnish with snipped chives and serve. —*Justin Chapple*

MAKE AHEAD The soup can be refrigerated overnight. The broccoli florets and croutons can be made early in the day and stored at room temperature.

Celery Root Bisque with Walnut-Parsley Gremolata

📷 PAGE 66

Active **45 min**; Total **1 hr 30 min**; Serves **8**

Sneaking a small piece of Parmesan cheese into this silky bisque gives it a boost of umami. Topping it with a vibrant walnut-and-parsley gremolata adds a terrific crunch.

- 1 Tbsp. unsalted butter
- 1 large leek, white and light green parts only, thinly sliced
- 5 garlic cloves, crushed
- 2½ lbs. celery root, peeled and cut into 1-inch dice (8 cups)

  One 2-inch chunk of Parmigiano-Reggiano cheese (1 oz.), plus ¼ cup freshly grated cheese
- 2 cups chicken stock or low-sodium broth
- ½ cup walnuts
- ¼ cup extra-virgin olive oil
- ½ cup coarsely chopped parsley
- ½ cup heavy cream

  Kosher salt and pepper

1. In a large saucepan, melt the butter. Add the leek and garlic and cook over moderate heat, stirring occasionally, until softened, about 5 minutes. Add the celery root, Parmesan chunk, stock and 5 cups of water and bring to a simmer. Cover and cook over moderately low heat, stirring occasionally, until the celery root is tender, about 40 minutes.

2. Meanwhile, preheat the oven to 375°. Spread the walnuts in a pie plate and toast for 5 to 7 minutes, until golden. Let cool, then finely chop and transfer to a bowl. Add the oil, parsley and grated cheese and mix well.

3. In a blender, puree the soup in 2 batches until very smooth. Pour into a clean saucepan and stir in the heavy cream; season with salt and pepper and reheat if necessary. Serve topped with the walnut gremolata. —*Kay Chun*

MAKE AHEAD The soup can be refrigerated for up to 2 days.

CREAMY SPINACH
SOUP WITH DILL

SWEET POTATO–
COCONUT SOUP
WITH THAI CURRY

Tom Kha Gai

⏱ Total **40 min**; Serves **4**

"Ask Americans to name a Thai dish they love, and they say, 'Pad thai...and that amazing chicken soup with coconut,'" says *Bizarre Foods* host Andrew Zimmern. "The soup has a name: tom kha gai." He gives his quick version tremendous flavor with fish sauce, chili paste, lemongrass and kaffir lime leaves.

- 1 **lb. skinless, boneless chicken thighs, trimmed and sliced crosswise ¼ inch thick**
- ¼ **cup Asian fish sauce**
- 3 **cups chicken stock or low-sodium broth**
- 3 **Tbsp. Thai chili paste (nam prik pao; see Note)**
- 2 **Tbsp. light brown sugar**
- 2 **fresh or frozen kaffir lime leaves**
- 1 **stalk of fresh lemongrass, tender inner white part only, minced (about 2 Tbsp.)**

  Two 14-oz. cans unsweetened coconut milk
- ½ **lb. shiitake mushrooms, stems removed and caps thinly sliced**
- ¼ **cup fresh lime juice**
- 2 **Thai chiles, seeded and very thinly sliced on the diagonal, plus more for garnish**

  Kosher salt
- ⅓ **cup cilantro leaves, for garnish**

  Limes wedges, for serving

1. In a medium bowl, toss the chicken with the fish sauce.

2. In a medium saucepan, combine the stock with the chili paste, sugar, lime leaves and lemongrass and bring to a boil over moderately high heat. Stir in the coconut milk and simmer for 5 minutes.

3. Add the chicken and fish sauce to the saucepan along with the shiitake; simmer, stirring occasionally, until the chicken is cooked through and the mushrooms are tender, about 5 minutes. Remove from the heat and discard the lime leaves. Stir in the lime juice and chiles and season with salt.

4. Ladle the soup into bowls, garnish with the cilantro and sliced chiles and serve with lime wedges. —*Andrew Zimmern*

NOTE Nam prik pao is a sweet and spicy Thai condiment. It's available at Asian markets and online at kalustyans.com.

WINE Briny, citrus-inflected white: 2014 Argyros Santorini Assyrtiko.

Sweet Potato–Coconut Soup with Thai Curry

Active **20 min**; Total **1 hr**; Serves **8 to 10**

Cookbook author Melissa Clark uses coconut in three forms—oil, milk and toasted flakes—in this fragrant and lovely twist on a classic fall soup.

- 3 **Tbsp. organic coconut oil**
- 2 **onions (1 lb.), chopped**
- 2 **medium green bell peppers, chopped**
- 2 **Tbsp. Thai red curry paste**
- 2 **Tbsp. minced fresh ginger**
- 2 **garlic cloves, minced**
- 3½ **lbs. sweet potatoes, peeled and cut into 1½-inch pieces**

  One 15-oz. can unsweetened coconut milk
- 3 **Tbsp. fresh lime juice**

  Toasted unsweetened coconut and cilantro sprigs, for garnish

1. In a large saucepan, heat the coconut oil. Add the onions and peppers and cook over moderate heat, stirring occasionally, until tender, about 10 minutes. Add the curry paste and cook, stirring, until lightly caramelized, about 2 minutes. Add the ginger and garlic and cook until fragrant, about 1 minute. Add the sweet potatoes and 2 quarts of water and bring to a simmer. Cook until the sweet potatoes are tender, about 25 minutes. Remove from the heat. Stir in the coconut milk and lime juice.

2. In batches, puree the soup until smooth. Serve hot, garnished with coconut flakes and cilantro sprigs. —*Melissa Clark*

MAKE AHEAD The soup can be refrigerated for up to 3 days.

Pumpkin Soup with Trumpet Mushrooms and Sour Cream

Active **45 min**; Total **1 hr 15 min**; Serves **8**

Chef Daniel Rose of NYC's Le Coucou serves this elegant soup for festive winter meals—it'll be a hit at your next party.

- 4 **Tbsp. unsalted butter**
- 1 **medium onion, thinly sliced**
- 3 **lbs. pumpkin or kabocha squash— peeled, seeded and cut into 1-inch pieces**
- 8 **cups chicken stock or low-sodium broth**

  Pinch of freshly grated nutmeg

  Kosher salt and pepper
- 4 **oz. trumpet mushrooms, rinsed and patted dry**
- 1 **Tbsp. minced shallot**
- 1 **Tbsp. chopped parsley, plus leaves for garnish**

  Sour cream, for garnish

1. In a large saucepan, melt 2 tablespoons of the butter. Add the onion and cook over moderate heat, stirring occasionally, until softened but not browned, about 5 minutes. Add the pumpkin, stock and nutmeg and bring to a boil. Cover and cook over moderately low heat until the pumpkin is tender, about 30 minutes. In batches, puree the soup in a blender until smooth. Return the soup to the saucepan, season with salt and pepper and keep warm.

2. Meanwhile, in a large skillet, melt the remaining 2 tablespoons of butter. Add the mushrooms and cook over moderately high heat, stirring occasionally, until tender, about 3 minutes. Add the shallot and cook, stirring, until softened, about 2 minutes. Season with salt and pepper and stir in the chopped parsley.

3. Ladle the soup into bowls. Top with a dollop of sour cream and some of the mushrooms. Garnish with parsley and serve. —*Daniel Rose*

MAKE AHEAD The soup can be refrigerated for up to 1 week.

DIY Chicken Pho

Bunker, a tiny Vietnamese restaurant in an industrial stretch of Queens, New York, is a cult favorite for its chicken-and-noodle soup. Chef **JIMMY TU** explains how to tackle it.

Chicken Pho

Active **1 hr;** Total **4 hr;** Serves **4**

PHO

    Kosher salt

    One 3½-lb. chicken

2 **star anise pods**

2 **cardamom pods**

1 **tsp. coriander seeds**

    One 2½-inch cinnamon stick

1 **tsp. black peppercorns**

½ **tsp. white peppercorns**

1 **tsp. goji berries**

2 **shallots, halved**

1 **small onion, quartered**

1 **leek, halved lengthwise and cut into 2-inch pieces**

1 **Tbsp. crushed rock sugar or dark brown sugar**

1 **Tbsp. Asian fish sauce**

GARNISHES

¼ **cup canola oil**

3 **medium shallots, thinly sliced (1 cup)**

6 **oz. dried rice noodles**

¼ **cup sliced scallions**

¼ **cup chopped cilantro**

    Bean sprouts, basil sprigs, mint sprigs, thinly sliced jalapeños and lime wedges, for serving

START THE PHO

1. In a large stockpot, bring 5 quarts of water to a boil. Add 1 tablespoon of salt and the chicken, breast side down. Place a heatproof plate over the chicken to keep it submerged and bring to a boil. Reduce the heat and simmer the chicken for 30 minutes; it will not be cooked through. Transfer the chicken to a bowl of ice water and let cool completely. Drain well and pat dry.

2. Meanwhile, in a large cast-iron skillet, combine the star anise, cardamom, coriander, cinnamon stick, black and white peppercorns and goji berries. Cook over moderately low heat, stirring, until very fragrant, about 3 minutes. Transfer to a small bowl.

3. In the same skillet, combine the shallots, onion and leek. Cook over moderate heat, stirring occasionally, until deep golden, about 10 minutes.

4. Remove all of the meat from the chicken and coarsely shred it.

SIMMER THE BROTH

5. Return all of the chicken skin and bones to the broth in the stockpot. Add the pan-roasted shallot, onion and leek mixture and bring to a boil. Cover and simmer over moderately low heat for 1 hour.

6. Stir the toasted spices and goji berries into the broth. Cover and simmer for 1 hour longer. Add the rock sugar and simmer for another 30 minutes.

7. Strain the broth into a large bowl, pressing on the solids; discard the solids. Pour the broth into a clean saucepan.

MAKE THE GARNISHES

8. In a large skillet, heat the oil. Add the shallots and cook over moderate heat, stirring, until golden brown, 5 to 7 minutes. Using a mesh skimmer, transfer the shallots to a paper towel–lined plate to drain. Let cool.

9. Soak the noodles in a large bowl of boiling water until pliable, 8 to 10 minutes.

10. Bring the broth to a simmer. Stir in the shredded chicken and cook until just white throughout, 1 to 2 minutes. Stir in the fish sauce and season the broth with salt.

11. Drain the rice noodles and transfer to large bowls. Ladle the broth and chicken over the noodles. Top with the scallions and cilantro. Garnish with the crispy shallots, bean sprouts, basil, mint and jalapeños and serve with lime wedges.

MAKE AHEAD The poached chicken and finished broth can be refrigerated separately overnight.

WINE Fragrant northern Italian white: 2013 J. Hofstätter Alto Adige Pinot Bianco.

STEP-BY-STEP PHO LESSON

PREPARE THE CHICKEN Poach the bird for 30 minutes, then chill it in an ice bath. The meat will finish cooking in the soup.

TOAST THE SPICES In a heavy skillet, toast the spices with goji berries over moderately low heat, stirring, until very fragrant.

SIMMER AND STRAIN THE BROTH Remove the skin and bones from the chicken. Simmer with alliums and spices, then strain.

FINISH THE PHO Add the chicken to the broth and simmer. Season with fish sauce and salt. Serve with noodles and garnishes.

For the most flavorful pho broth, use a high-quality natural or free-range bird. Poaching it before simmering the broth ensures the shredded meat is tender.

BLACK BEAN AND
CHORIZO SOUP

Black Bean and Chorizo Soup

Active **30 min**; Total **3 hr 15 min plus overnight soaking**; Serves **4 to 6**

One 16-oz. bag dried black beans (2¼ cups), rinsed and soaked overnight

1 bay leaf

1 thyme sprig

1 parsley sprig

3 onions—1 quartered and 2 finely chopped

Kosher salt and pepper

1½ Tbsp. extra-virgin olive oil

3 oz. Spanish-style dried chorizo, finely chopped

2 garlic cloves, minced

1 tsp. ground cumin

4 cups chicken stock or low-sodium broth

Mexican crema, sliced avocado, thinly sliced radishes, cilantro sprigs, lime wedges and warm tortillas, for serving

1. Drain the black beans, then, in a large enameled cast-iron casserole, combine them with enough water to cover by 3 inches. Add the bay leaf, thyme, parsley, quartered onion and 1 tablespoon of salt. Bring to a boil over moderately high heat. Reduce the heat to low, cover and cook until the beans are just tender, about 1 hour. Drain the beans and discard the bay leaf, thyme, parsley and onion. Wipe out the casserole.

2. In the casserole, heat the olive oil. Add the chorizo and cook over moderate heat, stirring occasionally, until starting to crisp, 4 minutes. Add the chopped onions, the garlic and cumin; season with salt and pepper. Continue cooking over moderate heat, stirring occasionally, until the onions are tender, 10 to 12 minutes. Add the stock and 2 cups of water and bring to a boil. Return the beans to the casserole, cover, reduce the heat to low and cook until the beans are very tender and the soup has thickened, about 1 hour and 45 minutes.

3. Ladle the soup into bowls and serve garnished with crema, avocado, radishes and cilantro. Pass lime wedges and warm tortillas at the table. —*Kathy Gunst*

Tangy Beef Soup

Active **1 hr**; Total **2 hr**; Serves **4**

BROTH

3 lbs. meaty beef bones

1 onion, peeled

1 bay leaf

10 black peppercorns

5 allspice berries

SOUP

3 Tbsp. canola oil

½ lb. fresh chorizo sausages

1 onion, finely chopped

1 Tbsp. tomato paste

1 carrot, peeled and coarsely grated

1 tsp. sugar

Kosher salt and pepper

4 oz. mushrooms, thinly sliced

2 Tbsp. finely chopped pickles plus ¼ cup pickle brine from the jar

⅓ cup pitted olives, thinly sliced

1 Tbsp. capers

Chopped parsley and thin lemon slices, for garnish

1. Make the broth In a large saucepan, combine all of the ingredients with 3 quarts of water. Bring to a boil, skimming off any foam from the surface. Simmer over low heat until reduced by half, about 1 hour. Strain the broth through a fine sieve; discard the solids. Pour the broth into a large saucepan.

2. Make the soup In a large nonstick skillet, heat 1 tablespoon of the oil. Add the chorizo and cook over moderate heat, turning, until golden, about 5 minutes. Add ¼ cup of water, cover and simmer over low heat until cooked through, about 5 minutes. Transfer the chorizo to a cutting board and slice ½ inch thick. Add to the broth.

3. In the same skillet, heat 1 tablespoon of the oil. Add the onion and cook over moderate heat, stirring occasionally, until softened, about 5 minutes. Add the tomato paste, grated carrot and sugar and cook until golden, about 5 minutes longer; season with salt and pepper. Scrape the mixture into the broth.

4. In the same skillet, heat the remaining 1 tablespoon of oil. Add the mushrooms, season with salt and pepper and cook over moderate heat, stirring occasionally, until

golden, about 5 minutes. Add to the broth along with the pickles, brine, olives and capers and bring to a simmer. Season the soup with salt and pepper. Ladle into shallow bowls, garnish with parsley and lemon slices and serve. —*Olia Hercules*

MAKE AHEAD The soup can be refrigerated for up to 2 days.

WINE Austrian Blaufränkisch: 2013 Anita & Hans Nittnaus Kalk und Schiefer.

Lentil Soup with Apple and Bacon

Total **1 hr 30 min**; Serves **4 to 6**

1 tsp. canola oil

6 slices of bacon, chopped

1 medium leek, white and tender green parts only, thinly sliced

2 celery ribs, cut into ¼-inch dice

1 medium carrot, cut into ¼-inch dice

2 garlic cloves, minced

2 Tbsp. minced peeled fresh ginger

Kosher salt and pepper

1 tsp. ground cumin

8 cups chicken stock, low-sodium broth or water

½ cup apple cider

1 cup green lentils

1 Granny Smith apple, peeled and cut into ¼-inch dice

½ tsp. finely chopped rosemary

Buttermilk, for serving

In a large saucepan, heat the oil. Add the bacon and cook over moderate heat, stirring occasionally, until crisp, about 8 minutes. Using a slotted spoon, transfer to a paper towel–lined plate to drain. Add the leek, celery, carrot, garlic and ginger to the saucepan and season with salt and pepper. Cook over moderate heat, stirring occasionally, until the vegetables are beginning to soften, about 8 minutes. Stir in the cumin and cook until fragrant, 30 seconds. Add the stock, cider and lentils and simmer, stirring occasionally, until the lentils are tender, about 40 minutes. Stir in the apple and rosemary and cook until the apple is just softened, about 3 minutes. Season with salt and pepper and ladle into bowls. Drizzle the soup with buttermilk, garnish with the bacon and serve. —*Vivian Howard*

WINE Earthy red: 2015 Fram Shiraz.

DIY Bouillabaisse

Chef **DANIEL BOULUD** makes an elegant, Americanized version of bouillabaisse that still captures every bit of the Provençal fish soup's classic flavor. Read on to learn his tricks.

Bouillabaisse à l'Américaine

Active **1 hr 45 min**; Total **3 hr**; Serves **6 to 8**

GARLICKY ROUILLE

- **1 baking potato, peeled and cut into 1-inch pieces**
- **Pinch of saffron threads**
- **Kosher salt**
- **Pinch of cayenne**
- **6 superfresh garlic cloves**
- **2 large egg yolks**
- **1 cup extra-virgin olive oil**

HERB-AND-SPICE SACHET

- **2 tsp. fennel seeds**
- **2 tsp. whole coriander seeds**
- **1 bay leaf**
- **4 thyme sprigs**
- **1 head of garlic, halved crosswise, or 6 large cloves, crushed**
- **Three 3-inch-long strips of orange zest**

BOUILLABAISSE

- **Two 2-lb. whole black sea bass, cleaned and filleted, heads and bones reserved**
- **One 4-lb. red snapper, cleaned and filleted, head and bones reserved**
- **¼ cup extra-virgin olive oil**
- **2 yellow onions, chopped**
- **3 celery ribs, chopped**
- **1 fennel bulb, trimmed and thinly sliced**
- **1 leek, white and light green parts only, coarsely chopped**
- **½ tsp. saffron threads**
- **¼ tsp. cayenne or crushed red pepper, plus more for seasoning**
- **¼ cup pastis**
- **2 Tbsp. tomato paste**
- **1 lb. large shrimp, shelled and deveined, shells reserved**
- **1 lb. plum tomatoes, quartered**
- **1 lb. German Butterball or small Yukon Gold potatoes, quartered**
- **Kosher salt and white pepper**
- **1 lb. mussels, scrubbed and debearded**
- **Crusty baguette, for serving**

MAKE THE GARLICKY ROUILLE

1. In a medium saucepan, combine the potato, saffron, a pinch of salt and 2 cups of water. Bring to a boil and cook until the saffron water is reduced by half and the potato is cooked through, about 20 minutes. Cool completely, then transfer the potato and saffron water to a blender.

Add the cayenne, garlic and egg yolks and pulse to combine. With the machine on, slowly drizzle in the oil until well blended. Season with salt. Transfer the rouille to a serving bowl and refrigerate.

MAKE THE HERB-AND-SPICE SACHET

2. Assemble all of the ingredients on a piece of cheesecloth, wrap into a bundle and tie with kitchen string.

MAKE THE BOUILLABAISSE

3. Rinse all of the fish heads and bones until the water runs clear. Cut the fillets into 2-inch pieces and transfer to a bowl; cover and refrigerate.

4. In a large enameled cast-iron casserole or pot, heat the olive oil. Add the onions, celery, fennel, leek, saffron and cayenne and cook over moderate heat until the vegetables soften, 8 minutes. Add the pastis and cook until evaporated. Add the tomato paste and cook, stirring, until beginning to caramelize, about 5 minutes.

5. Add the fish heads and bones, shrimp shells, herb-and-spice sachet and enough water to just cover, about 16 cups. Bring to a simmer and cook over moderately low heat for 20 minutes, skimming off the foam

STEP-BY-STEP BOUILLABAISSE LESSON

START THE ROUILLE Simmer a cubed baking potato in salted saffron water until tender. Let the potato and broth cool.

FINISH THE ROUILLE In a blender, pulse the potato and cooking water with cayenne, garlic and egg yolks, then blend in olive oil.

MAKE THE SACHET Bundle the herbs, spices, garlic and orange zest in cheesecloth tied with kitchen string.

COOK THE AROMATICS Cook vegetables with saffron and cayenne; add the fish bones and heads, shrimp shells and sachet.

Boulud swaps in black sea bass and red snapper fillets for small whole fish, making the dish much easier to eat. Feel free to use any local seafood.

that rises to the surface. Stir in the tomatoes and cook gently for 30 minutes.

6. Meanwhile, cook the potatoes in a large saucepan of salted boiling water until tender, about 15 minutes. Drain well.

7. Pick out and discard the herb-and-spice sachet, the fish head and any large fish bones. Working in batches, transfer the contents of the casserole to a blender and puree until smooth. Strain the soup through a fine-mesh sieve into a clean pot, pressing on the solids.

FINISH THE BOUILLABAISSE

8. Bring the soup to a simmer. Add the potatoes. Season the fish with salt and pepper and add to the soup. Cook over low heat for 3 minutes. Add the shrimp and mussels, cover and cook until the mussels open and the fish and shrimp are cooked through, 2 minutes longer. Season with salt, pepper and cayenne.

9. Stir 2 tablespoons of the hot soup into the rouille. Ladle the bouillabaisse into shallow bowls. Serve with the rouille and crusty bread.

MAKE AHEAD The rouille can be refrigerated for 2 days. The soup can be refrigerated for 3 days or frozen for 3 months.

WINE Bandol white: 2013 Domaine le Galantin.

SIMMER THE BROTH Add enough water to just cover the fish bones and cook, skimming off the foam as it rises to the surface.

FINISH THE BROTH Add tomatoes to the pot and cook gently. Pick out and discard the sachet and any large fish bones.

PUREE THE SOUP Ladle the broth–fish bones and all–into the blender and puree until smooth. Strain the soup.

ADD THE FISH Return the soup to a clean casserole and bring to a simmer. Add cooked potatoes, seasoned fish and shellfish.

Caldo Verde with Beef Shank and Sausage

Active **45 min**; Total **4 hr plus overnight soaking**; Serves **8**

Chicago chef Abraham Conlon's take on the Azorean soup *caldo verde* ("green broth") is great for a hungry crowd. It's a perfect one-pot meal featuring succulent bits of meat, kale, potatoes and beans in a richly flavored broth that's perked up with a hit of tangy sherry vinegar.

- 2 **Tbsp. extra-virgin olive oil**
- 1 **lb. meaty beef shank**
   Kosher salt and black pepper
- 1 **medium Spanish onion, halved and thinly sliced**
- 1 **bay leaf**
- 2 **Tbsp. minced garlic**
- ¼ **tsp. crushed red pepper**
- 1 **qt. chicken stock or low-sodium broth**
- ½ **cup dried kidney beans, soaked overnight and drained**
- 1 **lb. Yukon Gold potatoes, peeled and cut into 1-inch pieces**
- 1 **lb. kale or collard greens, stems discarded and leaves chopped (½ lb.)**
- ½ **lb. linguiça or Spanish chorizo, sliced ¼ inch thick**
- 2 **Tbsp. sherry vinegar, plus more for serving**

1. In a large pot, heat the olive oil. Season the beef shank with salt and black pepper and add it to the pot. Cook over moderately high heat, turning, until browned all over, about 8 minutes. Transfer to a plate. Add the onion, bay leaf and a generous pinch each of salt and black pepper to the pot and cook, stirring occasionally, until the onion is softened, about 5 minutes. Add the garlic and crushed red pepper and cook, stirring, until fragrant, about 2 minutes. Add the stock, beans and 2 cups of water and bring to a boil. Return the beef shank to the pot. Cover and cook over moderately low heat until the beef and beans are tender, about 2 hours and 30 minutes.

2. Add the potatoes to the pot and simmer uncovered, stirring occasionally, until tender, about 30 minutes. Using tongs, transfer the beef shank to a plate. Add the kale to the pot and cook, stirring occasionally, until wilted, about 10 minutes. Pick out and discard the bay leaf.

3. Using 2 forks, shred the beef into bite-size pieces. Discard the bone and any gristle. Add the beef and sausage to the pot and simmer for 5 minutes. Stir in the 2 tablespoons of vinegar and season with salt and black pepper. Ladle into bowls and serve, passing more vinegar at the table. —*Abraham Conlon*

Persian Split Pea and Rice Soup with Lamb Meatballs

Active **45 min**; Total **3 hr 30 min plus overnight soaking**; Serves **6**

This bright, herbaceous porridge, called *ash,* is from Naomi Duguid's *Taste of Persia* cookbook. A staple of Persian home cooking, it can be made days in advance and reheated beautifully; simply swirl in the pomegranate molasses and let the tiny lamb meatballs simmer for 10 minutes before serving.

SOUP

- 2 **Tbsp. extra-virgin olive oil**
- 1 **yellow onion, thinly sliced**
- ½ **tsp. ground cinnamon**
- ½ **tsp. ground turmeric**
- ¾ **cup short-grain white rice**
- ¾ **cup dried green split peas, soaked overnight and drained**
- 4 **scallions, thinly sliced**
- 2 **cups finely chopped parsley leaves and tender stems**
- 2 **cups finely chopped cilantro leaves and tender stems**
- ½ **cup finely chopped mint leaves**
- 2 **Tbsp. pomegranate molasses, plus more as needed**
   Kosher salt

MEATBALLS

- ½ **lb. ground lamb**
- 1 **small yellow onion, grated**
- ½ **tsp. kosher salt**
- ¼ **tsp. pepper**

TOPPINGS

- ¼ **cup canola oil**
- 2 **Tbsp. dried mint**
- 1 **large onion, thinly sliced**

1. Make the soup In a large enameled cast-iron casserole, heat the olive oil. Add the onion, cinnamon and turmeric and cook over moderate heat, stirring occasionally, until the onion is beginning to soften, 5 minutes. Add the rice, split peas and 10 cups of water and bring to a boil. Reduce the heat and simmer, stirring occasionally, until the rice and peas are tender and the soup is quite thick, 1½ to 2 hours. Add the scallions, parsley, cilantro and mint and simmer for 30 minutes. Stir in the pomegranate molasses and season with salt.

2. Make the meatballs In a medium bowl, combine all of the ingredients. Roll rounded teaspoons of the ground lamb into balls. Add the meatballs to the soup and simmer until cooked through, about 10 minutes. If the soup is getting too thick, add water.

3. Meanwhile, make the toppings In a small skillet, heat 2 tablespoons of the canola oil. Add the dried mint and cook until fragrant, 30 seconds. Scrape the mint oil into a bowl and wipe out the skillet. Heat the remaining 2 tablespoons of canola oil in the skillet. Add the onion and cook over moderate heat until golden and crisp, about 8 minutes; drain. Serve the soup garnished with the mint oil and fried onions. —*Naomi Duguid*

MAKE AHEAD The soup can be refrigerated for up to 3 days and reheated gently. Add the meatballs and simmer for 10 minutes before serving.

WINE Aromatic rosé: 2015 Copain Tous Ensemble.

Silken Tofu Stew

Active **45 min**; Total **1 hr 30 min**; Serves **4**

Tofu and runny egg yolks add luscious, creamy texture to this complex, spicy Korean stew. All kinds of seafood work well here, so use whatever is fresh and looks best, like clams, lump crabmeat or even cubes of firm white fish.

DASHI

½ cup dried anchovies (1 oz.), heads and guts removed

10 dried shiitake mushrooms (1 oz.)

8 garlic cloves, crushed

Two 4-inch squares of kombu

½ onion, thinly sliced

STEW

2 Tbsp. canola oil

1 cup thinly sliced fresh shiitake mushroom caps

⅓ cup finely chopped onion

1 Tbsp. minced garlic

3 scallions, white, light green and dark green parts thinly sliced separately

½ cup chopped kimchi, plus more for serving

2 Tbsp. gochugaru (Korean red pepper flakes)

1 Tbsp. soy sauce

1 Tbsp. Asian fish sauce

½ lb. medium shrimp, shelled and deveined

½ lb. mussels, scrubbed and debearded

4 oz. cleaned calamari, tentacles left whole and bodies cut crosswise into ¼-inch rings

1 lb. silken tofu, broken into chunks

4 large eggs

1 cup watercress leaves and tender stems

1. Make the dashi In a large saucepan, combine all of the ingredients with 10 cups of water and bring to a boil. Reduce the heat to low and simmer until reduced to 4 cups, about 30 minutes. Strain the dashi through a fine-mesh sieve set over a medium bowl; discard the solids and wipe out the saucepan.

2. Make the stew In the saucepan, heat the oil. Add the mushrooms, onion, garlic, the sliced white and light green scallions and the ½ cup of kimchi and cook over moderate heat, stirring, until the onion is beginning to brown, about 8 minutes. Add the dashi, gochugaru, soy sauce and fish sauce and bring to a simmer. Add the shrimp and mussels, cover and cook over low heat until the mussels open, about 2 minutes. Discard any mussels that don't open. Stir in the calamari and tofu. Carefully crack the eggs into the stew. Cover and cook until the egg whites are set but the yolks are still runny, 2 to 3 minutes.

3. Ladle the tofu stew into bowls and garnish with the watercress and sliced scallion greens. Serve with kimchi. —*Sohui Kim*

WINE Lime-scented, off-dry Riesling: 2014 Leitz Dragonstone Rheingau.

Lamb-and-Lemon Stew with Chickpeas

Active **45 min**; Total **3 hr 30 min**
Serves **6 to 8**

This terrific Middle Eastern–style lamb stew is fragrant with cumin, coriander and Aleppo pepper; a quartered lemon simmers alongside the lamb, adding a nice acidity.

4 lbs. trimmed boneless leg of lamb, cut into 1½-inch pieces

Kosher salt and black pepper

¼ cup extra-virgin olive oil

1 lemon, quartered lengthwise, plus wedges for serving

1½ Tbsp. ground cumin

1 Tbsp. ground coriander

1 Tbsp. Aleppo pepper

1 large onion, coarsely chopped

2 medium celery ribs, coarsely chopped

1 large carrot, coarsely chopped

3 garlic cloves, chopped

1 qt. chicken stock or low-sodium broth

Two 15-oz. cans chickpeas, rinsed and drained

Yogurt and chopped cilantro, for serving

1. Season the lamb with salt and black pepper. In a large enameled cast-iron casserole, heat 1 tablespoon of the olive oil. Add the quartered lemon and half of the lamb and cook over moderately high heat, turning occasionally, until the lamb is browned all over, about 8 minutes. Transfer the lamb and lemon quarters to a plate; repeat with the remaining lamb.

2. Pour off the fat in the casserole and heat the remaining 3 tablespoons of olive oil in it. Add the cumin, coriander, Aleppo pepper and 1 teaspoon of black pepper and cook over moderate heat until fragrant, about 1 minute. Stir in the chopped onion, celery, carrot and garlic, then add the chicken stock and 4 cups of water; bring to a boil. Return the lamb and lemon quarters to the casserole and simmer over moderately low heat, stirring occasionally, until the lamb is nearly tender, about 2 hours.

3. Add the chickpeas to the casserole and simmer, stirring occasionally, until the lamb is tender and the sauce has thickened, about 30 minutes. Discard the lemon quarters and season the stew with salt and black pepper. Ladle into bowls and serve with yogurt, chopped cilantro and lemon wedges. —*Anya Fernald*

MAKE AHEAD The stew can be refrigerated for up to 3 days. Reheat gently.

WINE Medium-bodied, savory Syrah: 2013 Kingston Family Vineyards Lucero.

GENIUS STORAGE TIP

Soup Portion Control

Instead of freezing leftover soup or stew in one large container, you can ladle it into jumbo muffin tins and freeze for single servings. Once the portions are frozen, pop them out and store in resealable freezer bags.

PASTA AND NOODLES

L.A. chef Bryant Ng gives Asian noodles an Italian twist with pecorino cheese and butter (p. 109). OPPOSITE Cavatelli with Sparerib Ragù (p. 94).

Spaghetti with Mushroom Bolognese

Active **1 hr;** Total **2 hr 30 min;** Serves **4**

Three kinds of mushroom plus eggplant and carrots come together in this satisfying vegetarian riff on ragù Bolognese. Miso is the secret ingredient that adds extra seasoning and depth.

- ¼ cup dried porcini mushrooms
- 6 Tbsp. extra-virgin olive oil
- 1 small onion, cut into ¼-inch dice
- 2 medium carrots, peeled and cut into ¼-inch dice
- 1 baby eggplant (8 oz.), peeled and cut into ¼-inch dice
- 1 lb. cremini mushrooms, one-fourth sliced, the rest cut into ¼-inch dice
- 8 oz. shiitake mushrooms, stemmed, caps cut into ¼-inch dice
  Kosher salt and pepper
- 5 garlic cloves, minced
- 2 Tbsp. tomato paste
- 1 Tbsp. white miso
  One 2-inch chunk of Parmigiano-Reggiano cheese, plus grated cheese for serving
  One 28-oz. can whole peeled tomatoes, crushed
- 1 thyme sprig
- ½ tsp. turbinado sugar
- 12 oz. spaghetti
- 2 Tbsp. chopped parsley

1. In a small bowl, cover the porcini with 1 cup of boiling water; soak until softened, about 30 minutes. Finely chop the porcini, discarding any tough bits. Pour off and reserve ½ cup of the soaking liquid.

2. In a large enameled cast-iron casserole, heat 2 tablespoons of the oil. Add the onion and carrots and cook over moderate heat until light golden, about 8 minutes. Add the eggplant and 2 tablespoons of the oil and cook, stirring occasionally, until softened, 8 minutes. Stir in the cremini, shiitake, chopped porcini and the remaining 2 tablespoons of oil and season with salt and pepper. Cook, stirring occasionally, until the mushrooms are golden, 8 to 10 minutes. Stir in the garlic, tomato paste and miso and cook for 2 minutes. Add the chunk of cheese, the tomatoes and their juices, the thyme, sugar and reserved mushroom soaking liquid and bring to a simmer.

3. Cover the casserole and cook over low heat, stirring occasionally, until the sauce is very thick, about 1 hour and 30 minutes. Discard the thyme sprig; season the sauce with salt and pepper.

4. In a pot of salted boiling water, cook the spaghetti until al dente. Drain, reserving ¼ cup of the pasta water.

5. Add the pasta, pasta water and parsley to the sauce; toss to coat. Serve in bowls, topped with grated cheese. —*Kay Chun*

MAKE AHEAD The mushroom Bolognese can be refrigerated for 2 days.

WINE Earthy, red currant–fruited Nebbiolo: 2013 Ar.Pe.Pe. Rosso di Valtellina.

Pink Peppercorn and Parmesan Spaghetti

Total **20 min;** Serves **6**

Crushed pink peppercorns star in this wonderful four-ingredient pasta, making it particularly fragrant. At her restaurant Lilia in Brooklyn, chef Missy Robbins uses curly-edged mafaldine for the dish, but any long noodle works well.

- 1 lb. spaghetti
- 6 Tbsp. unsalted butter
- 1 Tbsp. crushed pink peppercorns, plus more for garnish
- ¾ cup freshly grated Parmigiano-Reggiano cheese
  Kosher salt

1. In a pot of salted boiling water, cook the spaghetti until al dente. Drain, reserving 1 cup of the pasta water.

2. In a large skillet, melt the butter. Add the spaghetti, pasta water, the 1 tablespoon of crushed peppercorns and ½ cup of the cheese and cook over moderate heat, stirring, until a sauce forms, about 2 minutes. Season with salt. Transfer the spaghetti to bowls and top with the remaining ¼ cup of cheese. Garnish with crushed peppercorns and serve. —*Missy Robbins*

WINE Lush and aromatic white: 2014 Manni Nössing Alto Adige Kerner.

Spaghetti with Broccolini

Total **50 min;** Serves **4 to 6**

This simple pasta gets great flavor from garlicky Broccolini florets and crispy roasted Broccolini leaves.

- 1½ lbs. leafy Broccolini, leaves reserved, the rest cut into 2-inch lengths
- 3 Tbsp. plus 1 tsp. extra-virgin olive oil
  Fine sea salt and pepper
- 1 lb. spaghetti
- 4 garlic cloves, thinly sliced
- 4 Tbsp. unsalted butter, cut into tablespoons
- 3 Tbsp. fresh lemon juice
  Grated Parmigiano-Reggiano cheese, for serving

1. Preheat the oven to 375°. On a rimmed baking sheet, toss the Broccolini leaves with 2 teaspoons of the olive oil and season lightly with salt. Bake for 15 to 20 minutes, until lightly browned and crisp. Let cool completely.

2. Meanwhile, set up a large ice water bath. In a large saucepan of salted boiling water, blanch the rest of the Broccolini until crisp-tender, 2 to 3 minutes. Using a slotted spoon, transfer to the ice water bath to cool, then drain well and pat dry.

3. In the saucepan of salted boiling water, cook the spaghetti until al dente. Reserve 1 cup of the pasta water. Drain the pasta and toss with 2 teaspoons of the olive oil.

4. Wipe out the saucepan and heat the remaining 2 tablespoons of olive oil in it. Add the garlic and cook over moderate heat, stirring, until softened, about 1 minute. Add the blanched Broccolini and cook over moderately high heat, stirring frequently, until the garlic is golden, about 3 minutes. Add the spaghetti and the reserved pasta water and cook, tossing, until coated in a light sauce, 2 to 3 minutes. Remove from the heat. While tossing, add the butter 1 tablespoon at a time until incorporated. Stir in the lemon juice and season generously with salt and pepper. Transfer to bowls. Top with the crispy Broccolini leaves and more pepper and serve right away, passing Parmesan at the table. —*Paul Everett*

WINE Crisp, herbal Sauvignon Blanc: 2015 Whitehaven Marlborough.

SPAGHETTI WITH
MUSHROOM BOLOGNESE

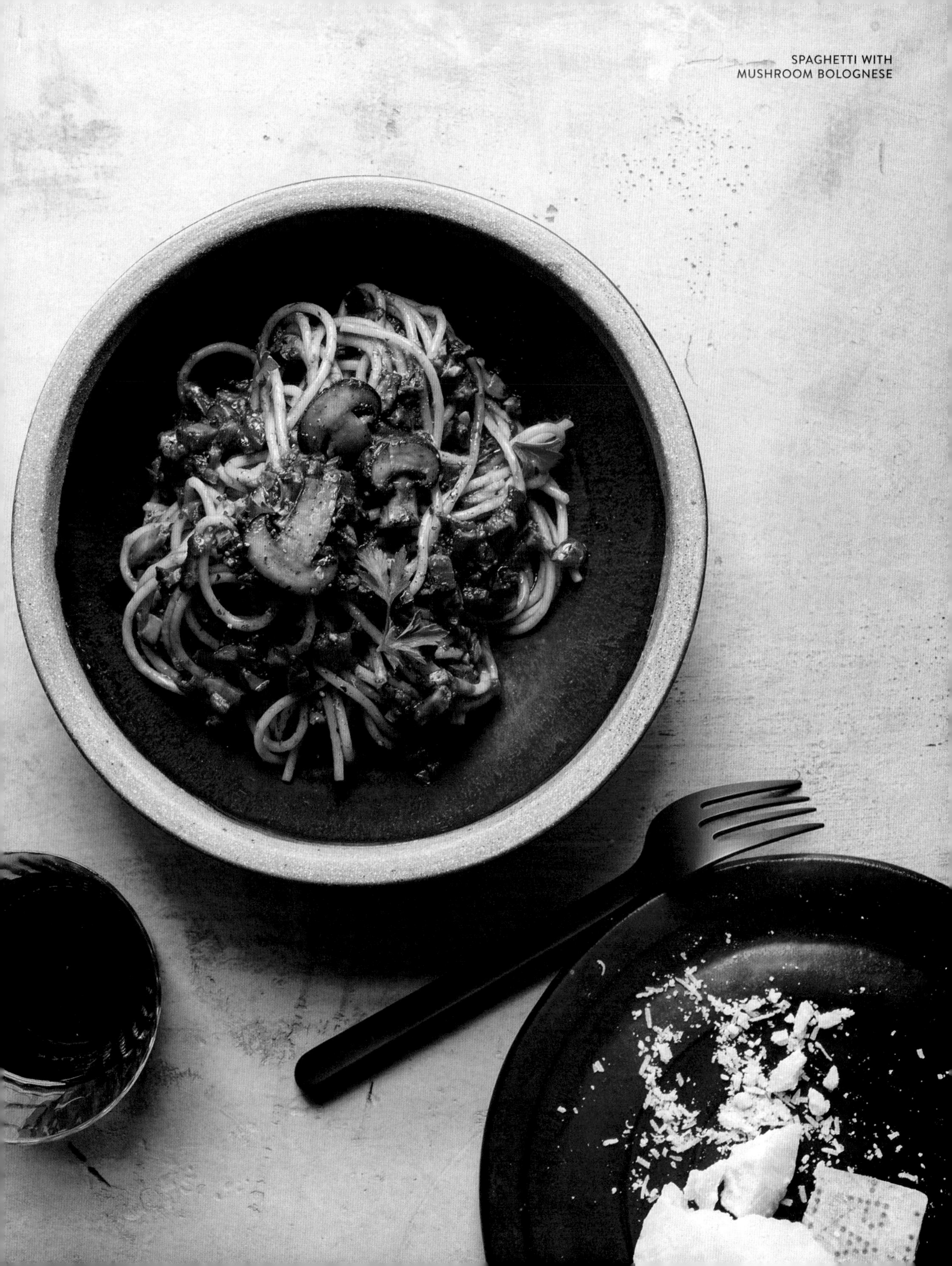

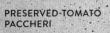
PRESERVED-TOMATO
PACCHERI

Pasta with Marinated Grilled Eggplant, Burrata and Chiles

Total **1 hr**; Serves **6**

At The Lunatic, The Lover & The Poet in Chicago, Simon Lamb tosses torn pieces of burrata into just-cooked orecchiette so the cheese melts ever so slightly into the pasta.

- **2 lbs. mixed eggplant (such as Italian and Japanese), trimmed and halved lengthwise**
- **¼ cup plus 2 Tbsp. extra-virgin olive oil**
- **Kosher salt and pepper**
- **2 Tbsp. fresh lemon juice**
- **1 Tbsp. red wine vinegar**
- **2 tsp. minced preserved lemon rind (see Note)**
- **2 garlic cloves, finely chopped**
- **2 oregano sprigs, plus leaves for garnish**
- **1 dried chile de árbol, crushed**
- **1 lb. orecchiette**
- **3 oil-packed Calabrian chiles, drained and finely chopped**
- **½ cup freshly grated Romano cheese, plus more for serving**
- **½ lb. burrata or buffalo mozzarella, torn into bite-size pieces**
- **Chopped parsley, for garnish**

1. Heat a grill pan. Rub the eggplant with ¼ cup of the olive oil and season with salt and pepper. Grill the eggplant over moderate heat, turning, until golden and tender, about 15 minutes. Transfer to a cutting board and let cool slightly. Cut into ¾-inch pieces and transfer to a bowl. Add the lemon juice, vinegar and 1 teaspoon of the preserved lemon rind and mix well.

2. In a small skillet, heat the remaining 2 tablespoons of oil. Add the garlic, oregano sprigs and chile de árbol and cook over moderately low heat, stirring, until the garlic is fragrant and starts to brown, 1 to 2 minutes. Add the mixture to the eggplant and toss to evenly coat.

3. In a large saucepan of salted boiling water, cook the pasta until al dente. Drain, reserving 1 cup of the cooking water.

4. Return the pasta and pasta water to the saucepan and add the eggplant and its marinade, the Calabrian chiles, the ½ cup of grated Romano and the remaining 1 teaspoon of preserved lemon rind. Season with salt and pepper and toss over moderately high heat until well combined and the pasta is saucy, about 2 minutes. Remove the pan from the heat and discard the oregano sprigs. Add the burrata, toss quickly and transfer to plates. Garnish with oregano leaves and chopped parsley and serve, passing grated Romano cheese at the table. —*Simon Lamb*

NOTE Preserved lemons, cured in lemon juice and salt, are available at specialty food stores.

MAKE AHEAD The marinated eggplant can be refrigerated overnight.

WINE Lemon-zesty Italian white: 2013 Palmina Honea Vineyard Tocai Friulano.

Preserved-Tomato Paccheri

Active **1 hr**; Total **6 hr**; Serves **6**

For her unconventional tomato sauce, Brooklyn chef Missy Robbins marinates canned tomatoes in a mix of garlic, spices, citrus and warm olive oil. The result is a supple coating for wide, tubular paccheri pasta that she serves al dente.

- **Four 28-oz. cans whole San Marzano tomatoes—drained, halved lengthwise and seeded**
- **4½ tsp. sugar**
- **Kosher salt**
- **1 Tbsp. fennel seeds**
- **1 Tbsp. coriander seeds**
- **2 cups plus 3 Tbsp. extra-virgin olive oil**
- **7 garlic cloves—2 crushed and 5 thinly sliced**
- **Wide strips of zest from 2 small lemons plus 1 tsp. finely grated zest**
- **Wide strips of zest from 1 small orange**
- **2 basil sprigs**
- **2 marjoram sprigs plus 2 tsp. marjoram leaves**
- **1½ tsp. crushed red pepper**
- **1 lb. paccheri or other wide, tubular pasta**
- **¼ cup freshly grated Pecorino Romano cheese, for garnish**

1. Put the tomato halves in a colander set over a bowl. Sprinkle with the sugar and 4½ teaspoons of kosher salt and toss gently. Let stand at room temperature for 2 hours.

2. Meanwhile, in a small skillet, toast the fennel and coriander seeds over moderately low heat, shaking the pan, until very fragrant, about 2 minutes. Transfer the seeds to a spice grinder or mortar and let cool slightly, then coarsely grind.

3. In a small saucepan, combine 2 cups of the olive oil, the ground seeds, crushed garlic, lemon and orange zest strips and the basil and marjoram sprigs. Warm over low heat until the oil begins to bubble, about 7 minutes. Transfer the drained tomatoes to a deep ceramic baking dish and pour the warm oil over them. Let stand at room temperature for about 3 hours.

4. Using a slotted spoon, transfer the preserved tomatoes to a bowl. (Reserve the oil for another use.) Using your hands or a metal spoon, coarsely crush them; you should have 3 cups.

5. In a large skillet, warm the remaining 3 tablespoons of olive oil over moderate heat. Add the sliced garlic and cook, stirring, until fragrant but not browned, about 2 minutes. Add the crushed tomatoes and crushed red pepper and cook until the tomatoes are warmed through, about 2 minutes; keep the sauce warm over low heat.

6. In a pot of salted boiling water, cook the paccheri until al dente. Drain well. Add to the skillet and stir to coat. Stir in the grated lemon zest and the marjoram leaves. Transfer the paccheri to a bowl, garnish with the cheese and serve. —*Missy Robbins*

MAKE AHEAD The tomatoes can be refrigerated in the oil for up to 4 days.

WINE Bright, juicy Barbera: 2013 La Miraja Le Masche Barbera d'Asti Superiore.

Busiate with Brussels Sprouts, Mint and Two Cheeses

⏱ Total **40 min**; Serves **6**

Chef Ignacio Mattos's first rule of pasta: "Make sure your cooking water is well salted, so it tastes like the sea." His second rule is to use just a few well-chosen ingredients, like the brussels sprouts, lemon, mint and pecorino that punch up this vegetarian pasta that has become a favorite at Café Altro Paradiso in New York City.

- **1** **lb. busiate or other corkscrew pasta**
- **½** **cup extra-virgin olive oil**
- **12** **oz. brussels sprouts, thinly sliced on a mandoline (6 cups)**
- **2** **shallots, thinly sliced**
- **1** **garlic clove, thinly sliced**
- **¼** **cup fresh ricotta cheese**
- **1** **tsp. finely grated lemon zest**
  Pinch of crushed red pepper
  Kosher salt and black pepper
- **¼** **cup chopped mint, plus more for garnish**
  Freshly grated Pecorino Romano cheese, for garnish

1. In a pot of salted boiling water, cook the busiate until al dente. Drain, reserving 2 cups of the pasta water. Wipe out the pot.

2. Meanwhile, in a large skillet, heat 3 tablespoons of the olive oil. Add the brussels sprouts and cook over moderate heat, stirring, until softened, about 3 minutes. Add the shallots, garlic and 1 tablespoon of the oil and cook until the brussels sprouts are lightly golden, about 3 minutes. Stir in the ricotta, lemon zest and crushed red pepper and season with salt and black pepper.

3. Return the pasta and pasta water to the pot. Add the brussels sprout mixture, the remaining ¼ cup of oil and the ¼ cup of mint and toss until a sauce forms, 2 minutes. Garnish with black pepper, pecorino and mint and serve. —*Ignacio Mattos*

WINE Minerally Sicilian white: 2008 Benanti Pietramarina Etna Bianco Superiore.

Tajarin with Grilled Kale Pesto

Active **1 hr 45 min**; Total **2 hr 45 min**
Serves **6 to 8**

A combination of kamut and finely milled 00 flour is key to getting the perfect texture in this pasta. The number of egg yolks called for here may sound extreme, but that's what gives tajarin noodles their signature yellow color and rich flavor.

PASTA

- **2½** **cups 00 flour (see Note), plus more for dusting**
- **¾** **cup kamut flour**
  Kosher salt
- **18** **large egg yolks**
- **1** **large egg**
- **1** **Tbsp. extra-virgin olive oil**

PESTO

- **½** **cup pecans**
- **½** **lb. Tuscan kale, stemmed**
- **1½** **cups extra-virgin olive oil, plus more for brushing**
- **3** **marinated white anchovy fillets**
- **2** **Tbsp. fresh lemon juice**
- **1** **small garlic clove**
- **¼** **cup finely grated pecorino cheese, plus shaved pecorino for serving**
  Kosher salt and pepper
  Chive flowers, for garnish

1. Make the pasta In a large bowl, whisk both flours with a generous pinch of salt and make a well in the center. Add the egg yolks, whole egg, olive oil and 1 tablespoon of water. Using a fork, gradually whisk the flours into the wet ingredients until a shaggy dough forms. Scrape the dough out onto a very lightly floured work surface and knead until stiff but smooth, about 5 minutes. Wrap in plastic and let rest at room temperature until soft and relaxed, 30 minutes to 1 hour.

2. Divide the dough into 4 pieces and work with 1 piece at a time; keep the rest covered. Press the dough to flatten. Using a pasta machine, starting at the widest setting, run the dough through successively narrower settings until you reach the second to thinnest; the dough should be a scant ⅛ inch thick. Cut the pasta sheet into 10-inch lengths, lay them on a lightly floured work surface and generously dust with 00 flour. Repeat with the remaining pieces of dough.

3. Working with 1 sheet at a time, loosely fold the pasta over itself 3 or 4 times like a ribbon. Using a very sharp knife, cut across the folds into ⅛-inch-wide noodles. Uncoil the tajarin and toss with flour. Transfer to a lightly floured baking sheet. Repeat with the remaining sheets of pasta.

4. Make the pesto Preheat the oven to 375°. Spread the pecans in a pie plate and toast for about 7 minutes, until golden. Let cool, then coarsely chop.

5. Set up an ice bath. In a large saucepan of salted boiling water, blanch the kale until barely tender, about 2 minutes. Drain; transfer to the ice bath. Drain again and pat dry.

6. Light a grill and oil the grate. Spread the kale on the grate and grill over high heat, turning occasionally, until charred in spots, about 3 minutes. Let cool slightly, then coarsely chop. In a blender, combine the kale with the anchovies, lemon juice, garlic, half of the toasted pecans and the ¼ cup of pecorino. With the machine on, gradually add the 1½ cups of olive oil and puree until smooth. Season the pesto generously with salt and pepper.

7. In a large saucepan of salted boiling water, cook the pasta until al dente, about 1 minute. Drain, reserving 1 cup of the cooking water.

8. Wipe out the saucepan and add the pesto to it. Cook over moderate heat, stirring, until just hot, about 2 minutes. Add the pasta along with ½ cup of the reserved cooking water and toss until hot and evenly coated with pesto, about 2 minutes. Add a little more pasta water if necessary. Transfer the tajarin to shallow bowls. Top with shaved pecorino, chive flowers and the remaining chopped pecans. Serve right away. —*Kevin Fink*

NOTE *Doppio zero* ("double zero," or 00) is a fine Italian flour available at specialty food shops and from amazon.com.

MAKE AHEAD The tajarin can be prepared earlier in the day and kept uncovered at room temperature. It may require additional cooking time. The pesto can be refrigerated overnight.

WINE Herb-inflected Sangiovese: 2014 Uccelliera Rosso di Montalcino.

TAJARIN WITH
GRILLED KALE PESTO

Spaghettini with Warm Bacon-Mushroom Vinaigrette

📷 COVER

Total **1 hr**; Serves **6**

According to Tim Cushman, the chef at Covina in New York City, what makes the mushroom topping here is a splash of balsamic, which gives the pasta both tang and subtle sweetness.

- ¼ cup extra-virgin olive oil
- 1 lb. sliced bacon, cut crosswise into ½-inch strips
- 1 large onion, finely chopped
- 8 oz. mixed mushrooms, such as cremini and stemmed shiitake, thinly sliced
- 2 tsp. finely grated garlic
  Kosher salt and pepper
- ¼ cup balsamic vinegar
- 1 lb. spaghettini
- ½ cup freshly grated Parmigiano-Reggiano cheese, plus more for garnish
- ½ cup thinly sliced basil, plus basil leaves for garnish
  White truffle oil, for drizzling (optional)

1. Bring a large pot of water to a boil. In a large nonstick skillet, heat the olive oil. Add the bacon and cook over moderate heat, stirring occasionally, until golden brown and the fat is rendered, about 8 minutes. Add the onion and cook, stirring occasionally, until softened, about 3 minutes. Add the mushrooms and garlic, season with salt and pepper and cook until the vegetables are tender, about 5 minutes. Stir in the balsamic vinegar.

2. Add salt to the boiling water. Add the pasta and cook until al dente. Drain, reserving 1 cup of the pasta water. Return the pasta and water to the pot. Add the bacon-mushroom vinaigrette and the ½ cup each of grated cheese and sliced basil and toss over moderate heat until the pasta is evenly coated. Season with salt and pepper. Transfer to plates and garnish with additional cheese and basil leaves. Drizzle with truffle oil if desired and serve.
—*Tim Cushman*

WINE Juicy Nero d'Avola: 2014 Tamì Terre Siciliane.

Orecchiette with Sweet Sausage and Escarole

Active **1 hr 15 min**; Total **2 hr**; Serves **4**

Garlicky escarole adds a pleasant bitter hit to this chunky sausage ragù from La Sirena restaurant in New York City.

- ¼ cup plus 2 Tbsp. extra-virgin olive oil
- 1 lb. sweet Italian sausage, casings removed
- 1 fennel bulb, minced
- 2 large yellow onions, finely chopped (4 cups)
- 4 garlic cloves—2 smashed and 2 minced
  Kosher salt and black pepper
- 2 cups dry red wine
  One 28-oz. can crushed tomatoes
- 2 heads of escarole (2 lbs.), coarsely chopped
- 1 cup dry white wine
  Crushed red pepper
- 1 lb. orecchiette
- 1 cup freshly grated Parmigiano-Reggiano cheese, plus more for serving

1. In a large enameled cast-iron casserole, heat 2 tablespoons of the olive oil. Add the sausage and cook over moderate heat, stirring, until browned, 5 minutes; transfer to a plate. Add the fennel, half of the onions and the smashed garlic to the casserole and season with salt and black pepper. Cook, stirring, until the vegetables are golden and softened, about 10 minutes. Add the sausage, red wine, tomatoes and 2 cups of water and bring to a simmer. Cook over low heat until the sauce is thickened, 45 minutes.

2. Meanwhile, in a large saucepan, heat 2 tablespoons of the olive oil. Add the remaining chopped onions and cook over moderate heat, stirring occasionally, until golden and softened, about 10 minutes. Add the chopped escarole in batches, stirring until each batch is wilted before adding more. Add 1 tablespoon of the olive oil and the minced garlic and cook, stirring, until fragrant, about 2 minutes. Add the white wine and a pinch of crushed red pepper and season with salt. Cook, stirring occasionally, until the escarole is tender, about 40 minutes. Stir the escarole mixture into the sausage ragù.

3. In a large pot of salted boiling water, cook the pasta until al dente. Drain, reserving ½ cup of the pasta water. Return the pasta to the pot and add the reserved water, 5 cups of the ragù, the remaining 1 tablespoon of olive oil and the 1 cup of grated cheese. Season with salt, black pepper and crushed red pepper and toss to coat. Serve with additional cheese. Reserve the remaining ragù for later use.
—*Josh Laurano*

WINE A fruity Nero d'Avola tinged with bitterness: 2009 Gulfi Nerobufaleffj Sicilia.

Rigatoni with Pecorino and Crispy Guanciale

⏲ Total **30 min**; Serves **6**

Chef Nabil Hassed of Rome's Salumeria Roscioli puts his own spin on *gricia*, the classic Roman pasta made with guanciale (cured pork jowl) and pecorino cheese. Instead of leaving the guanciale soft, he cooks it to a crisp, then tops the dish with different kinds of black pepper, including fragrant Malaysian Sarawak.

- 8 oz. guanciale, sliced ⅓ inch thick and 1 inch long
- 1 lb. rigatoni
- 1¾ cups grated Pecorino Romano cheese (5 oz.), plus shavings for garnish
  Kosher salt and ground black pepper, preferably Sarawak (see Note)

1. In a large nonstick skillet, cook the guanciale over moderately low heat, stirring, until crisp, 8 to 10 minutes. Using a slotted spoon, transfer to a paper towel–lined plate.

2. Meanwhile, in a large saucepan of salted boiling water, cook the pasta until al dente. Drain; reserve 1 cup of the pasta water. Return the pasta and reserved water to the saucepan and cook over moderate heat, stirring, until the liquid is slightly thickened, 2 minutes. Stir in the grated cheese. Fold in the guanciale; season with salt and pepper. Serve garnished with pecorino and more pepper.
—*Nabil Hassed*

NOTE Sarawak, a Malaysian black pepper, has flavors of fruit and chocolate. Look for it at specialty markets.

WINE A savory Lazio red: 2013 Damiano Ciolli Silene Cesanese di Olevano Romano.

Gemelli with Peach–and–Yellow Tomato Pork Ragù

Active **45 min**; Total **4 hr**; Serves **6**

- 2 Tbsp. extra-virgin olive oil
- One 3-lb. boneless pork shoulder roast
- Kosher salt and pepper
- 4 medium peaches (about 1½ lbs.), quartered
- 4 medium yellow tomatoes (about 2 lbs.), quartered
- 2 Tbsp. gin
- 1 rosemary sprig
- 1½ Tbsp. minced peeled fresh ginger
- 1 lb. gemelli
- 1 cup cherry tomatoes, halved
- ½ cup freshly grated Grana Padano cheese, plus more for serving
- Torn basil leaves, for garnish

1. Preheat the oven to 325°. In a large enameled cast-iron casserole, heat the olive oil. Season the pork with salt and pepper and cook over moderately high heat, turning, until golden brown all over, about 8 minutes. Add the peaches, yellow tomatoes, gin, rosemary, ginger and ½ cup of water and bring to a boil. Cover and braise in the oven until the pork is very tender, about 3 hours. Transfer the pork to a work surface and let cool slightly. When cool enough to handle, shred the meat into large pieces.

2. Meanwhile, working in 2 batches, puree the braising liquid in a blender until smooth; wipe out the casserole. Strain the sauce through a sieve set over the casserole. Simmer the sauce over moderate heat, stirring occasionally, until slightly thickened, about 10 minutes.

3. In a large pot of salted boiling water, cook the pasta until al dente. Drain, reserving ½ cup of the pasta water. Stir the shredded pork, pasta, pasta water, cherry tomatoes and the ½ cup of cheese into the sauce and cook until hot, about 3 minutes. Season with salt and pepper. Transfer the pasta to bowls, garnish with basil and pass extra cheese at the table. —*Matt Bolus*

MAKE AHEAD The ragù can be refrigerated for up to 2 days and gently reheated.

WINE Juicy Chilean Chardonnay: 2015 Viña Leyda.

Friulian Pasta with Zucchini and Zucchini Flowers

Active **30 min**; Total **1 hr**; Serves **4**

This traditional pasta from the northern Italian region of Friuli is called *girini* ("tadpoles"). It's made with a very soft egg batter that gets pushed through the holes of a colander like spaetzle. Friulian chef Alessandro Gavagna tosses the pasta with sliced zucchini and aged Montasio cheese.

- 4 large eggs
- 1¼ cups 00 flour (see Note on p. 88)
- Kosher salt and pepper
- 2 Tbsp. unsalted butter
- 2 Tbsp. extra-virgin olive oil, plus more for drizzling
- 4 oz. baby zucchini, sliced crosswise ⅛ inch thick (1 cup)
- 8 zucchini flowers (2 oz.), stamen or pistils discarded and flowers halved lengthwise (optional)
- ¼ cup small basil leaves
- Aged Montasio or Parmigiano-Reggiano cheese, for shaving

1. In a bowl, beat the eggs. Using a wooden spoon, mix in the flour and a pinch of salt until a smooth, thick pasta batter forms. Cover and let rest for 30 minutes.

2. Bring a large pot of salted water to a boil. Using a flexible spatula, carefully press ¼ cup of the pasta batter through the holes of a colander into the water and cook until the pasta is firm and floats to the surface, about 30 seconds. Using a slotted spoon, transfer the pasta to an ice water bath to cool. Repeat to cook the remaining 3 batches of pasta. Drain well and pat dry.

3. In a skillet, melt the butter in the 2 tablespoons of olive oil. Add the zucchini rounds and season with salt and pepper. Cook over moderate heat, stirring, until softened, about 2 minutes. Stir in the pasta and season with salt and pepper. Cook, stirring, until warmed through, 3 minutes. Off the heat, stir in the zucchini flowers, if using, and basil. Garnish the pasta with cheese shavings, drizzle with oil and serve. —*Trattoria al Cacciatore della Subida*

MAKE AHEAD The boiled pasta can be refrigerated for up to 2 days.

WINE Crisp, juicy Italian Friulano: 2015 Venica & Venica Ronco delle Cime.

Gluten-Free Penne with Curry-Roasted Cauliflower and Raisins

Active **40 min**; Total **1 hr**; Serves **4 to 6**

- One 2½-lb. head of cauliflower, cored and cut into 1-inch florets
- 2 Tbsp. Madras curry powder
- 2 Tbsp. garam masala
- ¼ cup plus 3 Tbsp. extra-virgin olive oil
- Kosher salt
- ⅓ cup sliced almonds
- 1 cup golden raisins, ½ cup soaked in hot water for 15 minutes and drained
- 3 Tbsp. fresh lemon juice
- ½ lb. gluten-free penne
- 1 leek, halved lengthwise and thinly sliced crosswise
- 1 large garlic clove, thinly sliced
- ½ cup chopped parsley leaves, plus more for garnish
- Yogurt, for topping

1. Preheat the oven to 450°. On a large rimmed baking sheet, toss the cauliflower with the curry powder, garam masala and ¼ cup of the olive oil. Season with salt and toss again. Roast the cauliflower for about 12 minutes, until tender.

2. Meanwhile, spread the almonds in a pie plate and toast for about 5 minutes, until they are golden. In a mini food processor, puree the soaked raisins with the lemon juice, 1 tablespoon of the olive oil and a pinch of salt until smooth.

3. In a large saucepan of salted boiling water, cook the pasta until al dente. Drain well, reserving ¾ cup of the cooking water.

4. Wipe out the saucepan and heat the remaining 2 tablespoons of olive oil in it. Add the leek and garlic and cook over moderate heat, stirring occasionally, until softened and lightly browned, 5 to 7 minutes. Stir in the raisin puree, then add the cauliflower, pasta and the reserved cooking water and cook over moderate heat, tossing, until the pasta is coated in the sauce. Remove from the heat and stir in the ½ cup of parsley and the remaining ½ cup of golden raisins. Transfer to shallow bowls. Garnish with the toasted almonds and chopped parsley and top with yogurt. Serve right away. —*Franklin Becker*

WINE Dry, fruit-forward German Riesling: 2014 Leitz Eins Zwei Dry 3.

SPAGHETTI WITH
SHRIMP, LEMON,
MINT AND PECORINO

Garlicky Mushroom Pasta with Parsley

Total **30 min**; Serves **4**

- 12 oz. orecchiette
- ¼ cup extra-virgin olive oil
- 1 lb. small cremini mushrooms, halved if large
- 5 garlic cloves, finely chopped
- 4 Tbsp. unsalted butter
- ¼ cup chopped parsley
  Kosher salt and pepper
  Lemon wedges, for serving

1. In a large pot of salted boiling water, cook the pasta until al dente. Drain, reserving ½ cup of the cooking water.

2. Meanwhile, in a large skillet, heat the olive oil. Add the mushrooms and garlic and cook over moderate heat, stirring occasionally, until golden and tender, about 8 minutes.

3. Stir the pasta, reserved cooking water and the butter and parsley into the mushrooms and cook, tossing, until saucy, about 2 minutes; season with salt and pepper. Serve with lemon wedges. —*Kay Chun*

WINE Minerally, lemon-zesty Sancerre: 2015 Pascal Jolivet.

Spaghetti with Shrimp, Lemon, Mint and Pecorino

Total **30 min**; Serves **4**

- ½ cup sliced almonds
- ½ lb. spaghetti
- ¼ cup extra-virgin olive oil
- 2 garlic cloves, halved
- ¾ lb. medium shrimp—shelled, deveined and halved lengthwise
  Kosher salt and pepper
- 1 tsp. finely grated lemon zest plus 1 Tbsp. fresh lemon juice
- ¼ cup chopped mint, plus small leaves for garnish
- 1 cup freshly grated Pecorino Romano cheese (3 oz.)
- 1 Fresno chile, thinly sliced

1. Preheat the oven to 425°. Spread the almonds in a cake pan and toast until golden, about 3 minutes. Let cool.

2. In a large saucepan of salted boiling water, cook the pasta until al dente. Drain, reserving ½ cup of the pasta water.

3. Meanwhile, in a large skillet, heat 2 tablespoons of the olive oil. Add the garlic and cook over moderately low heat, stirring, until golden, about 5 minutes; discard the garlic. Season the shrimp with salt and pepper, add to the skillet and cook, turning, until the shrimp are almost white throughout, about 2 minutes.

4. Add the pasta, pasta water, lemon zest, lemon juice, chopped mint, ⅔ cup of the cheese and the remaining 2 tablespoons of olive oil to the skillet and cook, stirring, until saucy, about 2 minutes; season with salt. Transfer the pasta to bowls, garnish with the toasted almonds, mint leaves, chile and remaining cheese and serve. —*Angelo Troiani*

WINE Crisp Tuscan white: 2015 Terenzuola Vigne Basse Colli di Luni Vermentino.

Whole-Wheat Spaghettini with Pork Meatballs and Corn Cream

Total **1 hr 30 min**; Serves **6**

- 1 stick plus 2 Tbsp. unsalted butter
- 4½ cups corn kernels (from 6 ears)
  Kosher salt and pepper
- 3 Tbsp. extra-virgin olive oil
- 1 tsp. minced sage
- 1 tsp. minced thyme
- ¼ cup whole milk
- 3 Tbsp. plain dry breadcrumbs
- 12 oz. ground pork
- 1 Tbsp. minced parsley
- 2 tsp. minced garlic
- ¼ tsp. ground coriander
  Pinch of ground allspice
- ½ cup freshly grated Parmigiano-Reggiano cheese, plus more for garnish
- 6 oz. chanterelle mushrooms, cleaned and cut into large pieces
- ½ cup thinly sliced shallots
- ¼ cup dry white wine
- 1 Tbsp. sherry vinegar
- 4 cups low-sodium chicken broth
- 1 lb. whole-wheat spaghettini

1. In a medium saucepan, melt 2 tablespoons of the butter. Stir in 2 cups of the corn and season with salt and pepper. Add ⅔ cup of water and bring to a simmer; remove from the heat. Transfer the corn and water to a blender and puree until smooth. Strain the corn cream through a fine sieve into a small bowl, pressing on the solids; discard the solids.

2. In a skillet, heat 1 tablespoon of the olive oil. Add ½ teaspoon each of the sage and thyme and cook over moderate heat until fragrant, 30 seconds. Scrape the oil into a bowl and stir in the milk and breadcrumbs. Add the pork, parsley, garlic, coriander, allspice, 2 tablespoons of the grated cheese, 2 teaspoons of salt and ½ teaspoon of pepper and mix well. Form the mixture into 12 meatballs and transfer to a plate.

3. In a nonstick skillet, heat the remaining 2 tablespoons of olive oil. Add the meatballs and cook over moderately high heat until browned all over, about 5 minutes. Transfer to a plate. Add 4 tablespoons of the butter and the mushrooms to the skillet and season with salt and pepper. Cook, stirring occasionally, until lightly browned, about 3 minutes. Using a slotted spoon, add the mushrooms to the meatballs.

4. Add the remaining 2½ cups of corn kernels to the skillet and cook over moderately high heat, stirring, for 1 minute. Add the shallots and the remaining ½ teaspoon each of sage and thyme, reduce the heat to moderate and cook, stirring occasionally, until the shallots are softened, about 3 minutes. Add the wine and vinegar and cook for 1 minute. Stir in the chicken broth and bring to a boil. Cook until the broth is reduced by half, about 15 minutes.

5. Add the meatballs and mushrooms to the skillet and cook, stirring, until the sauce is thickened and the meatballs are cooked through, 5 to 7 minutes. Transfer the meatballs to a plate and keep warm.

6. Meanwhile, cook the pasta in a pot of salted boiling water until al dente. Drain, reserving ½ cup of the pasta water.

7. Return the pasta and pasta water to the pot. Add the corn mixture, corn cream and the remaining 4 tablespoons of butter and 6 tablespoons of cheese and cook, tossing, until the pasta is coated with a thick sauce. Season with salt and pepper. Top with the meatballs, garnish with more cheese and serve at once. —*Carmen Quagliata*

WINE Vibrant Pinot Noir: 2011 Montebruno Crawford Beck Vineyard Eola–Amity Hills.

Cavatelli with Sparerib Ragù

📷 PAGE 82

Active **1 hr**; Total **3 hr**; Serves **10 to 12**

For this hearty ragù, Manhattan chef Josh Laurano enriches tomato sauce with both little riblets and tender chunks of sparerib meat. He simmers it with pork skin to make it next-level luscious.

- **One 4-lb. rack of pork spareribs, rack cut crosswise through the rib bones into 3 strips (have your butcher do this)**
- ¼ **cup plus 1 Tbsp. extra-virgin olive oil**
- **Kosher salt and pepper**
- 1 **large yellow onion, finely chopped**
- 5 **carrots, finely chopped**
- 4 **celery ribs, finely chopped**
- 4 **garlic cloves, crushed**
- 2 **Tbsp. chopped thyme**
- ½ **lb. pork skin, cut into small dice (optional)**
- 2 **cups dry red wine**
- **One 28-oz. can crushed tomatoes**
- 2 **lbs. cavatelli**
- 1 **cup freshly grated Parmigiano-Reggiano cheese, plus more for serving**

1. Preheat the oven to 450°. Cut the center strip of the spareribs into individual riblets and set on a baking sheet. Cut each outer strip into 3 equal pieces and add to the baking sheet. Drizzle the ribs with 2 tablespoons of the oil, season with salt and pepper and turn to coat. Roast until golden, 20 minutes. Let cool slightly, then tie the individual ribs in a cheesecloth bundle.

2. In a large enameled cast-iron casserole, heat 2 tablespoons of the oil. Add the onion, carrots, celery, garlic, thyme and pork skin, if using. Cook over moderate heat, stirring, until the vegetables are softened, 15 minutes. Add the wine and cook until reduced by half, 5 minutes. Stir in the tomatoes, 2 cups of water and the roasted rib strips and bring to a simmer. Cook over low heat for 45 minutes, stirring occasionally. Add the cheesecloth rib bundle. Cook, stirring, until the sauce is thick and all the ribs are tender, about 1 hour longer. Remove the cheesecloth bundle and reserve the riblets.

3. Transfer the rib strips to a work surface and remove the meat from the bones. Add the meat to the ragù; discard the bones.

4. In a large pot of salted boiling water, cook the pasta until al dente. Drain, reserving 1 cup of the pasta water. Return the pasta to the pot and add the reserved water, the ragù, the remaining 1 tablespoon of olive oil and the 1 cup of grated cheese. Season with salt and pepper and toss until well coated. Mound the pasta in bowls, garnish with the riblets and serve, passing additional cheese at the table.
—*Josh Laurano*

MAKE AHEAD The ragù can be refrigerated for up to 1 week or frozen for up to 1 month.

WINE Rich, vibrant, deeply fruity Tuscan red: 2012 Fattoria Fibbiano L'Aspetto Toscano.

Buckwheat Pasta Triangles with Lardo and Greens

Active **1 hr 15 min;** Total **2 hr 15 min** Serves **4**

This hand-rolled pasta, made with a mix of buckwheat and all-purpose flours, is called *blecs* in Friuli, Italy. The name refers to the unusual triangular shape, though the pasta can also be square.

PASTA DOUGH
- ¾ **cup plus 2 Tbsp. all-purpose flour, plus more for dusting**
- ⅓ **cup plus 2 Tbsp. buckwheat flour**
- ½ **tsp. kosher salt**
- 2 **large eggs**
- ½ **tsp. extra-virgin olive oil**

TOPPING
- 4 **oz. lardo (Italian cured pork back fat; see Note) or guanciale, finely chopped (⅔ cup)**
- 2 **garlic cloves, minced**
- 1 **large egg**
- 8 **oz. curly spinach, stemmed and coarsely chopped (4 cups)**
- 4 **oz. baby arugula (8 cups)**
- **Kosher salt and pepper**
- ½ **cup freshly grated Parmigiano-Reggiano cheese, plus more for garnish**
- **Extra-virgin olive oil, for drizzling**

1. Make the pasta dough In a medium bowl, whisk the 2 flours with the salt. Mound the flour mixture on a work surface and make a well in the center. Add the eggs and olive oil to the well and beat with a fork; gradually incorporate the flour, starting with the inner rim and maintaining the side of the well as long as possible. Once a soft dough forms, knead until elastic and smooth but still a little tacky, about 5 minutes. Wrap the pasta dough in plastic and refrigerate for 1 hour.

2. Divide the dough in half. On a floured work surface, using a lightly floured rolling pin, roll out 1 piece of dough 1/16 inch thick. With a sharp knife, cut the dough into 2-inch-wide strips, then cut each strip into 2- to 3-inch triangles. Transfer to a parchment paper–lined baking sheet and top with another sheet of parchment. Repeat with the second piece of dough.

3. Make the topping In a large skillet, cook the lardo over moderately low heat, stirring, until starting to crisp, 3 to 4 minutes. Add the garlic and cook until fragrant, 1 minute. Add the egg and cook, stirring, just until scrambled. Add the spinach and arugula and toss just until wilted, about 2 minutes. Season the topping with salt and pepper and set aside half in a bowl.

4. In a pot of salted boiling water, cook half of the pasta until al dente, about 3 minutes. Using a slotted spoon, add the triangles to the topping in the skillet with a little water clinging to the pasta. Add ¼ cup of the cheese. Cook over moderate heat, tossing, until well blended, 2 minutes. Transfer to a large serving bowl. Repeat with the remaining pasta, boiling it, then finishing it with the remaining topping and ¼ cup of cheese. Garnish the dish with cheese, drizzle with oil and serve.
—*Giampaolo Venica*

NOTE Lardo is available at specialty food shops and Italian markets.

MAKE AHEAD The pasta triangles can be refrigerated overnight, layered between sheets of parchment.

WINE Fragrant, minerally Pinot Grigio: 2015 Venica & Venica Jesera Collio.

Ricotta Gnocchi Gratin

Total **1 hr 45 min**; Serves **8**

Celebrity chef Geoffrey Zakarian sautés airy ricotta cheese gnocchi with sage and butter until golden, then sprinkles them with a generous amount of Parmigiano-Reggiano. For tips on mastering this delicate pasta, see Gnocchi Secrets (below right).

- **1½ lbs. ricotta cheese**
- **⅔ cup grated Parmigiano-Reggiano cheese, plus more for serving**
- **1 large egg plus 1 large egg yolk**
- **1½ tsp. grated lemon zest plus 6 tsp. fresh lemon juice**
- **½ tsp. freshly grated nutmeg**
- **Kosher salt and pepper**
- **1¼ cups all-purpose flour, plus more for dusting**
- **3 Tbsp. extra-virgin olive oil, plus more for greasing**
- **One 4 oz. piece of pancetta, finely chopped**
- **1 stick plus 1 Tbsp. unsalted butter**
- **30 sage leaves**
- **½ tsp. finely grated orange zest**

1. In the bowl of a stand mixer fitted with the dough hook, mix the ricotta with the ⅔ cup of Parmigiano, the whole egg, egg yolk, lemon zest, nutmeg, 2 teaspoons of salt and ½ teaspoon of pepper at medium speed until blended. With the machine on low, gradually add the 1¼ cups of flour until incorporated. Beat at medium speed until a tacky dough forms, about 1 minute. Scrape the dough out onto a floured work surface and pat into a mass. Dust the top with flour, then wrap in plastic and refrigerate for 30 minutes.

2. Line a baking sheet with wax paper and dust with flour. On a floured surface, cut the dough into 4 pieces; gently roll each into a ¾-inch-thick rope. Cut the ropes into 1-inch lengths and transfer to the prepared baking sheet.

3. Grease a large rimmed baking sheet with oil. In a large pot of simmering salted water, cook one-third of the gnocchi over moderate heat until they rise to the surface, then cook for 2 minutes longer. Using a slotted spoon, transfer to the prepared baking sheet. Repeat with the remaining gnocchi.

4. Preheat the oven to 200°. In a large skillet, cook one-third of the pancetta in 1 tablespoon of the oil over moderate heat, stirring occasionally, until the fat is rendered but the pancetta is not crisp, 3 to 5 minutes. Stir in 3 tablespoons of the butter and cook, stirring, until it just starts to brown and smell nutty, about 3 minutes. Add 10 sage leaves and cook until crisp, about 20 seconds.

5. Add one-third of the gnocchi to the skillet and cook, undisturbed, until golden on the bottom, 2 to 3 minutes. Using a metal spatula, flip the gnocchi and cook until browned, about 2 minutes longer. Stir in 2 teaspoons of the lemon juice and a pinch of the orange zest; season with salt and pepper. Using a spatula or slotted spoon, transfer the gnocchi, pancetta and sage to a large ovenproof serving dish. Spoon 2 tablespoons of the fat from the skillet over the gnocchi; keep warm in the oven. Pour off the remaining fat from the skillet. Repeat the whole process 2 more times. Sprinkle Parmesan over the gnocchi and serve. —*Geoffrey Zakarian*

WINE Rich, fruit-forward Chardonnay: 2012 Foxglove.

Calabrian Carbonara

Total **30 min**; Serves **4 to 6**

"I love this pasta mash-up," says chef Andrew Carmellini of Locanda Verde in New York City. "It's a Roman classic with Calabrian style, where I replace one pork product (bacon) with another ('nduja)."

- **6 large egg yolks**
- **1 large egg**
- **½ cup finely grated Pecorino Romano cheese, plus more for serving**
- **1 lb. spaghetti**
- **2 Tbsp. extra-virgin olive oil**
- **4 oz. 'nduja (see Note)**
- **Kosher salt and pepper**
- **Dried oregano, for sprinkling**

1. In a medium bowl, beat the egg yolks with the whole egg and the ½ cup of grated Pecorino Romano cheese.

2. In a large pot of salted boiling water, cook the spaghetti until al dente. Drain, reserving ¾ cup of the cooking water.

3. Meanwhile, in a medium skillet, heat the olive oil. Add the 'nduja and cook over moderate heat, breaking up the meat with a wooden spoon, until the fat is rendered, 3 to 5 minutes.

4. In a large bowl, toss the hot pasta with the 'nduja. Add the egg mixture and the reserved pasta cooking water and toss aggressively until the pasta is coated in a creamy sauce, about 1 minute. Season with salt and pepper. Transfer the pasta to shallow bowls or a platter and sprinkle with dried oregano. Serve, passing more cheese at the table. —*Andrew Carmellini*

NOTE 'Nduja is a spicy, spreadable Calabrian pork sausage. Look for it at Italian food shops and on amazon.com.

WINE Spice-inflected Calabrian red blend: 2013 Odoardi Savuto.

CHEF COMMANDMENTS

Gnocchi Secrets

Chef and Food Network personality Geoffrey Zakarian shares his tips for making perfectly fluffy gnocchi.

DON'T use a fork to mix gnocchi dough. You need a stand mixer to fully and evenly incorporate all of the ingredients and enough air to make them tender.

DO nudge the dough into a lumpy mass. It doesn't need to be a perfect ball.

DON'T roll the dough with your hands parallel. Instead, gently push out with your hands at an angle.

DON'T cut gnocchi unevenly. Different-size pieces of dough will need different cooking times.

DO keep the cooked gnocchi warm in a 200° oven while you finish the dish.

Potato Gnocchi with Chorizo Sauce

Active **1 hr 45 min**; Total **3 hr**; Serves **8 to 10**

Star Argentinean chef Francis Mallmann is a fan of contrasts in his food, as this pasta dish demonstrates. "The chorizo has a very peasant, strong flavor, and the delicate gnocchi melt in your mouth," he says. "When you have clashes of tastes in your mouth, it wakes you up."

GNOCCHI

- **3 lbs. baking potatoes**
- **6 large egg yolks, lightly beaten**
- **3 cups all-purpose flour, plus more for dusting**
- **1½ cups freshly grated Parmigiano-Reggiano cheese**
- **4 tsp. kosher salt**
- **1 tsp. freshly ground pepper**
- **¼ tsp. freshly grated nutmeg**

CHORIZO SAUCE

- **3 medium tomatoes**
- **1 lb. fresh chorizo, casings removed**
- **2 Tbsp. extra-virgin olive oil**
- **1 small yellow onion, minced**
  Kosher salt and black pepper
- **1 carrot, coarsely grated**
- **2 garlic cloves, minced**
- **1½ Tbsp. tomato paste**
- **½ cup dry white wine**
- **1 bay leaf**
- **1 Tbsp. sugar**
- **2 cups chicken stock**
- **¼ cup freshly grated Parmigiano-Reggiano, plus more for garnish**
- **1½ tsp. minced oregano, plus sprigs for garnish**
  Crushed red pepper, for garnish

1. Make the gnocchi Preheat the oven to 400°. Prick the potatoes with a fork, wrap in foil and bake until tender, 1 hour. Let stand until just cool enough to handle, about 10 minutes. Peel the potatoes and cut into large chunks. Press through a ricer onto a work surface; you should have about 6 loosely packed cups. Gently spread the potatoes into a 10-by-18-inch rectangle. Scrape the egg yolks on top and sprinkle with the 3 cups of flour, the cheese, salt, pepper and nutmeg. Using a pastry scraper, swiftly chop the ingredients

together. Knead gently until the dough comes together in a smooth ball. Cut into 8 wedges and cover with a kitchen towel.

2. Lightly dust 2 rimmed baking sheets with flour. Roll 1 wedge of gnocchi dough into a ¾-inch-thick rope, about 18 inches long. Using a knife, cut the rope into ¾-inch pieces and transfer to a prepared baking sheet. Repeat with the remaining dough. Cover the gnocchi with plastic wrap and refrigerate until firm, at least 30 minutes.

3. Make the chorizo sauce Working over a bowl, coarsely grate the tomatoes on a box grater; discard the skins. You should have about 1¾ cups of tomato puree.

4. In a deep medium skillet, cook the chorizo over moderate heat, breaking up any clumps, until beginning to brown, 8 to 10 minutes. Scrape the chorizo onto a plate.

5. Heat the oil in the skillet. Add the onion, season with a generous pinch each of salt and black pepper and cook over moderate heat until golden, 5 to 7 minutes. Add the carrot and garlic and cook, stirring, until softened, about 2 minutes. Stir in the tomato paste. Deglaze the skillet with the wine, scraping up any browned bits. Cook until the wine has reduced by two-thirds, about 3 minutes. Return the chorizo to the skillet with the fresh tomato puree, bay leaf, sugar and chicken stock. Bring the sauce to a boil, then simmer over moderately low heat, stirring, until reduced by half, about 45 minutes. Stir in the ¼ cup of cheese and the minced oregano and season with salt and black pepper. Keep warm.

6. In a pot of salted boiling water, cook the gnocchi in 3 batches until tender, about 6½ minutes per batch. The gnocchi will float to the top after 1 to 2 minutes; keep cooking them. Using a slotted spoon, transfer the gnocchi to a warm platter. Spoon the chorizo sauce on top and garnish with grated cheese, oregano sprigs and red pepper. —*Francis Mallmann*

MAKE AHEAD The uncooked gnocchi can be frozen for 1 month; boil without defrosting. The chorizo sauce can be refrigerated for 4 days and gently reheated.

WINE A smoky Argentinean Malbec: 2012 Bodega Colomé Estate.

Ricotta Gnocchi with Summer Herbs

⏱ Total **45 min**; Serves **4 to 6**

- **Kosher salt and pepper**
- **2 cups fresh ricotta cheese (1 lb.)**
- **1 large egg**
- **¼ cup freshly grated Parmigiano-Reggiano cheese**
- **¾ cup all-purpose flour**
- **2 Tbsp. extra-virgin olive oil, plus more for drizzling**
- **1½ tsp. finely grated lemon zest, plus more for garnish**
  Snipped chives, chopped parsley and small basil leaves, for garnish

1. Tie a length of thin kitchen twine tightly across a two-handled large saucepan. Fill the saucepan halfway with water and bring to a simmer. Add a generous pinch of salt.

2. Meanwhile, in a food processor, pulse the ricotta with the egg and Parmigiano-Reggiano until smooth; scrape down the side of the bowl as necessary. Add the flour and 1½ teaspoons of salt and pulse until just incorporated.

3. Scrape the gnocchi dough into a large, sturdy resealable plastic bag; press the dough into a corner of the bag to remove as much air as possible, then snip off the corner to make a ½- to ¾-inch opening.

4. Using steady pressure and carefully working over the pot of simmering water, pipe one-third of the gnocchi dough into ¾-inch lengths, using the twine to cut the gnocchi into the saucepan. Simmer until the gnocchi rise to the surface, then continue simmering until the gnocchi are plump and cooked through, about 5 minutes total. Using a slotted spoon, transfer the gnocchi to a lightly oiled rimmed baking sheet. Repeat the process with the remaining 2 batches of dough.

5. Transfer the gnocchi to a platter. Add the 2 tablespoons of olive oil and 1½ teaspoons of lemon zest and gently toss to coat. Season with salt and pepper and toss again. Serve in shallow bowls, garnished with a drizzle of olive oil, lemon zest, snipped chives, chopped parsley and small basil leaves. —*Justin Chapple*

WINE Bright, fruit-forward red from Sicily: 2014 Tamì Frappato.

RICOTTA GNOCCHI
WITH SUMMER HERBS

BAKED RIGATONI WITH
MILK-BRAISED PORK,
RICOTTA AND LEMON

Crusty Baked Shells and Cauliflower

Active **about 1 hr**; Total **about 1 hr 30 min**
Serves **6 to 8**

- **Kosher salt and freshly ground black pepper**
- ¾ **lb. medium shells, such as Barilla**
- **Good olive oil**
- 2½ **lbs. cauliflower, cut into small florets (1 large head)**
- 3 **Tbsp. roughly chopped fresh sage leaves**
- 2 **Tbsp. capers, drained**
- 1 **Tbsp. minced garlic (3 cloves)**
- ½ **tsp. grated lemon zest**
- ¼ **tsp. crushed red pepper flakes**
- 2 **cups freshly grated Italian Fontina Val d'Aosta cheese, lightly packed (10 oz. with rind)**
- 1 **cup (8 oz.) fresh ricotta**
- ½ **cup panko (Japanese bread flakes)**
- 6 **Tbsp. freshly grated Italian Pecorino cheese**
- 2 **Tbsp. minced fresh parsley leaves**

1. Preheat the oven to 400°.

2. Fill a large pot with water, add 2 tablespoons of salt and bring to a boil. Add the pasta and cook until al dente, according to the instructions on the package. Since it will be baked later, don't overcook it! Drain and pour into a very large bowl.

3. Meanwhile, heat 3 tablespoons of olive oil in a large (12-inch) sauté pan over medium-high heat, add half of the cauliflower in one layer and sauté for 5 to 6 minutes, tossing occasionally, until the florets are lightly browned and tender. Pour the cauliflower, including the small bits, into the bowl with the pasta. Add 3 more tablespoons of olive oil to the sauté pan, add the remaining cauliflower, cook until browned and tender and add to the bowl.

4. Add the sage, capers, garlic, lemon zest, red pepper flakes, 2 teaspoons salt and 1 teaspoon black pepper to the bowl and stir carefully. Stir in the Fontina. Transfer half of the mixture to a 10 x 13 x 2–inch rectangular baking dish. Spoon rounded tablespoons of ricotta on the pasta and spoon the remaining pasta mixture on top. Combine the panko, Pecorino, parsley and 1 tablespoon of olive oil in a small bowl and sprinkle it evenly on top. Bake for 25 to 30 minutes, until browned and crusty on top. Serve hot. —*Ina Garten*

WINE Light-bodied Pinot Noir: 2014 Angeline Reserve.

Baked Rigatoni with Milk-Braised Pork, Ricotta and Lemon

Active **45 min**; Total **4 hr 30 min**; Serves **8**

The secret to this sumptuous baked pasta is the tender milk-braised pork and its cooking liquid, which is pureed to create the sauce for the rigatoni.

- ¼ **cup extra-virgin olive oil**
- **One 4-lb. boneless pork shoulder roast**
- **Kosher salt and pepper**
- 12 **garlic cloves**
- ½ **cup dry white wine**
- 3 **qts. whole milk**
- 6 **rosemary sprigs, plus chopped rosemary for garnish**
- 1 **bay leaf**
- **Five 3-inch strips of lemon zest**
- 1 **lb. rigatoni**
- 2 **cups fresh ricotta cheese (1 lb.)**
- **Freshly grated pecorino cheese, preferably Pecorino di Fossa**

1. Preheat the oven to 375°. In a large enameled cast-iron casserole, heat 2 tablespoons of the olive oil. Rub the pork all over with the remaining 2 tablespoons of olive oil and season with salt and pepper. Add to the casserole and cook over moderately high heat until browned all over, about 8 minutes; transfer to a plate. Add the garlic to the casserole and cook, stirring, until golden, 1 to 2 minutes. Add the wine; cook until almost evaporated, about 2 minutes.

2. Add the milk, rosemary sprigs, bay leaf and lemon zest to the casserole and bring to a simmer. Add the pork and braise in the oven for about 3 hours, until the meat is very tender. Let the pork cool in the casserole to room temperature.

3. Transfer the pork to a work surface and cut in half. Coarsely chop 1 piece; reserve the remaining pork for another use. Working in 2 batches, puree the cooking liquid in a blender until smooth. Strain through a fine sieve, pressing down on the solids.

4. Increase the oven temperature to 425°. Lightly grease a 3½- to 4-quart baking dish. In a pot of salted boiling water, cook the pasta until barely al dente. Drain and transfer to a large bowl. Add the chopped pork and 3 cups of the strained cooking liquid, season with salt and pepper and toss to coat. Transfer the pasta to the prepared baking dish and dollop the ricotta on top. Cover with foil and bake for about 20 minutes, until the pasta is tender. Uncover and bake for about 15 minutes longer, until golden on top. Garnish with pepper and chopped rosemary. Serve with grated pecorino. —*Ryan Hardy and Tim Caspare*

WINE Supple, full-bodied white: 2013 J.L. Chave Selection Circa Saint-Joseph Blanc.

Pasta Bundt Loaf

Active **25 min**; Total **1 hr 15 min**; Serves **8**

Justin Chapple, star of F&W's Mad Genius Tips videos, creates a fun riff on mac and cheese that maximizes the crisp bits. He mixes spaghetti with three types of cheese, then bakes everything in a Bundt pan—its grooves deliver more crisp edges than a rectangular baking dish.

- **Unsalted butter, for greasing**
- 1 **lb. spaghetti**
- 6 **oz. Fontina cheese, shredded (2 cups)**
- 6 **oz. sharp white cheddar cheese, shredded (2 cups)**
- 1½ **cups whole milk**
- ¾ **cup grated Parmigiano-Reggiano cheese**
- 3 **large eggs, lightly beaten**
- 2½ **tsp. pepper**
- 2 **tsp. kosher salt**

1. Preheat the oven to 425°. Generously butter a 10-inch Bundt pan. In a pot of salted boiling water, cook the spaghetti until al dente. Drain well.

2. In a large bowl, mix the pasta with all of the remaining ingredients. Scrape into the prepared pan and bake until the cheese is melted and bubbling, 35 to 40 minutes.

3. Transfer the pan to a rack and let cool for 15 minutes. Invert the loaf onto a platter, cut into wedges and serve. —*Justin Chapple*

WINE Medium-bodied Italian white: 2015 Sartarelli Verdicchio Castelli di Jesi Classico.

Ricotta-Filled Handkerchief Pasta with Pesto and Marinara

Total **2 hr 15 min;** Serves **8**

Known as *mandilli di seta,* or silk handkerchiefs, this dish is a specialty of Genoa. Delicate sheets of pasta are coated with pesto, stuffed with ricotta, then set atop a pool of tomato sauce. To save time, you can use store-bought pasta sheets.

PASTA

1½ cups (8 oz.) 00 flour (see Note on p. 88)

½ cup durum semolina flour, plus more for dusting

1 tsp. kosher salt

10 large egg yolks

1 Tbsp. extra-virgin olive oil

PESTO

1¼ cups blanched almonds

4 garlic cloves

2¼ cups extra-virgin olive oil

4 cups basil leaves

2 cups freshly grated Parmigiano-Reggiano cheese (6 oz.)

1¼ cups freshly grated Pecorino Romano cheese, plus more for garnish

⅓ cup mascarpone cheese

Kosher salt

MARINARA

Two 28-oz. cans whole peeled San Marzano tomatoes

2 Tbsp. extra-virgin olive oil

1 garlic clove, minced

Pinch of sugar

Kosher salt

2 cups fresh ricotta cheese (1 lb.)

1. Make the pasta In a medium bowl, whisk the 00 flour and the ½ cup of semolina flour with the salt. In another bowl, whisk the egg yolks with the olive oil and ¼ cup of water. Mound the flour mixture on a work surface and make a well in the center. Add the beaten yolks to the well and gradually incorporate the flour with a fork, starting with the inner rim of the well and working your way out until all of the flour is incorporated and a soft dough forms. Knead the dough until smooth and elastic, about 10 minutes. Wrap in plastic and refrigerate for 1 hour.

2. Cut the dough into 8 equal pieces and cover with a kitchen towel. Lightly dust 1 piece of dough with semolina flour and flatten slightly. Run the dough twice through a pasta machine at the widest setting. Run the dough twice through successively narrower settings until it is ⅛ to 1/16 inch thick and 14 to 16 inches long. Lay the pasta sheet on a semolina-dusted baking sheet and generously dust with more semolina. Repeat with the remaining 7 pieces of dough. Keep the pasta sheets covered with a damp kitchen towel.

3. Make the pesto In a food processor, pulse the almonds with the garlic and olive oil until smooth. Add the basil and pulse until finely chopped. Add the Parmesan, the 1¼ cups of pecorino and the mascarpone and pulse until smooth. Season with salt and scrape into a large bowl.

4. Make the marinara In a food processor, pulse the tomatoes with their juices until almost smooth. In a large saucepan, heat the olive oil. Add the garlic and cook over moderate heat, stirring, until fragrant, 1 minute. Add the pureed tomatoes and the sugar, season with salt and bring to a simmer. Cook over moderately low heat, stirring occasionally, until thickened, about 30 minutes; keep warm.

5. Meanwhile, preheat the oven to 450°. Line 2 rimmed baking sheets with parchment paper. In a very large pot of salted boiling water, cook 2 pasta sheets until al dente, about 3 minutes. Using a slotted spoon, lift out the pasta sheets and let them drain slightly, then turn gently in the pesto to coat. Lay one of the pasta sheets on a prepared baking sheet and dollop ¼ cup of the ricotta near one end. Fold one-third of the pasta sheet over the ricotta, then fold the rest of the sheet over onto itself. Repeat to fill the second pesto-coated sheet, then repeat the entire process with the remaining pasta sheets, pesto and ricotta. Cover the folded handkerchief pasta with foil and bake for 10 minutes, until hot throughout.

6. Spoon the marinara sauce into shallow bowls. Top with the stuffed pasta handkerchiefs, garnish with pecorino and serve. —*Tim Cushman*

WINE Berry-rich Italian red: 2014 Piazzo Piemonte Barbera.

Corn-and-Zucchini Orzo Salad with Goat Cheese

Total **45 min;** Serves **4**

Take pasta salad to a new level with sweet grilled corn, zucchini and a creamy lime dressing spiked with chile powder. Then finish it off with tangy slivers of fresh goat cheese. To prevent clumping, borrow this chef hack: Freeze the cheese before shaving it.

3 ears of corn, shucked

1 lb. small zucchini or summer squash, halved lengthwise

¼ cup extra-virgin olive oil

Kosher salt and pepper

½ lb. orzo

¼ cup mayonnaise

3 Tbsp. fresh lime juice

1 Tbsp. minced shallot

½ tsp. guajillo or ancho chile powder

1½ cups coarsely chopped cilantro

2 oz. fresh goat cheese, frozen

1. Light a grill or heat a grill pan. In a large bowl, toss the corn and zucchini with 1 tablespoon of the olive oil and season with salt and pepper. Grill over moderate heat until charred and crisp-tender, about 10 minutes for the zucchini and 15 minutes for the corn. Transfer to a cutting board and let cool. Cut the kernels off the corncobs and coarsely chop the zucchini. Transfer to a large bowl.

2. Meanwhile, in a large saucepan of salted boiling water, cook the orzo until al dente. Drain and rinse under cold water to cool. Drain well and spread the orzo out on a baking sheet; pat dry with paper towels.

3. In a large bowl, whisk the mayonnaise with the remaining 3 tablespoons of olive oil and the lime juice, shallot, chile powder and ½ cup of the cilantro; season with salt and pepper. Add the orzo, corn, zucchini and the remaining chopped cilantro and mix well. Transfer to a platter. Using a vegetable peeler, shave the frozen goat cheese all over the top and serve. —*Kay Chun*

WINE Citrusy white: 2014 Mt. Beautiful North Canterbury Sauvignon Blanc.

RICOTTA-FILLED
HANDKERCHIEF PASTA WITH
PESTO AND MARINARA

DIY Ravioli

At Chicago's Monteverde, chef **SARAH GRUENEBERG** and her Italian pasta squad prepare *uovo in raviolo*—a giant pasta round stuffed with fresh ricotta, feta and a runny egg yolk. Here's how to #putanegginit at home.

Uovo in Raviolo with Hand-Grated-Tomato Sauce

Active **1 hr 15 min**; Total **2 hr**; Serves **8**

PASTA DOUGH

- 2 large eggs
- 4 large egg yolks
- 2 cups (10 oz.) 00 flour (see Note on p. 88)

FILLING

- 8 oz. soft sheep-milk feta cheese, such as Bulgarian or Spanish
- 8 oz. whole-milk ricotta
- ½ cup (1 oz.) freshly grated Pecorino Romano cheese
- ½ tsp. grated orange zest
- 1 Tbsp. chopped parsley
- 2 tsp. chopped oregano
- Kosher salt

TOMATO SAUCE

- 4 lbs. ripe tomatoes, halved
- 6 Tbsp. extra-virgin olive oil
- 1 garlic clove, minced
- 1 pinch of crushed red pepper
- Kosher salt

RAVIOLI

- Semolina, for dusting
- 8 large egg yolks
- 3 large egg whites, beaten
- 1 cup torn basil leaves, plus small leaves for garnish
- Shaved Pecorino Romano cheese, for garnish

MAKE THE PASTA DOUGH

1. In a small bowl, whisk the eggs with the egg yolks and ¼ cup of water. Mound the flour on a work surface, make a well in the center and add the eggs. Using a fork, gradually draw in the flour until a dough forms. Gather and knead the dough until smooth. Form into a ball, cover in plastic wrap and refrigerate for 1 hour.

MAKE THE FILLING

2. In a food processor, pulse the feta until smooth. Scrape into a medium bowl and add the next 5 ingredients. Mix until well blended and season with salt. Refrigerate until ready to use.

MAKE THE TOMATO SAUCE

3. Grate the tomato halves on the large holes of a box grater set in a bowl until only the skins remain; discard the skins. In a large saucepan, heat the olive oil. Add the garlic and cook over moderate heat, stirring, until fragrant, about 2 minutes. Add the grated tomatoes and crushed red pepper and season with salt. Cook over moderate heat, stirring occasionally, until the sauce has thickened and reduced to 3 cups, about 20 minutes.

MAKE THE RAVIOLI

4. Divide the pasta dough into 4 pieces. Work with 1 piece at a time; keep the rest covered. Press the dough to flatten it slightly. Run the dough twice through a pasta machine at the widest setting. Run the dough through 4 successively narrower settings, twice per setting, until it is about 1⁄16 inch thick. Dust a work surface with semolina and lay the pasta sheet on top; dust the pasta generously with semolina and cover with a damp kitchen towel. Repeat with the remaining 3 pieces of pasta dough, keeping the rolled-out sheets covered.

5. Lay 1 of the pasta sheets on a work surface and brush off the semolina. Spoon four ¼-cup mounds of the cheese filling onto the pasta sheet about 4 inches apart. Spread the mounds of filling into 3-inch rounds and make a small well in the center

STEP-BY-STEP RAVIOLI LESSON

MAKE THE TOMATO SAUCE Rub the tomatoes on a box grater set in a bowl until only the skins remain in your hand. Cook the tomato pulp.

GET ROLLING Starting at the pasta machine's widest setting, roll out the dough through successively narrower settings until you have thin sheets.

ADD CHEESE AND EGGS Spread the cheese filling into 3-inch rounds and make an indentation in each one. Gently set an egg yolk into each hollow.

SANDWICH THE FILLING Brush the pasta dough around the filling with egg white. Cover with another pasta sheet.

of the filling. Slip 1 egg yolk into each well. Brush around the filling with the beaten egg whites. Drape another sheet of pasta on top and press around the fillings to push any air pockets out of the ravioli. Using a 4-inch fluted cookie cutter, stamp out the ravioli. Press the edges to make sure they are sealed. Transfer the ravioli to a semolina-dusted baking sheet. Repeat to form another 4 ravioli; reserve any remaining filling for another use.

6. Bring a large pot of water to a boil and season generously with salt. Reheat the tomato sauce in the saucepan. Using a slotted spoon, add 4 of the ravioli to the boiling water and cook until al dente, about 3 minutes. Using a slotted spoon, transfer the ravioli to the sauce. Add half of the torn basil and cook, stirring gently, until nicely coated, about 1 minute. Transfer the ravioli to plates and spoon some of the sauce on top. Repeat with the remaining 4 ravioli and torn basil. Garnish with pecorino and basil leaves and serve.

MAKE AHEAD The filling and tomato sauce can be stored separately in the refrigerator for up to 3 days. The formed ravioli can be covered and refrigerated for 3 hours.

WINE A bright and smoky red from Sicily: 2013 Benanti Rosso di Verzella Etna Rosso.

FORM THE RAVIOLI Using your fingertips, press the pasta dough around the filling to release any air bubbles and to seal. The yolks are protected by the ricotta.

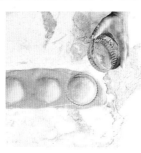

STAMP OUT NEAT ROUNDS Using a fluted or round biscuit cutter, press firmly around each ravioli and discard or reuse excess dough.

FINISH THE RAVIOLI Boil the ravioli until just al dente, then drain and transfer to the tomato sauce to coat thoroughly.

SPINACH-AND-
PROSCIUTTO RAVIOLI

Spinach-and-Prosciutto Ravioli

Active **1 hr 30 min**; Total **3 hr**; Serves **6 to 8**

FILLING

- ½ lb. prosciutto, sliced ½ inch thick
- 1 lb. curly spinach, stems discarded
- 6 oz. fresh ricotta cheese
- 6 oz. fresh mascarpone cheese
- 2 large egg yolks
- 1 cup freshly grated Parmigiano-Reggiano cheese
-   Kosher salt

PASTA

- 2½ cups 00 flour (see Note on p. 88)
- 1 tsp. kosher salt
- 12 large egg yolks
-   Semolina flour, for dusting
- 1 stick plus 2 Tbsp. unsalted butter, cut into thin slices
- 4 oz. curly spinach, coarsely chopped (4 cups)
- 2 tsp. fennel pollen or ½ tsp. ground fennel
- ½ cup freshly grated Parmigiano-Reggiano cheese

1. Make the filling Dice the prosciutto and transfer to a bowl. Freeze until very firm, 30 minutes. In a food processor, pulse the chilled prosciutto until finely chopped, about 30 seconds. Return to the bowl.

2. Meanwhile, in a pot of salted boiling water, blanch the spinach until just tender, about 1 minute. Transfer to a colander and let cool slightly. Press out all of the excess water and coarsely chop the spinach; you should have ½ cup.

3. In a medium bowl, whisk the ricotta until smooth. Add the prosciutto along with the chopped spinach, the mascarpone, egg yolks and Parmesan; stir well. Season with salt. Cover the filling with plastic wrap and refrigerate until firm, about 30 minutes.

4. Make the pasta In a large bowl, whisk the 00 flour with the salt; make a well in the center. Add the egg yolks and 1 tablespoon of water to the well and mix. Using a fork, gradually incorporate the flour into the wet ingredients until a shaggy dough forms. Scrape the dough out onto a work surface very lightly dusted with semolina flour and knead until stiff but smooth, 5 minutes. Wrap in plastic and let rest at room temperature until softened, 45 minutes.

5. Generously dust a work surface with semolina flour. Line a rimmed baking sheet with parchment paper and dust with semolina flour. Divide the pasta dough into 4 pieces and work with one at a time; keep the rest covered. Press the dough to flatten. Using a hand-cranked pasta machine and starting at the widest setting, run the dough twice through each of the first 5 settings, then run it once through the sixth setting. Cut the sheet in half; run each half through the thinnest setting one time. Transfer the sheets to the prepared work surface.

6. Lay 1 pasta sheet on a work surface with a long edge facing you. Spoon eight 1-teaspoon-size balls of filling in each of 2 rows on the sheet, allowing 1 inch of space between them. Very lightly brush the dough around the filling with water. Place the second pasta sheet on top. Using your fingers, press the dough around each mound of filling. Using a 2-inch fluted cutter, stamp out the ravioli; transfer to the semolina-dusted baking sheet. Cover with a clean tea towel. Repeat with the remaining dough and filling to make 64 ravioli.

7. In a pot of salted boiling water, cook the ravioli in 2 batches until the edges are tender, about 2 minutes. Using a slotted spoon, transfer to a shallow bowl. Reserve 1 cup of the cooking water.

8. Melt 4 tablespoons of the butter in each of 2 large skillets. Add ½ cup of the pasta water and half of the chopped spinach to each skillet and cook over moderately high heat until the spinach is just wilted, about 1 minute. Add half of the ravioli to each skillet and cook, stirring gently, until they are coated in butter. Using a slotted spoon, transfer the ravioli and spinach to a large serving bowl. Scrape the remaining liquid from 1 large skillet into the other. Add the remaining 2 tablespoons of butter to the skillet along with 1 teaspoon of the fennel pollen and ¼ cup of the cheese. Cook over moderate heat, swirling the pan gently, until the butter has melted and the sauce has thickened slightly, about 1 minute. Scrape the sauce over the ravioli. Sprinkle with the remaining fennel pollen and cheese and serve immediately. —*Missy Robbins*

WINE Vivacious sparkling wine: NV Ronco Calino Franciacorta Brut.

Risotto-Style Penne with Tomatoes and Zucchini Blossoms

Total **1 hr**; Serves **6**

- 1 qt. chicken stock
- ½ cup extra-virgin olive oil
- 1 shallot, minced
- 1 lb. slow-dried penne rigate
- 1 cup dry white wine
- 3 cups prepared marinara sauce
- 3 garlic cloves, thinly sliced
- ¾ lb. heirloom tomatoes, cut into 1-inch chunks
-   Kosher salt and pepper
- ¾ cup torn basil leaves, plus more for garnish
- 4 zucchini blossoms, stems and pistils removed, blossoms halved, for garnish (optional)
-   Freshly grated Parmigiano-Reggiano or pecorino cheese, for serving

1. In a medium saucepan, combine the stock and 1 cup of water and bring to a boil. Keep warm over very low heat.

2. In a large saucepan, heat ¼ cup of oil. Add the shallot and cook over moderate heat, stirring, until softened, about 3 minutes. Add the penne and stir constantly for 2 minutes. Add the wine and simmer, stirring, until absorbed, about 2 minutes. Add 1½ cups of the warm stock mixture and cook over moderate heat, stirring, until nearly absorbed. Stir in the marinara sauce; bring to a simmer. Continue adding the stock ½ cup at a time, stirring frequently, until nearly absorbed before adding more. The pasta is done when it's al dente and the sauce is thick, about 25 minutes total.

3. Meanwhile, in a skillet, heat the remaining ¼ cup of oil. Add the garlic and cook over moderately high heat, stirring, until fragrant but not browned, about 2 minutes. Add the tomatoes and a generous pinch each of salt and pepper and cook, stirring, until just starting to soften, 3 to 5 minutes.

4. Add the tomatoes to the pasta and cook over moderate heat, stirring, for 2 minutes. Stir in the ¾ cup of basil and season with salt and pepper. Transfer the pasta to bowls and garnish with the zucchini blossoms (if using) and basil. Serve right away, with cheese. —*Fabio Trabocchi*

WINE Cherry-rich Sangiovese: 2013 Altesino Rosso di Montalcino.

Bangkok Mall Pasta

Total **45 min**; Serves **2**

Kris Yenbamroong, the chef at L.A.'s Night + Market restaurants, calls this "mall pasta" because it reminds him of the spaghetti stir-fried with ketchup available in the '90s-era Italian joints in Bangkok's shopping plazas. He says that the holy trinity in this dish is the salty-pungent combination of fried garlic, anchovies and chile that permeates the noodles. He cautions: "Using dried pasta is crucial because a fresh noodle won't hold up in the hot wok."

- **4** oz. spaghetti
- **¼** cup extra-virgin olive oil
- One 2-oz. tin anchovies packed in oil, anchovies finely chopped and oil reserved
- **2** Tbsp. minced garlic plus 2 Tbsp. thinly sliced garlic
- **1** Tbsp. minced Thai bird chile with seeds
- **½** yellow bell pepper, thinly sliced
- **1½** Tbsp. oyster sauce
- **1½** Tbsp. low-sodium soy sauce
- **1** tsp. sugar
- **2** Tbsp. whole pink peppercorns
- Pinch of ground white pepper
- **¼** cup torn basil leaves, plus small whole leaves for garnish

1. In a large pot of salted boiling water, cook the pasta until al dente. Drain, reserving ¼ cup of the pasta water.

2. In a wok, heat the olive oil. Add the anchovies, anchovy oil, minced garlic, chile and bell pepper and stir-fry over moderately high heat until the bell pepper is softened, about 3 minutes. Add the pasta, reserved pasta water, oyster sauce, soy sauce and sugar and cook, tossing, until the sauce is slightly thickened, about 2 minutes. Add the sliced garlic, pink peppercorns, white pepper and torn basil leaves and toss. Serve topped with whole basil leaves. —*Kris Yenbamroong*

WINE Bright-fruited Gamay: 2014 Edmunds St. John Bone-Jolly El Dorado County.

Toasted Capellini with Clams and Dashi

Total **1 hr 15 min**; Serves **2**

At Nishi in New York City, chef Joshua Pinsky makes an Asian-accented version of classic Portuguese fideos by infusing noodles with a flavorful broth of dashi and soy sauce. See Ingredient Intel (below right) for tips on stocking an Asian pantry.

- **1** tsp. instant dashi powder
- **2** dozen littleneck clams, scrubbed
- **¾** cup fresh apple cider
- **2** Tbsp. Asian fish sauce
- **1** Tbsp. plus 1 tsp. white soy sauce
- **1** Tbsp. tobanjan
- **1** Tbsp. unsalted butter
- **4** oz. capellini, broken in half
- **1** cup coarsely chopped green cabbage
- **1** garlic clove, thinly sliced
- One 2-inch piece of fresh ginger, peeled and cut into matchsticks
- **1** small leek, white and light green parts only, thinly sliced
- **1** serrano chile—halved lengthwise, seeded and thinly sliced on the diagonal
- **1** cup coarsely chopped escarole
- **1** Tbsp. small oregano leaves

1. Preheat the oven to 450°. In a small saucepan, bring ¾ cup of water to a boil. Stir in the dashi powder until dissolved.

2. In a large pot, bring 2½ cups of water to a boil. Add the clams, cover and cook over moderately high heat for 5 to 7 minutes; transfer to a baking sheet as they open, and discard any that don't. Strain ¾ cup of the clam cooking liquid into a large saucepan. Add the dashi, apple cider, fish sauce, white soy sauce and tobanjan to make a clam broth.

3. In a medium skillet, melt the butter. Add the capellini and toast over moderately high heat, stirring, until golden, 3 to 4 minutes. Add half of the clam broth and layer the cabbage, garlic, ginger, leek and serrano chile on top; do not stir. Bake for about 15 minutes, until all of the broth is absorbed and the pasta is al dente.

4. Add the steamed clams to the remaining broth in the saucepan. Stir in the escarole and simmer until heated through. Stir in the oregano. Transfer the pasta and vegetables to bowls, top with the steamed clams and escarole and serve. —*Joshua Pinsky*

MAKE AHEAD The dashi can be refrigerated for up to 3 days.

WINE Aromatic Italian white: 2014 Punta Crena Vigneto Reiné Mataòssu.

INGREDIENT INTEL

Asian Noodle Redux

Read on for a guide to some of the harder-to-find Asian ingredients called for in recipes throughout this book. You can buy these at Asian markets and online from amazon.com.

CHINESE WHEAT NOODLES Linguine-like Cantonese noodles for stir-fries and soups; also known as pancit.

FURIKAKE A Japanese seasoning mix that includes nori, sesame seeds, sugar, salt and bonito (dried fish flakes).

INSTANT DASHI POWDER A Japanese soup base made from seaweed and bonito (dried fish flakes).

KUDZU A Japanese starch made from the root of this plant; also known as kuzu.

SHIO KOMBU Strips of the Japanese seaweed kombu boiled in soy sauce.

TOBANJAN A spicy, fermented Chinese bean paste; also known as doubanjiang.

WHITE SOY SAUCE A Japanese soy sauce with a golden hue, milder flavor and thinner consistency than regular soy sauce; also known as shiro shoyu.

YUZU KOSHO A Japanese mix of grated citrus, chiles and sweet-tangy yuzu juice.

BANGKOK MALL
PASTA

CHOW FUN WITH
ROAST PORK AND
KALE-TOMATO SALAD

Chow Fun with Roast Pork and Kale-Tomato Salad

⏱ Total **45 min**; Serves **4**

Sheldon Simeon, the chef at Tin Roof in Maui, makes his own chow fun noodles, but you can use store-bought as a base for this unconventional dish. The noodles are topped with roast pork and a tangy kale salad and served with a buttery broth.

- 12 oz. fresh wide rice noodles, such as chow fun, or 8 oz. dried noodles
- 3 Tbsp. canola oil, plus more for tossing
- 3 oz. torn curly kale
- 2 ripe tomatoes, cut into wedges
- ½ small red onion, thinly sliced
- 1½ Tbsp. fresh lime juice
- 1 Tbsp. Asian fish sauce
  Kosher salt
- 2 Tbsp. soy sauce
- 1 tsp. instant dashi powder (see Ingredient Intel, p. 106)
- 6 oz. warm Chinese-style roast pork, chopped (1½ cups)
  Brown Butter Broth (recipe follows), for serving

1. In a saucepan of salted boiling water, cook the noodles until al dente; drain well. Toss with a little canola oil.

2. In a saucepan of salted boiling water, blanch the kale until tender, about 5 minutes. Drain and cool in a bowl of ice water. Drain again and pat dry. Transfer to a bowl and toss with the tomatoes, onion, lime juice and fish sauce. Season with salt.

3. In a wok or very large skillet, heat the 3 tablespoons of canola oil until shimmering. Add the noodles and cook over moderately high heat, stirring occasionally, until lightly browned and hot, 3 to 5 minutes. Remove from the heat and toss with the soy sauce and dashi powder. Season with salt.

4. Transfer the noodles to shallow bowls and top with the kale-tomato salad and roast pork. Serve right away, with the Brown Butter Broth. —*Sheldon Simeon*

WINE Fruity, dry rosé: 2015 Martin Ray Rosé of Pinot Noir.

BROWN BUTTER BROTH
⏱ Total **15 min**; Makes **1 cup**

- 1 Tbsp. unsalted butter
- 1 cup chicken stock
- 1 tsp. Asian fish sauce
- ¼ tsp. ground annatto (see Note)

In a small skillet, cook the butter over moderate heat, stirring, until golden, 3 to 5 minutes. In a small saucepan, combine the chicken stock, fish sauce and the ground annatto and bring just to a boil. Transfer to a blender. With the machine on, gradually drizzle in the brown butter until incorporated. Keep warm. —*SS*

NOTE Mild-flavored ground annatto (also called achiote) gives dishes a bright-reddish color. You can find it at most supermarkets.

Scallion-Mushroom Mee

Active **1 hr 30 min**; Total **2 hr**; Serves **4**

Chef Bryant Ng creates this Chinese-Italian hybrid pasta at Cassia in Los Angeles. "This dish is crazy," says sommelier Kathryn Coker. "It's like what I would eat every day in college, but the best version of it."

MUSHROOM RAGÙ
- 1 oz. dried shiitake mushroom caps
- 4 Tbsp. unsalted butter
- 1 shallot, minced
- 2 garlic cloves, crushed
- 1 Tbsp. minced peeled fresh ginger
- 2 Tbsp. Chinese black bean sauce
- 1 Tbsp. Shaoxing or other Chinese cooking wine
- 1 lb. finely chopped mixed mushrooms, such as stemmed shiitake and cremini (7 cups)
- 1 Tbsp. oyster sauce
  Kosher salt

NOODLES AND SAUCE
- 12 oz. spaghetti
- 2 Tbsp. minced garlic
  Kosher salt
- ¼ cup canola oil
- 2 Tbsp. thinly sliced scallions, plus more for garnish
- 1 Tbsp. oyster sauce
- 1 tsp. Maggi sauce
- 1 Tbsp. Chinese black bean sauce
- 1 tsp. Chinese black vinegar
- ¼ cup grated pecorino cheese, plus more for serving
- 2 Tbsp. unsalted butter

1. Make the mushroom ragù In a small heatproof bowl, soak the dried shiitake in 2 cups of boiling water until softened, about 30 minutes. Remove the shiitake and finely chop. Pour the soaking liquid into a clean bowl, stopping before you reach the grit at the bottom.

2. In a large skillet, melt the butter. Add the shallot, garlic and ginger and cook over moderately low heat, stirring, until softened, about 3 minutes. Stir in the black bean sauce and wine. Add the fresh mushrooms and reconstituted shiitake along with the reserved soaking liquid and 1 cup of water and cook, stirring occasionally, until the mushrooms are softened and saucy, about 15 minutes. Stir in the oyster sauce and season with salt. Scrape the ragù into a large bowl and keep warm. Clean the skillet.

3. Make the noodles and sauce In a large saucepan of salted boiling water, cook the spaghetti until al dente. Drain well.

4. Using the flat side of a chef's knife, mash the garlic to a paste with a pinch of salt. In the skillet, heat the oil. Add the garlic paste and cook over low heat, stirring, until very fragrant and light golden, 3 minutes. Stir in the 2 tablespoons of scallions, the oyster sauce, Maggi sauce, black bean sauce and vinegar; warm over low heat. Add the spaghetti and toss to coat. Stir in the ¼ cup of cheese and the butter and toss well. Transfer to plates and top with the mushroom ragù. Garnish with more cheese and scallions and serve. —*Bryant Ng*

MAKE AHEAD The mushroom ragù can be refrigerated overnight. Reheat with a little water if it gets too thick.

WINE Light red from Sicily: 2013 Girolamo Russo 'a Rina Etna Rosso.

Spring Buckwheat Noodle Salad

Total **1 hr;** Serves **6**

Jasmine and Melissa Hemsley, the sisters behind the wellness blog Hemsley + Hemsley, dress this vegetable-packed noodle salad with a tangy sun-dried tomato pesto made with Brazil nuts instead of the usual pine nuts.

- 6 Brazil nuts
- ¼ cup drained oil-packed sun-dried tomatoes
- ¼ cup fresh lemon juice
- 2 small garlic cloves
  Pinch of crushed red pepper
- ½ cup extra-virgin olive oil
  Kosher salt and black pepper
- 12 oz. buckwheat noodles
- ½ lb. haricots verts, halved crosswise
- 1½ cups fresh young peas (8 oz.)
- 1½ cups shelled and peeled fava beans or thawed frozen lima beans
- 8 oz. arugula, thick stems discarded and leaves chopped
- ½ cup lightly packed parsley, chopped
- ½ cup lightly packed basil leaves, torn
- 1 Hass avocado, peeled and cubed
  Finely grated lemon zest and shaved Parmigiano-Reggiano cheese, for serving

1. Preheat the oven to 375°. Spread the nuts in a pie plate and bake for about 5 minutes, until lightly browned. Transfer to a food processor and let cool completely. Add the sun-dried tomatoes, lemon juice, garlic and crushed red pepper and pulse until a chunky paste forms. With the machine on, gradually add the oil until incorporated. Season the pesto with salt and black pepper.

2. In a large saucepan of salted boiling water, cook the noodles until just tender. Drain and cool under cold running water. Drain again. In a large bowl, toss the noodles with 2 tablespoons of the pesto.

3. In a large saucepan of salted boiling water, cook the haricots verts, peas and fava beans until crisp-tender, 3 to 4 minutes. Drain well and add to the noodles; toss well. Add the remaining pesto along with the arugula, parsley and basil; season with salt and black pepper and toss again. Transfer the noodles to shallow bowls and top with the avocado, lemon zest and cheese. Serve right away. *—Jasmine and Melissa Hemsley*

WINE Bright Sauvignon Blanc: 2015 Whitehaven Marlborough from New Zealand.

Shrimp-and-Pork Pan-Fried Noodles

Total **1 hr 15 min;** Serves **4 to 6**

Maui chef Sheldon Simeon gives his noodles an extra flavor boost with pork and shrimp that have been fried in garlic oil.

- Canola oil, for frying and tossing
- 9 garlic cloves—6 thinly sliced and 3 minced
- 8 oz. Chinese wheat noodles (see Ingredient Intel, p. 106)
- ⅔ cup chicken stock
- ¼ cup oyster sauce
- 1 Tbsp. plus 1 tsp. Asian fish sauce
- 2 tsp. instant dashi powder (see Ingredient Intel, p. 106)
- 1 tsp. ground annatto (see Note on p. 109)
- 12 large shrimp, shelled and deveined
- 4 oz. Chinese-style roast pork, chopped (1 cup)
- 4 oz. shiitake mushrooms, stems discarded and caps thinly sliced
- 2 medium carrots, thinly sliced
- 4 oz. baby bok choy, halved lengthwise and cut crosswise into 3-inch pieces
- ½ small red onion, thinly sliced
  Snipped chives, for garnish
  Lime wedges and hot sauce, for serving

1. In a small skillet, heat ¼ inch of canola oil. Add the sliced garlic and cook over moderate heat, stirring, until golden and crisp, about 5 minutes. Using a slotted spoon, transfer the fried garlic to paper towels. Reserve the garlic oil.

2. In a saucepan of salted boiling water, cook the noodles until al dente. Drain well and toss with 1 teaspoon of canola oil.

3. In a bowl, whisk the stock, oyster sauce, fish sauce, dashi powder and annatto.

4. In a wok or very large skillet, heat ¼ cup of the reserved garlic oil until shimmering. Add the shrimp, pork and minced garlic and stir-fry over high heat until the shrimp just start to turn pink, about 3 minutes. Add the shiitake and carrots and stir-fry until the mushrooms are softened and the shrimp are white throughout, about 3 minutes. Add the noodles, bok choy, onion and the oyster sauce mixture and stir-fry until the noodles are hot and the sauce is absorbed, about 3 minutes. Transfer to plates. Garnish with the fried garlic and snipped chives and serve with lime wedges and hot sauce. *—Sheldon Simeon*

BEER Crisp, lightly toasty lager: Kona Brewing Co. Longboard Island.

Asian Pork Noodles with Spinach

Total **25 min;** Serves **4**

Spaghetti is the base for this quick Thai-inspired pork stir-fry. It's a bright and satisfying meal ideal for breaking out of your weeknight dinner rut.

- 12 oz. spaghetti, broken into 3-inch pieces
- 2 Tbsp. canola oil
- 1 lb. ground pork
- 3 Tbsp. finely chopped garlic
- 3 Tbsp. finely chopped peeled fresh ginger
- 2 Tbsp. Asian fish sauce
- 2 Tbsp. fresh lime juice
- 8 oz. curly spinach (8 packed cups)
  Kosher salt and pepper
  Chopped basil, for garnish

1. In a pot of salted boiling water, cook the spaghetti until al dente. Drain.

2. In a large skillet, heat the oil. Add the pork, garlic and ginger and cook over moderate heat, stirring, until browned, about 5 minutes. Stir in the pasta, fish sauce, lime juice and spinach; season with salt and pepper and toss well. Transfer to bowls, garnish with basil and serve. *—Kay Chun*

WINE Ripe, fruit-forward, dry German Riesling: 2015 Fritz Haag Estate Riesling Trocken.

Stir-Fried Sweet Potato Noodles (Jap Chae)
Total **1 hr 15 min**; Serves **4**

Judy Joo, the chef at Jinjuu restaurant in London and Hong Kong, says jap chae, a traditional Korean dish of stir-fried glossy sweet potato starch noodles, is a great way to use whatever protein or vegetables you have in your fridge: Swap in bell peppers, alliums, tofu or even thinly sliced steak for the shrimp and vegetables in this recipe.

- 8 oz. Korean-style vermicelli noodles (see Note)
- 3 Tbsp. soy sauce
- 3 Tbsp. vegetable oil
- 2 Tbsp. toasted sesame oil
- 2 Tbsp. toasted white sesame seeds, crushed
- 1 Tbsp. sugar
  Kosher salt
- 1 large egg
- 1 lb. large shrimp, shelled and deveined
- 1 garlic clove, minced
- 1½ tsp. mirin
- 1 small red onion, sliced
- 2 carrots, julienned
- 3 oz. Broccolini, halved lengthwise
- 2 stalks of red Swiss chard, leaves chopped and stems thinly sliced
- 2 oz. oyster mushrooms, sliced ½ inch thick
- 1 cup sugar snap peas, halved on the bias
- ½ cup fresh English peas
- 1 scallion, julienned
  Black sesame seeds

1. In a large pot of salted boiling water, cook the noodles until just tender, about 6 minutes. Drain and rinse under cold water. Drain the noodles thoroughly and transfer to a rimmed baking sheet. Toss the noodles with 1 tablespoon of the soy sauce and 2 teaspoons of the vegetable oil and spread in an even layer.

2. In a small bowl, whisk the sesame oil with the crushed white sesame seeds, sugar and the remaining 2 tablespoons of soy sauce; season with salt.

3. In a small bowl, beat the egg with 1 teaspoon of water and a pinch of salt. In a small nonstick skillet, heat 1 teaspoon of the vegetable oil. Add the egg and cook over moderate heat, swirling the pan to coat the bottom but not stirring, until the egg is just set, 2 minutes. Using a spatula, carefully flip the omelet and cook until just set, about 15 seconds more. Carefully slide onto a work surface and gently roll into a log, then slice into ¼-inch-thick strips.

4. In a large wok, heat 1 tablespoon of the vegetable oil. Add the shrimp, garlic and a generous pinch of salt and stir-fry over moderately high heat until the shrimp begin to turn pink, about 2 minutes. Add the mirin and continue cooking until the shrimp are white throughout and the liquid has reduced, about 2 minutes more. Scrape the shrimp into a medium bowl. Wipe out the wok.

5. Heat the remaining 1 tablespoon of vegetable oil in the wok. Add the red onion and carrots and stir-fry over moderately high heat until the carrots are almost tender, about 4 minutes. Add the Broccolini, Swiss chard stems and a generous pinch of salt and stir-fry until all the vegetables are crisp-tender, about 5 minutes. Add the Swiss chard leaves, oyster mushrooms, sugar snaps and English peas and stir-fry until the mushrooms and peas are tender, about 2 minutes more.

6. Add the noodles to the wok in batches, stirring well after each addition. Add the sauce and stir-fry until the noodles are warmed through, 3 minutes. Add the cooked shrimp and their juices to the wok along with half of the sliced egg and toss gently. Transfer the jap chae to bowls; garnish with the remaining egg, the scallion and black sesame seeds and serve.
—*Judy Joo*

NOTE Korean-style vermicelli (sweet potato starch noodles) is available at Asian markets and on amazon.com.

WINE Aromatic Alsace white: 2014 Albert Mann Gewürztraminer.

Spicy Wok-Fried Ramen with Crab
Total **45 min**; Serves **4**

New Orleans chef Michael Gulotta uses fragrant Thai chile paste as well as crab paste to pack flavor into his fresh crab-and-mushroom noodle stir-fry. He makes the noodles from scratch at his restaurant MoPho, but using store-bought ramen (minus the seasoning packet) is a smart shortcut.

- Three 3.5-oz. packages ramen, seasoning packets reserved for another use
- ¾ cup canola oil
- ¼ cup minced peeled fresh ginger
- 4 garlic cloves, thinly sliced
- 1 Tbsp. crab paste (see Note)
- 1 tsp. Thai chile paste or sambal oelek
- ½ lb. shiitake mushrooms, stems discarded and caps thinly sliced (4 cups)
- 1 cup vegetable broth
- ½ lb. jumbo lump crabmeat, picked over
- ¼ cup chopped mint, plus small leaves for garnish
- 1 tsp. finely grated lime zest plus 3 Tbsp. fresh lime juice
  Kosher salt

1. In a large saucepan of boiling water, cook the ramen until al dente. Drain well and pat dry with paper towels.

2. In a large wok, heat ½ cup of the oil until smoking. Add the ginger, garlic, crab paste, chile paste and shiitake and cook over high heat, stirring, until the garlic is golden, about 3 minutes. Add the ramen and toss to coat. Spread the noodles in an even layer over the bottom and halfway up the side of the wok and drizzle with the remaining ¼ cup of oil. Cook over high heat, undisturbed, until the edges start to crisp, about 2 minutes. Toss the noodles, then spread them out again and cook until the edges start to crisp, about 2 minutes. Toss and repeat one more time. Stir in the broth, crabmeat, chopped mint, lime zest and lime juice, season with salt and toss well. Transfer to plates. Garnish with mint leaves and serve. —*Michael Gulotta*

NOTE Crab paste is available at Pan-Asian markets and from amazon.com.

WINE Juicy Chenin Blanc: 2015 L'Ecole No. 41 Columbia Valley.

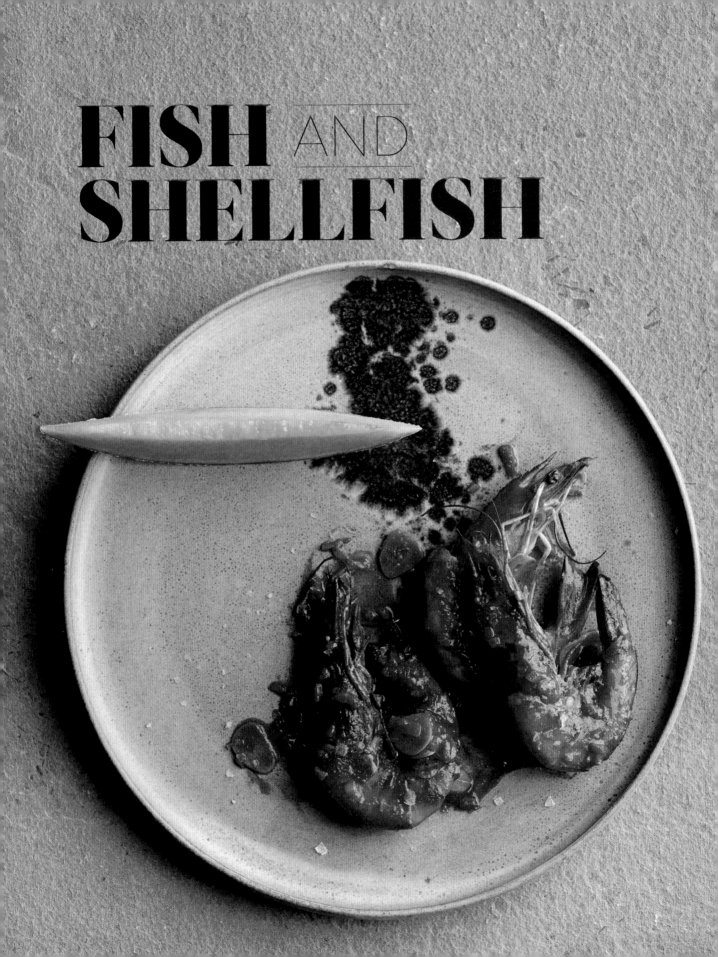

FISH AND SHELLFISH

Honolulu chef Mark Noguchi harvests seaweed from He'eia Fishpond, a source for sustainable seafood on Oahu. OPPOSITE Pepper Shrimp (p. 130).

Sole Meunière

Total **25 min plus 45 min soaking**
Serves **4 to 6**

"Even the squirmiest eater will love this delicate, white-fleshed fish," says *Bizarre Foods* host Andrew Zimmern. *Meunière* means "in the style of the miller's wife" and refers to the dredging of the fillets in flour before frying and serving with a lemony butter sauce.

¼ cup salt-packed capers, rinsed

  Eight 5-oz. sole fillets

  Kosher salt and pepper

1 cup all-purpose flour

¼ cup clarified butter or ghee

⅓ cup dry white wine

2 Tbsp. fresh lemon juice

6 Tbsp. cold unsalted butter, thinly sliced

2 Tbsp. minced parsley

1. In a small bowl, soak the capers in cold water for 45 minutes. Drain and pat dry.

2. Season the fish with salt and pepper. In a shallow bowl, whisk the flour with 1 teaspoon each of salt and pepper. Dredge the fillets in flour and shake off any excess; transfer to a platter.

3. In a large skillet, melt 2 tablespoons of the clarified butter over moderately high heat. Add 4 sole fillets to the skillet and cook, turning once, until golden brown on both sides, about 4 minutes total. Transfer to a platter. Repeat with the remaining clarified butter and sole fillets.

4. Add the capers to the skillet and cook over moderately high heat until lightly browned and fragrant, about 30 seconds. Add the white wine and lemon juice and cook over moderately high heat until reduced to 2 tablespoons, about 1 minute. Remove the skillet from the heat and add the butter, a few pieces at a time, whisking until the butter is melted before adding more. Add half of the parsley and season the sauce with salt and pepper. Pour the warm sauce over the sole and garnish with the remaining parsley. Serve immediately.
—*Andrew Zimmern*

WINE Elegant, mineral-laced Chablis: 2014 Gilbert Picq & Ses Fils Vieilles Vignes.

Whole Baked Trout with Fennel and Orange

Active **45 min**; Total **1 hr 30 min**; Serves **4**

Icelandic chef Victoria Elíasdóttir, whose father was a chef on a fishing boat, has a knack for cooking seafood. She offers a tip for getting trout skin nicely golden: Bake it on foil that's been well buttered.

4 Tbsp. unsalted butter, plus 3 Tbsp. melted

1 small onion, finely chopped

½ fennel bulb—trimmed, cored and thinly sliced crosswise

3 scallions, coarsely chopped

5 garlic cloves, crushed

2 tsp. chopped thyme

1 Tbsp. dried lovage or 1 tsp. celery seeds

  One 3-inch strip of orange zest plus 3 Tbsp. fresh orange juice

1 tsp. light brown sugar

1 cup dry white wine

  One 4-lb. steelhead trout or arctic char—cleaned, rinsed and patted dry

2 Tbsp. extra-virgin olive oil

  Flaky sea salt and pepper

2 Tbsp. honey-Dijon mustard

1 orange, thinly sliced

1. Preheat the oven to 350°. In a medium saucepan, melt the 4 tablespoons of butter. Add the onion, fennel, scallions, garlic, thyme, lovage, orange zest, orange juice and sugar and bring to a simmer. Cook over moderate heat, stirring occasionally, until the onion and fennel are softened but not browned, about 8 minutes. Stir in the wine and simmer for 5 minutes. Let cool to room temperature.

2. Rub the trout all over with the oil and season with salt and pepper. Drizzle the melted butter on a foil-lined baking sheet and set the trout on top. Spread the honey mustard all over the inside of the trout and fill the cavity with the orange slices, overlapping them slightly. Spoon the fennel mixture on top of the orange slices.

3. Tightly wrap the trout in the foil and roast in the oven for 30 minutes, until almost cooked through. Unwrap the trout and roast for about 10 minutes longer, until the skin is golden and the flesh is just cooked through and flakes easily. Scoop out the fennel filling and fillet the trout; discard the bones and oranges. Arrange the fish and fennel stuffing on a platter and serve.
—*Victoria Elíasdóttir*

WINE Rhône-inspired white: 2013 Tablas Creek Vineyard Roussanne.

Trout Francesca

Total **30 min**; Serves **4**

By day, Sadelle's in New York City offers bagels and babka; by night, it's a candlelit brasserie serving Russian-style dishes like this trout. Simply pan-fried, the fish is topped with nutty brown butter, capers and vibrant beet horseradish.

  Two 14-oz. butterflied brook trout, heads and pinbones removed

2 Tbsp. canola oil

  Kosher salt and pepper

10 Tbsp. unsalted butter

¼ cup coarsely chopped capers

2 Tbsp. chopped parsley

  Beet horseradish, for garnish

Heat a large nonstick skillet. Rub the fish all over with the oil and season with salt and pepper. Place 1 fish in the skillet, skin side down, and cook over moderately high heat until the skin is golden, about 3 minutes. Add 3 tablespoons of the butter and cook over moderate heat, basting the trout constantly, until the skin is crisp and the flesh is just white throughout, about 2 minutes. Transfer to a plate. Add 2 tablespoons each of the butter and capers to the skillet and cook, stirring, until the butter is deep golden, 1 to 2 minutes. Season with salt and stir in 1 tablespoon of the parsley. Spoon the brown butter sauce over the fish. Repeat with the remaining fish, butter, capers and parsley. Spoon beet horseradish over the trout and serve.
—*Sadelle's*

WINE European-style Georgian white: 2014 Kindzmarauli Marani Kisi.

SOLE
MEUNIÈRE

Jerk Trout with Collard Slaw

⏱ Total **45 min**; Serves **4**

Trout is an excellent sustainable seafood option. For an island spin, these fillets are crusted in jerk spices, then served alongside a tangy collard-and-cabbage slaw.

COLLARD SLAW

½ cup fat-free Greek yogurt

¼ cup extra-virgin olive oil

2 Tbsp. fresh lemon juice

1 tsp. finely grated garlic

12 oz. collard greens, stems discarded and leaves finely shredded (6 cups)

¼ head of red cabbage, finely shredded (4 cups)

2 celery ribs, thinly sliced

2 Tbsp. chopped dill

Kosher salt and pepper

JERK TROUT

1 Tbsp. crushed red pepper

2 tsp. dried oregano

1 tsp. dried thyme

½ tsp. ground allspice

½ tsp. ground cumin

¼ tsp. black pepper, plus more for seasoning

Four 6-oz. skin-on trout fillets, pinbones removed

6 Tbsp. extra-virgin olive oil

Kosher salt

1. Make the collard slaw In a large bowl, combine the yogurt, olive oil, lemon juice and garlic. Whisk until smooth. Add the collards, cabbage, celery and dill, season with salt and pepper and toss to coat.

2. Make the jerk trout In a small bowl, mix all of the seasonings. Rub the trout all over with 2 tablespoons of the olive oil and season with salt and pepper. Sprinkle the spice rub over the flesh side of the trout, patting gently to help it adhere.

3. In a large nonstick skillet, heat 2 tablespoons of the oil. Add 2 trout fillets, skin side down, and cook over moderately high heat until golden and crisp, about 3 minutes. Flip the fish and cook over moderate heat until golden and just cooked through, about 2 minutes longer. Transfer to plates. Wipe out the skillet and repeat with the remaining oil and trout fillets. Serve with the collard slaw. —*Kay Chun*

MAKE AHEAD The spice rub can be stored at room temperature for up to 2 weeks.

WINE Lush but vibrant Chardonnay: 2014 Porter-Bass Poco a Poco.

Citrus-Cured Trout with Meyer Lemon Vinaigrette

Total **1 hr**; Serves **4**

Trout is a regular feature on the menu at HH & Co., a hotel restaurant near the streams of Hampshire in southeastern England. The fish is smoked or seared and drizzled with a lemony vinaigrette.

1 lemon, preferably Meyer

¼ cup extra-virgin olive oil

1 Tbsp. minced preserved lemon rind (see Note)

Kosher salt and pepper

5 Tbsp. canola oil

½ cup panko

½ tsp. fennel seeds, crushed

1 Tbsp. chopped dill

1 Tbsp. finely grated grapefruit zest

1 tsp. finely grated lime zest

3 Tbsp. sugar

Four 6-oz. skin-on trout fillets

1. Finely grate the lemon zest and reserve it. Using a knife, peel the lemon, removing all of the bitter white pith. Working over a small saucepan, cut in between the membranes to release the sections. Squeeze any remaining juice from the membranes into the saucepan and bring to a gentle simmer. Cook over moderately low heat, stirring occasionally, until the lemon breaks down, about 15 minutes. Transfer to a small bowl and stir in the olive oil and preserved lemon. Season the vinaigrette with salt; let cool.

2. Meanwhile, in a large skillet, heat 1 tablespoon of the canola oil. Add the panko and fennel seeds and toast over moderately low heat, stirring occasionally, until golden and fragrant, about 5 minutes. Stir in the dill and season with salt. Transfer the breadcrumbs to a paper towel–lined plate to drain. Wipe out the skillet.

3. In a small bowl, combine the grapefruit and lime zests with the reserved lemon zest, the sugar and 3 tablespoons of kosher salt. Lay the trout fillets on a baking sheet skin side down and cover evenly with the citrus-salt cure. Let stand for 6 minutes. Rinse the trout and pat dry.

4. In the large skillet, heat 2 tablespoons of the canola oil. Lightly season the trout with salt and pepper. Add 2 fillets to the skillet skin side down and cook over moderately high heat until the skin is golden and crispy, about 3 minutes. Flip the fish and cook until golden and white throughout, 2 to 3 minutes longer. Briefly drain the fish on paper towels, then transfer to plates. Repeat with the remaining 2 tablespoons of oil and 2 trout fillets. Spoon some of the lemon vinaigrette over the trout and garnish with the fennel seed breadcrumbs. Serve with braised endives and pass the remaining vinaigrette at the table. —*HH & Co., Hampshire, England*

NOTE Jarred preserved lemon can be found at specialty food shops and stores like Whole Foods.

WINE Citrusy Riesling: 2014 Poet's Leap.

FLAVOR UPGRADE

Olive Brine on Grilled Seafood

"When you baste with it, the brine gives this magical whisper of flavor and a nice salinity that works with almost anything you would put on the grill." —*Chef Brad Farmerie, Public, Manhattan*

Grilled Snapper with Four-Herb Gremolata

Total **1 hr**; Serves **4**

For flavorful snapper fillets with perfectly crisp skin, Jennifer Carroll of Requin in Fairfax, Virginia, seasons only the flesh side before cooking on a very hot grill.

¼ cup each finely chopped chives, parsley, tarragon and chervil

⅓ cup plus ¼ cup extra-virgin olive oil, plus more for brushing

1 tsp. finely grated lemon zest plus ¼ cup fresh lemon juice

Kosher salt and pepper

1 red bell pepper—stemmed, peeled, quartered and seeded

1 yellow bell pepper—stemmed, peeled, quartered and seeded

12 scallions, trimmed

Four 6-oz. red snapper fillets

5 oz. baby lettuces (4 cups)

1 Fresno chile, thinly sliced

1. In a medium bowl, combine the herbs with ⅓ cup of the olive oil, the lemon zest and lemon juice; season the gremolata with salt and pepper and mix well.

2. Light a grill or heat a large cast-iron grill pan. In a large bowl, toss the bell peppers and scallions with 2 tablespoons of the olive oil and season with salt and pepper. Grill over moderately high heat, turning, until golden and tender, 5 to 8 minutes. Halve the scallions crosswise and cut the peppers lengthwise into ½-inch strips. Transfer to a large bowl.

3. Brush the grill with oil. Rub only the flesh side of the fish with the remaining 2 table-spoons of oil and season with salt and pep-per. Grill the snapper skin side down over moderately high heat until golden, 3 to 4 minutes. Flip and cook until opaque throughout, about 2 minutes lon-ger. Transfer to plates.

4. Add the lettuces, chile and ¼ cup of the gremolata to the bowl with the scallions and peppers and toss. Spoon the salad over the fish and serve the remaining gremolata on the side. —*Jennifer Carroll*

MAKE AHEAD The gremolata can be refrig-erated for up to 3 hours.

WINE Tangy New Zealand Sauvignon Blanc: 2015 Babich.

Red Snapper with Sweet and Spicy Pickled Grapes

Active **30 min**; Total **1 hr 30 min**; Serves **4**

This dish includes the pickled grapes that helped *Top Chef* Season 13 winner Jeremy Ford nab the coveted title. Just make them and you'll see why—they have the ideal balance of heat and sweet, plus they're juicy and very aromatic.

1½ tsp. coriander seeds

1 cup Champagne vinegar

⅓ cup sugar

2 thin strips of orange zest

½ tsp. dried lavender flowers

Kosher salt and pepper

½ cup fresh lime juice

¼ cup fresh clementine, mandarin or orange juice

1 serrano chile, thinly sliced (with seeds)

½ lb. seedless green grapes, thinly sliced

¼ cup plus 1 Tbsp. extra-virgin olive oil

Four 5-oz. red snapper fillets

1. In a small saucepan, toast the coriander seeds over moderate heat until fragrant, about 2 minutes. Add the vinegar, sugar, orange zest, lavender flowers and 1 table-spoon of salt and bring to a boil, stirring to dissolve the sugar and salt. Add the lime juice, clementine juice and chile. Let the brine cool completely, about 45 minutes.

2. Strain the brine into a bowl. Add the grapes and let pickle at room temperature for 15 minutes. Drain the grapes, return them to the bowl and stir in ¼ cup of the olive oil. Reserve the brine for another use.

3. Season the snapper fillets with salt and pepper. In a large nonstick skillet, heat the remaining 1 tablespoon of olive oil until shimmering. Add the fillets skin side down and gently press with a spatula to flatten. Cook over moderately high heat until the skin is crisp, about 3 minutes. Turn the fil-lets and cook until white throughout, about 2 minutes longer. Transfer to a platter or plates, spoon some of the pickled grapes on top and serve. —*Jeremy Ford*

MAKE AHEAD The drained pickled grapes can be refrigerated for up to 1 day.

WINE Bracing New Zealand Sauvignon Blanc: 2015 Greywacke Marlborough.

Fennel-and-Grapefruit-Rubbed Snapper

Total **45 min**; Serves **4**

F&W's Justin Chapple rubs a fragrant mix of crushed fennel seeds and grapefruit zest onto snapper before baking it on a bed of tender roasted fennel.

3 fennel bulbs, cut into ¾-inch wedges

¼ cup plus 1½ Tbsp. extra-virgin olive oil

1½ tsp. chopped thyme

¼ tsp. crushed red pepper

Kosher salt and black pepper

Two 12-oz. red snapper fillets

2 tsp. crushed fennel seeds

½ tsp. finely grated grapefruit zest

1 pink grapefruit, peeled and supremed

1. Preheat the oven to 400°. On a rimmed baking sheet, toss the fennel wedges with ¼ cup of the olive oil, the thyme and crushed red pepper. Season with salt and black pepper. Roast for about 20 min-utes, until just tender.

2. Make 5 or 6 slashes in each fillet. In a small bowl, whisk the remaining 1½ table-spoons of olive oil with the fennel seeds and grapefruit zest and rub all over the fil-lets and in the slashes; season with salt and black pepper. Arrange the snapper skin side up on the fennel wedges and roast for about 8 minutes, until the fish is just cooked through. Serve the fish and fennel with the grapefruit sections. —*Justin Chapple*

WINE Citrusy, medium-bodied white Bor-deaux: 2013 Clos Floridène.

Grilled Fish with Tapenade and Smoky Ratatouille

Total **1 hr 45 min**; Serves **4**

This wonderful fish was inspired by a signature dish at L'Estagnol in Provence. In the version here, fire-roasted tomatoes and smoked salt mimic the flavor imparted by the restaurant's wood-fired oven.

RATATOUILLE

- ½ cup extra-virgin olive oil
- 1 small red bell pepper, cut into ½-inch pieces
- 1 small zucchini, cut into ½-inch pieces
- 1 very small eggplant, cut into ½-inch pieces (1¼ cups)
- 1 medium onion, finely chopped
- 4 garlic cloves, minced
- ½ tsp. herbes de Provence
  Kosher salt and pepper
  Two 14-oz. cans fire-roasted diced tomatoes
  Pinch of sugar
- ¼ cup chopped parsley
  Smoked salt

TAPENADE

- ¼ cup pitted kalamata olives
- ¼ cup pitted oil-cured black olives
- 2 Tbsp. extra-virgin olive oil
- 2 garlic cloves, lightly crushed
- 2 oil-packed anchovies, drained
- 1 Tbsp. capers
- 1½ tsp. chopped thyme
- 1½ tsp. chopped rosemary

FISH

  Canola oil, for brushing
  Two 1½- to 2-lb. whole black bass, sea bass, porgy or dorade, cleaned
- 2 Tbsp. extra-virgin olive oil
  Kosher salt and pepper
- 2 lemons, halved

1. Make the ratatouille In a large saucepan, heat 1½ tablespoons of the oil. Add the pepper and cook over moderate heat, stirring occasionally, until softened, about 8 minutes. Transfer to a bowl. Repeat the process with the zucchini and then the eggplant, cooking each vegetable in 1½ tablespoons of oil until tender, about 8 minutes each.

2. Heat 1½ tablespoons more of the olive oil in the saucepan. Add the onion, garlic and herbes de Provence, season with kosher salt and cook over low heat, stirring, until the onion is softened, about 10 minutes. Add the tomatoes and sugar and season with kosher salt and pepper. Cook, partially covered, until the sauce thickens, about 20 minutes. Stir in the remaining 2 tablespoons of olive oil and all of the sautéed vegetables. Cover partially and cook for 5 minutes. Stir in the parsley and season the ratatouille with smoked salt.

3. Make the tapenade In a food processor, combine all of the ingredients and pulse until chunky.

4. Prepare the fish Light a grill and oil the grate. Rub the fish all over with the olive oil and season with salt and pepper. Grill, covered, over moderately high heat, turning once, until just opaque, 5 to 7 minutes per side. Transfer the fish to a work surface and remove the fillets. Transfer to plates and serve with the smoky ratatouille, tapenade and lemon halves. —*L'Estagnol, Bormes-Les-Mimosas, France*

MAKE AHEAD The ratatouille can be refrigerated for up to 3 days; the tapenade can be refrigerated for up to 2 days. Serve both at room temperature.

WINE Racy, fruit-tinged rosé: 2015 Sulauze Côteaux d'Aix-en-Provence Pomponette.

Roast Dorade with Figs, Olives and Almonds

Total **40 min**; Serves **4**

Simple and delicious roast fish is one of Venice-based blogger Skye McAlpine's go-tos for lazy weeknights and dinner parties alike. Make sure to use moist figs so they don't dry out during baking.

- ¼ cup extra-virgin olive oil
  Four 12-oz. dorade—scaled, cleaned and patted dry
  Kosher salt
- 5 dried Turkish figs, stemmed and quartered
- ½ cup each pitted Cerignola and Castelvetrano olives
- 3 Tbsp. rosemary leaves
- 2 Tbsp. coarsely chopped raw almonds
- ¼ cup dry white wine
  Lemon wedges, for serving

Preheat the oven to 350°. Drizzle 1 tablespoon of the oil in a large roasting pan. Set the dorade in the roasting pan. Season generously with salt. Scatter the figs, olives, rosemary and almonds over and around the fish and drizzle on the wine and the remaining 3 tablespoons of oil. Roast for about 30 minutes, until the fish just flakes. Serve with lemon wedges. —*Skye McAlpine*

WINE Plum-scented red blend: 2014 Le Salette Valpolicella Classico.

Marinated Tuna with Chickpeas and Shishitos

Active **30 min**; Total **3 hr 30 min**; Serves **4**

- 2 cups extra-virgin olive oil
- 3 garlic cloves, thinly sliced
- ½ cup tarragon leaves
- 2 tsp. crushed coriander seeds
  Three 3-inch strips of lemon zest plus 2 Tbsp. fresh lemon juice
- 2 tsp. kosher salt
- ½ tsp. pepper
- 4 oz. shishito peppers, halved lengthwise
  Two 7-oz. cans or jars good-quality tuna in olive oil, drained and broken into large chunks
  One 15-oz. can chickpeas, drained and rinsed
- 1 cup thinly sliced celery hearts plus ¼ cup celery leaves
- ½ cup chopped Castelvetrano olives
  Lemon wedges and crusty bread, for serving

In a large bowl, mix the olive oil, garlic, tarragon, coriander, lemon zest, lemon juice, salt and pepper. Add all of the remaining ingredients except the lemon wedges and bread and toss to coat. Cover and let stand for at least 3 hours or overnight. Serve with lemon wedges and crusty bread. —*Kay Chun*

MAKE AHEAD The marinated tuna can be refrigerated for up to 1 week.

WINE Minerally Greek white: 2015 Artemis Karamolegos Feredini Assyrtiko.

Steamed Snapper with Garlic-Ginger Sauce

Total **50 min**; Serves **4**

"Hawaii has always been known for great seafood; now we're getting sustainable fish that's world-class," says chef Chris Kajioka of Senia in Honolulu. He's partial to Hawaiian red snapper (you can substitute cod or halibut), which he steams and serves with a sweet and savory ginger sauce.

- 2 Tbsp. grapeseed or canola oil
- 3 Tbsp. minced shallot
- 2 Tbsp. sugar
- 1½ Tbsp. minced peeled fresh ginger
- 1½ tsp. minced garlic
- ¼ cup dark soy sauce
- 3 Tbsp. Chinese black vinegar (see Note) or balsamic vinegar
- 1 Tbsp. Asian fish sauce
- 1 Tbsp. shio kombu (see Ingredient Intel, p. 106)
- 1½ Tbsp. minced cilantro
- 1½ Tbsp. finely chopped scallion
- 4 green cabbage leaves, for steaming
- 1 Tbsp. toasted sesame oil
  Four 5-oz. skinless snapper fillets
  Kosher salt

1. In a small skillet, heat 1 tablespoon of the grapeseed oil. Add the shallot and cook over moderately low heat, stirring occasionally, until lightly browned, about 8 minutes. Add the sugar, ginger and garlic and cook, stirring, until fragrant and the sugar is melted, about 2 minutes. Add the soy sauce, vinegar, fish sauce and shio kombu and bring to a boil over moderately high heat, then simmer over moderately low heat until slightly reduced, about 3 minutes. Remove from the heat and stir in the cilantro and scallion.

2. Set a bamboo steamer in a wok or a large, deep skillet. Add 1 inch of water to the wok or skillet and bring to a boil. Line the inside of the steamer with the cabbage leaves. Combine the sesame oil and the remaining 1 tablespoon of grapeseed oil and brush all over the fish. Season the fish lightly with salt and set it on the cabbage leaves. Cover and steam over moderate heat for about 7 minutes, until just cooked through. Transfer the fish to plates and serve with the ginger-garlic sauce. —*Chris Kajioka*

NOTE Chinese black vinegar is a richly flavored, slightly sweet vinegar.

MAKE AHEAD The ginger sauce can be refrigerated overnight. Let stand at room temperature for 15 minutes before serving.

WINE Ripe, fruity Alsace Pinot Gris: 2012 Famille Hugel Classic.

Snapper with Black Beans and Bok Choy

Total **40 min**; Serves **4**

Chef Jonathan Waxman of Barbuto in New York City loves rustic dishes like this crisp-skinned snapper. The secret ingredient in the sauce is rosé wine.

- 3 Tbsp. extra-virgin olive oil
- 6 small heads of bok choy (1 lb.), halved lengthwise
  Kosher salt and pepper
- 1 Tbsp. unsalted butter
  Four 5-oz. skin-on red snapper fillets
- 1 Tbsp. fermented black beans
- 1 garlic clove, thinly sliced
- ½ cup dry rosé
- 1 Tbsp. dry sherry
- 1 tsp. low-sodium soy sauce
- ½ tsp. finely grated peeled fresh ginger
- ½ tsp. minced serrano chile
- ½ tsp. toasted sesame oil

1. In a large skillet, heat 2 tablespoons of the olive oil. Add the bok choy; season with salt and pepper. Cook over moderate heat, stirring, until golden and crisp-tender, 5 to 7 minutes. Transfer to a platter. Wipe out the skillet.

2. In the skillet, melt the butter in the remaining 1 tablespoon of oil. Season the fish with salt and pepper and add to the skillet skin side down. Cook over moderate heat until golden and crisp underneath, 3 minutes. Turn the fish and add the remaining ingredients to the skillet. Bring to a boil and cook, swirling the pan occasionally, until the sauce is slightly thickened and the fish is white throughout, 2 to 3 minutes longer. Spoon the sauce over the bok choy, top with the fish and serve. —*Jonathan Waxman*

WINE Full-bodied Alsace Pinot Gris: 2013 Kuentz-Bas Tradition.

Red Snapper with Korean Miso Vinaigrette

Total **1 hr 30 min**; Serves **4**

- 2 Tbsp. doenjang (fermented soybean paste; available at Korean markets)
- 2 Tbsp. mayonnaise
- 1½ Tbsp. finely chopped peeled ginger
- 1 Tbsp. fresh lime juice
- ½ cup canola oil
  Kosher salt and pepper
  One 8-inch piece of kombu
- 1 cup loosely packed bonito flakes
- ½ lb. parsnips, peeled and cut into 2-by-¼-inch matchsticks
- 1 medium onion, cut through the core into ¼-inch-thick wedges
  Four 6-oz. skin-on red snapper fillets
  Toasted white sesame seeds, shaved radishes and cilantro, for garnish

1. In a food processor, pulse the doenjang with the mayonnaise, ginger and lime juice. With the machine on, slowly drizzle in 6 tablespoons of the oil until well blended. Season the vinaigrette with salt.

2. In a saucepan, cover the kombu with 4 cups of water and bring to a simmer; discard the kombu. Simmer gently for 5 minutes. Add the bonito and simmer gently for 5 minutes longer. Strain the dashi (broth) through a cheesecloth-lined sieve into a saucepan; discard the solids. Add the parsnips to the dashi and bring to a simmer. Cook over moderately low heat until the parsnips are almost tender, 10 minutes.

3. Heat a large cast-iron skillet. Add the onion wedges and cook over moderate heat, turning, until lightly charred all over, about 5 minutes. Add the onion to the dashi and simmer until tender, about 5 minutes; keep warm. Wipe out the skillet.

4. Heat the remaining 2 tablespoons of oil in the skillet. Season the fish with salt and pepper. Cook skin side down over moderately high heat, turning once, until cooked through and the skin is crisp, about 3 minutes per side.

5. Ladle the dashi and vegetables into shallow bowls and top with the fish, skin side up. Spoon the vinaigrette over, garnish with sesame seeds, radishes and cilantro and serve. —*Cathal Armstrong*

WINE Crisp Sardinian Vermentino: 2015 Sella & Mosca La Cala.

Mochi-Crusted Snapper

Total **1 hr**; Serves **6**

Chef Wade Ueoka of Honolulu's MW Restaurant is an expert at using the Japanese rice cake called mochi (available at Asian markets) as a coating when frying foods—even Spam. Here, he wraps snapper in shredded mochi before cooking, creating a crust that's both chewy and crispy.

- ¼ **cup soy sauce**
- ¼ **cup rice vinegar**
- ¼ **cup sugar**
- 2 **tsp. kudzu (see Ingredient Intel, p. 106) or cornstarch**
- 2 **tsp. Asian sesame oil**
- 2 **tsp. toasted sesame seeds**
- 2 **tsp. yuzu kosho (see Ingredient Intel, p. 106)**
- ½ **cup plus 2 Tbsp. canola oil**
- **Three 1½- to 2-oz. blocks of mochi, coarsely shredded (2 cups)**
- 1 **Tbsp. furikake (see Ingredient Intel, p. 106)**
- **Six 5-oz. skinless red snapper fillets**
- **Kosher salt**
- **Thinly sliced scallions, for garnish**
- **Cooked somen noodles, for serving**

1. In a small saucepan, bring the soy sauce, rice vinegar, sugar and 3 tablespoons of water to a boil. In a small bowl, whisk the kudzu with 1 tablespoon of water, then whisk into the saucepan. Boil over moderately high heat until thickened, about 1 minute. Remove from the heat and whisk in the sesame oil, sesame seeds, yuzu kosho and 2 tablespoons of the canola oil; keep warm.

2. In a bowl, toss the mochi with the furikake. Season the snapper with salt. In a large nonstick skillet, heat ¼ cup of the canola oil. Using a ⅓ cup measuring cup, scoop 3 loose mounds of the mochi mixture into the skillet; flatten them slightly. Set 1 fillet on each mound. Spread another ⅓ cup of the mochi on each fillet. Cook over moderately high heat until golden, about 4 minutes. Using a spatula, carefully flip the fish and cook until golden and the fish is cooked through, 4 to 6 minutes. Drain on paper towels. Wipe out the skillet and repeat with the remaining ¼ cup of canola oil, mochi mixture and fish. Transfer the fish to plates and garnish with scallions. Serve with somen noodles and the sauce. —Wade Ueoka

WINE Full-bodied Chenin Blanc: 2013 Thierry Germain Cuvée Soliterre Saumur Blanc.

Halibut with Einkorn, Morels and Tempura Ramps

Total **1 hr 45 min**; Serves **4**

This elegant dish from Seattle chef Edouardo Jordan features high-in-protein einkorn, the oldest and smallest variety of wheat berry and the only one that's never been hybridized. Its inherent sweetness is perfect with the earthy morels. The fried ramps are more than just a flourish—they're spectacularly tasty, too.

HALIBUT

- ¼ **cup kosher salt, plus more for seasoning**
- **Four 5-oz. skinless halibut fillets**
- 2 **Tbsp. extra-virgin olive oil**
- 1 **Tbsp. fresh lemon juice**

EINKORN

- 1 **cup einkorn or wheat berries**
- ½ **yellow onion**
- 1 **bay leaf**

MORELS

- 2 **Tbsp. extra-virgin olive oil**
- ½ **lb. fresh morels, cleaned (4 cups)**
- ¼ **cup finely chopped onion**
- **Kosher salt**
- 2 **Tbsp. chopped parsley**
- 1 **tsp. chopped thyme, plus thyme leaves for garnish**

PRESERVED LEMON VINAIGRETTE

- 1 **preserved lemon, seeded and chopped (3 oz.)**
- 3 **Tbsp. water**
- 3 **Tbsp. extra-virgin olive oil**
- 3 **Tbsp. muscatel vinegar or sherry vinegar**

TEMPURA RAMPS

- **Canola oil, for frying**
- ¾ **cup (4 oz.) all-purpose flour**
- 2 **Tbsp. cornstarch**
- ½ **Tbsp. kosher salt**
- ½ **Tbsp. baking powder**
- **Pinch of cayenne**
- 1 **cup chilled soda water**
- 4 **ramps, trimmed**

1. Brine the halibut In a bowl, whisk 4 cups of water with the ¼ cup of salt. Add the halibut; refrigerate for 1 hour.

2. Meanwhile, make the einkorn In a medium saucepan, combine the einkorn, onion and bay leaf with enough water to cover by 2 inches. Bring to a boil and cook over moderate heat until tender, about 30 minutes. Drain and transfer to a bowl; discard the onion and bay leaf.

3. Make the morels In a large skillet, heat the oil. Add the morels and onion and season with salt. Cook over moderately high heat, stirring occasionally, until the morels are tender and dry, about 8 minutes. Reserve half of the morels in a bowl; add the rest to the einkorn and stir in the parsley and chopped thyme.

4. Make the vinaigrette In a blender, puree all of the ingredients until smooth. Add ¼ cup of the vinaigrette to the einkorn, season with salt and mix well.

5. Preheat the oven to 425°. Line a baking sheet with parchment paper. Remove the halibut from the brine and pat dry. Rub with the olive oil and season with salt. Arrange on the sheet and bake for about 8 minutes, until just cooked through but not browned. Drizzle with the lemon juice.

6. Meanwhile, fry the ramps In a large enameled cast-iron casserole, heat 3 inches of oil to 350°. Set a rack over a baking sheet and line with paper towels. In a bowl, whisk all of the ingredients except the soda and ramps. Whisk in the cold soda to form a batter. Dip the ramps in the batter, letting the excess drip off. Fry the ramps in batches, turning, until crisp, about 2 minutes. Transfer to the paper towels to drain.

7. Spread the vinaigrette in bowls. Top with the einkorn and halibut. Garnish with the morels, ramps and thyme leaves. —Edouardo Jordan

WINE Vibrant California Chardonnay: 2014 Au Bon Climat Santa Barbara County.

Grilled Swordfish with Fennel-Olive Relish

Active **1 hr**; Total **2 hr**; Serves **4**

SWORDFISH

- ¼ cup extra-virgin olive oil, plus more for brushing
- 1 tsp. finely grated lemon zest plus 1 Tbsp. fresh lemon juice
- ½ tsp. kosher salt
- ¼ tsp. pepper
- Four ½-inch-thick 8-oz. skinless swordfish steaks, skin and bloodline trimmed

ROSÉ MAYONNAISE

- ¾ cup dry rosé
- 2 Tbsp. minced shallot
- 1 Tbsp. unseasoned rice vinegar
- ½ tsp. finely grated lemon zest plus 2 tsp. fresh lemon juice
- ¼ tsp. grated garlic
- 1 cup mayonnaise

RELISH

- 5 oz. baby spinach (4 cups)
- 1 fennel bulb, cored and finely chopped, fronds reserved
- ½ cup thinly sliced radishes
- ¼ cup pitted kalamata olives, thinly sliced
- ¼ cup chopped chives
- 3 Tbsp. extra-virgin olive oil
- 1 Tbsp. unseasoned rice wine vinegar
- ½ tsp. finely grated lemon zest plus 1 Tbsp. fresh lemon juice
- Kosher salt and pepper

1. Marinate the swordfish In a large resealable plastic bag, combine all of the ingredients except the fish and mix well. Add the swordfish and turn to coat. Seal and refrigerate for 1 hour.

2. Meanwhile, make the mayonnaise In a small saucepan, simmer the rosé over moderate heat until reduced to 2 tablespoons, 10 minutes. Transfer to a bowl and let cool to room temperature. Whisk in the shallot, vinegar, lemon zest and juice, garlic and mayonnaise until smooth.

3. Make the relish In a medium bowl, combine all of the ingredients except the fennel fronds and season with salt and pepper. Add ⅓ cup of the rosé mayonnaise and toss to evenly coat the vegetables.

4. Heat a large cast-iron grill pan and brush with oil. Remove the swordfish from the marinade and season with salt and pepper. Grill over moderately high heat, turning once, until golden and cooked through, 3 to 4 minutes per side. Top the fish with fennel fronds and serve with the relish and remaining rosé mayonnaise.
—*Jennifer Carroll*

WINE A crisp but full-bodied Viognier: 2014 Barboursville Reserve from Virginia.

Grilled Swordfish with Herbs and Charred Lemon Salsa

Total **50 min**; Serves **4**

"Swordfish is so meaty and flavorful, it's like the steak of the sea," says F&W's Justin Chapple. The fish is hearty enough to stand up to assertive ingredients like the dried rosemary, thyme and oregano here.

- 1 lemon, preferably thin-skinned, very thinly sliced and seeded
- ¼ cup extra-virgin olive oil, plus more for brushing
- 1 medium celery rib, finely chopped
- 2 Tbsp. minced shallot
- ¼ cup finely chopped parsley
- 2 tsp. each dried rosemary, thyme and oregano
- Kosher salt and pepper
- Four 8-oz. skinless swordfish steaks, cut 1 inch thick

1. Light a grill or heat a grill pan. Brush the lemon slices with olive oil and grill over moderate heat, turning occasionally, until lightly charred and the rind is tender, about 8 minutes. Transfer to a work surface and let cool, then finely chop.

2. In a small bowl, whisk the chopped lemon with the celery, shallot, parsley, ¼ cup of olive oil and ½ teaspoon each of the rosemary, thyme and oregano. Season the salsa with salt and pepper.

3. Brush the swordfish with oil and season with salt, pepper and the remaining 1½ teaspoons each of the dried herbs. Grill the fish over moderately high heat, turning once, until lightly charred and just cooked through, 8 minutes. Transfer to plates and serve with the salsa. —*Justin Chapple*

WINE Full-bodied Napa Valley Chardonnay: 2014 Miner Family.

Swordfish with Romesco Sauce

Active **35 min**; Total **1 hr 15 min**; Serves **4**

To complement grilled swordfish, chef Jonathan Waxman of Barbuto and Jams in New York City makes a spicy romesco sauce with roasted vegetables, two kinds of nuts and Calabrian chiles.

- 1 pint grape or cherry tomatoes
- 1 medium onion, thinly sliced
- 1 jalapeño, thinly sliced with seeds
- 4 garlic cloves, crushed
- 3 Calabrian chiles in oil, drained
- 1 tsp. smoked paprika
- ¼ cup plus 2 Tbsp. extra-virgin olive oil
- Kosher salt and pepper
- ¼ cup hazelnuts
- ¼ cup almonds
- 2 Tbsp. sherry vinegar
- Four 6-oz. swordfish steaks

1. Preheat the oven to 450°. On a rimmed baking sheet, combine the tomatoes, onion, jalapeño, garlic, chiles, paprika and 2 tablespoons of the olive oil; season with salt and pepper and toss well. Roast for about 40 minutes, until the vegetables are caramelized.

2. Meanwhile, spread the hazelnuts and almonds in a pie plate and toast for about 12 minutes, until deep golden. Transfer the hazelnuts to a clean kitchen towel and rub off the skins.

3. In a food processor, pulse the toasted nuts until a paste forms. Add the caramelized vegetables, 2 tablespoons of the olive oil and the sherry vinegar and pulse until the romesco is slightly chunky.

4. Heat a grill pan. Rub the fish with the remaining 2 tablespoons of olive oil and season with salt and pepper. Add the fish to the pan and grill over moderate heat, turning once, until nicely charred and cooked through, 4 to 5 minutes per side. Serve with the romesco.
—*Jonathan Waxman*

SERVE WITH Steamed green beans.

MAKE AHEAD The romesco sauce can be refrigerated for up to 1 week. Bring to room temperature before serving.

WINE Toasty, apple-y, full-bodied white: 2013 Clos Julien Chardonnay.

GRILLED SWORDFISH
WITH HERBS AND
CHARRED LEMON SALSA

SALMON WITH
LENTIL-BEET SALAD

Salmon with Lentil-Beet Salad

Total **50 min**; Serves **4**

The buttery salmon fillet in this healthy dish is perfect with the tangy lentil salad, but the salad itself is so good, it could easily stand on its own. If you can't find frisée, use escarole and chicory instead.

- **1 cup French green lentils**
  Kosher salt and pepper
- **6 baby golden beets, scrubbed and cut into ½-inch wedges**
- **2 Tbsp. sherry vinegar**
- **2 Tbsp. minced shallot**
- **2 tsp. Dijon mustard**
- **¼ cup plus 1 Tbsp. extra-virgin olive oil**
- **3 cups torn frisée, white and light green parts only**
- **2 red endives—halved lengthwise, cored and sliced crosswise on the diagonal**
  Four 5- to 6-oz. skin-on salmon fillets

1. In a large saucepan, cover the lentils with at least 2 inches of water and bring to a boil. Simmer over moderate heat until just tender, about 20 minutes. Remove from the heat, add a generous pinch of salt and let stand for 5 minutes. Drain well and spread the lentils on a baking sheet to cool.

2. Rinse out the saucepan and put a steamer basket in it. Add 1 inch of water and bring to a boil. Scatter the beets in the basket, cover and steam until tender, about 10 minutes. Let the beets cool.

3. In a large bowl, whisk the vinegar with the shallot, mustard and ¼ cup of the olive oil. Season with salt and pepper. Add the lentils, beets, frisée and endives and toss to coat. Season the salad with salt and pepper and toss again.

4. Season the salmon with salt and pepper. In a large nonstick skillet, heat the remaining 1 tablespoon of olive oil until shimmering. Add the salmon, skin side down, and press gently with a spatula to flatten. Cook over moderately high heat until the skin is browned and crisp, about 3 minutes. Flip the salmon and cook until it is medium within, about 3 minutes longer. Transfer the salmon to plates and serve with the lentil salad. —*Justin Chapple*

MAKE AHEAD The lentil salad can be refrigerated overnight. Fold in the frisée and endive just before serving.

WINE Raspberry-scented Sonoma County Pinot Noir: 2014 Decoy.

Harissa-Spiced Salmon with Israeli Couscous

Total **50 min**; Serves **4**

Spicy harissa and sweet agave combine to make a delicious rub for crisp-skinned salmon fillet. The fish is paired with herbed Israeli couscous, which has larger, pearl-shaped grains than its North African counterpart.

- **1 cup Israeli couscous**
  Kosher salt and pepper
- **½ cup plus 1 Tbsp. chopped chives**
- **½ cup each chopped mint and parsley**
- **2½ Tbsp. fresh lemon juice**
- **2 Tbsp. extra-virgin olive oil**
- **1½ lbs. salmon fillet in 1 piece, cut from the tail end**
- **2 Tbsp. harissa**
- **1 Tbsp. agave nectar**

1. Preheat the oven to 400°. Bring a medium saucepan of water to a boil. Add the couscous and a pinch of salt and cook, stirring, until al dente, about 10 minutes. Drain well; let cool.

2. In a medium bowl, toss the couscous with ½ cup of the chives, the mint, parsley, lemon juice and oil. Season with salt and pepper.

3. Make 5 or 6 slashes in the salmon fillet about ½ inch deep. In a small bowl, whisk the harissa, agave and the remaining 1 tablespoon of chives. Rub all over the salmon and in the slashes; season with salt and pepper.

4. Transfer the fish, skin side up, to a foil-lined baking sheet. Roast for 8 minutes, until barely cooked. Turn on the broiler and broil for 3 to 5 minutes, until nearly cooked through and the skin is crisp. Cut the salmon into 4 pieces and serve with the couscous. —*Justin Chapple*

WINE Medium-bodied, spicy Lebanese red: 2012 Chateau Musar Jeune Rouge.

Spiced Arctic Char with Crushed Sunchokes, Capers and Lemon

Total **1 hr**; Serves **4**

F&W's Justin Chapple coats arctic char, a rich, sustainable fish, in an aromatic spice mix of caraway, fennel, coriander and smoky pimentón before pan-frying.

- **1½ lbs. sunchokes, half peeled and half left unpeeled, cut into 1-inch pieces**
  Kosher salt and pepper
- **¼ cup plus 1 Tbsp. extra-virgin olive oil**
- **⅓ cup finely chopped parsley**
- **2½ Tbsp. fresh lemon juice, plus lemon wedges for serving**
- **2½ Tbsp. capers, finely chopped**
- **¾ tsp. caraway seeds**
- **¾ tsp. fennel seeds**
- **¾ tsp. coriander seeds**
- **¾ tsp. sweet pimentón de la Vera**
  Four 5- to 6-oz. skin-on arctic char fillets

1. In a large saucepan, cover the sunchokes with water and bring to a boil. Add a generous pinch of salt and simmer over moderate heat until tender, about 10 minutes. Drain well. Return the sunchokes to the saucepan and add ¼ cup of olive oil along with the parsley, lemon juice and capers. Using a wooden spoon, gently crush the sunchokes. Season with salt and pepper and mix again. Cover the saucepan and keep warm.

2. Meanwhile, in a small skillet, toast the caraway, fennel and coriander seeds over moderate heat, stirring, until fragrant, about 2 minutes. Transfer to a spice grinder and let cool, then grind to a powder. Transfer the spice mix to a small bowl and stir in the pimentón. Season the fish all over with salt, pepper and the spice mix.

3. In a large nonstick skillet, heat the remaining 1 tablespoon of olive oil. Add the fish, skin side down, and cook over moderately high heat until the skin is golden and crisp, about 3 minutes. Flip the fish and cook until medium, 2 to 3 minutes longer. Drain briefly on paper towels, then transfer to plates. Pile the crushed sunchokes alongside and serve with lemon wedges. —*Justin Chapple*

WINE Quince-scented Loire Valley Chenin Blanc: 2014 Château d'Épiré Savennières.

Salmon Burgers with Harissa Mayonnaise

Total **1 hr plus 1 hr chilling**; Serves **6**

CUCUMBER RELISH

- 1 **English cucumber—halved lengthwise, seeded and sliced ¼ inch thick**
- ⅓ **cup rice vinegar**
- 1 **Tbsp. chopped dill**
- 1 **shallot, minced**
- 1 **tsp. sugar**
- 1 **tsp. kosher salt**

HARISSA MAYO

- ⅔ **cup mayonnaise**
- ¼ **cup Greek yogurt**
- 2 **Tbsp. harissa**
- 1 **tsp. finely grated lemon zest plus 1 Tbsp. fresh lemon juice**
- **Kosher salt and pepper**

SALMON BURGERS

- 5 **scallions, white and light green parts only, coarsely chopped**
- 1 **small red bell pepper, coarsely chopped (about ¾ cup)**
- 1 **small green bell pepper, coarsely chopped (about ¾ cup)**
- 1½ **lbs. skinless center-cut salmon fillet, cut into 1-inch cubes and frozen for 30 minutes**
- ½ **cup plain dry breadcrumbs**
- 1 **Tbsp. kosher salt**
- ½ **tsp. pepper**
- 2 **Tbsp. unsalted butter**
- ¼ **cup extra-virgin olive oil**
- 6 **brioche buns, split and toasted**
- **Lettuce and tomato slices, for serving**

1. Make the cucumber relish In a medium bowl, combine all of the ingredients. Cover and refrigerate for at least 1 hour.

2. Make the harissa mayo In a medium bowl, whisk together all of the ingredients. Season with salt and pepper.

3. Make the salmon burgers In a food processor, pulse the scallions and bell peppers until finely chopped; transfer to a medium bowl. Pulse the salmon in the food processor until finely chopped but with some bigger chunks remaining. Add the salmon to the bowl with the scallions and peppers and fold in the breadcrumbs,

salt, pepper and ⅓ cup of the harissa mayo. Using lightly oiled hands, shape the salmon mixture into six ¾-inch-thick patties. Transfer to a lightly oiled plate and refrigerate for 30 minutes.

4. Light a grill. Set a large cast-iron skillet on the grill and melt 1 tablespoon of the butter in 2 tablespoons of the olive oil. Add 3 of the salmon burgers and cook over moderately high heat, turning once, until golden brown and just cooked through, 4 to 5 minutes. Transfer to a plate and repeat with the remaining butter, olive oil and salmon burgers.

5. Spread some of the harissa mayo on the buns. Top with the salmon burgers, cucumber relish, lettuce and tomato slices and serve. —*Rick Moonen*

WINE Bold Sonoma Sauvignon Blanc: 2014 Banshee.

Norwegian Fish Cakes with Dill Mayonnaise

Total **30 min**; Makes **12**

- 1¼ **lbs. skinless hake fillet, cut into ½-inch pieces**
- 1 **Tbsp. baking powder**
- **Kosher salt and black pepper**
- ¾ **cup plus 2 Tbsp. heavy cream**
- 6 **Tbsp. unsalted butter**
- 1 **cup mayonnaise**
- ¼ **cup chopped dill, plus more for garnish**
- 1 **Tbsp. distilled white vinegar**
- **Freshly ground white pepper**

1. In a food processor, pulse the hake until minced. Add the baking powder, 2 teaspoons of salt and ¼ teaspoon of black pepper and pulse until combined. With the machine on, add the cream and puree until the fish mixture is smooth and light in texture, about 2 minutes.

2. In a large nonstick skillet, melt 2 tablespoons of the butter. Spoon ¼ cup of the fish mixture into the skillet and flatten to a ½-inch-thick cake. Repeat 3 more times to make 4 cakes. Cook over moderately low heat, turning once, until golden and cooked through, 4 to 5 minutes. Transfer the fish cakes to a platter and keep warm. Repeat with the remaining butter and fish mixture to make 8 more cakes.

3. Meanwhile, in a small bowl, stir the mayonnaise with the ¼ cup of dill and the vinegar and season with salt and white pepper. Serve the fish cakes with the dill mayonnaise and a sprinkling of chopped dill. —*Magnus Nilsson*

MAKE AHEAD The mayonnaise can be refrigerated overnight.

WINE A white with brisk acidity: the 2014 Robert Weil Tradition.

Citrus-and-Herb-Marinated Shrimp

Active **30 min**; Total **3 hr**; Serves **4**

To intensify their flavor, New York City chef Dan Kluger air-dries shrimp in the refrigerator for a couple of hours before marinating.

- 2 **lbs. large shrimp, shelled and deveined, tails left on**
- 1½ **cups extra-virgin olive oil**
- ¾ **cup chopped cilantro**
- ¾ **cup chopped parsley**
- ¼ **cup plus 2 Tbsp. fresh orange juice**
- 1 **Tbsp. finely grated orange zest**
- 1 **Tbsp. finely grated lemon zest plus 3 Tbsp. fresh lemon juice**
- **One 3-inch piece of fresh ginger, peeled and finely grated**
- ¼ **tsp. crushed red pepper**
- **Kosher salt**
- **Lemon wedges, for serving**

1. Spread the shrimp in an even layer on a large rimmed baking sheet. Refrigerate uncovered for 2 hours to air-dry.

2. In a large bowl, mix all of the remaining ingredients except the salt and lemon wedges. Add the shrimp and stir to coat. Refrigerate for 30 minutes, stirring the shrimp occasionally.

3. Remove the shrimp from the marinade; season with salt. Light a grill or heat a grill pan. Grill the shrimp over moderately high heat, turning once, until just white throughout, about 4 minutes. Transfer to a platter and serve with lemon wedges. —*Dan Kluger*

WINE Zesty Loire Sauvignon Blanc: 2015 Clos de la Grange Touraine.

SAUTÉED SHRIMP IN
FISH SAUCE CARAMEL

Sautéed Shrimp in Fish Sauce Caramel
⏲ Total **30 min**; Serves **4**

Chef Angela Dimayuga of Manhattan's Mission Chinese Food tosses a variety of seafood with her sweet-savory fish sauce; crushed red pepper and black pepper amp up the flavor of this quick weeknight meal.

- ¼ cup turbinado sugar
- 3 Tbsp. Asian fish sauce
- 2 Tbsp. soy sauce
- 1 Tbsp. canola oil
- 1 Tbsp. minced garlic
- ½ tsp. crushed red pepper
- Kosher salt and black pepper
- 1 lb. medium shrimp, shells intact
- One 6-oz. bunch of watercress, thick stems discarded

1. In a medium saucepan, combine the sugar with 1 tablespoon of water. Cook over moderately high heat, swirling the pan, until an amber caramel forms, 4 to 5 minutes. Remove from the heat and immediately add the fish sauce, soy sauce and 2 tablespoons of water.

2. Heat a large skillet over high heat until smoking. Add ½ tablespoon of the canola oil and stir in half of the garlic and crushed red pepper; season with salt and black pepper. Add half of the shrimp in an even layer and cook over moderately high heat, turning once, until crisp on the outside and just white throughout, about 3 minutes. Transfer to a plate. Repeat with the remaining oil, garlic, crushed red pepper and shrimp.

3. Return all of the shrimp to the skillet; add the caramel sauce. Cook over high heat, tossing, until the shrimp are hot and evenly coated, 1 to 2 minutes. Scatter the watercress on a platter, top with the shrimp and sauce and serve. Eat the shrimp with or without the shells. —*Angela Dimayuga*

WINE Bracing, zesty pink wine: 2015 Birichino California Vin Gris.

Grilled Shrimp with Lemony Potatoes
Total **1 hr**; Serves **4**

For this simple yet elegant dish, *Top Chef* star Jennifer Carroll dresses grilled shrimp and potatoes with a quick herb oil.

- 1½ lbs. fingerling potatoes, scrubbed but not peeled
- 1 cup extra-virgin olive oil
- Kosher salt and pepper
- 1¼ lbs. jumbo shrimp, shelled and deveined
- 2 Tbsp. fresh lemon juice
- ½ cup chopped dill
- ½ cup chopped chives
- 3 oz. baby arugula (4 cups loosely packed)
- 1 Tbsp. finely chopped preserved lemon peel

1. Heat a large cast-iron grill pan. In a medium bowl, toss the potatoes with 2 tablespoons of the olive oil and season with salt and pepper. Grill over moderate heat, turning, until golden and tender, about 20 minutes. Transfer to a work surface and let cool slightly, then coarsely chop and transfer to a large bowl.

2. In another large bowl, toss the shrimp with 2 tablespoons of the oil and season with salt and pepper. Grill over moderately high heat, turning once, until golden and just cooked through, about 4 minutes. Transfer to a plate and drizzle with 1 tablespoon of the lemon juice.

3. In a small bowl, whisk the remaining ¾ cup of olive oil with the dill and chives and season with salt and pepper.

4. Add ⅓ cup of the herb oil to the potatoes along with the arugula, preserved lemon peel and the remaining 1 tablespoon of lemon juice. Season with salt and pepper and toss to coat. Spoon the potato salad onto plates and top with the shrimp. Serve the remaining herb oil on the side. —*Jennifer Carroll*

MAKE AHEAD The herb oil can be made 3 hours ahead.

WINE An unoaked white Rhône-style blend: 2014 Unti Vineyards Cuvée Blanc.

Shrimp à l'Américaine
⏲ Total **30 min**; Serves **10 to 12**

L.A. restaurateur Stephane Bombet creates a truly luscious version of shrimp à l'Américaine—a classic dish made with tomatoes and wine—that includes Cognac, crème fraîche and a touch of cayenne.

- 2 lbs. large shrimp (about 40), shelled and deveined
- Kosher salt and pepper
- 6 Tbsp. unsalted butter
- 3 Tbsp. extra-virgin olive oil
- 4 shallots, very thinly sliced
- 2 garlic cloves, minced
- ¾ cup dry white wine
- 2 Tbsp. Cognac
- One 15-oz. can diced tomatoes
- 2 tsp. tomato paste
- ¼ tsp. cayenne
- ¼ cup crème fraîche
- Crusty bread, for serving

1. Season the shrimp with salt and pepper. In a large skillet, melt 3 tablespoons of the butter in the olive oil over moderately high heat. Add half of the shrimp and cook, turning once, until lightly browned but not cooked through, 1 to 2 minutes. Transfer to a plate. Repeat with the remaining shrimp.

2. In the skillet, melt the remaining 3 tablespoons of butter. Add the shallots and garlic and cook over moderate heat, stirring occasionally, until softened and just starting to brown, about 5 minutes. Add the wine and Cognac and simmer until slightly reduced, about 2 minutes. Stir in the tomatoes, tomato paste and cayenne and simmer for 5 minutes, stirring occasionally. Add the shrimp and cook, stirring, until just cooked through, 3 to 5 minutes. Stir in the crème fraîche; season with salt and pepper. Serve with bread. —*Stephane Bombet*

WINE Crisp Spanish white: 2015 Fillaboa Albariño.

Pepper Shrimp

📷 PAGE 112

Total **45 min plus 4 hr marinating**
Serves **4 to 6**

"The Liberian coast provides outstanding seafood for this spicy—I mean *very* spicy—dish," says *Bizarre Foods* host Andrew Zimmern. "Liberian cooks often use Maggi seasoning cubes and ground peanuts here, but I've skipped them for simplicity's sake." Zimmern likes to serve the dish with icy glasses of fresh mango pureed with yogurt and orange juice.

1¾ lbs. head-on large shrimp (24)

¼ cup canola oil

2 large yellow onions, finely chopped

3 Tbsp. sweet paprika

2 Scotch bonnet chiles—stemmed, seeded and minced

2 Tbsp. tomato paste

6 garlic cloves, thinly sliced

1 cup unsweetened coconut milk

3 Tbsp. fresh lime juice

Kosher salt

Steamed rice and sliced melon tossed with chopped mint, for serving (optional)

1. Using scissors, make a cut from just below the head of each shrimp to the base of the tail, cutting through the shell but not removing it. Use the tip of a knife to remove the intestinal vein.

2. In a large bowl, combine 2 tablespoons of the canola oil and 1¼ cups of the onions with the paprika, chiles and tomato paste. Add the shrimp and stir gently until they are evenly coated. Cover and refrigerate for 4 hours. Bring the shrimp to room temperature before proceeding.

3. In a very large skillet or in 2 large skillets, heat the remaining 2 tablespoons of oil until shimmering. Spread the shrimp and marinade in the pan in a single layer. Cook over moderately high heat, without stirring, until the shrimp begin to brown, about 2 minutes. Add the garlic and the remaining onions to the skillet and cook until the onions begin to brown, about 1 minute. Stir in the coconut milk and bring to a boil. Cook over moderately high heat until the shrimp are just cooked through, about 2 minutes. Remove from the heat and add the lime juice. Season with salt and serve with steamed rice and melon tossed with mint, if desired. *—Andrew Zimmern*

WINE A fresh, fruit-forward sparkling wine: NV Clément Klur Crémant d'Alsace Brut.

Squid and Summer Vegetable Salad with Preserved Lemon Dressing

Total **1 hr; Serves 4**

This seafood salad from the French Riviera combines simply poached squid, a piquant dressing and a mix of superthin vegetables crisped in an ice water bath.

4 red radishes, sliced paper-thin

½ small zucchini, sliced paper-thin

½ small yellow squash, sliced paper-thin

½ fennel bulb, halved lengthwise and sliced paper-thin

3 Tbsp. white balsamic vinegar

1 Tbsp. minced preserved lemon rind

1 Tbsp. minced shallot

½ cup plus 1 Tbsp. extra-virgin olive oil

Kosher salt and pepper

12 oz. cleaned squid, bodies sliced crosswise ¼ inch thick and tentacles left whole

8 cherry tomatoes, halved or quartered if large

12 niçoise olives, pitted

¼ cup chopped mixed herbs, such as parsley, basil and chives

Piment d'Espelette and fleur de sel, for garnish

1. Soak the radishes, zucchini, squash and fennel slices in a bowl of ice water.

2. In a large bowl, mix the vinegar with the preserved lemon and shallot. Slowly whisk in ½ cup of the olive oil. Season the vinaigrette with salt and pepper.

3. In a large skillet, combine the remaining 1 tablespoon of oil with 2 tablespoons of water and bring to a simmer. Add the squid and season with salt and pepper. Cover and cook over moderate heat until just opaque throughout, about 1 minute. Add the poached squid to the vinaigrette.

4. Drain the iced vegetables and pat thoroughly dry. Add the vegetables, tomatoes, olives and herbs to the squid and mix well. Arrange the salad on plates and drizzle with any remaining vinaigrette. Garnish with piment d'Espelette and fleur de sel. *—Cyrille Chaussade*

WINE A bright coastal white from Corsica: 2014 Yves Leccia Domaine d'E Croce Patrimonio Blanc.

SEAFOOD KNOW-HOW

How to Clean and Cut Squid

You may be able to find squid already cleaned, but it's supereasy to do yourself– and it will be less expensive, to boot.

STEP 1 Separate the body from the tentacles by slicing behind the eyes.

STEP 2 Hold the body and pull out the head and innards, which include the intestines and ink sac. Next, pull out the quill, which is the long, clear cartilage inside the body.

STEP 3 Starting from the cut end of the squid, peel away the skin and discard.

STEP 4 Slice the body into rings.

SQUID AND SUMMER
VEGETABLE SALAD WITH
PRESERVED LEMON DRESSING

CRAB AND CRISPY
CHEESE TACOS

Crab and Crispy Cheese Tacos

Active **50 min;** Total **1 hr 45 min;** Makes **12**

SALSA

- **4 dried guajillo chiles**
- **2 dried chipotle chiles**
- **Boiling water**
- **2 garlic cloves**
- **¼ cup toasted sesame seeds**
- **2 clementines, peeled**
- **2 Tbsp. honey**
- **2 Tbsp. apple cider vinegar**
- **Kosher salt**

CRAB FILLING

- **2 large shallots, minced**
- **1 jalapeño—stemmed, seeded and minced**
- **¼ cup plus 2½ Tbsp. fresh lime juice**
- **Kosher salt and pepper**
- **¼ cup Greek yogurt**
- **¼ cup mayonnaise**
- **1½ lbs. fresh lump crabmeat, picked over**
- **1 English cucumber, cut into thin 3-inch spears**
- **10 oz. sharp cheddar cheese, shredded (about 3 cups)**
- **12 corn tortillas, warmed**
- **Cilantro sprigs, toasted sesame seeds and lime wedges, for serving**

1. Make the salsa In a medium skillet, toast the guajillo and chipotle chiles until lightly browned and fragrant, about 2 minutes. Transfer to a heatproof bowl and cover with boiling water. Let stand at room temperature until the chiles have softened, about 20 minutes.

2. Drain the chiles, reserving ¼ cup of the soaking liquid. Stem and seed the chiles and transfer to a blender. Add the garlic, sesame seeds, clementines, honey, vinegar and the chiles' reserved soaking liquid and blend until smooth; season the salsa with salt.

3. Make the crab filling In a medium bowl, mix the shallots with the jalapeño and ¼ cup of the lime juice; season with salt. Let stand for 10 minutes. Whisk in the yogurt and mayonnaise, then fold in the crabmeat and season with salt and pepper. Refrigerate until ready to serve.

4. In a medium bowl, toss the cucumber with the remaining 2½ tablespoons of lime juice and 1 teaspoon of salt. Let stand at room temperature for 10 minutes. Drain the cucumber and refrigerate.

5. Preheat the oven to 350° and position racks in the top, middle and bottom. Line 3 rimmed baking sheets with parchment paper and lightly grease. Mound four ¼-cup portions of shredded cheese on each baking sheet; the mounds should be about 4 inches wide and 1 inch apart. Bake until melted and light golden brown, 12 to 14 minutes; shift the pans from front to back and top to bottom halfway through baking. Using a thin spatula, transfer the fricos to a rack and let them cool completely.

6. Top each warm tortilla with a crispy frico. Spread some of the salsa on each taco and top with the crab, some of the cucumber, cilantro and sesame seeds. Serve with lime wedges and the remaining salsa and cucumber. —*Nate Appleman*

BEER A hop-forward IPA with a kick: Ballast Point Habanero Sculpin.

Lobster with Fried Bread, Spinach and Tangy Pomegranate

Active **1 hr;** Total **1 hr 30 min;** Serves **4**

Key to this excellent dish is the lobster oil; Stockholm chef Petter Nilsson makes it with the lobster shells, then uses it to fry the bread and sauté the meat.

- **Two 1½-lb. live lobsters or 2 cooked lobsters in their shells**
- **½ cup canola oil**
- **4 oz. sourdough bread, torn into 1½-inch pieces (3 cups)**
- **2 Tbsp. extra-virgin olive oil**
- **6 garlic cloves, crushed**
- **½ lb. curly spinach, thick stems discarded (8 packed cups)**
- **5 Tbsp. salted butter**
- **1 tsp. fresh lemon juice**
- **Kosher salt and pepper**
- **½ cup fresh pomegranate seeds (3 oz.)**
- **3 umeboshi plums, pitted and finely chopped (see Note)**
- **1 tsp. low-sodium soy sauce**
- **1 tsp. apple cider vinegar**

1. If using live lobsters, bring a large pot of salted water to a boil. Add the lobsters headfirst and cook just until they turn bright red, about 9 minutes. Transfer to an ice bath and let cool. Remove the meat from the shells and chop coarsely. Rinse the shells and pat dry. Crush and reserve the shells.

2. In a medium saucepan, cook the lobster shells in the canola oil over low heat, covered, until the oil is orange-hued and very fragrant, about 30 minutes. Strain the oil through a fine sieve; discard the shells. You should have ¼ cup of lobster oil.

3. In a large skillet, heat 3 tablespoons of the lobster oil. Add the bread and cook over moderate heat, stirring, until golden and crisp, about 5 minutes. Drain on paper towels. Wipe out the skillet.

4. Heat the olive oil in the skillet. Add the garlic and cook over low heat until lightly golden. Add the spinach and cook, stirring, until just wilted, about 2 minutes. Stir in 1 tablespoon of the butter and the lemon juice and season with salt and pepper. Transfer to a bowl and keep warm. Wipe out the skillet.

5. Add the remaining 4 tablespoons of butter to the skillet and cook over low heat until browned, about 5 minutes. Stir in the pomegranate seeds, umeboshi, soy sauce and vinegar and cook until well combined, about 1 minute. Transfer to a bowl and season with salt. Wipe out the skillet.

6. Heat the remaining 1 tablespoon of lobster oil in the skillet. Add the lobster and cook over low heat until heated through, about 2 minutes. Transfer to plates and mound the spinach alongside. Spoon the pomegranate sauce on top, garnish with the bread and serve. —*Petter Nilsson*

NOTE Umeboshi are tangy pickled Japanese plums. They're available at Japanese markets and Whole Foods.

WINE A crisp, coastal white: 2014 Cantina Santa Maria la Palma Aragosta Vermentino.

Langoustines alla Busara

🕐 Total **30 min**; Serves **4**

Venice-based blogger Skye McAlpine loves the delicate flavor of langoustines, but to her the real magic of this dish is the superflavorful winey tomato sauce in which they simmer.

- **3 Tbsp. extra-virgin olive oil, plus more for drizzling**
- **1 garlic clove**
- **3 Tbsp. plain dry breadcrumbs**
- **8 medium langoustines (about 2 lbs.), rinsed and patted dry (see Note)**
- **¼ cup dry white wine**
  One 28-oz. can whole peeled tomatoes, drained and coarsely chopped, ¼ cup of juices reserved
- **1 tsp. crushed red pepper**
  Kosher salt and black pepper
- **2 Tbsp. chopped parsley**
  Lemon wedges and crusty bread, for serving

1. In a large, deep skillet, heat the 3 tablespoons of olive oil. Add the garlic and cook over moderate heat, stirring frequently, until just beginning to brown, about 3 minutes. Stir in the breadcrumbs and cook until beginning to brown, about 1 minute.

2. Add the langoustines to the skillet in a single layer. Pour the wine over them and cook until reduced by half, about 1 minute. Add the tomatoes and their juices, crushed red pepper and a generous pinch each of salt and black pepper. Cover and simmer over moderately low heat, stirring occasionally, until the tail meat is opaque, 16 to 18 minutes. Discard the garlic clove. Stir in the parsley and drizzle with a little more olive oil. Serve the langoustines with lemon wedges and crusty bread.
—*Skye McAlpine*

NOTE If langoustines are unavailable, use 1½ pounds of head-on unpeeled colossal shrimp. To prepare the shrimp, use scissors to make a cut through the shell from the base of the head to the tip of the tail and remove the intestinal veins. The shrimp will cook in about 10 minutes.

WINE Bold, citrusy white: 2015 Scarbolo Friuli Grave Sauvignon.

Scallops with Charred Scallions and Marcona Romesco

Total **1 hr**; Serves **4**

ROMESCO

- **1 large red bell pepper**
- **½ cup marcona almonds**
- **2 garlic cloves, crushed**
- **1 Tbsp. sherry vinegar**
- **½ tsp. crushed red pepper**
- **½ cup extra-virgin olive oil**
  Kosher salt and black pepper

SCALLOPS AND GREENS

- **¼ cup plus 1 Tbsp. extra-virgin olive oil**
- **24 scallions (10 oz.), halved crosswise**
  Kosher salt and pepper
- **12 large sea scallops**
- **2 Tbsp. unsalted butter**
- **3 garlic cloves**
- **1 thyme sprig**
- **2 oz. pea tendrils or shoots**
- **1½ tsp. fresh lemon juice**
  Chopped marcona almonds, for garnish

1. Make the romesco Roast the bell pepper directly over a gas flame or under the broiler, turning often, until charred all over, about 10 minutes. Transfer to a bowl, cover with plastic wrap and let steam for 15 minutes. Peel, core and seed the pepper.

2. In a food processor, pulse the roasted pepper with the almonds, garlic, vinegar and crushed red pepper until minced. With the machine on, drizzle in the oil until incorporated. Season with salt and black pepper.

3. Prepare the scallops and greens In a large cast-iron skillet, heat 2 tablespoons of the olive oil. Add the scallions, season with salt and pepper and cook over moderately high heat, turning, until lightly charred all over, about 5 minutes. Transfer to plates and wipe out the skillet.

4. Heat 2 more tablespoons of oil in the skillet. Season the scallops with salt and pepper and cook over moderately high heat until golden on the bottom, about 2 minutes. Add the butter, garlic and thyme and flip the scallops. Cook, basting with the butter, until just opaque throughout, about 2 minutes longer. Discard the garlic and thyme. Arrange the scallops on the scallions.

5. In a small bowl, toss the pea tendrils with the remaining 1 tablespoon of olive oil and the lemon juice; season with salt and pepper. Top the scallops with the pea tendrils, garnish with chopped almonds and serve with the romesco. —*Alex Knezevic*

MAKE AHEAD The romesco can be refrigerated for up to 2 days.

WINE Citrusy Sauvignon Blanc: 2014 Cliff Lede.

Penn Cove Mussels in Hard Cider

🕐 Total **25 min**; Serves **6**

- **3 Tbsp. unsalted butter**
- **2 large shallots, thinly sliced (1 cup)**
- **2 Tbsp. Dijon mustard**
- **3 cups dry hard cider**
- **3 lbs. mussels, scrubbed and debearded**
- **1 Tbsp. fresh lemon juice**
  Kosher salt
- **¾ cup crème fraîche**
- **⅓ cup tarragon leaves**
  Crusty bread, for serving

1. In a large enameled cast-iron casserole, melt the butter over moderate heat. When it has stopped foaming, add the shallots and cook, stirring occasionally, until softened, about 6 minutes. Whisk in the mustard and cider and increase the heat to moderately high.

2. Add the mussels to the casserole, cover and cook until they begin to open, about 5 minutes. Using a slotted spoon, transfer them to a large bowl as they open; discard any that do not.

3. Continue simmering the broth until reduced by a third, about 4 minutes. Stir in the lemon juice and season with salt. Reduce the heat to low and whisk in the crème fraîche. Return the mussels and any accumulated juices to the casserole and add the tarragon. Stir until the mussels are warmed through and coated with the cider cream, about 1 minute. Serve immediately, with crusty bread.
—*Renee Erickson*

WINE Robust, mineral-driven white Burgundy: 2013 Bouchard Aîné & Fils Mâcon-Villages.

SCALLOPS WITH CHARRED
SCALLIONS AND
MARCONA ROMESCO

PEPPER JELLY–
BRAISED CLAMS
WITH MINT

Mussels with Cava and Roasted Carrot Romesco

Total **50 min;** Serves **4**

- 2 Tbsp. extra-virgin olive oil
- 1 large carrot, cut into ½-inch pieces
- 1 orange bell pepper, cut into ½-inch pieces
- 2 scallions—white and light green parts sliced, dark green parts reserved
- 2 plum tomatoes, chopped
- 2 Tbsp. chopped salted roasted almonds
- 1 tsp. sherry vinegar
- ⅛ tsp. pimentón de la Vera
  Kosher salt
- 2 Tbsp. unsalted butter
- 2 lbs. mussels, scrubbed and debearded
- ¼ cup dry Cava
- ½ cup bottled clam juice
- 2 Tbsp. heavy cream
- 2 Tbsp. chopped parsley
  Toasted country bread brushed with olive oil, for serving

1. Preheat the oven to 425°. In a large ovenproof skillet, heat the olive oil. Add the carrot and bell pepper and cook over moderate heat, stirring occasionally, until lightly browned, about 8 minutes. Stir in the sliced scallions and tomatoes. Roast the vegetables in the oven until tender, about 10 minutes.

2. Scrape the vegetables into a food processor. Add the almonds, vinegar and pimentón and puree until smooth. Season the romesco with salt.

3. In an enameled cast-iron casserole, melt the butter. Thinly slice the reserved scallion greens and add to the casserole. Cook over moderate heat, stirring, until softened, 1 minute. Add the mussels, Cava, clam juice, cream and ½ cup of the carrot romesco and bring to a simmer. Cover and cook until the mussels open, about 3 minutes. Discard any that don't open. Season with salt and stir in the parsley. Serve the mussels with the toasts and the remaining romesco. —*Michael Serpa*

WINE Crisp Albariño: 2014 Granbazán Etiqueta Verde.

Pepper Jelly–Braised Clams with Mint

Total **35 min;** Serves **4**

F&W Best New Chef 2016 Michael Gulotta of MoPho in New Orleans uses a traditional Southern ingredient—pepper jelly—in a decidedly Asian preparation for braised clams. The result is a deeply fragrant dish that's a fantastic blend of briny, sweet and spicy. Gulotta likes draping the hot clams with lardo (seasoned fatback), but bits of crispy bacon work just as well.

- 8 slices of bacon (8 oz.)
- ¼ cup canola oil
- 1 Tbsp. minced garlic
- 1 Tbsp. minced peeled fresh ginger
- 1 Tbsp. crab paste (see Note, p. 111)
- 1 Tbsp. Thai chile paste or sambal oelek
- 4 dozen littleneck clams, scrubbed
- 1½ cups dry white wine
- 3 cups unsweetened coconut milk
- 5 Tbsp. hot pepper jelly
- 1 tsp. finely grated lime zest plus 2 Tbsp. fresh lime juice
- ¼ cup coarsely torn mint leaves, plus small whole leaves for garnish
  Kosher salt

1. Preheat the oven to 375°. Arrange the bacon slices side by side on a rack set over a baking sheet. Bake for about 20 minutes, until golden and crisp. Transfer the bacon to a paper towel–lined plate to cool. Break into large pieces.

2. Meanwhile, in a large enameled cast-iron casserole, heat the oil. Add the garlic, ginger, crab paste and chile paste and cook over moderately high heat, stirring, until the garlic is golden, about 3 minutes. Add the clams and wine, cover and simmer over high heat until all the clams have opened, 8 to 10 minutes. Discard any clams that don't open. Add the coconut milk and 3 tablespoons of the pepper jelly. Simmer for 1 minute, then stir in the lime zest and juice and torn mint and season with salt.

3. Ladle the clams and broth into bowls. Dollop the remaining 2 tablespoons of pepper jelly over the clams and garnish with mint leaves and the bacon. —*Michael Gulotta*

WINE Off-dry Riesling: 2015 Hexamer Quarzit Nahe.

Clam-and-Oyster Pan Roast

Total **45 min;** Serves **4**

Steamed clams meet New Orleans–style creamed oysters for a dish that's hearty but not heavy. The winter greens in the aromatic broth make it a full meal.

- 4 Tbsp. unsalted butter
- 2 small leeks, white and tender green parts only, thinly sliced (2 cups)
  Kosher salt
- 4 cups chopped mustard or turnip greens
- 4 thyme sprigs
- 2 garlic cloves, thinly sliced
- ¼ tsp. crushed red pepper
- 1 cup dry vermouth
- 2 dozen littleneck clams, scrubbed
- 2 dozen oysters, freshly shucked, with their liquor
- 2 Tbsp. heavy cream
- 2 Tbsp. chopped parsley
- 1 tsp. fresh lemon juice
- 2 dashes of hot sauce
  Crusty bread, for serving

In a large enameled cast-iron casserole, melt 2 tablespoons of the butter. Add the leeks, season with salt and cook over moderate heat, stirring occasionally, until softened, 8 minutes. Add the mustard greens, thyme, garlic and crushed red pepper and cook, stirring, until the greens are wilted, about 2 minutes. Add the vermouth and clams and bring to a boil. Cover and cook over moderate heat until the clams open, 5 to 10 minutes; transfer the clams to a bowl as they open, discarding any that do not. Add the oysters and their liquor, the cream, parsley, lemon juice, hot sauce and remaining 2 tablespoons of butter and cook just until the oysters start to curl around the edges, 1 to 2 minutes. Discard the thyme sprigs. Stir in the clams and any juices; serve immediately, with crusty bread. —*Vivian Howard*

WINE Crisp Chablis: 2015 Drouhin Vaudon.

Oysters Normande

⏱ Total **30 min**; Serves **8 as a first course**

Oysters Normande may sound like a big project, but Daniel Rose of Le Coucou in New York City debunks the notion quickly: "Shuck oysters, add cream, broil." As a finishing touch, he tops the oysters with pastis-spiked spinach, which adds a subtle licorice flavor.

- **1 lb. spinach, stemmed**
- **2 Tbsp. minced shallots**
- **1 Tbsp. pastis**
  Kosher salt and pepper
- **16 oysters (preferably Wellfleet), shucked, on the half shell**
- **½ cup (4 oz.) sour cream**

1. Preheat the broiler and position a rack 8 inches from the heat.

2. Fill a medium bowl with ice water. In a medium saucepan of salted boiling water, blanch the spinach just until wilted, about 1 minute. Drain, then transfer to the ice bath to cool completely, about 3 minutes. Drain, squeeze dry and finely chop. Transfer the spinach to another medium bowl and add the shallots and pastis. Season with salt and pepper and mix well.

3. Arrange the oysters on a baking sheet. Spoon the spinach on top and dot with the sour cream. Broil for about 10 minutes, until golden. Serve warm. —*Daniel Rose*

MAKE AHEAD The blanched spinach can be refrigerated for up to 2 days.

WINE Minerally, supercrisp Champagne: NV Laherte Frères Ultradition Brut.

Oysters with Green Apple and Wasabi Granita

Active **15 min;** Total **3 hr 45 min**
Makes **1 cup granita**

Chef Aaron Silverman of Rose's Luxury in Washington, DC, tops freshly shucked oysters with a sweet, spicy granita that's made with just apple juice, fresh wasabi and a dot of green food coloring. He loves using supersmall, superclean Kusshi oysters from British Columbia, but if they're unavailable, other small oysters from the Pacific Northwest will be equally fabulous.

- **½ cup fresh Granny Smith apple juice**
- **2 Tbsp. sugar**
  One ½-inch piece fresh wasabi, peeled and finely chopped
- **1 drop green food coloring**
  Shucked Kusshi oysters, for serving
  Micro nasturtium leaves, for garnish

In a blender, combine the apple juice, sugar and fresh wasabi and puree until smooth. Strain through a fine sieve into a pie plate; discard the solids. Stir in the food coloring, then freeze for 30 minutes. Using a fork, stir the granita; continue stirring every 30 minutes until frozen and fluffy, about 3 hours. To serve, spoon 1 teaspoon of the granita onto a shucked oyster and garnish with micro nasturtium leaves. —*Aaron Silverman*

MAKE AHEAD The granita can be frozen for up to 5 days.

Oysters on the Half Shell with Celery-and-Cucumber Mignonette

⏱ Total **5 min;** Makes **1¼ cups**

This refreshing cucumber mignonette for oysters on the half shell is from Seattle chef and oyster fanatic Renee Erickson.

- **1 cup Champagne vinegar**
  One 6-inch celery rib, coarsely chopped
  One 2-inch piece of English cucumber, coarsely chopped
  Freshly ground pepper
  Oysters on the half shell, for serving

In a blender, combine the vinegar, celery and cucumber and blend at medium speed until the vegetables are finely chopped. Season the mignonette with pepper and serve with oysters on the half shell. —*Renee Erickson*

MAKE AHEAD The mignonette can be refrigerated overnight.

PAIRING PRIMER

What to Sip When Slurping

Wine has *terroir;* oysters, according to experts, have "mer-roir" (*mer,* as in "sea"). In other words, like wine, oysters reflect in their taste the place they're from. Here's how chef Michael Serpa of Select in Boston pairs them with wine.

WELLFLEET Clean and supersalty; from Wellfleet, Massachusetts.
Drink Chardonnay with some weight, such as Liquid Farm Golden Slope.

KUSSHI Notes of cucumber and melon; from British Columbia.
Drink White from Alsace, such as Trimbach Riesling Cuvée Frédéric Emile.

PEMAQUID Refreshing, lemony; from Damariscotta River, Maine.
Drink Flinty Chablis, such as Gilbert Picq Dessus La Carrière.

BEAUSOLEIL Yeasty; from Miramichi Bay, New Brunswick, Canada.
Drink Bright and light Champagne, such as Jacquesson Cuvée 736.

KATAMA BAY Briny, buttery; from Katama Bay, Martha's Vineyard, Massachusetts.
Drink A rich Chenin, such as Ken Forrester The FMC.

OYSTERS ON THE HALF SHELL
WITH CELERY-AND-
CUCUMBER MIGNONETTE

POULTRY

Cookbook author
Melissa Clark (with
her daughter Dahlia)
prepares a stress-free
Thanksgiving dinner.
OPPOSITE Mustard-
and-Rosemary Roast
Turkey (p. 166).

Classic BBQ Chicken Drumsticks

Total **50 min**; Serves **6**

"My dad grew up in the Chicago suburbs in the '50s, when backyard barbecues were trending," says Ben Ford, the chef at Ford's Filling Station in L.A. "Of course he loves a classic barbecued drumstick. What red-blooded Midwestern kid doesn't?" In a nod to his famous father, actor Harrison Ford, Ben grills irresistibly sweet and sticky chicken drumsticks slicked with a homemade barbecue sauce.

- 1 **Tbsp. kosher salt**
- 1 **Tbsp. packed light brown sugar**
- 2 **garlic cloves, minced**
- 1½ **tsp. sweet paprika**
- 1 **tsp. ground black pepper**
- 1 **tsp. ground coriander**
- ½ **tsp. cayenne**
- 12 **chicken drumsticks (3 lbs.)**
  Classic BBQ Sauce (recipe follows), for brushing
  Bread-and-butter pickles, for serving

1. In a small bowl, whisk together the first 7 ingredients. Rub the chicken all over with the spice mix.

2. Set up a grill for direct and indirect cooking, then light the grill and oil the grate. Grill the chicken over moderately high heat, turning occasionally, until lightly charred all over, 8 to 10 minutes.

3. Move the chicken to indirect heat. Brush all over with some of the barbecue sauce. Cover and cook at 425°, basting and turning occasionally, until an instant-read thermometer inserted in the thickest part of each drumstick registers 165°, about 20 minutes. Transfer to a platter and serve with bread-and-butter pickles and the remaining barbecue sauce. —*Ben Ford*

WINE Juicy Zinfandel: 2013 Easton Amador County.

CLASSIC BBQ SAUCE

Active **35 min**; Total **1 hr 30 min**
Makes **2¾ cups**

- ½ **lb. plum tomatoes**
- 1 **medium onion, thinly sliced**
- 6 **large garlic cloves, crushed**
- ¼ **cup vegetable oil**
  Kosher salt and pepper
- 1 **cup ketchup**
- ¾ **cup apple cider vinegar**
- ½ **cup packed light brown sugar**
- 2 **Tbsp. unsulfured molasses**
- 1½ **Tbsp. Worcestershire sauce**
- 1 **Tbsp. chili powder**
- 1 **Tbsp. paprika**
- ¼ **tsp. ground coriander**
- ¼ **tsp. ground cumin**

1. Preheat the oven to 350°. On a large rimmed baking sheet, toss the tomatoes, onion and garlic with the oil; season with salt and pepper. Roast for about 40 minutes, until the tomatoes and onion are tender and browned in spots.

2. In a saucepan, bring the roasted tomatoes, onion and garlic and the remaining ingredients to a boil over moderately high heat. Cook over low heat, stirring often, until thick, about 30 minutes.

3. Scrape the mixture into a blender, add ½ cup of water and puree until smooth. Season with salt and pepper. —*BF*

Rosemary Chicken Breasts with Roasted Preserved Lemon

Active **35 min**; Total **1 hr 15 min**; Serves **6**

These chicken breasts get great flavor from homemade rosemary salt as well as garlic and strips of preserved Meyer lemon tucked under the skin.

- 6 **skin-on, bone-in chicken breast halves**
- 1 **Roasted Preserved Lemon (recipe follows), pulp discarded and peel cut into thin strips**
- 3 **garlic cloves, thinly sliced**
- 2 **Tbsp. kosher salt**
- 1 **Tbsp. lightly packed rosemary leaves**
- 1 **Tbsp. coarsely ground black pepper**
- 1 **tsp. garlic powder**
  Extra-virgin olive oil, for brushing

1. Carefully loosen the skin of the chicken breast halves and stuff the preserved lemon and garlic slices underneath.

2. In a mini food processor, combine the salt with the rosemary, black pepper and garlic powder and pulse until the rosemary is very finely chopped. Brush the chicken all over with olive oil and season with some of the rosemary salt.

3. Set up a grill for direct and indirect cooking, then light the grill and oil the grate. Set the chicken breasts skin side down and grill over moderately high heat, turning occasionally, until lightly charred all over, 10 to 12 minutes. Move the chicken to indirect heat, skin side up. Cover and cook at 425° until an instant-read thermometer inserted in the thickest part of each breast registers 160°, 25 to 30 minutes. Transfer to a platter and let rest for 5 minutes before serving with the remaining rosemary salt. —*Ben Ford*

WINE Minerally Chardonnay: 2014 Failla Sonoma Coast.

ROASTED PRESERVED LEMONS

Active **15 min**; Total **3 hr 15 min plus cooling**; Makes **2 cups**

Ford's take on preserved lemons calls for slow-roasting with salt, which concentrates their flavor.

- 3 **Meyer lemons, cut lengthwise into 6 wedges each**
- 2 **Tbsp. kosher salt**
- ½ **cup fresh lemon juice**

Preheat the oven to 200°. In an 8-inch-square glass or ceramic baking dish, toss the lemon wedges with the salt. Add the lemon juice and cover tightly with foil. Bake for about 3 hours, stirring occasionally, until the peels are tender. Let cool before using. —*BF*

MAKE AHEAD The preserved lemons can be refrigerated in an airtight container for up to 3 weeks.

Roast Chicken Breasts with Butternut Squash Puree and Seared Cabbage

Active **35 min**; Total **1 hr 30 min**; Serves **4**

- **1** small butternut squash (1¾ lbs.)—peeled, seeded and cut into 1-inch cubes (4 cups)
- **1** Tbsp. minced preserved lemon rind (see Note)

  Kosher salt and pepper

  Four 12-oz. skin-on, boneless chicken breast halves with the first wing joint attached (airline cut)
- **¼** cup extra-virgin olive oil
- **5** Tbsp. unsalted butter
- **1** small head of Savoy cabbage (1½ lbs.), cut into 4 wedges

1. Preheat the oven to 450°. In a medium saucepan of boiling water, cook the squash until tender, 20 to 25 minutes. Drain well. In a food processor, puree the squash with the preserved lemon rind until smooth. Season with salt and keep warm.

2. On a rimmed baking sheet, rub the chicken with 2 tablespoons of the olive oil; season with salt and pepper. In a large cast-iron skillet, melt 4 tablespoons of the butter in the remaining 2 tablespoons of oil. Add the cabbage cut side down and cook over moderately high heat until golden, about 3 minutes. Turn the cabbage onto the other cut side. Add the chicken skin side up, transfer to the oven and roast with the cabbage for about 30 minutes, until the cabbage is caramelized and tender and the chicken is golden and cooked through. Add the remaining 1 tablespoon of butter to the cabbage and toss to coat. Let the chicken rest for 10 minutes. Serve the chicken with the cabbage and squash puree. —*HH & Co., Hampshire, England*

SERVE WITH Barley with Walnuts and Bacon (p. 249).

NOTE Jarred preserved lemon can be found at specialty food shops and stores like Whole Foods.

MAKE AHEAD The squash puree can be refrigerated overnight. Reheat gently.

WINE Citrusy Napa Valley Sauvignon Blanc: 2014 Honig.

Ode to Hot-Star Fried Chicken

Active **45 min**; Total **1 hr 15 min**; Serves **8**

These highly seasoned fried chicken cutlets—coated in a mix of flour, spices and crushed bouillon cubes, then fried until supercrispy—are based on a popular snack at the Shilin Night Market in Taipei, Taiwan.

- **1** cup sliced scallions (from about 8 scallions)
- **½** cup chopped garlic (from about 1 head)
- **2** Tbsp. chopped peeled fresh ginger
- **½** cup soy sauce
- **½** cup mirin
- **¼** cup sugar
- **2** tsp. baking soda
- **2** tsp. Chinese five-spice powder

  Eight 6-oz. chicken cutlets, ¼ inch thick

  Canola oil, for frying
- **1½** cups all-purpose flour

  Four ½-oz. chicken bouillon cubes
- **1** tsp. paprika
- **½** tsp. guajillo or ancho chile powder

1. In a food processor, combine the scallions, garlic, ginger, soy sauce, mirin, sugar, baking soda, five-spice powder and 1½ cups of water and puree until smooth. Scrape the marinade into a large bowl, add the chicken and turn to coat. Cover and let marinate at room temperature for 30 minutes to 2 hours.

2. In a large enameled cast-iron casserole, heat 2 inches of oil to 300°. In a food processor, blend the flour, bouillon cubes, paprika and chile powder to a powder. Transfer to a shallow bowl.

3. Dredge 2 of the chicken cutlets in the seasoned flour. Fry, turning, until golden brown and cooked through, 4 to 5 minutes. Transfer to a rack to drain briefly and keep warm. Coat and fry the remaining chicken; serve hot. —*Bonjwing Lee*

WINE Off-dry Champagne: NV Laurent-Perrier Demi-Sec.

Devil's Chicken Breasts

Active **1 hr**; Total **4 hr 40 min**; Serves **6**

The "devil" in this spicy herbed chicken is two tablespoons of black pepper and one of crushed red pepper. To press the chicken into the grill, you'll need three standard-size bricks wrapped in foil or small cast-iron skillets.

- **8** garlic cloves, finely chopped
- **3** Tbsp. chopped thyme
- **3** Tbsp. finely chopped rosemary
- **2** Tbsp. finely chopped parsley
- **2** Tbsp. finely chopped basil
- **2** Tbsp. finely chopped oregano
- **1** tsp. finely grated lemon zest plus 3 Tbsp. fresh lemon juice
- **2** Tbsp. coarsely ground black pepper
- **1** Tbsp. kosher salt
- **½** cup extra-virgin olive oil
- **2** Tbsp. Dijon mustard
- **1** Tbsp. crushed red pepper

  Three 1½-lb. skin-on, boneless whole chicken breasts (you can have your butcher do this)

1. In a food processor, combine the garlic, thyme, rosemary, parsley, basil, oregano, lemon zest and juice, black pepper and salt; pulse until a paste forms. With the machine on, add the oil, then add the mustard and crushed red pepper and pulse to mix. Scrape the marinade into a large bowl. Add the chicken, cover and refrigerate for 3 hours.

2. Set up a grill for indirect cooking and heat to 425°. Cover 3 bricks with foil. Remove the chicken from the marinade, scraping off the excess. Oil the grill grate. Set the chicken breasts skin side down on the grill and press them down with the bricks. Cover and cook at 425° until browned on the bottom, 20 to 25 minutes. Remove the bricks and turn the chicken. Cover with the bricks, press down and cover the grill. Cook until an instant-read thermometer inserted in the thickest part of the breasts registers 160°, about 15 minutes longer. Transfer the chicken to a board to rest for 5 minutes. Serve. —*Ben Ford*

WINE Lightly spicy red: 2011 Sella & Mosca Cannonau di Sardegna Riserva.

Five-Alarm Drumsticks

Active **1 hr 15 min**; Total **3 hr 45 min**
Serves **6**

"I don't mind buffalo chicken wings, but I think the spicy sauce can transfer to drumsticks," says L.A. chef Ben Ford. "My five-alarm version is hot but balanced enough to show off the flavor of a good piece of chicken."

- **2 lbs. plum tomatoes, cored and quartered lengthwise**
- **5 garlic cloves, minced**
- **1 Tbsp. chopped thyme**
- **1 Tbsp. chopped oregano**
- **2 bay leaves**
  Kosher salt and pepper
- **2 Tbsp. extra-virgin olive oil, plus more for brushing**
- **2 roasted red bell peppers, seeded and chopped**
- **2 chipotle chiles in adobo, plus ¼ cup adobo sauce**
- **¼ cup plus 2 Tbsp. Sriracha**
- **12 chicken drumsticks (3 lbs.)**
- **4 Tbsp. unsalted butter**
  Blue cheese dressing, for serving

1. Preheat the oven to 300°. On a large rimmed baking sheet, toss the tomatoes, garlic, thyme, oregano, bay leaves, 1 teaspoon of salt, ½ teaspoon of pepper and the 2 tablespoons of oil. Bake for 2 hours and 30 minutes, until the tomatoes are soft and slightly dried. Discard the bay leaves.

2. Scrape the tomatoes and any juices into a food processor. Add the red peppers, chipotles, adobo sauce and Sriracha and puree until nearly smooth. Scrape into a large pot.

3. Set up a grill for direct and indirect cooking, then light the grill and oil the grate. Brush the chicken with oil and season with salt and pepper. Grill over moderately high heat, turning occasionally, until lightly charred, 8 to 10 minutes; move to indirect heat. Cover and cook at 425° until an instant-read thermometer inserted in the thickest part of each drumstick registers 165°, about 15 minutes. Transfer to a baking sheet.

4. Add the butter to the hot sauce and bring to a boil over moderately high heat, stirring. Remove from the heat. Add half of the drumsticks to the hot sauce and turn to coat. Transfer to a platter. Repeat with the remaining drumsticks. Serve with blue cheese dressing, passing the remaining hot sauce at the table. —*Ben Ford*

BEER Rich brown ale: Samuel Smith's Nut Brown Ale.

Grilled Chicken Thighs with Pickled Peaches

Active **1 hr**; Total **2 hr 30 min plus overnight brining and pickling**; Serves **4 to 6**

Sean Brock of Husk in Charleston, South Carolina, pickles fresh peaches in a ginger-lemongrass brine, then chars them on the grill to serve alongside his crispy, herb-marinated chicken thighs.

PICKLED PEACHES

- **6 firm-ripe medium peaches**
- **1½ cups distilled white vinegar**
- **1 cup sugar**
- **1 stalk of lemongrass, tender inner bulb only, thinly sliced**
  One 1-inch piece of fresh ginger, peeled and thinly sliced
- **½ tsp. whole black peppercorns**
- **5 allspice berries**
- **2 whole cloves**
  One 3-inch cinnamon stick

CHICKEN

- **1 Tbsp. sorghum syrup or molasses**
  Kosher salt and pepper
- **8 skin-on, bone-in chicken thighs (about 2 lbs.)**
- **½ cup plus 1 Tbsp. extra-virgin olive oil, plus more for brushing**
- **1 Tbsp. red wine vinegar**
- **2 garlic cloves, finely chopped**
- **¼ cup each chopped parsley, basil and tarragon**
- **4 cups arugula, thick stems discarded**

1. Pickle the peaches Bring a large saucepan of water to a boil. Fill a large bowl with ice water. Using a sharp paring knife, mark an X on the bottom of each peach. Add the peaches to the saucepan and blanch until the skins start to peel away, 1 to 2 minutes. Transfer the peaches to the ice bath and let cool completely. Peel, halve and pit the peaches and transfer to a large heatproof bowl. Wipe out the saucepan.

2. In the large saucepan, combine all of the remaining ingredients with 1½ cups of water and bring to a boil, stirring to dissolve the sugar. Let the brine cool slightly, then pour over the peaches and let cool completely. Cover and refrigerate overnight.

3. Meanwhile, prepare the chicken In a large bowl, whisk 8 cups of water with the sorghum syrup and 2 tablespoons of salt. Add the chicken, cover and refrigerate overnight.

4. Drain the chicken and wipe out the bowl. Return the chicken to the bowl and toss with ½ cup of the olive oil, the vinegar, garlic, chopped herbs and 1 teaspoon of pepper. Let stand at room temperature for 1 hour.

5. Light a grill and oil the grate. Remove the peaches from the brine and reserve the pickling liquid. Grill the peaches over moderate heat, turning once, until lightly charred, 4 to 5 minutes. Transfer to a work surface. Grill the chicken thighs over moderate heat, turning, until lightly charred and cooked through, 20 to 25 minutes. Transfer to the work surface and let rest for 5 minutes.

6. In a bowl, toss the arugula with 1 tablespoon of the peach pickling liquid and the remaining 1 tablespoon of olive oil; season with salt and pepper. Arrange the salad, chicken and grilled peaches on a platter and serve. —*Sean Brock*

WINE Fruit-rich California Chardonnay: 2014 Amici Cellars Olema Sonoma County.

GRILLED CHICKEN THIGHS
WITH PICKLED PEACHES

BRAISED CHICKEN THIGHS
WITH MARINATED ARTICHOKES

Braised Chicken Thighs with Marinated Artichokes

Active **30 min**; Total **1 hr 45 min**
Serves **4 to 6**

For maximum flavor, chef Naomi Pomeroy of Beast in Portland, Oregon, doesn't just roast chicken thighs: Instead, she crisps the skin by weighing down the meat with a pot lid, then braises the pieces in a sherry-spiked, umami-rich broth.

- 8 skin-on, bone-in chicken thighs (3¾ lbs.)
  Sea salt and pepper
- 1 Tbsp. extra-virgin olive oil
- 15 oz. marinated artichoke hearts, plus ¼ cup brine from the jar
- 1 cup Castelvetrano olives
- 1 head of garlic, halved crosswise
- 1 lemon, thinly sliced
- 6 thyme sprigs
- 1 cup chicken stock or low-sodium broth
- ½ cup semidry sherry, such as amontillado
- 1 Tbsp. Asian fish sauce

1. Preheat the oven to 375°. Season the chicken all over with salt and pepper. In a large cast-iron skillet or black steel pan, heat the oil. Add half of the chicken skin side down and top the pieces (not the pan) with a pot lid; cook over moderate heat until browned and crisp, 5 to 7 minutes. Transfer skin side up to a large baking dish. Repeat with the remaining chicken. Scatter the artichoke hearts, olives, garlic, lemon slices and thyme in the baking dish.

2. Pour off the fat from the skillet. Add the artichoke brine, stock, sherry and fish sauce; bring to a boil. Stir in 1 teaspoon of salt, then pour the mixture around the chicken. Cover tightly with foil and braise in the oven for 1 hour, until the chicken is very tender.

3. Uncover and increase the oven temperature to 400°. Roast the chicken for 15 minutes longer, until the skin is crisp. Discard the thyme. Transfer to plates and serve.
—*Naomi Pomeroy*

WINE California Dolcetto: 2013 Palmina Santa Barbara County.

Chicken Paprikash

Total **45 min**; Serves **4**

Molly Yeh, the blogger behind My Name is Yeh, loves the aroma that fills her kitchen as she makes this easy weeknight dish. She serves the chicken with crunchy pieces of sourdough toast, but feel free to substitute egg noodles or dumplings.

- 4 Tbsp. unsalted butter
- 2 large onions, thinly sliced
  Kosher salt and pepper
- 4 garlic cloves, minced
- 2 Tbsp. Hungarian sweet paprika
- ¼ tsp. cayenne
- 2 Tbsp. all-purpose flour
- 1½ cups low-sodium chicken broth
  Pinch of sugar
- 1 lb. skinless, boneless chicken thighs, trimmed and cut into ¾-inch pieces
- ¼ cup heavy cream
  Four 1-inch-thick slices of sourdough toast, torn into bite-size pieces

1. In a large saucepan, melt 3 tablespoons of the butter. Add the onions, season with salt and pepper and cook over moderate heat, stirring occasionally, until golden and tender, about 10 minutes. Add the garlic, paprika and cayenne and cook, stirring, until dark red in color, 2 minutes. Add the flour and the remaining 1 tablespoon of butter and cook, stirring, for 2 minutes. Stir in the broth and sugar and cook until the sauce is thickened, about 2 minutes. Add the chicken to the sauce and bring to a simmer. Cook over moderately low heat until the chicken is tender, about 15 minutes. Stir in the heavy cream and season with salt and pepper.

2. Divide the bread between bowls, spoon the chicken paprikash on top and serve.
—*Molly Yeh*

MAKE AHEAD The chicken paprikash can be refrigerated overnight.

WINE A dark, rich red: 2013 Joel Gott Zinfandel.

Butter Chicken

Total **1 hr plus overnight marinating**
Serves **4**

"This beloved Indian classic has plenty of onions, tomatoes and vibrant spices in a rich, creamy sauce," says *Bizarre Foods* host Andrew Zimmern. "It's possibly one of the tastiest chicken dishes ever."

- ¾ cup Greek yogurt
- ¼ cup plus 2 Tbsp. vindaloo spice (see Note)
- 3 Tbsp. fresh lemon juice
- 8 bone-in chicken thighs, skin removed
- 1 stick salted butter
- 2 large yellow onions, finely chopped
  Kosher salt and pepper
  One 15-oz. can crushed tomatoes
- ⅔ cup chicken stock or low-sodium broth
- 1 cup heavy cream
  Basmati rice, cilantro sprigs and chopped salted roasted cashews, for serving

1. In a large bowl, mix the yogurt with the vindaloo spice and lemon juice. Add the chicken and turn to coat. Cover with plastic wrap and refrigerate overnight.

2. In a large enameled cast-iron casserole, melt the butter over moderate heat. Add the onions, season with salt and pepper and cook, stirring occasionally, until golden brown, 12 to 15 minutes.

3. Add the chicken and its marinade along with the crushed tomatoes and stock to the casserole and bring to a simmer. Cook, stirring occasionally, until the sauce has thickened slightly, 20 minutes. Stir in the cream and simmer until the sauce is flavorful and the chicken is cooked through, 10 to 12 minutes longer. Season with salt and pepper and serve with basmati rice, cilantro sprigs and chopped cashews.
—*Andrew Zimmern*

NOTE Vindaloo spice is a blend of over 10 spices, including cumin, coriander, turmeric and Indian chiles. You can find it at penzeys.com and kalustyans.com.

MAKE AHEAD The butter chicken can be refrigerated for up to 2 days.

WINE Light, floral-inflected California red: 2014 J. Lohr Estates Wildflower Valdiguié.

Chicken Thighs with Charred Carrots, Yogurt and Nutty Dukka

⊘ Total **40 min**; Serves **4**

- 2 lbs. small multicolored carrots
- ¼ cup extra-virgin olive oil
  Kosher salt and pepper
- 8 skin-on, bone-in chicken thighs
- 1 cup full-fat Greek yogurt
- 1 Tbsp. honey
- 1 tsp. ground turmeric
  Cashew-Almond Dukka (recipe follows)
  Lemon wedges, for serving

1. Preheat the oven to 450° and position racks in the upper and lower thirds. On a rimmed baking sheet, toss the carrots with 2 tablespoons of the olive oil and season with salt and pepper.

2. Heat a large ovenproof nonstick skillet. Rub the chicken thighs all over with the remaining 2 tablespoons of olive oil and season with salt and pepper. Cook skin side down over moderately high heat until the skin is crisp and golden brown, about 5 minutes. Turn the chicken thighs and set the skillet on the upper rack of the oven. Set the carrots on the lower rack. Roast until the chicken is cooked through and the carrots are tender, about 15 minutes.

3. In a medium bowl, whisk the yogurt with the honey and turmeric and season with salt and pepper. Spoon some of the yogurt onto plates and top with the chicken thighs and carrots. Sprinkle with dukka and serve with the remaining yogurt and lemon wedges. —*Christopher Bates*

WINE Fruity Pinot Noir: 2013 Heart & Hands Finger Lakes.

CASHEW-ALMOND DUKKA

⊙ Total **10 min**; Makes **¾ cup**

- 1 Tbsp. sesame seeds
- 1½ tsp. coriander seeds
- ¾ tsp. cumin seeds
- ¼ cup unsalted roasted cashews
- ¼ cup unsalted roasted almonds
- ½ tsp. finely grated lemon zest
- ½ tsp. kosher salt

In a small skillet, toast the sesame, coriander and cumin seeds over moderately low heat until fragrant, about 3 minutes.

Transfer to a mini food processor and let cool slightly. Add the nuts, lemon zest and salt and pulse until finely chopped. —*CB*

Extra-Crispy Marinated Chicken Thighs

Total **30 min plus 1 hr marinating** Serves **6 to 8**

For perfectly crackly skin, make sure that the marinade doesn't cover the chicken completely; the skin exposed to the air dries out a little, which allows it to crisp up.

- 10 skin-on, boneless chicken thighs (3 lbs.)
  Kosher salt and pepper
  Citrus-Lemongrass Marinade or Soy-Ginger Marinade (recipes follow)
  Canola oil, for brushing

1. Season the chicken with salt and pepper. Pour the marinade into a 9-by-13-inch baking dish and add the chicken skin side up; the skin should not be submerged. Cover with plastic wrap and refrigerate for 1 hour.

2. Light a grill and oil the grate. Remove the chicken thighs from the marinade and pat dry; season the skin with salt. Grill the chicken skin side down over moderately low heat until the skin is golden brown and very crisp, 18 to 20 minutes. Turn the chicken over and grill until cooked through and a thermometer inserted in the thickest part registers 160°, about 3 minutes longer. Transfer the chicken to a work surface and let stand for 5 minutes before serving. —*Josiah Citrin*

WINE Fresh and fragrant rosé: 2015 Mas de Gourgonnier Les Baux de Provence.

CITRUS-LEMONGRASS MARINADE

⊙ Total **10 min**; Makes **about 2 cups**

- 1 cup fresh orange juice
- ¾ cup fresh lime juice
- 2 garlic cloves
- 1 stalk of fresh lemongrass, tender inner white bulb only, minced
- ½ cup chopped cilantro leaves
- ½ cup chopped mint leaves
- ¼ cup oregano leaves, tightly packed
  Kosher salt

In a blender, puree all of the ingredients until smooth, about 2 minutes. Season with salt. —*JC*

SOY-GINGER MARINADE

⊙ Total **10 min**; Makes **1¼ cups**

- ½ cup soy sauce
- ½ cup honey
- 3 Tbsp. Dijon mustard
- 2 Tbsp. toasted sesame oil
- 3 garlic cloves, finely grated
- 2 tsp. finely grated lemon zest
  One 2-inch piece of fresh ginger, peeled and finely grated
  Kosher salt and pepper

In a medium bowl, whisk all of the ingredients until smooth. Season with salt and pepper. —*JC*

Coriander-and-Almond-Crusted Chicken Legs

Active **25 min**; Total **1 hr**; Serves **4**

- ½ cup whole blanched almonds
- 2½ Tbsp. coriander seeds
- 2 tsp. white peppercorns
- 2 tsp. yellow mustard seeds
- 2¼ tsp. sea salt
- 1¼ tsp. finely grated lemon zest
- 4 whole chicken legs (2½ lbs.)
- ¼ cup extra-virgin olive oil, plus more for brushing
  Lemon wedges, for serving

1. Preheat the oven to 400°. In a spice grinder, pulse the almonds until finely ground. Transfer to a large bowl. In the spice grinder, grind the coriander, peppercorns and mustard seeds until coarsely ground. Add to the large bowl along with the salt and lemon zest and mix well. Brush the chicken with olive oil, then dredge in the almond mixture, pressing to help it adhere.

2. In a large cast-iron skillet, heat the ¼ cup of olive oil over moderate heat. When the oil is hot, add the chicken, skin side down, and cook until lightly browned, 8 to 10 minutes. Flip and cook until very lightly browned on the bottom, about 5 minutes. Transfer the skillet to the oven and roast the chicken until an instant-read thermometer inserted in the thickest part of each thigh registers 165°, 15 to 20 minutes. Serve with lemon wedges. —*Seamus Mullen*

WINE Vibrant Côtes du Rhône red: 2013 Éric Texier Chat Fou.

CORIANDER-AND-ALMOND-
CRUSTED CHICKEN LEG;
CHINESE-STYLE BRAISED
MUSHROOMS AND MUSTARD
GREENS (P. 228)

POULET BASQUAISE WITH
CURRANT COUSCOUS

Poulet Basquaise with Currant Couscous

Active **1 hr 15 min**; Total **2 hr 30 min**
Serves **4**

This hearty, slow-braised chicken with peppers and tomatoes is a standout among the French country dishes served at Les Clos wine bar in San Francisco. The sauce is enhanced with pimentón, the smoky Spanish paprika, and a splash of sherry vinegar.

CHICKEN

- 2 **Tbsp. canola oil**
- 6 **whole chicken legs, separated into thighs and drumsticks**
  Kosher salt and pepper
- 1 **small red onion, minced**
- 1 **poblano chile, chopped**
- 1 **red bell pepper, chopped**
- 1 **lb. tomatoes, chopped**
- 1 **tsp. pimentón de la Vera**
- ½ **cup dry white wine**
- 2 **Tbsp. sherry vinegar**
- 3 **thyme sprigs**
- 2 **bay leaves**

COUSCOUS

- 1 **cup dry white wine**
- 6 **Tbsp. extra-virgin olive oil**
  Small pinch of saffron threads
- 2½ **cups couscous (about 14 oz.)**
- ½ **cup dried currants**
- ¼ **cup minced red onion**
- 1 **tsp. kosher salt**

1. Make the chicken Preheat the oven to 350°. In a large enameled cast-iron casserole, heat the canola oil. Season the chicken with salt and pepper. Add half of the pieces to the casserole and cook over moderately high heat until browned all over, about 8 minutes. Transfer to a plate. Brown the remaining chicken.

2. Pour off all but 2 tablespoons of the oil from the casserole. Add the onion, poblano and bell pepper. Cook over moderate heat, stirring, until softened, 8 to 10 minutes. Stir in the tomatoes and cook until broken down, about 8 minutes. Add the pimentón and cook for 1 minute. Add the wine, vinegar, thyme and bay leaves and simmer until the liquid is reduced by half, 2 minutes.

Nestle the chicken in the sauce, cover and braise in the oven until cooked through, about 1¼ hours; discard the thyme and bay leaves.

3. Make the couscous In a saucepan, combine the wine, olive oil, saffron and 1 cup of water and bring to a boil. In a large heatproof bowl, combine the couscous, currants, onion and salt. Pour the hot wine mixture over, cover and let stand until the couscous is tender and the liquid is absorbed, 30 minutes. Fluff the couscous and serve with the chicken. —*Shawn Gawle*

WINE Savory, elegant red Burgundy: 2012 Domaine Hudelot-Noëllat Bourgogne Rouge.

Braised Chicken with Fava Beans

Active **45 min**; Total **3 hr**; Serves **6**

The warm, toasty notes of baharat (a cumin-scented spice blend) contrast with the fresh pops of fava beans, herbs and lemon in this surprisingly light braised chicken dish.

- 2½ **tsp. baharat (see Note)**
  Kosher salt and pepper
- 6 **whole chicken legs (3½ lbs.)**
- 1 **Tbsp. canola oil**
- 1 **small onion, halved through the root**
- 1 **lemon, halved**
- 1 **bay leaf**
- ⅓ **cup dry sherry**
- 3¾ **cups chicken stock or low-sodium broth**
- 3 **lbs. fava beans, shelled**
- ½ **cup chopped parsley, plus more for garnish**

1. In a small bowl, mix 1½ teaspoons of the baharat with 1 tablespoon of salt. Rub the mixture all over the chicken legs and let stand at room temperature for 1 hour.

2. Preheat the oven to 250°. In a large enameled cast-iron casserole, heat the oil. Add 3 of the chicken legs and cook over moderately high heat, turning once, until browned, about 10 minutes; transfer to a plate. Repeat with the remaining chicken, then pour off the fat.

3. Add the onion and 1 lemon half to the casserole cut side down and cook over moderately high heat until browned, 1 to 2 minutes. Add the bay leaf and sherry and scrape up any browned bits with a wooden spoon. Return the chicken and its juices to the casserole. Add the stock, the remaining 1 teaspoon of baharat and ¾ teaspoon of salt; bring to a simmer. Cover and braise in the oven until the chicken is very tender, about 1 hour and 45 minutes.

4. Transfer the chicken legs to a plate and let cool slightly; discard the onion, lemon half and bay leaf. Skim the fat off the braising liquid, then simmer over moderately high heat until reduced by one-fourth, 8 to 10 minutes; season with salt and pepper. Discard the chicken skin and bones and pull the meat into large chunks; return the meat to the braising liquid and keep warm.

5. Meanwhile, fill a large bowl with ice water. In a large saucepan of salted boiling water, blanch the fava beans for 1 minute. Drain and transfer to the ice bath to cool. Drain the fava beans and peel off the skins.

6. Fold the fava beans and the ½ cup of parsley into the braised chicken and reheat if necessary. Garnish the chicken with more parsley. Cut the remaining lemon half into wedges and serve with the chicken. —*Sara Hymanson and Sarah Kramer*

SERVE WITH Crispy Rice with Dried Mint and Lemon (p. 246).

NOTE *Baharat* (pronounced BAH-ha-ROT) is the Arabic word for "spices." This all-purpose blend commonly includes black pepper, cumin and cinnamon. It's available at Middle Eastern markets and online from amazon.com.

MAKE AHEAD The recipe can be prepared through Step 4 and refrigerated for up to 4 days. Reheat gently before finishing.

WINE Full-bodied South African white blend: 2014 Thorne & Daughters Rocking Horse.

Green Chile–Chicken Enchiladas

Active **1 hr 15 min;** Total **3 hr**
Serves **10 to 12**

Modern Family star Jesse Tyler Ferguson hails from New Mexico, which explains his penchant for these cheesy and spicy chicken enchiladas. They're often made with canned cream of chicken soup, but they're even better with his quick and easy homemade sauce.

- **4** skin-on, bone-in chicken breast halves (4½ lbs.)
- **1** qt. chicken stock or low-sodium broth
  Kosher salt and pepper
- **6** Tbsp. unsalted butter, plus more for greasing
- **⅓** cup all-purpose flour
- **1½** cups whole milk
- **18** corn tortillas
- **12** oz. sharp white cheddar cheese, shredded (3 cups)
- **12** oz. jarred or canned chopped roasted Hatch chiles
- **½** cup minced white onion
  Cilantro leaves and thinly sliced jalapeño, for garnish

1. In a large saucepan, cover the chicken breast halves with the stock and 1 quart of water and bring to a boil. Simmer over moderately low heat, turning the chicken occasionally, until an instant-read thermometer inserted in the thickest part of each piece registers 160°, 30 to 35 minutes. Using tongs, transfer the chicken to a plate to cool. Discard the skin and bones. Shred the meat and season generously with salt and pepper. Transfer 2 cups of the chicken cooking broth to a large heatproof measuring cup and reserve the remaining broth for another use.

2. Wipe out the saucepan and melt the 6 tablespoons of butter in it. Whisk in the flour and cook over moderate heat, whisking constantly, until bubbling and just starting to change color, about 2 minutes. Gradually whisk in the milk and the 2 cups of cooking broth and bring to a boil. Simmer over moderately low heat, whisking frequently, until the sauce is thickened and no floury taste remains, about 10 minutes. Remove the sauce from the heat and season generously with salt and pepper. Let cool slightly.

3. Preheat the oven to 375°. Grease a 9-by-13-inch baking dish. Line the dish with 6 slightly overlapping tortillas. Spread one-third of the sauce over the tortillas, then top with 1 cup of the cheese and half each of the chicken, chiles and onion. Repeat the layering with 6 more tortillas, one-third of the sauce, 1 cup of the cheese and the remaining chicken, chiles and onion. Lay the remaining 6 tortillas on top and spread the remaining sauce over them.

4. Bake the enchiladas for about 45 minutes, until the filling is bubbling. Sprinkle the remaining 1 cup of cheese on top and bake for 15 minutes more. Turn on the broiler and broil for 1 to 2 minutes, until lightly browned in spots. Let the enchiladas stand for 20 minutes. Garnish with cilantro leaves and jalapeño slices and serve. —*Jesse Tyler Ferguson*

MAKE AHEAD The assembled, unbaked enchiladas can be refrigerated overnight. Bring to room temperature before baking.

WINE Full-bodied, ripe California Chardonnay: 2014 Spellbound.

Lentil and Chicken Cassoulet

Active **15 min;** Total **1 hr;** Serves **4**

- **2** Tbsp. extra-virgin olive oil
- **6** whole chicken legs (3 lbs.)
- **8** garlic cloves, crushed
- **1** lb. sausages, such as Italian or merguez
- **3** cups low-sodium chicken broth
- **1** tarragon sprig, plus chopped tarragon for garnish
- **2** cups beluga lentils
  Kosher salt and pepper

In a large enameled cast-iron casserole, heat the oil. Add the chicken and garlic and cook over moderate heat, turning, until browned, about 8 minutes. Add the sausages, broth and tarragon sprig and bring to a boil. Simmer for 15 minutes. Stir in the lentils, cover and cook over moderate heat until tender, about 30 minutes. Remove the tarragon sprig. Season the cassoulet with salt and pepper, garnish with chopped tarragon and serve. —*Kay Chun*

WINE Substantial Rhône Valley red: 2014 Domaine Charvin Côtes du Rhône Le Poutet.

Chicken Tinga Tacos

Active **40 min;** Total **1 hr 30 min;** Serves **6**

Justin Chapple, F&W's Mad Genius, has a brilliant hack for making hard taco shells without deep-frying: He folds tortillas in half and stuffs them between the cups of an inverted muffin tin, then bakes them until they're crisp.

- **2** Tbsp. extra-virgin olive oil
- **1** white onion, thinly sliced
- **4** garlic cloves, sliced
- **1½** tsp. cumin seeds
- **1½** tsp. ground coriander
- **2** cups chicken stock
- **14** oz. tomato puree
- **1** oregano sprig
- **2** bay leaves
- **4½** lbs. skinless whole chicken legs
  Twelve 5-inch flour tortillas
- **3** Tbsp. distilled white vinegar
  Kosher salt and pepper
  Cilantro, lime wedges and sliced onion, for serving

1. In a large enameled cast-iron casserole, heat the oil. Add the onion, garlic, cumin and coriander. Cook over moderately high heat until the onion is softened. Add the chicken stock, tomato puree, oregano and bay leaves; bring to a boil. Add the chicken, cover partially and simmer until cooked through, 35 to 40 minutes.

2. Meanwhile, preheat the oven to 400°. In batches, fold the tortillas in half and stuff them between the cups of an inverted muffin tin to form shells. Bake for 15 minutes, until crisp.

3. Remove the chicken from the sauce and shred the meat. Return the meat to the sauce and simmer for 10 minutes. Discard the bay leaves and oregano sprig. Stir in the vinegar and season with salt and pepper. Serve in the taco shells with cilantro, lime and onion. —*Justin Chapple*

WINE Earthy, focused red Burgundy: 2014 Maison Roche de Bellene Vieilles Vignes Bourgogne Pinot Noir.

CHICKEN TINGA TACOS

TANDOORI CHICKEN WINGS
WITH YOGURT SAUCE

Hill Country Smoked Chicken Wings with Texas Ranch Dressing

Active **1 hr**; Total **3 hr 40 min**; Serves **6**

"My wife is from Texas Hill Country, and I've spent a lot of time there," says Ben Ford, chef at Ford's Filling Station in L.A. "I know I'll never be a real cowboy, but I can have a killer pair of boots and a chicken wing recipe that may be remembered in song." He rubs his wings with a mix of sweet and spicy seasonings before smoking to give them incredible flavor.

WINGS

- ¼ cup unrefined cane sugar, such as turbinado
- ¼ cup packed dark brown sugar
- 2 Tbsp. kosher salt
- 1½ Tbsp. chili powder
- 1½ tsp. chipotle chile powder
- 1 tsp. ground cumin
- 1 tsp. cayenne
- 1 tsp. smoked paprika
- 1 tsp. onion powder
- 1 tsp. garlic powder
- 1 tsp. mustard powder
- 18 whole chicken wings
- 2 cups hardwood chips, such as hickory or applewood, soaked in water for 1 hour and drained

DRESSING

- ⅔ cup mayonnaise
- ⅓ cup buttermilk
- 1 Tbsp. packed torn basil leaves
- 1 Tbsp. packed parsley leaves
- 1 tsp. finely chopped thyme
- 1 tsp. sugar
- ¼ tsp. apple cider vinegar
- 1 pickled jalapeño with seeds, minced
- 2 small garlic cloves, minced
- 2 tsp. minced onion
  Kosher salt and pepper

1. Smoke the wings In a food processor, combine all of the ingredients except the chicken wings and hardwood chips and pulse until well blended. In a large bowl, toss the wings with the spice rub until well coated. Refrigerate for 2 hours or overnight.

2. Set up a grill for indirect cooking, then heat to 425° and oil the grate. Wrap the wood chips in a double layer of heavy-duty foil and poke holes in the top. Place the packet directly on the flames of the grill. When the chips are smoking, add the chicken wings to the grill, cover and smoke the wings, turning occasionally, until an instant-read thermometer inserted in the thickest part of a wing registers 165°, about 40 minutes.

3. Meanwhile, make the dressing In a food processor, combine the first 7 ingredients and puree until nearly smooth. Add the jalapeño, garlic and onion and pulse to mix; it will still be slightly chunky. Scrape into a bowl and season the dressing with salt and pepper.

4. Transfer the chicken wings to a platter and serve with the ranch dressing.
—*Ben Ford*

BEER Smoky lager: Shiner Bock.

Tandoori Chicken Wings with Yogurt Sauce

Active **45 min**; Total **7 hr**; Serves **6**

WINGS

- ½ cup Greek yogurt
- 6 garlic cloves, minced
- 3 Tbsp. garam masala
- 2 Tbsp. minced peeled fresh ginger
- 2 Tbsp. vegetable oil, plus more for brushing
- 1 tsp. finely grated lemon zest plus 2 Tbsp. fresh lemon juice
- 1 Tbsp. hot paprika
- 2½ tsp. kosher salt
- 1 tsp. turmeric
- 18 whole chicken wings
  Cilantro sprigs and thinly sliced white onion, for garnish
  Lemon wedges, for serving

YOGURT SAUCE

- 1 cup Greek yogurt
- ¼ cup cream cheese, softened
- ½ cup finely chopped mint
- 3 Tbsp. fresh lemon juice
- 2 garlic cloves, minced
- 1 tsp. ground cumin
  Kosher salt and pepper

1. Marinate the wings In a large bowl, whisk together all of the ingredients except the wings, cilantro, onion and lemon wedges. Add the chicken wings and toss to coat. Cover and refrigerate for at least 6 hours or overnight.

2. Meanwhile, make the yogurt sauce In a medium bowl, whisk together all of the ingredients and season with salt and pepper.

3. Set up a grill for direct and indirect cooking, then light the grill and oil the grate. Remove the wings from the marinade, scraping off all but a thin layer. Grill over moderately high heat, turning, until the wings are lightly charred all over, about 8 minutes. Move to indirect heat, cover and cook at 425° until an instant-read thermometer inserted in the thickest part of a wing registers 165°, about 15 minutes.

4. Transfer the wings to a platter and garnish with cilantro sprigs and thinly sliced white onion. Serve with the yogurt sauce and lemon wedges. —*Ben Ford*

MAKE AHEAD The yogurt sauce can be refrigerated for up to 3 days.

BEER Crisp pilsner: Victory Prima Pils.

Cold Fried Chicken

Active **1 hr;** Total **2 hr 15 min plus overnight brining;** Serves **4**

"Double-dredging chicken in a spiced mix of wheat and rice flours means you get really crunchy bits that stay crisp in the refrigerator," says chef Justin Yu, who created this addictive fried chicken to be served cold at Public Services in Houston.

CHICKEN

- **2 Tbsp. kosher salt**
- **2 Tbsp. pimentón de la Vera**
- **1 Tbsp. granulated garlic**
- **1 Tbsp. coarsely ground black pepper**
- **One 4-lb. chicken, cut into 8 pieces**
- **1 quart buttermilk**

COATING

- **2 Tbsp. coriander seeds**
- **2 Tbsp. cumin seeds**
- **1 Tbsp. caraway seeds**
- **1 Tbsp. dried oregano**
- **1 Tbsp. black peppercorns**
- **1 tsp. crushed red pepper**
- **2 Tbsp. pimentón de la Vera**
- **1 Tbsp. granulated garlic**
- **1 Tbsp. kosher salt**
- **4 cups all-purpose flour**
- **1 cup rice flour**
- **2 Tbsp. cornstarch**
- **Canola oil, for frying**

1. Make the chicken In a bowl, combine the salt, pimentón, garlic and pepper. Add the chicken and rub all over with the spices. Add the buttermilk and turn to coat. Cover with plastic wrap; refrigerate overnight.

2. Make the coating In a small skillet, toast the coriander, cumin, caraway, oregano, peppercorns and red pepper over low heat, stirring, until very fragrant, 3 minutes. Transfer to a spice grinder, let cool slightly, then finely grind. Transfer to a bowl and whisk in the pimentón, garlic, salt and all-purpose flour. Transfer half of the flour mixture to another bowl and whisk in the rice flour and cornstarch.

3. Drain the chicken, reserving the buttermilk. Coat the chicken in the seasoned all-purpose flour, shaking off any excess. Set on a rack and refrigerate for 1 hour. Let stand at room temperature for 15 minutes.

4. In a large enameled cast-iron casserole, heat 3 inches of oil to 325°. Dip the chicken in the reserved buttermilk, then dredge in the rice flour mixture. Fry in 2 batches, turning, until the dark meat registers 155° on an instant-read thermometer and the breast meat registers 150°, about 15 minutes for the dark meat and 20 minutes for the breast. Transfer to a rack and let cool, then refrigerate until cold. —*Justin Yu*

WINE Slightly off-dry Riesling: 2014 Peter Lauer Barrel X.

Gochujang Chicken Wings with Daikon Pickles

Total **1 hr 15 min plus overnight brining and 5 days pickling;** Serves **4**

PICKLES

- **1 lb. daikon, peeled and cut into 1-inch cubes**
- **1 Tbsp. kosher salt**
- **½ cup unseasoned rice vinegar**
- **¾ cup sugar**

CHICKEN WINGS

- **½ cup kosher salt**
- **¼ cup granulated sugar**
- **3 lbs. chicken wings**
- **¾ cup gochujang (red pepper paste)**
- **¾ cup light brown sugar**
- **¾ cup unseasoned rice wine vinegar**
- **⅓ cup soy sauce**
- **⅓ cup light corn syrup**
- **Canola oil, for frying**
- **1 cup potato starch**
- **Sesame seeds and thinly sliced scallions, for garnish**

1. Make the pickles In a colander set in the sink, toss the daikon with 2 teaspoons of the salt; let stand for 1 hour.

2. In a medium bowl, whisk ¼ cup of water with the vinegar, sugar and the remaining 1 teaspoon of salt. Add the daikon, cover and let stand at room temperature for 24 hours, then refrigerate for 5 days.

3. Prepare the wings In a large bowl, whisk the salt and granulated sugar with 8 cups of water until dissolved. Add the wings, cover and refrigerate overnight.

4. In a medium saucepan, combine the gochujang, brown sugar, vinegar, soy sauce and corn syrup with ¾ cup of water and simmer over moderate heat, whisking often, until reduced to 2 cups, 15 to 20 minutes. Scrape into a large bowl and let cool.

5. In a large enameled cast-iron casserole, heat 3 inches of oil to 350°. Set a rack over a baking sheet. Rinse and dry the wings. In a large bowl, toss the wings with the potato starch until coated. Fry the wings in batches until golden and just cooked through, about 12 minutes per batch. Transfer the wings to the rack and let them cool to room temperature.

6. Increase the oil temperature to 375°. Fry the wings until browned, about 8 minutes. Using a wire skimmer, transfer the wings to the glaze; toss to coat. Transfer to a platter. Sprinkle with sesame seeds and scallions. Serve with the pickles. —*Brandon Kirksey*

WINE Off-dry Riesling: 2014 Charles Smith Kung Fu Girl.

Ginger-and-Honey Chicken Wings

Total **45 min;** Serves **4**

- **One 4 oz. piece of fresh ginger, peeled**
- **¼ cup honey**
- **Kosher salt and pepper**
- **2 Tbsp. canola oil, plus more for brushing**
- **2¼ lbs. chicken wings**
- **2 Tbsp. crushed salted roasted peanuts**
- **2 Tbsp. finely chopped cilantro**
- **Lime wedges, for serving**

1. Finely grate the ginger into a fine sieve set over a bowl. Press the juice from the ginger; you should have ⅓ cup. Discard the solids. Whisk in the honey and a generous pinch each of salt and pepper.

2. Light a grill and oil the grate. In a large bowl, toss the chicken with the 2 tablespoons of oil and season generously with salt and pepper. Grill over moderate heat, turning, until lightly browned on both sides, about 7 minutes. Continue to grill, turning and brushing with the ginger-honey mixture occasionally, until lightly charred and cooked through, about 8 minutes longer. Transfer to another large bowl and toss with the peanuts and cilantro. Serve with lime wedges. —*Justin Chapple*

BEER Crisp and aromatic ale: Montauk Offland IPA.

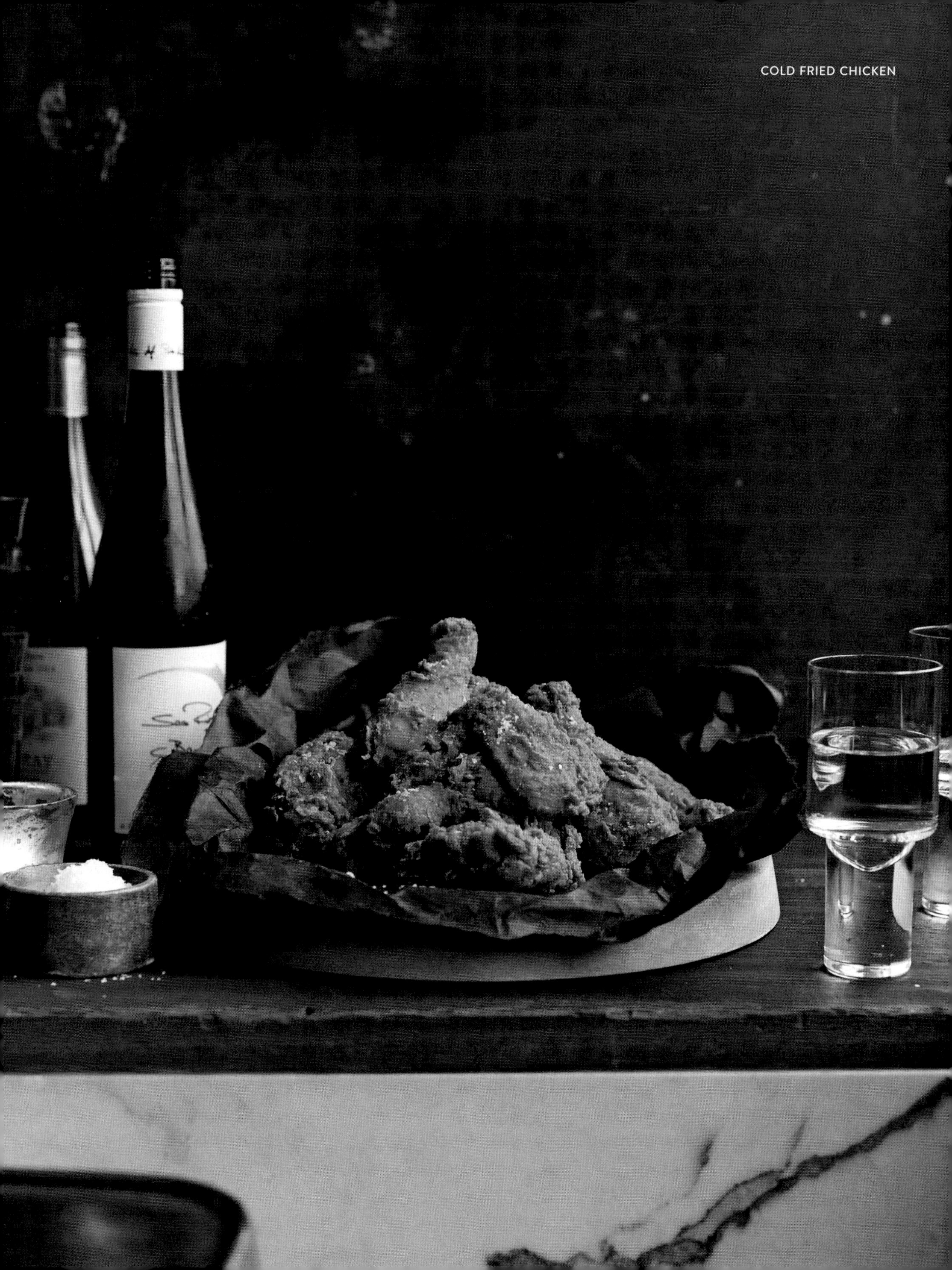

Garlic Fried Chicken

Active **1 hr**; Total **2 hr**; Serves **4**

F&W's Justin Chapple bakes his chicken at low heat before battering and deep-frying it. The benefit: The chicken can be fried quickly at high heat to finish cooking and to develop an uber-crispy crust.

- 2 **Tbsp. canola oil, plus more for frying**
- 2 **garlic cloves, finely grated**
- 1½ **Tbsp. granulated garlic**
- 1½ **Tbsp. dried parsley**
  One 3½- to 4-lb. chicken, cut into 10 pieces and patted dry (2 drumsticks, 2 thighs, 2 wings and 4 breast quarters)
  Kosher salt and pepper
- 1 **cup cornstarch**
- 3 **large eggs**
- 1½ **cups all-purpose flour**
- 1½ **cups panko, finely crushed**
  Lemon wedges, for serving

1. Preheat the oven to 250°. In a small bowl, whisk the 2 tablespoons of canola oil with the grated garlic cloves and ½ tablespoon each of the granulated garlic and dried parsley. Rub the mixture all over the chicken and under the skin. Season the chicken with salt and pepper and set on a large rimmed baking sheet. Bake for about 1 hour, until an instant-read thermometer inserted in the thickest piece registers 150°. Let cool slightly.

2. Spread the cornstarch in a pie plate. In another pie plate, beat the eggs with a pinch of salt. In a large resealable plastic bag, mix the flour with the panko, 1½ teaspoons of salt, ½ teaspoon of pepper and the remaining 1 tablespoon each of granulated garlic and dried parsley.

3. Line a baking sheet with wax paper. Working in batches, dredge the baked chicken in the cornstarch and shake off the excess, then dip in the egg and coat thoroughly with the panko flour. Transfer the chicken to the prepared baking sheet.

4. In a large saucepan, heat 2 inches of canola oil to 375°. Add half of the chicken and fry over moderately high heat, turning once, until deep golden brown and an instant-read thermometer inserted in the thickest part of each piece registers 165°, about 6 minutes for the breasts and 8 minutes for the drumsticks, thighs and wings. Transfer the fried chicken to paper towels to drain. Let the oil return to 375° and fry the remaining chicken. Transfer all of the fried chicken to a platter and serve with lemon wedges. —*Justin Chapple*

SERVE WITH Coleslaw.

WINE Fresh, juicy Gamay: 2015 Michel Guignier Beaujolais.

Buffalo-Style Roast Chicken with Potatoes

Active **30 min**; Total **1 hr 45 min**; Serves **4**

Roasting a chicken on top of a Bundt pan exposes the whole bird to even heat, as with a rotisserie. Plus, the drippings flavor the potatoes at the bottom of the pan.

- 6 **Tbsp. unsalted butter, melted**
- ¼ **cup hot sauce, such as Frank's RedHot**
  Kosher salt and pepper
- 2 **lbs. mixed baby red and Yukon Gold potatoes**
- 6 **large shallots, halved lengthwise**
- 2 **Tbsp. extra-virgin olive oil**
  One 4-lb. chicken

1. Preheat the oven to 450°. In a small bowl, blend the butter, hot sauce and 1 teaspoon each of salt and pepper. Refrigerate until spreadable, about 10 minutes.

2. Wrap the center pillar of a 10-inch Bundt pan with foil. In a medium bowl, toss the potatoes and shallots with the olive oil and season generously with salt and pepper. Add to the pan.

3. Run your fingers under the breast and thigh skin of the chicken to loosen. Spread the chilled butter under the skin, over the breast and thighs. Season with salt and pepper. Perch the chicken on the pan by inserting the center pillar into the cavity.

4. Roast the chicken in the center of the oven for about 1 hour, until browned and an instant-read thermometer inserted in an inner thigh registers 155°. Transfer to a carving board and let rest for 15 minutes. Carve the chicken and serve with the potatoes and shallots. —*Justin Chapple*

SERVE WITH A big green salad.

WINE Bold Spanish white: 2014 Venus La Universal Dido Macabeu i Garnatxa.

Pan-Roasted Chicken with Warm Farro Salad

Active **30 min**; Total **1 hr 15 min**; Serves **4**

- **One 4-lb. chicken, backbone removed and chicken cut in half**
- 5 **Tbsp. extra-virgin olive oil**
  Kosher salt and pepper
- 2 **Tbsp. unsalted butter**
- 3 **sage sprigs**
- ½ **lb. small (not baby) carrots**
- 1 **lb. mixed mushrooms, chopped, any tough stems discarded**
- 1½ **cups farro**
- 1 **Tbsp. fresh lemon juice, plus wedges for serving**
- ½ **cup chopped toasted hazelnuts**
  Chopped parsley, for garnish

1. Preheat the oven to 450°. Set racks in the middle and lower thirds of the oven. Rub the chicken all over with 2 tablespoons of the olive oil and season with salt and pepper. In a large cast-iron skillet, melt the butter. Add the sage sprigs, then add the chicken, skin side down, and cook over moderately high heat until golden, about 5 minutes. Turn the chicken over and roast in the middle of the oven, basting occasionally, until cooked through, about 40 minutes. Transfer the chicken to a cutting board and let rest for 10 minutes. Reserve the pan juices but discard the sage.

2. While the chicken is cooking, on a rimmed baking sheet, toss the carrots and mushrooms with the remaining 3 tablespoons of olive oil; season with salt and pepper. Roast the vegetables on the lower rack of the oven until golden and tender, about 20 minutes. Let cool slightly, then slice the carrots. Transfer the carrots and mushrooms to a large bowl.

3. Meanwhile, in a medium saucepan of salted boiling water, cook the farro until al dente, 15 to 20 minutes. Drain well. Add the farro to the vegetables along with the lemon juice, half of the hazelnuts and ½ cup of the reserved chicken pan juices; mix well. Transfer to plates, top with the remaining hazelnuts and garnish with parsley. Carve the chicken and serve it with the farro and lemon wedges. —*Kay Chun*

WINE Spicy California Pinot Noir: 2013 Rodney Strong Sonoma Coast.

Pan-Roasted Chicken with Green Olives and Garlic

Active **40 min**; Total **1 hr 10 min**; Serves **4**

- 3 Tbsp. extra-virgin olive oil
- 4 oz. thinly sliced pancetta, cut into ½-inch-wide strips
- One 3½- to 4-lb. chicken, cut into 8 pieces
- Kosher salt and pepper
- 12 unpeeled garlic cloves, crushed
- 6 thyme sprigs, plus chopped thyme for garnish
- 3 rosemary sprigs
- 1 cup dry white wine
- ½ cup (3 oz.) pitted green olives, such as Cerignola
- 6 Tbsp. unsalted butter
- Baby arugula and fleur de sel, for serving

1. Preheat the oven to 450°. In a large enameled cast-iron casserole, heat 1 table-spoon of the olive oil. Add the pancetta and cook over moderate heat, stirring occasionally, until golden, about 5 minutes. Using a slotted spoon, transfer the pancetta to a paper towel–lined plate.

2. Rub the chicken with the remaining 2 tablespoons of olive oil and season with salt and pepper. Add half of the chicken to the casserole, skin side down, along with half each of the garlic, thyme sprigs and rosemary. Cook over moderately high heat, turning, until golden brown all over, about 5 minutes. Transfer the chicken to a large plate. Repeat with the remaining chicken, garlic, thyme and rosemary. Return all of the chicken and aromatics to the casserole.

3. Roast the chicken until the breasts are just cooked through, about 15 minutes. Transfer the breasts to a platter. Roast the chicken legs for 10 minutes longer, until cooked through. Add the chicken legs and garlic to the platter; discard the herb sprigs and garlic skins.

4. Pour off all of the fat from the casserole. Add the white wine, olives and pancetta and cook over moderately high heat, scraping up the browned bits on the bottom, until the wine is reduced by half, 2 to 3 minutes. Whisk in the butter and season with salt and pepper. Spoon the sauce over the chicken and top with arugula, chopped thyme and fleur de sel. —*Jane Sigal*

WINE Spice-driven Côtes du Rhône: 2014 Château de Saint Cosme Les Deux Albion.

Chicken and Wild Rice Casserole

Active **1 hr 45 min**; Total **2 hr 30 min**
Serves **8 to 10**

WILD RICE
- ½ lb. wild rice (1½ cups)
- 1 medium carrot, finely chopped
- 1 small onion, finely chopped
- 1 celery rib, finely chopped
- 1 bay leaf
- 1 thyme sprig
- Kosher salt and pepper

SWISS CHARD
- 3 Tbsp. grapeseed or canola oil
- 1 large shallot, minced
- 2 large garlic cloves, minced
- 3 lbs. Swiss chard, stems discarded and leaves coarsely chopped

MUSHROOM SAUCE
- ¼ cup grapeseed or canola oil
- 1½ lbs. cremini mushrooms, sliced
- 2 Tbsp. unsalted butter
- ½ small onion, finely chopped
- 1 small celery rib, finely chopped
- 2 garlic cloves, minced
- 3 thyme sprigs
- 1½ tsp. minced rosemary
- Kosher salt and pepper
- ¼ cup all-purpose flour
- 4 cups chicken stock or low-sodium broth
- ½ cup heavy cream
- 2 lbs. thinly sliced chicken scaloppine, pounded ¼ inch thick
- 1½ cups panko
- 3 Tbsp. unsalted butter, melted
- Chopped parsley, for serving

1. **Make the wild rice** In a large saucepan, combine all of the ingredients with a generous pinch each of salt and pepper. Cover with water and bring to a boil over high heat. Simmer over moderate heat until the rice is tender, about 1 hour. Drain well. Discard the bay leaf and thyme sprig.

2. **Meanwhile, cook the Swiss chard** Set a rack over a large rimmed baking sheet. In a pot, heat the oil. Add the shallot and garlic and cook over moderately high heat, stirring, until softened, 1 to 2 minutes. Add the Swiss chard in large handfuls, letting each batch wilt slightly before adding more. Cook, stirring occasionally, until all of the chard is wilted, 8 to 10 minutes. Spread the chard out on the rack to drain and let cool completely. Squeeze out any excess water.

3. **Make the mushroom sauce** In a large, deep skillet, heat 2 tablespoons of the oil until shimmering. Add half of the mushrooms and cook over moderately high heat, undisturbed, until browned on the bottom, 5 minutes. Cook, stirring, until the mushrooms are tender and browned all over, 5 minutes longer; transfer to a plate. Repeat with the remaining oil and mushrooms.

4. Wipe out the skillet and melt the 2 tablespoons of butter in it. Add the onion, celery, garlic, thyme, rosemary and a generous pinch each of salt and pepper. Cook over moderate heat, stirring occasionally, until the vegetables are just starting to brown, 8 minutes. Stir in the mushrooms. Sprinkle over the flour and cook, stirring, until incorporated, 2 minutes. Gradually whisk in the stock and bring to a boil, stirring frequently. Reduce the heat to moderate and simmer, stirring occasionally, until the sauce is thickened and no floury taste remains, about 7 minutes. Stir in the cream and season with salt and pepper. Discard the thyme sprigs.

5. Preheat the oven to 375°. Arrange half of the chicken in the bottom of a 9-by-13-inch or 4-quart baking dish that's at least 2 inches deep. Scatter half of the Swiss chard over the chicken, followed by half of the wild rice and half of the mushroom cream sauce. Repeat the layering once more with the remaining chicken, greens, rice and sauce.

6. In a medium bowl, toss the panko with the 3 tablespoons of melted butter and sprinkle evenly over the casserole. Cover with foil and bake for about 35 minutes, until bubbling. Uncover the casserole and turn on the broiler. Broil 6 inches from the heat until the panko is lightly browned, about 3 minutes. Let stand for 10 minutes. Garnish with chopped parsley and serve. —*Gavin Kaysen*

WINE Ripe, full-bodied California Chardonnay: 2014 Truchard Vineyards.

ROAST CHICKEN WITH
PICKLED FENNEL AND
CANDIED WALNUTS

Roast Chicken with Pickled Fennel and Candied Walnuts

Active **1 hr 30 min**; Total **3 hr 30 min plus overnight chilling**; Serves **4**

ROAST CHICKEN

- 2 Tbsp. plus 2 tsp. fine sea salt
- One 3-lb. chicken, refrigerated uncovered overnight (see Note)
- Kosher salt
- 4 thyme sprigs
- 4 dill sprigs
- Wide strips of zest from 1 medium orange
- 2 tsp. canola oil

PICKLED FENNEL

- ¾ cup rice vinegar
- 3 Tbsp. sugar
- 2 tsp. kosher salt
- 2 whole cloves
- 1 fennel bulb—halved, cored and thinly sliced lengthwise

ORANGE DRESSING

- 1 cup fresh orange juice
- ¼ cup Chardonnay vinegar
- 2 Tbsp. sugar
- 2 Tbsp. fresh lemon juice
- ⅓ cup canola oil
- 1 Tbsp. walnut oil
- Kosher salt and pepper
- 1 medium navel orange
- 2 small heads of radicchio, torn into bite-size pieces
- ¼ cup minced dill, plus more for garnish
- Candied Walnuts (recipe follows), for serving

1. **Prepare the chicken** In a large bowl, whisk the sea salt into 4½ cups of water until dissolved. Add the chicken and cover with a plate, pressing so the chicken is submerged in the brine. Refrigerate for 1 hour. Transfer the chicken to a rack, pat dry with paper towels and refrigerate for 1 hour more.

2. Preheat the oven to 425°. Season the chicken inside and out with kosher salt. Fill the cavity with the thyme, dill and orange zest. Tie the legs with kitchen twine. In a large cast-iron skillet, heat the oil. Add the chicken, breast side down, and cook over moderately high heat, turning, until

the bird is browned on all sides, about 8 minutes total; spoon off the excess fat. Roast in the oven for 45 to 50 minutes, until an instant-read thermometer inserted in the thickest part of a thigh registers 165°. Tent with foil; let rest for 15 minutes.

3. **Meanwhile, pickle the fennel** In a small saucepan, combine the rice vinegar, sugar, salt and cloves. Cook over moderate heat, stirring occasionally, until the sugar dissolves, 5 minutes. Transfer the sliced fennel to a heatproof bowl and pour the hot brine over it. Press plastic wrap on the fennel so it's submerged; marinate at room temperature for 1½ hours.

4. **Make the orange dressing** In a small saucepan, simmer the orange juice over moderately high heat until reduced by half, about 15 minutes. Add the vinegar and sugar and simmer, stirring occasionally, until reduced to ⅓ cup, 7 to 8 minutes. Remove from the heat and whisk in the lemon juice. Transfer to a bowl and whisk in the oils in a slow, steady stream. Season the dressing with salt and pepper.

5. Using a sharp knife, peel the orange, being sure to remove any bitter pith. Cut between the membranes to release the sections into a bowl. Add the radicchio and the ¼ cup of dill. Season with salt and pepper. Drain the pickled fennel and add to the radicchio with the Candied Walnuts and ¼ cup of the orange dressing; toss well.

6. Transfer the salad to a platter. Carve the chicken and arrange on the salad. Garnish with dill and serve, passing the remaining dressing at the table. —*Ben Devlin*

NOTE Refrigerating the chicken uncovered overnight dries out the skin so it's crisper once it's roasted. Refrigerate the bird on a rack set on a rimmed baking sheet.

WINE Restrained California Chardonnay: 2014 Copain Tous Ensemble.

CANDIED WALNUTS

Total **30 min**; Makes **1 cup**

- 1 cup walnuts
- ¼ cup sugar
- Kosher salt

1. Preheat the oven to 350°. In a small pie plate, toast the walnuts until lightly browned, about 10 minutes. Let cool; leave the oven on.

2. In a small bowl, toss the walnuts with 1 tablespoon of water. Add the sugar and 2 generous pinches of salt and toss to coat. Spread the nuts on a parchment paper–lined baking sheet. Bake, stirring once, until brown and crisp, 12 to 14 minutes. Let cool. —*BD*

Roast Chicken with Sausage and Peppers

Active **30 min**; Total **1 hr 45 min**; Serves **4**

Another reason to roast chicken in a Bundt pan: The juices drip down and baste the vegetables so they won't dry out like they do in a baking pan.

- ¾ lb. hot Italian sausages, halved crosswise
- 3 Italian frying peppers or Cubanelles, halved lengthwise and seeded
- 2 large red bell peppers, cut into large strips
- 2 large red onions, cut into 1-inch wedges
- 2 Tbsp. extra-virgin olive oil, plus more for brushing
- 2 Tbsp. dried oregano
- Kosher salt and pepper
- One 4-lb. chicken
- 2 tsp. finely grated lemon zest

1. Preheat the oven to 450°. Wrap the center pillar of a 10-inch Bundt pan with foil.

2. In a large bowl, toss the sausages with all of the peppers, the onions, the 2 tablespoons of olive oil and 1 tablespoon of the oregano. Season with salt and pepper and add to the pan.

3. Brush the chicken with olive oil and season with salt, pepper, the remaining 1 tablespoon of oregano and the lemon zest. Perch the chicken on the pan by inserting the center pillar into the cavity.

4. Roast the chicken for about 1 hour, until an instant-read thermometer inserted in an inner thigh registers 155°. Transfer to a cutting board and let rest for 15 minutes.

5. Transfer the sausages, peppers, onions and pan juices to a platter. Carve the chicken, arrange on the platter and serve right away. —*Justin Chapple*

SERVE WITH Crusty bread.

WINE Juicy Barbera: 2013 Marchesi di Barolo Maraia.

Spatchcock Chicken with Marinated Peach Salad

Active **30 min**; Total **2 hr 15 min plus overnight seasoning**; Serves **4 to 6**

Spatchcocking a chicken, a technique that promotes fast and even grilling, calls for removing the backbone and flattening the bird. Star chef Michael Symon pairs his grilled spatchcock chicken with a summery salad of peaches marinated in honey and white wine vinegar.

> One 4-lb. chicken, backbone removed
>
> Kosher salt and pepper
>
> ½ cup plus 2 Tbsp. extra-virgin olive oil
>
> 2 Tbsp. white wine vinegar
>
> 2 tsp. honey
>
> 4 tsp. Dijon mustard
>
> 4 peaches, cut into ¼-inch-thick wedges
>
> 4 cups baby arugula
>
> ½ cup torn basil leaves
>
> ¼ cup roasted salted peanuts, coarsely chopped

1. Set the chicken skin side up on a rack set over a baking sheet. Press down firmly on the breastbone to flatten the bird. Season the chicken all over with 2 teaspoons of salt and refrigerate uncovered overnight. Let the chicken stand at room temperature for 30 minutes before roasting.

2. Preheat the oven to 425°. Rub the chicken with 2 tablespoons of the olive oil and season with pepper. Roast for about 1 hour, until golden and an instant-read thermometer inserted in a thigh registers 160°. Transfer to a rack and let rest for 15 minutes.

3. Meanwhile, in a large bowl, whisk the vinegar with the honey and mustard. Whisking constantly, drizzle in the remaining ½ cup of olive oil and season with salt and pepper. Transfer half of the dressing to a small bowl. Add the peaches to the large bowl and toss to coat. Let the peaches marinate at room temperature for 30 minutes.

4. Cut the chicken into 8 pieces and arrange on a platter. Add the arugula and basil to the marinated peaches and toss to coat. Transfer the peach salad to a bowl, top with the chopped peanuts and serve with the chicken, passing the reserved dressing at the table. —*Michael Symon*

MAKE AHEAD The dressing can be refrigerated overnight.

WINE Aromatic Viognier: 2014 Cristom Estate.

Zucchini Noodles with Chicken and Ginger Dressing

Total **40 min**; Serves **4**

A spiralizing gadget makes quick work of the long, noodle-like strands of zucchini in this dish. Tossed with roast chicken and an aromatic Asian dressing, the "zoodles" are a healthy alternative to pasta.

> 6 Tbsp. canola oil
>
> 3 Tbsp. fresh lemon juice
>
> ¼ cup finely grated peeled fresh ginger
>
> ½ tsp. finely grated garlic
>
> 2 Tbsp. chopped scallions, plus more for garnish
>
> 2 Tbsp. toasted sesame seeds, plus more for garnish
>
> Kosher salt and pepper
>
> 4 zucchini (1¾ lbs.), spiralized
>
> 1 bunch of watercress, thick stems discarded (8 cups)
>
> 2 cups shredded cooked chicken

1. In a large bowl, whisk the oil with the lemon juice, ginger, garlic and the 2 tablespoons each of scallions and sesame seeds; season with salt and pepper.

2. Fill a bowl with ice water. In a large saucepan of salted boiling water, blanch the zucchini for 30 seconds. Drain, then transfer to the ice water to cool. Drain well and pat thoroughly dry with paper towels. Add the zucchini, watercress and chicken to the dressing in the bowl and season with salt and pepper. Toss to coat. Garnish with scallions and sesame seeds and serve.—*Kay Chun*

MAKE AHEAD The dressing can be refrigerated overnight.

WINE Fruit-driven Oregon white: 2014 Adelsheim Vineyard Pinot Gris.

Roast Chicken with Salsa Verde and Roasted Lemons

Active **40 min**; Total **1 hr**; Serves **4**

Chef Jonathan Waxman is justly famous for his roast chicken. This salsa verde–topped bird is one of our all-time favorites.

> One 4-lb. chicken, backbone removed, chicken halved lengthwise
>
> 1 cup plus 2 Tbsp. extra-virgin olive oil
>
> Kosher salt and pepper
>
> 2 lemons, halved crosswise
>
> ¼ cup capers, rinsed
>
> 4 anchovy fillets in oil, drained
>
> 3 garlic cloves, crushed
>
> ½ cup coarsely chopped arugula
>
> ½ cup coarsely chopped parsley
>
> ½ cup coarsely chopped basil
>
> ½ cup coarsely chopped cilantro
>
> ¼ cup coarsely chopped tarragon
>
> ¼ cup coarsely chopped chives
>
> ¼ cup coarsely chopped sage

1. Preheat the oven to 450°. Arrange the chicken skin side up on a rack set over a baking sheet. Rub with 2 tablespoons of the olive oil; season with salt and pepper. Place the lemons cut side down on the rack. Roast the chicken for about 40 minutes, until golden and cooked through. Let rest for 10 minutes.

2. Meanwhile, in a mortar or blender, mash the capers with the anchovies and garlic until a paste forms. Transfer to a medium bowl and whisk in the remaining 1 cup of olive oil. Stir in the herbs; season with salt.

3. Carve the chicken; arrange on a platter with the lemons. Serve with the salsa verde. —*Jonathan Waxman*

MAKE AHEAD The salsa verde can be refrigerated overnight; serve at room temperature.

WINE Lemony, medium-bodied Sicilian white: 2014 Graci Etna Bianco.

ZUCCHINI NOODLES
WITH CHICKEN AND
GINGER DRESSING

POACHED CHICKEN
WITH FRAGRANT
HERB VINAIGRETTE

Filipino Chicken Inasal

Total **1 hr plus 4 hr marinating**
Serves **6 to 8**

According to *Bizarre Foods* host Andrew Zimmern, this tangy grilled chicken marinated with lemongrass and ginger originated in the Philippine province of Negros Occidental and is famously associated with its capital, Bacolod City. Zimmern serves the chicken with plenty of rice and small bowls of coconut vinegar seasoned with slivers of garlic and minced hot chiles.

DIPPING SAUCE

- ¼ cup coconut vinegar (see Note)
- 2 garlic cloves, thinly sliced
- 2 serrano chiles, seeded and minced

CHICKEN

- ¾ cup coconut vinegar
- 9 garlic cloves, finely grated
- 3 stalks of fresh lemongrass, tender inner white parts only, minced
- ¼ cup fresh lime juice
- ¼ cup firmly packed light brown sugar
- ¼ cup minced peeled fresh ginger
  Two 3-lb. chickens, quartered
- ¼ cup annatto seeds (see Note)
- 1 stick unsalted butter
  Kosher salt and pepper
  Steamed white rice and lime wedges, for serving

1. Make the dipping sauce In a small bowl, mix the coconut vinegar with the garlic and chiles. Cover and set aside.

2. Make the chicken In a large bowl, whisk the coconut vinegar with two-thirds of the grated garlic, the lemongrass, lime juice, brown sugar and ginger. Put each quartered chicken in a large resealable plastic bag. Add the marinade and seal the bags. Refrigerate for 4 to 6 hours.

3. Meanwhile, in a spice grinder or mortar, crush the annatto seeds to a fine powder. In a small saucepan, melt the butter with the annatto powder over very low heat and cook until fragrant and deep red, 25 to 30 minutes. Remove the saucepan from the heat and stir in 1 teaspoon each of salt and pepper along with the remaining grated garlic.

4. Preheat the oven to 425°. Heat a grill pan over moderately high heat. Scrape the marinade off the chicken; reserve the marinade. Transfer the chicken to a plate and season with salt and pepper. Grill the chicken in batches over moderately high heat, basting twice with the marinade, until lightly browned on all sides, 10 minutes.

5. Transfer the chicken to a rimmed baking sheet and baste with the annatto butter. Roast, basting once more with the annatto butter, until an instant-read thermometer inserted into the thickest part registers 165°, about 12 minutes for the breasts and 15 minutes for the legs. Transfer to a platter and serve with steamed rice, lime wedges and the coconut vinegar dipping sauce. —*Andrew Zimmern*

NOTE Coconut vinegar is a key ingredient in Filipino cooking. It is available at some Asian markets and from amazon.com. Annatto (also called achiote) seeds are used to add a distinctive red color to dishes; they are available at supermarkets.

WINE Fresh and fruity rosé: 2015 Château Pradeaux Le Côtes de Provence.

Poached Chicken with Fragrant Herb Vinaigrette

Active **45 min**; Total **1 hr 45 min**; Serves **4**

The gingery vinaigrette for this chicken is so dense with herbs, it's practically a salad. Serve the dish with the nourishing poaching broth alongside for sipping.

CHICKEN

- One 3½- to 4-lb. chicken, backbone removed and reserved
- One 5-inch piece of ginger, thinly sliced
- 2 heads of garlic, halved crosswise
- 1 whole star anise
  One 3-inch cinnamon stick
- 2 Tbsp. dry green peppercorns
- 1 Tbsp. kosher salt

HERB VINAIGRETTE

- ½ cup chopped cilantro, plus sprigs for garnish
- ½ cup chopped scallions, plus more for garnish
- ½ cup coarsely chopped parsley
- ⅓ cup chopped basil, plus small leaves for garnish
- 1 serrano chile, minced with seeds
- 2 Tbsp. finely grated peeled fresh ginger
- ½ cup extra-virgin olive oil
- 2 Tbsp. fresh lime juice
  Kosher salt and pepper
  Steamed brown rice and lime wedges, for serving

1. Poach the chicken In a large pot, combine the chicken and the backbone with enough water to cover by 1 inch. Add the ginger, garlic, star anise, cinnamon stick, peppercorns and salt and bring to a rolling boil. Place a heatproof plate on top of the chicken to completely submerge it. Cover the pot and remove from the heat. Let stand for 1 hour.

2. Transfer the chicken to a cutting board and let stand for 10 minutes. Carve the chicken and arrange on a platter; discard the skin if desired. Strain the poaching liquid through a sieve and keep warm.

3. Make the vinaigrette In a bowl, combine the chopped cilantro, scallions, parsley, basil and serrano with the ginger, olive oil and lime juice; mix well. Season with salt and pepper.

4. Spoon the vinaigrette over the chicken and garnish with cilantro sprigs, scallions and basil leaves. Serve with rice and lime wedges, passing the hot broth for sipping. —*Kay Chun*

MAKE AHEAD The herb vinaigrette can be refrigerated for up to 3 hours.

WINE Fresh, stony Chablis: 2013 Domaine Servin Premier Cru Vaucoupin.

Mustard-and-Rosemary Roast Turkey

📷 PAGE 140

Active **30 min**; Total **2 hr 15 min plus overnight marinating**; Serves **8 to 10**

- ¼ cup Dijon mustard
- 2 Tbsp. extra-virgin olive oil
- 4 garlic cloves, finely grated
- 2 Tbsp. finely chopped rosemary
- 2 Tbsp. kosher salt
- 2 tsp. black pepper
  One 12-lb. turkey, cut into breasts, wings and legs/thighs (have your butcher do this)
- 1 large onion, halved and thinly sliced
- ½ cup dry white wine
  Port and Black Pepper Gravy (recipe follows), for serving

1. In a bowl, combine the mustard, olive oil, garlic, rosemary, salt and pepper and blend well. Rub the mixture all over the turkey. Arrange the breasts on a large rimmed baking sheet and the wings and legs/thighs on another. Refrigerate uncovered overnight.

2. Preheat the oven to 450°; set the racks in the upper and lower thirds. Let the turkey stand at room temperature for 30 minutes.

3. Divide the onion and wine around the turkey on the baking sheets. Roast the white meat in the lower third of the oven and the dark meat in the upper third for 30 minutes. Reduce the oven temperature to 350° and roast the white meat for 20 minutes longer and the dark meat for 30 minutes longer, until an instant-read thermometer inserted in the thickest part of the meat registers 165°. Discard the onion. Let the turkey rest for 15 minutes before carving. Serve with the port gravy. —*Melissa Clark*

WINE Earthy, spicy Rhône red: 2014 Château de Saint Cosme Gigondas.

PORT AND BLACK PEPPER GRAVY

⏱ Total **40 min**; Makes **5 cups**

- 1 stick unsalted butter
- ½ cup finely chopped onion
- 1 tsp. freshly ground black pepper
  Kosher salt
- ½ cup all-purpose flour
- 2 Tbsp. port
- 5 cups turkey stock

In a medium saucepan, melt the butter. Add the onion and pepper and season with salt. Cook over moderate heat, stirring occasionally, until tender and golden, about 10 minutes. Add the flour and cook, stirring, until deep golden in color, about 5 minutes. Whisk in the port and stock and bring to a simmer. Cook over low heat, stirring occasionally, until thickened, about 10 minutes. —*MC*

Turkey Posole

Active **1 hr**; Total **3 hr 30 min**
Serves **10 to 12**

- 4½ lbs. turkey drumsticks
- 1 large onion, cut into chunks
- 10 garlic cloves, crushed
- 2 qts. turkey stock
  Kosher salt
- ½ cup pepitas (hulled pumpkin seeds)
- 3 Tbsp. extra-virgin olive oil
- 1½ lbs. tomatillos—husked, rinsed and halved
- 3 serrano chiles, halved lengthwise and seeded
- 1 cup lightly packed cilantro, plus leaves for serving
- ¼ cup chopped epazote (optional)
- 1½ tsp. finely chopped oregano
- 1½ tsp. ground cumin
- ¾ tsp. crushed red pepper
  Four 15-oz. cans hominy, drained and rinsed
  Diced avocado, thinly sliced radishes, Mexican crema or sour cream, lime wedges and oregano leaves, for serving

1. In a large pot, cover the turkey, onion and garlic with the stock and 3 quarts of water; bring to a boil over high heat. Add a generous pinch of salt and simmer over moderately low heat until the turkey is very tender, about 2 hours and 30 minutes.

2. Meanwhile, in a large cast-iron skillet, toast the pepitas in the olive oil over moderately high heat until golden, about 3 minutes. Transfer to a small bowl. Add the tomatillos and chiles to the skillet cut side down and cook over high heat until charred on the bottom, about 5 minutes. Transfer to the bowl with the pepitas.

3. Using tongs, transfer the turkey to a plate; let cool. Discard the skin and bones, then shred the meat. Using a slotted spoon, transfer the onion and garlic to a blender. Add the tomatillos, chiles and pepitas along with the 1 cup of cilantro, the epazote (if using), oregano, cumin, crushed red pepper and 2 cups of the broth and puree until the salsa verde is smooth.

4. Stir the salsa verde into the broth in the pot and season generously with salt. Stir in the turkey and hominy and cook over moderate heat until hot, 5 minutes. Serve the posole with avocado, radishes, crema, lime wedges, oregano and cilantro. —*Ellen Bennett*

WINE Lightly tart New Zealand Pinot Noir: 2014 Giesen Estate Marlborough.

Roast Hens with Yassa Marinade

Active **15 min**; Total **2 hr 25 min**; Serves **4**

- 1½ cups tamari
- 1½ cups grapeseed or canola oil
- ¼ cup mint leaves with stems
- 1 medium onion, chopped
- 1 fresh Thai bird chile with stem
- 1 Tbsp. finely grated lemon zest
- 1 Tbsp. Dijon mustard
- 1 tsp. thyme leaves with stems
- ½ tsp. kosher salt, plus more for seasoning
  Four 1¼- to 1½-lb. Cornish game hens

1. In a blender or food processor, pulse all of the ingredients except the hens until chunky.

2. In a large bowl, season the hens with salt. Add the marinade and rub it all over the hens and in the cavities. Cover and refrigerate for 1 to 3 hours.

3. Preheat the oven to 375°. Set a rack over a large rimmed baking sheet. Arrange the hens on the rack, leaving some of the marinade in the cavities. Roast for about 1 hour, or until an instant-read thermometer inserted in the inner thighs registers 165° and the juices run clear. Transfer the hens to a cutting board and let rest for 10 minutes before serving. —*Joseph Johnson*

WINE Savory Sicilian red: 2013 Tascante Ghiaia Nera.

ROAST HENS
WITH YASSA MARINADE

PAN-ROASTED DUCK WITH
CHERRIES AND OLIVES

Pan-Roasted Duck with Cherries and Olives

Total **1 hr**; Serves **8**

- **4** cups ruby port
- **1½** sticks unsalted butter, diced and chilled
- **¼** cup chopped dried cherries
- **¼** cup pitted and chopped Taggiasca olives

  Kosher salt and pepper

  Four 1-lb. magret duck breasts
- **1½** lbs. fresh duck foie gras—veins removed, liver sliced 1 inch thick and chilled

  Marcona almonds and watercress sprigs, for garnish

1. In a medium saucepan, simmer the port over moderate heat until syrupy and reduced to 1 cup, about 15 minutes. Whisk in the butter, cherries and olives and season with salt and pepper. Keep the sauce warm.

2. Meanwhile, preheat the oven to 425°. Set a rack over a rimmed baking sheet.

3. In a large ovenproof skillet, cook 2 of the duck breasts skin side down over moderately low heat until the fat renders and the skin is browned and crispy, about 10 minutes. Transfer the duck to the rack skin side up. Discard the fat. Repeat with the remaining 2 duck breasts. Transfer the duck to the oven and roast until an instant-read thermometer inserted in the thickest part of the breasts registers 130° for medium-rare, about 15 minutes. Transfer to a cutting board and let rest for 10 minutes. Slice the duck breasts ⅓ inch thick. Leave the oven on.

4. Clean the skillet, wipe it dry and heat until very hot. Add half of the foie gras and cook over high heat until deep golden, about 30 seconds. Flip the foie gras and roast in the oven until just cooked through, about 3 minutes longer. Transfer to a paper towel–lined plate to drain. Repeat with the remaining foie gras.

5. Arrange the duck and foie gras on a platter and spoon over the sauce. Garnish with almonds and watercress and serve.
—*Daniel Rose*

WINE Savory Rhône red: 2014 Alain Graillot Crozes-Hermitage.

Seared Duck with Date Jus and Piave Foam

Active **35 min**; Total **1 hr 15 min**; Serves **4**

The sweet date jus served with this succulent duck is made simply by cooking Medjool dates with rosemary and water until they become a sauce.

- **12** oz. Medjool dates, pitted and halved
- **1** rosemary sprig
- **1¼** cups heavy cream
- **½** cup finely grated Piave cheese (about 1 oz.)

  Kosher salt and pepper

  Two 12-oz. Moulard duck breasts

1. In a saucepan, bring the dates, rosemary and 4 cups of water to a boil. Simmer over moderate heat, mashing the dates with a wooden spoon, until very soft and the sauce is thick, 15 minutes. Strain, pressing on the solids; keep the date jus warm.

2. In a small saucepan, bring the cream to a simmer. Slowly whisk in the cheese until well blended. Transfer the Piave sauce to a bowl, season with salt and let cool until lukewarm.

3. Preheat the oven to 425°. Using a sharp knife, score the duck fat in a crosshatch pattern at ½-inch intervals. Heat a 12-inch ovenproof nonstick skillet. Season the duck with salt and pepper and add to the skillet skin side down. Cook over moderate heat until most of the fat is rendered and the skin is deep golden and crisp, about 8 minutes. Turn the duck over and roast in the oven until medium-rare within and an instant-read thermometer inserted in the center registers 130°, about 12 minutes. Transfer the breasts to a cutting board and let stand for 10 minutes. Slice the duck crosswise ¼ inch thick and arrange on plates.

4. Whisk the Piave sauce until slightly thickened, about 1 minute. Serve the duck with the date jus and the Piave sauce.
—*Evan Algorri*

WINE Peppery Loire red: 2012 Olga Raffault Chinon.

Gratin of Celery Root, Duck Confit and Pears

Active **1 hr 15 min**; Total **1 hr 40 min**
Serves **8**

Instead of the usual bacon or sausage, Daniel Rose, the chef at Le Coucou in New York City and Spring in Paris, flavors this gratin with luscious duck confit.

- **¼** cup raisins
- **4** Tbsp. salted butter, plus more for brushing
- **1** large celery root (3 lbs.), peeled and cut into 1-inch pieces
- **½** cup heavy cream
- **1** large egg yolk

  Kosher salt and pepper
- **4** Bosc pears (2 lbs.)—peeled, cored and cut into 1-inch pieces
- **4** confit duck legs, skin discarded and meat shredded
- **½** tsp. finely grated orange zest

  Pinch of ground cinnamon

1. In a small bowl, combine the raisins with water to cover by 2 inches and let stand for 1 hour. Drain.

2. Meanwhile, preheat the oven to 425°. Brush a 3-quart shallow baking dish with butter.

3. In a large saucepan of salted boiling water, cook the celery root until tender, about 15 minutes. Drain well. In a food processor, puree half of the celery with the cream, egg yolk and 2 tablespoons of the butter until smooth. Season with salt and pepper. Scrape the mixture into a large bowl and stir in the remaining celery root.

4. In a large skillet, melt the remaining 2 tablespoons of butter. Add the pears and cook over moderately high heat, stirring occasionally, until golden, about 3 minutes. Fold into the celery root.

5. In a medium bowl, combine the duck confit with the orange zest, cinnamon and 3 tablespoons of the raisins. Spread the duck in the prepared dish and spoon the celery root mixture evenly over it. Bake for about 15 minutes, until heated through; remove the dish from the oven. Position a rack in the oven 8 inches from the heat and preheat the broiler on high. Broil the gratin for about 5 minutes, until golden. Top with the remaining 1 tablespoon of raisins and serve warm. —*Daniel Rose*

PORK AND VEAL

Cult winemaker
Giampaolo Venica in
the prosciutto-aging
room at D'Osvaldo in
Italy's Friuli region.
OPPOSITE Crispy
Shake-and-Bake
Pork (p. 172).

Pork Milanese with Gribiche Sauce

Total **1 hr**; Serves **4**

At Manhattan's Wildair, chefs Jeremiah Stone and Fabián von Hauske serve their breaded and fried pork shoulder cutlets with gribiche—a tangy sauce studded with chopped hard-boiled eggs and pickles.

GRIBICHE SAUCE

- **4 large eggs**
- **6 Tbsp. extra-virgin olive oil**
- **2 Tbsp. finely chopped shallot**
- **2 Tbsp. finely chopped capers**
- **2 Tbsp. finely chopped cornichons**
- **2 Tbsp. finely chopped parsley**
- **1½ Tbsp. Dijon mustard**
- **1 Tbsp. red wine vinegar**
   Kosher salt and pepper

PORK

   Four 3-oz. pork shoulder cutlets
- **½ cup all-purpose flour**
- **2 large eggs, lightly beaten**
- **1½ cups plain breadcrumbs**
   Kosher salt and pepper
   Canola oil, for frying

1. Make the gribiche sauce In a small saucepan, cover the eggs with 2 inches of water and bring to a boil. Cover, remove from the heat and let stand for 10 minutes. Transfer the eggs to an ice bath to cool. Peel the eggs, finely chop and transfer to a bowl. Add all of the remaining ingredients and mix well. Stir in 1 tablespoon of water; season with salt and pepper.

2. Make the pork Using a wooden meat mallet, pound each pork cutlet to an ⅛-inch thickness. Put the flour, eggs and breadcrumbs in 3 separate shallow bowls. Season the pork with salt and pepper and dip in the flour. Dip the cutlets in the egg and then in the breadcrumbs, pressing to help the crumbs adhere.

3. In a large cast-iron skillet, heat ¼ inch of canola oil until shimmering. Working in batches, fry the pork cutlets over moderately high heat, turning once, until golden and crispy, about 3 minutes. Transfer to paper towels to drain. Serve warm with the gribiche sauce. —*Jeremiah Stone and Fabián von Hauske*

MAKE AHEAD The gribiche sauce can be refrigerated overnight.

WINE Light, herbal Pinot Noir: 2014 Pierre-Olivier Bonhomme Vercheny.

Crispy Shake-and-Bake Pork

PAGE 170

Active **10 min**; Total **30 min**; Serves **4**

In an updated version of the packaged breadcrumb coating, these pork chops are tossed with unsweetened shredded wheat cereal and lots of seasonings, then baked until crispy.

- **7 oz. unsweetened shredded wheat cereal, crushed (3 cups)**
   Kosher salt
- **2 tsp. dried oregano**
- **2 tsp. dried parsley**
- **2 tsp. celery salt**
- **1 tsp. garlic powder**
- **1 tsp. granulated onion**
- **1 tsp. paprika**
- **1 tsp. pepper, plus more for seasoning**
- **7 Tbsp. canola oil**
   Four ½-inch-thick boneless rib pork chops (about 6 oz. each)
   Lemon wedges, for serving

1. Preheat the oven to 450°. Set a rack over a baking sheet. In a medium bowl, combine the shredded wheat, 2 teaspoons of salt, all of the spices and 5 tablespoons of the oil. Mix well and transfer to a resealable plastic bag.

2. Rub the pork all over with the remaining 2 tablespoons of oil; season lightly with salt and pepper. Put each slice of pork in the bag; shake to evenly coat and press to help the crumbs adhere. Transfer to the rack.

3. Bake the chops for about 20 minutes, until golden and cooked through. Serve with lemon wedges. —*Kay Chun*

VARIATION Crispy Shake-and-Bake Fish Sticks Use flaky white fish, such as cod, cut into ¾-inch-thick sticks. Follow the recipe through Step 2, then bake for 12 to 15 minutes.

MAKE AHEAD The shredded wheat coating can be refrigerated overnight.

WINE Fruit-forward Cal-Italian red: 2013 Palmina Dolcetto.

Pork Chops with Almond Salmuera

Total **35 min**; Serves **4**

Brushing pork chops with salmuera—a flavorful Argentinean brine—while they cook adds moisture and seasons the meat to its core. Chef Tory Miller of Madison, Wisconsin's Estrellón also makes a "finishing" salmuera with toasty nuts and herbs to give the meat one more layer of flavor before it's served. This technique can be used for all kinds of meat and fish, and also works beautifully on vegetables.

- **½ cup extra-virgin olive oil**
- **¼ cup plus 2 Tbsp. sherry vinegar**
- **1 shallot, minced**
- **1 garlic clove, minced**
   Kosher salt and pepper
- **¼ cup marcona almonds, chopped**
- **1 tsp. minced chives**
- **1 tsp. minced parsley**
- **1 tsp. minced mint**
- **1 tsp. minced cilantro**
   Canola oil, for brushing
   Four 8-oz. bone-in pork rib chops, cut 1 inch thick
   Flaky sea salt, for finishing

1. In a medium bowl, whisk ¼ cup of the olive oil and 2 tablespoons of the vinegar with the shallot, garlic, 1 tablespoon of kosher salt, 1 teaspoon of pepper and 1 cup of water. Stir in the almonds, chives, parsley, mint and cilantro.

2. Light a grill and oil the grate. In a small bowl, whisk the remaining ¼ cup each of olive oil and vinegar with 2 tablespoons of kosher salt, 2 teaspoons of pepper and ¼ cup of water. Grill the pork chops over moderately high heat, basting frequently with the seasoning salmuera, until browned and an instant-read thermometer inserted in the thickest part registers 140°, 6 to 7 minutes per side.

3. Transfer the chops to a platter and top with some of the marcona almond salmuera. Sprinkle with flaky salt and serve the rest of the salmuera alongside. —*Tory Miller*

MAKE AHEAD Both salmueras can be refrigerated overnight. Stir in the marcona almonds just before serving.

WINE A bold, fruit-forward Spanish Garnacha blend: 2013 Giné Giné Priorat.

PORK CHOPS WITH
ALMOND SALMUERA

PORK CHOPS IN SAGE
BUTTER WITH BEET PUREE
AND SWISS CHARD

Pork Chops in Sage Butter with Beet Puree and Swiss Chard

Active **1 hr**; Total **1 hr 30 min**; Serves **4**

The vibrant magenta puree served alongside these juicy pork chops is made with almost equal parts beets and creamy Yukon Gold potatoes.

- **2 large red beets (1 lb.), halved**
- **2 medium Yukon Gold potatoes (½ lb.)**
- **1 stick unsalted butter**
- **Kosher salt and pepper**
- **Four 12-oz. bone-in pork rib chops, cut 1 inch thick**
- **¼ cup extra-virgin olive oil**
- **3 garlic cloves, crushed**
- **1 sage sprig**
- **1 tsp. fresh lemon juice**
- **2 lbs. Swiss chard, stems discarded and leaves chopped**

1. In a large saucepan, combine the beets and potatoes. Add enough water to cover by 2 inches and bring to a boil over high heat. Cook until the beets and potatoes are tender, 35 to 40 minutes. Drain well. When cool enough to handle, peel the beets and potatoes, then coarsely chop; transfer to a food processor. Add 2 tablespoons of the butter and puree until smooth. Season with salt and pepper and keep warm.

2. Heat a large cast-iron skillet. Rub the pork chops all over with 2 tablespoons of the olive oil; season with salt and pepper. Cook over moderately high heat until golden brown on the bottom, 7 to 8 minutes. Turn the chops and add the garlic, sage and 2 tablespoons of the butter. Cook until the chops are golden and an instant-read thermometer inserted in the thickest part registers 135°, about 7 minutes longer. Transfer the pork chops to plates and let stand for 5 minutes. Whisk the lemon juice and 2 tablespoons of the butter into the skillet; season with salt. Strain the sage butter through a fine sieve over the pork chops. Reserve the crispy sage leaves and discard the garlic.

3. Meanwhile, in a large nonstick skillet, melt the remaining 2 tablespoons of butter in the remaining 2 tablespoons of olive oil.

Add the chard in large handfuls; let each batch wilt slightly before adding more. Cook, stirring occasionally, until all of the chard is wilted, about 5 minutes. Season with salt and pepper.

4. Serve the pork chops with the beet puree and Swiss chard and garnish with the crispy sage leaves. —*Kamil Oseka*

MAKE AHEAD The beet puree can be refrigerated overnight. Reheat gently.

WINE A lightly earthy Burgundy: the 2013 Domaine Faiveley Mercurey Rouge.

Pork Chops with Burnt Applesauce and Greens

Active **1 hr**; Total **1 hr 30 min**; Serves **4**

Chef James Lowe of Lyle's in London was inspired to char apples as an accompaniment to his pork chops after watching a cook in Mexico make salsa with blackened vegetables for added flavor.

- **¾ cup apple juice**
- **¼ cup plus 3 Tbsp. extra-virgin olive oil**
- **2 Tbsp. fresh lemon juice**
- **Kosher salt and pepper**
- **2 Braeburn or other sweet-tart apples (1 lb.)—peeled, cored and sliced ¼ inch thick**
- **3 Tbsp. unsalted butter**
- **Four 12-oz. bone-in pork rib chops, cut 1 inch thick**
- **1 cup chicken stock**
- **8 cups torn mixed bitter lettuces, such as chicory, radicchio and Treviso**

1. Preheat the oven to 450°. In a small saucepan, simmer ½ cup of the apple juice over moderate heat until reduced to ¼ cup, about 5 minutes. Transfer to a small bowl to cool. Whisk in ¼ cup of the oil and the lemon juice; season the dressing with salt and pepper.

2. In a large cast-iron skillet, heat 1 tablespoon of the oil. Add the apples and cook over moderate heat until blackened all over, about 10 minutes. Transfer to a blender, add the remaining ¼ cup of apple juice and puree until smooth; keep the applesauce warm. Wipe out the skillet.

3. In the skillet, melt 1 tablespoon of the butter in 1 tablespoon of the oil. Season the pork with salt and pepper. Cook 2 of the chops over moderately high heat, turning

once, until golden, about 6 minutes; transfer to a plate. Cook the remaining 2 chops in 1 tablespoon each of the butter and oil.

4. Return all of the chops to the skillet and roast in the oven for 8 to 10 minutes, until an instant-read thermometer inserted in the center registers 140°. Let the chops rest for 15 minutes.

5. Pour off the oil from the skillet. Add the stock and simmer until slightly thickened, about 3 minutes. Whisk in the remaining 1 tablespoon of butter and cook until the sauce thickens, about 2 minutes.

6. In a large bowl, toss the greens with half of the apple dressing and season with salt and pepper. Mound the salad on plates and spoon a dollop of the applesauce alongside. Cut the chops off the bones; cut the meat into thick slices. Add the meat to the plates and drizzle with the pan sauce. Pass the remaining apple dressing at the table. —*James Lowe*

WINE Oregon Pinot Noir: 2013 Bethel Heights Estate.

SUPEREASY FLAVOR BOOST

Amp Up Your Pork

Take pork chops (or any other cut) to the next level with Chinese five-spice powder, a bold mix of cinnamon, clove, fennel seed, star anise and Sichuan peppercorn. Before cooking, mix these exotic, fragrant spices with brown sugar and a few other ingredients and rub on the meat for a flavorful crust.

ASIAN FIVE-SPICE RUB In a small bowl, combine 3 Tbsp. **Chinese five-spice powder** with 1 Tbsp. **light brown sugar,** 1 Tbsp. **kosher salt,** 1 tsp. **cayenne** and ½ tsp. **garlic powder,** pressing out any lumps of brown sugar.

Pork Tonkatsu

Total **30 min; Serves 4**

"Tonkatsu is one of my top-five favorite dishes," says *Bizarre Foods* host Andrew Zimmern. "The crucial ingredient is possibly the best processed food on planet Earth: tonkatsu sauce. It's sweet and pungent, with apple and raisin notes, a hint of fermentation and a whisper of Worcestershire." He recommends three brands, all available at Asian markets: Bull-Dog, Ikari and Kikkoman (Japanese label only).

> **Four 6- to 7-oz. boneless pork loin chops, pounded ½ inch thick**
> 2 **cups all-purpose flour**
> 2 **large eggs, lightly beaten**
> 3 **cups panko**
> **Kosher salt and pepper**
> **Canola oil, for frying**
> 3 **Tbsp. Japanese mustard powder (see Note) or Colman's mustard powder**
> ½ **lb. green cabbage, thinly sliced, preferably on a mandoline (4 cups)**
> **Tonkatsu sauce (see Note) and lemon wedges, for serving**

1. Using kitchen shears or a knife, score the fat at the edges of the chops at 1-inch intervals, about ¼ inch deep.

2. Put the flour, eggs and panko in 3 separate shallow bowls. Season the flour with 1 teaspoon each of salt and pepper. Season the pork cutlets with salt and pepper and coat them with flour, tapping off the excess. Dip the cutlets in the beaten eggs and then in the panko, pressing to help the crumbs adhere.

3. In a large skillet, heat 1 inch of oil to 360°. Fry 2 pork cutlets over moderate heat, turning once, until golden brown and white throughout, about 4 minutes. Drain on paper towels. Transfer to a cutting board and season with salt. Repeat with the remaining cutlets.

4. In a small bowl, whisk the mustard powder with 3 tablespoons of water until smooth.

5. Slice the tonkatsu into ¾-inch strips and transfer to plates. Serve with the cabbage, Japanese mustard, tonkatsu sauce and lemon wedges. —*Andrew Zimmern*

NOTE Japanese mustard, which you make by combining equal parts Japanese mustard powder and water, is spicier and more pungent than most other prepared mustards. Tonkatsu sauce is available at Asian markets and from amazon.com.

WINE Aromatic white blend from Austria: 2014 Neumeister Gemischter Satz.

Penang-Style Pork with Soft Tofu

Total **1 hr;** Serves **4**

On his menu at Restaurant Eve in Alexandria, Virginia, chef Cathal Armstrong calls this "Warning: You Must be Brave to Order This Dish." He gives the pork tenderloin curry plenty of fire with Korean chile flakes, black pepper and Thai chile. To keep the heat level in check, reduce the amount of chile flakes.

SPICE PASTE

> 1 **tsp. coriander seeds**
> 1 **tsp. cumin seeds**
> 1½ **Tbsp. Korean chile flakes (gochugaru)**
> 1 **Tbsp. minced peeled fresh ginger**
> 1 **Tbsp. minced shallot**
> 1 **Tbsp. finely chopped lemongrass, tender inner bulb only**
> 2 **tsp. finely grated lime zest**
> 2 **garlic cloves, chopped**
> ½ **tsp. Asian shrimp paste (see Note)**
> ½ **tsp. kosher salt**
> ½ **tsp. black pepper**
> ¼ **tsp. ground mace**
> ⅛ **tsp. ground cardamom**

CRISPY GARLIC

> **Canola oil, for frying**
> 3 **garlic cloves, thinly sliced**

PORK CURRY

> 12 **oz. pork tenderloin, sliced crosswise ¾ inch thick**
> **Kosher salt and pepper**
> 1 **Tbsp. minced peeled fresh ginger**
> 1 **Tbsp. minced garlic**
> 2 **Tbsp. minced shallot**
> 1 **tsp. minced Thai chile**
> 1½ **cups low-sodium chicken broth**
> 6 **Tbsp. prepared Penang curry sauce**
> 3 **Tbsp. soy sauce**
> 2 **Tbsp. cornstarch mixed with 2 Tbsp. water**
> 8 **oz. soft tofu, cut into ½-inch dice**
> **Steamed jasmine rice, for serving**
> **Cilantro, for garnish**

1. Make the spice paste In a spice grinder, pulse the coriander and cumin until coarsely ground; transfer to a food processor. Add the remaining ingredients and puree until a smooth paste forms.

2. Make the crispy garlic In a medium nonstick skillet, heat ¼ inch of canola oil. Add the garlic and fry over moderately high heat, stirring, until golden and crisp, about 1 minute. Using a slotted spoon, transfer the garlic to a paper towel–lined plate to drain. Pour off all but 2 tablespoons of the oil in the skillet.

3. Make the pork curry Season the pork with salt and pepper. Cook in the skillet over moderately high heat, turning once, until browned, 2 minutes per side. Transfer the pork to a cutting board and quarter each slice. Add the ginger, garlic, shallot, chile and spice paste to the skillet and cook over low heat, stirring, until very fragrant, about 5 minutes. Add the broth, curry sauce and soy sauce and bring to a simmer. Whisk in the cornstarch slurry and bring to a simmer, then add the pork and tofu and cook just until the sauce thickens, about 2 minutes.

4. Spoon jasmine rice into bowls and top with the pork curry. Garnish with the crispy garlic and cilantro and serve. —*Cathal Armstrong*

NOTE Southeast Asian shrimp paste is made with fermented ground shrimp. Look for it at Asian markets.

WINE Fruity cru Beaujolais: 2014 Julien Sunier Fleurie.

PORK TONKATSU

Porchetta-Spiced Pork Shoulder

Active **45 min**; Total **2 hr 30 min**
Serves **4 to 6**

This Italian-inflected recipe for pork rubbed with spices, herbs, lemon zest and garlic makes clever use of the delectable pan juices: They're whisked into a fantastic vinaigrette for the butter bean and spinach salad that's served alongside.

- **7 garlic cloves, crushed**
- **2 Tbsp. fennel seeds**
- **1 Tbsp. dried sage**
- **1 Tbsp. dried rosemary**
- **1 tsp. crushed red pepper**
- **Kosher salt and black pepper**
- **1 tsp. finely grated lemon zest plus 3 Tbsp. fresh lemon juice**
- **2 Tbsp. extra-virgin olive oil**
- **One 3-lb. trimmed boneless pork shoulder roast**
- **½ cup low-sodium chicken broth**
- **1½ tsp. Dijon mustard**
- **2 Tbsp. minced shallot**
- **Three 15-oz. cans butter beans, drained and rinsed**
- **8 oz. spinach (not baby), coarsely chopped (6 cups)**
- **½ cup shaved Parmigiano-Reggiano cheese**
- **Chopped parsley, for garnish**

1. Preheat the oven to 425°. In a spice grinder or mortar, grind the garlic, fennel seeds, sage, rosemary and crushed red pepper. Season with salt and black pepper. Stir in the lemon zest and olive oil.

2. Make a few 1-inch-deep slits in the top and bottom of the roast. Rub the spice mixture all over the meat, pushing some into the slits. Transfer to an enameled medium cast-iron casserole and roast for 30 minutes.

3. Reduce the oven temperature to 350°. Add the broth, cover the casserole and roast the pork for 1 hour and 15 minutes, until deep golden. Transfer to a cutting board and let rest for 15 minutes. Strain the juices in the casserole into a bowl.

4. In a large bowl, whisk 6 tablespoons of the pan juices with the mustard, lemon juice and shallot; set aside 2 tablespoons. Add the beans, spinach and cheese to the large bowl; season with salt and black pepper. Slice the pork and arrange on a platter. Spoon the salad alongside. Drizzle with the reserved dressing, garnish with parsley and serve. —*Kay Chun*

WINE Firm, tannic, aromatic Nebbiolo from Piedmont: 2014 Produttori di Barbaresco Langhe Nebbiolo.

Pork-and-Pineapple Coconut Curry

Active **35 min**; Total **2 hr 45 min**; Serves **6**

Paris-based cookbook author David Lebovitz smartly stirs a little peanut butter into his curry to cut the sweetness of the coconut milk. He likes making big batches to have leftovers the next day.

- **2 lbs. well-trimmed boneless pork shoulder, cut into 1-inch chunks**
- **¼ cup kosher salt**
- **2 cups unsweetened coconut milk**
- **¼ cup Thai red curry paste**
- **2 Tbsp. creamy peanut butter**
- **1 medium sweet potato, peeled and cut into 1-inch chunks**
- **One 1½-inch piece of fresh galangal or ginger, peeled**
- **3 lemongrass stalks, inner bulbs only, halved and crushed with a rolling pin**
- **1 tsp. Thai shrimp paste or 2 minced oil-packed anchovies**
- **5 oz. Thai eggplants, cut into wedges, or 1 small eggplant, cut into 1-inch dice (2 cups)**
- **3 Thai chiles, seeded and minced**
- **8 oz. fresh pineapple, cut into ½-inch chunks (1½ cups)**
- **1 cup loosely packed basil leaves**
- **Steamed white rice, for serving**

1. In a large enameled cast-iron casserole, cover the pork chunks with 1 inch of cold water (about 12 cups). Add the salt and bring to a boil over moderately high heat. Reduce the heat to moderate and simmer until the pork is tender, about 1 hour and 15 minutes. Using a slotted spoon, transfer the pork to a bowl. Set aside 2 cups of the pork stock; reserve the remaining pork stock for another use.

2. Wipe out the casserole. Add 1 cup of the coconut milk and simmer over moderate heat until reduced by half, about 5 minutes. Stir in the curry paste and peanut butter and cook for 1 minute more. Add the remaining 1 cup of coconut milk and the reserved 2 cups of pork stock along with the sweet potato, galangal, lemongrass and shrimp paste. Cover partially and bring to a simmer over moderate heat. Cook until the sweet potato is almost tender, about 10 minutes. Add the eggplant and simmer until just tender, about 10 minutes.

3. Add the pork and chiles to the casserole and simmer over moderate heat until the pork is heated through and the vegetables are tender, 10 minutes. Discard the galangal and lemongrass. Stir in the pineapple and cook until heated through, 1 to 2 minutes. Remove from the heat and stir in the basil. Serve with steamed white rice. —*David Lebovitz*

MAKE AHEAD The pork can be cooked 3 days ahead. Refrigerate it in the stock.

WINE A Riesling with a little bit of sweetness and great acidity: the 2014 Charles Smith Kung Fu Girl.

Sichuan-Style Green Beans with Pork

Total **30 min**; Serves **4**

Three key ingredients go into this fiery stir-fry from F&W's Justin Chapple: ground pork, green beans and dried hot red chiles. To round things out, Chapple adds just garlic, soy sauce and lime juice. The stir-fry is fantastic served over steamed white or brown rice, or rice noodles.

- **2 Tbsp. canola oil**
- **½ lb. ground pork**
- **¾ lb. green beans, thinly sliced crosswise**
- **7 to 10 dried Chinese hot red chiles, cracked**
- **2 garlic cloves, minced**
- **1½ Tbsp. soy sauce**
- **1½ Tbsp. fresh lime juice**
- **Kosher salt and white pepper**
- **Steamed rice, for serving**

In a large skillet, heat the oil until shimmering. Add the ground pork and cook over moderately high heat, breaking it up with a fork, until nearly cooked through, about 5 minutes. Add the green beans, red chiles and garlic and stir-fry over high heat until the green beans are crisp-tender, about 7 minutes. Stir in the soy sauce and lime juice and season with salt and white pepper. Serve with steamed rice. —*Justin Chapple*

WINE Tropical fruit–scented, off-dry German Riesling: 2015 Leitz Dragonstone.

Sausage-and-Potato Pan Roast

Active **20 min**; Total **55 min**; Serves **4 to 6**

We love one-pan dishes for cold-weather weeknight dinners. Simply roast sweet Italian sausages with potatoes and shallots, then toss with arugula and lemon juice before serving.

- 2 **large red potatoes, cut into 1½-inch pieces**
- 2 **Yukon Gold potatoes, cut into 1-inch wedges**
- 1 **large baking potato, cut into 1½-inch pieces**
- 10 **medium unpeeled shallots, halved**
- ⅓ **cup extra-virgin olive oil, plus more for brushing**

  Kosher salt and pepper
- 1½ **lbs. sweet Italian sausage, cut into 3-inch lengths**

  One 8-oz. bunch of arugula, stemmed and chopped
- 1 **Tbsp. fresh lemon juice**

1. Preheat the oven to 425°. On a large rimmed baking sheet, toss all of the potatoes with the shallots and the ⅓ cup of olive oil. Season generously with salt and pepper. Roast for about 15 minutes, until the potatoes are lightly browned. Brush the sausage with olive oil and add to the baking sheet. Roast for 20 to 25 minutes longer, until the potatoes are tender and the sausage is cooked through.

2. Transfer everything on the baking sheet to a platter. Fold in the arugula and lemon juice, season with salt and pepper and serve. —*Justin Chapple*

WINE Cherry-scented, old-school Rioja: 2011 Marqués de Murrieta Rioja Reserva.

Steamed Bok Choy with Mapo-Style Pork

Total **30 min**; Serves **4**

This recipe is great for anyone looking to eat less meat. Crisp steamed bok choy is the star, with just a modest topping of sweet-and-spicy pork reminiscent of the fiery Sichuan specialty mapo tofu.

- 2½ tsp. cornstarch
- 1 Tbsp. canola oil
- ½ lb. ground pork
- ½ tsp. ground Sichuan peppercorns

  Kosher salt
- 1 Tbsp. Asian chile-bean sauce
- 1 Tbsp. hoisin sauce
- 1 Tbsp. soy sauce
- ¼ cup thinly sliced scallions, plus more for garnish

  Four 6- to 8-oz. heads of baby bok choy, halved lengthwise

1. In a small bowl, whisk the cornstarch with 1¼ cups of water. In a large skillet, heat the oil. Add the pork, peppercorns and a generous pinch of salt and cook over high heat, stirring and breaking up the meat, until crumbly and lightly browned, about 3 minutes. Stir in the chile-bean, hoisin and soy sauces and cook, stirring, until fragrant, about 2 minutes. Stir in the cornstarch slurry and simmer until thickened, about 2 minutes. Stir in the ¼ cup of sliced scallions and season with salt. Keep warm over very low heat.

2. Meanwhile, set a steamer basket in a large saucepan. Add 1 inch of water and bring to a boil. Add the bok choy to the basket, cover and steam until crisp-tender, 4 to 6 minutes. Transfer to plates or a platter.

3. Spoon the pork over the bok choy, garnish with sliced scallions and serve right away. —*Justin Chapple*

MAKE AHEAD The pork can be refrigerated overnight. Reheat gently.

WINE Bright, peachy Riesling: 2014 Hermann J. Wiemer Finger Lakes Dry.

Sausage Choucroute

Active **10 min**; Total **55 min**; Serves **4**

Choucroute is a classic Alsatian comfort food made with sauerkraut, boiled potatoes and half a dozen types of sausage and smoked meat. It can take hours to cook, but our shortcut version is ready in less than 60 minutes.

- 1 **lb. mixed sausages, such as bratwurst and fresh chorizo**
- 1 **lb. small Yukon Gold potatoes, quartered**

  One 25-oz. jar sauerkraut, drained (3 cups)
- 2 **Tbsp. extra-virgin olive oil**
- 1 **tsp. caraway seeds**

  Kosher salt and pepper

  Crusty bread and grainy mustard, for serving

Preheat the oven to 425°. In a large cast-iron skillet, toss the sausages with the potatoes, sauerkraut, olive oil and caraway seeds; season with salt and pepper. Roast until the potatoes are golden and cooked through, about 45 minutes. Serve the sausage choucroute with crusty bread and mustard. —*Kay Chun*

WINE Ripe, lightly off-dry Alsace Riesling: 2015 Domaine Weinbach Cuvée Theo Riesling.

FOOLPROOF COOKING

Grill Sausages Like A Pro

Too often when sausages come off the heat they're over- or undercooked. No one wants to be that person who cuts into the meat to tell if it's done (losing juices in the process). Instead, char the sausages, then poach them in beer in a skillet set on the grill–which lets the sausages cook all the way through and infuses them with a smoky flavor–then char again to crisp. The method works with all kinds of sausage. —*Chef Tim Wiechmann, Bronwyn, Somerville, Massachusetts*

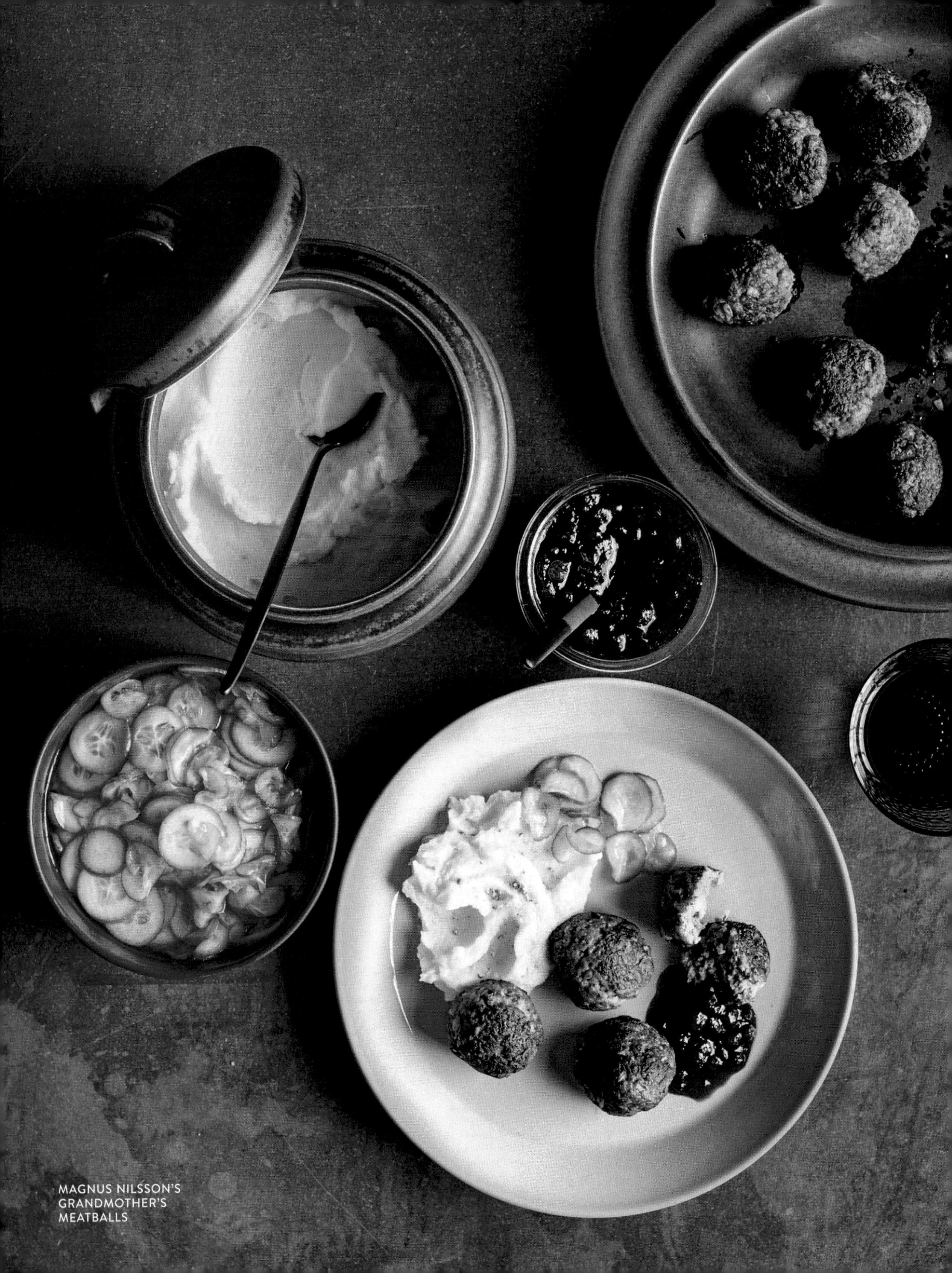

MAGNUS NILSSON'S
GRANDMOTHER'S
MEATBALLS

Spiced Brown Sugar Ham with Apple Jus

Active **20 min**; Total **5 hr 30 min**
Serves **8 to 10**

Make sure to keep the ham wrapped in foil while resting (two hours is ideal) so the meat can reabsorb any moisture released during cooking. "If you can't pick up the foil-wrapped ham without burning yourself, then it's not done resting!" says Georgia chef Kevin Gillespie.

> **One 1-lb. box light brown sugar**
> 2 **Tbsp. freshly ground black pepper**
> 1½ **tsp. ground cloves**
> 1½ **tsp. ground cinnamon**
> **One 8- to 10-lb. bone-in smoked ham, skin removed**
> 3 **medium Fuji apples—peeled, cored and thinly sliced**
> 2 **Tbsp. apple cider vinegar**
> **Kosher salt**

1. Preheat the oven to 350°. In a medium bowl, mix the sugar with the pepper, cloves and cinnamon.

2. Place the ham fat side up on 2 large pieces of aluminum foil and, using your hands, rub the sugar mixture all over the top and side; it should form a thick layer. Wrap the ham tightly in the foil and transfer to a large roasting pan. Bake for about 3 hours, until glossy on the outside and a thermometer inserted in the thickest part of the meat registers 125°. Transfer the ham to a work surface and let rest in the foil at room temperature until cool enough to handle, about 2 hours.

3. Unwrap the ham and slice the meat; transfer to a large platter and tent with foil to keep warm. Pour the accumulated juices into a large measuring cup and spoon off any fat. You should have about 3¼ cups.

4. In a medium saucepan, combine the sliced apples with 2 tablespoons of water. Cover and cook over moderate heat, stirring occasionally, until tender, about 10 minutes. Using a slotted spoon, transfer the apples to a blender and puree with the ham juices and vinegar until smooth. Strain the apple jus through a fine-mesh sieve set over a gravy boat and season with salt. Serve the ham, passing the apple jus at the table. —*Kevin Gillespie*

WINE Fruit-forward, luscious Zinfandel: 2014 Seghesio Sonoma County.

Sausages with Peaches and Pickled Chiles

Active **30 min**; Total **1 hr 30 min**; Serves **4**

Use your best peaches for this supersimple grilled main dish from Tandy Wilson, the chef at City House in Nashville. They add a pleasantly sweet contrast to the spicy sausages and tangy pickles.

> ¼ **cup apple cider vinegar**
> ¼ **cup distilled white vinegar**
> 3 **Tbsp. sorghum syrup or molasses**
> 1½ **tsp. kosher salt**
> 2 **jalapeños, seeded and thinly sliced**
> 1 **small onion, thinly sliced**
> **Canola oil, for brushing**
> **Six 4-oz. hot Italian sausages**
> 2 **medium peaches, pitted and sliced ¼ inch thick**

1. In a 1-quart jar, shake both vinegars with the sorghum syrup, salt and ½ cup of water until the salt dissolves. Add the jalapeños and onion, cover and let stand at room temperature for at least 1 hour.

2. Light a grill and oil the grate. Grill the sausages over moderate heat, turning, until lightly charred and cooked through, 10 to 12 minutes. Transfer to a cutting board and let rest for 5 minutes, then thinly slice on the bias.

3. Arrange the sliced peaches on a platter. Top with the sausages and some of the pickled jalapeños and onion. Drizzle with some of the pickling liquid and serve the remaining pickles on the side.
—*Tandy Wilson*

MAKE AHEAD The drained pickles can be refrigerated for up to 1 week.

WINE Fresh Provençal rosé: 2015 Bieler Père et Fils Sabine.

Magnus Nilsson's Grandmother's Meatballs

Total **50 min**; Makes **18**

Milk-and-cream-soaked breadcrumbs and a cooked potato are the secrets to these ultratender Swedish meatballs from chef Magnus Nilsson of Fäviken in Järpen, Sweden. Serve them as he does, with lingonberry jam and mashed potatoes.

> 1 **medium baking potato (8 oz.), peeled and cut into 2-inch pieces**
> 1 **large egg, beaten**
> ⅓ **cup plus 1 Tbsp. whole milk**
> ⅓ **cup plus 1 Tbsp. heavy cream**
> ¾ **cup plus 2 Tbsp. plain dry breadcrumbs**
> 12 **oz. ground pork**
> 12 **oz. ground beef**
> 1 **small onion, finely chopped**
> 2 **tsp. kosher salt**
> ½ **tsp. ground white pepper**
> 4 **Tbsp. unsalted butter**
> **Quick-Pickled Sweet Cucumbers (p. 218)**
> **Mashed potatoes and lingonberry jam, for serving**

1. In a small saucepan, cook the potato in salted boiling water until tender, about 12 minutes. Drain well, then pass through a ricer into a bowl. Let cool.

2. Meanwhile, preheat the oven to 425°. In a large bowl, whisk the egg with the milk and cream. Stir in the breadcrumbs and let stand for 5 minutes to soften. Add the pork, beef, onion, salt, pepper and riced potato and mix just until combined. Shape the mixture into 18 meatballs.

3. In a large ovenproof nonstick skillet, melt 2 tablespoons of the butter. Add half of the meatballs and cook over moderate heat, turning, until golden all over, about 8 minutes. Transfer to a plate and wipe out the skillet. Repeat with the remaining 2 tablespoons of butter and meatballs.

4. Return all of the meatballs to the skillet and bake until cooked through, about 10 minutes. Transfer to a platter and serve with the Quick-Pickled Sweet Cucumbers, mashed potatoes and lingonberry jam.
—*Magnus Nilsson*

WINE A generously fruity Zinfandel: the 2012 Buehler Vineyards Napa Valley.

Veal Chops with Sage and Plums

Active **30 min**; Total **1 hr**; Serves **4**

Italy-based blogger Skye McAlpine dusts her veal chops with flour before sautéing to give them a light, crisp coating. If you can't find firm plums, she suggests grapes as a good alternative.

> **Four 15-oz. bone-in veal rib chops, cut about 1 inch thick**
>
> **Kosher salt and pepper**
>
> ¼ **cup all-purpose flour**
>
> 3 **Tbsp. unsalted butter**
>
> ¼ **cup plus 2 tsp. extra-virgin olive oil**
>
> 4 **sage sprigs plus ¼ cup sage leaves**
>
> 6 **firm plums, quartered**

1. Pat the veal chops dry with paper towels and let them stand at room temperature for 30 minutes.

2. Generously season the chops with salt and pepper. Coat the chops with the flour, tapping off the excess. In each of 2 large skillets, melt 1½ tablespoons of the butter in 2 tablespoons of the olive oil over moderately high heat. Add 2 chops to each skillet and cook until golden brown on one side, about 9 minutes. Add 2 sage sprigs to each skillet and turn the chops. Continue cooking, basting occasionally with the sage butter, until the chops are golden brown and an instant-read thermometer inserted in the thickest part registers 125° for medium-rare or 135° for medium, 8 to 10 minutes longer. Transfer the veal chops to a platter and cover loosely with foil to keep warm. Discard the sage sprigs.

3. Add the sage leaves to one of the skillets and cook over moderately high heat until crisp, about 2 minutes. Drain on paper towels. Add the plums to the skillet along with the remaining 2 teaspoons of olive oil and season with salt and pepper. Cook, stirring occasionally, until the plums are just softened and lightly caramelized, 3 to 4 minutes. Scrape the plums and any accumulated pan juices over the chops, garnish with the crisp sage leaves and serve. —*Skye McAlpine*

WINE Richly textured Soave Classico: 2014 Suavia Monte Carbonare.

Wiener Schnitzel with Potato-Cucumber Salad

Active **50 min**; Total **1 hr 15 min**; Serves **4**

At San Luis, a mountain retreat in Italy's Alto Adige, the regional cuisine is heavily influenced by neighboring Austria and Germany. This classic schnitzel is a perfect example, though chef Arturo Spicocchi lightens up the traditional potato salad by folding in thinly sliced cucumber.

> 1½ **lbs. fingerling potatoes**
>
> **Kosher salt and pepper**
>
> ⅓ **cup apple cider vinegar**
>
> 2 **Tbsp. finely chopped dill, plus sprigs for garnish**
>
> 1 **Tbsp. whole-grain mustard**
>
> ¼ **cup plus 2 Tbsp. canola oil, plus more for frying**
>
> 1 **English cucumber, halved lengthwise and sliced ¼ inch thick**
>
> ⅓ **cup minced red onion**
>
> 1 **cup all-purpose flour**
>
> 2 **large eggs, beaten**
>
> 1½ **cups plain dry breadcrumbs**
>
> **Four 5-oz. veal cutlets, pounded ¼ inch thick**
>
> **Lemon wedges, for serving**

1. In a large saucepan, cover the potatoes with cold water and bring to a boil. Add a generous pinch of salt and simmer until tender, 15 to 20 minutes. Drain and let cool, then halve lengthwise.

2. In a large bowl, whisk the vinegar with the chopped dill and mustard. Gradually whisk in the ¼ cup plus 2 tablespoons of oil. Add the potatoes, cucumber and red onion and toss to coat.

3. Put the flour, beaten eggs and breadcrumbs in 3 separate shallow bowls. Season the veal cutlets with salt and pepper, then dredge in the flour and shake off the excess. Dip the cutlets in the eggs, then gently dredge in the breadcrumbs.

4. In a large skillet, heat ¼ inch of oil until shimmering. Add half of the veal cutlets in a single layer and cook over moderately high heat, turning once, until golden brown and crisp, about 5 minutes. Drain the schnitzels on a paper towel–lined plate, sprinkle with salt and transfer to a platter. Repeat with the remaining veal. Garnish the schnitzels with dill sprigs and serve with the potato-cucumber salad and lemon wedges. —*Arturo Spicocchi*

WINE Aromatic Alto Adige white: 2014 Alois Lageder Vogelmaier Moscato Giallo.

RECIPE IMPROV

Switch Up Your Schnitzel

Wiener schnitzel is the ultimate comfort food: juicy, tender veal cutlets coated with crispy breadcrumbs. After mastering the classic version, try your hand at these five equally delicious variations.

PANKO These Japanese crumbs made from white bread have large flakes; when fried, they offer a satisfying crunch.

POTATO CHIPS Instead of breadcrumbs, dredge your cutlets in finely crushed potato chips. Go classic with plain or sea salt varieties, or for an unexpected hit of tang, try salt-and-vinegar chips.

LAMB Swap in thinly pounded lamb leg steaks for a more robust alternative to milder veal, pork or chicken schnitzel.

FISH Skinless fillets of firm fish like trout also benefit from the schnitzel treatment. Bonus: Since fish fillets are already thin, you don't need to pound them.

ITALIAN With just a few more ingredients, transform schnitzel into veal Parmesan: Smother the fried cutlets with tomato sauce, top with shredded mozzarella and bake until the cheese is bubbling.

BEEF AND LAMB

In her home kitchen, Seattle chef Renee Erickson butter-bastes her steaks for the best crust (p. 187). OPPOSITE Aussie Burgers (p. 201).

BONE-IN RIB EYES
WITH GRILLED ONION
JAM

Bone-In Rib Eye Steaks with Grilled Onion Jam

Total **1 hr;** Serves **4**

Chef Dan Kluger of Loring Place in New York City starts his rib eyes at room temperature and turns them often so they cook evenly. When they're done, he brushes the steaks with a garlicky herb butter and serves them with a tangy-sweet onion jam.

ONION JAM

- 3 red onions, sliced

  Extra-virgin olive oil, for brushing

  Kosher salt and pepper
- 1 cup apple cider vinegar
- ¼ cup pure maple syrup
- ¼ tsp. finely chopped thyme

STEAKS

- Two 1½-lb. bone-in rib eye steaks (1½ inches thick), at room temperature

  Extra-virgin olive oil, for brushing

  Kosher salt and pepper
- 2 Tbsp. unsalted butter, softened
- 2 tsp. minced rosemary
- 2 tsp. minced thyme
- 2 garlic cloves, grated

1. Make the onion jam Light a grill or heat a grill pan. Brush the onions with olive oil and season with salt and pepper. Grill over moderate heat, turning once, until lightly charred and tender, about 7 minutes.

2. In a saucepan, bring the vinegar and maple syrup to a boil. Add the onions and simmer over moderately low heat until tender, about 8 minutes. Transfer to a bowl; let cool. Stir in the thyme. Season with salt and pepper.

3. Make the steaks Light a grill or heat a grill pan. Brush the steaks with oil and season with salt and pepper. Stand the steaks on their fatty edges (bone side up) and cook over moderate heat until the fat has started to render and is lightly charred, 5 minutes. Lay the steaks flat. Grill, turning often, until an instant-read thermometer inserted in the thickest part registers 120°, 12 to 15 minutes. If using a grill pan, carefully blot excess fat with paper towels to prevent flare-ups. Transfer to a cutting board; let rest for 10 minutes. Leave the grill on.

4. In a bowl, blend the butter, rosemary, thyme and garlic. Brush the herb butter on the steaks and grill over high heat, turning once, until sizzling, 1 minute per side. Transfer to a carving board. Slice the steaks and serve with the onion jam. —*Dan Kluger*

WINE Blackberry-scented Shiraz: 2014 Clonakilla Hilltops.

New York Steaks with Roasted Chiles

Active **40 min;** Total **1 hr;** Serves **4**

Simplicity is the key to this recipe from chef Jonathan Waxman. The perfectly grilled steaks need no embellishment beyond roasted chiles and sautéed onions.

- 8 Hatch or Anaheim chiles (1 lb.)
- 2 Tbsp. unsalted butter
- ¼ cup extra-virgin olive oil
- 2 medium onions, thinly sliced

  Kosher salt and pepper

  Four 10-oz. New York strip steaks (¾ inch thick)

1. Roast the chiles over a gas flame or broil them, turning with tongs, until charred all over, about 10 minutes. Transfer to a bowl and cover with plastic wrap; let steam for 15 minutes. Slip off and discard the skins. Stem and seed the chiles, then thinly slice lengthwise.

2. Meanwhile, in a large cast-iron skillet, melt 1 tablespoon of the butter in 2 tablespoons of the olive oil. Add the onions, season with salt and pepper and cook over moderate heat, stirring occasionally, until deep golden, 15 minutes. Stir in the roasted chiles and the remaining 1 tablespoon of butter. Keep warm.

3. Heat a grill pan. Rub the steaks with the remaining 2 tablespoons of olive oil; season with salt and pepper. Cook over moderately high heat, turning once, until nicely charred and medium-rare, about 3 minutes per side. Transfer to plates and let rest for 5 minutes. Serve with the chile-onion mixture. —*Jonathan Waxman*

WINE Juicy, herb-scented California red: 2013 Bebame Red.

Rib Eye Steaks with Togarashi-Lime Butter

Active **25 min;** Total **1 hr 15 min;** Serves **4**

Seattle chef Renee Erickson declares this steak would be her last meal. Basting the rib eyes with a delicious butter spiked with lime and the Japanese spice mix togarashi gives them an incredible caramelized crust.

- Two 1½-lb. bone-in rib eye steaks (1½ inches thick)
- 1 stick plus 5 Tbsp. unsalted butter, softened
- 1½ Tbsp. shichimi togarashi
- 1 tsp. finely grated lime zest plus 1 Tbsp. fresh lime juice

  Kosher salt

  Flaky sea salt, lime wedges and crusty bread, for serving

1. Place the steaks on a platter and let stand at room temperature for 45 minutes. Meanwhile, in a medium bowl, using a hand mixer, beat the stick of butter at medium speed until light and fluffy. Beat in the togarashi, lime zest and juice and ¼ teaspoon of kosher salt. Keep the togarashi butter at room temperature while you cook the steaks.

2. Melt 1½ tablespoons of the butter in each of 2 large cast-iron skillets over moderately high heat. Season the steaks generously with kosher salt. When the butter has stopped foaming, add 1 steak to each skillet and cook undisturbed until deeply browned on one side, about 6 minutes. Flip the steaks and add 1 tablespoon of butter to each pan. Continue cooking the steaks, basting frequently with butter, until they are well browned on both sides and an instant-read thermometer inserted into the thickest part registers 125° for medium-rare, 7 to 9 minutes longer. Transfer to a cutting board, cover with foil and let rest for 10 minutes.

3. Spread half of the togarashi butter on each steak and sprinkle with flaky salt. Thinly slice the steaks across the grain and serve with lime wedges and crusty bread. —*Renee Erickson*

MAKE AHEAD The togarashi butter can be refrigerated for up to 4 days. Bring to room temperature before serving.

WINE French Cabernet Franc: 2015 Domaine Philippe Alliet Chinon.

Grilled Hanger Steak with Spring Vegetables and Hazelnuts

Active **1 hr;** Total **3 hr 15 min;** Serves **4 to 6**

San Francisco chef Trevor Krunk includes a surprise ingredient in the salad that accompanies this grilled marinated steak: rhubarb. It adds a delicious tartness to the watercress, asparagus and peas.

1½ Tbsp. smoked sweet paprika

2 medium shallots, halved and thinly sliced

6 Tbsp. extra-virgin olive oil

 Kosher salt and pepper

 Two ¾- to 1-lb. hanger steaks

1 cup hazelnuts

1 cup fresh English peas (5 oz.)

½ lb. asparagus, cut into 1-inch lengths

4 oz. watercress, large stems trimmed (about 6 cups)

2 Tbsp. minced rhubarb

1 Tbsp. minced peeled fresh ginger

½ tsp. finely grated lemon zest plus 2 Tbsp. fresh lemon juice

1. In a small bowl, mix the paprika with the shallots, 3 tablespoons of the olive oil and 1½ tablespoons each of salt and pepper. Rub the marinade all over the steaks and refrigerate for 2 to 6 hours. Let return to room temperature before grilling.

2. Meanwhile, preheat the oven to 375°. In a pie plate, bake the hazelnuts for about 8 minutes, until lightly browned. Transfer to a clean kitchen towel and rub the nuts together to remove the skins. Coarsely chop the nuts.

3. In a medium saucepan of salted boiling water, blanch the peas until crisp-tender, 2 to 3 minutes. Using a slotted spoon, transfer the peas to an ice bath to cool. Add the asparagus to the boiling water and cook until crisp-tender, 1 to 2 minutes; transfer to the ice bath to cool. Drain the peas and asparagus and pat dry.

4. Light a grill or heat a grill pan. Scrape the marinade off the steaks. Grill the steaks over moderately high heat, turning occasionally, until lightly charred all over and medium-rare within, about 10 minutes. Transfer to a cutting board and let rest for 5 minutes.

5. In a large bowl, toss the watercress with the peas, asparagus, hazelnuts, rhubarb, ginger, lemon zest, lemon juice and the remaining 3 tablespoons of olive oil. Season with salt and pepper. Slice the steaks across the grain and serve with the salad. —*Trevor Kunk*

WINE Oregon Pinot Noir: 2014 St. Innocent Villages Cuvée.

Lemon-Garlic-Marinated Flank Steak

Active **40 min;** Total **2 hr 15 min** Serves **6 to 8**

20 garlic cloves, peeled

2¼ cups extra-virgin olive oil

 Kosher salt and pepper

 Two 1¼-lb. flank steaks

1½ cups fresh lemon juice (from about 8 lemons)

2 Tbsp. dried oregano

1. In a small saucepan, cover the garlic cloves with 1½ cups of the olive oil; cook over low heat until the garlic is tender and golden brown, 35 to 40 minutes. Strain the garlic through a fine sieve set over a bowl; reserve the garlicky oil for another use. In a small bowl, mash the garlic with 1½ tablespoons of salt and 1½ teaspoons of pepper. Rub 3 tablespoons of the garlic paste all over the steaks.

2. In a medium bowl, whisk the lemon juice with the remaining ¾ cup of olive oil and the oregano. Place the steaks in a 9-by-13-inch baking dish and coat with 1½ cups of the lemony marinade. Reserve the marinade remaining in the bowl. Let the steaks stand at room temperature for 1 hour.

3. Light a grill. Remove the steaks from the marinade, pat dry and season with salt and pepper. Discard the marinade in the baking dish. Grill the steaks over moderately high heat, turning once, until lightly charred and an instant-read thermometer inserted in the thickest part registers 125°, 8 to 10 minutes. Dip the grilled steaks in the reserved marinade in the bowl and transfer to a carving board. Spread the remaining garlic paste on the steaks and let stand for 5 minutes. Thinly slice the meat against the grain and serve. —*Jimmy Bannos, Jr.*

WINE Spicy Côtes du Rhône: 2014 Domaine de la Bastide Cuvée les Figues.

Beef Tenderloin Steaks with Mushroom Sauce

Total **1 hr;** Serves **4**

Store-bought demiglace, a concentrated stock, is a go-to in traditional French kitchens. It adds instant depth and richness to the silky mushroom sauce served with these tenderloins.

6 Tbsp. unsalted butter

12 oz. mixed mushrooms, coarsely chopped

 Kosher salt and pepper

2 cups chicken stock or low-sodium broth

2 Tbsp. demiglace (1.5 oz.)

 Four 6-oz. center-cut beef tenderloin steaks

2 Tbsp. extra-virgin olive oil

1. Preheat the oven to 450°. In a large cast-iron skillet, melt 2 tablespoons of the butter. Add the mushrooms and cook over moderate heat, stirring occasionally, until golden brown, about 10 minutes. Season with salt and pepper. Add the stock and demiglace and bring to a boil. Simmer the sauce until thickened, about 10 minutes. Whisk in the remaining 4 tablespoons of butter and season with salt and pepper. Transfer the mushroom sauce to a medium bowl or saucepan and keep warm. Clean the skillet.

2. Heat the skillet. Rub the steaks with the olive oil and season with salt and pepper. Sear over moderately high heat until browned, about 2 minutes per side. Transfer the skillet to the oven and cook the steaks until an instant-read thermometer inserted in the thickest part registers 125°, 6 to 8 minutes. Transfer the steaks to a work surface and let rest for 5 minutes. Serve the steaks with the mushroom sauce. —*John Besh and Chris Lusk*

SERVE WITH Mashed potatoes and sautéed Broccolini.

MAKE AHEAD The mushroom sauce can be refrigerated for up to 2 days and reheated gently before serving.

WINE Herb-inflected red blend: 2012 Robert Sinskey Vineyards Los Carneros POV.

POUNDED BEEF
TENDERLOIN
WITH HEARTS OF
PALM SALAD

Pounded Beef Tenderloin with Hearts of Palm Salad

◔ Total **30 min;** Serves **4**

If you're trying to eat less meat, you can stretch a small amount creatively. This recipe calls for pounding beef tenderloin fillets thin and grilling them superquickly, so they stay tender and juicy.

- **1 lb. center-cut beef tenderloin, cut crosswise into 4 slices and lightly pounded ⅛ inch thick**
- **2 Tbsp. extra-virgin olive oil, plus more for brushing**
- **Kosher salt and pepper**
- **1½ Tbsp. fresh lemon juice, plus lemon wedges for serving**
- **2 Tbsp. minced shallot**
- **1½ tsp. Dijon mustard**
- **4 oz. watercress, thick stems discarded (6 cups)**
- **One 15-oz. can hearts of palm, drained and sliced ¼ inch thick on the diagonal**
- **1 Hass avocado, peeled and cut into 1-inch pieces**
- **⅓ cup snipped chives**

1. Heat a large grill pan for 10 minutes. Brush the steaks with oil; season with salt and pepper. Grill over high heat until lightly charred, 45 seconds. Flip and grill until medium-rare, 30 seconds. Transfer to plates.

2. In a large bowl, whisk the 2 tablespoons of oil with the lemon juice, shallot and mustard; season with salt and pepper. Add the watercress, hearts of palm and avocado, season with salt and pepper and toss. Mound the salad beside the steaks, top with the chives and serve with lemon wedges. —*Justin Chapple*

WINE Minerally, light red: 2013 Domaine Robert Chevillon Bourgogne Passetoutgrain.

Flatiron Steaks with Poblano Mash and Tomatillo Sauce

Active **45 min;** Total **2 hr 15 min;** Serves **4**

L.A. chef Jeremy Fox reinvents a staple side for steak, folding charred poblanos into mashed potatoes and serving the indulgent dish with a bold tomatillo sauce.

TOMATILLO SAUCE

- **1½ lbs. tomatillos, husked and rinsed**
- **1 medium onion, quartered**
- **1 Tbsp. extra-virgin olive oil**
- **½ tsp. finely chopped garlic**
- **1 tsp. chopped parsley**
- **1 tsp. chopped cilantro**
- **1½ tsp. sugar**
- **Kosher salt**

POBLANO MASH

- **2 baking potatoes (1¼ lbs.), scrubbed but not peeled**
- **1 lb. poblano chiles**
- **4 Tbsp. unsalted butter, at room temperature**
- **½ cup heavy cream, warmed**
- **Kosher salt**

STEAKS

- **Four 10-oz. flatiron steaks (1 inch thick), kept at room temperature for 30 minutes**
- **2 Tbsp. canola oil**
- **Kosher salt and pepper**
- **Lemon wedges, for serving**

1. Make the tomatillo sauce Preheat the oven to 450°. Put the tomatillos and onion on a foil-lined baking sheet and roast for about 20 minutes, stirring occasionally, until charred in spots and blistered. Scrape the vegetables into a medium saucepan and cook over moderate heat, stirring and mashing with a wooden spoon occasionally, until almost all of the liquid has evaporated, about 15 minutes. Scrape the mixture into a medium bowl. Stir in the olive oil, garlic, parsley, cilantro and sugar; season the sauce with salt.

2. Make the poblano mash Put the potatoes in a large saucepan and add enough water to cover them by 2 inches. Bring to a simmer and cook until the potatoes are tender, about 45 minutes. Drain and cool slightly, then peel. Return the potatoes to the saucepan.

3. Meanwhile, cook the poblanos directly over a gas flame or under the broiler, turning, until they are charred all over, 8 to 10 minutes. Transfer to a heatproof bowl, cover with plastic wrap and let steam for about 15 minutes. Peel, seed and chop the poblanos.

4. Mash the potatoes with the butter and cream until well blended. Fold in the poblanos and season with salt. Keep the poblano mash warm.

5. Cook the steaks Heat a large cast-iron skillet. Coat the steaks with the canola oil and season with salt and pepper. Cook until browned outside and medium-rare within, 5 to 7 minutes per side. Transfer to a cutting board and let rest for 10 minutes. Thinly slice against the grain and serve with the tomatillo sauce, poblano mash and lemon wedges for squeezing over the steaks. —*Jeremy Fox*

WINE Gamay-like California red: 2013 Cruse Wine Co. Napa Valley Valdiguié.

CHEF POINTERS

Steak Tips from the Pros

HEAT THE PAN "Get the pan as hot as you can, then get it twice as hot. When you put a cold steak in a pan that's not hot enough, you'll just have gray steak." —*Grant Achatz, Alinea, Chicago*

FLIP THE MEAT "It's OK to turn the steak a few times in the skillet–it gets the blood moving." —*Alex Guarnaschelli, Butter, New York City*

LET IT REST "A good steak should rest in a warm spot near the grill for at least half the time it took to cook, in order for the juices to settle inside. Otherwise, when you slice the meat, the juices will run out onto the cutting board." —*Lee Hefter, CUT, Beverly Hills*

Brisket with Apricots and Prunes

Active **30 min;** Total **3 hr 40 min**
Serves **6 to 8**

To keep the meat moist in the dry heat of the oven, Julia Turshen, author of *Small Victories,* covers it with a damp piece of crumpled parchment. "In this case, a wet blanket is a good thing!" she says.

One 3½- to 4½-lb. brisket, preferably second cut

Kosher salt

2 **Tbsp. extra-virgin olive oil**

1 **large yellow onion, thinly sliced**

6 **thyme sprigs**

4 **garlic cloves, crushed**

2 **Tbsp. tomato paste**

1 **tsp. hot smoked paprika (pimentón)**

¼ **tsp. ground cinnamon**

One 15-oz. can whole peeled tomatoes

1½ **cups chicken stock or low-sodium broth**

12 **pitted prunes**

12 **dried Turkish apricots**

1. Preheat the oven to 325°. Season the brisket with salt. In a large enameled cast-iron casserole, heat the olive oil. Add the brisket and cook over moderately high heat until browned all over, 4 to 5 minutes. Transfer to a large plate.

2. Add the onion to the casserole and cook over moderate heat, stirring occasionally, until softened, about 5 minutes. Add the thyme, garlic, tomato paste, paprika and cinnamon and cook, stirring, until the tomato paste is deep red in color, 1 to 2 minutes. Add the tomatoes and chicken stock and bring to a boil. Remove from the heat and stir in the prunes and apricots. Return the brisket and its juices to the casserole.

3. Scrunch up a large piece of parchment paper and moisten it with water. Spread the wet parchment over the brisket, cover and braise in the oven until tender, about 3 hours. Transfer to a work surface and let rest for 10 minutes. Discard the thyme sprigs. Slice the brisket across the grain and serve with the sauce. —*Julia Turshen*

MAKE AHEAD The brisket can be cooled to room temperature and refrigerated in its sauce for up to 5 days. Reheat gently in a 350° oven or on the stovetop before serving.

WINE Spicy Pinot Noir: 2014 Lazy Creek Middleridge Ranch.

Pepper-Crusted Skirt Steak with Charred Leeks

Active **45 min;** Total **3 hr 45 min**
Serves **4 to 6**

Chef Alex Guarnaschelli says that the easiest way to crack the peppercorns and coriander seeds for this recipe is to crush them under a flat-bottomed skillet. Put the heel of your hand in the skillet, then push down and out away from you.

4 **Tbsp. unsalted butter**

2 **tsp. coarsely cracked coriander seeds**

2 **tsp. coarsely cracked black peppercorns**

2 **tsp. coarsely cracked white peppercorns**

¾ **tsp. crushed red pepper**

1 **Tbsp. packed dark brown sugar**

Kosher salt

2 **lbs. skirt steak, cut into 5-inch lengths**

4 **medium leeks (2½ lbs.), white and light green parts only, halved lengthwise and cleaned**

2 **Tbsp. Dijon mustard**

2 **Tbsp. balsamic vinegar**

3 **Tbsp. canola oil**

2 **Tbsp. fresh lemon juice**

1. In a small skillet, melt the butter. Add the coriander, all the peppercorns and the crushed red pepper and cook over moderately low heat for 1 minute. Scrape into a medium bowl and stir in the brown sugar and 1½ tablespoons of salt. Rub the mixture all over the steak and transfer to a baking dish. Cover with plastic wrap and refrigerate for 3 hours.

2. In a large saucepan of salted boiling water, blanch the leeks until just tender, 3 to 4 minutes. Using tongs, transfer them cut side down to a paper towel–lined baking sheet to drain.

3. In a small bowl, whisk the mustard with the vinegar.

4. In a large cast-iron skillet, heat 1 tablespoon of the oil over high heat until smoking. Add half of the steak and cook over high heat, turning a few times, until lightly charred on the outside and medium-rare within, 4 to 5 minutes. Transfer to a carving board, spread with some of the Dijon vinegar and let rest for 10 minutes. Repeat with 1 tablespoon of the oil and the remaining steak and Dijon vinegar.

5. Wipe out the skillet and heat the remaining 1 tablespoon of oil in it. Add the leeks cut side down and cook over high heat until lightly charred on the bottom, about 3 minutes. Transfer to a platter and drizzle with the lemon juice. Slice the steak against the grain and serve with the leeks. —*Alex Guarnaschelli*

WINE French Cabernet Franc: 2013 Béatrice et Pascal Lambert Les Terrasses Chinon.

Pinot Noir–Braised Pot Roast with Root Vegetables

Active **1 hr;** Total **2 hr 30 min;** Serves **4**

This recipe from Ben Dailey of Cebo in Geneva, New York, is for anyone who loves wine, since that's the only liquid the meat braises in. Be sure to pick a bottle that's rich and fruity; Dailey is a fan of the 2013 Pinot Noir from nearby Finger Lakes wine pioneer Dr. Konstantin Frank.

POT ROAST

2 **Tbsp. extra-virgin olive oil**

2 **lbs. chuck roast, cut into 1½-inch cubes**

Kosher salt and pepper

All-purpose flour, for dredging

6 **medium carrots, peeled and cut into 1-inch pieces**

3 **medium parsnips, peeled and cut into 1-inch pieces**

2 **leeks, white and light green parts only, cut into 1-inch pieces**

1 **lb. celery root, peeled and cut into 1-inch pieces**

One 750-ml bottle fruity Pinot Noir

4 **Tbsp. unsalted butter**

1 **tsp. white balsamic vinegar**

PICKLED RED ONION

- 1 red onion, thinly sliced
- ½ cup white balsamic vinegar
- 1 bay leaf
- 1 Tbsp. sugar
- 1 Tbsp. kosher salt
- 1 tsp. whole pink peppercorns

MASHED POTATOES

- 1½ lbs. Yukon Gold potatoes, peeled and cut into 2-inch pieces
- 1 sweet onion, chopped
- Kosher salt and pepper
- 4 Tbsp. unsalted butter
- Chopped parsley, for garnish
- Extra-virgin olive oil, for drizzling

1. Make the pot roast In a large enameled cast-iron casserole, heat the olive oil. Season the meat with salt and pepper and dredge in flour. Working in 2 batches, sear the meat over moderately high heat until browned all over, 5 minutes per batch; transfer to a plate. Add the vegetables to the casserole and cook over moderate heat for 5 minutes. Return the meat and juices to the pot, add the wine and bring to a boil. Cover and cook over low heat, stirring occasionally, until the meat is tender, 1 hour and 30 minutes. Stir in the butter and vinegar; season with salt and pepper.

2. Make the pickled red onion Pack the sliced red onion into a 1-quart jar. In a saucepan, combine the vinegar, bay leaf, sugar, salt, peppercorns and 1½ cups of water and bring to a boil until the sugar is dissolved. Pour the brine over the red onion and let cool; drain well.

3. Make the mashed potatoes In a medium saucepan, cover the potatoes and onion with cold water and bring to a boil. Add a big pinch of salt and simmer until the potatoes are very tender, 40 minutes. Drain the potatoes; return to the saucepan. Add the butter, season with salt and pepper and whisk until a chunky puree forms.

4. Spoon the mashed potatoes into shallow bowls. Top with the pot roast, garnish with the pickled red onion and parsley and drizzle with olive oil; serve. —*Ben Dailey*

MAKE AHEAD The pot roast can be refrigerated for up to 2 days.

WINE Peppery Syrah: 2011 Element Winery Finger Lakes.

Rib Eye Roast with Black Garlic–Red Wine Gravy

Active **1 hr**; Total **5 hr 30 min**; Serves **8**

Grant Achatz, the visionary chef at Alinea in Chicago, gives his elegant roast unexpected flavor with an ultrasavory shallot-and-prune marinade. His pro tip: Using a spoonful of soy sauce in the gravy adds incredible umami.

ROAST

- 1 cup canola oil
- ½ cup pitted prunes
- 4 shallots, chopped
- ⅓ cup rosemary leaves
- 3 Tbsp. juniper berries
- 3 garlic cloves, crushed
- 1½ Tbsp. kosher salt
- 1 tsp. pepper
- One 5- to 6-lb. cap-on boneless rib eye roast

GRAVY

- 1 stick unsalted butter
- ½ cup finely chopped shallots
- 2 heads of black garlic, peeled (⅓ cup; see Note)
- 1 garlic clove, crushed
- ½ cup plus 2 Tbsp. all-purpose flour
- 1½ Tbsp. light brown sugar
- 1 cup plus 1 Tbsp. dry red wine
- 1 Tbsp. soy sauce
- 1 qt. beef broth
- 3 thyme sprigs
- 1 rosemary sprig
- 1 tsp. red wine vinegar
- Kosher salt and pepper

1. Make the roast In a blender, combine all of the ingredients except the rib eye and puree until smooth. Set a rack in a roasting pan. Set the roast on the rack and rub the marinade all over. Let stand at room temperature for 2 hours.

2. Preheat the oven to 350°. Roast the beef for about 2 hours, until an instant-read thermometer inserted in the center registers 120°. Transfer the roast to a rack and let stand for 30 minutes.

3. Meanwhile, make the gravy In a medium saucepan, melt the butter. Add the shallots and cook over moderate heat, stirring occasionally, until golden, about 5 minutes. Stir in the black garlic, crushed garlic, flour and sugar and cook, stirring often, until a golden-brown paste forms, about 5 minutes longer. Stir in 1 cup of the wine and the soy sauce and simmer for 2 minutes, then add the broth, thyme and rosemary. Bring to a simmer and cook, stirring occasionally, until thickened and reduced to 4 cups, about 30 minutes.

4. Stir the remaining 1 tablespoon of wine and the vinegar into the gravy and season with salt and pepper. Strain into a gravy boat. Thinly slice the roast across the grain and serve the gravy alongside. —*Grant Achatz*

NOTE Black garlic is prized for its sweet and savory, deep molasses-like flavor; its jelly-like texture makes it perfect for adding to sauces because it dissolves so easily. It's available at specialty shops and from blackgarlic.com.

MAKE AHEAD The gravy can be refrigerated for up to 3 days.

WINE Rich Rhône red: 2014 André Brunel Côtes du Rhône.

RECIPE IMPROV

Leftover Roast Beef Hacks

EMPANADAS Finely chop the beef and mix with chopped onion, garlic and spices. Use store-bought pizza dough to fold around the beef filling.

NEGIMAKI ROLLS Thinly slice the beef and wrap it around roasted asparagus or scallions. Brush with soy sauce and broil until browned and crispy in spots.

SCALOPPINE Bread and pan-fry thin slices of beef until crispy, then top with fresh herbs or a chopped vegetable salad.

HASH Sauté potatoes, onions and beef for a hearty weekend breakfast.

Braised Short Ribs with Root Vegetable Mash

Active **2 hr**; Total **4 hr**; Serves **4**

This twist on the British Sunday roast swaps the traditional roast beef and potatoes for red-wine-braised short ribs and a mash of root vegetables and squash.

SHORT RIBS

- 2 lbs. trimmed boneless beef short ribs, cut into 8 equal pieces
  Kosher salt and pepper
  All-purpose flour, for dusting
- 2 Tbsp. canola oil
- 4 Tbsp. unsalted butter
- 3 slices of bacon, cut into 1-inch pieces
- 1 head of garlic, halved crosswise
- 2 onions, quartered
- 4 shallots, quartered
- 3 thyme sprigs
- 2 bay leaves
- 2 cups dry red wine
- ¼ cup ruby port
- 4 cups chicken stock or low-sodium broth

ROOT VEGETABLE MASH

- 5 Tbsp. unsalted butter
- ½ lb. carrots, peeled and cut into ½-inch pieces
- ½ lb. rutabaga, peeled and cut into ½-inch pieces
- ½ lb. butternut squash, peeled and cut into ½-inch pieces
- ½ lb. parsnips, peeled and cut into ½-inch pieces
- ½ lb. celery root, peeled and cut into ½-inch pieces
- 6 garlic cloves, crushed
- 3 thyme sprigs
- 2 bay leaves
- 3 Tbsp. honey
- 1 Tbsp. chopped parsley, plus more for garnish
  Kosher salt and pepper

1. Make the short ribs Season the short ribs with salt and pepper and lightly dust with flour. In a large enameled cast-iron casserole, heat the oil. Add the ribs and cook over moderately high heat, turning, until browned all over, about 8 minutes. Transfer the ribs to a plate. Add the butter, bacon, garlic, onions, shallots, thyme and bay leaves to the casserole and cook over moderate heat, stirring occasionally, until the bacon fat is partially rendered and the vegetables are golden, about 5 minutes. Stir in the red wine and port and cook over moderate heat until reduced by half, about 5 minutes longer.

2. Return the short ribs and their juices to the casserole, add the stock and bring to a simmer. Cover and cook over low heat until the meat is very tender, about 2 hours. Transfer the short ribs to a plate. Strain the sauce through a fine sieve set over a bowl, pressing on the solids; discard the solids. Return the sauce to the casserole and simmer until reduced by one-third, about 15 minutes. Add the ribs and simmer gently until warmed through, 5 minutes.

3. Meanwhile, make the mash In a large saucepan, melt 4 tablespoons of the butter. Add the vegetables, garlic, thyme and bay leaves and cook over moderately low heat, stirring occasionally, until the vegetables begin to soften, 10 minutes. Stir in the honey, cover and cook until softened, 15 minutes. Add 1 cup of water, cover and cook, stirring occasionally, until almost all of the liquid is absorbed, 20 minutes longer. Discard the bay leaves and thyme sprigs. Stir in the remaining 1 tablespoon of butter and mash with a fork until chunky. Fold in the 1 tablespoon of parsley and season with salt and pepper. Keep warm.

4. Spoon the root vegetable mash onto plates and top with the short ribs. Garnish with chopped parsley and pass the remaining sauce at the table.
—Soho Farmhouse, Oxfordshire, England

MAKE AHEAD The braised short ribs and mash can be refrigerated for up to 3 days. Reheat gently.

WINE A tannic red: the 2012 De Martino Legado Cabernet Sauvignon from Chile.

Standing Beef Rib Roast with Pimentón

Active **30 min**; Total **3 hr 30 min**; Serves **10**

It's hard to believe that this showstopping roast is so incredibly simple. Be sure to use freshly ground pink peppercorns, good-quality Spanish pimentón and a flavorful, flaky pink salt. Also, ask your butcher to keep the long frenched rib bones on for a truly jaw-dropping presentation. If you have any leftovers, pile them into the Thai Beef Sandwiches with Green Curry Mayo on page 275.

- One 4-rib, 9-lb. prime rib roast, frenched and tied
  Himalayan pink salt
  Freshly ground pink peppercorns
- ½ cup extra-virgin olive oil
- 3 Tbsp. pimentón de la Vera (sweet smoked Spanish paprika)

Preheat the oven to 350°. Let the rib roast stand at room temperature for 1 hour. Season generously with pink salt and pepper. In a small bowl, whisk the oil with the pimentón, then brush the oil all over the roast. Set the meat in a large roasting pan bone side down and cover tightly with foil. Roast for 2 hours, basting with the pan juices halfway through. Uncover and roast, basting occasionally, until the outside is browned and an instant-read thermometer inserted in the thickest part registers 115°, 30 minutes longer. Transfer to a carving board and let rest for 30 minutes. Discard the string, carve the meat and serve. Pass additional pink salt and pepper at the table. *—Justin Chapple*

WINE Powerful Cabernet Sauvignon: 2013 La Jota Vineyard Howell Mountain.

BRAISED SHORT RIBS
WITH ROOT
VEGETABLE MASH

SHORT RIBS WITH
SERRANO CHIMICHURRI AND
JICAMA-RADISH SALAD

Short Ribs with Serrano Chimichurri and Jicama-Radish Salad

Active **1 hr 50 min**; Total **4 hr 25 min plus marinating**; Serves **4 to 6**

The chefs at Three Blue Ducks in Byron Bay, Australia, season short ribs with Chinese five-spice powder before grilling. Serve the beef with a vibrant radish salad tossed with yuzu dressing.

SHORT RIBS

- 1 Tbsp. Chinese five-spice powder
- 1½ tsp. kosher salt
- 3½ lbs. English-cut short ribs (3-inch pieces)
- 1 Tbsp. canola oil
- 3 garlic cloves, lightly crushed
- One 1½-inch piece of fresh ginger, peeled and thinly sliced
- 1 serrano chile, halved and seeded
- 4½ cups beef stock or low-sodium broth
- 2 cups Shaoxing wine (see Note) or dry sherry
- 2 Tbsp. soy sauce
- 2 Tbsp. honey
- 1 Tbsp. Asian fish sauce

SALAD

- 1 Tbsp. yuzu juice (see Note) or fresh lemon juice
- 2 Tbsp. plus ½ tsp. rice vinegar
- One ½-inch piece of fresh ginger, peeled and finely grated
- 2 Tbsp. grapeseed oil
- 2 Tbsp. extra-virgin olive oil
- 2 tsp. soy sauce
  Kosher salt and pepper
- 9 oz. radishes, trimmed and cut into ¼-inch wedges
- 1 medium cucumber—peeled, halved and cut into ¼-inch wedges
- ½ medium jicama, peeled and cut into ¼-inch wedges
- 1 medium shallot minced (¼ cup)
- 1 cup each chopped cilantro and parsley
  Pickled Chiles and Serrano Chimichurri (recipes follow), for serving

1. Make the short ribs In a bowl, combine the five-spice powder and salt. Season the ribs generously with the seasoned salt. Set the ribs in a 9-by-13-inch baking dish, cover and refrigerate for 4 hours.

2. Preheat the oven to 375°. In a large enameled cast-iron casserole, heat the canola oil. Working in batches, brown the short ribs on all sides over moderate heat, 8 to 10 minutes. Return the browned short ribs to the baking dish. Tilt the casserole and spoon off most of the fat from the pan.

3. Add the garlic, ginger and serrano to the casserole. Cook over moderate heat, stirring occasionally, until the garlic is lightly browned and fragrant, about 3 minutes. Add the beef stock, Shaoxing, soy sauce, honey and fish sauce and bring to a boil, scraping up any browned bits from the bottom of the casserole. Return the short ribs and any accumulated juices to the casserole. Cover and braise in the oven until the ribs are tender, 2¼ to 2½ hours.

4. Make the salad In a small bowl, whisk the yuzu juice with the rice vinegar and ginger. Whisk in the grapeseed and olive oils in a slow, steady stream. Whisk in the soy sauce; season with salt and pepper. In a large bowl, toss the radishes, cucumber, jicama, shallot, cilantro and parsley. Just before serving, toss with the dressing.

5. Transfer the ribs to a deep platter. Strain the braising liquid into a medium saucepan and skim off the fat. Add ½ cup of water and cook the sauce over moderately high heat until reduced by half, about 15 minutes. Pour over the ribs. Serve with the radish salad, Pickled Chiles and Serrano Chimichurri. —*Three Blue Ducks, Byron Bay, Australia*

SERVE WITH Steamed jasmine rice.

NOTE Shaoxing wine is an aged Chinese rice wine often used in cooking. It's available at Asian markets. Tart yuzu juice is available at specialty food stores.

MAKE AHEAD The braised short ribs can be refrigerated for up to 4 days. Reheat gently.

WINE Fruit-forward Pinot Noir: 2013 Merry Edwards Sonoma Coast.

PICKLED CHILES

Total **10 min plus 2 hr pickling**; Makes **1 cup**

This all-purpose condiment—spicy serranos in a sweet-tangy brine—is also fantastic on pizza, grilled meat and poultry.

- 7 Tbsp. apple cider vinegar
- 2 tsp. light brown sugar
- 1 tsp. kosher salt
- 7 serrano chiles, thinly sliced and seeded

In a medium bowl, whisk the vinegar, brown sugar and salt until the sugar and salt have dissolved. Stir in the sliced chiles. Cover with plastic wrap and let stand at room temperature for 2 hours. —*Three Blue Ducks*

MAKE AHEAD The pickled chiles can be refrigerated in the vinegar mixture for up to 2 weeks.

SERRANO CHIMICHURRI

Total **25 min**; Makes **1⅓ cups**

It's worth the short time it takes to make chimichurri instead of buying it; the flavors are much fresher. The zesty herb sauce would also be great with grilled meat or poultry as well as shellfish or firm, white-fleshed fish.

- ½ cup minced cilantro
- ½ cup minced parsley
- ¼ cup minced red onion
- 2 garlic cloves, peeled and minced
- ¼ cup plus 1 Tbsp. extra-virgin olive oil
- 2 tsp. finely grated lemon zest plus ⅓ cup fresh lemon juice
- 2 serrano chiles—halved, seeded and minced
- 1 tsp. Dijon mustard
  Kosher salt and pepper

In a medium bowl, combine the cilantro, parsley, red onion and garlic. In another bowl, whisk the olive oil with the lemon zest and juice, the minced serranos and the mustard. Stir into the herb mixture and season with salt and pepper. —*Three Blue Ducks*

MAKE AHEAD The chimichurri can be refrigerated for up to 2 days.

Soy-Braised Short Ribs

Active **45 min;** Total **2 hr 45 min**
Serves **4 to 6**

- 2 Tbsp. canola oil
- 5 lbs. English-cut short ribs
  (4- to 5-inch pieces)
  Kosher salt and pepper
- 1 yellow onion, chopped
- 3 garlic cloves, crushed
  One 2-inch piece of fresh ginger, peeled
- 2 cups dry red wine
- 2 cups chicken stock, low-sodium broth or water
- ¾ cup soy sauce
- ½ cup mirin
- ½ cup packed brown sugar
- ½ cup chopped kimchi, plus more for serving
  Sliced scallions and toasted sesame seeds, for garnish
  Steamed short-grain rice, for serving

1. In a large enameled cast-iron casserole, heat the oil. Season the short ribs with salt and pepper. Working in 2 batches, sear over moderately high heat, turning, until browned all over, 5 minutes per batch. Transfer to a plate.

2. Add the onion, garlic and ginger to the casserole and cook over moderate heat, stirring occasionally, until softened, about 5 minutes. Add the wine, bring to a boil and simmer until reduced by half, 3 minutes. Stir in the stock, soy sauce, mirin, brown sugar and the ½ cup of kimchi. Return the ribs to the casserole bone side up along with any accumulated juices. Bring to a boil, cover and reduce the heat to low. Simmer gently until the ribs are very tender, about 2 hours.

3. Transfer the ribs to a shallow serving bowl. Strain and degrease the sauce. Spoon some of the sauce over the ribs and garnish with scallions and sesame seeds. Serve with steamed rice and more kimchi. —*Sohui Kim*

MAKE AHEAD The short ribs can be refrigerated for up to 2 days.

WINE Smoky, savory red blend: 2011 McEvoy Ranch Red Piano.

Dried-Cherry-and-Miso-Braised Short Ribs

Active **1 hr 10 min;** Total **3 hr 30 min**
Serves **10 to 12**

- 6 lbs. boneless English-cut short ribs (about 5 oz. each), at room temperature
  Kosher salt
- ¼ cup canola oil
- 8 cups beef stock or low-sodium broth
- 2 cups dry sherry
- 1 large onion, cut into chunks
- 1 medium leek, halved lengthwise and cut into 3-inch pieces
- 8 scallions, halved crosswise, plus thinly sliced scallions for garnish
- ½ cup mirin
- 4 oz. fresh ginger, rinsed and thinly sliced
- 1 head of garlic, halved crosswise
- ¼ cup soy sauce
- ¼ cup red miso paste
- ¼ cup sugar
- 3 whole star anise pods
  One 3-inch cinnamon stick
- 1 tsp. ground mace
- 1 cup dried sour cherries, wrapped in cheesecloth and tied
- 6 shallots, halved and thinly sliced

1. Preheat the oven to 275°. Season the short ribs all over with salt. In a large enameled cast-iron casserole, heat 2 tablespoons of the oil until shimmering. In batches, cook the short ribs over moderately high heat, turning occasionally, until browned all over, about 8 minutes per batch. Transfer the ribs to a plate.

2. Spoon off the fat from the casserole. Add the stock, sherry, onion, leek, halved scallions, mirin, ginger, garlic, soy sauce, miso, sugar, star anise, cinnamon stick and mace; bring to a boil over high heat. Add the short ribs and the cherry bundle, cover and braise in the oven for about 2 hours, until the beef is tender.

3. Using tongs, transfer the short ribs and the cherry bundle to a plate. Strain the braising liquid through a fine sieve into a large heatproof bowl; discard the solids. Remove the cherries from the cheesecloth and transfer to a blender. Add 7 cups of the strained braising liquid and puree until smooth. Reserve the remaining braising liquid for another use.

4. Wipe out the casserole and heat the remaining 2 tablespoons of oil in it. Add the shallots and cook over moderate heat, stirring occasionally, until softened and browned, about 8 minutes. Add the braising puree and boil over high heat until reduced to 6 cups, about 10 minutes. Add the short ribs to the sauce, cover and cook over low heat until they are hot and tender, about 10 minutes.

5. Transfer the ribs and some of the sauce to bowls. Garnish with sliced scallions and serve. —*Kris Morningstar*

MAKE AHEAD The short ribs can be refrigerated in the sauce overnight. Reheat gently to serve.

WINE Intense Napa Valley Cabernet: 2013 Black Stallion.

Shredded Beef Taco Bar

Active **2 hr 15 min;** Total **8 hr 30 min**
Serves **4 to 6**

BEEF SHANK TACO FILLING

- 5 dried guajillo chiles, stemmed and seeded
- 5 dried ancho chiles, stemmed and seeded
- ¼ cup extra-virgin olive oil
  One 4-lb. bone-in beef shank, trimmed and tied by the butcher
  Kosher salt and pepper
- 1 yellow onion, finely chopped
- 5 garlic cloves, thinly sliced
- 2 tsp. dried oregano
- 2 tsp. ground cumin
  Two 12-oz. bottles light Mexican beer
  One 28-oz. can crushed tomatoes
- 2 cups chicken stock or low-sodium broth
- 2 Tbsp. apple cider vinegar
- 2 Tbsp. unsalted butter

PICKLED RED ONION

- 1 cup red wine vinegar
- ¾ cup sugar
- 1 tsp. kosher salt
- 1 medium red onion, halved and thinly sliced

LIME CREMA

- **1 cup sour cream**
- **1 tsp. finely grated lime zest plus 2 Tbsp. fresh lime juice**
- **Kosher salt and pepper**

CABBAGE SLAW

- **½ cup mayonnaise**
- **2 Tbsp. hot sauce**
- **Kosher salt and pepper**
- **1¼ lbs. red cabbage (½ medium head), cored and very thinly sliced (6 cups)**
- **Canola oil, for brushing**
- **Warm flour tortillas, chopped cilantro and lime wedges, for serving**

1. Make the taco filling Preheat the oven to 325°. In a mortar, pound the dried chiles until finely ground. In a large enameled cast-iron casserole, heat the olive oil. Season the beef shank generously with salt and pepper, add to the casserole and cook over moderately high heat until browned on all sides, about 25 minutes. Transfer the shank to a plate.

2. Add the onion, garlic and a generous pinch of salt to the casserole and cook over moderately high heat, stirring occasionally, until the onion is beginning to brown, about 8 minutes. Add the ground chiles, oregano and cumin and cook, stirring, until fragrant, about 1 minute. Add the beer and bring to a boil, scraping up any browned bits with a wooden spoon. Cook until the beer is reduced by half, about 6 minutes. Add the crushed tomatoes and chicken stock and return to a boil. Return the beef shank and any accumulated juices to the casserole. Cover and braise in the oven for about 3½ hours, basting the shank with sauce every hour, until the meat is very tender. Remove the casserole from the oven and let the beef shank stand at room temperature in the braising liquid, uncovered, until ready to grill, at least 2 hours.

3. Meanwhile, make the pickled red onion In a medium bowl, whisk the red wine vinegar, sugar and salt until the sugar is dissolved. Add the sliced red onion, cover and let stand at room temperature, stirring occasionally, for at least 1 hour.

4. Make the lime crema In a small bowl, whisk all of the ingredients together and season with salt and pepper. Refrigerate until ready to serve.

5. Make the cabbage slaw In a large bowl, whisk the mayonnaise with the hot sauce and season with salt and pepper. Add the red cabbage and toss to coat. Refrigerate until ready to serve.

6. Carefully remove the cooled shank from the braising liquid and transfer to a plate. Transfer the braising liquid to a medium saucepan and bring to a simmer over low heat, skimming off any accumulated fat. Stir in the cider vinegar and butter and season with salt and pepper; keep warm.

7. Meanwhile, light a grill. Fold a 24-inch sheet of foil in half and brush lightly with canola oil. Set the foil oiled side up on the grill. Place the cooled shank on the foil, cover and grill over moderately high heat, basting with the warm braising liquid every 10 minutes, until the shank is lightly charred and warmed through, 35 to 40 minutes. Transfer the shank to a platter and let rest for 10 minutes. Discard the strings and serve the shank warm with the pickled red onion, lime crema, cabbage slaw, warm flour tortillas, chopped cilantro, lime wedges and the remaining braising liquid. Set out tongs or a fork so guests can pull the meat themselves. —*Rob Levitt*

MAKE AHEAD The braised shank can be refrigerated in the braising liquid in the casserole for up to 4 days. Rewarm gently over moderately low heat, covered, before proceeding. The pickled red onion can be refrigerated for up to 2 weeks.

BEER Classic Mexican lager: Negra Modelo.

Taco Pie

Active **25 min**; Total **2 hr**
Makes **one 9-inch deep-dish pie**

In the 1980s, spice companies began exporting taco seasoning packets to Sweden, according to Swedish chef Magnus Nilsson. Today, home cooks throughout the country use taco spices to flavor savory pies like this one. You can swap in ¼ cup of store-bought seasoning mix for the homemade blend here if you prefer.

CRUST

- **5½ Tbsp. cold unsalted butter, cut into ½-inch cubes**
- **2½ cups plus 1 Tbsp. all-purpose flour**
- **1½ tsp. baking powder**
- **1 tsp. kosher salt**
- **½ cup plus 1 Tbsp. milk**

FILLING

- **2 Tbsp. chili powder**
- **1 Tbsp. ground cumin**
- **Kosher salt and black pepper**
- **1 tsp. onion powder**
- **1 tsp. cornstarch**
- **½ tsp. cayenne**
- **½ tsp. ground coriander**
- **1 Tbsp. unsalted butter**
- **1 lb. ground beef**
- **1¼ cups crème fraîche**
- **4½ oz. cheddar cheese, grated**
- **1 large egg, beaten**
- **2 Tbsp. mayonnaise**

1. Make the crust In a food processor, combine the butter, flour, baking powder and salt and pulse just until the mixture resembles coarse meal. Add the milk and pulse just until the dough comes together. Press the dough evenly over the bottom and halfway up the side of a 9-inch springform pan. Cover with plastic wrap and refrigerate until firm, about 45 minutes.

2. Make the filling In a small bowl, whisk the chili powder with the cumin, 2 teaspoons of salt, the onion powder, cornstarch, cayenne and coriander. In a medium skillet, melt the butter. Add the beef and cook over moderately high heat, stirring, until browned and cooked through, about 5 minutes. Add the spice blend and ⅔ cup of water and cook, stirring occasionally, until the water has evaporated, about 3 minutes. Remove from the heat.

3. Preheat the oven to 350°. In a medium bowl, whisk the crème fraîche with the cheddar, egg and mayonnaise. Season with a pinch each of salt and black pepper. Set the crust on a rimmed baking sheet. Using a slotted spoon, spread the ground meat over the crust and cover with the cheddar topping. Bake until the topping is set and the crust is golden brown, about 45 minutes. Let cool for 15 minutes before serving. —*Magnus Nilsson*

MAKE AHEAD The taco pie can be refrigerated for up to 2 days. Rewarm before serving.

WINE Substantial Syrah from Washington state: 2013 Waterbrook.

Peking-Style Short Rib Tacos

Total **45 min** plus **2 hr marinating**; Serves **6**

The secret to the insanely tender and cara-melized meat: adding onion juice to the marinade. The recipe calls for flanken-cut beef short ribs, which are sliced across the bone about ⅓ inch thick, so each piece has about four small sections of bone. If you can't find this cut, ask your butcher to pre-pare the ribs for you.

- ½   large onion, grated on a box grater
- ¼   cup soy sauce
- 2   Tbsp. finely grated peeled fresh ginger
- 1½ Tbsp. sugar
- 2   garlic cloves, finely grated
   Kosher salt and pepper
- 3½ lbs. flanken-style beef short ribs, cut ⅓ inch thick
   Warm small flour tortillas, for serving
   Hoisin sauce, julienned cucumbers, grilled yellow squash, sliced hot red chiles, scallions and lime wedges, for serving

1. In a large resealable plastic bag, mix the onion with the soy sauce, ginger, sugar, garlic and 1 teaspoon each of salt and pepper. Add the short ribs, seal the bag and turn to coat all the ribs well. Let marinate in the refrigerator for at least 2 hours or overnight.

2. Light a grill. Scrape some of the mari-nade off the meat. Season the ribs with salt and pepper. Grill over high heat, turn-ing once, until lightly charred in spots, about 5 minutes. Transfer to a platter and let rest for 2 minutes. Use scissors to snip off the bones and cut the meat into bite-size pieces. Serve in tortillas with hoisin sauce, julienned cucumbers, grilled yellow squash, sliced chiles and scallions, and lime wedges for squeezing.
—*Justin Chapple*

WINE Brisk and fruity Riesling: 2014 Her-mann J. Wiemer Finger Lakes Semi-Dry.

Aussie Burgers with Pickled Beets, Pineapple and Fried Eggs

📷 PAGE 184

Active **50 min**; Total **3 hr**; Serves **4**

Unconventional toppings—earthy pickled beets, grilled pineapple and runny fried eggs—push chef April Bloomfield's Essen-tial Burgers (recipe at right) over the top.

- 1   red beet (8 oz.), scrubbed
- 2   tsp. extra-virgin olive oil
   Kosher salt
- 1   small white onion, thinly sliced
- 1¼ cups distilled white vinegar
- ½   cup rice vinegar
- 2   Tbsp. sugar
   Four ¼-inch-thick slices of fresh pineapple
   Crushed red pepper
- 2½ Tbsp. unsalted butter
- 4   large eggs
   April's Essential Burgers (recipe at right)

1. Preheat the oven to 350°. In a small bowl, coat the beet with 1 teaspoon of the olive oil and sprinkle with a generous pinch of salt. Wrap the beet in foil and roast in a pie plate until tender, 1 hour. Let cool, then peel the beet and slice it ¼ inch thick. Transfer to a heatproof bowl and add the onion.

2. In a medium saucepan, combine the white vinegar, rice vinegar, sugar and 2½ tablespoons of salt. Bring to a boil over moderate heat, stirring to dissolve the sugar. Pour the brine over the beet and onion and let cool, about 1 hour.

3. Light a grill or heat a grill pan. Coat the pineapple slices with the remaining 1 tea-spoon of olive oil and a pinch each of salt and crushed red pepper. Grill the pineapple until warm and lightly charred, 2 minutes per side. Transfer to a plate and keep warm.

4. In a large nonstick skillet, melt the butter. Add the eggs and cook over moderate heat until the whites are set and the yolks are slightly runny, 3 minutes. Remove from the heat and season with salt.

5. Layer the pickled beets and onions on April's Essential Burgers. Top with the grilled pineapple rings and the fried eggs and serve. —*April Bloomfield*

MAKE AHEAD The pickled beets can be refrigerated for up to 2 weeks.

WINE Ripe Oregon white: 2014 Underwood Pinot Gris.

April's Essential Burgers

Active **15 min**; Total **2 hr 20 min**
Serves **4**

For her casual Manhattan burger spot, Salvation Burger, April Bloomfield uses a secret beef blend; she created this version with home cooks in mind. The key to an extra-juicy burger is to ask your butcher for freshly ground meat with a good amount of fat. And don't pack the patties too firmly or the burgers will be tough.

- 6   oz. ground fatty brisket (see Note)
- 6   oz. ground short rib
- 6   oz. ground bottom round
- 6   oz. ground chuck
   Kosher salt
- 4   hamburger buns, split and toasted

1. In a bowl, combine the ground meats, mixing gently with your hands. Divide the meat into 4 pieces and gently shape each into a ¾-inch-thick patty. Set the burgers on a baking sheet, cover with plastic wrap and refrigerate until firm, at least 2 hours.

2. Light a grill or heat a grill pan. Generously season the burgers on both sides with salt. Grill over high heat until browned outside and medium-rare within, about 3 minutes per side. Transfer to a rack and let rest for 3 minutes, then set the burgers on the buns and serve. —*April Bloomfield*

NOTE Ground skirt steak can replace the ground brisket, the ground short rib or both.

WINE Structured Napa Valley red: 2011 White Rock Vineyards Claret.

Mexican Avocado Burgers

Active **25 min**; Total **2 hr 30 min**
Serves **4**

- **6** oz. ground fatty brisket (see Note on p. 201)
- **6** oz. ground short rib
- **6** oz. ground bottom round
- **6** oz. ground chuck
- **1½** tsp. ground coriander
- **1½** tsp. ancho chile powder
- **¾** tsp. ground cumin
- **¾** tsp. sweet smoked paprika
- **¾** tsp. ground oregano
- **¾** tsp. chipotle chile powder
  Kosher salt
- **8** oz. queso fresco, crumbled
- **4** hamburger buns, split and toasted
- **3** Tbsp. Mexican crema or sour cream
- **1** large avocado—peeled, pitted and thinly sliced
  Thinly sliced red onion and cilantro leaves, for serving

1. In a bowl, combine the ground meats, mixing gently with your hands. Divide the meat into 4 pieces and gently shape each into a ¾-inch-thick patty. Set the burgers on a baking sheet, cover with plastic wrap and refrigerate until firm, at least 2 hours.

2. In a small bowl, whisk the ground coriander with the ancho powder, cumin, smoked paprika, oregano and chipotle powder to combine.

3. Light a grill or heat a grill pan. Generously season the burgers on both sides with salt. Grill over high heat until browned on the bottom, about 3 minutes. Flip and top each burger with 1 teaspoon of the spice blend; reserve the remaining spice blend for another use. Continue grilling the burgers until browned outside and medium-rare within, about 3 minutes. Transfer the burgers to a rack, top each with 2 ounces of the crumbled queso fresco and let rest for 3 minutes. Spread the toasted buns with the crema. Set the burgers on the buns, top with the avocado, red onion slices and cilantro and serve. —April Bloomfield

BEER Dark and smoky beer: Shiner Bock.

Classic Blue Cheese Burgers

Active **15 min**; Total **2 hr 20 min**
Serves **4**

This juicy burger topped with melted blue cheese is based on the one that April Bloomfield is famous for at her New York City gastropub, The Spotted Pig.

- **6** oz. ground fatty brisket (see Note on p. 201)
- **6** oz. ground short rib
- **6** oz. ground bottom round
- **6** oz. ground chuck
  Kosher salt
- **8** oz. Roquefort cheese, crumbled
- **4** hamburger buns, split and toasted

1. In a bowl, combine the ground meats, mixing gently with your hands. Divide the meat into 4 pieces and gently shape each into a ¾-inch-thick patty. Set the burgers on a baking sheet, cover with plastic wrap and refrigerate until firm, at least 2 hours.

2. Light a grill or heat a grill pan. Generously season the burgers on both sides with salt. Grill over high heat until browned outside and medium-rare within, 3 minutes per side. Transfer the burgers to a rack and top each with 2 ounces of the crumbled Roquefort. Let rest for 3 minutes, then set on the toasted buns and serve. —April Bloomfield

WINE Earthy Languedoc red: 2012 Domaine Leon Barral Jadis Faugères.

Spicy Italian Cheeseburgers

Active **20 min**; Total **2 hr 25 min**
Serves **4**

- **6** oz. ground fatty brisket (see Note on p. 201)
- **6** oz. ground short rib
- **6** oz. ground bottom round
- **6** oz. ground chuck
  Kosher salt
- **8** oz. Taleggio cheese, rind discarded, cheese coarsely grated
- **4** hamburger buns, split and toasted
- **4** spicy pickled cherry peppers, seeded and minced (¼ cup)

1. In a bowl, combine the ground meats, mixing gently with your hands. Divide the meat into 4 pieces and gently shape each into a ¾-inch-thick patty. Set the burgers on a baking sheet, cover with plastic wrap and refrigerate until firm, at least 2 hours.

2. Light a grill or heat a grill pan. Generously season the burgers on both sides with salt. Grill over high heat until browned on the bottom, 3 minutes. Flip and top the burgers with the grated Taleggio. Continue grilling until browned outside and medium-rare within, 3 minutes more. Transfer the burgers to a rack and let rest for 3 minutes. Set the burgers on the toasted buns, top with the minced peppers and serve. —April Bloomfield

WINE Rich, peppery Puglian red: 2013 Leone de Castris Maiana Salice Salentino.

Atomic Chile Jack Cheeseburgers

Total **20 min**; Serves **4**

Chef Michael Symon serves this spicy burger at his popular Ohio chain B Spot. It gets its name from the incendiary ghost chile that seasons the meat as well as the pickled jalapeños and hot sauce that top the patties. Grill these outside: The ghost chile powder is powerful.

- **½** tsp. ghost chile powder (see Note)
- **2** tsp. kosher salt
- **1½** lbs. ground chuck
- **4** pepper jack cheese slices
- **4** soft potato rolls, toasted
  Mayonnaise, sliced red onion, pickled jalapeños and cilantro, for serving

1. In a small bowl, mix the ghost chile powder and salt.

2. Light a grill and oil the grate. Form the meat into four 5-inch patties and season with the chile salt. Grill over moderately high heat until lightly charred on the bottom, 3 minutes. Flip the burgers, top with the cheese and grill until medium-rare, about 3 minutes more.

3. Set the burgers on the buns. Spread the tops with mayonnaise and garnish with sliced red onion, pickled jalapeños and cilantro; serve. —Michael Symon

NOTE Ghost chiles, also called bhut jolokia, are about 150 times hotter than jalapeños.

BEER Lightly toasty ale: Bell's Amber Ale.

ATOMIC CHILE JACK
CHEESEBURGERS

Bacon-Cheeseburger Sliders with Hickory Sauce

Active **1 hr**; Total **1 hr 30 min**; Serves **12**

An ode to New Orleans burger joint Bud's Broiler, these incredibly juicy sliders are topped with a tangy and superversatile barbecue-style sauce. Slather it on ribs, mix it into your shrimp cocktail sauce or use it as a dip for fries.

HICKORY SAUCE

- 2 Tbsp. canola oil
- 1 cup finely chopped yellow onion
- ¾ cup ketchup
- ⅓ cup apple cider vinegar
- ¼ cup light brown sugar
- 2 Tbsp. Worcestershire sauce
- 2 tsp. black pepper
- ½ tsp. crushed red pepper
  Kosher salt

SLIDERS

- 12 slices of bacon
- 1 sweet onion, thinly sliced
- ¼ cup cane or apple cider vinegar
  Kosher salt and pepper
- 4 Tbsp. unsalted butter, melted
- 2¼ lbs. ground beef, formed into twelve ½-inch-thick patties
- 1½ cups shredded sharp cheddar cheese (6 oz.)
  Mayonnaise
- 12 slider buns, toasted
  Sliced tomatoes, pickles and shredded lettuce, for serving

1. Make the hickory sauce In a medium saucepan, heat the oil. Add the onion and cook over moderate heat, stirring occasionally, until golden brown, about 10 minutes. Add the next 6 ingredients and cook, stirring occasionally, until thick, about 5 minutes. Transfer the sauce to a blender and puree until smooth; season with salt. Transfer to a medium bowl and let cool to room temperature.

2. Make the sliders Preheat the oven to 400°. Arrange the bacon on a rack set over a baking sheet. Bake until golden and crisp, 25 minutes. Transfer to a paper towel–lined plate to drain, then break the slices in half. In a medium bowl, toss the onion with the vinegar and a pinch of salt.

3. In a large ovenproof skillet, heat 2 tablespoons of the butter. Season the beef patties with salt and pepper and add half of them to the skillet. Cook until browned on the bottom, about 2 minutes. Flip, then top each with 1 tablespoon of the hickory sauce and 2 tablespoons of the cheese. Transfer the skillet to the oven and cook until the cheese melts and the patties are just cooked through, 1 to 2 minutes. Transfer the burgers to a work surface, cover with foil and repeat the process to make 6 more burgers.

4. Spread mayonnaise on the buns and top with the sliders, tomatoes, bacon, pickled onion, pickles and shredded lettuce. Close the sliders and serve with the remaining hickory sauce on the side. —*John Besh and Chris Lusk*

WINE Fruit-rich Zinfandel: 2014 Dashe Dry Creek Valley.

Loaded Hot Dogs with Chipotle Mayo

Total **20 min**; Makes **8**

These next-level hot dogs from chef Christopher Bates of FLX Wienery in New York's Finger Lakes region have everything going for them. They're cheesy, spicy, tangy—and even crunchy, from a topping of Fritos.

- ½ cup mayonnaise
- 1 canned chipotle chile in adobo
  Kosher salt and pepper
- 1 Tbsp. canola oil
- 8 beef hot dogs
- 8 hot dog buns, toasted
- 4 oz. crumbled cheddar cheese curds or sharp cheddar cheese
- ½ cup piccalilli or pickle relish
- 2 cups corn chips (3 oz.), preferably Fritos, crushed
- ½ cup chopped mixed herbs, such as parsley, dill and cilantro

In a food processor, puree the mayonnaise with the chipotle until smooth. Season with salt and pepper. In a large nonstick skillet, heat the oil. Cook the hot dogs over moderate heat until lightly browned, 4 minutes. Spread the mayo on the buns and top with the hot dogs, cheese curds, piccalilli, chips and herbs; serve. —*Christopher Bates*

WINE Dry Riesling: 2013 Bloomer Creek Tanzen Dame Auten Vineyard.

Spicy Glazed Meatloaf

Active **30 min**; Total **1 hr 50 min**; Serves **8**

Justin Chapple, F&W's resident Mad Genius, bakes meatloaf in a Bundt pan. The result? A striking presentation, neat slices and (best of all) plenty of crispy edges.

- 2 Tbsp. canola oil
- 1 red onion, finely chopped
- ¼ cup minced peeled fresh ginger
- 6 garlic cloves, minced
- 3 Tbsp. minced lemongrass, white inner bulb only
- 1¾ lbs. ground chuck
- 1¾ lbs. ground pork
- 1¼ cups panko
- 1 cup finely chopped scallions
- 2 large eggs, beaten
- 1½ Tbsp. kosher salt
- 2 tsp. pepper
- 1¾ cups ketchup
- 5 Tbsp. Sriracha

1. Preheat the oven to 375°. In a large skillet, heat the oil. Add the onion, ginger, garlic and lemongrass and cook over moderate heat, stirring occasionally, until softened, about 8 minutes. Scrape into a large bowl. Add the chuck, pork, panko, scallions, eggs, salt, pepper, ¾ cup of the ketchup, ½ cup of water and 2 tablespoons of the Sriracha and knead until combined.

2. Press the meat mixture evenly into a 10-inch Bundt pan. Bake for about 50 minutes, until firm. Let rest for 15 minutes, then invert onto a large rimmed baking sheet.

3. Preheat the broiler. In a medium bowl, mix the remaining 1 cup of ketchup and 3 tablespoons of Sriracha. Spoon the glaze over the meatloaf and down the side. Broil the meatloaf 8 inches from the heat until glazed, about 2 minutes; rotate the baking sheet occasionally during broiling. Cut the meatloaf into wedges and serve. —*Justin Chapple*

WINE Substantial Malbec: 2014 Valentin Bianchi.

Garlicky Lamb and Rice Pilaf

Total **1 hr 45 min**; Serves **6 to 8**

Plov (lamb and rice pilaf) is the national dish of Uzbekistan and very popular across all of Central Asia. It's hearty and rich, with an irresistible topping of lamb cracklings.

- 6   oz. lamb fat, cut into ½-inch strips (see Note)
-    Kosher salt and pepper
- 2   lbs. boneless leg of lamb, cut into ¾-inch cubes
- 2   large yellow onions, chopped
- 20 garlic cloves
- 3   medium carrots, shredded
- 2   Tbsp. cumin seeds
- 2   Tbsp. za'atar
- 7   cups low-sodium beef broth
- 2   cups long-grain white rice
-    Chopped parsley, for serving

1. In a large enameled cast-iron casserole, cook the lamb fat over moderately low heat until rendered and the cracklings are golden brown, about 10 minutes. Remove the cracklings with a slotted spoon and drain on paper towels. Season with salt. Leave the fat in the casserole.

2. In a medium bowl, season the lamb with 2 teaspoons of salt and 1 teaspoon of pepper. Add one-third of the lamb to the casserole and cook over moderate heat until browned, 5 to 7 minutes. Using a slotted spoon, transfer the browned meat to a plate. Repeat with the remaining lamb.

3. Add the onions to the casserole and season with salt and pepper. Cook, stirring occasionally, until golden brown, 8 to 10 minutes. Stir in the garlic and cook until fragrant and lightly browned, 2 to 3 minutes. Add the shredded carrots to the casserole along with the cumin and za'atar and cook, stirring occasionally, until the carrots are just softened, about 2 minutes.

4. In a saucepan, bring the beef broth to a simmer. Return the lamb and any accumulated juices to the casserole along with the rice. Add 2 cups of the broth to the rice and cook, stirring, until it is absorbed, about 4 minutes. Repeat with another 2 cups of broth, cooking until absorbed. Stir in the remaining broth. Cover and simmer over moderately low heat until the rice is tender, about 10 minutes. Remove the casserole from the heat and let stand uncovered for 10 minutes before serving. Garnish with the cracklings and parsley and serve. —*Andrew Zimmern*

NOTE Ask your butcher for lamb fat.

WINE Spice-inflected Chianti Classico: 2013 Monteraponi.

Thai-Spiced Lamb Shoulder

Active **20 min**; Total **3 hr 15 min**
Serves **8 to 10**

"I favor long-cooked meat, especially for dinner parties," says Paris-based cookbook author David Lebovitz. "The cuts are less expensive and you don't have to pay so much attention to the cooking—or when to put it in the oven, because in France, people always come late to dinner parties."

- ½   cup granulated sugar
- ¼   cup finely grated palm sugar or light brown sugar
- ¼   cup Asian fish sauce
- 2   tsp. Chinese five-spice powder
-    One 2-inch piece of fresh ginger, peeled and finely grated
- 2½ cups warm water
- 3   Tbsp. Chinese black vinegar or aged balsamic vinegar
- 2   Tbsp. soy sauce
- 2   tsp. Thai red chile paste
- 2   tsp. Thai shrimp paste or 3 minced oil-packed anchovies
- 4   lbs. well-trimmed boneless lamb shoulder

1. Preheat the oven to 325°. In a small bowl, combine the granulated sugar with the palm sugar, fish sauce, five-spice powder and ginger. In another bowl, combine the water with the vinegar, soy sauce, chile paste and shrimp paste; whisk until no lumps of chile paste or shrimp paste remain.

2. Using a sharp knife, score the fat cap of the lamb shoulder crosswise at 1-inch intervals, making the cuts ½ inch deep. Lay the lamb flat on a work surface and rub the sugar mixture all over the meat. Roll up the roast, wrapping the flaps of fat around the outside to form a neat cylinder, then tie at 1-inch intervals with kitchen string.

3. Set the trussed lamb in a small roasting pan, fat side up, and pour the vinegar mixture over it. Roast the lamb for 1 hour, basting after 30 minutes. Turn the lamb shoulder over and roast for 1 hour longer, basting again after 30 minutes. Turn the lamb once more and cook for about 45 minutes longer, basting once, until an instant-read thermometer inserted in the center of the roast registers 140° for medium-rare. Transfer to a carving board and let rest for 15 minutes. Skim the excess fat from the juices. Discard the kitchen strings and thinly slice the meat against the grain. Serve with the juices. —*David Lebovitz*

SERVE WITH Lebovitz's Kale-and-Shiitake Fried Rice (p. 243) or steamed white rice.

WINE A peppery, robust Zinfandel: the 2012 Stuhlmuller Estate.

SUPERFAST DINNER IDEA

Lamb Chops with Garlic and Olive Oil

Light a grill or heat the broiler. In a shallow dish, combine 4 Tbsp. **olive oil** with 2 minced **garlic cloves**, ½ tsp. **salt** and ¼ tsp. **pepper**. Add 8 **lamb rib chops** and turn to coat. Grill over high heat or broil for 5 minutes, basting with 2 more Tbsp. **olive oil**. Turn and cook until the chops are done, about 5 minutes longer.

VARIATIONS Add to the garlic-oil mixture: 4 tsp. chopped **fresh rosemary** or 3 Tbsp. chopped **fresh sage** and an additional 1 Tbsp. **olive oil**.

RACK OF LAMB WITH
ARTICHOKES, PURPLE
POTATOES AND LICORICE

Rack of Lamb with Artichokes, Purple Potatoes and Licorice

Active **1 hr**; Total **1 hr 40 min**; Serves **6**

Baby lamb roasted over yellow potatoes is as rustic a Roman dish as you can get. At Trattoria Epiro in Rome, chef Marco Mattana makes a refined version with carefully sliced and plated lamb accompanied by a puree of purple potatoes. The dish may seem New American, but the artichokes and licorice powder are proudly Italian.

½ **lemon**

6 **large artichokes**

1 **cup plus 2 Tbsp. extra-virgin olive oil**

1 **head of garlic, halved crosswise**

3 **mint sprigs**

3 **oregano sprigs, plus oregano leaves for garnish**

   Kosher salt and pepper

   Two 2-lb. frenched racks of lamb

2 **lbs. baby purple potatoes, scrubbed**

½ **tsp. licorice powder (optional)**

1. Preheat the oven to 350°. Squeeze the lemon half into a bowl of cold water; add it to the water. Snap off the outer leaves of 1 artichoke. Using a sharp knife, cut off the top half and peel the base and stem. Using a melon baller or a spoon, scoop out the furry choke; halve the artichoke lengthwise and add to the lemon water. Repeat with the remaining artichokes.

2. Drain the artichokes; transfer to a medium saucepan. Add ½ cup of the oil, the garlic, mint, oregano sprigs and ¼ cup of water; season with salt and pepper. Bring to a simmer, cover and cook over low heat until just tender, about 20 minutes. Keep warm in the saucepan.

3. Set a rack over a baking sheet. Heat a large cast-iron skillet. Rub the lamb all over with 2 tablespoons of the olive oil and season with salt and pepper. Sear 1 rack of lamb at a time over moderately high heat, turning, until golden, about 5 minutes. Transfer to the baking sheet and roast for about 30 minutes for medium-rare; an instant-read thermometer inserted in the center will register 120°. Transfer to a cutting board and let rest for 10 minutes.

4. Meanwhile, in a large saucepan, cover the potatoes with 2 inches of water, season with salt and bring to a boil. Cook over moderate heat until tender, about 20 minutes. Drain, reserving ½ cup of the cooking water. Return the potatoes to the saucepan and add the remaining ½ cup of oil and ¼ cup of the reserved cooking water. Season with salt and coarsely mash with a fork; add more cooking water if necessary. Stir in the licorice powder, if using.

5. Transfer the artichokes to 6 plates. Carve the lamb into individual chops and serve with the artichokes and crushed purple potatoes. Garnish with oregano leaves. —*Marco Mattana*

WINE Rich and smoky red: 2012 Salvatore Molettieri Cinque Querce Irpinia Aglianico.

Thyme-Roasted Lamb with Caramelized Vegetables

Active **30 min**; Total **3 hr plus overnight marinating**; Serves **6**

The fresh thyme, juniper berries and dried lavender in the marinade permeate the lamb, giving it an amazing fragrance as it roasts. If you don't have lavender, you can substitute herbes de Provence.

4 **garlic cloves**

1½ **Tbsp. chopped thyme, plus 5 thyme sprigs**

½ **Tbsp. dried lavender or herbes de Provence**

8 **juniper berries**

2 **Tbsp. honey**

½ **cup canola oil**

   Five 3-inch strips of lemon zest

3 **bay leaves**

   One 5-lb. bone-in leg of lamb, excess fat trimmed

2 **medium yellow onions, cut into wedges**

2 **medium parsnips, peeled and cut into 2-inch pieces**

3 **medium carrots, peeled and cut into 2-inch pieces**

4 **Tbsp. unsalted butter, melted**

   Sea salt

1. In a blender, puree the garlic, chopped thyme, lavender, juniper berries, honey and oil to a smooth paste. Stir in the lemon zest and bay leaves. On a rimmed baking sheet, rub the marinade all over the lamb. Cover with plastic wrap and refrigerate for at least 6 hours or overnight. Let stand at room temperature for 30 minutes.

2. Preheat the oven to 325°. In a roasting pan, toss the onions, parsnips, carrots and thyme sprigs with the butter. Season with salt. Set the lamb on the vegetables and roast for about 1 hour and 45 minutes, basting occasionally, until an instant-read thermometer inserted in the thickest part of the leg registers 140° for medium-rare.

3. Increase the oven temperature to 450° and roast for 10 minutes, until the lamb is deep golden brown. Transfer to a cutting board and let rest for 20 minutes. Carve the lamb and transfer to a serving platter. Sprinkle with sea salt and serve with the vegetables. —*Victoria Elíasdóttir*

WINE Medium-bodied, spice-driven red: 2014 Château La Canorgue Luberon Rouge.

Oregano-Scented Lamb Shoulder Chops with Tomatoes and Olives

Total **30 min**; Serves **4**

At the avant-garde restaurant Trattoria Al Cacciatore in the Friuli region of Italy, this lamb is served in a sealed jar to maximize the aromas. Our version requires just 30 minutes in a skillet; the potato chip garnish adds a wonderful crunch.

3 **Tbsp. extra-virgin olive oil**

1 **Tbsp. oregano leaves**

   Four 10-oz. meaty lamb shoulder chops

   Kosher salt and pepper

1½ **cups cherry tomatoes (8 oz.), halved**

½ **cup pitted kalamata olives, halved**

   Thick-cut potato chips, for serving

In a large nonstick skillet, heat 1 tablespoon of the olive oil. Add the oregano and cook over moderate heat, stirring, until fragrant, 1 minute. Rub the lamb with the remaining 2 tablespoons of oil and season with salt and pepper. Add to the skillet and cook over moderately high heat, turning once, until golden brown, 3 to 4 minutes per side. Add the tomatoes and olives and cook, stirring, until they start to soften and the lamb is medium-rare within, about 2 minutes longer. Transfer to plates and scatter potato chips around the lamb. Spoon the pan juices over the meat and serve. —*Trattoria Al Cacciatore, Cormòns, Italy*

WINE Spice-laden red: 2013 Ronchi di Cialla Colli Orientali del Friuli Cialla Refosco dal Peduncolo Rosso.

Harissa-Spiced Cassoulet

Active **1 hr 30 min**; Total **3 hr plus overnight soaking**; Serves **10 to 12**

This North African–inspired cassoulet is chef Gavin Kaysen's nod to the broad spectrum of cultures in Minneapolis, home to his restaurant Spoon and Stable. "I wanted to showcase new flavors, but in a familiar format," says Kaysen. "I like seeing another culture's view of comfort food."

- **½ lb. thick-cut bacon, finely chopped**
- **1 large onion, finely diced**
- **1 celery rib, finely diced**
- **2 medium carrots, finely diced, plus 2 large carrots, cut into 2½-inch lengths**
- **14 oz. dried cannellini beans (2 cups), soaked overnight and drained**
   Kosher salt and black pepper
- **1½ tsp. cumin seeds**
- **1½ tsp. coriander seeds**
- **1½ tsp. yellow mustard seeds**
- **1 tsp. smoked paprika**
- **¾ tsp. crushed red pepper**
- **¼ cup plus 1 Tbsp. extra-virgin olive oil**
   Twelve 2-oz. merguez sausages
- **2 large sweet potatoes (1¼ lbs.), peeled and cut into 2½-inch pieces**
- **3 turnips (¾ lb.), peeled and cut into 2½-inch pieces**
- **4 oz. rustic peasant bread, crusts removed, bread cut into ¼-inch dice (2 cups)**
- **2 Tbsp. minced parsley**
- **1 tsp. finely grated lemon zest**
   Plain yogurt, for serving

1. In a large enameled cast-iron casserole, cook the bacon over moderately high heat, stirring occasionally, until the fat is rendered. Add the onion, celery and diced carrots and cook, stirring occasionally, until beginning to soften, about 8 minutes. Add the beans, cover with water and bring to a boil. Reduce the heat to moderately low and simmer until the beans are al dente, about 20 minutes. Remove from the heat, add a generous pinch of salt and let stand for 30 minutes. Drain and transfer the beans, bacon and vegetables to a bowl; reserve 2 cups of the cooking liquid.

2. Meanwhile, preheat the oven to 350°. In a small skillet, toast the cumin, coriander and mustard seeds over moderate heat, shaking the pan, until fragrant and the mustard seeds begin to pop, 3 to 5 minutes. Transfer to a spice grinder and let cool. Add the smoked paprika and crushed red pepper and grind the harissa blend into a powder.

3. Wipe out the casserole and heat 2 tablespoons of the olive oil in it. Add the merguez and cook over moderate heat until lightly browned all over, about 5 minutes. Transfer to a plate. Do not wipe out the casserole.

4. Add the sweet potatoes, turnips and large carrots to the casserole. Season with salt and black pepper and cook over moderately high heat, stirring occasionally, until the vegetables begin to soften, about 5 minutes. Add the harissa spice blend and cook until fragrant, about 2 minutes. Stir in the bean mixture and the reserved 2 cups of cooking liquid and bring just to a simmer. Arrange the merguez on top. Cover and bake the cassoulet until the beans are tender and most of the liquid has been absorbed, about 1 hour. Remove from the oven and uncover the cassoulet.

5. Preheat the broiler. In a bowl, toss the bread, parsley, lemon zest and the remaining 3 tablespoons of olive oil; season with salt and black pepper. Sprinkle the bread over the cassoulet; broil until golden and crisp. Let the cassoulet stand for about 10 minutes before serving. Pass yogurt at the table. —*Gavin Kaysen*

WINE Red-berried, medium-bodied Côtes du Rhône: 2011 Chateau des Tours.

Grilled Lamb Ribs with Quick Preserved Lemons

Active **1 hr 15 min**; Total **3 hr 45 min** Serves **6**

Cleveland chef Michael Symon, who grew up in a Greek and Sicilian family, often adds Mediterranean flourishes when he cooks. He seasons these lamb ribs with oregano and coriander before grilling and serves them with tangy, quick preserved lemons.

PRESERVED LEMONS
- **2 lemons, scrubbed and quartered lengthwise**
- **2 Tbsp. kosher salt**

RIBS
- **1 Tbsp. garlic salt**
- **1 Tbsp. smoked sweet paprika**
- **1 Tbsp. ground coriander**
- **1 tsp. black pepper**
- **1 Tbsp. minced oregano**
- **2½ tsp. kosher salt**
- **2 racks well-trimmed meaty lamb spareribs (5 lbs. total)**
   Lemon juice, for brushing

1. Make the preserved lemons In a small saucepan, combine the lemon quarters with 1 cup of water and the salt and cook over moderately low heat until the lemon peels are tender and the liquid is reduced by half, about 30 minutes. Let the lemons cool in the brine.

2. Transfer the lemons to a work surface; finely chop. Return the chopped lemons to the brine and refrigerate until chilled.

3. Make the ribs Set up a grill for indirect cooking by lighting only one side of a gas grill or raking hot coals to one side of a charcoal grill. In a bowl, whisk together all of the spices. Brush the lamb ribs with lemon juice; season all over with the rub.

4. Arrange the ribs on the grill. Cover and cook for about 1 hour, until well browned, maintaining a temperature of about 300°; add more coals if needed.

5. Layer 2 large sheets of heavy-duty aluminum foil on a work surface and set 1 rack of ribs, meat side up, in the center. Fold the foil tightly around the ribs. Repeat with the second rack of ribs. Arrange the rib packets meat side up on the grill. Cover and grill for 1 hour, until tender but not falling apart, turning the packets over after 30 minutes. Transfer to a baking sheet and let rest for 15 minutes, then unwrap.

6. Set the grill up for direct cooking by lighting all of the burners or raking the hot coals. Grill the rib racks meat side down over moderately high heat, turning once, until lightly charred all over, about 6 minutes total. Transfer to a carving board, tent with foil and let rest for 10 minutes. Cut the ribs between the bones; serve with the preserved lemons. —*Michael Symon*

MAKE AHEAD The lemons can be refrigerated for up to 1 week.

WINE Smoky Syrah: 2013 Foxen Toasted Rope.

GRILLED LAMB RIBS
WITH QUICK
PRESERVED LEMONS

VEGETABLES
AND TOFU

At Kismet in L.A., chefs Sara Kramer (left) and Sarah Hymanson highlight vegetables on their small-plates menu. OPPOSITE Crispy Tofu Steaks (p. 233).

Broccoli with Preserved Lemon Yogurt

Active **20 min**; Total **50 min**; Serves **4**

To jazz up broccoli, chef Laurent Tourondel of the BLT restaurant empire roasts "steaks" cut from the vegetable and serves them with a cool, tangy yogurt sauce. To get steaks that hold their shape, slice from the core to the edges to avoid crumbling florets.

- 1½ lbs. broccoli (2 small heads)
- ¼ cup extra-virgin olive oil
- ¼ tsp. crushed red pepper
  Kosher salt and black pepper
- 6 Tbsp. Greek yogurt
- 2 Tbsp. mayonnaise
- 1 small garlic clove, minced
- 1 tsp. minced preserved lemon rind, plus julienned rind for garnish
- 2 tsp. fresh lemon juice
- 2 Tbsp. freshly grated Parmigiano-Reggiano cheese

1. Preheat the oven to 475°. Place a baking sheet on the center rack and allow to heat for 10 minutes. Meanwhile, cut the broccoli lengthwise into ⅓-inch-thick slabs, reserving any florets that fall off; trim the florets to form mini steaks that lie flat.

2. In a large bowl, toss the broccoli, olive oil and crushed red pepper and season with salt and black pepper. Carefully arrange in a single layer, cut side down, on the hot baking sheet. Roast for about 20 minutes, turning halfway, until golden and tender.

3. Meanwhile, in a small bowl, mix the yogurt, mayonnaise, garlic, minced lemon rind and lemon juice and season with salt and black pepper.

4. Transfer the broccoli to plates and top with the cheese. Garnish with julienned lemon rind. Spoon the yogurt sauce on the side and serve. —*Laurent Tourondel*

MAKE AHEAD The preserved lemon yogurt can be refrigerated overnight.

Coriander-Roasted Broccoli

Total **35 min**; Serves **4**

- 2 garlic cloves
- 1 Tbsp. cumin seeds
- 2 tsp. coriander seeds
  Kosher salt
- ¼ cup plus 2 Tbsp. extra-virgin olive oil
- 2 heads of broccoli (1¾ lbs.), sliced lengthwise through the stems ¼ inch thick

1. Preheat the oven to 450°. In a mini food processor, combine the garlic, cumin, coriander, 1 teaspoon of salt and ¼ cup of the olive oil; puree until smooth.

2. Arrange the broccoli on 2 large rimmed baking sheets. Drizzle with the remaining 2 tablespoons of olive oil, season with salt and toss to coat. Roast for 5 minutes. Spoon the coriander oil over the broccoli, toss and roast until just tender, 10 minutes longer, shifting the baking sheets halfway through. Serve hot. —*Joseph Johnson*

Grilled Broccoli Rabe with Salsa Rossa

Active **50 min**; Total **1 hr 15 min**
Serves **4 to 6**

New York City chef Andrew Carmellini blanches and then grills broccoli rabe so it's both tender and slightly charred. He serves it with a killer sun-dried tomato and roasted red pepper sauce kicked up with pickled hot peppers.

SALSA ROSSA

- 1 cup sun-dried tomatoes (not oil-packed)
  Pinch of crushed red pepper
- 1 roasted red bell pepper, chopped
- ¼ cup finely chopped pickled hot peppers, plus ¼ cup brine from the jar
- 3 Tbsp. red wine vinegar
- ½ cup extra-virgin olive oil
- 1 tsp. dried oregano
- 1 tsp. sugar
  Kosher salt and black pepper

BROCCOLI RABE

- 1 lb. broccoli rabe, trimmed
- 2 Tbsp. extra-virgin olive oil
  Kosher salt and black pepper
  Shaved Pecorino Sardo, for serving

1. Make the salsa rossa In a small saucepan, bring 1 cup of water to a boil. Remove from the heat and add the tomatoes and crushed red pepper. Let stand until the tomatoes are softened, about 15 minutes.

2. Transfer the tomatoes and their liquid to a blender. Add the roasted pepper, pickled peppers, brine and vinegar and puree until very smooth. With the machine on, gradually add the olive oil until incorporated. Transfer to a bowl and stir in the oregano and sugar. Season the salsa rossa with salt and black pepper.

3. Make the broccoli rabe Set up an ice bath. In a large saucepan of salted boiling water, blanch the broccoli rabe for 2 minutes. Transfer to the ice bath, then drain and pat dry.

4. Light a grill or heat a grill pan. In a bowl, toss the broccoli rabe with the oil; season with salt and pepper. Grill over high heat, turning once, until lightly charred, 4 minutes. Serve with the salsa rossa and pecorino. —*Andrew Carmellini*

Roasted Brussels Sprouts with Cumin and Coriander

Total **45 min**; Serves **8**

- 1½ tsp. coriander seeds
- 1½ tsp. cumin seeds
- 2 lbs. brussels sprouts, trimmed and halved
- ¼ cup extra-virgin olive oil
  Kosher salt and pepper
  Finely grated lemon zest, for garnish

1. Preheat the oven to 450°. In a mortar, lightly crush the coriander and cumin seeds until coarsely ground.

2. On a large rimmed baking sheet, toss the brussels sprouts with the olive oil and season with salt and pepper. Arrange them in a single layer. Roast for 8 minutes, then add the crushed coriander and cumin and toss to coat the sprouts evenly. Roast for 10 to 15 minutes longer, until golden and crisp in spots. Transfer the sprouts to a serving platter, garnish with lemon zest and serve. —*Melissa Clark*

MAKE AHEAD The brussels sprouts can be made 3 hours ahead. Serve warm or at room temperature.

Charred Brussels Sprouts with Brown Butter and Shiso

Total **50 min;** Serves **4**

Most people who say they don't like brussels sprouts are won over when the vegetables are deeply browned. Andrew Le of The Pig & the Lady in Honolulu's Chinatown does just that, then tosses the sprouts with garlic-infused brown butter, clementines and the fragrant Japanese herb shiso.

- **6 Tbsp. unsalted butter, cut into tablespoons**
- **1 large shallot, thinly sliced**
- **4 garlic cloves, crushed**
- **⅓ cup sliced blanched almonds**
  Kosher salt
- **1 lb. medium brussels sprouts, halved**
- **2 Tbsp. fresh lemon juice**
- **2 Tbsp. Asian fish sauce**
- **1 clementine, peeled and separated into sections**
- **½ cup torn shiso leaves**
- **2 Tbsp. finely chopped parsley**
- **2 Tbsp. snipped chives**

1. In a small saucepan, cook the butter over moderate heat, stirring, until golden brown and nutty-smelling, about 5 minutes. Add the shallot and garlic and cook over very low heat until the shallot is very soft, about 20 minutes. Remove from the heat.

2. In a small skillet, heat ½ tablespoon of the infused brown butter. Add the almonds and cook over moderate heat, stirring, until golden, 3 to 5 minutes. Transfer to a small bowl and season lightly with salt.

3. In a very large cast-iron skillet, heat 2 tablespoons of the brown butter. Add the brussels sprouts cut side down and season lightly with salt. Cook over moderately high heat until browned on the bottom, 3 to 5 minutes. Add ½ cup of water, cover and cook over moderate heat, stirring occasionally, until just tender and the water is evaporated, 5 to 7 minutes. Remove from the heat and stir in the lemon juice, fish sauce and the remaining brown butter. Transfer to a platter and top with the clementine sections, shiso, parsley, chives and almonds. Serve right away. —*Andrew Le*

Grilled Cabbage with Two Sauces

⏱ Total **45 min;** Serves **8**

Honolulu chef Chris Kajioka is obsessed with local ingredients. He sources a conical variety of cabbage called conehead, grills it in wedges and serves it with a creamy herb sauce as well as a pungent, ginger-spiked Asian-style dressing. For the recipe here, Savoy cabbage is an excellent substitute.

SEAWEED ANCHOÏADE

- **½ cup extra-virgin olive oil**
- **¼ cup unseasoned rice vinegar**
- **2 Tbsp. shio kombu (see Note)**
- **1 Tbsp. minced shallot**
- **1 Tbsp. minced peeled fresh ginger**
- **1 Tbsp. minced garlic**
- **1 Tbsp. dark soy sauce**

HERB SAUCE

- **½ cup mayonnaise**
- **2 Tbsp. unseasoned rice vinegar**
- **2 Tbsp. honey**
- **2 Tbsp. each packed dill, parsley and tarragon**
- **2 Tbsp. Dijon mustard**
- **½ Tbsp. fresh lemon juice**
- **½ Tbsp. extra-virgin olive oil**
  Kosher salt and pepper

CABBAGE

- **One 2½-lb. head of Savoy cabbage, cut through the core into 8 wedges**
- **Extra-virgin olive oil, for brushing**
- **Kosher salt and pepper**

1. Make the seaweed anchoïade In a medium bowl, whisk all of the ingredients together. Let stand at room temperature for about 20 minutes.

2. Make the herb sauce In a blender, combine all of the ingredients except the salt and pepper and puree until smooth. Scrape into a bowl and season with salt and pepper.

3. Cook the cabbage In a large saucepan, steam the cabbage over boiling water, covered, until just tender, about 12 minutes. Transfer to a plate.

4. Light a grill or heat a grill pan. Brush the cabbage wedges with olive oil and season generously with salt and pepper. Grill over high heat, turning once, until lightly charred, about 8 minutes. Transfer the cabbage wedges to a platter and serve with the seaweed anchoïade and herb sauce. —*Chris Kajioka*

NOTE Shio kombu, strips of the Japanese seaweed kombu boiled in soy sauce, can be found at Asian markets and from amazon.com.

WINE Herb- and citrus-scented Sauvignon Blanc: 2014 Hanna.

Blackened Carrots

Total **50 min;** Serves **4 to 6**

Food Network star Alex Guarnaschelli dips carrots in butter before coating them in spices to roast. She says an uneven coating on the blackened carrots is a good thing: It helps avoid flavor overload.

- **2 tsp. sweet paprika**
- **2 tsp. dried oregano**
- **1 tsp. cayenne**
- **1 tsp. garlic powder**
- **4 Tbsp. unsalted butter, melted**
- **1¼ lbs. medium carrots, halved lengthwise**
- **2 Tbsp. canola oil**
  Kosher salt and pepper
- **2 Tbsp. red wine vinegar**
- **1 Tbsp. honey**
- **¼ cup extra-virgin olive oil**

1. Preheat the oven to 375°. In a small bowl, whisk the paprika with the oregano, cayenne and garlic powder. Spread on a rimmed baking sheet and toast in the oven for 2 minutes, until the spices are fragrant.

2. Put the butter in a shallow bowl. Dip the cut side of each carrot in the butter and then coat in the spice mixture, pressing to help the spices adhere; transfer to a plate.

3. In a large cast-iron skillet, heat the canola oil until shimmering. Working in batches if necessary, add the carrots cut side down in a single layer and season with salt and pepper. Cook over high heat until blackened on the bottom, about 2 minutes. Transfer the skillet to the oven and roast for 12 to 15 minutes, until the carrots are just tender.

4. Meanwhile, in a small bowl, whisk the vinegar and honey. Whisk in the olive oil, then season with salt and pepper. Transfer the carrots to a platter and drizzle with the vinaigrette. —*Alex Guarnaschelli*

Glazed Carrots with Goat Cheese and Honey

Total **1 hr**; Serves **4**

CARROTS

- 2 Tbsp. unsalted butter
- 2 Tbsp. extra-virgin olive oil
- 1½ lbs. medium carrots, peeled
- 6 garlic cloves, crushed
- 3 tarragon sprigs
- 2 thyme sprigs
- 1 rosemary sprig
- 2 bay leaves
- 2 star anise pods
- ⅛ tsp. each cumin seeds, fennel seeds and mustard seeds

  Kosher salt and pepper
- 2 Tbsp. honey, plus more for serving
- 2 Tbsp. apple cider vinegar
- 1½ cups chicken stock

GREMOLATA

- 1 cup chopped parsley
- ¼ cup chopped tarragon
- 1 tsp. finely grated garlic
- 1 tsp. finely grated lemon zest
- ½ cup extra-virgin olive oil

  Kosher salt and pepper
- 6 oz. fresh goat cheese and flaky sea salt, for serving

1. Cook the carrots In a large, deep skillet, melt the butter in the olive oil. Add the carrots, garlic, tarragon, thyme, rosemary, bay leaves, star anise and the cumin, fennel and mustard seeds and season with salt and pepper. Cook over moderate heat, stirring occasionally, until the carrots are golden, about 12 minutes. Add the 2 tablespoons of honey and cook, stirring, until the honey is lightly caramelized, about 3 minutes. Stir in the vinegar and cook until the carrots are evenly coated, about 2 minutes. Add the stock, cover and cook over moderately low heat, stirring occasionally, until the carrots are tender and the liquid is syrupy, about 20 minutes; discard the herb sprigs, bay leaves and star anise. Transfer the carrots to a plate and let cool slightly; halve lengthwise.

2. Make the gremolata In a medium bowl, combine the parsley, tarragon, garlic, lemon zest and olive oil; season with salt and pepper.

3. Spread the goat cheese on plates and drizzle with honey. Top each plate with the glazed carrots and gremolata, sprinkle with flaky sea salt and serve.
—Soho Farmhouse, Oxfordshire, England

Root-Vegetable Hot Dish with Parsnip Puree

Active **1 hr 45 min**; Total **3 hr**; Serves **8 to 10**

SORGHUM

- 2 Tbsp. grapeseed or canola oil
- 1 small onion, finely chopped
- 2 garlic cloves, minced

  Kosher salt and pepper
- 2 cups pearled sorghum (13 oz.), rinsed (see Note)
- 4 cups chicken stock or low-sodium chicken or vegetable broth

ROOT VEGETABLES

- ¾ lb. rutabaga, peeled and cut into ½-inch dice
- ¾ lb. carrots, peeled and cut into ½-inch dice
- ¾ lb. celery root, peeled and cut into ½-inch dice
- ¾ lb. turnips, peeled and cut into ½-inch dice
- ¼ cup extra-virgin olive oil

  Kosher salt and pepper

PARSNIP PUREE

- 2 Tbsp. unsalted butter
- 1 small onion, finely chopped
- 1 lb. parsnips, peeled and cut into 1-inch pieces
- 3 cups chicken stock or low-sodium chicken or vegetable broth

  Kosher salt

CRISPY SHALLOTS

  Grapeseed or canola oil, for frying
- 3 large shallots, sliced into thin rings
- 1 Tbsp. all-purpose flour

  Kosher salt

  Snipped chives, for serving

1. Cook the sorghum Preheat the oven to 400°. In a large saucepan, heat the oil. Add the onion, garlic and a generous pinch of salt and cook over moderate heat, stirring occasionally, until the onion begins to soften, 3 to 5 minutes. Add the sorghum and stock and bring to a boil over high heat. Reduce the heat to low, cover and simmer, stirring occasionally, until the sorghum is tender and the stock is absorbed, about 1 hour. Season the sorghum with salt and pepper.

2. Meanwhile, cook the root vegetables In a very large bowl, toss all of the vegetables with the olive oil and season generously with salt and pepper. Spread the vegetables in an even layer on 2 large rimmed baking sheets. Roast until tender and lightly browned, 30 to 35 minutes; stir the vegetables halfway through roasting.

3. Make the parsnip puree In a medium saucepan, melt the butter. Add the onion and cook over moderate heat, stirring occasionally, until just softened, about 5 minutes. Add the parsnips, stock and a generous pinch of salt and bring to a boil. Simmer over moderately high heat until the parsnips are tender and the stock is slightly reduced, about 20 minutes. Let cool slightly, then transfer the parsnips and their cooking liquid to a food processor and puree until smooth. Season with salt.

4. Fold the cooked sorghum into the parsnip puree and spread evenly in a 9-by-13-inch or 4-quart baking dish that's at least 2 inches deep. Scatter the roasted vegetables evenly over the puree. Cover with foil and bake for about 25 minutes, until bubbling.

5. Meanwhile, make the crispy shallots In a large saucepan, heat ½ inch of oil until shimmering. In a bowl, toss the shallots with the flour. Working in batches, fry the shallots over moderately high heat, stirring, until lightly browned and crisp. Using a slotted spoon, transfer the fried shallots to a paper towel–lined plate to drain; season with salt. Garnish the casserole with the crispy shallots and chives and serve.
—Gavin Kaysen

NOTE Sorghum is a grain that grows in the Midwest and the South. If you can't find pearled sorghum, use unpearled (whole) sorghum—soak the grain overnight and increase the cooking time to about 1 hour and 45 minutes.

MAKE AHEAD The casserole can be prepared through Step 4 and refrigerated overnight. Bring to room temperature and reheat gently before topping with the shallots and chives.

WINE Earthy, fruit-forward cru Beaujolais: 2013 Georges Descombes Morgon.

GLAZED CARROTS
WITH GOAT
CHEESE AND HONEY

GRILLED SUMMER SQUASH WITH
BLUE CHEESE AND PECANS

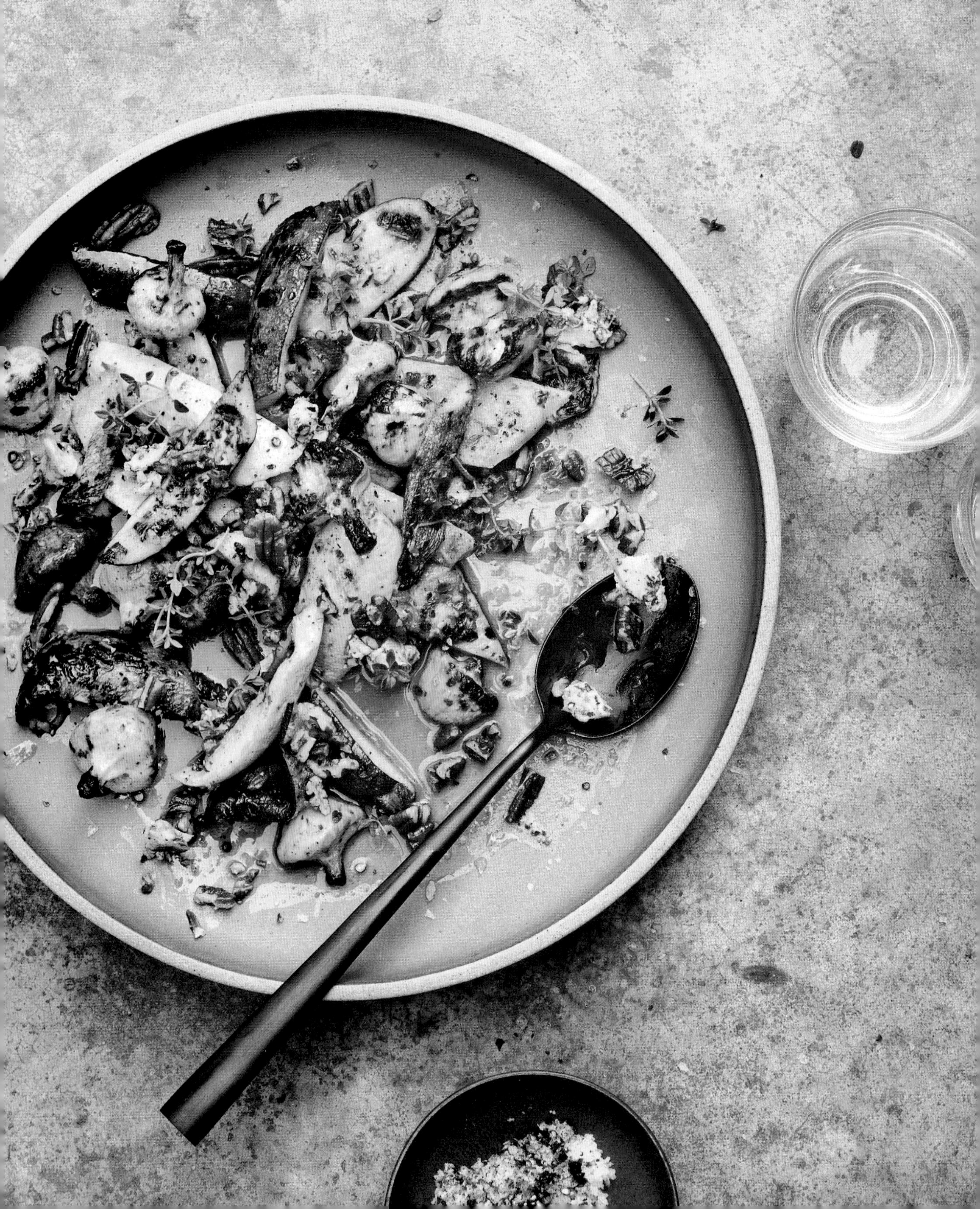

Honey-Mustard-Braised Radishes and Mustard Greens

Total **1 hr 15 min**; Serves 8

In this surprisingly easy side dish, star chef Grant Achatz showcases mustard three ways, including the nose-tingling condiment, the greens and the seeds.

½ Tbsp. yellow mustard seeds

½ Tbsp. brown mustard seeds

1 stick unsalted butter

¾ cup finely grated peeled fresh horseradish

2 garlic cloves, minced

2 shallots, minced

¼ cup plus 2 Tbsp. white wine vinegar

2 Tbsp. honey

1½ Tbsp. Dijon mustard

1 small bunch of radishes (5 oz.)—tops coarsely chopped (1 cup), 1 radish thinly sliced and remaining radishes quartered

2 bunches of mustard greens (1¼ lbs.), stemmed and chopped (16 cups)

Kosher salt and pepper

2 Tbsp. chopped chives

1. In a small dry skillet, toast the mustard seeds over low heat until they are fragrant, about 5 minutes.

2. In a large saucepan, combine the butter, horseradish, garlic, shallots, vinegar, honey and mustard with 2 cups of water. Bring to a simmer over moderately high heat and cook over moderate heat, stirring occasionally, until reduced by half, about 10 minutes. Add the quartered radishes and cook until beginning to soften, about 3 minutes. In batches, add the radish tops and mustard greens and cook, stirring, until wilted, about 2 minutes. Season with salt and pepper. Transfer to a shallow serving bowl and top with the sliced radish. Sprinkle with the chives and mustard seeds and serve. —*Grant Achatz*

Butternut Squash Steaks au Poivre

Total **50 min**; Serves 4

In a meat-free play on steak au poivre, F&W's Justin Chapple swaps in slabs of butternut squash for the beef and serves them with the go-to steakhouse green, sautéed spinach.

1 neck of a 3¼-lb. butternut squash, peeled and cut lengthwise into 4 steaks

2 Tbsp. extra-virgin olive oil, plus more for brushing

Kosher salt and coarsely cracked black pepper

1 Tbsp. unsalted butter

1 large shallot, thinly sliced

1 garlic clove, very finely chopped

1 thyme sprig

¼ cup brandy

1¼ cups low-sodium vegetable broth

½ tsp. sweet paprika

2 Tbsp. Greek yogurt

Chopped parsley, for garnish

1. Preheat the oven to 375°. Using a paring knife, score one side of each squash steak in a crosshatch pattern. Brush the steaks with olive oil and season all over with salt and cracked black pepper.

2. In a large cast-iron skillet, heat the 2 tablespoons of olive oil until shimmering. Add the squash steaks, scored side down, and cook over moderately high heat until well browned on the bottom, about 5 minutes. Flip and cook until browned on the second side, about 3 minutes. Transfer the skillet to the oven and roast the squash for about 7 minutes, until just tender. Transfer to a platter and tent with foil to keep warm.

3. In the same skillet, melt the butter. Add the shallot, garlic and thyme and cook over moderate heat, stirring, until softened, about 2 minutes. Add the brandy and cook until almost evaporated, about 1 minute. Whisk in the broth and paprika and cook, scraping up any browned bits, until slightly reduced, about 3 minutes. Discard the thyme sprig. Whisk in the yogurt and season with salt and pepper. Spoon the sauce over the squash, garnish with chopped parsley and serve. —*Justin Chapple*

WINE Earthy Côtes du Rhône: 2013 Domaine Charvin Le Poutet.

Grilled Summer Squash with Blue Cheese and Pecans

Total **45 min**; Serves 4

Summer squash can turn spongy on the grill. To give it a uniformly crisp texture, chef Vivian Howard of Chef & the Farmer in North Carolina quarters squash lengthwise and removes the watery seeds.

½ cup pecan halves

1 Tbsp. unsalted butter, melted

Kosher salt and pepper

2 lbs. mixed zucchini, summer squash and pattypan squash

¼ cup extra-virgin olive oil

1 tsp. finely grated lemon zest plus 3 Tbsp. fresh lemon juice

1 Tbsp. honey

1 tsp. thyme leaves

2 oz. blue cheese, crumbled

Grilled bread, for serving

1. Preheat the oven to 375°. On a rimmed baking sheet, toss the pecans with the butter and ½ teaspoon of salt and roast until fragrant and browned, about 10 minutes. Let cool completely, then coarsely chop.

2. Quarter the zucchini and summer squash lengthwise and cut off the soft, seedy centers. Cut any large pattypans in half lengthwise—you'll want all of the pieces to be roughly the same size. In a large bowl, toss all of the squash with 2 tablespoons of the olive oil and season with salt and pepper. Thread the pattypan squash onto metal skewers for easy grilling.

3. Light a grill. Grill all of the squash over moderately high heat, turning once, until lightly charred and tender, about 10 minutes. Cut the zucchini and summer squash into 2-inch lengths; transfer to a large bowl. Remove the pattypans from the skewers and add to the bowl.

4. In a small bowl, whisk the lemon zest and juice with the honey, thyme and the remaining 2 tablespoons of olive oil; season with salt and pepper. Add the vinaigrette to the grilled squash and toss. Transfer to a serving bowl and top with the blue cheese and toasted pecans. Serve with grilled bread. —*Vivian Howard*

Roasted Kabocha with Maple Syrup and Ginger

⏱ Total **45 min**; Serves **8 to 10**

- **3 lbs. kabocha squash**—peeled, seeded and cut into 1-inch-thick wedges
- **3 Tbsp. pure maple syrup**
- **3 Tbsp. extra-virgin olive oil**
- **1 Tbsp. finely grated peeled fresh ginger**
- **6 thyme sprigs, plus thyme leaves for garnish**
- **Kosher salt**

Preheat the oven to 450°. On a rimmed baking sheet, toss the squash wedges with the maple syrup, olive oil, ginger, thyme sprigs and salt. Arrange the squash in a single layer and roast for 15 minutes. Flip and roast for 15 minutes longer, until golden and tender. Discard the thyme sprigs. Transfer the squash to a serving platter and garnish with thyme leaves. —*Melissa Clark*

MAKE AHEAD The squash can be made up to 6 hours ahead.

Quick-Pickled Sweet Cucumbers

📷 PAGE 180

Active **15 min**; Total **2 hr 45 min**
Makes **1 quart**

- **1 cup sugar**
- **½ cup distilled white vinegar**
- **2 unpeeled medium cucumbers, very thinly sliced**
- **1 Tbsp. kosher salt**

1. In a medium saucepan, combine the sugar with 1½ cups of water and bring to a simmer over moderate heat, stirring to dissolve the sugar. Remove the pan from the heat and stir in the vinegar. Transfer the brine to a heatproof bowl and let cool to room temperature.

2. In a colander set over a bowl, toss the cucumbers with the salt. Let stand at room temperature for 15 minutes. Press down on the cucumbers to release any excess liquid, then transfer the cucumbers to the brine. Cover and refrigerate for at least 2 hours. —*Magnus Nilsson*

MAKE AHEAD The pickles can be refrigerated for up to 1 week.

Spinach-and-Ricotta-Stuffed Tomatoes with Piquillo Peppers

Active **1 hr**; Total **1 hr 50 min**; Serves **4**

At the exquisite Provence winery Commanderie de Peyrassol, chef Guillaume Delaune uses ingredients from his kitchen garden to make dishes like these beautiful stuffed tomatoes. He uses a melon baller to hollow out the tomatoes, leaving sturdy cups to hold the cheesy filling. The accompanying sauce is made from the scooped-out tomato seeds and juices.

- **2 slices of sourdough bread, cut into ¼-inch cubes**
- **9 Tbsp. extra-virgin olive oil, plus more for drizzling**
- **4 firm-ripe medium tomatoes, top ½ inch cut off and reserved**
- **Kosher salt and pepper**
- **½ medium onion, halved and thinly sliced**
- **½ cup rosé**
- **8 oz. baby spinach**
- **4 oz. fresh ricotta cheese**
- **3 piquillo peppers, drained and diced**
- **1½ oz. freshly grated Parmigiano-Reggiano cheese**
- **¼ cup chopped basil**
- **¼ cup chopped parsley**
- **1 garlic clove, minced**
- **¼ tsp. minced thyme**
- **¼ tsp. minced rosemary**
- **7 pitted kalamata olives, quartered lengthwise**
- **Pinch of piment d'Espelette**
- **Baby arugula, for garnish**

1. Preheat the oven to 350°. On a rimmed baking sheet, toss the bread cubes with 2 tablespoons of the olive oil. Bake until golden and crisp, 8 to 10 minutes. Let cool. Leave the oven on.

2. Using a medium melon baller, scoop the insides of the tomatoes into a small gratin dish, leaving a ¼-inch wall on the sides. Lightly sprinkle the insides of the tomato cups with salt and drain upside down on a paper towel–lined plate.

3. In a large nonstick skillet, heat 2 tablespoons of the olive oil. Add the onion and cook over moderate heat, stirring occasionally, until softened, about 5 minutes. Add the rosé and cook until almost completely evaporated, about 5 minutes. Scrape the mixture into a medium bowl and wipe out the skillet.

4. Heat 1 tablespoon of the olive oil in the skillet. Add the spinach and cook over moderately high heat, stirring, just until wilted; transfer to the bowl with the onion. Add the ricotta, piquillos, Parmigiano-Reggiano, basil, parsley, garlic, thyme, rosemary, olives and piment d'Espelette. Season with salt and pepper.

5. Set the tomatoes in the gratin dish in their juices and stuff with the ricotta filling. Bake until the tomatoes are softened, about 20 minutes. Set the tops on the tomatoes and bake for 10 minutes longer.

6. Using a slotted spoon, transfer the stuffed tomatoes to a plate; cover to keep warm. Transfer the cooking juices to a blender, add the remaining ¼ cup of oil and puree until smooth. Strain the sauce into a small saucepan and season with salt and pepper. Simmer over moderately low heat, stirring occasionally, until slightly thickened, about 10 minutes.

7. Spoon the sauce into shallow bowls and set a stuffed tomato in each one. Garnish with the croutons and arugula, drizzle with olive oil and serve. —*Guillaume Delaune*

MAKE AHEAD The filling can be refrigerated for up to 2 days.

WINE Herb-inflected Provence white: 2014 Domaine Le Galantin Bandol Blanc.

ROASTED KABOCHA WITH
MAPLE SYRUP AND GINGER

Creamed Spinach with Fried Cheese Curds

Total **1 hr**; Serves **8**

Chef Gavin Kaysen serves this incredibly decadent curd-topped spinach at Spoon and Stable in Minneapolis. Wonder just how much Minnesotans love cheese curds? The restaurant sold some 8,500 orders of the dish in its first 10 months.

- ½ **cup grapeseed or canola oil, plus more for frying**
- 4 **medium shallots, minced**
- 6 **garlic cloves, minced**
  Kosher salt and pepper
  Four 10-oz. bags curly spinach, stems discarded
- 2 **cups crème fraîche**
- 2 **cups panko**
- 1 **cup all-purpose flour**
- 2 **large eggs**
- ½ **lb. cheddar cheese curds**

1. Set a rack over a large rimmed baking sheet. In a large pot, heat the ½ cup of oil until shimmering. Add the shallots, garlic and a generous pinch of salt and cook over moderately high heat, stirring, until softened, 1 to 2 minutes. Add the spinach in large handfuls, letting each batch wilt slightly before adding more. Cook, stirring occasionally, until all of the spinach is wilted, 7 minutes. Spread the spinach on the rack to drain and cool completely.

2. Preheat the oven to 375°. Squeeze the spinach dry and return it to the pot. Stir in the crème fraîche and season with salt and pepper. Transfer to individual 6-ounce gratin dishes or a 2-quart baking dish. Bake the spinach until bubbling, 15 minutes.

3. Meanwhile, in a large saucepan, heat 1½ inches of oil to 350°. Spread the panko and flour in 2 separate shallow bowls. In another shallow bowl, beat the eggs with a pinch each of salt and pepper. Dredge the cheese curds in the flour, tapping off any excess. Coat the curds in the beaten egg, then dredge in the panko, pressing lightly on the curds to help the crumbs adhere.

4. Working in 2 batches, fry the cheese curds until golden and crisp, 2 to 3 minutes. Using a slotted spoon, transfer the fried curds to paper towels to drain. Top the spinach with the fried cheese curds and serve. —*Gavin Kaysen*

Roasted Sunchokes and Swiss Chard with Chili Ricotta

Total **45 min**; Serves **4 to 6**

Josh Lewis, the chef at Fleet in Australia's Byron Bay, gives sunchokes and Swiss chard the spicy-and-sweet treatment: He dollops the vegetables with chili powder–spiked ricotta, then drizzles them with a lightly reduced balsamic dressing.

- 1 **cup balsamic vinegar**
- 1½ **Tbsp. grapeseed oil**
- 1 **lb. sunchokes, scrubbed and halved lengthwise**
  Kosher salt and pepper
- 2 **medium bunches of Swiss chard, stems discarded**
- 1 **cup fresh ricotta cheese**
  Chili powder, for garnish

1. In a small saucepan, simmer the balsamic vinegar over moderately high heat until reduced to ½ cup, about 10 minutes. Remove the saucepan from the heat.

2. Preheat the oven to 425°. In a large oven-proof skillet, heat the grapeseed oil. Add the sunchokes cut side down and season with a generous pinch each of salt and pepper. Cook over moderately high heat until golden, 4 to 5 minutes. Turn the sunchokes, transfer to the oven and roast until tender, 12 to 15 minutes.

3. Meanwhile, in a medium saucepan of salted boiling water, blanch the Swiss chard until just tender, 1 to 2 minutes. Using tongs, transfer the chard to a colander. Let cool slightly, then squeeze dry.

4. Arrange the roasted sunchokes and blanched Swiss chard on a platter. Dollop the ricotta over the vegetables and drizzle with half of the reduced balsamic. Sprinkle with chili powder and season with salt and pepper. Serve with the remaining balsamic. —*Josh Lewis*

Swiss Chard with Aleppo Pepper and Buttermilk

Total **40 min**; Serves **4 to 6**

Sara Kramer and Sarah Hymanson of L.A.'s Kismet spoon these tender steamed greens over a pool of seasoned buttermilk, but you can swap in kefir, a fermented milk frequently used in Middle Eastern cooking, or plain yogurt. Serve these greens alongside the duo's Crispy Rice with Dried Mint and Lemon (p. 246) and Braised Chicken with Fava Beans (p. 151)—the creamy buttermilk doubles as a delicious sauce.

- ⅔ **cup buttermilk**
- ¼ **cup extra-virgin olive oil, plus more for drizzling**
  Kosher salt and black pepper
- 1½ **lbs. Swiss chard, stems sliced ¼ inch thick and leaves chopped**
- 2 **tsp. Aleppo pepper (see Note)**
- ½ **tsp. ground sumac**
- 1 **garlic clove, finely grated**
- ½ **lemon, for serving**

1. In a large, shallow bowl, whisk the buttermilk with 2 tablespoons of the olive oil and season with salt and black pepper.

2. In a large skillet, heat the remaining 2 tablespoons of olive oil. Add the chard stems and season with the Aleppo pepper, sumac and a generous pinch each of salt and black pepper. Cook the chard over moderately high heat, stirring occasionally, until the stems begin to soften, about 5 minutes.

3. Add the chard leaves and the garlic to the skillet. Cover and cook over moderately high heat, stirring once, until the leaves are tender and wilted, about 4 minutes. Season the chard with salt and black pepper and let cool to room temperature.

4. Spoon the Swiss chard over the buttermilk. Squeeze the lemon half over the greens, drizzle with olive oil and serve. —*Sarah Hymanson and Sara Kramer*

NOTE Aleppo pepper is a dried ground pepper from Syria and Turkey; it's mildly spicy, tart and fruity.

MAKE AHEAD The steamed Swiss chard can be refrigerated overnight. Bring to room temperature before serving.

Asparagus with Speck and Chopped Egg

⏱ Total **30 min**; Serves **4**

In the Friuli region of northern Italy, this dish is called *asparagi paparot* (*paparot* means "to squash"), referring to the hard-boiled eggs crumbled on top. This recipe is based on one from Trattoria Al Grop, which uses the asparagus that grows wild in the surrounding hills.

- **2 large eggs**
- **¼ cup extra-virgin olive oil**
- **1 oz. thinly sliced speck or prosciutto, cut into ¼-inch-wide strips**
- **1 garlic clove, minced**
- **1 lb. medium asparagus, trimmed**
  Kosher salt and pepper
- **2 Tbsp. red wine vinegar**
- **1 Tbsp. chopped parsley**

1. In a medium saucepan, cover the eggs with 2 inches of water and bring to a boil. Cover, remove from the heat and let stand for 10 minutes. Drain the eggs and let cool in an ice water bath, then peel and chop them.

2. Meanwhile, in a large nonstick skillet, heat 1 tablespoon of the olive oil. Add the speck and cook over moderate heat, stirring occasionally, for 2 minutes. Stir in the garlic and cook until golden and the speck is crispy, about 2 minutes. Using a slotted spoon, transfer the speck and garlic to a paper towel–lined plate.

3. Add the asparagus and 1 tablespoon of olive oil to the skillet, season with salt and pepper and cook, turning, until golden and crisp-tender, 3 to 4 minutes. Transfer the asparagus to a platter.

4. Remove the skillet from the heat and whisk in the red wine vinegar, parsley and the remaining 2 tablespoons of olive oil; season with salt and pepper. Spoon the warm dressing over the asparagus and top with the speck and chopped eggs. Serve the dish hot or warm. —*Trattoria Al Grop, Tavagnacco, Italy*

WINE Pear-scented Friulano: 2014 Marco Felluga Collio.

Flash-Grilled Beans with Lemon-Dill Aioli

⏱ Total **45 min**; Serves **6**

Ben Ford, the chef at Ford's Filling Station in L.A., takes green and yellow wax beans to a new level, charring them just enough so they're still a little crunchy and serving them with a lemony, chive-laced aioli.

- **1 large egg**
- **1 tsp. finely grated lemon zest plus 1 Tbsp. fresh lemon juice**
- **1 tsp. Dijon mustard**
- **2 garlic cloves**
- **¼ cup vegetable oil**
- **¾ cup plus 1 Tbsp. extra-virgin olive oil**
- **1 Tbsp. minced chives**
- **1 Tbsp. minced dill**
  Kosher salt and pepper
- **¾ lb. green beans**
- **¾ lb. yellow wax beans**
- **2 shallots, sliced into rings**
  Dill and parsley sprigs, for serving

1. In a blender, combine the egg with the lemon zest and juice, Dijon mustard, garlic and 1 teaspoon of water and puree until smooth. With the machine on, drizzle in the vegetable oil and ¾ cup of the olive oil until emulsified. Scrape the aioli into a bowl and stir in the minced chives and dill. Season the aioli with salt and pepper. Refrigerate until chilled, about 30 minutes.

2. Meanwhile, in a large saucepan of salted boiling water, blanch the green and yellow beans until they are just crisp-tender, about 2 minutes. Drain and cool under running water; pat thoroughly dry.

3. Light a grill and put a perforated grill pan on it to heat. In a large bowl, toss the beans with the shallots and the remaining 1 tablespoon of olive oil; season with salt and pepper. Spread the beans on the grill pan and grill over high heat until lightly charred on the bottom, about 3 minutes. Toss and grill for 30 seconds longer. Transfer the beans to a bowl and garnish with dill and parsley sprigs. Serve with the aioli. —*Ben Ford*

Blistered Snap Peas with Everything-Bagel Seasonings

⏱ Total **25 min**; Serves **4 to 6**

At their restaurant Ox in Portland, Oregon, Greg Denton and Gabrielle Quiñónez Denton have a clever trick for keeping small vegetables from slipping through the grill grate: They place a cross-hatched cooling rack upside down on the grill—no grill basket needed.

- **1 Tbsp. toasted sesame seeds**
- **1 Tbsp. salted roasted sunflower seeds**
- **¾ tsp. flaky sea salt**
- **½ tsp. nigella seeds or poppy seeds**
- **½ tsp. dried onion flakes**
- **½ tsp. dried garlic flakes**
- **¼ tsp. caraway seeds**
- **1 lb. snap peas, trimmed**
- **¼ cup toasted sesame oil**
  Kosher salt and pepper
- **2 Tbsp. unsalted butter, melted**
- **⅓ cup mascarpone**
  Snipped chives and salmon roe, for serving

1. In a small bowl, mix the sesame seeds with the sunflower seeds, flaky sea salt, nigella seeds, onion and garlic flakes and the caraway seeds.

2. Light a grill. Place a latticed wire cooling rack upside down on top of the grill (or set a rack with parallel bars perpendicular to the grate). In a medium bowl, toss the snap peas with 2 tablespoons of the sesame oil and season with kosher salt and pepper. Grill the snap peas on the rack over moderately high heat, turning occasionally, until lightly charred and tender, 3 to 4 minutes. Return the snap peas to the bowl and toss with the melted butter and the remaining 2 tablespoons of sesame oil. Add the seed mixture and toss to coat; let cool slightly.

3. Spread the mascarpone on a platter or plates. Mound the snap peas on top and drizzle with any remaining sesame butter. Garnish with chives and salmon roe; serve immediately. —*Greg Denton and Gabrielle Quiñónez Denton*

GREEN VEGETABLES
WITH DUKKA AND
TAHINI DRESSING

Blistered Okra with Dill-Coriander Lebneh

Total **40 min** plus **2 hr** brining
Serves **4 to 6**

Okra lovers will rejoice in this elevated take on the vegetable. Brining gives the dish extra depth, while the bright, tangy sauce made with dill and lebneh (Greek yogurt's thicker, richer Middle Eastern cousin) brings the dish together.

- **Kosher salt and cracked black pepper**
- 1 **head of garlic, halved crosswise, plus ¾ tsp. finely grated garlic**
- 1 **cup coarsely chopped dill sprigs plus ¼ cup chopped dill fronds, plus small sprigs for garnish**
- 1 **lb. okra**
- ¾ **cup lebneh or Greek yogurt**
- 1 **tsp. crushed coriander seeds**
- ¼ **cup plus 2 Tbsp. extra-virgin olive oil**
- **Lemon wedges, for serving**

1. In a large bowl, whisk 8 cups of hot water with ½ cup of salt, the halved garlic head and the chopped dill sprigs until the salt is dissolved. Let cool to lukewarm.

2. Using a paring knife, pierce each piece of okra in a few spots to help it absorb the brine. Add the okra to the brine and place a plate on top to keep them completely submerged. Let stand at room temperature for 2 hours.

3. Meanwhile, in a small bowl, combine the lebneh with the crushed coriander, grated garlic, chopped dill fronds and ¼ cup of the olive oil. Add 2 tablespoons of water and season with salt and cracked pepper. Whisk until smooth.

4. Light a grill or heat a grill pan. Drain the okra and pat dry; discard the garlic and dill sprigs. In a medium bowl, toss the okra with the remaining 2 tablespoons of olive oil and season with pepper. Grill the okra over moderately high heat, turning, until charred in spots and crisp-tender, about 5 minutes. Spread the lebneh on plates and top with the blistered okra. Garnish with small dill sprigs and serve with lemon wedges. —*Kay Chun*

MAKE AHEAD The dill lebneh can be refrigerated overnight.

Green Vegetables with Dukka and Tahini Dressing

Total **50 min**; Serves **4**

The Egyptian nut-and-spice blend dukka is a fantastic garnish for steamed vegetables. The dish gets extra crunch from activated almonds (nuts sprouted in water). You can find them at Whole Foods, health food stores and online from amazon.com.

DUKKA

- 3 **Tbsp. hazelnuts**
- 1 **Tbsp. coriander seeds**
- 1½ **tsp. cumin seeds**
- 1 **Tbsp. toasted sesame seeds**
- ¾ **tsp. pepper**
- ½ **tsp. Maldon salt**

DRESSING

- ¼ **cup tahini**
- ¼ **cup tamari**
- ¼ **cup apple cider vinegar**
- ¼ **cup extra-virgin olive oil**
- 1 **small garlic clove, thinly sliced**
- ¼ **cup parsley leaves**
- ½ **tsp. honey**
- **Kosher salt and pepper**

STEAMED VEGETABLES

- 8 **oz. sugar snap peas, trimmed**
- 1 **bunch of Broccolini or broccoli, trimmed and cut into 2-inch lengths**
- 8 **oz. asparagus, trimmed and cut into 3-inch pieces**
- ½ **cup sprouted almonds**

1. Make the dukka Preheat the oven to 350°. Spread the hazelnuts in a pie plate; toast until golden and the skins blister, 10 to 12 minutes. Let cool slightly. Transfer to a clean kitchen towel and rub off the skins.

2. In a small skillet, toast the coriander and cumin seeds over moderate heat, shaking the pan, until fragrant, 2 to 3 minutes. In a mortar or mini food processor, pound the seeds until finely ground. Add the hazelnuts, sesame seeds, pepper and Maldon salt to the mortar and crush the hazelnuts into ¼-inch bits.

3. Make the dressing In a blender, combine the tahini, tamari, vinegar, olive oil, garlic, parsley and honey. Blend until smooth and season with salt and pepper.

4. Cook the vegetables Set a steamer basket over, but not in, a large saucepan of boiling water. Add the snap peas, cover and steam until tender, 2 minutes. Using a slotted spoon, transfer the snap peas to a rack set over a rimmed baking sheet to cool slightly. Add the Broccolini to the steamer basket, cover and cook until tender, about 5 minutes. Transfer the Broccolini to the rack to drain. Add the asparagus to the steamer basket, cover and cook until tender, about 5 minutes.

5. In a large bowl, toss the peas, Broccolini and asparagus with ½ cup of the tahini dressing and 3 tablespoons of the dukka. Garnish with the sprouted almonds and more dukka. Serve the remaining dressing on the side. —*Adam Coates*

MAKE AHEAD The dukka can be kept in an airtight container for 2 weeks. The tahini dressing can be refrigerated for 4 days.

Grilled Sweet Corn with Coconut Glaze

Total **40 min**; Serves **6**

Kris Yenbamroong of L.A.'s Night + Market restaurants says this grilled corn is one of his favorite summer treats because it's "high pleasure, low hassle." The coconut milk and sugar in the glaze intensify the sweet corn flavor.

- One 15-oz. can unsweetened coconut milk
- 1 **Tbsp. coconut sugar**
- 2 **tsp. kosher salt**
- 2 **tsp. ground turmeric**
- 6 **ears of corn, shucked**

1. In a small saucepan, combine the coconut milk, coconut sugar, salt and turmeric. Bring to a boil, stirring to dissolve the sugar. Cook until slightly thickened, about 10 minutes.

2. Light a grill or heat a grill pan over moderate heat. Brush the corn with some of the coconut glaze and grill, turning and basting occasionally, until slightly charred and crisp-tender, about 20 minutes. Brush the corn with more glaze and serve warm. —*Kris Yenbamroong*

MAKE AHEAD The coconut glaze can be refrigerated overnight.

Grilled Spring Onions with Pistachio Butter

Total **1 hr** plus **2 hr** pickling; Serves **4 to 6**

- 1 cup rice vinegar
- ¼ cup sugar
- 1 bay leaf
- Kosher salt
- 1 cardamom pod
- 1 tsp. black peppercorns
- 1 tsp. coriander seeds
- 1½ cups whole pitted prunes
- 1¼ cups unsalted pistachios
- 1 garlic clove, finely grated
- 1 tsp. finely grated lemon zest
- 6 Tbsp. extra-virgin olive oil, plus more for drizzling
- 25 young spring onions or large scallions, trimmed
- 1 cup Greek yogurt
- ½ tsp. Urfa or Aleppo pepper (see Note)
- Mint leaves, for garnish

1. In a small saucepan, combine the rice vinegar, sugar, bay leaf, ½ teaspoon of salt and ¾ cup of water. Wrap the cardamom, peppercorns and coriander seeds in a cheesecloth bundle and add to the saucepan. Simmer the brine over moderate heat for 10 minutes. Put the prunes in a heatproof bowl, pour the brine over them and let stand for 2 hours.

2. Drain the prunes, reserving the brine. Discard the spice bundle and bay leaf. Simmer the brine until it coats the back of a spoon, 10 minutes, then pour over the prunes in the bowl.

3. Preheat the oven to 300°. Spread the pistachios on a baking sheet and bake until lightly browned, 12 to 15 minutes. Transfer to a food processor and let cool. Add the garlic and lemon zest and process until finely chopped, 1 minute. Add 2 tablespoons of the olive oil and ½ cup plus 2 tablespoons of water and process until a smooth paste forms; season with salt.

4. Light a grill. In a large bowl, toss the spring onions with the remaining ¼ cup of olive oil and season with salt. Grill the onions over moderately high heat until tender and lightly charred, 6 to 8 minutes.

5. Quarter 8 of the prunes. (Save the rest for another use.) Spread the yogurt and pistachio butter on a platter. Top with the grilled onions and season with the Urfa pepper. Garnish with the prunes, mint leaves and a drizzle of olive oil; serve immediately. —*Sarah Hymanson and Sara Kramer*

NOTE Urfa pepper is a smoky, coarsely ground Turkish chile. Aleppo pepper is a dried ground pepper from Syria and Turkey; it's mildly spicy, tart and fruity.

Parmesan Leek Gratin

:D Active **15 min**; Total **30 min**; Serves **4**

According to Magnus Nilsson, the chef at Fäviken in Järpen, Sweden, it's simply too cold too much of the time in Scandinavia to cultivate a lot of produce. "So we take advantage of sturdy vegetables," he explains. Here, he glazes leeks under the broiler with a light Parmesan cream.

- 8 small leeks, root ends trimmed
- 6 Tbsp. heavy cream
- ½ cup freshly grated Parmigiano-Reggiano cheese
- Kosher salt and white pepper
- Freshly grated nutmeg

1. Preheat the broiler. Cut off all but 3 inches of the dark green portion of the leeks. Make a lengthwise slice from the green ends, stopping at the firm white bulb. Rinse the leeks very well.

2. In a pot of salted boiling water, blanch the leeks until just tender, about 8 minutes. Drain and transfer to a bowl of ice water to stop the cooking. Drain very well and pat dry. Halve the leeks lengthwise and arrange cut side up in a 2½-quart gratin dish.

3. In a medium bowl, mix the cream with the cheese and season with salt, white pepper and nutmeg. Spoon the cream mixture over the leeks. Broil 6 inches from the heat for 7 to 8 minutes, until golden and bubbling. Season with salt and white pepper and serve. —*Magnus Nilsson*

Roman Fried Artichokes

Total **1 hr 15 min**; Serves **4 to 6**

Double-frying the artichokes is the secret to getting supercrisp edges while keeping the insides tender.

- 3 large egg yolks
- 1 tsp. finely grated lemon zest
- ¼ cup plus 1 Tbsp. fresh lemon juice
- 1½ tsp. fine sea salt
- 1½ cups extra-virgin olive oil
- 12 small salt-packed anchovy fillets, rinsed and minced (1 Tbsp.)
- 24 baby artichokes (about 3 lbs.)
- Canola oil, for frying
- Maldon sea salt
- Lemon wedges, for serving

1. In a medium bowl, whisk the egg yolks, lemon zest, 1 tablespoon of the lemon juice and the fine sea salt. Whisking constantly, slowly stream in the olive oil until the aioli is thick and glossy. Whisk in 1 more tablespoon of the lemon juice and the anchovies. Cover and refrigerate.

2. Add the remaining 3 tablespoons of lemon juice to a large bowl of cold water. Working with 1 artichoke at a time, trim the stem. Snap off the leaves until you reach the tender light green inner leaves. Cut off the top third of the artichoke and trim off any tough leaves near the base. Halve the artichoke lengthwise, scoop out the fuzzy choke if necessary and drop the artichoke in the lemon water. Repeat with the remaining artichokes.

3. In a medium, straight-sided skillet, heat 2 inches of canola oil to 250°. Line a rimmed baking sheet with paper towels and top with a rack. Drain the artichokes well and pat dry. Fry in 3 batches over moderately high heat until tender and just beginning to brown, about 5 minutes. Using a slotted spoon, transfer the artichokes to the wire rack to drain.

4. Heat the oil to 375°. Fry the artichokes again in 3 batches until crispy, about 1 minute per batch. This time, drain on the paper towels. Season generously with Maldon sea salt and serve hot, with the aioli and lemon wedges. —*Andrew Zimmern*

WINE Fragrant Italian white: 2014 Principe Pallavicini Poggio Verde Frascati Superiore.

GRILLED EGGPLANT
INVOLTINI

Leeks in Riesling Butter with Cheese Sauce

⏱ Total **45 min**; Serves **4**

Scottish chef Isaac McHale of The Clove Club in London has a deft hand with vegetables, as these outstanding leeks show. He bathes them in Riesling butter and serves them with a light cheese sauce, watercress and pickled onions.

- **6 medium leeks, white and light green parts only, halved lengthwise**
- **1 cup dry Riesling wine**
- **2 sticks cold unsalted butter, cubed**
  Kosher salt
- **½ cup whole milk**
- **½ lb. sharp cheddar cheese, preferably Montgomery's, grated (2 cups)**
- **1 cup chopped watercress leaves and small sprigs**
  Sliced pickled onions, for garnish

1. In a large skillet of salted boiling water, blanch the leeks just until fork-tender, 8 to 10 minutes. Transfer to an ice bath to cool; drain well and pat dry. Wipe out the skillet.

2. Meanwhile, in a small saucepan, bring the wine to a simmer. Cook over moderately low heat until reduced by half, about 10 minutes. Off the heat, whisk in the butter, a few cubes at a time, until smooth. Season with salt.

3. In another small saucepan, bring the milk to a boil. Add the cheese, cover and let stand off the heat for 3 minutes. Scrape the mixture into a blender and puree until smooth. Season with salt. Keep warm.

4. Return the leeks to the skillet and pour the Riesling butter over. Cook over moderately low heat, stirring, just until warmed through, 2 minutes. Spoon a little cheese sauce onto each of 4 plates. Top with the leeks and spoon some Riesling butter on top. Garnish with the watercress and pickled onions and serve. —*Isaac McHale*

Grilled Eggplant Involtini

Active **1 hr**; Total **2 hr 20 min**
Serves **10 to 12**

For a lighter take on classic involtini, this rustic dish calls for grilling the eggplant first instead of deep-frying it. The lightly charred slices are rolled around a filling of rice and mozzarella, then baked in fresh tomato sauce.

- **6 lbs. tomatoes**
- **2 Tbsp. extra-virgin olive oil, plus more for brushing**
- **1 small yellow onion, finely chopped**
  Kosher salt and pepper
- **1 basil sprig plus ½ cup chopped basil**
- **1 cup long-grain white rice, rinsed and drained**
  Three 1¼-lb. Italian eggplants, sliced lengthwise ¼ inch thick (about 36 slices)
- **2 cups shredded fresh mozzarella cheese (8 oz.)**
- **1½ cups freshly grated Parmigiano-Reggiano cheese, plus more for sprinkling**

1. Bring a large saucepan of water to a boil. Using a paring knife, core the tomatoes and mark an X on the bottom of each one. Add half of the tomatoes to the saucepan at a time and blanch them until they begin to soften and the skins are wrinkled, 3 to 5 minutes. Transfer the hot tomatoes to a work surface and let cool slightly, then peel and coarsely chop. Working in 2 batches, puree the tomatoes in a food processor; you should have about 9½ cups of puree.

2. In the saucepan, heat the 2 tablespoons of olive oil. Add the onion and a generous pinch of salt and cook over moderate heat, stirring occasionally, until the onion is softened and beginning to brown, about 8 minutes. Add the tomato puree and basil sprig and bring to a boil. Simmer over moderately high heat, stirring frequently, until the tomato sauce is thickened and reduced to 5½ cups, about 45 minutes. Discard the basil and season the sauce with salt and pepper. Let cool slightly.

3. Meanwhile, in a medium saucepan, bring 1½ cups of water to a boil. Add the rice and a generous pinch of salt and stir once. Cover and simmer over low heat until the rice is tender and the water is absorbed, about 20 minutes. Remove from the heat and let steam, covered, for 20 minutes. Fluff the rice with a fork and let cool.

4. Light a grill or heat a grill pan. Brush the eggplant slices with oil and grill over moderately high heat, turning once, until tender and lightly charred, about 4 minutes per batch. Transfer the eggplant to a work surface and season with salt and pepper.

5. Preheat the oven to 350°. In a large bowl, combine the cooled rice with 2 cups of the tomato sauce. Fold in the mozzarella, chopped basil and 1 cup of the Parmesan, then season the filling with salt and pepper.

6. Spread ¾ cup of the tomato sauce in the bottom of each of two 9-by-13-inch baking dishes. Dollop 2 tablespoons of the rice filling near one end of each eggplant slice and roll into a tight cylinder; arrange in the prepared baking dishes. Spoon 1 cup of the sauce over the involtini in each baking dish and top with the remaining ½ cup of Parmesan. Bake the involtini until the filling is hot and the sauce is just bubbling, 15 to 20 minutes. Let stand for 5 minutes before serving with additional Parmesan. —*Giuseppe Angelini*

MAKE AHEAD The tomato sauce can be refrigerated for up to 3 days; the grilled eggplant can be refrigerated overnight.

WINE Fruit-rich Italian white: 2015 Cantina del Taburno Falanghina del Sannio.

Chinese-Style Braised Mushrooms and Mustard Greens

📷 PAGE 149

Active **30 min**; Total **1 hr 15 min**; Serves **4**

Seamus Mullen of Tertulia in New York City braises vegetables in a fragrant broth of rice wine, dried shiitake, star anise and Chinese five-spice powder.

- ½ oz. small dried shiitake mushrooms
- 2 cups boiling water
- ¼ cup extra-virgin olive oil
- 2 king oyster mushrooms or white button mushrooms (6 oz.), cut into 1-inch pieces
- 4 medium shallots, quartered lengthwise
- Fine sea salt and pepper
- 2 garlic cloves, thinly sliced
- 1 star anise pod
- 1 tsp. Chinese five-spice powder
- ½ cup dry rice wine or dry white wine
- One 10-oz. bunch of mustard greens, stems discarded and leaves torn (4 cups)

1. In a medium heatproof bowl, cover the shiitake with the boiling water and top with a heatproof plate to keep them submerged. Let stand until softened, about 25 minutes. Using a slotted spoon, transfer the shiitake to a work surface and cut them in half. Reserve the soaking liquid.

2. In a large saucepan, heat the oil. Add the king oyster mushrooms, shallots and a generous pinch of salt and cook over moderately high heat until just starting to soften, about 3 minutes. Stir in the shiitake, garlic, star anise and five-spice powder. Add the wine and simmer until it has evaporated, about 2 minutes.

3. Add the shiitake soaking liquid to the saucepan and bring to a boil. Simmer over moderate heat, stirring occasionally, until the soaking liquid is slightly reduced, about 10 minutes. Add the greens and cook, stirring occasionally, until just tender, about 5 minutes. Discard the star anise. Season with salt and pepper. Serve. —*Seamus Mullen*

Roasted Mushrooms with Red Wine Butter

Total **1 hr**; Serves **8**

Instead of cooking mushrooms in a skillet, Food Network fixture Geoffrey Zakarian roasts them in the oven until tender before tossing them in a buttery red wine sauce with garlic and fresh herbs. Be sure not to salt the mushrooms before roasting; they'll release a lot of liquid and steam instead of brown.

- 3 lbs. mixed mushrooms, such as cremini, oyster and chanterelle, halved if large
- ¾ cup plus 1 Tbsp. canola oil
- 1 Tbsp. thyme leaves
- 1 tsp. minced rosemary
- 1 large shallot, minced
- 1 Tbsp. minced garlic
- 1 cup dry red wine
- 3 Tbsp. cold unsalted butter, cubed
- Kosher salt and pepper
- ¼ cup chopped tarragon
- ¼ cup chopped parsley

1. Position racks in the upper and lower thirds of the oven and preheat to 400°. Heat 2 large rimmed baking sheets in the oven for at least 10 minutes.

2. In a large bowl, toss the mushrooms with ¾ cup of the oil, the thyme and rosemary. Remove the baking sheets from the oven and immediately spread the mushrooms on them in an even layer. Roast for 25 to 30 minutes, until tender and browned, stirring halfway through roasting.

3. Meanwhile, in a medium skillet, heat the remaining 1 tablespoon of oil. Add the shallot and garlic and cook over moderately high heat, stirring, until softened, about 3 minutes. Add the wine and simmer until reduced to a glaze, 3 to 5 minutes. Swirl in the butter and season with salt and pepper.

4. Scrape all the mushrooms onto 1 baking sheet. Add the red wine butter and toss well. Season with salt and pepper and toss again. Transfer to a bowl, top with the tarragon and parsley and serve. —*Geoffrey Zakarian*

Beet Socca with Yogurt and Bitter Greens

Total **50 min**; Serves **4**

These Provençal chickpea flour pancakes are great for weekend brunch, weekday lunch or a light supper. You can dress them up with smoked fish, horseradish crème fraîche and poached or fried eggs. Or make minis and serve with cocktails.

- 1 lb. golden beets, peeled and coarsely shredded
- 2 large eggs
- 1 cup chickpea flour
- 2 Tbsp. each minced parsley, dill and scallion
- 1 garlic clove, finely grated
- ¼ cup fresh lemon juice
- Fine sea salt
- Canola oil, for brushing
- 3 cups lightly packed spicy greens, such as arugula or watercress
- 1 Tbsp. extra-virgin olive oil
- ½ cup lebneh

1. In a large saucepan of salted boiling water, blanch the beets for 30 seconds. Drain and transfer to an ice water bath to cool completely. Drain well, then squeeze and pat dry.

2. In a large bowl, beat the eggs with the chickpea flour, herbs, garlic, 3 tablespoons of the lemon juice, ¾ teaspoon of salt and ½ cup of water. Add the beets.

3. Heat a large cast-iron griddle until smoking. Brush it generously with canola oil. Spoon 4 mounds of the batter on the griddle and spread each into a 5-inch round. Cook the socca over moderately high heat until lightly browned, 2 to 3 minutes per side. Transfer to plates.

4. In a medium bowl, toss the greens with the olive oil and the remaining 1 tablespoon of lemon juice. Season with salt. Dollop the lebneh on the socca, top with the greens and serve. —*Jessica Koslow*

ROASTED MUSHROOMS
WITH RED WINE BUTTER

GREEN-MARKET TACOS
WITH CORN CREMA

Wild Mushroom Shepherd's Pie with Potato-Chestnut Topping

Active **1 hr 30 min**; Total **4 hr 45 min**
Serves **8 to 10**

SAUCE

- 3 lbs. white mushrooms, coarsely chopped
- 1 lb. leeks, white and light green parts only, chopped
- 1 carrot, chopped
- 3 garlic cloves, crushed
- 2 bay leaves
- 1½ Tbsp. kosher salt
- 1 Tbsp. thyme leaves
- 1 Tbsp. black peppercorns
- ½ tsp. hot curry powder
- 2 cups heavy cream
- 6 Tbsp. unsalted butter
- ¼ cup plus 2 Tbsp. all-purpose flour

FILLING

- 6 Tbsp. unsalted butter
- 1 large shallot, finely chopped
- 2 garlic cloves, minced
- 8 oz. rutabaga, peeled and cut into ⅓-inch dice
- 8 oz. turnips, peeled and cut into ⅓-inch dice
- ¼ lb. sunchokes, peeled and cut into ⅓-inch dice
- 1 small carrot, cut into ⅓-inch pieces
- 1 small parsnip, peeled and cut into ⅓-inch pieces
  Kosher salt and pepper
- 1 lb. shiitake mushrooms, stemmed and caps quartered
- 2 lbs. mixed cremini, oyster, maitake and portobello mushrooms, cut into bite-size pieces
- ½ cup finely chopped parsley
- ½ cup chopped chives
- 2 Tbsp. chopped thyme

TOPPING

- 2 lbs. Yukon Gold potatoes, peeled and cut into large chunks
  One 5-oz. package roasted chestnuts
- 1 small parsnip, peeled and cut into 1-inch pieces
- 1 qt. heavy cream
- ½ tsp. freshly grated nutmeg
  Kosher salt
- 4 large egg yolks
- ¼ cup chopped mixed parsley, chives and thyme

1. Make the sauce In a food processor, pulse the mushrooms in 4 batches until finely chopped; transfer to a 12-quart pot. Add the leeks, carrot, garlic, bay leaves, salt, thyme, peppercorns and curry powder to the food processor and pulse until very finely chopped; transfer to the pot. Add the cream and 1 quart of water to the pot and bring to a boil over high heat, then simmer over moderate heat, stirring occasionally, for 1 hour.

2. Strain the stock through a fine sieve set over a large heatproof bowl, pressing on the solids; discard the solids. Return the stock to the pot and boil over moderately high heat until reduced to 3 cups, about 10 minutes. Pour the stock into the bowl.

3. Wipe out the pot and melt the butter in it. Whisk in the flour and cook over moderate heat, whisking often, until well browned, about 7 minutes. Gradually whisk in the stock until smooth and bring to a boil. Simmer over moderately low heat, whisking often, until thickened and no floury taste remains, about 15 minutes. Scrape the sauce into the bowl.

4. Make the filling Wipe out the pot and melt the butter in it. Add the shallot and garlic and cook over moderately high heat, stirring, until softened, about 2 minutes. Add the rutabaga, turnips, sunchokes, carrot, parsnip and a generous pinch of salt. Cook, stirring occasionally, until just softened, about 7 minutes. Add all of the mushrooms and cook, stirring occasionally, until tender and their liquid evaporates, 10 to 12 minutes. Add the sauce and cook over moderately low heat, stirring often, until the vegetables are coated in a creamy sauce, 10 to 15 minutes. Remove the pot from the heat and stir in the herbs. Season with salt and pepper. Spread the filling in a 9-by-13-inch gratin dish.

5. Make the topping In a large saucepan, cover the potatoes, chestnuts and parsnip with the cream and 1 quart of water and bring to a boil over moderately high heat. Stir in the nutmeg and 1 tablespoon of salt and simmer over moderate heat, stirring occasionally, until the vegetables are tender, about 30 minutes.

6. Drain the vegetables in a colander set over a heatproof bowl. Transfer half of the vegetables to a food processor, add ¾ cup of the cooking liquid and puree until smooth. Scrape into a large bowl. Repeat with the remaining vegetables and another ¾ cup of the cooking liquid. Let the vegetable puree cool slightly, then stir in the egg yolks and chopped herbs and season with salt. Spread the topping over the filling and swirl decoratively.

7. Preheat the oven to 375°. Bake the pie for about 40 minutes, until the filling bubbles. Turn on the broiler and broil 8 to 10 inches from the heat for 2 to 3 minutes, until the top is lightly browned. Let stand for 20 minutes. Sprinkle with salt and serve. —*Grant Achatz*

Green-Market Tacos with Corn Crema

Total **45 min**; Serves **4**

- 3 ears of corn, shucked
- 1 lb. mixed haricots verts, green beans and yellow wax beans, halved lengthwise
- 1 cup Greek yogurt
- ¼ cup extra-virgin olive oil
- 2 oz. creamy feta cheese
- 3 Tbsp. finely chopped cilantro
- ½ tsp. ground cumin
  Kosher salt and pepper
  Eight 6-inch flour tortillas
  Avocado wedges, sliced radishes and cilantro sprigs, for garnish

1. Working in a large bowl, cut the corn kernels off the cobs. Add the beans and toss.

2. Using the back of a knife, scrape all of the corn milk from the cobs into a medium bowl. Add the yogurt, olive oil, cheese, chopped cilantro and cumin, season with salt and pepper and mix the corn crema until smooth. Add all but ½ cup of the corn crema to the corn and beans, season with salt and pepper and toss to coat.

3. Spoon the corn and beans onto the tortillas and top with avocado, radishes and cilantro sprigs. Fold in half and serve with the remaining corn crema. —*Kay Chun*

WINE Medium-bodied Chardonnay: 2014 Porter-Bass Poco a Poco Mendocino.

Double Drive-Thru Veggie Burgers

Total **45 min**; Makes **4**

Vegan chef Chloe Coscarelli of the By Chloe restaurants in New York City and beyond is known for her deliciously charred veggie burgers. For her "special sauce," she creates a tangy-sweet vegan take on Thousand Island dressing with silken tofu.

SAUCE

- 6 oz. soft silken tofu, cubed
- 3 Tbsp. ketchup
- 1 Tbsp. yellow mustard
- 1 tsp. agave nectar
- 1 garlic clove
- 2 Tbsp. sweet pickle relish
- 1 Tbsp. chopped fresh dill
  Kosher salt

BURGERS

- 5 Tbsp. canola oil
- 1 onion, finely chopped
- 2 garlic cloves, minced
  Kosher salt and pepper
- 1 cup cooked brown rice
  One 15-oz. can cooked lentils, rinsed and drained
- 1 cup toasted walnuts
- ½ cup all-purpose flour
- 1 tsp. dried basil
- 4 hamburger buns plus 4 bun bottoms, toasted
  Tomato slices, dill pickle chips, lettuce and thinly sliced red onion, for topping

1. Make the sauce In a blender, puree the tofu with the ketchup, mustard, agave and garlic until smooth. Transfer the sauce to a bowl and stir in the pickle relish and dill; season with salt and refrigerate.

2. Make the burgers In a large nonstick skillet, heat 2 tablespoons of the oil. Add the onion and cook over moderate heat until lightly browned, 6 minutes. Add the garlic and cook until softened, 2 minutes; season with salt. Scrape the onion and garlic into a food processor. Add the rice, lentils, walnuts, flour and dried basil and pulse until the mixture just comes together and whole grains of rice are still visible; season with salt and pepper. Using lightly oiled hands, press ⅓ cup of the mixture into a ½-inch-thick patty; transfer to a plate. Repeat with the remaining mixture for a total of 8 patties.

3. Wipe out the skillet and heat 1½ tablespoons of the oil in it. Arrange 4 burger patties in the pan and cook over moderately high heat until browned on the bottom, about 5 minutes. Flip the patties and continue cooking until browned and heated through, about 5 minutes longer. Transfer the patties to a work surface. Repeat with the remaining oil and burger patties.

4. Spread the sauce on 4 of the bun bottoms and top with 4 patties and half of the burger toppings; top with the remaining bun bottoms. Repeat the layering once more, with more sauce and the remaining patties, toppings and the bun tops; serve. —*Chloe Coscarelli*

WINE Bright and spicy Zinfandel: 2013 Stuhlmuller Vineyards.

Zucchini Burgers with Roasted Garlic Tzatziki

Active **40 min**; Total **3 hr**; Makes **8**

- 3 lbs. zucchini, sliced into ½-inch-thick rounds
- 3 lbs. yellow squash, sliced into ½-inch-thick rounds
- ½ cup extra-virgin olive oil
  Kosher salt and pepper
- 1 Tbsp. smoked paprika
- 1 tsp. sweet paprika
- 1 tsp. cayenne
- 2 garlic cloves, minced
- 4 cups panko
- ½ cup chopped parsley
  Potato rolls, kale leaves, sliced tomato and Roasted Garlic and Sumac Tzatziki (recipe follows), for serving

1. Preheat the oven to 425°. In a large bowl, toss the zucchini and yellow squash with 6 tablespoons of the olive oil. Season with salt and pepper and spread on 2 baking sheets in a single layer. Roast until golden, turning the squash and rotating the baking sheets halfway through, about 1 hour. Let cool to room temperature.

2. In a small bowl, combine both paprikas with the cayenne, garlic and 1 tablespoon of salt. In a food processor, pulse the squash and zucchini with the paprika spice mix in 2 batches until finely chopped. Transfer to a large bowl. Stir in the panko and parsley and mix gently.

3. Form the squash mixture into eight 4-inch burgers about 1 inch thick. Arrange the burgers on a parchment-lined baking sheet and refrigerate for 1 hour.

4. On a griddle, heat the remaining 2 tablespoons of olive oil. Cook the burgers over moderately high heat until well browned and heated through, 5 to 7 minutes per side. Set the zucchini burgers on the rolls and serve with the toppings. —*Eli and Max Sussman*

BEER Light-bodied, summery ale: Evil Twin Bikini Beer.

ROASTED GARLIC AND SUMAC TZATZIKI

Active **20 min**; Total **2 hr 30 min** Makes **3½ cups**

- 1 head of garlic
- ¼ cup extra-virgin olive oil
- 1 European cucumber
  Kosher salt
- 3 cups full-fat Greek yogurt
- 2 Tbsp. chopped dill
- 1½ Tbsp. sumac
- 1 Tbsp. red wine vinegar
- ½ tsp. garlic powder

1. Preheat the oven to 425°. Cut 1 inch off the top of the garlic. Drizzle with 1 teaspoon of the olive oil and wrap in foil. Roast for 45 minutes, until tender. Let cool. Squeeze out the cloves and mash until smooth.

2. Peel the cucumber and grate it on the smallest holes of a box grater. Squeeze out all of the liquid. In a small bowl, mix the cucumber with 1 teaspoon of salt and let stand for 10 minutes. Squeeze out all of the liquid again. Combine the garlic and cucumber in a bowl. Add the remaining olive oil as well as all of the remaining ingredients, season with salt and mix well. Refrigerate the tzatziki for at least 1 hour before serving. —*ES & MS*

Crispy Tofu Steaks with Ginger Vinaigrette

📷 PAGE 210

🕐 Total **30 min**; Serves **4**

- 3 **Tbsp. minced peeled fresh ginger**
- 3 **Tbsp. minced scallion**
- 1 **Tbsp. distilled white vinegar**
- ²⁄₃ **cup canola oil**
- **Kosher salt**
- 1 **large egg**
- 1 **cup panko**
- **One 14-oz. package firm tofu, drained and sliced 1 inch thick**

1. In a small bowl, mix the ginger with the scallion, vinegar and ⅓ cup of the oil; season the vinaigrette with salt.

2. Beat the egg in a medium bowl. Spread the panko on a plate. Dip the tofu slices in the egg, then coat in the panko. In a large nonstick skillet, heat the remaining ⅓ cup of oil. Fry the tofu over moderate heat, turning, until golden and crispy, about 8 minutes. Season with salt and serve with the ginger vinaigrette. —*Kay Chun*

WINE Fruity Alsace Pinot Gris: 2013 Hugel Classic.

Tofu Masala

🕐 Total **30 min**; Serves **4**

This riff on the Indian dish chana masala swaps in cubes of firm tofu for the usual chickpeas. The tofu has a wonderful way of soaking up the vibrant gingery sauce.

- 3 **Tbsp. canola oil**
- 1 **small onion, chopped**
- 1 **serrano chile, chopped**
- ¼ **cup finely chopped garlic**
- ¼ **cup finely chopped peeled fresh ginger**
- 4 **tsp. ground coriander**
- 4 **tsp. garam masala**
- 2 **medium tomatoes, chopped (4 cups)**
- **One 14-oz. package firm tofu, drained and cubed**
- **Chopped cilantro, for garnish**
- **Steamed basmati rice, for serving**

In a large nonstick skillet, heat the oil. Add the onion, serrano, garlic, ginger, coriander, garam masala and tomatoes and cook over moderate heat, stirring, until fragrant and saucy, about 8 minutes. Stir in the tofu and 1 cup of water and bring to a simmer. Garnish with cilantro and serve with basmati rice. —*Kay Chun*

WINE Juicy, tropical fruit–inflected South African Chenin Blanc: 2015 Indaba.

Savory Galette with Radicchio and Endive

Active **50 min**; Total **1 hr 45 min**
Serves **10 to 12**

When she's entertaining a big group, Hedley & Bennett founder Ellen Bennett loves making savory galettes with seasonal ingredients. In the colder months, she opts for radicchio and endive, which she sautés with a touch of honey and vinegar before scattering over the creamy ricotta filling.

CRUST

- 2 **cups all-purpose flour, plus more for dusting**
- ¾ **tsp. sugar**
- ¾ **tsp. kosher salt**
- 1½ **sticks unsalted butter, cubed and chilled**
- ½ **cup ice water**

FILLING

- 2 **Tbsp. unsalted butter**
- 2 **Tbsp. extra-virgin olive oil**
- **One 8-oz. head of radicchio—halved, cored and sliced ¾ inch thick**
- **Kosher salt and pepper**
- 1 **Tbsp. honey**
- 1 **Tbsp. red wine vinegar**
- ¾ **lb. Belgian endives (4 small), cut lengthwise into ½-inch wedges**
- ¾ **cup fresh ricotta**
- ¼ **cup freshly grated Parmigiano-Reggiano cheese, plus shredded cheese for sprinkling**
- ¼ **cup crème fraîche**
- 1 **large egg yolk**
- ½ **tsp. finely grated lemon zest plus 1½ Tbsp. fresh lemon juice**
- 1 **large egg beaten with 1 Tbsp. water**
- **Chopped pistachios, for sprinkling**

1. Make the crust In a food processor, pulse the 2 cups of flour with the sugar and salt. Add the butter and pulse until the mixture resembles coarse meal. Drizzle the ice water all over the mixture and pulse until the dough just starts to come together. Scrape the dough out onto a work surface, gather up any crumbs and pat the dough into a disk. Wrap in plastic and refrigerate until well chilled, about 1 hour.

2. Make the filling Preheat the oven to 425°. In a large skillet, melt 1 tablespoon of the butter in 1 tablespoon of the olive oil. Add the radicchio and a pinch each of salt and pepper and cook over moderately high heat, tossing, until just starting to wilt, about 2 minutes. Stir in the honey and vinegar. Transfer to a large bowl.

3. In the skillet, melt ½ tablespoon of the butter in ½ tablespoon of the olive oil. Add half of the endive and a pinch each of salt and pepper. Cook over moderately high heat, tossing, until browned in spots and just starting to wilt, about 2 minutes. Transfer to the large bowl. Repeat with the remaining butter, olive oil and endive. Let cool.

4. In a medium bowl, mix the ricotta with the ¼ cup of Parmesan, the crème fraîche, egg yolk, lemon zest, lemon juice, ½ teaspoon of salt and ¼ teaspoon of pepper.

5. On a lightly floured work surface, roll out the dough to a 14-inch round. Slide the pastry onto a parchment paper–lined baking sheet. Spread the ricotta mixture evenly on the pastry, leaving a 1-inch border. Scatter the cooled radicchio and endive on the ricotta mixture, then fold the pastry edge up over the vegetables to create a border.

6. Brush the edge of the galette with the egg wash and bake for about 25 minutes, until the pastry is nicely browned and crisp. Let cool slightly, then sprinkle with shredded Parmesan and pistachios. Serve warm or at room temperature. —*Ellen Bennett*

MAKE AHEAD The galette can be made earlier in the day and kept at room temperature.

WINE Crisp Italian white: 2015 Poggio al Tesoro Solesole Vermentino.

POTATOES, GRAINS AND BEANS

At Spoon and Stable, chef Gavin Kaysen reinvents classic hot dish for Minnesotans. OPPOSITE Risotto with Anchovy and Ginger (p. 242).

Mashed-Potato Casserole with Sage and Fontina

Active **20 min**; Total **1 hr**; Serves **8 to 10**

To take mashed potatoes up a few notches, cookbook author Melissa Clark folds in a creamy, tangy mix of crème fraîche, butter, parsley and sage. She finishes with cheesy breadcrumbs and bakes until crisp.

- 6 **Tbsp. unsalted butter, at room temperature, plus more for greasing**
- 3 **lbs. baking potatoes, peeled and cut into 2-inch pieces**
- ½ **cup crème fraîche**
- 2 **Tbsp. chopped parsley**
- 1 **Tbsp. chopped sage plus 12 sage leaves**
- 8 **oz. imported Fontina cheese, shredded**

  Kosher salt and pepper
- ⅓ **cup plain dry breadcrumbs**
- ⅓ **cup freshly grated Parmigiano-Reggiano cheese**

  Olive oil, for frying

1. Preheat the oven to 400°. Lightly grease a 2-quart shallow baking dish. In a large saucepan, combine the potatoes with enough water to cover by 2 inches. Bring to a boil and cook until fork-tender, 15 to 20 minutes. Drain well and transfer to a large bowl. Mash the potatoes with 4 tablespoons of the butter, the crème fraîche, parsley and chopped sage. Fold in the Fontina and season with salt and pepper. Spread the potato mixture in the prepared dish in an even layer.

2. In a small bowl, using your fingers, blend the remaining 2 tablespoons of butter with the breadcrumbs and Parmesan until coarse crumbs form. Top the potatoes with the breadcrumb mixture. Bake until golden and crisp on top, about 30 minutes.

3. Meanwhile, in a small skillet, heat ¼ inch of olive oil over low heat. Add the sage leaves and cook, stirring occasionally, until crisp, about 3 minutes. Transfer the sage to paper towels to drain. Scatter the fried sage over the casserole and serve. —*Melissa Clark*

MAKE AHEAD The assembled unbaked casserole can be refrigerated overnight.

Aunt Elsie's Texas Potatoes

Active **30 min**; Total **1 hr 30 min**
Serves **10 to 12**

Modern Family actor Eric Stonestreet got this rich, cornflake-topped potato casserole recipe from his great-aunt Elsie Ball. The original uses canned cream of chicken soup, but taking a few extra minutes to prepare a homemade sauce makes this already delicious side dish even better.

- 2½ **sticks unsalted butter— 1½ sticks cubed, 1 stick melted**
- 1 **large onion, finely chopped**

  Kosher salt and pepper
- ¼ **cup plus 2 Tbsp. all-purpose flour**
- 2½ **cups chicken stock or low-sodium broth**
- 2½ **cups cornflakes**
- 1 **cup plain dry breadcrumbs**
- 4 **lbs. baking potatoes—peeled, shredded and squeezed dry**
- 16 **oz. sour cream**

1. Preheat the oven to 350°. In a large skillet, melt the 1½ sticks of cubed butter. Add the onion and a generous pinch of salt and cook over moderate heat, stirring occasionally, until softened, about 7 minutes. Whisk in the flour and cook, whisking constantly, until bubbling, about 2 minutes. Gradually whisk in the stock and bring to a boil over moderately high heat, then simmer over moderately low heat until the sauce is thickened and no floury taste remains, 8 to 10 minutes.

2. In a medium bowl, toss the cornflakes with the breadcrumbs and the 1 stick of melted butter. Season with salt and pepper.

3. In a large bowl, combine the sauce with the potatoes, sour cream, 2 teaspoons of salt and 1 teaspoon of pepper and mix well. Scrape into a 9-by-13-inch baking dish and bake for about 20 minutes, until bubbling. Sprinkle the cornflake mixture evenly over the potatoes and bake for 20 to 25 minutes longer, until the topping is browned and crisp. Let stand for 10 minutes before serving. —*Eric Stonestreet*

MAKE AHEAD The casserole can be baked earlier in the day and kept at room temperature. Reheat to serve.

Raclette-and-Potato Gratin

Active **30 min**; Total **1 hr 40 min**
Serves **4 to 6**

Raclette is the name of both a Swiss cow's milk cheese and an Alpine dish of melted cheese served with potatoes and cornichons. Chef Jeremy Fox of L.A.'s Rustic Canyon uses those ingredients as inspiration for an over-the-top gratin.

- 2 **Tbsp. unsalted butter**
- 2 **Tbsp. all-purpose flour**
- 1 **cup whole milk**
- 1½ **Tbsp. whole-grain mustard**

  Kosher salt and pepper
- 1 **lb. fingerling potatoes, scrubbed but not peeled, then sliced ⅛ inch thick (4 cups)**
- ¾ **cup heavy cream**
- 1 **tsp. chopped rosemary**
- ¼ **lb. raclette cheese, coarsely shredded (1 cup)**
- 12 **cornichons, sliced**

1. In a medium saucepan, melt the butter. Add the flour and cook over moderately low heat, whisking, until light golden, about 3 minutes. Whisk in the milk and bring to a simmer, whisking frequently. Cook the sauce, whisking, until it is thick enough to coat the back of a spoon, about 5 minutes. Scrape the béchamel into a medium bowl, whisk in the mustard and season with salt. Let cool completely.

2. Preheat the oven to 350°. In an 8-by-11-inch baking dish, toss the potatoes with the cream, rosemary, 2 teaspoons of salt and ¼ teaspoon of pepper; mix well. Cover and bake until the potatoes are tender when pierced, about 30 minutes. Uncover and bake until the cream reduces and thickens, about 15 minutes.

3. Spoon the béchamel over the potatoes and bake for about 10 minutes, until golden and bubbly. Scatter the raclette cheese on top and bake for 5 minutes longer, until melted. Let stand for 10 minutes, then top with the cornichons and serve hot. —*Jeremy Fox*

WINE Earthy Spanish Tempranillo: 2013 Antídoto Ribera del Duero.

MASHED-POTATO
CASSEROLE WITH
SAGE AND FONTINA

Campfire Potato Salad

Total **1 hr 15 min**; Serves **6**

POTATOES

- **2 lbs. medium white potatoes, cut into 1-inch pieces**
- **6 slices of meaty applewood-smoked bacon**
- **2 rosemary sprigs**
- **5 thyme sprigs**
- **6 garlic cloves**
- **2 bay leaves**
- **¼ cup plus 2 Tbsp. extra-virgin olive oil**
  Kosher salt and pepper
- **1½ cups thinly sliced leeks, white and light green parts only**

DRESSING

- **¼ cup chicken stock or broth**
- **½ cup mayonnaise**
- **¼ cup white wine vinegar**
- **2 Tbsp. Dijon mustard**
- **2 Tbsp. capers, finely chopped**
- **1 garlic clove, minced**
  Pinch of crushed red pepper
  Kosher salt and black pepper
- **4 hard-boiled eggs, sliced ¼ inch thick**
- **¼ cup finely chopped red onion**
- **¼ cup finely chopped parsley**
- **¼ cup finely chopped dill**
- **2 Tbsp. minced chives**

1. Make the potatoes Light a grill and heat it to 400°. Layer 3 large sheets of heavy-duty foil on a work surface. On the foil, toss the potatoes with the bacon, rosemary, thyme, garlic, bay leaves and ¼ cup of the olive oil and season with salt and pepper. Seal the packet tightly and grill for about 45 minutes, turning once, until the potatoes are tender.

2. Meanwhile, in a medium skillet, heat the remaining 2 tablespoons of oil. Add the leeks and a pinch of salt and cook over moderate heat, stirring occasionally, until tender, about 8 minutes. Scrape into a large bowl.

3. Make the dressing In the same skillet, warm the chicken stock over moderate heat. Whisk in the mayonnaise, vinegar, mustard, capers, garlic and crushed red pepper. Season with salt and black pepper.

4. Open the potato packet and discard the herb sprigs, bay leaves and garlic. Coarsely chop the bacon and add to the bowl with the leeks. Add the potatoes and dressing and toss well. Fold in the eggs, onion, parsley, dill and chives. Season with salt and black pepper and serve warm. —*Ben Ford*

Warm Smashed Potatoes with Miso Walnuts and Cheddar

Active **30 min**; Total **1 hr**; Serves **6 to 8**

Chefs Jeremiah Stone and Fabián von Hauske of Contra and Wildair in New York City put a unique spin on potato salad. They boil Yukon Gold potatoes with garlic and bay leaves, smash them with cheddar, onion and miso-coated walnuts and top them with maple syrup and fragrant mint.

- **3 lbs. small Yukon Gold potatoes**
- **1 head of garlic, left whole**
- **2 bay leaves**
- **1 Tbsp. extra-virgin olive oil**
- **½ cup walnuts, finely chopped**
- **1 Tbsp. white miso**
- **4 oz. aged cheddar cheese, preferably Cabot Clothbound, grated**
- **¼ cup thinly sliced onion**
- **1 Tbsp. pure maple syrup**
- **1 Tbsp. white wine vinegar**
  Torn mint, for garnish

1. In a large saucepan, cover the potatoes, garlic and bay leaves with 2 inches of water and bring to a boil. Cook until the potatoes are tender, about 30 minutes. Drain the potatoes; discard the garlic and bay leaves.

2. Meanwhile, in a small skillet, heat the olive oil. Add the walnuts and toast, stirring, until golden, about 5 minutes. Add the miso and stir until coated. Transfer to a plate to cool.

3. Transfer the potatoes to a large bowl and mash with a fork until chunky. Add the walnuts, cheese and onion and mix well. Transfer to a platter and drizzle with the maple syrup and vinegar. Garnish with mint and serve. —*Jeremiah Stone and Fabián von Hauske*

Potato-and-Tuna Salad with Sorrel Vinaigrette

⏱ Total **45 min**; Serves **6**

SORREL VINAIGRETTE

- **5 Tbsp. extra-virgin olive oil**
- **½ sweet onion, thinly sliced (1 cup)**
- **½ hothouse cucumber, peeled and cut into ¾-inch pieces**
- **2 cups packed sorrel leaves (see Note), stemmed**
- **¼ cup canola oil**
- **2 Tbsp. crème fraîche**
  Kosher salt

SALAD

- **1 lb. small potatoes, such as Yukon Gold or Carola**
  Kosher salt and pepper
- **2 Tbsp. extra-virgin olive oil**
- **1 hothouse cucumber (1 lb.), thinly sliced crosswise**
- **8 oz. arugula, thick stems discarded**
- **8 oz. best-quality tuna packed in olive oil, drained and flaked into large pieces**

1. Make the vinaigrette In a small non-stick skillet, heat 1 tablespoon of the olive oil. Add the onion and cook over low heat, stirring occasionally, until very soft but not browned, about 12 minutes. Scrape into a blender and let cool.

2. Add the cucumber and sorrel to the blender and puree until smooth. With the machine on, drizzle in the remaining ¼ cup of olive oil and the canola oil. Strain the vinaigrette into a small bowl, pressing on the solids. Whisk in the crème fraîche and season with salt. Cover and refrigerate.

3. Make the salad In a medium saucepan, cover the potatoes with 2 inches of water and season with salt. Bring to a simmer and cook until tender, about 30 minutes. Drain and let cool slightly. Thinly slice the potatoes and transfer to a medium bowl. Toss with the olive oil and season with salt.

4. In another bowl, combine the sliced cucumber and arugula with ¾ cup of the vinaigrette and season with salt and pepper; toss to coat. Mound the salad on plates and top with the potatoes and tuna. Garnish with pepper and serve the remaining vinaigrette on the side. —*Katy Millard*

NOTE If sorrel is unavailable, you can substitute 2 cups baby spinach plus 1 tablespoon fresh lemon juice.

Oven-Baked Potatoes Hasselbacken

Total **1 hr**; Serves **4**

Thinly sliced and impressively fanned-out butter-basted potatoes Hasselbacken (named for the Stockholm restaurant where they were invented in the 1940s) are beloved in Sweden.

- 1½ lbs. small white potatoes, such as Yukon Golds, peeled
- 4 Tbsp. unsalted butter
  Kosher salt
- 2 Tbsp. plain dry breadcrumbs

1. Preheat the oven to 425°. Using a sharp paring knife, slice each potato crosswise at ¼-inch intervals, cutting straight down but not all the way through the potato. Transfer the potatoes to a large cast-iron skillet.

2. Add the butter to the skillet and set over moderate heat; as the butter melts, spoon it over the potatoes. Season the potatoes with salt and transfer to the oven. Roast for about 40 minutes, basting occasionally, until golden and tender. Sprinkle the breadcrumbs on top and roast for 10 minutes longer, until golden and crisp. Serve hot. —*Magnus Nilsson*

Salt-and-Vinegar French Fries

Active **10 min**; Total **30 min**; Serves **4**

These no-fry french fries are baked in a very hot oven for a supertender interior and an extra-crispy crust.

- 2 large baking potatoes, peeled and cut into ¼-inch-thick sticks
- 3 Tbsp. extra-virgin olive oil
  Kosher salt
  Malt vinegar, for serving

Preheat the oven to 425°. In a medium bowl, toss the potatoes with the olive oil and a generous pinch of salt. Spread the potatoes on a rimmed baking sheet in a single layer. Bake until golden brown and tender, 20 to 25 minutes, stirring halfway through. Sprinkle with salt and malt vinegar and serve immediately, passing more vinegar at the table. —*Chloe Coscarelli*

Sweet Potato Poutine with Maitake Mushrooms

Active **15 min**; Total **1 hr**; Serves **4**

You may never go back to classic poutine after trying this delicious new take: Frozen sweet potato fries are baked, then smothered with meaty maitake mushrooms and a quick Fontina cheese sauce.

- 1 lb. maitake mushrooms, torn into large pieces
- 7 oz. store-bought frozen sweet potato fries, such as Alexia
- ¼ cup extra-virgin olive oil
- 2 Tbsp. unsalted butter
- 2 Tbsp. all-purpose flour
- ¾ cup whole milk
  Kosher salt and pepper
- 3½ oz. Fontina cheese, shredded (1 cup)

1. Preheat the oven to 425°. In a 3-quart baking dish, toss the mushrooms with the fries and olive oil. Bake until the fries are crispy, about 45 minutes. Remove from the oven and turn on the broiler.

2. Meanwhile, in a small saucepan, melt the butter. Add the flour and cook, whisking, until golden, 5 minutes. Whisk in the milk and cook until thickened, about 3 minutes. Season with salt and pepper. Spoon the gravy over the mushrooms and fries and top with the cheese. Broil 6 inches from the heat until golden, about 5 minutes. —*Kay Chun*

BEER Nutty, malty brown ale: Smuttynose Old Brown Dog.

Tater Tots with Spicy Aioli

Total **20 min**; Serves **4 to 6**

The aioli here approximates the top-secret recipe at Augustine wine bar in Sherman Oaks, California.

- 1 lb. frozen Tater Tots
- ½ cup Sriracha
- ¼ cup chipotle Tabasco sauce
- 6 Tbsp. Lemon Aioli (recipe follows)

1. Cook the Tater Tots according to the package directions.

2. In a medium bowl, mix the Sriracha with the Tabasco. Stir in the aioli and serve with the tots. —*Evan Algorri*

LEMON AIOLI

Total **10 min**; Makes **about 1 cup**

- 3 large egg yolks
- 1 Tbsp. fresh lemon juice
- 1 Tbsp. Champagne vinegar
- 1 Tbsp. Dijon mustard
- 2 garlic cloves, crushed
- ¾ cup extra-virgin olive oil
  Kosher salt and pepper

In a food processor, pulse the egg yolks, lemon juice, vinegar, mustard and garlic to blend. With the machine on, slowly drizzle in the oil until incorporated. Season with salt and pepper. —*Ramon Siewert*

Chickpea and Swiss Chard Chili

Total **30 min**; Serves **6**

Chickpeas and Swiss chard replace the usual meat and beans in this smoky, robust and satisfying chili.

- 6 slices of bacon, chopped
- 1 large onion, chopped
- 1 large carrot, cut into ½-inch pieces
- 2 garlic cloves, thinly sliced
  Kosher salt and pepper
  One 28-oz. can crushed tomatoes
- 2 cups chicken stock or low-sodium broth
  Two 15-oz. cans chickpeas, rinsed
- 1 lb. Swiss chard, leaves and stems chopped
- 3 chipotles in adobo, minced
  Shredded Monterey Jack cheese, for serving

In a large saucepan, cook the bacon over moderately high heat, stirring occasionally, until the fat is rendered, about 7 minutes. Add the onion, carrot, garlic and a generous pinch each of salt and pepper and cook, stirring occasionally, until softened, 8 to 10 minutes. Add the tomatoes, stock, chickpeas, Swiss chard and chipotles and bring to a boil. Simmer over moderately low heat until the chili is thickened and the Swiss chard is wilted and just tender, about 8 minutes. Serve in bowls topped with shredded cheese. —*Justin Chapple*

MAKE AHEAD The chili can be refrigerated overnight. Reheat gently.

VEGETARIAN BLACK
BEAN CHILI WITH
ANCHO AND ORANGE

Vegetarian Black Bean Chili with Ancho and Orange

Active **20 min**; Total **50 min**; Serves **4 to 6**

A hit of fresh orange adds a warm, sweet note to the aromatic spices in this healthy chili from TV chef Ellie Krieger. To turn the chili into a dip for corn chips on game night, layer it with chopped avocado, shredded cheddar, salsa and sour cream.

- 2 Tbsp. canola oil
- 1 medium onion, cut into ¼-inch dice
- 1 medium red bell pepper, cut into ¼-inch dice
- 4 garlic cloves, minced
- 2 Tbsp. tomato paste
- 1 Tbsp. ancho chile powder
- 2 tsp. ground cumin
- 1 tsp. dried oregano
- ½ tsp. cayenne
   Kosher salt and pepper
   One 15-oz. can crushed tomatoes
   Three 15-oz. cans black beans, rinsed and drained
- 1 Tbsp. honey
- 1 tsp. finely grated orange zest plus 2 Tbsp. fresh orange juice
   Cilantro leaves, for garnish
   Greek yogurt, for serving

In a large saucepan, heat the oil. Add the onion and bell pepper and cook over moderate heat, stirring occasionally, until softened, about 8 minutes. Stir in the garlic, tomato paste, chile powder, cumin, oregano and cayenne and season with salt and pepper. Cook, stirring, for 1 minute. Add the crushed tomatoes, black beans, honey, ½ teaspoon of the orange zest and 2 cups of water and bring to a simmer. Cover and cook over low heat, stirring occasionally, until all the flavors meld and the liquid is slightly reduced, about 20 minutes. Stir in the orange juice and season with salt and pepper. Ladle the chili into bowls and garnish with cilantro leaves and the remaining ½ teaspoon of orange zest. Serve with yogurt. —*Ellie Krieger*

MAKE AHEAD The chili can be refrigerated overnight and reheated with more water if it's too thick.

BEER Toasty, malty beer: Anchor Steam.

Spanish-Style Chickpea Quesadillas

Total **45 min**; Serves **4 to 6**

For a quick and tasty vegetarian meal, F&W's Justin Chapple revamps classic Tex-Mex bean-and-cheese quesadillas by mashing canned chickpeas with Manchego cheese and sweet piquillo peppers.

   One 15-oz. can chickpeas, rinsed
- ½ lb. Manchego cheese, shredded (2 cups)
- 4 piquillo peppers, chopped
- ¼ cup thinly sliced scallions, plus more for garnish
   Kosher salt and pepper
   Canola oil, for brushing
   Eight 8-inch flour tortillas
   Hot sauce, for serving

1. In a large bowl, mash the chickpeas with a fork. Stir in the cheese, piquillos and the ¼ cup of scallions and season with salt and pepper.

2. Heat a large nonstick skillet and brush it with oil. Place 1 tortilla in the skillet and scatter one-fourth of the chickpea mixture evenly on top. Cover with another tortilla and cook over moderately high heat until crisp on the bottom, about 3 minutes. Flip the quesadilla and cook until the cheese is melted, 2 to 3 minutes longer. Transfer the quesadilla to a platter. Repeat with the remaining tortillas and chickpea mixture. Cut the quesadillas into wedges, garnish with sliced scallions and serve with hot sauce. —*Justin Chapple*

MAKE AHEAD The chickpea mixture can be refrigerated overnight. Let stand at room temperature for 30 minutes before making the quesadillas.

BEER Light, slightly bitter pilsner: Tröegs Sunshine Pils.

Falafel with Israeli Pickles

Active **45 min**; Total **2 hr plus overnight soaking**; Serves **4 to 6**

- 2 cups dried chickpeas, soaked overnight in cold water
- 2 large yellow onions, finely chopped
- ⅓ cup minced parsley
- ¼ cup plus 1 Tbsp. all-purpose flour
- 3 garlic cloves, minced
- 2 tsp. ground coriander
- 2 tsp. ground cumin
   Kosher salt and pepper
   Canola oil, for frying
   Butter lettuce, tomato slices, sliced red onion, tahini, Israeli zhoug (see Note), Israeli pickles and warm pita, for serving

1. Drain the chickpeas and transfer to a large pot. Cover with cold water and bring to a boil over moderately high heat. Reduce the heat to moderately low and simmer until tender, about 1 hour. Drain the chickpeas and spread them out on a rimmed baking sheet; let cool to room temperature, about 20 minutes.

2. In a large bowl, combine the cooled chickpeas with the onions, parsley, flour, garlic, coriander and cumin. Transfer to a food processor and pulse until finely chopped but not pureed, about 2 minutes. Scrape the falafel mixture into the large bowl and season with salt and pepper.

3. Shape the falafel mixture into twenty-four 3-tablespoon-size balls. Flatten into 1½-inch rounds, about ¾ inch thick. Transfer the falafel to a rimmed baking sheet.

4. In a medium saucepan, heat 2 inches of oil to 375° over moderately high heat. Fry the falafel in batches until golden brown and cooked through, about 3 minutes per batch. Drain on a wire rack lined with paper towels and season with salt. Serve the falafel warm as a sandwich with lettuce, tomato, red onion, tahini, zhoug, Israeli pickles and pita. —*Andrew Zimmern*

NOTE Zhoug (or schug) is a spicy sauce made with chiles, garlic and spices. It's available at Middle Eastern markets.

WINE Lime-scented Chilean Sauvignon Blanc: 2015 Matetic Vineyards EQ Coastal Casablanca Valley.

Rock Shrimp Risotto

Total **1 hr**; Serves **4**

At Alter restaurant in Miami, this lush shrimp risotto is so popular, chef Brad Kilgore can't take it off the menu. Creamy Boursin cheese gives the risotto its irresistible flavor; Meyer lemon juice and dill balance the richness.

PICKLED SHALLOTS

- **2** cups thinly sliced shallots (about 8 medium shallots)
- **¾** cup Champagne vinegar
- **¾** cup sugar
- **2** Tbsp. kosher salt

RISOTTO

- **4½** cups chicken stock or low-sodium broth
- **⅓** cup extra-virgin olive oil
- **1** cup carnaroli rice
- **½** cup dry white wine
- **5** oz. garlic-and-herb Boursin cheese
- **4** oz. Grana Padano cheese, finely grated (1½ cups)
- **2** tsp. finely grated Meyer lemon zest plus ¼ cup fresh Meyer lemon juice
- **2** Tbsp. minced dill, plus dill sprigs for garnish
- **6** oz. rock shrimp

1. Pickle the shallots Place the shallots in a heatproof bowl. In a small saucepan, combine the vinegar, sugar, salt and 1 cup of water and bring to a boil, stirring to dissolve the sugar. Pour the brine over the shallots and let cool to room temperature.

2. Make the risotto In a medium saucepan, bring the stock to a simmer and keep warm. In a large saucepan, heat the olive oil. Add the rice and cook over moderate heat, stirring, for 2 minutes. Add the wine and cook, stirring occasionally, until almost evaporated, about 2 minutes. Add ½ cup of the hot stock and cook, stirring constantly, until the liquid is absorbed, about 2 minutes. Continue adding the hot stock ½ cup at a time and stirring until almost absorbed before adding more. The risotto is done when the rice is just al dente and suspended in a creamy sauce, about 18 minutes total. Stir in both cheeses along with the lemon zest, lemon juice and minced dill. Remove the saucepan from the heat and stir in the shrimp. Let stand until the shrimp are just cooked through, about 2 minutes. Spoon the risotto into bowls and serve garnished with dill sprigs and the drained pickled shallots. —*Brad Kilgore*

MAKE AHEAD The drained pickled shallots can be refrigerated for up to 3 days.

WINE Minerally Greek Assyrtiko: 2014 Hatzidakis Santorini.

Fennel Risotto

Total **40 min**; Serves **4 to 6**

- **6** cups low-sodium chicken broth
- **6** Tbsp. unsalted butter
- **1** medium yellow onion, finely chopped
- **2** medium fennel bulbs, cored and thinly sliced lengthwise
   Kosher salt
- **1½** cups arborio rice (14 oz.)
- **1½** cups freshly grated Parmigiano-Reggiano cheese, plus more for serving
- **2** Tbsp. fennel fronds, plus more for serving

1. In a medium saucepan, bring the chicken broth to a simmer; keep warm. In a medium enameled cast-iron casserole, melt 4 tablespoons of the butter over moderately high heat. Add the onion and fennel, season with salt and cook over moderately high heat, stirring, until softened, about 10 minutes.

2. Add the rice to the casserole and cook for 1 minute, stirring constantly to coat the rice with butter. Add 1 cup of the warm broth and cook over moderately high heat, stirring constantly, until nearly absorbed. Continue adding the broth 1 cup at a time and stirring constantly until it is nearly absorbed between additions. The risotto is done when the rice is al dente and suspended in a thick, creamy sauce, about 20 minutes total. Stir in the remaining 2 tablespoons of butter, the 1½ cups of Parmigiano-Reggiano and the 2 tablespoons of fennel fronds. Garnish with more fennel fronds and serve immediately, passing grated cheese at the table. —*Skye McAlpine*

WINE Lively, medium-bodied Italian red: 2012 Le Vigne di Zamò Il Refosco.

Risotto with Anchovy and Ginger

📷 PAGE 234

Active **1 hr**; Total **2 hr**; Serves **4**

FISH STOCK

- **2** Tbsp. extra-virgin olive oil
- **1** large onion, chopped
- **2** carrots, chopped
- **2** celery ribs, chopped
- **3** lbs. fish bones and heads from white fish, such as snapper or sea bass
- **¼** cup dry white wine
- **8** cups ice

RISOTTO

- **7** salt-packed anchovy fillets, rinsed and patted dry
- **2** cups carnaroli rice (12 oz.)
- **¼** cup dry white wine
- **1** stick unsalted butter
- **2** Tbsp. salted butter
- **4** tsp. colatura (see Note)
   Kosher salt
   Slivered candied ginger and chopped chives, for garnish

1. Make the fish stock In a large stockpot, heat the olive oil. Add the chopped onion, carrots and celery and cook over moderate heat, stirring occasionally, until the vegetables are golden, about 5 minutes. Add the fish bones and heads and cook until white, about 5 minutes. Stir in the wine and cook for 1 minute. Stir in the ice and 8 cups of water and bring to a simmer. Cook over low heat until reduced by half, about 45 minutes. Strain the stock through a cheesecloth-lined sieve and keep warm.

2. Make the risotto On a work surface, using the side of a chef's knife, mash 3 of the anchovy fillets to a paste. In a large saucepan, cook the rice over moderately low heat, stirring, until translucent around the edges, 5 minutes. Stir in the wine and cook over moderate heat until absorbed, 1 minute. Add 1 cup of the warm stock and cook, stirring, until all of the stock is absorbed, 3 minutes. Add another 1 cup of stock and the anchovy paste and cook, stirring, until the stock is absorbed, about 3 minutes. Repeat 5 more times with the remaining stock; cook until the rice is al dente and suspended in a creamy liquid (reserve any remaining stock for another use). Stir in the unsalted butter until the risotto is creamy. Remove from the heat and let stand for 2 minutes.

3. Stir in the salted butter and the colatura; season with salt. Spoon the risotto into bowls and garnish with the remaining anchovies. Sprinkle with candied ginger and chives and serve. —*Alba Esteve Ruiz*

NOTE Colatura is an Italian fish sauce made from anchovies. Look for it at specialty markets and on amazon.com.

WINE Flinty, briny white: 2015 Terradora di Paolo Fiano di Avellino.

Kale-and-Shiitake Fried Rice

Total **40 min;** Makes **6 cups**

¼ cup vegetable oil

One ½-inch piece of fresh ginger, peeled and minced

6 scallions, thinly sliced

Kosher salt

¾ lb. shiitake mushrooms, stemmed and sliced

6 cups coarsely chopped curly kale leaves (about half of a medium bunch)

2 garlic cloves, minced

4 cups day-old cooked short-grain white rice

3 large eggs, lightly beaten

1½ Tbsp. rice wine vinegar

1 Tbsp. oyster sauce

1. In a wok or very large skillet, heat 3 tablespoons of the oil. Add the ginger, scallions and a pinch of salt. Cook over moderately high heat, stirring constantly, until the ginger and scallions are tender, about 2 minutes. Add the shiitake and a generous pinch of salt and cook, stirring frequently, until tender, about 5 minutes. Add the kale, season with salt and stir-fry until wilted, 2 to 3 minutes. Add the garlic and cook for 1 minute more. Add the cooked rice and stir-fry until heated through, about 3 minutes.

2. Make a well in the rice and add the remaining 1 tablespoon of oil. When the oil is shimmering, add the eggs. Cook without stirring until the eggs begin to set at the edge. Using a spatula, scramble the eggs until just set. Stir the eggs into the rice along with the vinegar and oyster sauce and season with salt. Serve immediately. —*David Lebovitz*

Warm Lentil and Carrot Salad with Feta Dressing

Total **45 min;** Serves **4 to 6**

1 lb. carrots—peeled, halved lengthwise and cut into 3-inch pieces

7 Tbsp. extra-virgin olive oil

¾ cup French green (Le Puy) lentils

1 cup chopped cucumber

¼ cup chopped dill

Kosher salt and pepper

½ cup crumbled feta cheese

1. Preheat the oven to 450°. On a baking sheet, toss the carrots with 2 tablespoons of the olive oil and roast until tender, about 30 minutes. Scrape into a large serving bowl.

2. Meanwhile, in a small saucepan of boiling water, cook the lentils until al dente, about 15 minutes. Drain well.

3. Add the lentils to the carrots along with the cucumber, dill and 2 tablespoons of the oil; season with salt and pepper.

4. In a blender, puree the feta with 2 tablespoons of water and the remaining 3 tablespoons of oil until smooth. Season with salt. Spoon the dressing over the lentil salad and serve. —*Kay Chun*

WINE Crisp, lightly herbal Sauvignon Blanc: 2015 Giesen Sauvignon Blanc.

Yellow Lentil Dal with Tofu

Active **20 min;** Total **50 min;** Serves **4 to 6**

Dal, a thick stew or puree of lentils, is an Indian staple. This boldly spiced version is fortified with soft tofu, transforming it into a substantial vegan meal.

2 Tbsp. canola oil

½ red onion, minced (⅓ cup)

½ tomato, minced (⅓ cup)

2 Tbsp. minced garlic

2 Tbsp. minced peeled fresh ginger

1 tsp. coriander seeds

1 tsp. cumin seeds

1 cup yellow lentils

12 oz. soft tofu, cubed

Chopped cilantro, for garnish

In a large saucepan, heat the oil. Add the onion, tomato, garlic, ginger, coriander and cumin and cook over moderate heat, stirring, until the aromatics are golden, about 5 minutes. Stir in the lentils and 6 cups of water and bring to a boil. Cover and simmer gently over moderately low heat until the lentils are tender and the dal is thickened, about 30 minutes. Fold in the tofu and cook until warmed through. Garnish with cilantro and serve. —*Kay Chun*

WINE Creamy, yellow apple–inflected California Chardonnay: 2015 Hess Select.

All of the Alliums Fried Rice

Total **35 min;** Serves **4**

Blogger Molly Yeh prefers seasoning her fried rice with salt rather than soy sauce. "I love having the flavor of the alliums and ginger front and center," she says.

1 Tbsp. canola oil

4 large eggs, beaten

Kosher salt and pepper

3 Tbsp. unsalted butter

4 cups finely chopped alliums, such as onions, shallots, leeks and scallions

4 garlic cloves, minced

2 Tbsp. minced fresh ginger

4 cups cooked white or brown rice

1 Tbsp. distilled white vinegar

2 Tbsp. Sriracha

2 Tbsp. mayonnaise

Sliced scallions, for garnish

1. In a large nonstick skillet, heat the oil. Add the eggs, season with salt and pepper and cook over moderate heat, stirring, until just set, about 2 minutes. Transfer to a cutting board and coarsely chop.

2. Wipe out the skillet and melt the butter in it. Add the alliums and season with salt. Cook over moderate heat, stirring occasionally, until golden and tender, about 12 minutes. Add the garlic and ginger and cook, stirring, for 2 minutes. Add the rice, vinegar and eggs, season with salt and pepper and cook, stirring, until well mixed. Spread the rice evenly in the skillet and cook without stirring until golden and crispy on the bottom, 4 to 5 minutes.

3. In a bowl, stir the Sriracha with the mayonnaise. Top the rice with scallions and serve with the Sriracha mayo. —*Molly Yeh*

Crispy Coconut Sticky Rice

Active **15 min**; Total **3 hr**; Serves **4**

"I totally hated rice as a kid!" says Joseph "JJ" Johnson, chef at The Cecil in New York City's Harlem neighborhood. "All I ever ate was the instant kind. Now that I've learned how to make rice properly, I eat it almost every day." Here, he flavors it with Thai curry–spiked coconut milk.

1½ cups short-grain sushi rice

 1 cup unsweetened coconut milk

 ¼ cup sugar

 1 Tbsp. Massaman or red curry paste

 Three 2-by-½-inch strips of lime zest

 One 2-by-1-inch piece of peeled fresh ginger, chopped

 ½ fresh Thai bird chile

 ½ tsp. kosher salt

 2 Tbsp. chopped cilantro leaves and stems

 2 tsp. grapeseed or canola oil

1. Put the rice in a large bowl and add enough warm water to cover by 2 inches. Let soak at room temperature for 2 hours, swirling occasionally. Drain well.

2. Meanwhile, in a medium saucepan, combine the coconut milk with the sugar, curry paste, lime zest, ginger, chile and salt and bring to a simmer over moderate heat, whisking to dissolve the curry paste and sugar. Strain through a fine sieve into a small bowl; discard the solids. Clean the saucepan.

3. In the saucepan, combine the drained rice with 2¼ cups of water and bring to a boil. Cover and simmer over low heat until the rice is tender and the water is absorbed, about 15 minutes. Transfer the rice to a large bowl and slowly drizzle the infused coconut milk on top. Fold the rice until the liquid is absorbed, then let stand for 15 minutes. Stir in the cilantro.

4. In a large nonstick skillet, heat the oil. Scrape the rice into the skillet, press it into an even layer and cook over moderate heat until the edge and bottom are golden and crisp, 12 to 15 minutes. Invert the rice onto a platter and serve. —*Joseph Johnson*

Bacon Fried Rice with Avocado and Fried Eggs

Total **1 hr 30 min**; Serves **6**

 One 10-oz. bag of curly spinach (16 cups), thick stems discarded

 2 tsp. toasted sesame seeds

 1 tsp. toasted sesame oil

 Kosher salt and pepper

12 thick slices of bacon

 Canola oil, for frying

 2 large shallots, thinly sliced crosswise

 4 cups cold cooked medium-grain white rice

 4 cups cold cooked medium-grain brown rice

 3 Tbsp. oyster sauce

 3 Tbsp. low-sodium soy sauce

 2 Tbsp. Sriracha

 4 Tbsp. unsalted butter

 1 small yellow onion, halved and thinly sliced

 1 medium celery rib, julienned

 4 scallions, thinly sliced

 6 large eggs

 1 Hass avocado—peeled, pitted and sliced

 Pickled vegetables, such as okra, long beans and radishes, for serving

1. In a large saucepan of salted boiling water, blanch the spinach until wilted, 1 to 2 minutes. Drain well and let cool slightly, then squeeze dry. In a medium bowl, toss the spinach with the sesame seeds and sesame oil. Season with salt.

2. In a very large skillet, cook the bacon over moderately high heat, turning, until crisp, about 5 minutes. Transfer to a paper towel–lined plate to drain. Pour off the fat from the skillet and heat ¼ inch of canola oil. Add the shallots and cook over moderate heat, stirring, until golden and crisp, about 5 minutes. Using a slotted spoon, transfer the shallots to a paper towel–lined plate to drain.

3. In a bowl, toss the white and brown rice with the oyster sauce, soy sauce and Sriracha until well coated. In a wok or the wiped-out very large skillet, melt the butter. Add the onion and celery and cook over moderate heat until just starting to soften, about 2 minutes. Add the rice and stir-fry over

high heat until hot, about 5 minutes. Stir in half of the scallions and season with salt and pepper; keep warm.

4. Heat a large nonstick skillet and brush with oil. Crack 3 of the eggs into the skillet and cook sunny side up, about 4 minutes. Transfer the eggs to a plate. Brush the skillet with oil and fry the remaining 3 eggs.

5. Spoon the fried rice into shallow bowls and top with the spinach, avocado, bacon, fried shallots, fried eggs and the remaining scallions. Serve with pickled vegetables. —*Ed Kenney*

WINE Zesty, white-peach-scented Albariño: 2014 Santiago Ruiz.

Kimchi-and-Kale Fried Rice

⟳ Total **15 min**; Serves **2**

 1 Tbsp. gochujang (Korean red pepper paste)

 2 tsp. soy sauce

 3 Tbsp. toasted sesame oil

 1 cup chopped kale leaves

 ½ cup kimchi, chopped, plus more for serving

 2 cups cooked white rice

 2 large eggs

 Kosher salt and pepper

 Thinly sliced scallions and toasted sesame seeds, for garnish

1. In a small bowl, whisk the gochujang with the soy sauce.

2. In a large nonstick skillet, heat 2 tablespoons of the sesame oil. Add the kale and the ½ cup of kimchi and stir-fry over moderately high heat until the kale is softened, about 2 minutes. Fold in the cooked rice. Add the gochujang sauce and stir-fry until the rice is starting to brown, about 2 minutes more. Divide the fried rice between 2 bowls and wipe out the skillet.

3. In the skillet, heat the remaining 1 tablespoon of sesame oil. Crack the eggs into the skillet and cook over moderate heat until the whites are firm and the yolks are still runny, about 5 minutes. Season with salt and pepper. Top the rice with the fried eggs and garnish with scallions and sesame seeds. Serve with additional kimchi. —*Rachel Yang*

BACON FRIED RICE
WITH AVOCADO AND
FRIED EGGS

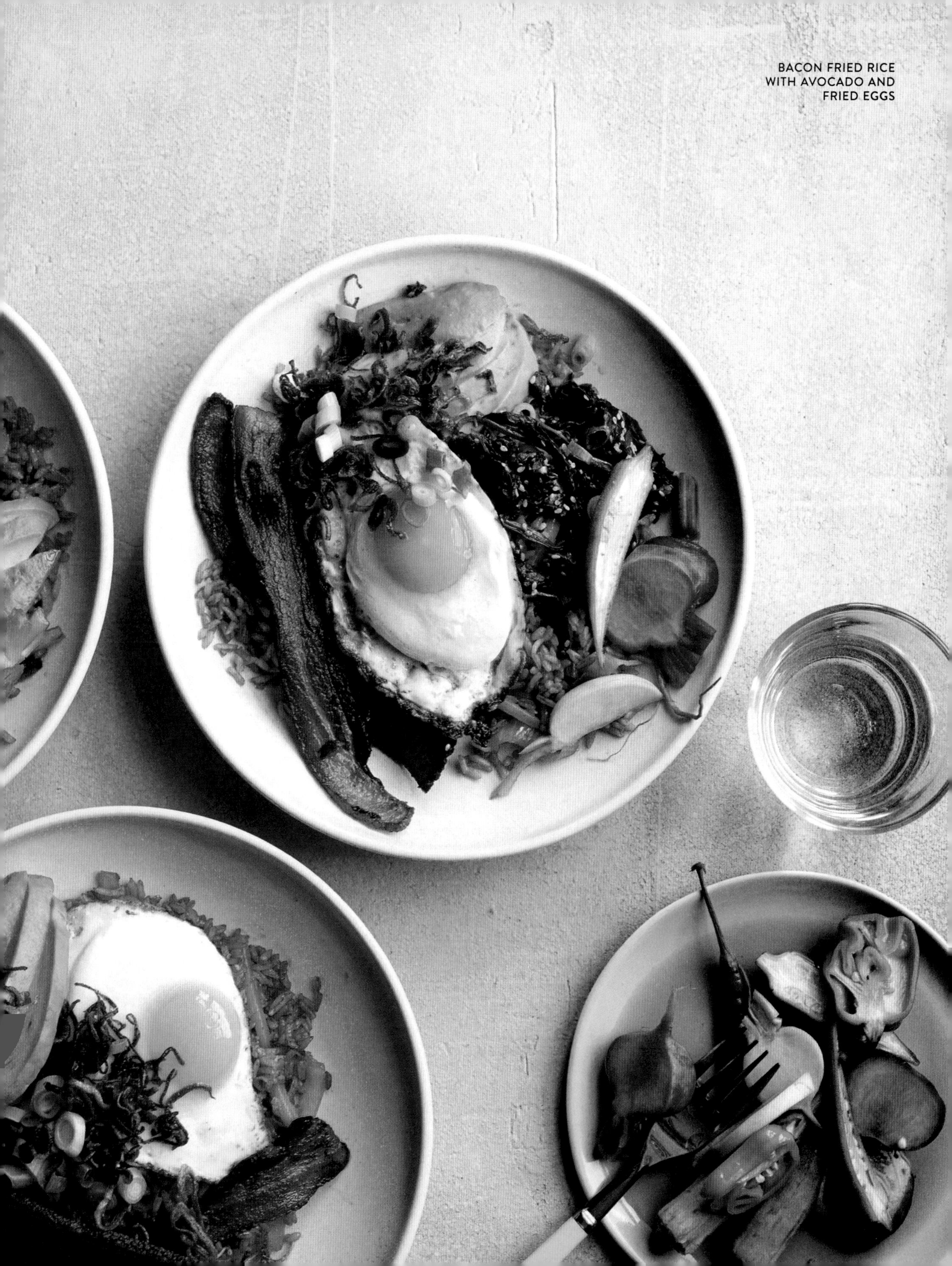

Crispy Rice with Dried Mint and Lemon

Total **1 hr**; Serves **4 to 6**

This lemony, aromatic rice dish from L.A. chefs Sara Kramer and Sarah Hymanson is for crispy food lovers. Simply pack the rice in an even layer in a skillet and let it cook undisturbed in butter until an amazing golden crust forms on the bottom.

- **2 bay leaves**
- **Kosher salt**
- **2¼ cups basmati rice, rinsed**
- **4½ Tbsp. unsalted butter**
- **3 Tbsp. extra-virgin olive oil**
- **2 tsp. finely grated lemon zest plus 6 Tbsp. fresh lemon juice**
- **2 tsp. dried mint**

1. In a medium saucepan, boil 8 cups of water with the bay leaves and 2 tablespoons of salt. Add the rice, stir once and cook over moderately high heat until it begins to soften but still has a bite, about 6 minutes. Drain the rice, rinse with cold water and transfer to a large bowl. Discard the bay leaves.

2. In the saucepan, melt 2½ tablespoons of the butter in the olive oil. Add the lemon zest and mint and cook over low heat until fragrant, 5 minutes. Remove from the heat and stir in the lemon juice, 2 teaspoons of salt and 3 tablespoons of water. Fold the lemon butter into the rice.

3. In a large nonstick skillet, melt the remaining 2 tablespoons of butter. Mound one-fourth of the rice in the center of the skillet. Spread it in an even layer, pressing firmly with a spatula to pack it ⅛ inch thick. Spread the remaining rice on top in an even layer.

4. Cover and cook over moderate heat until the rice smells toasty and is beginning to brown on the bottom, 10 minutes. Reduce the heat to low and cook until the rice is tender and golden brown on the bottom, 10 minutes more. Remove from the heat and let steam, covered, for 5 minutes.

5. Invert a large platter on the skillet and carefully turn the rice out onto it. Serve hot. —*Sara Kramer and Sarah Hymanson*

Kedgeree with Mango Chutney and Soft-Boiled Eggs

Active **1 hr**; Total **2 hr**; Serves **4**

Kedgeree, an Anglo-Indian favorite, is a curried rice dish studded with chunks of smoked fish. The homemade mango chutney here is exceptional, but you can use store-bought.

MANGO CHUTNEY

- **3 cups finely chopped mango (from 2 mangoes)**
- **1 medium yellow onion, finely chopped**
- **1 medium Granny Smith apple— peeled, cored and coarsely grated**
- **½ serrano chile, seeded and minced**
- **½ cup red wine vinegar**
- **¼ cup plus 2 Tbsp. light brown sugar**

KEDGEREE

- **2 cups basmati rice**
- **3 star anise pods**
- **One 3-inch cinnamon stick**
- **Kosher salt and pepper**
- **3 Tbsp. extra-virgin olive oil**
- **2 tsp. brown mustard seeds**
- **1 small yellow onion, finely chopped**
- **1 large garlic clove, minced**
- **2 Tbsp. curry powder**
- **¼ cup dried currants**
- **3 smoked trout fillets (9 oz.), skinned, meat flaked into large pieces**
- **½ cup heavy cream**
- **2 Tbsp. chopped parsley**
- **4 large eggs**

1. Make the mango chutney In a medium saucepan, combine the mango, onion, apple, chile, vinegar and brown sugar. Cover with a parchment paper round or lid and cook over moderately low heat, stirring occasionally, until the apple and onion are very soft, 45 minutes. Let cool completely.

2. Make the kedgeree In a medium saucepan, combine the basmati rice with the star anise, cinnamon stick, 2 teaspoons of salt and 3 cups of water. Bring to a boil, cover and cook over low heat until the rice is tender, about 15 minutes. Let stand, covered, for 5 minutes. Discard the star anise and cinnamon stick.

3. In a large skillet, heat the olive oil. Add the mustard seeds and cook over moderate heat, stirring occasionally, until the seeds begin to pop, 1 to 2 minutes. Add the onion and garlic, season with salt and cook, stirring occasionally, until softened, about 8 minutes. Stir in the curry powder and cook until fragrant, 2 minutes. Add the rice along with the currants and smoked trout. Cook over moderate heat, stirring a few times, until the trout is warm, 3 minutes. Add the cream and 1½ tablespoons of the parsley and cook, stirring occasionally, until heated through. Season with salt and pepper.

4. Bring a medium saucepan of water to a boil. Add the eggs and simmer over moderate heat for 6 minutes. Pour off the hot water and gently shake the eggs in the pan to crack the shells. Fill the pan with cold water and let stand for 1 minute. Peel the eggs. Add 2 inches of water to the saucepan and bring to a simmer. Add the peeled eggs and warm them for 2 minutes. Carefully drain and pat dry. Cut the eggs in half.

5. Top the kedgeree with the soft-boiled eggs, garnish with the remaining ½ tablespoon of parsley and serve with the mango chutney. —*Aneka Sidoti*

WINE Juicy, herb-inflected Spanish white: 2014 Telmo Rodríguez Gaba do Xil Godello.

Basmati Rice with Dill and Barberries

Active **15 min**; Total **1 hr**; Serves **6 to 8**

- **2 cups basmati rice, rinsed and drained well**
- **Fine sea salt and pepper**
- **4 Tbsp. unsalted butter, softened**
- **¾ cup chopped dill**
- **½ cup dried barberries or dried cranberries**
- **3 Tbsp. fresh lemon juice**
- **1 medium shallot, minced**

1. In a medium saucepan, combine the rice with 3 cups of water and bring to a boil. Add a generous pinch of salt. Stir once, cover and cook over low heat until the water is absorbed and the rice is tender, about 20 minutes. Remove from the heat and let steam, covered, for 20 minutes, then fluff with a fork.

2. In a large bowl, mix the rice with the butter. Fold in the dill, barberries, lemon juice and shallot. Season with salt and pepper and serve. —*Jessica Koslow*

Fragrant Crab Rice

Active **20 min**; Total **1 hr**; Serves **4**

Chef Angela Dimayuga of Mission Chinese Food in New York City gives her buttery crab rice a double dose of flavor with jasmine rice and toasted black tea leaves.

- **1½ cups jasmine rice**
- **Kosher salt and pepper**
- **3 Tbsp. black breakfast tea, preferably Japanese**
- **6 Tbsp. unsalted butter**
- **1 cup minced white onion**
- **½ lb. jumbo lump crabmeat, picked over**
- **Black sesame seeds, for garnish**

1. In a medium saucepan, bring 2¼ cups of water to a boil. Add the rice and a generous pinch of salt. Stir once, cover and simmer over low heat until the water is absorbed and the rice is tender, about 20 minutes. Remove from the heat and let steam, covered, for 20 minutes. Fluff the rice with a fork and spread it out on a plate to cool slightly.

2. Meanwhile, in a large skillet, toast the tea over moderately low heat, stirring, until fragrant, about 1 minute. Transfer the tea to a plate and let cool, then finely crumble with your fingers.

3. In the skillet, melt the butter. Add the onion and cook over moderately low heat, stirring occasionally, until very soft but not browned, about 12 minutes; season with salt. Add the rice and tea and cook over moderate heat, stirring gently, until the rice is hot and the tea is evenly distributed, about 2 minutes. Gently fold in the crabmeat and cook until warmed through, about 2 minutes. Season generously with pepper. Transfer to a platter and garnish with sesame seeds. Serve right away.
—*Angela Dimayuga*

WINE Dry, minerally white: 2014 Vietti Roero Arneis.

One-Pot Thai Curry Rice with Pork

Active **30 min**; Total **1 hr 15 min**
Serves **4 to 6**

Hot dish is a staple at potlucks and church suppers throughout the Midwest. By substituting coconut milk for the more commonly used creamed soup, Minnesota food blogger Molly Yeh makes hers slightly less heavy than the classic.

- **1 cup basmati rice**
- **1 cup chicken or vegetable stock or low-sodium broth**
- **2 Tbsp. canola oil**
- **1 lb. ground pork or chicken**
- **Kosher salt and pepper**
- **2 Tbsp. Thai red curry paste**
- **One 13.5-oz. can unsweetened coconut milk**
- **2 Tbsp. light brown sugar**
- **1 Tbsp. Asian fish sauce**
- **1 red bell pepper, cut into ¾-inch pieces**
- **1 small onion, cut into ½-inch pieces**
- **1 carrot, sliced into ½-inch-thick rounds**
- **4 oz. snap peas, cut into ½-inch pieces**
- **Lime wedges, chopped cilantro and crushed roasted peanuts, for serving**

1. Preheat the oven to 400°. In a medium saucepan, combine the rice and stock and bring to a boil. Cover and cook over moderately low heat until all of the liquid is absorbed, about 6 minutes; the rice will not be completely cooked.

2. In a medium enameled cast-iron casserole, heat the oil. Add the pork or chicken, season with salt and pepper and cook over moderate heat, stirring occasionally, until browned and cooked through, about 5 minutes. Stir in the curry paste and cook until very fragrant, about 2 minutes. Add the parcooked rice, the coconut milk, sugar, fish sauce, bell pepper, onion, carrot and snap peas and mix well. Cover and bake for 30 minutes. Uncover and bake for about 10 minutes longer, until the rice is tender and all of the coconut milk has been absorbed. Serve warm with lime wedges, cilantro and crushed peanuts. —*Molly Yeh*

WINE Moderately tannic red: 2013 Benovia Russian River Valley Pinot Noir.

Beets and Berries

Active **30 min**; Total **1 hr 15 min**; Serves **4**

Chef Jeremy Fox of Rustic Canyon in L.A. first gained fame for his stellar vegetarian food, like this lemony quinoa with roasted beets, smashed berries and creamy avocado. It's an unexpected combination that works brilliantly.

- **10 small beets (1 lb.)**
- **7 Tbsp. extra-virgin olive oil**
- **Kosher salt and pepper**
- **1 tsp. red wine vinegar**
- **1 cup quinoa, rinsed and drained**
- **½ tsp. finely grated lemon zest plus 3 Tbsp. fresh lemon juice**
- **1 cup blackberries or raspberries**
- **1 Hass avocado, peeled**
- **Chopped toasted pistachios**

1. Preheat the oven to 425°. On a large sheet of foil, toss the beets with 1 tablespoon of the oil; season with salt and wrap in the foil. Roast for about 45 minutes, until tender. Unwrap and let the beets cool, then peel them. Cut into wedges and transfer to a bowl. Add the vinegar, season with salt and toss.

2. Meanwhile, in a medium saucepan, cover the quinoa with 2 cups of water; bring to a boil. Cover and cook over moderately low heat for about 15 minutes, until all the water is absorbed. Fluff the quinoa and transfer to a bowl to cool slightly. Add the lemon zest and 2 tablespoons each of the lemon juice and oil; season with salt and pepper.

3. In a bowl, using a fork, smash the berries with 3 tablespoons of the olive oil until a chunky sauce forms. Season with salt.

4. In a small bowl, mash the avocado with the remaining 1 tablespoon each of olive oil and lemon juice; season with salt and pepper.

5. Spoon the quinoa into bowls. Arrange the beets on top and spoon the berry sauce over the beets. Dollop with the avocado, garnish with pistachios and serve.
—*Jeremy Fox*

WINE Dry Riesling; 2013 Leitz Rüdesheimer Trocken.

Wild Rice Salad with Beets, Grapes and Pecans

Active **30 min**; Total **1 hr**; Serves **8 to 10**

Nutty wild rice salad is a great make-ahead dish for dinner parties since it holds up well in the fridge overnight. Just fold in the arugula and pecans before you serve it.

- 2 cups wild rice (12 oz.), rinsed and drained
  Kosher salt and pepper
- 12 baby golden beets
- ¼ cup extra-virgin olive oil, plus more for rubbing
- 1½ cups pecans
- ¼ cup plus 1 Tbsp. apple cider vinegar
- 1 small shallot, minced
- 2 cups seedless green grapes (10 oz.), halved
- 5 oz. arugula (not baby), thick stems discarded, leaves chopped

1. Preheat the oven to 400°. In a large saucepan, cover the rice with at least 3 inches of water and bring to a boil. Add a generous pinch of salt and simmer over moderate heat until the rice is tender, about 45 minutes. Drain well, then spread on a large baking sheet to cool; stir occasionally.

2. Meanwhile, rub the beets with olive oil and season with salt and pepper. Roast for about 30 minutes, until just tender. Let cool, then rub off the skins and cut into ½-inch wedges.

3. Spread the pecans in a pie plate. Bake for about 10 minutes, until fragrant and browned. Let cool, then coarsely chop.

4. In a large serving bowl, whisk the vinegar with the shallot and let stand for 5 minutes. Whisk in the ¼ cup of olive oil. Add the rice, beets and grapes and toss well. Season with salt and pepper; toss again. Fold in the arugula and pecans and serve. —*Justin Chapple*

Quinoa with Spinach and Roasted Almonds

Total **40 min**; Serves **6**

- 1⅓ cups quinoa, rinsed and drained
- 8 oz. curly spinach (8 packed cups), stemmed and finely chopped (4 cups)
- 3 radishes, thinly sliced
- 6 Tbsp. extra-virgin olive oil
- 2 Tbsp. fresh lemon juice
  Kosher salt and pepper
- ½ cup chopped roasted almonds

1. In a medium saucepan of boiling water, cook the quinoa until tender, about 10 minutes. Drain and return the quinoa to the pan. Cover and let stand for 10 minutes; fluff with a fork.

2. In a large bowl, toss the quinoa with the spinach, radishes, olive oil and lemon juice. Season with salt and pepper and toss again. Garnish with the almonds and serve. —*Kay Chun*

MAKE AHEAD The recipe can be kept at room temperature for up to 3 hours.

Warm Barley-Shiitake Salad

Total **50 min**; Serves **4**

Barley and mushrooms are familiar partners in soup, but they're also a compelling duo in a salad—especially when you use robust fresh shiitake.

- 1 cup barley
- ¼ cup extra-virgin olive oil
- 12 oz. shiitake mushrooms, stemmed and thinly sliced
- 5 shallots, thinly sliced (2 cups)
- 2 Tbsp. fresh lemon juice
  Kosher salt and pepper
  Sliced scallions, for garnish

1. In a large saucepan of boiling water, cook the barley until tender, about 30 minutes. Drain.

2. Meanwhile, in a large skillet, heat the oil. Add the mushrooms and shallots and cook over moderate heat, stirring, until golden and tender, 5 to 7 minutes. Stir in the lemon juice and barley and season with salt and pepper. Transfer to a serving dish and garnish with sliced scallions. —*Kay Chun*

Barley with Walnuts and Bacon

Active **20 min**; Total **1 hr 20 min**; Serves **4**

Serve this hearty dish as a side for roast chicken or transform it into a meal-in-one grain bowl by topping the barley with a poached egg and fresh herbs.

- 1 Tbsp. extra-virgin olive oil
- 3 slices of bacon, finely chopped
- ⅓ cup finely chopped onion
- ⅓ cup finely chopped carrot
- ⅓ cup finely chopped celery
- 3 garlic cloves, minced
- 1¼ cups pearled barley (½ lb.)
- 4 cups chicken stock or low-sodium broth
- ½ cup chopped toasted walnuts

In a medium saucepan, heat the olive oil. Add the bacon and cook over moderate heat, stirring occasionally, until the fat has rendered, about 5 minutes. Add the onion, carrot, celery and garlic and cook, stirring occasionally, until softened, about 3 minutes. Stir in the barley and chicken stock and bring to a boil. Cover and cook over moderately low heat until all of the stock has been absorbed and the barley is tender, about 1 hour. Transfer to a bowl and garnish with the toasted walnuts. —*HH & Co., Hampshire, England*

UP YOUR GRAINS GAME

Quinoa Pointers

RINSE Quinoa can have a bitter residue, so make sure to rinse it well in a fine-mesh strainer.

MIX IN Quinoa's light texture makes it great for combining with heavier grains like rice and barley.

PICK A COLOR Red and black quinoa are slightly earthier than white, but they can be substituted for one another in recipes. —*Kristin Donelly, author of* Modern Potluck

DIY Lamb Biryani

Chef **MANEET CHAUHAN** of Nashville's Chauhan Ale & Masala House shares how to make the iconic Indian dish of saffron-laced rice and spiced lamb baked under a dough lid.

Hyderabadi Lamb Biryani

Active **2 hr**; Total **7 hr**; Serves **4**

LAMB

- ¼ cup canola oil
- 2 onions (1 lb.), thinly sliced
- ¾ cup finely chopped mint
- ½ cup finely chopped cilantro
- ¼ cup yogurt
- 3 Tbsp. fresh lemon juice
- 2 to 3 Thai chiles, minced
- 1 Tbsp. finely grated garlic
- 1 Tbsp. finely grated peeled ginger
- 1 Tbsp. kosher salt
- 2 tsp. cayenne
- 1½ tsp. ground coriander
- 1½ tsp. ground cumin
- 1 tsp. Garam Masala (opposite)
- ¼ tsp. ground turmeric
- 1½ lbs. trimmed boneless lamb shoulder, cut into 1-inch cubes
- 2 Tbsp. ghee or clarified butter

RICE

- 4 whole black peppercorns
- 2 whole cloves
- 2 green cardamom pods
- 1 black cardamom pod
- One 2-inch cinnamon stick
- 1 bay leaf
- Pinch of freshly grated nutmeg
- Small piece of mace
- 1 Tbsp. canola oil
- 1 Tbsp. kosher salt
- 1 tsp. caraway seeds
- 2 cups basmati rice
- Pinch of saffron threads
- ½ cup whole milk

BIRYANI

- 3 Tbsp. ghee or clarified butter, plus more for brushing
- 2 Tbsp. chopped cilantro
- 2 Tbsp. chopped mint
- ½ tsp. rosewater
- ½ tsp. Garam Masala (opposite)

DOUGH LID

- 1½ cups whole-wheat flour
- ½ cup plus 2 Tbsp. water

TOMATO-ONION RAITA

- 1 cup yogurt
- ½ cup finely chopped tomato
- 1 small Thai chile, minced
- 1 Tbsp. minced red onion
- 2 tsp. chopped mint, plus small leaves for garnish
- 2 tsp. chopped cilantro
- 1 tsp. ground cumin
- ⅛ tsp. cayenne
- Pinch of sugar
- Kosher salt

PREPARE THE LAMB

1. In a large nonstick skillet, heat the oil. Add the onions and cook over moderate heat, stirring occasionally, until golden brown, 10 to 12 minutes. Reserve one-third of the onions in a small bowl. Scrape the remaining onions into a large bowl and let cool to room temperature. Add all of the remaining ingredients except the lamb and ghee and mix well. Stir in the lamb until evenly coated. Cover and refrigerate for at least 3 hours or overnight.

2. In a large enameled cast-iron casserole, heat the ghee. Add the lamb mixture and cook over moderate heat, stirring occasionally, until browned, about 8 minutes. Add ½ cup of water, cover and cook over moderately low heat until the lamb is tender, about 1 hour and 15 minutes.

PREPARE THE RICE

3. In a large saucepan, bring 4 cups of water to a boil. Wrap the peppercorns, cloves, cardamom pods, cinnamon stick, bay leaf, nutmeg and mace in a piece of cheesecloth and tie into a secure bundle. Add to the saucepan along with the oil, salt and caraway; stir in the rice. Bring to a simmer and cook over moderate heat, stirring occasionally, until the rice is cooked three-quarters of the way, 8 to 10 minutes. Drain well, reserving ¼ cup of the cooking liquid. Discard the spice bundle.

STEP-BY-STEP BIRYANI LESSON

MARINATE THE LAMB Combine marinade ingredients. Add cubed lamb shoulder and refrigerate for at least 3 hours or overnight.

COOK THE LAMB Sauté the lamb mixture in ghee until well browned. Add water, cover and braise gently until tender.

PARCOOK THE RICE Simmer basmati rice with spices bundled in cheesecloth. Drain when the rice is three-quarters cooked.

FINISH THE BIRYANI Layer the biryani ingredients in a casserole. Cover with a dough lid, press to seal all around, then bake.

The dough "lid," which seals in flavor and absorbs moisture as the rice steams, is not meant to be eaten. Crack it off and discard before serving the biryani.

4. Meanwhile, in a small saucepan, toast the saffron over moderately low heat, stirring, until fragrant, about 2 minutes. Remove from the heat and stir in the milk.

ASSEMBLE THE BIRYANI

5. Preheat the oven to 350°. Drizzle 1 tablespoon of the ghee in a large enameled cast-iron casserole. Spoon half of the lamb mixture into the casserole in an even layer. Spread half of the rice over the lamb. Top with half each of the remaining cooked onions, saffron milk, ghee, cilantro, mint, rosewater and garam masala and 2 tablespoons of the reserved rice cooking water. Repeat the layering once more.

FINISH & BAKE

6. Make the dough lid In a medium bowl, mix the flour and water until a rough dough forms. On a lightly floured work surface, knead the dough until it is smooth and pliable, about 5 minutes. Gather into a ball and roll out to a ⅛-inch-thick round that's a few inches larger than your casserole.

7. Drape the dough over the top of the casserole, pressing to seal it around the edge. Bake the biryani for 20 to 25 minutes, until the dough is golden and the rice is hot. Brush the crust with ghee and let stand for 5 minutes.

8. Make the tomato-onion raita Combine all of the ingredients in a bowl and garnish with mint leaves.

9. Crack off and discard the dough lid and serve the lamb biryani hot, with the cooling raita.

WINE Juicy Cabernet Franc: 2013 Domaine de L'Oubliée Bourgueil Notre Histoire.

GARAM MASALA

In a small skillet, combine 10 **black peppercorns**, 2 whole **cloves**, one 4-inch **cinnamon stick**, ¼ tsp. **caraway seeds**, a pinch of freshly grated **nutmeg**, a piece of **mace** and the seeds from 4 **green cardamom pods**. Toast over moderate heat until very fragrant. Let cool and grind to a powder. *Makes 1 Tbsp.*

BULGUR AND HERB
SALAD WITH
SUNFLOWER SEEDS

Wheat Berry and Squash Salad

Active **45 min**; Total **1 hr 15 min**
Serves **10 to 12**

- 3 cups wheat berries
- One 2-lb. kabocha squash—halved, seeded, peeled and cut into 1½-inch pieces
- One 1½-lb. acorn squash—scrubbed, halved, seeded and cut into 1½-inch pieces
- 12 oz. parsnips (2 large), peeled and cut into 1-inch pieces
- ¾ cup extra-virgin olive oil
- Kosher salt and pepper
- 1 shallot, minced
- 3 Tbsp. fresh lemon juice
- 3 Tbsp. red wine vinegar
- 8 oz. Tuscan kale, thinly sliced crosswise
- ½ cup pomegranate seeds
- ½ cup dried sour cherries
- 1 persimmon, halved and thinly sliced (optional)
- 4 oz. feta cheese, crumbled
- ½ cup lightly packed mint leaves

1. In a large saucepan of salted boiling water, cook the wheat berries until tender, about 45 minutes. Drain well, then spread on a baking sheet to cool completely.

2. Meanwhile, preheat the oven to 425°. In a large bowl, toss the kabocha, acorn squash and parsnips with ¼ cup of the olive oil and season with salt and pepper. Spread on 2 large rimmed baking sheets and roast for about 25 minutes, until tender but not falling apart. Let cool completely.

3. In a large bowl, whisk the shallot with the lemon juice, vinegar and the remaining ½ cup of oil. Season with salt and pepper. Add the wheat berries, squash, parsnips, kale, pomegranate seeds, cherries and persimmon (if using) and toss well. Season with salt and pepper and toss again. Scatter the feta and mint on top and serve.
—Ellen Bennett

MAKE AHEAD The salad can be made up to 2 hours ahead and kept at room temperature. Add the feta and mint just before serving.

Freekeh with Grilled Tofu and Miso-Lime Dressing

Total **45 min**; Serves **4**

The base for this potluck-friendly salad is freekeh, a roasted and cracked green wheat. Not only is it high in fiber and protein, it also cooks in just 20 minutes.

- 1½ cups cracked freekeh
- 8 oz. haricots verts, trimmed and halved crosswise
- 3 Tbsp. unseasoned rice vinegar
- 1½ tsp. finely grated lime zest plus 1½ Tbsp. fresh lime juice
- 1½ Tbsp. white miso
- 2 tsp. packed finely grated peeled fresh ginger
- 3 scallions, white and green parts thinly sliced separately
- 1½ tsp. toasted sesame oil
- ½ cup plus 1 Tbsp. canola oil
- Kosher salt and pepper
- One 14-oz. package firm tofu—drained, sliced ½ inch thick and patted dry with paper towels
- 3 Persian cucumbers, thinly sliced
- Mint and furikake (see Note) or toasted sesame seeds, for garnish

1. Cook the freekeh in a large saucepan of salted boiling water until tender, about 20 minutes; add the haricots verts for the last 2 minutes. Drain and rinse the freekeh and beans under cold running water until cool. Drain well and transfer to a large bowl.

2. Meanwhile, in a medium bowl, whisk the rice vinegar with the lime zest, lime juice, miso, ginger and scallion whites. While whisking constantly, slowly drizzle in the toasted sesame oil and canola oil. Season with salt and pepper.

3. Heat a grill pan. Season the tofu with salt and pepper and brush with ¼ cup of the dressing. Grill over moderately high heat, turning once, until grill marks form and the tofu is heated through, about 3 minutes per side.

4. Add the remaining dressing, the cucumbers and two-thirds of the scallion greens to the freekeh, season with salt and pepper and toss. Mound the freekeh salad on plates and top with the grilled tofu. Garnish with the remaining scallion greens, mint and furikake and serve. —Kristin Donnelly

NOTE Furikake is a Japanese condiment made from dried seaweed, sesame seeds and fish. It's available at Asian markets and on amazon.com.

MAKE AHEAD The cooked freekeh and haricots verts and the dressing can all be refrigerated overnight. Bring to room temperature before using.

WINE Fragrant and minerally Pinot Bianco: 2015 Erste + Neue Alto Adige.

Bulgur and Herb Salad with Sunflower Seeds

Total **35 min**; Serves **6**

F&W's Justin Chapple dresses up humble bulgur with a lemony dressing, crunchy roasted sunflower seeds and a bounty of fresh herbs—cleverly snipped with scissors to avoid dirtying a cutting board.

- 1 cup medium bulgur
- 2 cups boiling water
- Kosher salt and pepper
- One 2-oz. bunch of parsley
- One 2-oz. bunch of cilantro
- One 1-oz. bunch of chives
- One 1-oz. bunch of dill
- ½ cup salted roasted sunflower seeds
- ¼ cup fresh lemon juice
- 3 Tbsp. extra-virgin olive oil

1. In a large heatproof bowl, cover the bulgur with the boiling water. Add a generous pinch of salt, cover with plastic wrap and let stand until the bulgur is tender and the water is absorbed, about 20 minutes. Fluff with a fork.

2. Hold the herb bunches together in one hand. Using scissors, snip the herbs over the bulgur until you reach the thick stems (you should have about 1½ cups each of parsley and cilantro and ¾ cup each of chives and dill); discard the stems. Add the sunflower seeds, lemon juice and olive oil to the bulgur and toss very well. Season with salt and pepper and toss again. Serve the salad at room temperature.
—Justin Chapple

MAKE AHEAD The bulgur salad can be made early in the day. The cooked bulgur can be refrigerated for up to 3 days.

Beet and Chard Polenta with Ricotta Salata

⏱ Total **45 min;** Serves **6**

This two-tone polenta is incredibly easy to make: Just mix half of the polenta with pureed raw chard and the rest with pureed raw beet. The resulting dish, topped with thinly sliced ricotta salata, echoes the colors of the Italian flag.

1½ cups stone-ground white polenta

6 Tbsp. unsalted butter

2 Tbsp. extra-virgin olive oil, plus more for drizzling

1 cup freshly grated Parmigiano-Reggiano cheese

Kosher salt and pepper

1½ cups chopped stemmed Swiss chard leaves

1 small red beet, peeled and chopped

3 oz. ricotta salata cheese, thinly sliced or crumbled

Baby arugula, for garnish

1. In a saucepan, bring 6 cups of water to a boil. Slowly drizzle in the polenta, whisking constantly. Bring to a simmer and cook over moderately low heat, stirring, until tender and thickened, 20 minutes. Stir in the butter, 2 tablespoons of oil and the grated cheese; season with salt and pepper.

2. In a blender, puree the Swiss chard with ½ cup of water until smooth. Scrape into a small bowl. Wipe out the blender. Add the beet and ½ cup of water and puree until smooth. Scrape into another small bowl.

3. Pour half of the polenta into a bowl. Add the chard puree to the remaining polenta in the saucepan and cook over low heat, stirring, until well blended, 2 minutes. Mound the chard polenta on one side of each of 6 shallow bowls. Rinse out the saucepan; add the reserved polenta and beet puree. Cook over low heat, stirring, until blended, 2 minutes. Spoon the beet polenta next to the chard polenta. Top with the ricotta salata, garnish with arugula and drizzle with oil. Season with pepper and serve. —*Giampaolo Venica*

MAKE AHEAD The chard and beet polentas can be refrigerated separately for up to 2 days. Reheat before serving, adding water if necessary.

WINE Brisk Friulian white: 2014 I Clivi delle Venezie Ribolla Gialla.

Jeweled Millet Salad with Crispy Chickpeas

Active **50 min;** Total **1 hr 15 min;** Serves **6**

½ cup millet

Kosher salt and pepper

One 15-oz. can chickpeas, rinsed and patted dry

2 Tbsp. harissa

½ cup extra-virgin olive oil

½ cup slivered blanched almonds

1 medium onion, thinly sliced

1 cup julienned carrots

¼ cup thinly sliced scallions

½ cup chopped cilantro

¼ cup chopped mint

¼ cup chopped basil

2 tsp. finely grated lemon zest plus 3 Tbsp. fresh lemon juice

1. Preheat the oven to 400°. In a medium saucepan, combine the millet with 1½ cups of water and bring to a boil. Add a generous pinch of salt, cover and simmer over low heat until the millet is tender and the water is absorbed, 20 minutes. Let steam, covered, for 10 minutes, then fluff with a fork.

2. Meanwhile, on a large rimmed baking sheet, toss the chickpeas with the harissa and 2 tablespoons of the olive oil and season with salt and pepper. Bake for about 25 minutes, until crisp. Let cool slightly.

3. In a medium skillet, heat the remaining 6 tablespoons of olive oil until shimmering. Add the almonds and cook over moderately high heat, stirring, until golden. Using a slotted spoon, transfer to a plate and season with salt and pepper. Add the onion to the skillet and cook over moderately low heat, stirring occasionally, until well browned, 12 to 15 minutes.

4. In a large bowl, toss the millet with the onion, almonds, carrots, scallions, cilantro, mint, basil and lemon zest and juice. Fold in the chickpeas, season with salt and pepper and serve. —*Ben Ford*

Farro with Vinegar-Glazed Sweet Potato and Apples

Total **1 hr;** Serves **6**

Tossing sweet potatoes and apples in sherry vinegar creates a tangy glaze during roasting. The combo is especially good with the farro, dried cherries and roasted cashews in this thoroughly satisfying grain salad from chef Michael Scelfo of Alden & Harlow in Cambridge, Massachusetts.

¼ cup plus 3 Tbsp. extra-virgin olive oil

1 small fennel bulb, finely chopped

1 small onion, finely chopped

5 garlic cloves, minced

Kosher salt and pepper

4 cups chicken stock or low-sodium broth

2 cups farro

¾ lb. sweet potato (1 large), scrubbed and cut into 1½-inch pieces

¼ cup sherry vinegar

2 Granny Smith apples—peeled, cored and cut into 1½-inch pieces

¾ cup dried cherries, soaked in warm water for 10 minutes and drained

1 cup roasted cashews, coarsely chopped

¾ cup coarsely chopped parsley

Shaved pecorino cheese, for serving

1. In a large saucepan, heat ¼ cup of the olive oil. Add the fennel, onion, garlic and a generous pinch of salt. Cook over moderate heat, stirring occasionally, until the fennel is softened, about 8 minutes. Add the stock and farro and bring to a boil over high heat. Reduce the heat to moderate and simmer, stirring occasionally, until the farro is tender and the stock is absorbed, 25 to 30 minutes.

2. Meanwhile, preheat the oven to 425°. On a large rimmed baking sheet, toss the sweet potato with the remaining 3 tablespoons of olive oil and season with salt and pepper. Drizzle with the sherry vinegar and roast for about 15 minutes, until just starting to soften. Add the apples and toss to coat. Roast for about 20 minutes longer, until the sweet potato and apples are tender but not falling apart. Let cool slightly.

3. In a large bowl, toss the farro mixture with the dried cherries, cashews, parsley and the roasted sweet potato and apples. Season with salt and pepper. Transfer to plates, top with shaved pecorino cheese and serve. —*Michael Scelfo*

MAKE AHEAD The farro salad can be refrigerated overnight. Stir in the cashews and parsley just before serving at room temperature.

WINE Light-bodied, fragrant Italian red: 2014 G.B. Burlotto Verduno Pelaverga.

Seared Tofu Tabbouleh

⏱ Total **40 min**; Serves **4 to 6**

Tabbouleh is a Middle Eastern salad typically made with bulgur and chopped vegetables. Adding bits of seared tofu to the mix quickly converts it into a vibrant vegan entrée.

- **4 cups bulgur**
- **5 Tbsp. extra-virgin olive oil**
- **One 14-oz. package firm tofu, drained and cubed**
- **5 scallions, chopped, plus more for garnish**
- **1 small tomato, chopped**
- **1 Kirby cucumber, chopped**
- **1 Tbsp. fresh lemon juice**
- **Kosher salt and pepper**

1. In a medium saucepan of boiling water, cook the bulgur until tender, about 12 minutes. Drain and return the bulgur to the pan. Cover and let stand for 10 minutes; fluff with a fork. Spread the bulgur on a baking sheet and let cool to room temperature.

2. In a large cast-iron skillet, heat 2 tablespoons of the oil. Add the tofu and 5 chopped scallions and cook over high heat, stirring, until golden and crisp in spots, about 5 minutes. Transfer to a large bowl. Stir in the bulgur, tomato, cucumber, lemon juice and the remaining 3 tablespoons of oil and season with salt and pepper. Garnish with more chopped scallions and serve. —*Kay Chun*

Barley and Tomato Salad

Active **45 min**; Total **1 hr 45 min**; Serves **4**

Victoria Elíasdóttir, chef at Dóttir in Berlin, creates a main-course salad brimming with contrasting flavors and textures: chewy barley, tender honey-roasted cherry tomatoes and crisp, tart green tomatoes—all tossed with a sweet and tangy anise-scented vinaigrette.

BARLEY

- **2 Tbsp. canola oil**
- **¼ cup finely chopped shallots**
- **1 celery rib, finely chopped**
- **1¼ cups pearled barley (8 oz.)**
- **2 garlic cloves, crushed**
- **2 bay leaves**
- **1 cup apple juice**
- **Kosher salt**

TOMATOES

- **1 lb. cherry tomatoes, halved**
- **¼ cup extra-virgin olive oil**
- **¼ cup honey**
- **2 garlic cloves, minced**
- **Kosher salt**
- **3 Tbsp. pure maple syrup**
- **3 Tbsp. apple juice**
- **3 Tbsp. apple cider vinegar**
- **8 oz. green tomatoes, coarsely chopped**

DRESSING

- **2 Tbsp. apple cider vinegar**
- **1½ Tbsp. extra-virgin olive oil**
- **1½ Tbsp. apple juice**
- **1 Tbsp. honey**
- **½ tsp. finely grated lemon zest**
- **1 Tbsp. chopped tarragon, plus leaves for garnish**
- **Kosher salt**

1. Cook the barley In a saucepan, heat the oil. Add the shallots and celery and cook over moderate heat, stirring, until softened, about 5 minutes. Stir in the barley, garlic and bay leaves. Add the apple juice and 2½ cups of water and season with salt. Bring to a simmer, cover and cook over low heat until the water is absorbed and the barley is tender, 45 minutes. Spread the barley on a baking sheet to cool. Discard the bay leaves.

2. Prepare the tomatoes Preheat the oven to 425°. On a rimmed baking sheet, toss the cherry tomatoes with the oil, honey and garlic. Season with salt. Roast for 20 minutes, stirring, until soft and caramelized. Transfer the baking sheet to a rack.

3. In a large bowl, whisk the maple syrup with the apple juice and vinegar. Season with salt. Add the green tomatoes, toss to coat and let stand at room temperature for at least 30 minutes, stirring occasionally.

4. Make the dressing In a bowl, whisk the vinegar, oil, apple juice, honey, lemon zest and chopped tarragon. Add the barley and toss. Season with salt. Spoon into shallow bowls and top with the roasted cherry tomatoes and marinated green tomatoes. Garnish with tarragon leaves and serve. —*Victoria Elíasdóttir*

WINE Dry, savory white: 2014 Stadlmann Grüner Veltliner.

INGREDIENT SWAPS

New Uses for Ancient Grains

WHEAT BERRIES For a twist on fried rice, add cooked wheat berries to the wok with your vegetables.

FARRO Treat it like oatmeal: Simmer in a combo of water and milk, stir in honey and sprinkle with chopped nuts.

MILLET Use this high-protein, gluten-free grain as a substitute for oats, or for rice in risotto. Finish with sautéed broccoli rabe, butter and Parmesan.

BREADS, SANDWICHES AND PIZZAS

Blogger Molly Yeh keeps cozy during long Minnesota winters by baking halvah-stuffed challah (p. 261). OPPOSITE Extra-Rich Brioche (p. 261).

Goat Cheese, Bacon and Olive Quick Bread

Active **35 min**; Total **1 hr 15 min plus cooling**
Makes **one 9-inch loaf**

Quick breads are popular in France, where they're known as savory cakes. Paris-based cookbook author David Lebovitz packs this one with olives, cheese and bacon, and infuses it with cayenne.

- **6** slices of thick-cut bacon, cut crosswise into ½-inch strips
- **1½** cups all-purpose flour
- **2** tsp. baking powder
- **1 to 2** tsp. cayenne
- **¼** tsp. kosher salt
- **4** large eggs, at room temperature
- **½** cup buttermilk
- **¼** cup extra-virgin olive oil
- **2** tsp. Dijon mustard
- **6** oz. fresh goat cheese, crumbled
- **1⅓** cups freshly grated Parmigiano-Reggiano cheese
- **½** cup pitted kalamata olives, halved lengthwise
- **2** scallions, thinly sliced
- **1** red serrano chile, seeded and minced
- **2** tsp. minced thyme leaves

1. Preheat the oven to 350°. Coat a 9-inch loaf pan with cooking spray; line the bottom with parchment paper. In a skillet, cook the bacon over moderate heat until crispy, 8 to 10 minutes. Drain on paper towels.

2. In a bowl, whisk the flour with the baking powder, cayenne and salt. In another bowl, whisk the eggs with the buttermilk, olive oil and mustard. Make a well in the center of the dry ingredients and stir in the egg mixture until just combined. Fold in the goat cheese, Parmigiano, olives, bacon, scallions, chile and thyme. Scrape the batter into the prepared loaf pan and smooth the surface.

3. Bake the bread until golden on top and a toothpick inserted in the center comes out clean, 35 to 40 minutes. Let cool for 15 minutes, then run a knife around the loaf to loosen it from the pan. Invert onto a plate and let cool completely. Cut the loaf into thick slices and serve. —*David Lebovitz*

MAKE AHEAD The bread can be wrapped in plastic wrap and refrigerated for 1 week.

Caraway Rolls with Garlic-Parsley Butter

Active **45 min**; Total **3 hr 30 min**; Makes **16**

ROLLS
- **1½** cups lukewarm whole milk (100°–105°)
- **2** tsp. active dry yeast
- **½** tsp. sugar
- **4** cups bread flour
- **1** Tbsp. caraway seeds
- **2** Tbsp. unsalted butter, at room temperature, plus more for greasing
- **2** tsp. kosher salt

GARLIC-PARSLEY BUTTER
- **2** sticks unsalted butter
- **¼** cup minced garlic
- **1** cup chopped parsley
  Flaky sea salt, for sprinkling

1. Make the rolls In a stand mixer fitted with the dough hook, whisk the warm milk, yeast and sugar and let stand until foamy. With the machine at medium-low speed, beat in the flour, caraway seeds, 2 tablespoons of butter and the kosher salt. Knead the dough until smooth but a little tacky, 5 minutes. Transfer to a lightly oiled bowl, cover with plastic wrap and let stand in a warm place until doubled in bulk, 1 hour.

2. Meanwhile, make the garlic-parsley butter In a small saucepan, melt the butter with the garlic. Scrape into a medium bowl and let cool, then stir in the parsley.

3. Butter a 12-inch cast-iron or ovenproof nonstick skillet. Divide the dough in half; keep 1 piece covered with a kitchen towel. Cut the other into 8 pieces; form each into a ball, then roll in the garlic-parsley butter. Arrange in concentric circles in the prepared skillet about ¼ inch apart. Repeat with the second piece of dough. Cover loosely with plastic and let stand in a warm place until doubled in bulk, 1 hour.

4. Preheat the oven to 350°. Brush the rolls with more of the garlic-parsley butter and bake for about 30 minutes, until golden. Brush with the remaining butter, sprinkle with sea salt and serve. —*Kay Chun*

Dinner Rolls with Nigella Seeds and Flaky Sea Salt

Active **40 min**; Total **3 hr 45 min**; Makes **18**

These crave-worthy rolls, from Jessica Koslow of Sqirl in L.A., are easy to make and have just the right light texture for eating alone or in a sandwich. The fragrant nigella seeds (also called black onion seeds) add a nutty, peppery flavor.

- **1½** cups warm whole milk, plus more for brushing
  One ¼-oz. package active dry yeast
- **¼** cup sugar
- **1** stick unsalted butter, melted and cooled, plus more for greasing
- **1** large egg, at room temperature and lightly beaten
- **2** tsp. fine sea salt
  About 4½ cups all-purpose flour
  Nigella seeds and flaky sea salt, for sprinkling

1. In a stand mixer fitted with the dough hook, mix the 1½ cups of milk with the yeast and 1 tablespoon of the sugar. Let stand until foamy, about 5 minutes. Mix in the stick of melted butter, the egg, fine sea salt and the remaining 3 tablespoons of sugar. At low speed, mix in 4½ cups of flour until the dough comes together; add more flour by the teaspoon if the dough is sticking to the side of the bowl. Mix at medium speed until the dough is soft and forms a loose ball around the hook, about 5 minutes. Transfer the dough to a buttered bowl. Cover with plastic wrap and let stand in a warm spot until doubled in bulk, about 1½ hours.

2. Line 2 large baking sheets with parchment paper. Scrape the dough out onto a work surface and cut into 18 equal pieces. Shape each piece into a ball, pinching the bottoms to seal. Arrange the balls 3 inches apart on the prepared sheets. Cover the rolls loosely with plastic wrap and let stand in a warm spot until doubled in bulk, about 1 hour.

3. Preheat the oven to 350°. Brush the rolls with milk and sprinkle with nigella seeds and flaky sea salt. Bake for about 25 minutes, until browned. Serve warm or at room temperature. —*Jessica Koslow*

CARAWAY ROLLS WITH
GARLIC-PARSLEY BUTTER

HALVAH-STUFFED
CHALLAH

Extra-Rich Brioche

📷 PAGE 256

Active **1 hr**; Total **5 hr plus overnight chilling**
Makes **one 10-by-5-inch loaf**

Iliana Regan of Chicago's Elizabeth restaurant is a whiz with bread. She has mastered brioche—a time-intensive bread that's well worth the wait. With a golden crust and buttery, tender crumb, this is one of the most delicious breads you can make.

> One ¼-oz. packet active dry yeast
> ⅓ cup plus 1 Tbsp. lukewarm buttermilk (100°–105°)
> 3 cups bread flour
> 3 Tbsp. sugar
> 1 Tbsp. kosher salt
> 5 large eggs
> 2½ sticks unsalted butter, melted and cooled
> Canola oil, for greasing

1. In a small bowl, whisk the yeast with the buttermilk until it dissolves. Let stand for 10 minutes, until foamy.

2. In the bowl of a stand mixer fitted with the dough hook, mix the bread flour with the sugar and salt. With the machine at medium speed, add the yeast mixture, then add 4 of the eggs, 1 at a time, beating well after each addition. Drizzle in the butter and beat for 10 minutes; the dough will look slightly greasy. Transfer to an oiled bowl, cover with plastic wrap and refrigerate overnight. Let the dough stand at room temperature for 1 hour before proceeding.

3. Lightly oil a 10-by-5-inch loaf pan. On a work surface, roll out the dough to a 10-by-8-inch rectangle. With a long side facing you, fold the dough in thirds and fit seam side down in the prepared loaf pan. Cover with plastic wrap and let rise in a warm place until doubled in bulk, about 2½ hours.

4. Preheat the oven to 425° and set a rack in the center. In a small bowl, beat the remaining egg. Brush the top of the brioche with some of the egg wash and make a ¼-inch-deep slit down the center of the loaf. Bake for 20 minutes. Brush the top again with egg wash and bake for 20 minutes longer, until the top is deep golden and an instant-read thermometer inserted in the center of the loaf registers 182°.

5. Transfer the brioche to a rack to cool for 30 minutes, then unmold and let cool completely. —*Iliana Regan*

SERVE WITH Regan's Cultured Butter (p. 364) and Fresh Raspberry Preserves (p. 366).

MAKE AHEAD The brioche can be wrapped tightly in plastic wrap and foil and kept at room temperature for up to 2 days.

Halvah-Stuffed Challah

Active **1 hr**; Total **3 hr 45 min**
Makes **2 loaves**

This brilliant challah is filled with halvah—the confection made with crushed sesame seeds and honey—and sweet tahini spread. Blogger Molly Yeh recommends using an extra-smooth, pourable tahini (such as Whole Foods' 365 brand). If yours is cakey and thick, she advises mixing it with warm water until spreadable.

DOUGH
> 1½ cups warm water
> 1½ Tbsp. active dry yeast
> ½ cup plus 1 tsp. sugar
> 4 large eggs
> ⅔ cup canola oil
> 1 Tbsp. pure vanilla extract
> 8¼ cups all-purpose flour
> 2 tsp. kosher salt
> 2 tsp. ground cinnamon
> ⅛ tsp. ground cardamom

FILLING AND TOPPING
> 1 cup tahini
> ⅓ cup plus 1 Tbsp. honey
> 1½ tsp. pure vanilla extract
> ½ tsp. ground cinnamon
> Pinch of kosher salt
> 1 large egg
> 1½ cups finely chopped halvah (6½ oz.)
> Sesame seeds and turbinado sugar, for sprinkling

1. Make the dough In a small bowl, whisk the water with the yeast and 1 teaspoon of the sugar. Let stand for 10 minutes, until foamy.

2. In a medium bowl, whisk the eggs with the oil and vanilla. In the bowl of a stand mixer fitted with the dough hook, combine the flour, salt, cinnamon, cardamom and the remaining ½ cup of sugar. Mix to blend. Add the egg and yeast mixtures and knead until the dough comes together, scraping down the side and bottom of the bowl, about 3 minutes. Scrape the dough out onto a work surface and knead until smooth and slightly sticky, 8 to 10 minutes. Transfer the dough to an oiled large bowl and cover with plastic wrap. Let stand at room temperature until doubled in bulk, about 2 hours.

3. Meanwhile, make the filling and topping In a medium bowl, stir the tahini with ⅓ cup of the honey, the vanilla, cinnamon, salt and 2 tablespoons of water until smooth. In a small bowl, beat the egg with the remaining 1 tablespoon of honey and 1 tablespoon of water.

4. Preheat the oven to 375° and line 2 baking sheets with parchment paper. Divide the dough into 2 equal pieces. Transfer 1 piece to a lightly floured work surface and keep the other piece covered with a damp kitchen towel. Divide the dough on the work surface into 3 equal pieces. Using a rolling pin, roll out 1 piece into a 14-by-6-inch rectangle. Spread ¼ cup of the tahini mixture on top, leaving a ½-inch border. Sprinkle ¼ cup of the halvah over the tahini in an even layer. With a long side facing you, tightly roll up the dough into a log, pressing the seam and ends together to seal in the filling. Repeat with the other 2 pieces of dough, ½ cup of the tahini mixture and ½ cup of the halvah. Arrange the 3 logs on one of the prepared sheets and braid them together. Brush with the egg wash and sprinkle with sesame seeds and turbinado sugar. Repeat with the second piece of dough and the remaining filling, egg wash and toppings. Bake the challahs for about 30 minutes on the middle and bottom racks of the oven, shifting and rotating halfway through, until deep golden. Transfer to racks to cool. —*Molly Yeh*

MAKE AHEAD The stuffed challahs can be stored at room temperature overnight.

Andouille Bread Pudding

Active **30 min**; Total **1 hr 15 min**
Serves **4**

Every Thanksgiving since star chef Marcus Samuelsson opened Red Rooster in New York City, he has been serving this savory, bacon-studded bread pudding, which is a favorite among guests. The recipe is featured in *The Red Rooster Cookbook*.

   Butter, for greasing

3 oz. bacon, cut into ½-inch pieces (4 slices)

6 oz. andouille sausage, cut into ¼-inch pieces

1 medium red onion, finely chopped

1 cup chopped collard greens

¼ cup dry-roasted peanuts, finely chopped

½ tsp. smoked hot paprika (pimentón)

   Kosher salt

3 large eggs

½ cup heavy cream

½ cup milk

4 oz. day-old peasant bread, cut into 1-inch cubes (2 cups)

½ cup coarsely shredded sharp cheddar cheese (2 oz.)

3 Tbsp. raisins

1. Preheat the oven to 375°. Generously butter an 8-inch-square baking dish. In a medium skillet, cook the bacon with the andouille over moderate heat, stirring occasionally, until the bacon is crisp, about 13 minutes. Using a slotted spoon, transfer to a medium bowl. Return the skillet to the heat.

2. Add the onion to the skillet along with the collards, peanuts, smoked paprika and a generous pinch of salt. Cook over moderate heat, stirring occasionally, until the onion has softened, about 5 minutes. Scrape the vegetables into the bowl with the bacon and andouille.

3. In a large bowl, whisk the eggs with the cream and milk. Add the bread to the bowl along with the cheddar cheese and raisins. Using a rubber spatula, stir gently until the bread is evenly moistened. Let stand for 5 minutes, then add the bacon, andouille and cooked vegetables and stir until just combined. Transfer to the prepared dish.

4. Bake for 30 minutes, until the bread pudding is puffed and golden brown. Transfer to a wire rack and let stand for 15 minutes before serving.
—*Marcus Samuelsson*

MAKE AHEAD The unbaked bread pudding can be refrigerated overnight. Bring to room temperature before baking.

Khachapuri Adjaruli

Active **1 hr**; Total **4 hr**; Makes **4**

This traditional Georgian cheese bread is a specialty of chef Maia Acquaviva at Oda House in New York City. The boat-shaped bread comes to the table piping hot, with a gooey cheese filling topped with a runny egg. Diners mix the egg into the cheese to finish cooking, then tear off pieces of the bread to scoop it all up.

DOUGH

1 Tbsp. active dry yeast

1 tsp. sugar

1 cup whole milk

1 large egg

3 Tbsp. canola oil, plus more for greasing

6 cups all-purpose flour (1 lb. 14 oz.), plus more for dusting

1 Tbsp. kosher salt

FILLING

1 lb. Bulgarian feta cheese, crumbled

6 large eggs

½ tsp. kosher salt

1 lb. mozzarella cheese, shredded

2 egg yolks beaten with 1½ tsp. water

4 Tbsp. salted butter, plus melted butter for brushing

1. Make the dough In a large bowl, whisk the yeast with the sugar and 1 cup of warm water. Let stand until foamy, about 10 minutes. In a small bowl, whisk the milk with the egg and 3 tablespoons of oil.

2. Add the milk mixture, the flour and salt to the foamy yeast and mix until a dough forms. Form the dough into a ball and transfer to a lightly oiled large bowl. Cover the bowl with plastic wrap and let the dough rise in a warm place until doubled in bulk, about 1½ hours.

3. Line 2 baking sheets with parchment paper. On a lightly floured work surface, divide the dough into 4 equal pieces and form into smooth balls. Set 2 balls of dough 5 inches apart on each sheet. Cover loosely with plastic wrap and let rest in a warm place for 45 minutes.

4. Make the filling In a blender, puree the feta with 2 of the eggs, 2 tablespoons of water and the salt. Transfer the mixture to a bowl and stir in the mozzarella.

5. Preheat the oven to 450°. Transfer the dough balls to a lightly floured work surface. Line the baking sheets with clean parchment. Roll out 1 ball of dough to a 10-inch round. Scoop one-fourth of the cheese filling onto one side of the dough round and fold the other side over; press the edges firmly to seal. Transfer the khachapuri seam side down to a baking sheet and form into an elongated oval with tapered ends. Repeat with the remaining balls of dough and filling. Brush all over with the beaten egg yolks.

6. Using scissors, cut a 6-inch slit down the center of each khachapuri; widen the slit to expose about 2½ inches of the filling. Bake for about 30 minutes, shifting and rotating the pans halfway through, until the breads are puffed and golden and the cheese is melted.

7. Stir the cheese filling and crack an egg in the center of each bread. Bake for 8 to 10 minutes, until the egg whites are almost set and the yolks are runny. Tuck 1 tablespoon of butter into each khachapuri, brush the breads with melted butter and serve hot. Mix the butter and egg into the filling before eating. —*Maia Acquaviva*

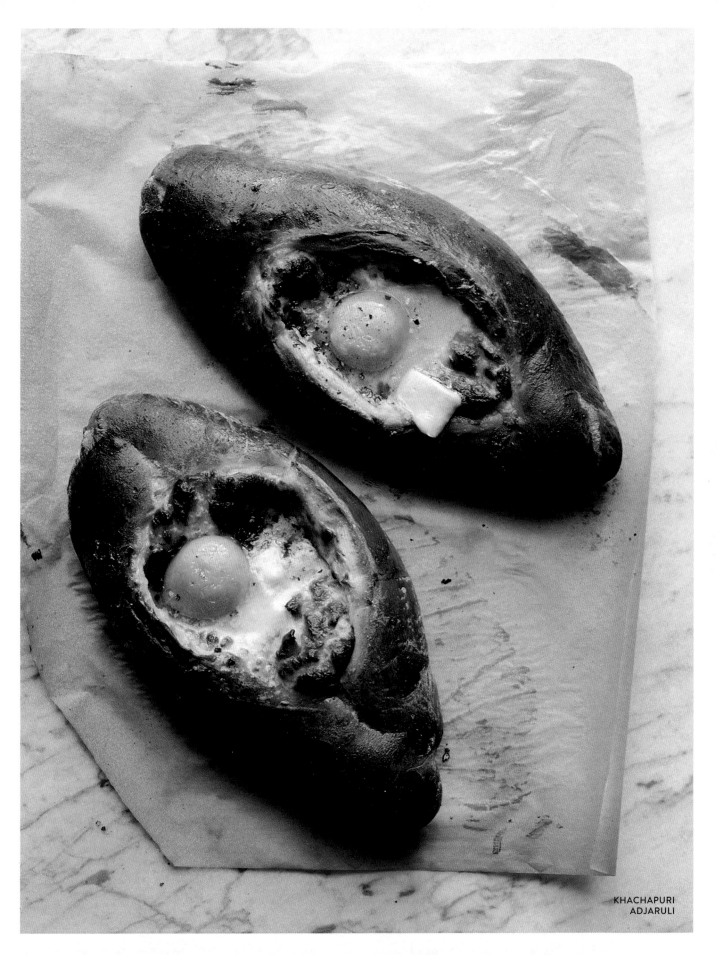

KHACHAPURI
ADJARULI

Egg Salad with Lovage on Seeded Quick Bread

Active **40 min**; Total **1 hr 20 min**
Makes **1 loaf and egg salad for 4**

Buttermilk makes this quick bread moist and tangy, while sunflower and pumpkin seeds give it crunch. Use it as a base for the egg salad or simply spread it with good salty butter and your favorite jam.

BREAD

2½ cups all-purpose flour
2½ cups barley flour (see Note)
½ cup salted roasted sunflower seeds
½ cup raw pumpkin seeds
4 tsp. baking powder
1½ tsp. sea salt
1½ cups buttermilk
1½ cups hot water

EGG SALAD

8 large eggs
4 Tbsp. mayonnaise
4 Tbsp. sour cream
2 tsp. Dijon mustard
1 tsp. honey
1 Tbsp. minced shallot
2 Tbsp. minced scallion
2 Tbsp. coarsely chopped lovage or pale green inner celery leaves
Kosher salt and pepper

1. Make the bread Preheat the oven to 400°. In a large bowl, whisk both flours with the sunflower seeds, pumpkin seeds, baking powder and salt. Stir in the buttermilk and hot water just until the dough comes together. Scrape the dough onto a parchment paper–lined baking sheet and shape into an 8-inch round. Bake until golden and cooked through and the bread sounds hollow when tapped, about 40 minutes. Transfer the bread to a rack to cool completely.

2. Meanwhile, make the egg salad In a medium saucepan, cover the eggs with 2 inches of water and bring to a rolling boil. Cover, remove from the heat and let stand for 10 minutes. Transfer the eggs to ice water to cool, then drain, peel and lightly mash them.

3. In a large bowl, whisk the mayonnaise with the sour cream, mustard and honey. Stir in the shallot, scallion and lovage and season with salt and pepper. Add the eggs and mix well, mashing with the back of a fork. Spread on the bread and serve. *—Victoria Elíasdóttir*

NOTE Barley flour is available at health food stores and from bobsredmill.com.

Garlic Aioli BLTs

Total **30 min**; Serves **4**

Gjelina Take Away in L.A. serves this excellent sandwich only when tomatoes are at their peak. Chef Travis Lett puts his own spin on the classic, substituting arugula for lettuce and garlic aioli for mayo.

8 slices of thick-cut bacon
¾ cup vegetable oil
¼ cup extra-virgin olive oil
1 garlic clove
Kosher salt and pepper
1 large egg yolk
2½ tsp. fresh lemon juice
1 sourdough boule, cut into eight ½-inch-thick slices and toasted
3 heirloom tomatoes (1½ lbs.), sliced ¼ inch thick
4 cups arugula

1. Preheat the oven to 400°. Set a rack over a foil-lined rimmed baking sheet. Arrange the bacon strips on the rack and bake until browned and crisp, about 25 minutes. Drain on paper towels.

2. In a measuring cup, combine the vegetable oil with the olive oil. On a work surface, top the garlic with a generous sprinkle of salt and smash to a paste with the flat side of a knife; scrape into a bowl. Whisk in the egg yolk, 1½ teaspoons of the lemon juice and 1 teaspoon of water, then slowly whisk in the oil mixture so the aioli thickens. Season with salt, pepper and the remaining 1 teaspoon of lemon juice.

3. Spread the aioli on each slice of toast. Arrange the tomatoes and arugula on 4 of the toasts; sprinkle with salt and pepper. Top with the bacon, close and serve. *—Travis Lett*

WINE Fruit-forward Prosecco: NV Zardetto Superiore Conegliano Valdobbiadene Brut.

Bacon-and-Butter Sandwiches

Total **15 min**; Serves **4**

At the London offshoot of his eponymous bakery, pastry chef Dominique Ansel gives the beloved English "bacon butty" a French accent by subbing baguette for the standard white toast. Instead of dousing the sandwich in HP sauce, Ansel stirs a bit of sherry into the butter.

8 slices of back bacon (see Note)
4 Tbsp. unsalted butter, softened
2 tsp. dry sherry
Four 4-inch-long baguette pieces, split and lightly toasted

1. In a large cast-iron skillet, cook half of the bacon over moderately high heat, turning once, until browned and the edges are crisp, 5 to 7 minutes. Transfer to paper towels. Repeat with the remaining bacon.

2. In a small bowl, blend the butter with the sherry. Spread it on the baguette bottoms. Top each with 2 slices of bacon, close the sandwiches and serve. *—Dominique Ansel*

NOTE Back bacon includes a portion of both the loin and the belly. It's available from British butchers and amazon.com, or try a combination of Canadian bacon and thick-cut bacon.

Chickpea Salad Sandwiches

Total **20 min**; Serves **4**

Canned chickpeas stand in brilliantly for tuna fish in these wholesome, satisfying sandwiches.

One 15-oz. can chickpeas, rinsed
2 Tbsp. mayonnaise
2 Tbsp. minced red onion
1 Tbsp. fresh lemon juice
1 Tbsp. chopped dill
Kosher salt and pepper
4 slices of multigrain bread, toasted
Sliced avocado and radish or alfalfa sprouts, for topping

In a large bowl, gently mash the chickpeas with a fork. Stir in the mayonnaise, onion, lemon juice and dill. Season with salt and pepper. Spoon the chickpea salad onto the toasts and top with sliced avocado and sprouts. Serve. *—Justin Chapple*

Fish Kofta Sandwiches

Active **1 hr**; Total **1 hr 30 min**; Serves **8**

Chopped fresh cod is mixed with lots of seasonings for a supertasty take on grilled Middle Eastern meat patties.

KOFTA

- 2 lbs. skinless cod fillets, cut into 1-inch pieces
- 2 garlic cloves, minced
- ½ cup minced red onion
- 2 Fresno chiles, minced
- ½ cup chopped curly parsley
- 2 Tbsp. ground coriander
- 2 Tbsp. ground cumin
- 2 Tbsp. za'atar
- 2 Tbsp. Asian fish sauce
- 2 tsp. kosher salt
- 1 tsp. black pepper
- 2 large eggs, beaten
- 1 cup dry breadcrumbs

GLAZE

- ¼ cup extra-virgin olive oil
- ¼ cup rice wine vinegar
- 1 Tbsp. Asian fish sauce
- ½ tsp. za'atar
- ½ tsp. smoked paprika
  Canola oil
- 8 top-split hot dog buns (preferably brioche) and Kohlrabi Slaw (p. 58)

1. Make the kofta In a food processor, pulse the fish until chopped and chunky. Scrape into a bowl, add all of the remaining ingredients and mix well. Form into eight 6-inch-long cylinders and refrigerate on a parchment-lined baking sheet for at least 30 minutes.

2. Make the glaze In a small bowl, whisk together all of the ingredients except the canola oil, buns and slaw.

3. Light a grill. Brush the kofta with 2 table-spoons of canola oil. Grill over moderate heat until golden, about 8 minutes. Cover and grill over low heat, brushing with the glaze and turning occasionally, until cooked through, about 15 minutes more. Serve the kofta in the hot dog buns, topped with the kohlrabi slaw. —Eli and Max Sussman

WINE Dry Riesling: 2014 Tatomer Vandenberg.

Tofu Banh Mi Sandwiches

📷 PAGE 4

Active **30 min**; Total **1 hr**; Serves **4**

Tofu makes a surprise appearance in this light riff on the traditional Vietnamese sub. Ham, liverwurst and thinly sliced firm tofu are sandwiched with crunchy quick-pickled vegetables, cilantro and two kinds of chiles.

- 1 cup distilled white vinegar
- 1 Tbsp. kosher salt
- 1 tsp. sugar
- 3 garlic cloves, crushed
- 3 oz. hothouse cucumber, julienned
- 4 oz. daikon, peeled and julienned
- 4 oz. multicolored carrots, peeled and julienned
  One 14-oz. package firm tofu, drained and sliced ⅛ inch thick
- ½ cup mayonnaise
- 1 baguette (about 20 inches long), halved lengthwise
- ½ cup liverwurst (4 oz.)
- 8 oz. sliced ham
  Thinly sliced serrano or jalapeño chiles and cilantro sprigs, for garnish

1. In a medium bowl, combine the vinegar, salt, sugar, garlic and ½ cup of water and whisk until the salt is dissolved. Add the cucumber, daikon and carrots and mix well. Let stand for 30 minutes, tossing occasionally. Drain the pickled vegetables and pick out and discard the garlic.

2. Meanwhile, line a baking sheet with paper towels. Arrange the tofu slices on the sheet in a single layer and top with more paper towels. Gently press to remove excess water.

3. Spread the mayonnaise on the top half of the split baguette; spread the liverwurst on the bottom. Arrange the ham slices on the liverwurst, slightly overlapping them, then top with the tofu and pickled vegetables. Garnish with chiles and cilantro sprigs. Close the sandwiches, cut into 4 pieces and serve. —Kay Chun

MAKE AHEAD The drained pickled vegetables can be refrigerated for up to 3 days.

BEER Summery sour-style beer: West-brook Brewing Co. Gose.

Grilled Cabbage Cemitas

⏱ Total **45 min**; Serves **4**

Tyler Kord of No. 7 Subs in New York City makes this delicious vegetarian version of the classic Mexican sandwich. He suggests quickly steaming the cabbage before grilling to ensure that it's tender.

- ½ medium green cabbage (1 lb.), cut through the core into 1½-inch wedges
- ½ medium red cabbage (1 lb.), cut through the core into 1½-inch wedges
- ¼ cup extra-virgin olive oil, plus more for brushing
- 2 large garlic cloves, minced
- ½ tsp. cumin seeds
  Kosher salt
- 4 cemita buns, kaiser rolls or hoagie rolls, split
- 1 Hass avocado, halved and pitted
- 1 cup shredded fresh mozzarella (4 oz.)
- ½ cup lightly packed cilantro leaves
  Hot sauce, for serving

1. Arrange the green and red cabbage wedges in 2 separate large skillets. Divide the olive oil, garlic and cumin between the skillets. Add 1 teaspoon of salt and ⅓ cup of water to each skillet and bring to a boil. Flip the cabbage wedges, cover and cook over moderately high heat until tender, about 8 minutes. Remove from the heat and let steam, covered, for 10 minutes. Transfer the cabbage wedges to a plate, keeping them intact.

2. Light a grill or heat a grill pan. Grill the cabbage wedges over high heat, turning once, until lightly charred all over, about 2 minutes. Transfer to the plate.

3. Brush the cut sides of the buns with olive oil and grill over high heat until lightly golden, about 1 minute. Transfer to a work surface.

4. Scoop the avocado into a small bowl. Add a generous pinch of salt and mash with a fork. Spread the avocado on the cut sides of the buns. Top with the cabbage wedges, mozzarella and cilantro and serve with hot sauce. —Tyler Kord

WINE Light, herbal Grüner Veltliner: 2014 Hiedler Löss.

GRILLED CABBAGE
CEMITAS

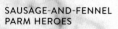

SAUSAGE-AND-FENNEL
PARM HEROES

Mortadella Reubens with Lemon Aioli

Active **30 min**; Total **50 min**; Serves **4**

This European spin on a classic Reuben is enriched with gooey brie and a garlicky aioli. At Union Larder in San Francisco, chef Ramon Siewert uses housemade corned pork loin, but mortadella is a great store-bought alternative.

LEMON AIOLI

3 large egg yolks
1 Tbsp. fresh lemon juice
1 Tbsp. Champagne vinegar
1 Tbsp. Dijon mustard
2 garlic cloves, crushed
¾ cup extra-virgin olive oil
  Kosher salt and pepper

SANDWICHES

  Eight ½-inch-thick slices of sourdough bread
4 Tbsp. unsalted butter, softened
8 oz. brie cheese, thinly sliced
1 cup sauerkraut
12 oz. thinly sliced mortadella
2 Tbsp. Dijon mustard
  Pickles, for serving

1. Make the lemon aioli In a food processor, pulse the egg yolks, lemon juice, vinegar, mustard and garlic to blend. With the machine on, slowly drizzle in the oil until incorporated. Season with salt and pepper.

2. Make the sandwiches Preheat the oven to 375°. Spread one side of each bread slice with ½ tablespoon of the butter. Arrange buttered side up on a baking sheet and toast until golden, 6 to 8 minutes. Top 4 of the toasts with the brie, sauerkraut and mortadella.

3. In a small bowl, mix ¼ cup of the aioli with the mustard. Spread the mustard aioli on the remaining 4 toasts and close the sandwiches. Bake until the mortadella is warm and the brie is melted, 8 to 10 minutes. Serve with pickles and extra lemon aioli. —*Ramon Siewert*

MAKE AHEAD The aioli can be refrigerated for up to 1 week.

WINE Bright California white: 2014 Matthiasson Tendu.

Sausage-and-Fennel Parm Heroes

Total **30 min**; Serves **4**

These heroes are like chicken parm sandwiches—but with Italian sausage instead of cutlets—topped with tomato sauce and smothered in melty mozzarella cheese.

4 hoagie rolls, split
2 Tbsp. extra-virgin olive oil
1 lb. sweet Italian sausage
3 fennel bulbs—halved, cored and thinly sliced (4 cups)
  Kosher salt and pepper
1½ cups jarred marinara sauce
8 oz. fresh mozzarella cheese, sliced
  Basil leaves, for garnish

1. Preheat the broiler. Place the rolls cut side up on a baking sheet. In a large skillet, heat the olive oil. Add the sausage and fennel and season with salt and pepper. Cook over moderate heat, stirring occasionally, until the fennel is deep golden and the sausage is cooked through, 12 to 15 minutes.

2. Mound the mixture on the bottom halves of the rolls, then top with the marinara and mozzarella. Broil 6 inches from the heat until the cheese is melted, about 3 minutes. Top with basil leaves, close the sandwiches and serve. —*Kay Chun*

BEER Fresh, mild Italian lager: Peroni.

Chorizo Hoagies with Tangy Cabbage-Pepper Relish

Total **45 min** plus overnight pickling
Serves **6**

Chef Tim Wiechmann of T.W. Food in Cambridge, Massachusetts, tops his sandwich with čalamada, a spicy Eastern European pickled-cabbage-and-pepper-relish. The relish is ready to eat after pickling overnight, but it's best after three or four days, when the flavors have melded.

CABBAGE-PEPPER RELISH

1 small head of green cabbage, thinly sliced (10 cups)
1 red bell pepper, thinly sliced
1 yellow onion, thinly sliced
1 carrot, shredded
1½ Tbsp. distilled white vinegar
1½ Tbsp. crushed red pepper
1 Tbsp. kosher salt

REMOULADE

1 cup mayonnaise
¼ cup minced chives
2 Tbsp. sweet smoked paprika
2 Tbsp. fresh lemon juice
1 small shallot, minced
  Kosher salt and pepper

CHORIZO

  Two 12-oz. bottles light beer or lager, plus more as needed
  Canola oil, for brushing
  Six 6-oz. fresh chorizo sausages, pricked all over with a paring knife
6 hoagie rolls, split

1. Make the relish In a large bowl, combine all of the ingredients. Mix by hand, squeezing the vegetables until the cabbage begins to soften and releases some liquid, about 3 minutes. Pack the cabbage-pepper relish into a 2-quart jar, cover tightly and refrigerate overnight, shaking once or twice.

2. Make the remoulade In a medium bowl, whisk all of the ingredients together and season with salt and pepper.

3. Grill the chorizo Light a grill. In a large cast-iron skillet placed directly on the grate, bring 3 cups of the beer to a simmer; it should be at least ½ inch deep.

4. Meanwhile, oil the grate and grill the chorizo over moderately high heat until lightly charred all over, about 6 minutes. Add the chorizo to the beer in the skillet and simmer, turning occasionally, until cooked through, 8 to 10 minutes; add more beer to the skillet as needed.

5. Return the chorizo to the grill and cook until well browned, about 6 minutes. Transfer to a work surface and let rest for 5 minutes. Grill the hoagie rolls cut side down until lightly toasted, about 2 minutes. Spread some of the remoulade on the buns and top with the chorizo and relish. Pass the remaining remoulade and relish at the table. —*Tim Wiechmann*

MAKE AHEAD The remoulade can be refrigerated overnight and the relish can be refrigerated for up to 2 weeks.

BEER Refreshing pilsner: SingleCut Beersmiths 19-33 Queens Lagrrr!

Shrimp Banh Mi Sliders

Total **1 hr 30 min;** Makes **12**

These sliders can easily be made into six larger sandwiches. Save any leftover nuoc cham; the herby, savory sauce is excellent drizzled over a cold rice noodle salad with shredded chicken.

PICKLED CARROTS

- ½ cup rice vinegar
- ½ cup sugar
- 4 medium carrots, julienned

NUOC CHAM

- ½ cup finely chopped cilantro
- ½ cup finely chopped mint
- ½ cup extra-virgin olive oil
- 1 tsp. finely grated lime zest plus ¼ cup fresh lime juice
- ¼ cup minced shallots
- 3 garlic cloves, minced
- 2 Tbsp. Asian fish sauce
- 1½ tsp. sambal oelek (Indonesian chile paste)
- 1 tsp. sugar
  Kosher salt

SRIRACHA MAYO

- ½ cup mayonnaise
- 1½ Tbsp. Sriracha
  Kosher salt

SLIDERS

- 24 jumbo shrimp, shelled and deveined (2 lbs.)
- 2 Tbsp. extra-virgin olive oil
  Kosher salt and pepper
- 12 mini baguette rolls or 3-inch pieces of baguette, split and toasted
- ½ English cucumber, thinly sliced
  Cilantro sprigs, for garnish

1. Make the pickled carrots In a medium saucepan, combine the vinegar, sugar and ½ cup of water and bring to a boil, stirring to dissolve the sugar. Remove from the heat and stir in the carrots. Let cool; drain.

2. Make the nuoc cham In a medium bowl, whisk all the ingredients together and season with salt.

3. Make the Sriracha mayo In a small bowl, whisk the mayonnaise with the Sriracha and season with salt.

4. Make the sliders Heat a grill pan. In a large bowl, toss the shrimp with the olive oil and season with salt and pepper. Working in 2 batches, grill the shrimp over moderately high heat, turning once, until lightly charred and cooked through, 2 to 3 minutes per side. Transfer to a medium bowl. Add half of the nuoc cham to the shrimp and toss to coat.

5. Spread the Sriracha mayo on the baguettes. Arrange 2 shrimp on the bottom half of each baguette and top with the pickled carrots, cucumber slices and cilantro sprigs. Close the sandwiches and serve the remaining nuoc cham on the side. —*John Besh and Chris Lusk*

MAKE AHEAD The drained pickled carrots, nuoc cham and Sriracha mayo can all be refrigerated separately overnight.

WINE Peach-scented dry Riesling: 2014 Robert Weil Rheingau Trocken.

Polish Boy Kielbasa Sandwiches

Active **1 hr;** Total **1 hr 30 min;** Serves **4**

At his Cleveland barbecue spot, Mabel's BBQ, star chef Michael Symon tops his version of the city's famed kielbasa sandwich with a spicy napa cabbage slaw and french fries. He makes his barbecue sauce with the local favorite brand of brown mustard: Stadium.

SLAW

- 2 Tbsp. spicy brown mustard
- 2 Tbsp. mayonnaise
- 1 Tbsp. Champagne vinegar
- 2 tsp. Worcestershire sauce
- 1 tsp. sugar
- 1 lb. napa cabbage, cored and shredded (6 cups)
- ½ red onion, thinly sliced
- 1 garlic clove, minced
- ½ jalapeño, minced
  Kosher salt

BARBECUE SAUCE

- ½ tsp. whole coriander seeds
- 1 cup apple cider vinegar
- 1 red onion, quartered
- 1 garlic clove, crushed
- 1 canned chipotle in adobo, plus 2 tsp. adobo sauce
- 2 Tbsp. bourbon
- ½ cup spicy brown mustard
- ¼ cup yellow mustard
- 2½ Tbsp. pure maple syrup
- ¾ tsp. black pepper
  Kosher salt
- 2 Tbsp. canola oil
- 4 kielbasa (1 lb.)
- 4 hoagie rolls, toasted
  French fries, for garnish

1. Make the slaw In a large bowl, whisk the mustard, mayonnaise, vinegar, Worcestershire sauce and sugar. Add the cabbage, red onion, garlic and jalapeño, season with salt and toss. Cover and refrigerate the slaw for 1 hour.

2. Make the barbecue sauce In a small saucepan, toast the coriander seeds over moderate heat, stirring, until fragrant, about 2 minutes. Add the vinegar, red onion, garlic, chipotle and bourbon and bring to a boil. Simmer over moderate heat until slightly reduced, about 5 minutes. Strain the sauce into a heatproof bowl and let cool. Whisk in the adobo sauce, mustards, maple syrup and pepper and season with salt.

3. In a nonstick skillet, heat the canola oil. Add the kielbasa and cook over moderate heat, turning occasionally, until golden and cooked through, about 10 minutes. Spread some of the mustard-barbecue sauce on the cut sides of the rolls and set a sausage in each roll. Top with the slaw and french fries and serve warm with the remaining barbecue sauce. —*Michael Symon*

BEER Lightly hoppy pilsner: Great Lakes Brewing Co. Turntable.

SHRIMP BANH MI
SLIDERS

THAI-STYLE PULLED
PORK SANDWICHES

Pork Sandwiches with Garlicky Red Pepper Jus

Active **1 hr**; Total **2 hr**; Makes **12**

For these succulent pork sandwiches, Chicago chef Abraham Conlon braises thin slices of pork shoulder in a red pepper–white wine broth until tender, then piles the spiced meat on Portuguese rolls. Whatever rolls you use, they should be crispy outside and tender inside to hold those delectable braising juices.

- 3½ **lbs. well-trimmed boneless pork shoulder**
- 1 **Tbsp. hot paprika**
  Kosher salt and black pepper
- ¼ **cup extra-virgin olive oil**
- 1 **bay leaf**
- 1 **Spanish onion, halved and sliced ¼ inch thick**
- ¼ **cup minced garlic**
- 1 **oregano sprig**
- 1 **tsp. crushed red pepper**
- 1 **cup Portuguese white wine, such as Vinho Verde**
- 1 **qt. chicken stock or low-sodium broth**
- 2 **roasted red bell peppers**
- 1 **lb. Petit Basque cheese, rind removed, cheese thinly sliced**
- 12 **small Portuguese or kaiser rolls, split and toasted**

1. Slice the pork across the grain ¼ inch thick. Arrange the slices on 2 large rimmed baking sheets in a single layer. In a small bowl, mix the paprika with 2 tablespoons of salt and 2 teaspoons of black pepper. Sprinkle the seasoning mix evenly on the meat and let stand at room temperature for 30 minutes.

2. Meanwhile, in a large enameled cast-iron casserole, heat the oil. Add the bay leaf and cook over moderate heat until lightly browned, about 2 minutes. Add the onion and a generous pinch of salt and cook, stirring occasionally, until the onion is browned, about 10 minutes. Using a slotted spoon, transfer the onion to a bowl; leave the bay leaf in the casserole.

3. Add the garlic, oregano and crushed red pepper to the casserole and cook over moderately high heat, stirring, until fragrant, 1 to 2 minutes. Add the wine and simmer until evaporated, 5 minutes. Add the stock and roasted bell peppers and bring to a boil. Discard the bay leaf and oregano. Transfer the mixture to a blender and puree until smooth.

4. Return the red pepper broth to the casserole. Add 4 cups of water and bring to a boil. Season with salt and black pepper. Add the pork and simmer over moderately low heat until very tender, about 1 hour.

5. Put the cheese on the roll bottoms. Top with the pork and onion and drizzle with some of the red pepper jus. Close the sandwiches and serve. —*Abraham Conlon*

Thai-Style Pulled Pork Sandwiches

Active **1 hr 15 min**; Total **5 hr**; Serves **8 to 10**

To make the complex sauce for this pulled pork, Boston chef Jamie Bissonnette mimics an indoor smoker by wrapping the spices and aromatics in foil, then cooking the packet directly on the stovetop burner until the contents are charred and smoky.

- ⅓ **cup Thai red curry paste**
- ¼ **cup Asian fish sauce**
- 6 **Tbsp. finely grated palm sugar or dark brown sugar**
  One 4-lb. boneless pork shoulder roast with fat cap
  Kosher salt and pepper
- 2 **cups chopped cilantro stems**
- 4 **garlic cloves**
- 2 **large shallots, halved**
- 2 **kaffir lime leaves**
- 1 **Thai bird chile**
- 1 **stalk of lemongrass, inner light green and white parts only, cut into 3 pieces**
  One ½-inch piece of fresh ginger, peeled and thinly sliced
- 24 **cardamom seeds**
- 1½ **tsp. ground turmeric**
  One 15-oz. can unsweetened coconut milk, chilled
- ⅓ **cup chicken stock or low-sodium broth**
- ½ **cup each finely chopped cilantro, Thai basil and mint leaves**
  Mayonnaise, for spreading
- 8 **brioche buns, split and toasted**
  Thinly sliced cucumber and red onion, cilantro, Thai basil and lime wedges, for serving

1. Preheat the oven to 325°. In a small skillet, simmer the curry paste with the fish sauce and ¼ cup of the palm sugar over moderate heat, stirring occasionally, until the sugar is dissolved and a smooth paste forms. Let cool slightly.

2. Season the pork with salt and rub it all over with the paste. Set the roast in a large enameled cast-iron casserole. Cover and roast, basting occasionally with the pan juices, until the meat is very tender, about 3½ hours. Uncover and roast until a golden-brown crust forms, about 15 minutes.

3. Transfer the pork to a large bowl and let rest for 15 minutes. Using 2 forks, shred the meat. Skim the fat from the pan juices, then stir the juices into the shredded pork. Cover with foil and keep warm.

4. Make a large double layer of foil. Wrap the cilantro stems, garlic, shallots, lime leaves, chile, lemongrass, ginger, cardamom and turmeric in the foil and seal the sides. Set the packet seam side up directly on a burner or in a cast-iron skillet. Cook over moderate heat until aromatic and beginning to smoke, about 5 minutes. Using tongs, transfer the packet to a rack; let cool slightly. The cilantro stems should be tender and the ingredients on the bottom should be lightly charred.

5. Scrape the contents of the packet into a food processor. Add the remaining 2 tablespoons of palm sugar and process to a smooth paste.

6. Open the can of coconut milk and spoon the thick cream on the surface into a large saucepan. Bring to a simmer over moderately high heat and whisk in the cilantro paste. Whisk in the coconut milk and chicken stock and bring to a simmer. Stir in the pulled pork and season with salt and pepper. Cook until the sauce has thickened slightly, about 10 minutes. Stir in the chopped herbs and season with salt and pepper. Keep warm.

7. Spread mayonnaise on the buns and top with the pulled pork, cucumber, red onion, cilantro and basil leaves. Serve with lime wedges. —*Jamie Bissonnette*

BEER Crisp Thai pale lager: Singha.

Roast Pork Sandwiches with Three-Cabbage Slaw and Aioli

Active **45 min**; Total **3 hr 45 min plus 2 days marinating**; Serves **8 to 10**

Jessica Koslow, the chef at Sqirl in Los Angeles, browns the pork first, then wraps it in heavy-duty foil to roast. Her trick traps in all the great flavor and keeps the meat incredibly juicy.

1½ cups kosher salt

1½ cups packed light brown sugar

5 chiles de árbol

2 Tbsp. dried oregano

5 garlic cloves, crushed

2 bay leaves

2 star anise pods

2 Tbsp. fennel seeds

5½ lbs. boneless pork shoulder in 1 piece

3 Tbsp. coriander seeds

2 Tbsp. cumin seeds

½ cup extra-virgin olive oil

8 Thai chiles, very thinly sliced

1 Tbsp. apple cider vinegar

Fine sea salt

Three-Cabbage Slaw (recipe follows) and Dinner Rolls with Nigella Seeds and Flaky Salt (p. 258), for serving

Aioli, for serving

1. In a very large pot, whisk the kosher salt and brown sugar with 6 quarts of water until dissolved. Wrap the árbol chiles, oregano, garlic, bay leaves, star anise and 1 tablespoon of the fennel seeds in cheesecloth and tie the bundle with kitchen twine; add to the brine.

2. Submerge the pork in the brine, cover and refrigerate overnight.

3. In a medium saucepan, combine the coriander, cumin and the remaining 1 tablespoon of fennel seeds. Toast over moderately high heat until fragrant and just starting to brown, 3 minutes. Transfer to a spice grinder; let cool, then grind to a powder. In a small bowl, whisk the oil with the spices, Thai chiles, vinegar and 1½ teaspoons of sea salt.

4. Remove the pork from the brine and pat dry. Put the pork on a rack set over a large rimmed baking sheet. Rub the seasoning mixture all over the meat and shape it into a tight roast. Refrigerate uncovered overnight. Let the pork stand at room temperature for 30 minutes before roasting.

5. Preheat the oven to 425°. Roast the pork until well browned, about 45 minutes. Remove the pork from the oven and reduce the oven temperature to 350°. Lay 2 very large sheets of heavy-duty foil on a work surface, set the pork in the center and wrap up tightly. Return the pork to the rack and roast until very tender, about 2 hours longer. Let rest in the foil for 30 minutes.

6. Unwrap the pork and transfer to a carving board. Thinly slice against the grain. Pile the sliced pork and the slaw on the dinner rolls, slather with aioli and serve.
—*Jessica Koslow*

MAKE AHEAD The sliced roast pork can be refrigerated overnight. Reheat gently.

WINE Savory Rhône-style red: 2013 Qupé Los Olivos Cuvée.

THREE-CABBAGE SLAW WITH TOASTED PUMPKIN SEED AND ÁRBOL VINAIGRETTE

Total **30 min**; Serves **8 to 10**

Shred the cabbages in a food processor using the slicing disk and no pressure.

1 lb. green cabbage, cored and finely shredded

1 lb. red cabbage, cored and finely shredded

½ lb. brussels sprouts, finely shredded

1 small red onion, halved and very thinly sliced

1 cup Toasted Pumpkin Seed and Árbol Vinaigrette (p. 58)

½ cup chopped cilantro

Fine sea salt and pepper

In a large bowl, toss the cabbages with the brussels sprouts, onion and vinaigrette. Fold in the cilantro, season with salt and pepper and serve. —*JK*

Smoky Kalua Pork Sandwiches with Spiced Pineapple Jam

Active **35 min**; Total **7 hr**; Makes **12**

Chef Lee Anne Wong of Koko Head Cafe in Honolulu kicks up her Hawaiian take on a pulled pork sandwich with a zesty pineapple jam loaded with spices. She also loves the pork in omelets, quesadillas and fried rice.

PORK

One 5-lb. boneless pork shoulder with the fat cap, trussed (optional)

3 Tbsp. kosher salt

2 Tbsp. liquid smoke

3 large thawed frozen banana leaves (sold at Asian and Latin markets)

JAM

5 cups diced (½ inch) fresh pineapple (about 3 lbs.)

3 cups cane or turbinado sugar

1 cup diced sweet onion

¼ cup fresh lime juice

5 whole cloves

3 whole allspice berries

2 garlic cloves, minced

1 Thai red chile, seeded and minced

1 large cinnamon stick

1 bay leaf

1 tsp. kosher salt

12 potato slider buns and lime wedges, for serving

1. Make the pork Preheat the oven to 300°. Using a sharp knife, score the pork shoulder all over with ½-inch-deep crosshatch cuts. In a small bowl, combine the salt with the liquid smoke; rub all over the pork shoulder. Spread 1 banana leaf lengthwise on a work surface; arrange the remaining 2 leaves crosswise on top, overlapping them slightly. Set the pork in the center of the leaves and wrap tightly. Wrap the package in 2 layers of heavy-duty foil and transfer to a large roasting pan. Add 2 cups of water to the pan. Roast the pork shoulder until very tender, about 5½ hours. Let rest without unwrapping for at least 30 minutes.

2. Meanwhile, make the jam In a medium saucepan, combine all of the ingredients except the slider buns and lime wedges and bring to a simmer over moderate heat.

Reduce the heat to moderately low and cook, stirring occasionally, until the pineapple is softened and the juices are syrupy, about 50 minutes. Discard the spices; let the jam cool to room temperature.

3. Unwrap the pork and transfer to a large platter; reserve the juices. Using 2 forks, shred the pork, discarding any large pieces of fat. Skim the fat from the pan juices; toss the shredded pork with ¼ cup of the pan juices. Serve the pork on the buns with the spiced pineapple jam and lime wedges. —*Lee Anne Wong*

MAKE AHEAD The jam can be refrigerated for up to 3 days.

BEER Citrusy wheat beer: Allagash White.

Thai Beef Sandwiches with Green Curry Mayo

Total **25 min**; Serves **4**

F&W's Justin Chapple packs the flavors of a Thai beef salad into this sandwich. It's an excellent vehicle for any leftover beef roast or store-bought roast beef.

- ½ cup mayonnaise
- ¼ cup Thai green curry paste
- 1 cup lightly packed mesclun greens
- 1 Persian cucumber, julienned
- ½ cup julienned carrot
- ½ cup lightly packed cilantro leaves
- ¼ cup very thinly sliced red onion
- 3 Tbsp. crushed roasted salted peanuts
- 1½ Tbsp. fresh lime juice
  Kosher salt
  One 24-inch baguette, split and toasted
- 12 oz. leftover beef roast (p. 194) or store-bought roast beef, thinly sliced

1. In a small bowl, whisk the mayonnaise with the curry paste. In a medium bowl, toss the greens with the cucumber, carrot, cilantro, onion, peanuts and lime juice; season with salt.

2. Spread some of the curry mayonnaise on the cut sides of the baguette. Top with the sliced beef and the vegetables. Close the baguette, slice into 4 sandwiches and serve. —*Justin Chapple*

WINE Spicy Pinot Noir: 2014 Calera Central Coast.

Grilled Steak Sandwiches with Dried Shrimp–Chile Jam

Total **1 hr 40 min**; Serves **4**

At Taberna do Mercado in London, chef Nuno Mendes channels his Portuguese childhood with prego (steak sandwiches) spread with mustard and a savory jam made from chiles and dried shrimp.

- 1 lb. skirt steak, cut into 2 equal pieces
- 3 Tbsp. canola oil
  Kosher salt and pepper
- 4 cups baby spinach
- 1 Tbsp. fresh lemon juice
  Dried Shrimp–Chile Jam (recipe follows)
- 4 Portuguese rolls or brioche buns, split and toasted (see Note)
- 2 Tbsp. salted butter, softened
  Yellow mustard (optional)

1. Heat a grill pan. Rub the steak all over with 2 tablespoons of the oil and season with salt and pepper. Grill over moderately high heat, turning once, until medium-rare, about 3 minutes per side. Transfer to a cutting board and let rest for 10 minutes.

2. In a bowl, toss the spinach with the lemon juice and the remaining 1 tablespoon of oil. Season with salt.

3. Thinly slice the steak against the grain. Spread a heaping tablespoon of the shrimp-chile jam on the bottom half of each roll and spread ½ tablespoon of the butter on each of the top halves. Spread with mustard, if using. Mound the spinach mixture on the rolls, top with the steak and serve. —*Nuno Mendes*

NOTE Pleasantly sweet Portuguese rolls are available at specialty food stores.

BEER English-style pale ale: Left Hand Brewing Company Sawtooth Ale.

DRIED SHRIMP–CHILE JAM

Active **45 min**; Total **1 hr 15 min**
Makes 1¾ cups

- ¾ cup canola oil
- ¼ cup minced peeled fresh ginger
- 5 garlic cloves, minced
- 3 shallots, minced
- 1 white onion, minced
- 2 Fresno chiles, seeded and minced
- 1 cup (5 oz.) dried shrimp (see Note)
- ¼ cup white wine vinegar
- ¼ cup tamarind concentrate (see Note)
- 1½ tsp. ground cumin
- ½ tsp. ancho chile powder
- 3 bay leaves

1. In a large nonstick skillet, heat ¼ cup of the oil. Add the ginger and garlic and cook over moderate heat, stirring, until golden, 10 minutes. Scrape into a bowl.

2. Heat another ¼ cup of the oil in the skillet. Add the shallots, onion and chiles; cook over moderately low heat, stirring, until golden, 15 minutes. Scrape into the bowl.

3. In the skillet, cook the dried shrimp in the remaining ¼ cup of oil over moderately low heat, stirring, until golden, 10 minutes. Add the contents of the bowl to the skillet along with the vinegar, tamarind, cumin, chile powder and bay leaves. Cook over low heat, stirring, until slightly thickened, 15 minutes. Discard the bay leaves and let cool. —*NM*

NOTE Dried shrimp and tamarind concentrate are Thai ingredients that are available at Asian markets.

MAKE AHEAD The dried shrimp–chile jam can be refrigerated for up to 1 month.

LEFTOVERS UPGRADE

Roast Beef Sloppy Joes

Finely chop **leftover roast beef**, then simmer with chopped **onions**, minced **garlic, tomato sauce** and **light brown sugar**. Serve on **toasted buns**.

Smoked Brisket Sandwiches with Pickled Vegetables

Active **1 hr**; Total **8 hr 30 min**; Serves **8**

Despite the many hours it takes to slow cook, this luscious applewood-smoked brisket is much easier to make at home than most barbecued meats. Star chef Michael Symon turns it into a fun sandwich, topping it with cilantro and pickled vegetables to cut the richness of the meat.

One 4-lb. beef brisket

Kosher salt and pepper

2½ cups applewood chips, soaked in water for 1 hour and drained

8 brioche buns, toasted

Mayonnaise, cilantro and chopped pickled vegetables, for serving

1. Season the brisket well with salt and pepper and let stand at room temperature for 1 hour.

2. Light a charcoal grill and set it up for indirect cooking by raking the hot coals to one side. Close the grill and, using the air vents to control the heat, bring the temperature to 300°.

3. Scatter 1 cup of the wood chips over the hot coals. Set the brisket fat side up on the grill opposite the coals. Close the grill and smoke the meat at 275° to 300° until an instant-read thermometer inserted in the thickest part of the meat registers 160°, about 4 hours. Add hot coals as necessary to maintain the temperature. Each hour, add ½ cup of the wood chips to the coals and turn the brisket over.

4. Wrap the brisket tightly in a double layer of heavy-duty foil and set on the grill opposite the coals. Close the grill and cook the brisket at 275° to 300° for 2 hours longer, until an instant-read thermometer inserted in the meat registers 190°; add coals as necessary to maintain the heat. Remove the brisket from the heat and let rest in the foil for 30 minutes.

5. Thinly slice the brisket against the grain. Spread the buns with mayonnaise, top with the brisket, cilantro and pickled vegetables and serve. —*Michael Symon*

MAKE AHEAD The brisket can be refrigerated for up to 3 days. Reheat gently in the foil.

WINE Substantial Cabernet Sauvignon: 2013 Sebastiani Sonoma County.

Bresaola-Arugula Tramezzini

Total **10 min**; Serves **4**

Every bar in Venice serves *tramezzini*, little triangular sandwiches you'll see locals snacking on mid-morning, spritz in hand. What differentiates a *tramezzino* from a run-of-the-mill sandwich is the thin white bread—not the fancy, artisanal kind, but the squishy packaged bread you get at the supermarket. *Tramezzini* might be filled with anything from baby artichokes, boiled eggs and tuna to grilled eggplant and prosciutto—and always lashings of mayonnaise. The key is to use very good-quality mayo, ideally homemade. If that seems too daunting, then go with the very best store-bought type you can find.

¼ cup mayonnaise

8 thin slices of white sandwich bread, crusts removed

2 cups arugula

12 thin slices of bresaola (2 oz.)

Spread the mayonnaise on the bread. Top 4 slices with the arugula and bresaola. Close the sandwiches, cut in half on the diagonal and serve. —*Skye McAlpine*

Pizza with Prosciutto and Sheep-Milk Cheese

Active **45 min**; Total **2 hr 30 min**
Makes **four 10-inch pizzas**

The secret to achieving a perfect, crackerlike crust is to preheat your pizza stone for at least 30 minutes before baking your pie.

DOUGH

1 cup lukewarm water

One ¼-oz. package active dry yeast

½ tsp. sugar

3 cups (1 lb.) 00 flour (see Note), plus more for dusting

1 Tbsp. kosher salt

Extra-virgin olive oil

Cornmeal, for dusting

TOMATO SAUCE

1 cup canned diced tomatoes

1 Tbsp. extra-virgin olive oil

Kosher salt and pepper

TOPPINGS

8 oz. semisoft sheep-milk cheese, in bite-size pieces

6 oz. thinly sliced prosciutto

Baby arugula, for garnish

1. Make the dough In a small bowl, whisk the water with the yeast and sugar. Let stand until foamy, 10 minutes. In a large bowl, whisk the 3 cups of flour with the salt. Stir in the yeast mixture and 1 tablespoon of oil until a dough forms. Turn the dough out onto a lightly floured work surface and knead until smooth. Lightly oil a large bowl and transfer the dough to it. Cover and let stand in a warm place until doubled in bulk, about 1 hour.

2. Preheat the oven to 450° with a pizza stone set on the middle rack. Roll the dough into 4 balls and arrange them on a parchment-lined baking sheet spaced a few inches apart. Cover the dough loosely with plastic wrap and let stand in a warm place for 30 minutes.

3. Meanwhile, make the sauce In a food processor, pulse the tomatoes with the oil until a chunky puree forms. Season with salt and pepper.

4. Dust an inverted baking sheet with cornmeal. On a lightly floured work surface, using a lightly floured rolling pin, roll out 1 piece of dough to a 10-inch round. Transfer to the inverted baking sheet. Spread ¼ cup of the tomato sauce on the dough, leaving a 1-inch border, then top with one-fourth of the cheese. Carefully slide the pizza onto the hot stone and bake until the crust is golden and crisp and the cheese is melted, about 10 minutes. Transfer the pizza to a work surface, top with one-fourth of the prosciutto and garnish with arugula. Slice and serve immediately. Repeat to make 3 more pizzas. —*Andrea Mattei*

NOTE Doppio zero, or 00, is a fine Italian flour that's available at specialty food shops and from amazon.com.

WINE Vibrant Tuscan red: 2014 La Poderina Rosso di Montalcino.

PIZZA WITH PROSCIUTTO
AND SHEEP-MILK CHEESE

CACIO E PEPE PIZZA

Grilled Pizza with Peaches and Aged Cheddar

Active **40 min**; Total **3 hr 40 min plus overnight resting**; Makes **two 10-inch pizzas**

Once the dough is fully proofed, this grilled pizza comes together in minutes. Bring your prepped toppings out to the grill with you for quick assembly (and quick eating).

- **1¾ cups all-purpose flour, plus more for dusting**
- **1 cup bread flour**
- **1½ tsp. kosher salt**
- **1 cup lukewarm water (about 105°–110°)**
- **1 tsp. active dry yeast**
- **¼ cup plus 1 Tbsp. extra-virgin olive oil, plus more for brushing**
- **2 medium peaches, thinly sliced**
- **8 oz. aged white cheddar cheese, shredded (2 cups)**
- **½ small red onion, thinly sliced**
- **Parsley leaves and snipped chives, for serving**

1. In a medium bowl, whisk both of the flours with the salt. In a large bowl, whisk the water with the yeast until the yeast dissolves. Whisk in 1 tablespoon of the olive oil. Add the flours and stir with a wooden spoon until a dough forms. Turn out onto a lightly floured work surface and knead until smooth, about 10 minutes. Transfer the dough to a lightly oiled bowl and press a sheet of plastic wrap directly on the surface. Refrigerate overnight.

2. Line a baking sheet with parchment paper. Cut the dough in half and form each piece into a ball; set them about 3 inches apart on the prepared sheet and cover with plastic wrap. Let stand at room temperature until doubled in bulk, 3 hours.

3. Light a grill. On a lightly floured work surface, using a lightly floured rolling pin, roll out each piece of dough into a 10-inch round and brush the tops with 2 tablespoons of the olive oil. Oil the grate and grill the dough oiled side down over moderate heat until lightly charred, 2 to 3 minutes. Brush the tops with the remaining 2 tablespoons of olive oil and flip. Arrange the peaches, cheddar cheese and red onion on top, cover and grill until the cheese is melted and the pizzas are lightly charred

on the bottom, 2 to 3 minutes more. Transfer to a work surface. Garnish with parsley and chives, slice and serve immediately. —*Tandy Wilson*

WINE Rich, Rhône-inspired white: 2014 Tablas Creek Vineyard Paso Robles Côtes de Tablas Blanc.

Cacio e Pepe Pizza

Active **1 hr 30 min**; Total **2 days** Makes **six 10- to 12-inch pizzas**

At Sbanco restaurant in Rome, chef Stefano Callegari has come up with rule-breaking methods for making his brilliant pizzas. He scatters a bit of crushed ice on the dough as it goes into the hot oven to keep the center moist and tender and the bottom and rim crisp and crackling. Then come the toppings, including this one inspired by cacio e pepe pasta. It's worth noting that this recipe is largely about the dough—the topping, while delicious, is relatively scant.

- **⅛ tsp. active dry yeast**
- **7¼ cups all-purpose flour**
- **1 Tbsp. kosher salt**
- **Canola oil, for greasing and brushing**
- **Cornmeal, for sprinkling**
- **Crushed ice**
- **1½ cups finely grated Pecorino Romano cheese (4 oz.)**
- **Extra-virgin olive oil, for drizzling**
- **Freshly ground black pepper**

1. In a medium saucepan, heat 3 cups of water to 80°. Transfer 2 tablespoons of the warm water to a small bowl and whisk in the yeast. In a large bowl, combine the flour with the remaining warm water; stir with a wooden spoon until a shaggy dough forms. Cover both bowls with plastic wrap and let stand for 30 minutes.

2. Mix the salt into the yeast and add to the dough in the large bowl. Knead until all of the liquid is absorbed; the dough will be quite wet. Cover with plastic wrap and let stand at room temperature for 30 minutes.

3. With a dampened hand, lift one edge of the dough, stretch it up and fold it over the top of the dough. Turn the bowl a quarter turn, lift up the edge of the dough, stretch it up and fold it over the top. Repeat until you've turned the bowl all the way around. Cover the bowl with plastic wrap and let the dough stand for 30 minutes. Repeat the lifting and folding one more time, then transfer the dough to a large oiled bowl. Cover with plastic wrap and let stand at room temperature until tripled in bulk, about 12 hours.

4. Turn the dough out onto a lightly floured work surface and cut into 6 equal pieces. Take 1 piece of dough and pull the edge into the center, then place seam side down on the work surface. Roll the dough into a ball and set on an oiled baking sheet. Repeat with the remaining 5 pieces of dough, arranging them 3 inches apart on the sheet. Brush the rounds with canola oil and cover with plastic wrap. Refrigerate for at least 8 or up to 12 hours.

5. Let the dough stand at room temperature for 30 minutes. Preheat the broiler. Place an inverted baking sheet or a pizza stone in the oven 8 inches from the heat. Invert a second baking sheet and dust liberally with cornmeal.

6. On a lightly floured surface, use your fingertips to press 1 ball of dough into a 6-inch round, leaving a border around the edge and keeping the center slightly thicker than the rest. Use your palms to press the dough into a 10- to 12-inch round. Transfer to the cornmeal-dusted sheet and slide onto the hot sheet in the oven. Place 2 tablespoons of ice in the center of the dough and bake for about 8 minutes, until golden. Immediately sprinkle ¼ cup of the cheese all over the pizza, drizzle with olive oil and season with pepper. Serve immediately. Repeat to make 5 more pizzas. —*Stefano Callegari*

WINE Spicy Italian red: 2012 Cantina Roccafiore Montefalco Rosso.

BREAKFAST
AND BRUNCH

Boston chef Jamie Bissonnette indulges in his ultimate egg and cheese sandwich (p. 282).
OPPOSITE Mexican Baked Eggs (p. 285).

Egg-and-Cheese Sandwiches with Scallion-Tomato Sauce

📷 PAGE 281

🕐 Total **30 min**; Serves **4**

A scallion-tomato sauce made with the Middle Eastern spice blend baharat adds great flavor to a cheesy scrambled egg sandwich. The sauce—also terrific on grilled fish, poultry and steak—can be served warm or at room temperature.

SCALLION-TOMATO SAUCE

- **2 Tbsp. extra-virgin olive oil**
- **8 scallions, white and green parts thinly sliced separately**
- **1 garlic clove, minced**
- **1 tsp. baharat, garam masala or Madras curry powder**
- **2 cups chopped plum tomatoes Kosher salt and pepper**

SANDWICHES

- **3 Tbsp. unsalted butter, at room temperature**
- **4 tsp. extra-virgin olive oil**
- **8 large eggs Kosher salt and pepper**
- **8 slices of aged cheddar cheese (12 oz.)**
- **4 English muffins, split and toasted**

1. Make the scallion-tomato sauce In a large skillet, heat the olive oil. Add the scallion whites and garlic and mix well. Cover and cook over low heat, stirring occasionally, until tender, about 5 minutes. Add the baharat and cook, stirring, for 1 minute. Add the tomatoes, season with salt and pepper and bring to a simmer. Cook over moderately low heat, stirring occasionally, until softened and saucy, about 10 minutes. Add the scallion greens and cook until tender, 2 minutes longer. Scrape the sauce into a small bowl and let cool to room temperature.

2. Make the sandwiches Heat a large nonstick skillet. Melt 1½ tablespoons of the butter in the olive oil. In a medium bowl, beat the eggs with a fork. Add them to the skillet, season with salt and pepper and cook over moderately low heat, stirring, until curds start to form, 4 to 5 minutes. Stir in the remaining 1½ tablespoons of butter and cook until the eggs are just set, 1 to 2 minutes longer.

3. Place 1 slice of cheese on the bottom half of each English muffin. Spoon 1 tablespoon of the scallion-tomato sauce on the cheese and top with half of the eggs. Repeat with the remaining cheese, sauce and eggs. Close the sandwiches and serve. —*Jamie Bissonnette and Ken Oringer*

MAKE AHEAD The scallion-tomato sauce can be refrigerated for up to 4 days.

Biscuit Breakfast Sandwiches with Peach-Ginger Jam

Active **1 hr**; Total **1 hr 45 min plus cooling**
Serves **4**

PEACH JAM

- **2 small peaches (about 8 oz.)**
- **2 cups sugar**
- **1 Tbsp. fresh lemon juice**
- **½ Tbsp. unsalted butter**
- **½ tsp. finely grated peeled fresh ginger**
- **3 Tbsp. pectin**

BISCUITS

- **2½ cups all-purpose flour, plus more for dusting**
- **1 Tbsp. sugar**
- **1 tsp. baking powder**
- **¼ tsp. kosher salt**
- **5 Tbsp. cold unsalted butter, cubed**
- **5 Tbsp. cold lard (2½ oz.), cubed**
- **1 cup buttermilk**
- **1 large egg, lightly beaten**

SANDWICHES

- **1 Tbsp. unsalted butter**
- **6 oz. thinly sliced country ham**
- **4 large eggs Kosher salt and pepper**
- **1 cup shredded aged cheddar cheese (3 oz.)**

1. Make the peach jam Bring a medium saucepan of water to a boil. Fill a bowl with ice water. Using a sharp paring knife, mark an X on the bottom of each peach. Add the peaches to the saucepan and blanch until the skins start to peel away, 1 to 2 minutes. Transfer to the ice bath and let cool completely. Peel, pit and thinly slice the peaches. Wipe out the saucepan.

2. Add the sugar, lemon juice, butter, ginger and ⅓ cup of water to the saucepan and simmer over moderate heat, stirring occasionally, until the sugar has dissolved, about 5 minutes. Stir in the pectin and peaches and bring to a boil. Cook, stirring occasionally, until the peaches begin to soften, about 2 minutes. Transfer the jam to a heatproof jar and let cool completely at room temperature. Cover and refrigerate until ready to use.

3. Make the biscuits Preheat the oven to 350° and line a baking sheet with parchment paper. In a large bowl, whisk the 2½ cups of flour with the sugar, baking powder and salt. Scatter the cubed butter and lard over the dry ingredients and pinch the fat into the flour with your fingers until the mixture resembles very coarse crumbs, with some pieces the size of small peas. Stir in the buttermilk until a shaggy dough forms.

4. Turn the dough out onto a lightly floured work surface and knead gently until it just comes together. Pat into a 1-inch-thick round. Using a 3-inch biscuit cutter, stamp out 3 biscuits. Gather the scraps and cut out one more biscuit. Arrange the 4 biscuits about 2 inches apart on the prepared baking sheet and brush the tops with the beaten egg. Bake for about 40 minutes, until golden brown. Transfer to a rack and let cool.

5. Make the sandwiches In a large nonstick skillet, melt ½ tablespoon of the butter. Working in 2 batches, cook the country ham over moderately high heat, turning once, until golden and crisp around the edges, about 1 minute per batch. Transfer to a plate and wipe out the skillet. In a medium bowl, beat the eggs and season with salt and pepper. Melt the remaining ½ tablespoon of butter in the skillet. Add the eggs and cook over low heat, stirring occasionally, until almost set, 4 minutes. Sprinkle with the cheese, then fold the omelet in half. Cook until set in the center, 1 to 2 minutes longer. Transfer the omelet to a work surface and cut into 4 equal pieces. Split the biscuits and top each bottom half with a piece of omelet and a few slices of ham. Drizzle with the peach jam, close the sandwiches and serve immediately. —*Andy Mumma*

Cumin Oil–Fried Egg and Avocado Toasts

⏱ Total **15 min**; Serves **4**

Avocado toast, the darling of the breakfast world, gets a fun revamp here. It serves as the base for eggs fried in fragrant cumin and crushed red pepper for a healthy and satisfying meal.

Four ½-inch-thick slices of toasted rustic bread

1 **Hass avocado, sliced ½ inch thick**

Kosher salt

3 **Tbsp. extra-virgin olive oil**

1 **tsp. cumin seeds**

1 **tsp. crushed red pepper**

4 **large eggs**

Top the toasts with the avocado and season with salt. In a large nonstick skillet, heat the olive oil. Add the cumin seeds and crushed red pepper and crack the eggs into the skillet. Fry over moderate heat until the whites are set and the yolks are slightly runny, about 3 minutes. Set the eggs on the toasts, drizzle with the cumin-pepper oil and serve. —*Kay Chun*

Soft Green-Herb Omelet

⏱ Total **15 min**; Serves **2**

4 **large eggs**

½ **cup finely chopped mixed herbs, such as mint, parsley, dill, chives, tarragon, chervil and basil**

Kosher salt and pepper

1 **Tbsp. unsalted butter**

½ **cup chopped raw spinach**

¼ **cup crumbled feta cheese**

½ **tsp. finely grated lemon zest**

In a medium bowl, beat the eggs with the herbs and a generous pinch each of salt and pepper. In a large nonstick skillet, melt the butter over moderate heat until it begins to foam. Add the eggs and cook undisturbed until they just start to set on the bottom, about 30 seconds. Using a fork, gently pull the cooked eggs at the edge into the center, tilting to allow the uncooked eggs to run onto the pan. When most of the omelet is set, let it cook undisturbed for 1 minute longer. Remove from the heat. Sprinkle the chopped spinach, feta and lemon zest over half of the omelet. Using a spatula, fold the omelet over to form a half-moon, slide it onto a plate and serve immediately. —*Anna Jones*

Greens Frittata with Mixed Herbs

⏱ Total **45 min**; Serves **6**

"These are the flavors of our *cucina povera*," says Friulian winemaker Giampaolo Venica about this frittata made with spring greens, chives and mint.

4 **oz. curly spinach, stemmed and leaves coarsely chopped (2 cups)**

½ **cup parsley leaves**

¼ **cup baby arugula**

2 **Tbsp. snipped chives**

2 **Tbsp. mint leaves**

2 **Tbsp. extra-virgin olive oil, plus more for drizzling**

1 **medium yellow onion, finely chopped**

Kosher salt and pepper

1 **dozen large eggs, lightly beaten**

1. Preheat the oven to 375°. In a food processor, pulse the spinach, parsley, arugula, chives and mint until finely chopped. Scrape into a small bowl.

2. In a 10-inch ovenproof nonstick skillet, heat the 2 tablespoons of olive oil. Add the onion, season with salt and pepper and cook over moderately low heat, stirring occasionally, until softened, about 8 minutes. Add the eggs and stir in all but 2 tablespoons of the chopped herbs; season with salt and pepper. Cook over moderately low heat, stirring occasionally, until the eggs start to set on the bottom and side, about 5 minutes. Transfer the frittata to the oven and bake until set, about 10 minutes. Slide onto a serving plate and garnish with the reserved chopped herbs. Drizzle with olive oil and serve warm. —*Giampaolo Venica*

MAKE AHEAD The herb mixture can be refrigerated overnight.

WINE Bright, tangy Sauvignon Blanc: 2015 Venica & Venica Ronco del Cerò.

Sausage and Apple Frittata with Dill

⏱ Active **15 min**; Total **45 min**
Serves **4 to 6**

Instead of serving breakfast sausages alongside eggs, this recipe calls for baking them right into a delicious frittata. Sweet bites of apple and sharp cheddar give the eggs even more flavor. This is the perfect brunch dish with a simple salad.

1 **Tbsp. extra-virgin olive oil**

½ **lb. breakfast sausage links**

1 **dozen large eggs, beaten**

¼ **cup whole milk**

1 **Granny Smith apple, peeled and cut into ¼-inch pieces**

1 **cup grated sharp cheddar cheese**

½ **cup chopped dill**

Kosher salt and pepper

Preheat the oven to 375°. In a 9-inch ovenproof nonstick skillet, heat the oil. Add the sausage and cook over moderate heat, turning, until golden, about 5 minutes. Stir in the eggs, milk, apple, cheese and dill and season with salt and pepper. Bake until golden and set, about 30 minutes, then serve. —*Kay Chun*

WINE Fresh, green apple–scented Cava: NV Gramona Gran Cuvee.

GENIUS CHEF HACK

Savory Oatmeal

"You can add just about anything to oatmeal and eat it any time of day. Instead of brown sugar and milk, I like to add tomato sauce and Parmesan or cook the oatmeal in dashi and add miso paste."
—*Chef Sang Yoon, Lukshon, Los Angeles*

SESAME BAGELS WITH
SOPPRESSATA AND BURRATA

Grits with Yogurt and Vegan Chorizo Oil

Total **1 hr;** Serves **6**

Chef Brad Kilgore of Alter in Miami calls this a "show-off" dish that's not really much work. He drizzles creamy grits with a smoky, fragrant oil that tastes like chorizo but is actually vegan.

VEGAN CHORIZO OIL

- ½ cup plus 2 Tbsp. canola oil
- ¼ cup thinly sliced garlic
- 1 Tbsp. smoked paprika
- 1 Tbsp. sweet paprika
- 1 tsp. cumin seeds
- ½ tsp. fennel seeds
- ½ tsp. whole black peppercorns
- ¼ tsp. whole coriander seeds
- ¼ tsp. crushed red pepper
- ⅛ tsp. curry powder

GRITS

- 3 cups whole milk
- ½ cup heavy cream
- ⅔ cup stone-ground white grits (4 oz.), preferably Anson Mills
- 4 oz. fresh goat cheese
- ⅓ cup full-fat Greek yogurt
- 4 Tbsp. unsalted butter
- 1 Tbsp. fresh lemon juice
  Kosher salt
  Coarsely chopped cilantro or small cilantro sprigs, for garnish

1. Make the vegan chorizo oil In a small saucepan, heat the oil. Add the garlic and cook over moderately low heat, stirring frequently, until light golden, about 5 minutes. Remove the pan from the heat and whisk in all of the remaining ingredients. Scrape the mixture into a heatproof bowl and let cool to room temperature, 30 minutes. Strain the oil through a cheesecloth-lined sieve, pressing on the solids.

2. Meanwhile, make the grits In a medium saucepan, combine the milk and cream and bring to a simmer. Whisk in the grits and cook over moderately low heat, whisking occasionally, until tender, smooth and porridge-like, about 25 minutes. Whisk in the goat cheese, yogurt, butter and lemon juice and season with salt.

3. Spoon the grits into bowls and drizzle with some of the vegan chorizo oil. Garnish with cilantro and serve warm. —*Brad Kilgore*

MAKE AHEAD The vegan chorizo oil can be refrigerated for up to 2 weeks.

Sesame Bagels with Soppressata and Burrata

Total **10 min;** Serves **4**

These supereasy bagel sandwiches are an ideal make-ahead dish for picnics or even work lunches. If you can't find burrata, use a quality buffalo mozzarella instead.

- ¼ cup oil-packed Calabrian chiles plus 1 tsp. oil from the jar
- 2 Tbsp. fresh orange juice
  Kosher salt
- 4 sesame bagels, split and toasted
- 6 oz. thinly sliced soppressata
- 8 oz. burrata or fresh mozzarella, sliced
  Basil leaves
  Extra-virgin olive oil, for drizzling

In a food processor, puree the chiles with the oil from the jar and the orange juice; season with salt. Spread the chile paste on the cut sides of the bagels and top with the soppressata, burrata and basil leaves; drizzle with olive oil. Close the sandwiches and serve. —*Missy Robbins*

Egg Salad with Herbs and Pickles

Total **20 min;** Serves **4**

Amped up with herbs, tangy capers and crunchy cornichons, this mayo-less egg salad is excellent on crackers or in a sandwich. To dress it up, serve it piled on a bed of crisp lettuce or over juicy tomatoes.

- 8 large eggs
- ½ cup Greek yogurt
- ¼ cup chopped capers
- ¼ cup chopped cornichons
- ¼ cup chopped parsley
- ¼ cup chopped tarragon
- ¼ cup extra-virgin olive oil
  Kosher salt and pepper

1. In a large saucepan, cover the eggs with 1 inch of water. Bring to a full boil, then cover and remove the pan from the heat. Let stand for 10 minutes. Drain and cool the eggs under cold running water. Peel and chop the eggs.

2. In a large bowl, combine the chopped eggs with all of the remaining ingredients, mashing with a fork, and season with salt and pepper. —*Kay Chun*

Mexican Eggs Baked in Tomato Sauce

PAGE 280
Total **40 min;** Serves **4**

This Mexican riff on Middle Eastern shakshuka (eggs baked in tomato sauce) is a terrific one-pot breakfast or brunch. It gets a double dose of heat from poblano chiles and jalapeños.

- 2 Tbsp. extra-virgin olive oil
- 3 poblano chiles, seeded and sliced ½ inch thick
- 3 garlic cloves, chopped
- 2 cups jarred tomato sauce
- 2 cups halved cherry tomatoes (12 oz.)
- 1 tsp. dried oregano
- 4 large eggs
- 1 cup crumbled queso fresco (5 oz.)
  Chopped cilantro and sliced jalapeños, for garnish
  Warm corn tortillas, for serving

Preheat the oven to 425°. In a large cast-iron skillet, heat the olive oil. Add the poblanos and garlic and cook over moderate heat, stirring, until golden, 5 minutes. Stir in the tomato sauce, tomatoes and oregano and cook over low heat until thickened, about 10 minutes. Crack the eggs into the tomato sauce and top with the cheese. Bake until set, about 12 minutes. Garnish with cilantro and jalapeños and serve with corn tortillas. —*Kay Chun*

Johnnycake Porridge

⏱ Total **45 min**; Serves **4**

Chefs Jamie Bissonnette and Ken Oringer of Little Donkey in Cambridge, Massachusetts, use stone-ground New England cornmeal enriched with almond milk in their creamy porridge. Don't skip any of the garnishes here: The hazelnuts, maple syrup, butter and salt all play their part in this delicious breakfast.

- 1 qt. unsweetened almond milk
- 2 Tbsp. turbinado sugar
- ¼ vanilla bean, seeds scraped and pod reserved
- ¾ cup stone-ground white cornmeal (5 oz.), preferably Kenyon's Grist Mill or Gray's Grist Mill
- ½ cup blanched hazelnuts
- 4 Tbsp. salted butter
  Pure maple syrup, for drizzling
  Himalayan pink salt or flaky sea salt, for garnish

1. In a large saucepan, combine the almond milk with the sugar, vanilla seeds and bean and 2 cups of water; bring to a boil. Gradually whisk in the cornmeal until smooth. Cook over moderately low heat, whisking frequently, until the cornmeal is tender and has thickened to a porridge-like consistency, 35 to 40 minutes. Discard the vanilla bean.

2. Meanwhile, preheat the oven to 425°. Spread the hazelnuts on a baking sheet and toast for about 8 minutes, until golden. Let cool slightly, then smash using the bottom of a pan.

3. Spoon the porridge into bowls and top with the butter and hazelnuts. Drizzle with maple syrup, garnish with salt and serve immediately. —*Jamie Bissonnette and Ken Oringer*

MAKE AHEAD The porridge can be refrigerated for up to 2 days; reheat and add a little water if too thick.

Cacio e Pepe Soufflé

⏱ Active **20 min**; Total **45 min**; Serves **2**

Copious amounts of finely grated Parmesan make this heavenly cheese soufflé sturdier than most.

- 4 Tbsp. unsalted butter—1 Tbsp. softened
- 2 oz. Parmigiano-Reggiano cheese, grated using a superfine grater such as a Microplane (1½ cups plus 3 Tbsp.)
  Coarsely ground black pepper
- 4 large eggs, separated
- 5 Tbsp. all-purpose flour
- 1 cup whole milk
- ¼ tsp. kosher salt

1. Preheat the oven to 350° and place a rack in the center. Use the 1 tablespoon of softened butter to grease the inside of a 3-cup soufflé dish. Add 2 tablespoons of the grated Parmigiano and turn the dish to coat it with the cheese. Wipe any cheese off the rim of the dish. Sprinkle the bottom of the dish with black pepper; refrigerate.

2. In a medium bowl, whisk the egg yolks with 3 tablespoons of the flour. In a medium saucepan, bring the milk to a simmer with the remaining 3 tablespoons of butter. While whisking constantly, slowly drizzle the hot milk into the egg yolk mixture until incorporated. Working off the heat, scrape this mixture into the saucepan. Whisk in the remaining 2 tablespoons of flour until incorporated, then whisk in 1½ cups of the cheese and the salt. Cook the mixture over moderately low heat, whisking constantly, until very thick, about 3 minutes. Scrape into a large bowl to cool slightly.

3. In a medium bowl, beat the egg whites at medium speed until medium-firm peaks form, about 3 minutes. Whisk the soufflé base to loosen, then stir in one-third of the egg whites just until blended; fold in the remaining egg whites until incorporated. Spoon the mixture into the prepared dish to reach three-quarters of the way up the side (you may have some left over). Smooth the top of the soufflé but avoid spreading the mixture up the edge of the dish. Sprinkle with the remaining 1 tablespoon of grated cheese and black pepper. Bake in the middle of the oven for about 22 minutes, until golden and puffed. Serve hot. —*Laurent Tourondel*

Oatmeal Soufflé

⏱ Active **30 min**; Total **1 hr**; Serves **4**

Oatmeal makes for a surprising, flavorful soufflé base. We love that much of the prep for this healthy, elegant and satisfying dish can be done the night before.

- 1 cup extra-thick rolled oats
- 3 cups whole milk
- 2 Tbsp. turbinado sugar
  Pinch of kosher salt
- 3 large eggs, separated
- 2 cups mixed raspberries and blueberries
- ½ tsp. finely grated lemon zest
  Confectioners' sugar, for dusting
  Pure maple syrup, for serving (optional)

1. Preheat the oven to 350°. Butter a 2-quart baking dish.

2. In a large saucepan, combine the oats, milk, turbinado sugar and salt and bring to a simmer. Cook the oatmeal over moderate heat, stirring occasionally, until thickened to a porridge consistency, about 15 minutes. Remove from the heat; let cool slightly.

3. Working quickly, stir the egg yolks into the oatmeal until well blended. Fold in 1 cup of the berries and the lemon zest.

4. In a large bowl, using a hand mixer, beat the egg whites at medium speed until medium-stiff peaks form, about 3 minutes. Gently fold the whites into the oatmeal just until combined. Scrape the mixture into the prepared dish and bake until golden and puffed, about 30 minutes. Dust with confectioners' sugar and serve hot with the remaining 1 cup of berries and maple syrup, if desired. —*Kay Chun*

MAKE AHEAD The oatmeal can be prepared through Step 2 and refrigerated for up to 3 days. Rewarm with some milk to loosen the oatmeal to a porridge consistency before proceeding.

JOHNNYCAKE
PORRIDGE

Broccoli-and-Cheddar Soufflé

Active **40 min**; Total **1 hr 40 min**
Serves **4 to 6**

- **7 Tbsp. unsalted butter, at room temperature**
- **¼ cup plain dry breadcrumbs**
- **Kosher salt**
- **One 6-oz. head of broccoli, finely chopped (1½ cups)**
- **1 cup packed baby spinach leaves (1½ oz.)**
- **3 Tbsp. minced shallots**
- **5 Tbsp. all-purpose flour**
- **1¾ cups whole milk**
- **¼ tsp. cayenne**
- **¼ tsp. black pepper**
- **6 large egg yolks**
- **4 oz. extra-sharp cheddar cheese, shredded (1 cup)**
- **7 large egg whites**
- **¼ tsp. cream of tartar**

1. Preheat the oven to 400°. Grease a 2-quart soufflé dish with 2 tablespoons of the butter and coat with the breadcrumbs, shaking out the excess.

2. In a medium saucepan, combine 1½ cups of water with ¾ teaspoon of salt and bring to a boil. Add the broccoli, cover and simmer over moderate heat until very soft, 8 to 10 minutes. Stir in the spinach and cook until just wilted, about 30 seconds. Using a slotted spoon, transfer the broccoli and spinach to a food processor and puree until nearly smooth; let cool.

3. Meanwhile, wipe out the saucepan and melt the remaining 5 tablespoons of butter in it. Add the shallots and cook over moderate heat, stirring, until softened, about 2 minutes. Add the flour and cook, whisking, until the roux starts to change color, about 3 minutes. Gradually whisk in the milk and bring to a boil. Cook over moderately low heat, whisking constantly, until thick, about 3 minutes. Scrape the mixture into a large bowl and whisk in the cayenne, black pepper and 1¼ teaspoons of salt; let cool completely, 15 minutes. Whisk in the cooled broccoli puree. Whisk in the egg yolks 1 at a time, then fold in the cheese.

4. In a large stainless steel bowl, using a hand mixer, beat the egg whites with the cream of tartar at medium-high speed until firm peaks form, about 2 minutes. Fold one-third of the whites into the soufflé base to lighten it, then fold in the remaining whites until no streaks remain.

5. Scrape the mixture into the prepared soufflé dish. Run your thumb around the dish's inside rim to wipe away any crumbs. Bake for 45 to 50 minutes, until the soufflé is puffed and well browned. Serve right away. —*Naomi Pomeroy*

WINE Pear-scented Oregon white: 2014 Adelsheim Willamette Chardonnay.

Sesame Bagel Breakfast Casserole

Active **45 min**; Total **6 hr 30 min**
Serves **8 to 10**

This casserole, studded with pieces of sesame bagels, is best assembled the night before, allowing the bread to soak up the egg custard. Simply pop it in the oven the next morning to bake.

- **2 Tbsp. extra-virgin olive oil, plus more for greasing**
- **10 large eggs**
- **2½ cups half-and-half**
- **6 oil-packed Calabrian chiles— drained, seeded and minced**
- **Kosher salt and pepper**
- **1 lb. day-old sesame bagels (3 large), cut into 1-inch pieces (9 cups)**
- **10 oz. button mushrooms, stemmed and sliced ¼ inch thick**
- **1 small bunch of curly kale, stemmed and chopped (5 cups)**
- **1 pint cherry tomatoes, quartered**
- **¼ cup finely chopped basil**
- **2 Tbsp. minced rosemary**
- **2 scallions, thinly sliced**
- **8 oz. fresh mozzarella cheese, shredded**
- **1 cup shredded Parmigiano-Reggiano cheese (2 oz.)**

1. Lightly grease a 3-quart oval baking pan. In a large bowl, whisk the eggs with the half-and-half, Calabrian chiles, 2 teaspoons of salt and 1 teaspoon of pepper. Stir in the bagel pieces and let stand at room temperature for 20 minutes.

2. Meanwhile, in a large skillet, heat the 2 tablespoons of olive oil. Add the mushrooms and kale and season with salt and pepper. Cook over moderately high heat, stirring occasionally, until tender and wilted, about 7 minutes. Stir in the cherry tomatoes, basil and rosemary and cook until the tomatoes start to soften, about 3 minutes. Remove the skillet from the heat and stir in the scallions; season with salt and pepper. Let cool slightly.

3. Fold the vegetables and shredded cheeses into the bagel mixture, then transfer to the prepared baking pan. Cover with plastic wrap and refrigerate for at least 4 hours or overnight.

4. Preheat the oven to 350°. Remove the plastic wrap and cover the baking pan with foil. Bake for 40 minutes, remove the foil and bake for 45 minutes more, until the top is puffed and golden and a toothpick inserted in the center comes out clean. Let stand for 20 minutes before serving. —*Anna Painter*

MAKE AHEAD The casserole can be prepared through Step 3 and refrigerated overnight.

Deep-Dish Spinach-and-Feta Quiche

Active **1 hr**; Total **3 hr**
Makes **one 9-inch quiche**

- **One 14-oz. package refrigerated double piecrust dough**
- **5 jalapeños, stemmed and seeded**
- **8 garlic cloves—4 cloves crushed, 4 cloves minced**
- **1 cup parsley leaves**
- **1 cup cilantro leaves**
- **1 tsp. ground cumin**
- **½ tsp. ground coriander**
- **¼ tsp. cayenne**
- **½ cup extra-virgin olive oil**
- **Kosher salt and pepper**
- **1 Tbsp. unsalted butter**
- **1 large onion, finely chopped**
- **10 large eggs**
- **2¾ cups heavy cream**
- **10 oz. thawed frozen chopped spinach, squeezed dry**
- **1½ cups crumbled feta cheese**

1. Preheat the oven to 450°. On a lightly floured work surface, stack the 2 rounds of pie dough and roll together into a 16-inch round. Ease the round into a 9-inch spring-form pan, pressing into the bottom and up the side. Trim the dough, leaving ¼ inch of overhang. Tuck the dough under itself and crimp the edge decoratively. Line the dough with parchment paper and fill with pie weights or dried beans. Bake for about 15 minutes, until lightly golden. Transfer to a rack to cool. Reduce the oven temperature to 375°. Remove the paper and weights.

2. Meanwhile, in a food processor, pulse the jalapeños and crushed garlic until finely chopped. Add the parsley, cilantro, cumin, coriander, cayenne and olive oil, season with salt and pepper and pulse the zhoug (a Yemeni hot sauce) until blended.

3. In a large nonstick skillet, melt the butter. Add the onion, season with salt and pepper and cook over moderate heat, stirring occasionally, until softened, about 8 minutes. Add the minced garlic and cook for 2 minutes. Scrape the onion mixture into a large bowl and let cool to room temperature.

4. Add the eggs and cream to the onion and beat until combined, then mix in the spinach, feta, ¾ teaspoon of salt, ⅛ teaspoon of pepper and ¼ cup of the zhoug. (Refrigerate or freeze the remaining zhoug.) Pour the filling into the quiche shell and bake until the center is set, about 1 hour and 10 minutes. Tent the crust with foil if the edge starts to get too dark. Transfer the quiche to a rack to cool for about 30 minutes before serving with extra zhoug, if desired. —Molly Yeh

MAKE AHEAD The zhoug can be refrigerated for up to 3 days or frozen for up to 3 months. The quiche can be refrigerated for up to 2 days; reheat before serving.

WINE A fruity sparkling wine like Prosecco: 2014 Bisol Crede.

Sausage-and-Cheddar Muffins
⏲ Active **10 min;** Total **40 min**
Makes **12**

- 2 cups all-purpose flour
- 1 Tbsp. baking powder
- ¾ tsp. kosher salt
- ½ tsp. baking soda
- 4 Tbsp. unsalted butter, melted
- 1 large egg, beaten
- 1 cup whole milk
- 1 cup shredded sharp cheddar cheese
- 1 cup chopped cooked breakfast sausage

Preheat the oven to 375°. In a large bowl, whisk the flour with the baking powder, salt and baking soda. Stir in the butter, egg, milk, cheese and sausage. Spoon the batter into 12 greased muffin cups and bake for 25 to 30 minutes, until golden. Transfer to a rack to cool before serving. —Kay Chun

MAKE AHEAD The muffins can be refrigerated overnight. Reheat in a 350° oven for about 10 minutes before serving.

Rye Pancakes with Caramelized Pears and Maple Syrup
⏲ Total **40 min;** Serves **4**

- 5 Tbsp. melted unsalted butter, plus more for brushing
- 2 Bartlett pears—peeled, cored and cut into ¾-inch pieces
- ¾ cup pure maple syrup
  Kosher salt
- 2 cups whole milk
- 2 large eggs
- 1 cup rye flour
- ¾ cup all-purpose flour
- 3 Tbsp. sugar
- 2 tsp. baking powder

1. In a large skillet, heat 2 tablespoons of the butter. Add the pears and cook over moderately high heat, stirring occasionally, until just tender and golden, about 5 minutes. Stir in the maple syrup, season with salt and keep warm.

2. Set a large resealable plastic bag in a tall bowl to hold it upright. In the bag, whisk the milk with the eggs and the remaining melted butter, then add both flours, the sugar, baking powder and ¾ teaspoon of salt; stir until incorporated.

3. Preheat a griddle and brush lightly with melted butter. Gently twist the bag and hold it upright. Using scissors, snip off ¼ inch from a bottom corner. For each batch of pancakes, pipe 4-inch rounds of batter onto the griddle. Cook over moderate heat until bubbles appear on the surface of the pancakes, 2 to 3 minutes. Flip and cook until risen and golden brown, 2 minutes longer. Serve topped with the maple pears. —Justin Chapple

Whole-Wheat Pancakes with Roasted Berries
⏲ Total **35 min;** Serves **4**

- 3 cups mixed berries, such as blueberries, raspberries and halved strawberries
- ¼ cup plus 3 Tbsp. granulated sugar
- 1½ cups whole milk
- 2 large eggs
- 3 Tbsp. melted unsalted butter, plus more for brushing
- 1 cup all-purpose flour
- ¾ cup whole-wheat flour
- 2 tsp. baking powder
- ¾ tsp. kosher salt
  Confectioners' sugar and whipped cream, for topping

1. Preheat the oven to 350°. On a rimmed baking sheet, toss the berries with ¼ cup of the granulated sugar. Bake until the berries are just softened, about 10 minutes.

2. Meanwhile, set a large resealable plastic bag in a tall bowl to hold it upright. In the bag, whisk the milk with the eggs and the 3 tablespoons of melted butter, then add both flours, the remaining 3 tablespoons of granulated sugar, the baking powder and salt; stir until incorporated.

3. Preheat a griddle and brush lightly with melted butter. Gently twist the bag and hold it upright. Using scissors, snip off ¼ inch from a bottom corner. For each batch of pancakes, pipe 4-inch rounds of batter onto the griddle. Cook over moderate heat until bubbles appear on the surface of the pancakes, 2 to 3 minutes; flip and cook until risen and golden brown, 2 minutes longer. Transfer to plates and top with the berries, whipped cream and confectioners' sugar. —Justin Chapple

JAM-STUFFED BRIOCHE
FRENCH TOAST

Pancetta, Cheddar and Sauerkraut Johnnycakes

Active **1 hr**; Total **1 hr 45 min**; Makes **3 dozen**

- 1¼ cups whole milk
- 2 tsp. active dry yeast
- 2 Tbsp. unsalted butter, melted
- 1¼ cups all-purpose flour
- ¾ cup stone-ground cornmeal
- ½ tsp. kosher salt
- 5 oz. pancetta, sliced ¼ inch thick and cut into ¼-inch dice (1 cup)
- 5 oz. drained sauerkraut (1 cup) plus ¼ cup brine from the jar
- 5 oz. sharp white cheddar, cut into ¼-inch dice
- Canola oil, for frying
- Crème fraîche, for serving

1. In a medium saucepan, warm the milk and ⅔ cup of water over low heat until it registers 82° on an instant-read thermometer. Whisk in the yeast and let stand for 15 minutes.

2. Whisk the butter into the yeast mixture. In a medium bowl, whisk the flour with the cornmeal and salt. Gently whisk the dry ingredients into the saucepan just until combined. Cover and let stand in a warm place for 30 minutes.

3. Meanwhile, in a small nonstick skillet, cook the pancetta with ½ cup of water over moderate heat, stirring occasionally, until all the water has evaporated, 6 to 8 minutes. Continue to cook until the pancetta is golden brown, about 2 minutes longer. Pour off all the fat in the skillet. Stir in the sauerkraut and brine and remove from the heat. Let cool.

4. Add the cooled pancetta mixture and the cheese to the batter and gently mix in.

5. Preheat the oven to 300°. Set a rack over a baking sheet and place in the oven. In a large nonstick skillet, heat 1 tablespoon of oil. In batches of 6, ladle 2 tablespoons of johnnycake batter into the skillet and cook over moderate heat, turning once, until golden and cooked through, about 3 minutes. Transfer the cakes to the rack to keep warm in the oven. Repeat with more oil and the remaining batter to make 36 johnnycakes. Serve warm, topped with crème fraîche. —*Kevin Fink*

WINE Bold Grüner Veltliner: 2015 Bründlmayer Kamptal Terrassen.

Strawberry Crème Fraîche Biscuits

Active **35 min**; Total **1 hr 35 min**; Makes **12**

Atlanta baker Abigail Quinn laces her buttery biscuits with fresh strawberries and serves them with a tangy crème fraîche swirled with even more sweet strawberries.

STRAWBERRY SWIRL

- 1 cup diced strawberries (6 oz.)
- 2 Tbsp. sugar
- 2 tsp. fresh lemon juice

BISCUITS

- 2½ cups all-purpose flour
- 5 Tbsp. sugar
- 2½ tsp. baking powder
- ½ tsp. baking soda
- ¼ tsp. kosher salt
- 1 stick plus 2 Tbsp. cold unsalted butter, cut into ½-inch cubes
- ½ cup crème fraîche
- 1 large egg
- ¼ cup buttermilk
- ¼ tsp. pure vanilla extract
- 1 cup diced strawberries (6 oz.)

WHIPPED CRÈME FRAÎCHE

- ¾ cup crème fraîche
- ½ cup heavy cream
- 2 Tbsp. sugar
- ½ tsp. pure vanilla extract
- ⅛ tsp. kosher salt

1. Make the strawberry swirl In a small saucepan, cook the strawberries with the sugar and lemon juice over moderate heat until the berries break down and the juices thicken, about 12 minutes. Let cool completely.

2. Make the biscuits Preheat the oven to 350°. Line 2 rimmed baking sheets with parchment paper. In a medium bowl, whisk the flour with the sugar, baking powder, baking soda and salt. Using a pastry cutter or 2 knives, cut the butter into the dry ingredients until pea-size pieces form. In another medium bowl, whisk the crème fraîche with the egg, buttermilk and vanilla. Stir the crème fraîche mixture into the dry ingredients until a dough just comes together. Fold in the diced strawberries, being careful not to overmix.

3. Scoop twelve ¼-cup mounds of the biscuit dough onto the prepared baking sheets, about 3 inches apart. Bake the biscuits for about 30 minutes, until browned; shift the pans from top to bottom and front to back halfway through baking. Transfer the biscuits to a rack and let cool slightly.

4. Make the whipped crème fraîche In a large bowl, using a hand mixer, whip the crème fraîche with the cream, sugar, vanilla and salt at moderate speed until medium peaks form. Fold in the cooled strawberry swirl until just combined. Serve with the warm biscuits. —*Abigail Quinn*

MAKE AHEAD The strawberry swirl can be refrigerated for up to 3 days. Fold into the whipped crème fraîche before serving.

Jam-Stuffed Brioche French Toast

Total **45 min**; Serves **4**

- Four 1½-inch-thick slices of brioche
- ¼ cup strawberry jam, plus more for serving
- 3 large eggs
- ¼ cup heavy cream
- 1½ tsp. granulated sugar
- Fleur de sel
- 4 Tbsp. unsalted butter
- Confectioners' sugar
- Crème fraîche, for serving
- ½ lemon

1. Preheat the oven to 350°. Cut a 2-inch pocket in the side of each brioche slice; spoon 1 tablespoon of jam in each one.

2. In a shallow bowl, whisk the eggs with the cream, granulated sugar and ½ teaspoon of fleur de sel.

3. In a large skillet, melt 2 tablespoons of the butter. Dip 2 slices of the stuffed brioche in the egg mixture and soak until saturated. Add to the skillet and cook over moderate heat until nicely browned on both sides, 2 minutes. Transfer the French toast to a baking sheet. Repeat with the remaining butter, brioche and egg mixture.

4. Bake the French toast for about 5 minutes, until cooked through. Transfer to plates and sift confectioners' sugar on top. Dollop crème fraîche and strawberry jam on the French toast. Squeeze a little lemon juice over each slice and sprinkle with fleur de sel. Serve right away. —*Jessica Koslow*

DIY Babka

Master baker **MELISSA WELLER** has a cult following for her glazed modern take on babka at Sadelle's in New York City. Learn how she makes two varieties of the Jewish bakery classic—chocolate (below) and raisin-nut (p. 295)—and her special twisting technique.

Chocolate Babka

Active **1 hr 15 min**; Total **6 hr plus overnight resting**; Makes **two 9-inch babkas**

DOUGH

- **4 cups all-purpose flour, preferably King Arthur**
- **⅓ cup plus 2 Tbsp. sugar**
- **2 tsp. fine sea salt**
- **1 cup whole milk, warmed**
- **1 packet dry active yeast**
- **1 large egg plus 1 large egg yolk**
- **1 stick plus 2 Tbsp. unsalted butter, cut into tablespoons, at room temperature**

FILLING

- **9 oz. milk chocolate, finely chopped**
- **3 oz. bittersweet chocolate, finely chopped**
- **1½ sticks unsalted butter, cubed**
- **1½ cups finely ground chocolate wafer cookies**
- **3 Tbsp. honey**

GLAZE

- **12 oz. bittersweet chocolate, finely chopped**
- **4 oz. milk chocolate, finely chopped**
- **1½ sticks unsalted butter, cubed**
- **2 Tbsp. light corn syrup**

PREP THE DOUGH

1. In a bowl, whisk the flour, sugar and salt. In a stand mixer fitted with the dough hook, combine the milk with the yeast and let stand until foamy, 5 minutes. Add the egg and egg yolk and sprinkle the dry ingredients on top. Mix at low speed for 2 minutes. Scrape down the side of the bowl and mix at medium speed until all of the dry ingredients are incorporated and the dough is smooth, 5 minutes. Add all of the butter at once and mix at low speed until it is fully incorporated and a tacky dough forms, 3 minutes; scrape down the side of the bowl as needed during mixing. Cover the bowl with plastic wrap and let the dough stand at room temperature for 1 hour.

2. Line a large baking sheet with parchment paper and coat the paper generously with nonstick baking spray. Scrape the dough out onto the paper and cut the dough in half. Pat each piece into a square. Cover with plastic and refrigerate overnight.

FILL & ROLL

3. Make the filling In a heatproof bowl set over a saucepan of simmering water, melt both chocolates with the butter, stirring, until smooth. Let cool to room temperature, then stir in the crumbs and honey.

4. Coat two 9-by-4-inch loaf pans with nonstick baking spray and line with parchment paper, allowing 2 inches of overhang on each of the long sides.

5. Roll out each square of dough to a 16-inch square. Using an offset spatula, spread all but ½ cup of the filling in an even layer over the dough squares to within ½ inch of the edges. Starting at the edge nearest you, tightly roll up each square of dough jelly roll–style into a tight log.

TWIST, BAKE & GLAZE

6. Using a sharp knife, cut the logs in half crosswise. Using an offset spatula, spread ¼ cup of the reserved filling on the top and sides of 2 of the halves. Set the other halves on top in the opposite direction to form a cross. Twist to form spirals and transfer to the prepared pans. Cover the loaves with a towel and let stand in a warm place until doubled in bulk, about 2 hours.

7. Preheat the oven to 375°. Bake the loaves in the center of the oven for about 45 minutes, until puffed and well browned. Let cool slightly, then use the parchment paper to lift the babkas out of the pans and onto a rack set over a baking sheet. Discard the paper.

8. Make the glaze In a heatproof bowl set over a saucepan of simmering water, melt both chocolates with the butter; stir until smooth. Stir in the corn syrup. Spread the glaze on top of the warm babkas and let stand until set, about 30 minutes.

STEP-BY-STEP BABKA-TWISTING LESSON

ROLL UP THE DOUGH Beginning at the edge closest to you, tightly roll up the dough jelly roll–style into a tight log.

PREPARE THE TWIST Cut the log in half crosswise and spread filling on the outside of one half; crisscross the two halves.

TWIST THE LOGS Carefully twist the coated and uncoated logs together to create the dough spirals.

LET THE BABKA RISE Transfer the twist to a loaf pan lined with parchment. Cover with a towel and let rise until doubled in size.

To guarantee an ample swirl, baker Melissa Weller spreads the filling on the inside and outside of the dough before twisting.

MISO BANANA BREAD

Raisin-Walnut Babka

📷 PAGE 293

Active **1 hr 30 min**; Total **6 hr plus overnight resting**; Makes **two 9-inch babkas**

Light and buttery babkas are swirled with a golden raisin puree, studded with dark raisins and walnuts and topped with a cinnamon glaze. (For our babka-twisting tutorial, see p. 292.)

DOUGH

- **4 cups all-purpose flour, preferably King Arthur**
- **⅓ cup plus 2 Tbsp. sugar**
- **2 tsp. fine sea salt**
- **1 cup whole milk, warmed**
- **1 packet dry active yeast**
- **1 large egg plus 1 large egg yolk**
- **1 stick plus 2 Tbsp. unsalted butter, cut into tablespoons, at room temperature**

FILLING

- **3 cups golden raisins, soaked in warm water for 10 minutes and drained**
- **¾ cup granulated sugar**
- **6 Tbsp. unsalted butter, softened**
- **1 Tbsp. ground cinnamon**
- **1½ tsp. fine sea salt**
- **½ cup dark raisins, soaked in warm water for 10 minutes and drained**
- **¾ cup walnuts, toasted and coarsely chopped**

GLAZE

- **1 stick unsalted butter**
- **6 Tbsp. whole milk**
- **2 Tbsp. ground cinnamon**
- **¼ tsp. fine sea salt**
- **1½ cups confectioners' sugar**

1. Make the dough In a medium bowl, whisk the flour with the sugar and salt. In a stand mixer fitted with the dough hook, combine the milk with the yeast and let stand until foamy, about 5 minutes. Add the egg and egg yolk and sprinkle the dry ingredients on top. Mix at low speed for 2 minutes. Scrape down the side of the bowl and mix at medium speed until all of the dry ingredients are incorporated and the dough is smooth, about 5 minutes. Add all of the butter at once and mix at low speed until it is fully incorporated and a tacky dough forms, about 3 minutes; scrape down the side of the bowl as needed during mixing. Cover the bowl with plastic wrap and let the dough stand at room temperature for 1 hour.

2. Line a large baking sheet with parchment paper and coat the paper generously with nonstick baking spray. Scrape the dough out onto the parchment paper and cut the dough in half. Pat each piece into a neat square. Cover with plastic wrap and refrigerate overnight.

3. Make the filling In a food processor, combine all of the ingredients except the dark raisins and walnuts and puree until smooth.

4. Coat two 9-by-4-inch loaf pans with nonstick baking spray and line with parchment paper, allowing 2 inches of overhang on the long sides. Roll out each square of dough to a 16-inch square. Using an offset spatula, spread all but ½ cup of the raisin puree in an even layer over the dough squares to within ½ inch of the edges. Sprinkle the dough evenly with the dark raisins and walnuts. Starting at the edge nearest you, tightly roll up each dough square jelly roll–style into a tight log.

5. Using a sharp knife, cut the logs in half crosswise. Using an offset spatula, spread ¼ cup of the reserved filling on the top and sides of 2 of the halves. Set the other halves on top in the opposite direction to form a cross. Twist to form spirals and transfer to the prepared pans. Cover the loaves with a towel and let stand in a warm place until doubled in bulk, about 2 hours.

6. Preheat the oven to 375°. Bake the loaves in the center of the oven for about 45 minutes, until puffed and well browned. Let cool slightly, then use the parchment paper to lift the babkas out of the pans and onto a rack set over a large rimmed baking sheet. Discard the paper.

7. Make the glaze In a small saucepan, melt the butter in the milk. Whisk in the remaining ingredients. Spread the glaze on the warm babkas and let stand until set, about 30 minutes. —*Melissa Weller*

Miso Banana Bread

Active **30 min**; Total **2 hr plus cooling**
Makes **one 10-by-5-inch loaf**

Ken Oringer and Jamie Bissonnette of Little Donkey in Cambridge, Massachusetts, add miso to their supremely addictive banana bread to give it a more robust flavor. The bread is fantastic right after it cools, but it tastes even better the following day—if it lasts that long.

- **5 medium overripe bananas**
- **1¾ cups all-purpose flour**
- **1 tsp. baking soda**
- **½ tsp. baking powder**
- **¼ tsp. kosher salt**
- **1 stick unsalted butter, softened**
- **1 cup sugar**
- **¼ cup white miso**
- **½ cup buttermilk**
- **2 large eggs**

1. Preheat the oven to 350°. Butter and flour a 10-by-5-inch metal loaf pan. In a medium bowl, using a fork, mash 4 of the bananas until chunky. In another medium bowl, whisk the flour, baking soda, baking powder and salt.

2. Using a stand mixer fitted with the paddle, cream the butter, sugar and miso at medium speed until fluffy, about 5 minutes. At low speed, slowly add the buttermilk, then beat in the eggs 1 at a time until incorporated. Beat in the mashed bananas; the batter will look curdled. Add the dry ingredients and mix until just blended. Scrape into the prepared pan.

3. Slice the remaining banana lengthwise and arrange the halves on top of the batter side by side, cut side up. Bake for 90 minutes, until a toothpick inserted in the center comes out clean. Let the bread cool on a rack for 30 minutes before turning out to cool completely. —*Jamie Bissonnette and Ken Oringer*

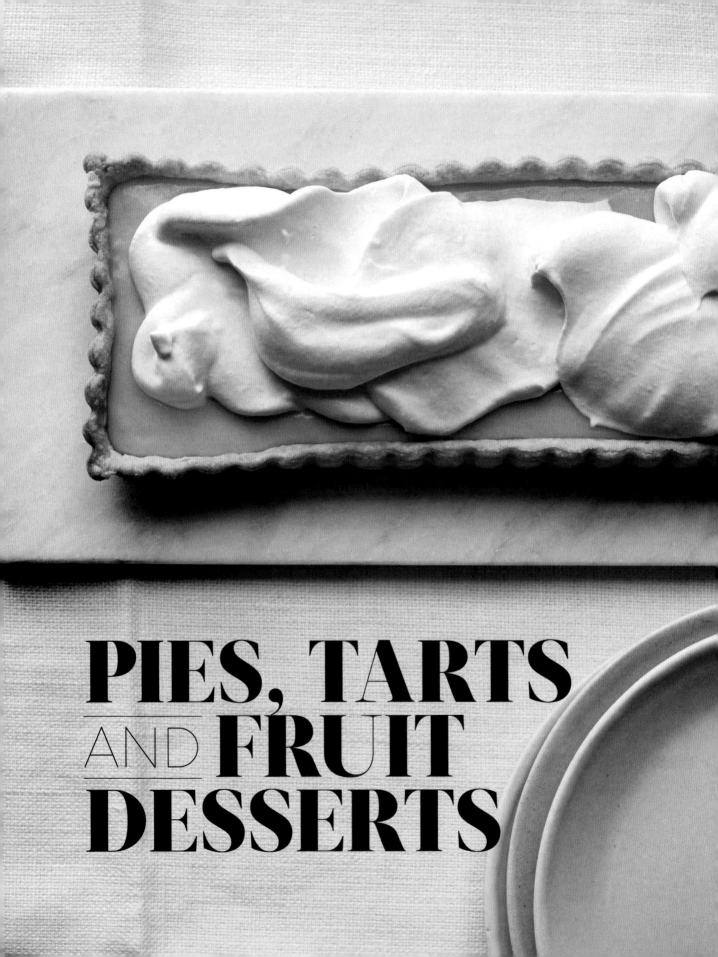

PIES, TARTS AND FRUIT DESSERTS

To upgrade day-old doughnuts, warm them on the grill and serve with tangy-sweet blueberry sauce (p. 313). OPPOSITE Tangerine Curd Tart (p. 305).

Pumpkin Cream Pie in a Chocolate Crust

Active **30 min;** Total **2 hr 15 min plus cooling;** Serves **8 to 10**

When she cooks for a crowd, author Melissa Clark sticks to sure things—a.k.a. recipes everyone is going to love. She dollops this silky pumpkin pie in a crispy chocolate cookie crust with a sweet-tangy crème fraîche topping.

CRUST

- **8** oz. chocolate wafer cookies (33 cookies)
- **1** stick unsalted butter, melted
- **2** Tbsp. granulated sugar

FILLING

- One 15-oz. can pure pumpkin puree
- **¾** cup heavy cream
- **½** cup packed light brown sugar
- **2** large eggs
- **1** Tbsp. bourbon, brandy or apple cider
- **1½** tsp. ground ginger
- **1½** tsp. ground cinnamon
- **1** tsp. finely grated peeled fresh ginger
- **½** tsp. fine sea salt
- **¼** tsp. freshly grated nutmeg
- **⅛** tsp. ground allspice

TOPPING

- **1** cup crème fraîche
- **½** cup heavy cream
- **2** Tbsp. confectioners' sugar
- Chocolate curls (see Note), for garnish

1. Make the crust In a food processor, pulse the cookies until finely ground. Transfer to a medium bowl and add the butter and granulated sugar. Mix until well combined, then press the crumbs into a 9-inch metal pie plate. Refrigerate for 30 minutes.

2. Preheat the oven to 350°. Bake the crust for 8 to 10 minutes, until set. Transfer to a rack and let cool.

3. Make the filling In a large bowl, whisk the pumpkin puree with all of the remaining ingredients until smooth. Scrape the filling into the piecrust and bake for 50 minutes to 1 hour, until the filling is set but slightly jiggly in the center. Transfer to a rack and let cool completely.

4. Make the topping In a medium bowl, using a hand mixer, beat the crème fraîche with the cream and confectioners' sugar until soft peaks form. Spoon the topping over the pie, garnish with chocolate curls and serve. —*Melissa Clark*

NOTE To make chocolate curls, use a vegetable peeler to shave them right off a large block of chocolate.

MAKE AHEAD The pie can be refrigerated overnight. Garnish with the chocolate curls before serving.

Blueberry-and-Nectarine Hand Pies

Active **45 min;** Total **3 hr;** Makes **8**

Atlanta baker Abigail Quinn is a hand-pie fanatic. "For me, pie is all about the crust," she says. With these beauties, you get a bite of crust in every bite of fruit. The pies are best once they've cooled a good bit but are still a little warm in the center.

DOUGH

- **3½** cups all-purpose flour
- **2** tsp. kosher salt
- **2** tsp. sugar, plus more for sprinkling
- **2** sticks unsalted butter, cut into ¼-inch cubes and chilled
- **½** cup plus 2 Tbsp. ice water

FILLING

- **2** ripe nectarines—peeled, pitted and sliced ¼ inch thick
- **1½** cups blueberries
- **⅔** cup sugar
- **1** Tbsp. fresh lemon juice
- **1** tsp. ground cinnamon
- **½** tsp. pure vanilla extract
- **¼** tsp. finely grated peeled fresh ginger
- Pinch of freshly grated nutmeg
- Pinch of kosher salt
- **2** Tbsp. cornstarch
- **1** large egg lightly beaten with 1 tsp. water, for brushing

1. Make the dough In a food processor, pulse the flour with the salt and 2 teaspoons of sugar. Add the butter and pulse until pea-size pieces form. Drizzle in the ice water as you pulse until the dough just comes together, about 1 minute. Turn the dough out onto a work surface and pat into a square about 1 inch thick. Wrap in plastic and refrigerate until firm, at least 1 hour or up to 2 days.

2. Make the filling In a medium bowl, toss the nectarines with the blueberries, sugar, lemon juice, cinnamon, vanilla, ginger, nutmeg and salt. Sift the cornstarch over the fruit and stir until coated, making sure no clumps of cornstarch remain.

3. Preheat the oven to 375°. Line 2 large baking sheets with parchment paper. Cut the chilled dough in half. Work with 1 piece at a time and keep the other half chilled. On a lightly floured work surface, roll out the dough ⅛ inch thick. Using a 4-inch round cookie cutter, stamp out 8 rounds and arrange on one of the baking sheets, 2 inches apart. Refrigerate the rounds. Roll out the remaining dough ⅛ inch thick. Using a 4½-inch round cookie cutter, stamp out 8 rounds; using a thin knife, cut three ½-inch slits in each round, then transfer to the second baking sheet.

4. Brush the edges of the 4-inch rounds with the egg wash. Using a slotted spoon, mound ⅓ cup of the fruit filling in the center of each round. Cover with the 4½-inch rounds and crimp and seal the edges with a fork. Brush the pies with egg wash and sprinkle with sugar. Bake the pies for 30 to 35 minutes, until bubbling and deeply golden brown; rotate the baking sheets from top to bottom and front to back halfway through baking. Let the pies cool on the baking sheets for 10 minutes, then transfer to a rack and let cool before serving. —*Abigail Quinn*

MAKE AHEAD The hand pies will keep in an airtight container overnight. Rewarm slightly in a 350° oven for 5 to 10 minutes before serving.

PUMPKIN CREAM PIE IN
A CHOCOLATE CRUST

BROWN BUTTER PECAN PIE
WITH ESPRESSO DATES

Pear-and-Cranberry Slab Pie

Active **50 min**; Total **3 hr plus cooling**
Serves **8 to 10**

Instead of making a traditional pie in a pie plate, F&W's Justin Chapple makes this free-form, fruit-filled, ginger-laced pie on a baking sheet.

2¾ cups all-purpose flour

½ cup plus 1 Tbsp. granulated sugar
Kosher salt

2 sticks unsalted butter, cubed and chilled

½ cup ice water

4 firm Bartlett or Anjou pears—peeled, cored and cut into ¾-inch wedges

1½ cups frozen cranberries

1 tsp. ground ginger

1 large egg beaten with 1 Tbsp. water
Turbinado sugar, for sprinkling

1. In a food processor, combine 2½ cups of the flour with 1 tablespoon of the granulated sugar and 1 teaspoon of kosher salt and pulse to mix. Add the butter and pulse in 1-second bursts until the mixture resembles coarse meal. Drizzle the ice water over the mixture and pulse in 1-second bursts until the dough just comes together. Turn the dough out onto a work surface, gather any crumbs and pat into 2 squares. Wrap the squares in plastic and refrigerate until chilled, about 45 minutes.

2. Preheat the oven to 400°. On a floured work surface, roll out 1 piece of the dough to a 12-inch square. Slide the dough onto a large sheet of parchment paper, then slide onto a large baking sheet. Repeat with the second piece of dough. Refrigerate for 15 minutes.

3. Slide 1 square of dough onto a work surface. In a large bowl, toss the pears with the cranberries, ginger, ½ teaspoon of salt and the remaining ½ cup of granulated sugar and ¼ cup of flour. Spread the fruit on the dough square on the baking sheet, leaving a 1-inch border. Ease the other square of dough on top of the fruit. Fold over the edge and crimp decoratively all around to seal. Brush the pie with the egg wash and sprinkle with turbinado sugar. Cut 16 small slits in the top and freeze for 15 minutes.

4. Bake the pie for about 50 minutes, until golden and the pears are tender; rotate halfway through baking. Let cool. Cut the pie into squares and serve.
—*Justin Chapple*

SERVE WITH Vanilla ice cream.

MAKE AHEAD The slab pie can be stored at room temperature for up to 2 days.

Brown Butter Pecan Pie with Espresso Dates

Active **1 hr**; Total **5 hr 15 min plus cooling**
Makes **one 9-inch pie**

This not-too-sweet pecan pie is a terrific alternative to the often syrup-laden classic. The filling is swirled with toasty brown butter and studded with rich and chewy dates cooked in pleasantly bitter espresso. The recipe was adapted from the *Soframiz* cookbook by Maura Kilpatrick and Ana Sortun of Sofra bakery in Boston.

PIECRUST

1¼ cups all-purpose flour

1½ tsp. sugar

½ tsp. kosher salt

1 stick unsalted butter, cubed and frozen
Ice water

FILLING

2 cups pecan halves (7 oz.)

½ lb. Medjool dates, pitted and chopped (1 cup)

3 Tbsp. brewed espresso or strong coffee

1 stick unsalted butter

1 cup packed light brown sugar

1 cup Lyle's Golden Syrup or light corn syrup

1½ tsp. instant espresso powder

1½ tsp. kosher salt

3 large eggs
Whipped cream, for serving

1. Make the piecrust In a food processor, pulse the flour with the sugar and salt. Add the butter and pulse until it is the size of small peas. Add ¼ cup of ice water and pulse until the dough is evenly moistened. Gradually add more water if needed. Turn out the dough onto a work surface and knead it 2 or 3 times, just until it comes together. Form into a disk, wrap in plastic and refrigerate until firm, about 1 hour.

2. On a lightly floured work surface, roll out the dough to a 12-inch round; transfer to a 9-inch pie plate. Fold the edge of the dough under itself and crimp the edge. Freeze the piecrust for at least 2 hours or overnight.

3. Preheat the oven to 375°. Line the piecrust with parchment paper and fill with pie weights or dried beans. Bake for about 25 minutes, or until lightly browned around the edge. Remove the paper and weights and bake until the bottom is lightly browned, about 10 minutes. Let cool completely.

4. Meanwhile, make the filling Reduce the oven temperature to 350°. Spread the pecans on a rimmed baking sheet and toast until fragrant, 8 to 10 minutes. Let cool completely.

5. In a small skillet, cook the dates in the brewed espresso over moderate heat, stirring, until very soft, 3 to 5 minutes. Scrape the mixture into a small bowl and wipe out the skillet.

6. Add the butter to the skillet and cook over moderate heat, swirling, until the milk solids turn a deep golden brown, about 5 minutes. Let cool slightly.

7. In a large bowl, whisk the brown sugar with the golden syrup, espresso powder and salt. Whisk in the eggs, then gradually whisk in the brown butter until the filling is smooth.

8. Set the pie plate on a rimmed baking sheet. Spread the espresso dates in the crust and scatter the pecans on top. Pour the filling over the pecans. Bake for about 1 hour and 15 minutes, or until the filling is set around the edge and slightly jiggly in the center. Transfer the pie to a rack and let cool completely. Serve with whipped cream. —*Maura Kilpatrick and Ana Sortun*

MAKE AHEAD The pecan pie can be covered and kept at room temperature for up to 3 days. The unbaked piecrust can be wrapped in plastic and frozen for 1 month.

WHISKEY Spice- and toffee-scented small-batch bourbon: Smooth Ambler Old Scout Straight Bourbon Whiskey.

DIY Lemon Meringue Pie

People wait in line for hours to try the mile-high lemon meringue pie at **REVIVAL** in Minneapolis. Here, the chefs reveal the secret to their exceptionally silky custard: homemade sweetened condensed milk.

Lemon Meringue Pie

Active **1 hr;** Total **4 hr plus chilling**
Makes **one 9-inch pie**

SWEETENED CONDENSED MILK

- **2 cups whole milk**
- **⅔ cup granulated sugar**
- **½ tsp. pure vanilla extract**

GRAHAM CRACKER CRUST

- **9 graham crackers**
- **¼ cup lightly packed light brown sugar**
- **6 Tbsp. unsalted butter, melted**

LEMON CUSTARD

- **8 large egg yolks**
- **¼ cup cornstarch**
- **2 tsp. finely grated lemon zest plus 1 cup fresh lemon juice**
- **4 Tbsp. unsalted butter**

MERINGUE

- **1 cup granulated sugar**
- **4 large egg whites**
- **¼ tsp. cream of tartar**

MAKE THE CONDENSED MILK

1. In a small saucepan, combine the milk and sugar and bring to a simmer, whisking constantly, until the sugar dissolves. Cook over very low heat (the mixture should not bubble), stirring occasionally, until thickened and reduced to 1¼ cups, 2½ hours. Stir in the vanilla and scrape the sweetened condensed milk into a medium bowl.

MAKE THE CRUST

2. Meanwhile, in a food processor, pulse the graham crackers with the brown sugar until fine crumbs form. Add the butter and pulse until incorporated. Press the crumbs evenly over the bottom and up the side of a glass pie plate to form a ½-inch-thick crust; use the bottom of a measuring cup to help form an even layer of crumbs. Refrigerate the crust for at least 45 minutes.

3. Preheat the oven to 350°. Bake the crust for about 12 minutes, until fragrant and browned. Transfer to a rack and let cool completely.

MAKE THE LEMON CUSTARD

4. In a medium bowl, beat the egg yolks. In a medium saucepan, whisk the sweetened condensed milk with the cornstarch until well blended. Add the lemon zest and lemon juice and bring to a simmer. Cook over moderately low heat, whisking, until thickened, 1 to 2 minutes. While whisking constantly, drizzle half of the milk mixture into the egg yolks. Add the egg yolk mixture to the saucepan and cook over moderately low heat, whisking, until very thick, about 3 minutes. Whisk in the butter. Pour the custard into the crust and let it cool to room temperature.

MAKE THE MERINGUE

5. Preheat the oven to 325°. In a saucepan, combine the sugar and ¼ cup of water and bring to a boil. Cook over moderate heat until the syrup reaches 243° on a candy thermometer, 8 to 10 minutes.

6. Meanwhile, in the bowl of a stand mixer fitted with the whisk, beat the egg whites with the cream of tartar at medium speed until soft peaks form. With the machine on, drizzle in the hot syrup and beat the meringue at medium-high speed until stiff and glossy, about 10 minutes. Scoop the meringue onto the pie, spreading and swirling it decoratively; make sure the meringue covers the filling completely and touches the crust all around.

7. Bake the pie on the middle rack of the oven for 10 minutes. Turn on the broiler; broil the meringue 6 inches from the heat until golden brown in spots, about 3 minutes (or use a blowtorch). Transfer the pie to a rack to cool completely. Refrigerate until chilled, 3 hours. —*Thomas Boemer and Tess Bouska*

STEP-BY-STEP MERINGUE PIE LESSON

MAKE THE SWEETENED CONDENSED MILK Cook milk with sugar and vanilla until thickened.

MAKE THE CRUST In a pie plate, press the graham cracker crumbs into an even layer.

FILL THE PIE Cook the thickened milk with egg yolks, lemon and cornstarch, then pour the custard into the baked crust.

ADD THE MERINGUE Cover the filling with billowy Italian meringue, make pretty swirls, then torch or broil the top.

This billowy Italian
meringue is more
stable than the
simple egg-white-
and-sugar kind, and
much less likely
to weep (dissolve)
or slide off.

APPLE-GINGER
CROSTATA

Tangerine Curd Tart

📷 PAGE 296

Active **1 hr 30 min**; Total **3 hr 30 min plus cooling and chilling**; Serves **8**

This beautiful sunny-yellow tart delivers the perfect balance of tangy and sweet. Any fresh citrus will work in the creamy filling.

TART SHELL

1½ **cups all-purpose flour**
½ **tsp. granulated sugar**
½ **tsp. kosher salt**
1 **stick unsalted butter, cubed and chilled**
¼ **cup ice water**

TANGERINE CURD

2 **tsp. finely grated tangerine zest plus 1 cup freshly squeezed tangerine juice (not bottled)**
5 **Tbsp. fresh lemon juice**
1 **cup granulated sugar**
12 **large egg yolks**
Pinch of kosher salt
1½ **sticks unsalted butter, cubed and at room temperature**

WHIPPED CREAM

1 **cup heavy cream**
2 **tsp. confectioners' sugar**

1. Make the tart shell In a small bowl, whisk the flour, sugar and salt. Add the butter and, using your fingertips, blend it in until pea-size pieces remain. Stir in the ice water until the dough comes together; add another tablespoon if the dough seems too dry. Turn the dough out onto a lightly floured surface and pat into a 1-inch-thick disk. Wrap in plastic; refrigerate for 1 hour.

2. On a lightly floured work surface, roll out the dough to an 8-by-18-inch rectangle, about ⅛ inch thick. Fit the dough into a 13-by-4-inch fluted tart pan with a removable bottom. Trim the overhang. Cover with plastic wrap and freeze for 30 minutes.

3. Preheat the oven to 400°. Line the tart shell with parchment paper and fill with pie weights. Bake for 40 minutes, until set. Remove the paper and pie weights and bake for 10 minutes, until cooked through. Transfer to a rack and let cool completely.

4. Make the tangerine curd In a medium saucepan, whisk the tangerine zest with the citrus juices, sugar, egg yolks and salt. Cook over moderately low heat, stirring often with a spatula, until the curd is very thick but pourable, about 30 minutes. Strain through a fine sieve into a medium bowl and whisk in the butter. Scrape the curd into the tart shell and press a sheet of plastic wrap directly onto the surface. Refrigerate until set and chilled, 3 hours.

5. Make the whipped cream In a medium bowl, beat the cream with the confectioners' sugar until medium peaks form. Dollop on top of the tart and serve. —*Kay Chun*

MAKE AHEAD The tart (without the whipped cream) can be refrigerated for up to 2 days.

Mixed-Fruit Cornmeal Cobbler

Active **45 min**; Total **2 hr 30 min**; Serves **8**

The cornmeal-biscuit dough that tops this cobbler is light and not too sweet. Cut the biscuits in any size rounds, or in fanciful shapes if you prefer.

CORNMEAL BISCUITS

1¾ **cups all-purpose flour**
¼ **cup corn flour**
¼ **cup fine cornmeal**
¼ **cup granulated sugar**
2 **tsp. finely grated lemon zest**
1½ **tsp. baking powder**
⅛ **tsp. baking soda**
1 **tsp. kosher salt**
1 **stick cold unsalted butter, cubed**
½ **cup plus 2 Tbsp. buttermilk**

COBBLER

½ **cup honey**
½ **cup light brown sugar**
¼ **cup fresh lemon juice**
1 **Tbsp. ground cinnamon**
½ **tsp. kosher salt**
⅓ **cup cornstarch mixed with ¼ cup water**
8 **cups raspberries, pitted cherries and sliced plums**
Heavy cream, for brushing
2 **Tbsp. turbinado sugar**
Lemon thyme sprigs
Whipped cream, for serving

1. Make the biscuits In a food processor, combine the all-purpose flour, corn flour, cornmeal, sugar, lemon zest, baking powder, baking soda and salt; pulse to blend. Add the butter and pulse until the mixture resembles coarse meal. With the machine on, drizzle in the buttermilk. Turn the dough out onto a work surface and knead just until it comes together. Pat into a 1-inch-thick disk, wrap in plastic and refrigerate until firm, at least 1 hour.

2. Preheat the oven to 350°. Butter a 3-quart baking dish. On a lightly floured work surface, roll out the dough ½ inch thick. Using a 2-inch biscuit cutter, stamp out rounds, rerolling the scraps.

3. Make the cobbler In a large bowl, mix the honey, brown sugar, lemon juice, cinnamon and salt. Stir and add the cornstarch mixture, then add the fruit and toss gently. Spread the fruit in the dish and top with the biscuits. Brush the biscuits with cream and sprinkle with the turbinado sugar. Bake until the fruit is bubbling and the biscuits are golden, about 45 minutes. Garnish with lemon thyme and serve warm, with whipped cream. —*Megan Garrelts*

Apple-Ginger Crostata

Active **20 min**; Total **1 hr**; Serves **8**

One 14- to 16-oz. sheet of puff pastry, thawed if frozen
2 **red apples, such as Honeycrisp or Pink Lady, thinly sliced crosswise and seeded**
3 **Tbsp. sugar**
2 **Tbsp. fresh lemon juice**
2 **tsp. finely grated peeled fresh ginger**
Pinch of kosher salt
3 **Tbsp. apricot preserves mixed with 1 tsp. water**

1. Preheat the oven to 375°. Line a large baking sheet with parchment paper.

2. Unfold the sheet of puff pastry on the prepared baking sheet. In a large bowl, toss the apple slices with the sugar, lemon juice, ginger and salt until well coated. Arrange the slices in slightly overlapping rows on the pastry, leaving a ½-inch border all around.

3. Bake in the center of the oven for about 30 minutes, until the pastry is puffed and golden. Immediately brush the crostata with the apricot preserves. Serve warm. —*Justin Chapple*

Plum-Cherry Crostata

Active **45 min;** Total **3 hr;** Serves **6**

PASTRY

2 **cups (10 oz.) all-purpose flour**

4 **tsp. sugar**

1 **tsp. kosher salt**

1 **stick plus 2 Tbsp. unsalted butter, cubed and chilled**

¾ **cup cold buttermilk**

1 **tsp. distilled white vinegar**

FILLING

1 **lb. black plums—halved, pitted and cut into ⅓-inch wedges**

3 **Tbsp. sugar, plus more for sprinkling**

1½ **Tbsp. cornstarch**

½ **tsp. finely grated lemon zest**

¼ **cup cherry jam**

2 **Tbsp. finely chopped Luxardo cherries (see Note), optional**

Heavy cream, for brushing

Lightly sweetened whipped cream or vanilla ice cream, for serving

1. Make the pastry In a large bowl, whisk the flour with the sugar and salt. Using your fingertips, blend in the butter until pea-size pieces form. Add the buttermilk and vinegar and mix with a wooden spoon until a dough forms. Pat the dough into a 1-inch-thick disk, wrap in plastic and refrigerate for 30 minutes.

2. On a sheet of lightly floured parchment paper, using a lightly floured rolling pin, roll out the pastry dough to a 14-inch round that's ⅛ inch thick. Transfer to a baking sheet and freeze for 15 minutes.

3. Make the filling In a large bowl, combine the plums with the 3 tablespoons of sugar, the cornstarch and lemon zest and toss to coat.

4. Preheat the oven to 425°. Spread the cherry jam in an 8-inch square in the center of the dough round, leaving about 3 inches around. Scatter the Luxardo cherries, if using, on top. Layer the plums, slightly overlapping, over the jam. Fold the rim of dough over the filling, leaving the center exposed and tucking in the corners to create a square crostata. Brush the dough with cream; sprinkle with sugar. Bake for 15 minutes, then lower the oven temperature to 375° and bake for about 30 minutes

longer, until the pastry is deep golden and the filling is bubbling and slightly runny. Transfer to a rack to let cool until warm. Serve with whipped cream or ice cream.
—*Tiffany MacIsaac*

NOTE Unlike cloyingly sweet, electric-red maraschinos, Luxardo cherries are dark brown and tart, and they have a deep cherry flavor. They're available at specialty food shops and from amazon.com.

MAKE AHEAD The crostata can be wrapped in foil and kept at room temperature overnight.

Peach Hand Pies

Active **1 hr;** Total **4 hr;** Makes **16**

These adorable individual pies are a fun alternative to a traditional pie. Freeze them up to a month in advance and pop in the oven for an impressive last-minute dessert.

FILLING

3 **small peaches (about 12 oz.)**

¼ **cup granulated sugar**

¼ **cup light brown sugar**

1 **tsp. finely grated lemon zest plus 1 Tbsp. fresh lemon juice**

¼ **tsp. kosher salt**

¼ **tsp. ground cinnamon**

½ **vanilla bean, split lengthwise and seeds scraped, pod reserved for another use**

DOUGH

2½ **cups all-purpose flour**

1 **tsp. kosher salt**

2 **sticks cold unsalted butter, cubed**

½ **cup ice water**

1 **large egg, lightly beaten**

Turbinado sugar, for sprinkling

1. Make the filling Bring a medium saucepan of water to a boil. Fill a bowl with ice water. Using a sharp paring knife, mark an X on the bottom of each peach. Add the peaches to the saucepan and blanch until the skins start to peel away, 1 to 2 minutes. Transfer to the ice bath and let cool completely. Peel, halve and pit the peaches and cut them into ¼-inch pieces; you should have about 2 cups. Wipe out the saucepan.

2. In the same saucepan, combine the peaches with all the remaining ingredients and bring to a boil. Cook over moderate heat, stirring occasionally, until thickened and syrupy, about 12 minutes. Scrape the filling into a small bowl; let cool to room temperature. Cover and refrigerate until cold, 2 hours.

3. Meanwhile, make the dough In a large bowl, whisk the flour with the salt. Scatter the butter over the flour and pinch it in with your fingers until the mixture resembles very coarse crumbs, with some pieces the size of small peas. Stir in the ice water just until a dough forms. Turn the dough out onto a lightly floured work surface and knead gently to form a ball. Pat into a 1-inch-thick round, wrap in plastic and refrigerate for 1 hour.

4. Preheat the oven to 450° and line a baking sheet with parchment paper. Cut the dough in half. On a lightly floured work surface, using a lightly floured rolling pin, roll out 1 piece of dough ⅛ inch thick. Using a 4-inch biscuit cutter, stamp out 6 rounds and transfer to the prepared baking sheet. Gather the scraps and form into a ball; roll out again and stamp out 2 more rounds. Transfer to the baking sheet. Top with a layer of parchment paper. Repeat with the second piece of dough, placing the 8 rounds on the parchment. Refrigerate for 30 minutes.

5. Line 2 baking sheets with parchment paper. Working with 1 dough round at a time, brush the rim with the beaten egg. Spoon 2 teaspoons of the filling into the center and fold the round in half to enclose. Press the edge firmly to seal and transfer to a prepared baking sheet. Repeat with the remaining dough and filling, arranging the hand pies 2 inches apart on the sheets. Brush the tops with the remaining beaten egg and sprinkle with turbinado sugar. Using a paring knife, cut 2 small slits in each pie. Bake the pies until puffed and golden brown, shifting the pans from top to bottom and back to front halfway through baking, 18 minutes. Transfer the hand pies to a rack and let cool slightly.
—*Lisa Donovan*

MAKE AHEAD The unbaked hand pies can be frozen for up to 1 month. Brush with the egg wash, sprinkle with sugar and bake from frozen according to the recipe.

Happy Marriage Rhubarb Jam Tart with Whipped Skyr

Active **45 min**; Total **2 hr 15 min**; Serves **8**

Called Happy Marriage cake in Iceland, this tart-like dessert is made with a rolled oat dough that doubles as both the tart shell and the crumb topping. It's accompanied by whipped skyr, Iceland's creamy yogurt. Any leftover rhubarb jam is great spread on toast.

RHUBARB JAM

- **1 lb. rhubarb, cut into 2-inch pieces**
- **1 cup granulated sugar**
- **1 cup elderflower syrup (see Note)**
- **2 to 3 Tbsp. fresh lemon juice**

TART

- **1½ sticks unsalted butter, cubed, plus more for greasing**
- **2¼ cups old-fashioned rolled oats**
- **¾ cup barley flour**
- **¾ cup barley flakes**
- **1 cup packed dark brown sugar**
- **1 tsp. baking powder**
- **¼ tsp. kosher salt**
- **½ tsp. thyme leaves**

TOPPING

- **1¼ cups skyr (Icelandic yogurt) or Greek yogurt**
- **¼ cup granulated sugar**
- **½ tsp. finely grated lemon zest**
- **1 tsp. rosewater (optional)**
- **1 cup heavy cream**

1. Make the rhubarb jam In a medium saucepan, combine the rhubarb, granulated sugar and elderflower syrup and bring to a simmer. Cook over moderately low heat, stirring occasionally, until thick, 50 minutes to 1 hour. Scrape the jam into a heatproof bowl; let cool to room temperature. Stir in the lemon juice.

2. Make the tart Preheat the oven to 350°. Butter a 10-inch fluted tart pan with a removable bottom. In a large bowl, whisk the oats with the barley flour, barley flakes, brown sugar, baking powder, salt and thyme. Using your fingers, blend the cubed butter into the oat mixture; blend in 1 tablespoon of water until well incorporated. Firmly press two-thirds of the mixture evenly over the bottom and up the side of the tart pan.

3. Spread 1½ cups of the rhubarb jam in the tart shell; reserve the remaining jam for another use. Pinch the remaining dough into large crumbs and scatter over the jam. Bake the tart for about 40 minutes, until the topping is deep golden. Transfer to a rack to cool completely.

4. Meanwhile, make the topping In a bowl, whisk the skyr with the granulated sugar, lemon zest and rosewater, if using. In another bowl, beat the heavy cream to stiff peaks. Fold the whipped cream into the skyr. Serve the tart with the whipped skyr. —*Victoria Elíasdóttir*

NOTE Elderflower syrup is available at many specialty food stores and from kalustyans.com. Alternatively, substitute St-Germain elderflower liqueur.

MAKE AHEAD The jam can be refrigerated overnight; bring to room temperature before using. The baked tart can be kept covered at room temperature overnight.

Hazelnut-Rosemary Caramel Tart

Active **1 hr**; Total **4 hr**
Makes **one 10-inch tart**

PASTRY

- **1 cup plus 2 Tbsp. all-purpose flour**
- **¼ cup confectioners' sugar**
- **¾ tsp. baking powder**
- **½ tsp. fine sea salt**
- **1½ sticks cold unsalted butter, cubed**
- **2 large egg yolks**
-     **Ice water**

FILLING

- **1½ sticks unsalted butter**
- **1 Tbsp. chopped rosemary**
- **1½ cups hazelnuts**
- **3 large eggs**
- **3 large egg yolks**
- **1 cup packed light brown sugar**
- **¾ cup brown rice syrup**
- **¼ cup honey**
- **1 tsp. fine sea salt**
- **2 Tbsp. heavy cream**
- **1 Tbsp. all-purpose flour**
- **1 tsp. pure vanilla extract**
-     **Flaky sea salt, for sprinkling**
-     **Whipped crème fraîche, for serving**

1. Make the pastry In a food processor, pulse the flour with the confectioners' sugar, baking powder and fine sea salt. Add the butter and pulse until the mixture resembles coarse meal. Add the egg yolks and 1 tablespoon of ice water and pulse until the pastry just comes together; add another tablespoon of ice water if it seems dry. Turn the pastry out onto a work surface and pat into a disk. Wrap in plastic and refrigerate until chilled, 1 hour.

2. On a floured work surface, roll out the pastry to a 12-inch round. Ease the round into a 10-inch fluted tart pan with a removable bottom, pressing it into the corners and up the side, patching any tears. Trim off any overhang. Freeze the tart shell for 30 minutes.

3. Preheat the oven to 375°. Line the tart shell with parchment paper and fill it with pie weights or dried beans. Bake in the center of the oven for 20 minutes. Remove the parchment and weights. Bake the shell for 10 to 15 minutes longer, until lightly browned. Let cool completely. Leave the oven on.

4. Meanwhile, make the filling In a small saucepan, melt the butter over moderate heat. Remove from the heat, add the rosemary and let steep for 20 minutes. Strain the butter into a small bowl and let cool.

5. Spread the hazelnuts on a rimmed baking sheet and toast in the oven until fragrant and golden and the skins are splitting, about 12 minutes. Let cool slightly, then transfer to a kitchen towel and rub together to remove the skins; let cool. Coarsely chop the hazelnuts and spread them in the cooled tart shell. Put the tart shell on a rimmed baking sheet. Reduce the oven temperature to 300°.

6. In a large bowl, beat the whole eggs and yolks with the brown sugar, brown rice syrup, honey and fine sea salt. Gradually whisk in the rosemary butter, then whisk in the cream, flour and vanilla. Pour the filling into the tart shell and sprinkle flaky sea salt on top. Bake the tart for 50 minutes, until the filling is set at the edge but slightly jiggly in the center. Let cool completely. Serve at room temperature or slightly chilled, with a dollop of whipped crème fraîche. —*Jessica Koslow*

MAKE AHEAD The tart can be refrigerated for up to 3 days.

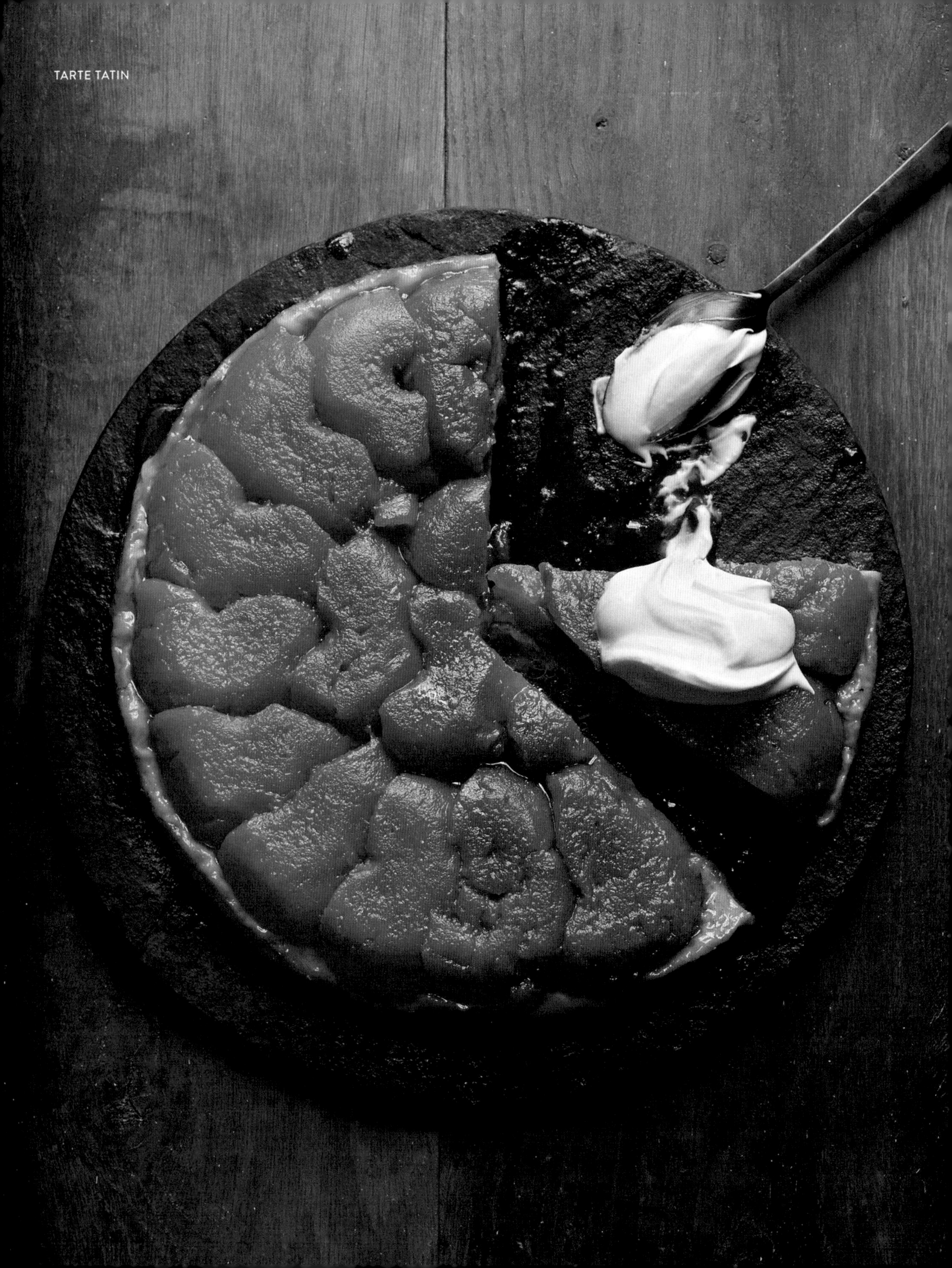

Plum Tartlets with Plum Cream

Active **1 hr**; Total **4 hr 30 min**; Makes **18**

What makes these plum-puree tartlets so good is the whipped cream topping that's infused with the plum pits. Note: You'll need eighteen 1-ounce tartlet molds to make this recipe.

PASTRY

- **1 stick salted butter, at room temperature**
- **¼ cup sugar**
- **1 cup plus 2 Tbsp. whole-wheat flour, sifted**
- **½ cup plus 2 Tbsp. almond flour**
- **⅛ tsp. pure almond extract**
- **1 large egg, beaten**

PLUM TOPPINGS

- **1½ lbs. red plums, chopped, pits crushed**
- **¼ cup sugar**
- **1 Tbsp. fresh lemon juice**
- **1½ cups heavy cream**

1. Make the pastry In a large bowl, using a hand mixer, beat the butter with the sugar at medium speed until fluffy. Fold in both flours, the almond extract and half of the beaten egg; reserve the rest of the egg for another use. Cover the bowl with plastic wrap and refrigerate for 30 minutes.

2. Preheat the oven to 350°. Divide the pastry into 18 equal pieces. Press each piece evenly into the bottom and up the side of a 1-ounce tartlet mold (our molds were 4-by-1¾-by-⅓ inches). Bake for 18 to 20 minutes, until the pastry is golden and set. Transfer to a rack to cool completely. Remove the tartlet shells from the molds.

3. Meanwhile, make the plum toppings In a medium saucepan, combine two-thirds of the chopped plums with the sugar and 2 tablespoons of water; bring to a boil. Simmer over moderately low heat, stirring occasionally, until very thick, about 30 minutes. Stir in the lemon juice and cook until slightly reduced, 5 minutes. Transfer to a blender and puree until smooth. Scrape the puree into a bowl and let cool; cover and refrigerate until firm and cold.

4. In a small saucepan, combine the heavy cream with the remaining plums and all of the crushed plum pits. Bring just to

a simmer and cook over low heat until the plum cream is reduced to 1¼ cups, about 30 minutes. Strain the plum cream into a medium bowl and let cool to room temperature, about 30 minutes. Cover and refrigerate until chilled, 1 hour.

5. Beat the plum cream to soft peaks. Spoon about 1 tablespoon of the plum puree into each tartlet. Top with a dollop of the plum cream and serve. —*Petter Nilsson*

Pain Perdu with Roasted Plums

Active **35 min**; Total **1 hr 15 min**; Serves **4**

Los Angeles pastry chef Karen Hatfield sprinkles her egg-soaked bread with cinnamon sugar before cooking it, creating a delicious crispy crust. She tops the French toast with vanilla-roasted plums and whipped crème fraîche for the ultimate dessert or breakfast.

- **¾ cup plus 2 Tbsp. sugar**
- **4 medium red plums, halved and pitted**
- **½ vanilla bean, split lengthwise, seeds scraped**
- **½ tsp. ground cinnamon**
- **2 cups heavy cream**
- **2 large eggs**
- **Four 1-inch-thick slices of challah or brioche**
- **3 Tbsp. unsalted butter**
- **Confectioners' sugar and whipped crème fraîche, for serving**

1. In a small saucepan, combine ¾ cup of the sugar and ¾ cup of water and bring to a boil over moderately high heat, stirring occasionally, until the sugar is dissolved, about 3 minutes. Remove the simple syrup from the heat; let cool slightly.

2. Preheat the oven to 350°. In an 8-inch-square baking dish, toss the halved plums with ½ cup of the simple syrup and the vanilla bean and seeds. Let the plums stand for 20 minutes.

3. Bake the plums for 20 to 25 minutes, turning once, until softened. Let the plums cool slightly in the syrup, then discard the vanilla bean. Cut each plum half into 4 wedges.

4. In a small bowl, whisk the remaining 2 tablespoons of sugar with the cinnamon.

5. In a shallow glass pie plate, whisk the remaining ½ cup of simple syrup with

the heavy cream and eggs. Add the bread slices 1 at a time and soak until evenly moistened but not soggy, 2 to 3 minutes per side; transfer the slices to a plate while you soak the remaining bread.

6. In a large skillet, melt the butter over moderately low heat. Sprinkle half of the cinnamon sugar on one side of each bread slice and cook sugared side down until the bread is browned, about 5 minutes. Sprinkle with the remaining cinnamon sugar, then flip and cook until browned on the other side, about 5 minutes more. Transfer the French toast to plates and dust with confectioners' sugar. Serve with the plums and their syrup and whipped crème fraîche. —*Karen Hatfield*

MAKE AHEAD The roasted plums can be refrigerated in their syrup for up to 3 days. Reheat gently before serving.

Tarte Tatin

Active **45 min**; Total **2 hr 15 min**; Serves **8**

- **One 14-oz. package all-butter puff pastry**
- **1 stick unsalted butter**
- **¾ cup sugar**
- **12 Golden Delicious apples—peeled, halved lengthwise and cored**
- **Crème fraîche, for serving**

1. On a lightly floured work surface, roll out the puff pastry ⅛ inch thick. Cut out a 12-inch round, transfer to a baking sheet and refrigerate; reserve the pastry scraps for another use.

2. In a 10-inch cast-iron skillet, melt the butter. Add the sugar and cook over moderately low heat, stirring occasionally, until the sugar is dissolved and the mixture comes to a simmer, about 2 minutes. Remove from the heat. Arrange the apple halves standing upright in the skillet in 2 snug concentric circles. Return to the heat and cook undisturbed until an amber caramel forms, about 30 minutes.

3. Preheat the oven to 375°. Top the apples with the puff pastry and bake for about 40 minutes, until the pastry is golden and the apples are tender. Let cool for 15 minutes.

4. Place a large plate on top of the skillet and carefully invert the tart. Serve warm, with crème fraîche. —*Jonathan Waxman*

Ultimate Pandowdy

Pie-obsessed residents of Kansas City, Missouri, flock to **MEGAN GARRELTS**'s Bluestem and Rye. At home, however, Garrelts favors simpler desserts like this pandowdy. It's easier to make and an even better showcase for the juiciest farm-stand finds.

Blueberry-Nectarine Pandowdy

Active **45 min**; Total **3 hr**; Serves **8**

Nectarines are Garrelts's favorite summer fruit. Here she tosses slices with blueberries, sweet spices and ginger and tops them with a lemon-lime sugar cookie dough.

SUGAR COOKIE DOUGH

- ¾ cup all-purpose flour
- ¼ tsp. baking powder
- ¼ tsp. kosher salt
- 4½ Tbsp. unsalted butter, softened
- ½ cup sugar
- ¼ tsp. pure vanilla extract
- 1½ tsp. finely grated lemon zest plus 1½ tsp. fresh lemon juice
- 1½ tsp. finely grated lime zest plus 1½ tsp. fresh lime juice
- 2 Tbsp. beaten egg (½ large egg)

PANDOWDY

- Unsalted butter, for greasing
- ½ cup sugar
- ½ tsp. ground cinnamon

- 4 cups sliced nectarines (4 to 5)
- 4 heaping cups blueberries
- ¼ cup cornstarch
- 1 Tbsp. finely grated orange zest plus ½ cup fresh orange juice
- 2 tsp. finely grated peeled fresh ginger
- 2 tsp. brandy
- 1 tsp. ground ginger
- ½ tsp. ground cardamom
- ½ tsp. freshly grated nutmeg
- Heavy cream, for brushing
- Ice cream, for serving

1. Make the sugar cookie dough In a medium bowl, sift the flour with the baking powder and salt. In a large bowl, beat the butter and sugar with a hand mixer at medium-high speed until light and fluffy, about 3 minutes. Beat in the vanilla, lemon zest, lemon juice, lime zest and lime juice, scraping down the side of the bowl as necessary. Beat in the egg. With the mixer at low speed, beat in the dry ingredients, scraping down the side of the bowl as necessary; the dough will be very soft.

2. Scrape the dough out onto a sheet of plastic wrap and roll into a 9-inch log. Flatten the log into a 2-inch-wide rectangle, about 1 inch tall. Refrigerate until very firm, at least 2 hours.

3. Make the pandowdy Preheat the oven to 350°. Butter a 9-by-13-inch glass, ceramic or metal baking dish and sprinkle with 2 tablespoons of the sugar; turn to coat the pan with sugar.

4. In a small bowl, mix 2 tablespoons of the sugar with the cinnamon. In a large bowl, toss the nectarines and blueberries with the remaining ¼ cup of sugar and the cornstarch, orange zest, orange juice, grated ginger, brandy, ground ginger, cardamom and nutmeg. Spread the fruit in the prepared dish.

5. Using a sharp knife, cut the rectangle of cookie dough into ¼-inch-thick slices. Arrange the slices over the fruit in a graphic or random pattern; they will spread during baking. Brush the dough with heavy cream and sprinkle with the cinnamon sugar. Bake the pandowdy until the dough is golden brown and the fruit is bubbling, about 45 minutes. Serve warm, with ice cream.

MAKE AHEAD The cookie dough can be refrigerated for up to 2 days.

STEP-BY-STEP PANDOWDY LESSON

MAKE THE TOPPING Prepare sugar cookie dough, pat into a rectangle and chill until firm. Slice the dough ¼ inch thick.

PREP THE FRUIT In a large bowl, combine nectarines and berries with sugar, spices, cornstarch and fresh orange juice. Toss well.

FILL THE PAN Spread the nectarines and berries in an even layer in a baking pan or a glass or ceramic baking dish.

ARRANGE THE TOPPING Place the dough on the fruit; it will spread during baking. Brush with cream and sprinkle on cinnamon sugar.

This pandowdy (you've got to love the name) bursts with bubbling fruit under a crisp cookie topping. Vanilla ice cream is the perfect accompaniment.

BAKED STUFFED PEACHES
WITH SAFFRON ZABAGLIONE

Baked Stuffed Peaches with Saffron Zabaglione

Active **25 min**; Total **1 hr**; Serves **4**

Venice-based blogger Skye McAlpine re-creates the baked stuffed peaches served at Alla Maddalena, a trattoria on the nearby island of Mazzorbo. Use fragrant but slightly underripe peaches—they're more likely to hold their shape as they bake. McAlpine sometimes adds chunks of dark chocolate or slivered almonds to the peach-and-amaretti-cookie filling.

- **5** large, firm freestone peaches
- **20** amaretti cookies, crushed into pea-size pieces
  Unsalted butter, for greasing
- **4** large egg yolks
- **¼** cup superfine sugar
- **¼** cup dry Marsala
- **7** saffron threads
  Kosher salt

1. Preheat the oven to 350°. Using a knife, halve 4 of the peaches lengthwise and remove the pits. Using a melon baller or a teaspoon, scoop about 2 teaspoons of flesh out of each peach half, leaving a ½-inch-thick shell all around. Coarsely chop the peach flesh and transfer it to a bowl. Peel and coarsely chop the remaining whole peach and add it to the bowl. Stir in the crushed amaretti cookies.

2. Lightly butter an 8-inch-square baking dish and arrange the peach halves in it, cut side up. Stuff each peach half with 2 tablespoons of the peach-amaretti filling. Bake for about 40 minutes, until the peaches are tender and the filling is golden brown.

3. Meanwhile, bring a medium saucepan of water to a simmer over moderately low heat. Fill a large bowl with ice water. In a large stainless steel bowl, using a hand mixer, beat the egg yolks with the sugar at medium speed for about 1 minute. Add the Marsala, saffron and a small pinch of salt. Continue beating at medium speed until the mixture is thick and very frothy, about 3 minutes longer.

4. Set the stainless steel bowl over the saucepan of simmering water and beat the zabaglione until doubled in volume and the consistency resembles softly beaten egg whites, about 8 minutes. Transfer the bowl to the ice water bath and continue beating the zabaglione at medium speed until it holds very soft peaks, about 2 minutes. Serve immediately, with the warm peaches. —*Skye McAlpine*

Grilled Doughnuts with Blueberry Sauce

Total **25 min**; Serves **6**

Something extraordinary happens to a day-old doughnut when you cook it on the grill: It becomes incredibly tender on the inside and nicely crisp on the outside. This technique works for other leftover breads and pastries, too, such as challah, pound cake or cinnamon buns.

- **2** pints blueberries (4 cups)
- **½** cup Chambord
- **⅓** cup sugar
  Kosher salt
- **1** tsp. fresh lemon juice
- **6** day-old large glazed doughnuts, halved horizontally
- **2** Tbsp. unsalted butter, softened
  Vanilla ice cream, for serving

1. Light a grill. In a small stainless steel saucepan set directly on the grate, simmer 3 cups of the blueberries with the Chambord, sugar and a pinch of salt, stirring occasionally, until the blueberries begin to burst, about 15 minutes. Add the remaining blueberries and the lemon juice. Move the saucepan to a cooler part of the grill.

2. Spread the cut side of each doughnut with softened butter. Grill the doughnuts cut side down over moderate heat until lightly charred, 2 to 3 minutes. Serve warm with the blueberry sauce and ice cream. —*Matt Louis*

Strawberry Millefoglie

Total **45 min** plus 1 hr chilling; Serves **4**

- **1** cup whole milk
- **1** cup heavy cream
- **1** vanilla bean, halved lengthwise and seeds scraped, pod reserved for another use
- **½** cup granulated sugar
- **2** Tbsp. 00 or all-purpose flour
- **2** Tbsp. cornstarch
  Pinch of kosher salt
- **3** large egg yolks
- **5** sheets of phyllo dough
  Melted unsalted butter, for brushing
  Confectioners' sugar, for dusting
- **8** oz. strawberries, hulled and thinly sliced
  Dark chocolate shavings, for garnish

1. In a medium saucepan, combine the whole milk with the heavy cream and vanilla bean seeds and bring to a bare simmer over moderately low heat.

2. Meanwhile, in a medium bowl, whisk the granulated sugar with the flour, cornstarch and salt. Add the egg yolks and mix well. While whisking constantly, slowly drizzle in half of the warm milk mixture. Scrape the egg mixture into the saucepan and stir over moderately low heat until thickened to a pudding consistency, about 5 minutes. Strain through a fine-mesh sieve into a medium bowl. Press a sheet of plastic wrap directly on the surface of the pastry cream and refrigerate until cold, about 1 hour.

3. Preheat the oven to 400°. Line a baking sheet with parchment paper. Set 1 phyllo sheet on it and brush all over with melted butter. Top with another phyllo sheet and brush with butter. Continue layering and buttering until you have a stack of 5 buttered phyllo sheets. Using a large, sharp knife, cut the stack into 32 equal pieces. Dust with confectioners' sugar and bake for about 8 minutes, until lightly golden and crisp. Transfer to a rack and let cool completely.

4. Spoon some of the pastry cream onto 4 plates. Top each with some of the phyllo crisps and strawberries and dust with confectioners' sugar. Garnish with chocolate shavings and serve immediately. —*Paul Pansera*

Babas au Rhum with Mixed Citrus Fruits

Active **40 min**; Total **3 hr 30 min**; Serves **4**

"My preference for dessert is a lot of fruit with a little something," says star blogger and baker David Lebovitz. And so he came up with these wonderful mini vanilla cakes, which he douses with rum syrup, then piles high with three kinds of citrus and whipped cream.

BABAS

- **2 Tbsp. milk**
- **1 Tbsp. plus ½ tsp. sugar**
- **½ tsp. fine sea salt**
- **½ vanilla bean, split lengthwise, seeds scraped**
- **1 tsp. active dry yeast**
- **1 Tbsp. lukewarm water (105°–115°)**
- **¾ cup plus 2 Tbsp. all-purpose flour**
- **2 large eggs**
- **4 Tbsp. unsalted butter at room temperature, cut into ½-inch cubes, plus more for greasing**

RUM SYRUP

- **1 cup sugar**
- **½ cup dark rum**

CITRUS SALAD

- **1 ruby red grapefruit**
- **1 blood orange**
- **1 navel orange**

WHIPPED CREAM

- **½ cup heavy cream, chilled**
- **1½ tsp. sugar**
- **¼ tsp. pure vanilla extract**
- **Thinly sliced lime wheels and grapefruit zest, for garnish (optional)**

1. Make the babas In a small saucepan, combine the milk with 1 tablespoon of the sugar, the salt and vanilla bean and seeds. Cook over low heat, stirring constantly, until the sugar is dissolved, 2 to 3 minutes. Remove from the heat and let cool to room temperature. Discard the vanilla bean.

2. In a stand mixer fitted with the paddle, stir the yeast with the remaining ½ teaspoon of sugar and the water. Let stand until small bubbles appear, about 10 minutes. At low speed, mix in one-third of the flour. Mix in the milk until just incorporated, then mix in the remaining flour until just a few white streaks remain. Add the eggs and beat at medium-high speed for 5 minutes. Scatter the cubed butter over the dough. Cover the bowl with a clean tea towel and let the dough rise at room temperature until doubled in bulk, about 1 hour.

3. Butter four ½-cup baba molds or muffin cups. Beat the dough at medium speed until the butter is fully incorporated and the dough is smooth and silky, 5 minutes. With moistened hands, fill the prepared baba molds halfway with dough, about ⅓ cup per mold. Set the molds in a warm place and let the dough rise until it reaches the top of the molds, about 1 hour.

4. Preheat the oven to 350°. Bake the babas until puffed and golden brown, about 20 minutes. Immediately turn out onto a rack and let cool slightly.

5. Make the rum syrup In a small saucepan, combine the sugar with 2 cups of water and cook over moderate heat, stirring occasionally, until the sugar has dissolved. Remove from the heat and stir in the rum; keep warm.

6. Make the citrus salad Using a very sharp knife, peel the grapefruit, blood orange and navel orange, removing all of the bitter white pith. Thinly slice the citrus fruits crosswise, discarding any seeds. In a medium bowl, toss the sliced citrus with ½ cup of the rum syrup.

7. Make the whipped cream In a medium bowl, beat the cream with the sugar and vanilla until soft peaks form. Refrigerate until ready to serve.

8. Using a skewer or fork, prick the babas all over. Dip each baba in the warm rum syrup; squeeze the baba gently so it absorbs the syrup. Set the babas on a platter and let rest for 5 minutes. Dip each baba in the syrup a second time. Cut the warm babas in half lengthwise and transfer them to plates. Drizzle with the remaining rum syrup and serve with the citrus salad and whipped cream. Garnish with lime wheels and grapefruit zest, if desired.
—David Lebovitz

Apricot Parfaits with Mascarpone Whipped Cream

Total **40 min**; Serves **4**

There are three simple but spectacular layers in these summery parfaits—none of which involve any cooking whatsoever: fresh apricots soaked in brandy, creamy whipped mascarpone and a buttery graham cracker crumble.

- **2 Tbsp. Cognac or other brandy**
- **2 Tbsp. fresh lemon juice**
- **3½ Tbsp. superfine sugar**
- **Kosher salt**
- **12 apricots—halved, pitted and cut into ½-inch wedges**
- **½ cup graham cracker crumbs (from 4 to 5 crackers)**
- **3 Tbsp. unsalted butter, softened**
- **½ cup mascarpone**
- **½ cup heavy cream**
- **2 Tbsp. confectioners' sugar**
- **½ vanilla bean, split lengthwise and seeds scraped**
- **2 Tbsp. chopped mint**

1. In a medium bowl, whisk the Cognac with the lemon juice, 2 tablespoons of the superfine sugar and a pinch of salt until the sugar dissolves. Add the apricots and mix well; let stand at room temperature for 15 minutes.

2. In another medium bowl, using a fork, mix the graham cracker crumbs with the butter, ¼ teaspoon of salt and the remaining 1½ tablespoons of superfine sugar until evenly moistened. Press the mixture into clumps and refrigerate until just firm, about 10 minutes.

3. Meanwhile, in a large bowl, using a hand mixer, beat the mascarpone with the heavy cream, confectioners' sugar and vanilla seeds until stiff peaks form.

4. Stir the chopped mint into the apricots. Spoon the apricots and their juices into four 4- to 6-ounce glasses. Top with the mascarpone whipped cream and the crumble and serve right away.
—Justin Chapple

MAKE AHEAD The apricots, mascarpone whipped cream and the crumble can be refrigerated separately overnight.

APRICOT PARFAIT WITH
MASCARPONE WHIPPED CREAM

PANNA COTTA WITH BERRY
GRANITA AND CARAMEL

Blood Orange Soufflés

Active **30 min**; Total **1 hr 15 min**; Serves **8**

New York City pastry chef Jen Yee uses blood oranges at the height of their season to make her tangy warm soufflés. She serves them in hollowed-out orange cups.

- **8   medium blood oranges**
- **¼   cup granulated sugar**
- **3   large eggs, separated**
- **1   Tbsp. cornstarch**
- **1   Tbsp. blood orange marmalade**
    Confectioners' sugar, for dusting

1. Preheat the oven to 400°. Line a baking sheet with parchment paper.

2. Cut a very thin slice off the bottom of each orange so it stands upright; be careful not to pierce the pith. Slice 1 inch off the tops to expose the fruit. Using a superfine citrus zester, such as a Microplane, grate ½ teaspoon of zest from the orange tops and reserve; discard the remaining tops.

3. Using a sharp paring knife or grapefruit spoon, scoop out the fruit into a medium bowl. Hollow out the oranges, being careful not to pierce through the skin and collecting all the juice in the bowl. Arrange the orange shells on the prepared baking sheet.

4. Squeeze the juice from the fruit and strain into a bowl. Transfer ½ cup of the juice to a medium saucepan; reserve the rest for another use. Add 2 tablespoons of the granulated sugar to the saucepan and bring to a simmer over moderate heat; cook until the sugar is dissolved.

5. Meanwhile, in a medium bowl, whisk the egg yolks with the remaining 2 tablespoons of granulated sugar and the cornstarch until smooth. While whisking constantly, slowly drizzle in the hot orange juice. Add the mixture to the saucepan and cook over moderately low heat, whisking constantly, until thickened to a pudding consistency, about 1 minute. Whisk in the reserved ½ teaspoon of grated zest and the marmalade. Scrape the mixture into a medium bowl and let cool until lukewarm, about 30 minutes.

6. In a medium bowl, beat the egg whites with a hand mixer at medium speed until soft peaks form. Fold the whites into the cooled orange mixture until well blended. Spoon the filling into the orange shells, leaving ¼ inch at the top. Run the tip of a sharp paring knife just around the inner rim of the oranges to help the soufflés rise evenly.

7. Bake for 12 to 13 minutes, until the soufflés are risen and golden on top. Transfer to serving plates, dust with confectioners' sugar and serve immediately. —*Jen Yee*

MAKE AHEAD The soufflés can be prepared through Step 6 and kept at room temperature for 1 hour before baking.

WINE Lightly sparkling, orange blossom–scented Moscato d'Asti: 2014 Ceretto.

Panna Cotta with Berry Granita and Caramel

Total **1 hr 30 min** plus overnight chilling and freezing; Serves **8**

"At Wildair [in New York City], I wanted to do a dessert of creamy panna cotta with something cold. I hate sorbet, but I love granita—it reminds me of Mexico City's shaved ice," says Fabián von Hauske, an F&W Best New Chef 2016.

STRAWBERRY GRANITA

- **1   lb. strawberries, hulled and quartered (4 cups)**
- **½   cup sugar**

PANNA COTTA

- **1   Tbsp. powdered gelatin**
- **4   cups heavy cream**
- **3   Tbsp. sugar**
- **1½   vanilla beans, seeds scraped and pods reserved for another use**

CARAMEL SAUCE

- **1   cup sugar**
- **1   cup heavy cream**
- **1   stick unsalted butter, cut into tablespoons and at room temperature**
    Kosher salt

MILK CRUMBLE

- **½   cup powdered milk**
- **½   cup all-purpose flour**
- **¼   cup sugar**
- **6   Tbsp. unsalted butter, at room temperature**

1. Make the strawberry granita In a blender, puree the strawberries, sugar and ¼ cup plus 2 tablespoons of water until smooth. Scrape into a 9-by-13-inch metal baking pan and freeze overnight. Using a fork, scrape the granita until icy and flaky.

2. Meanwhile, make the panna cotta In a small bowl, whisk the gelatin with ¼ cup plus 2 tablespoons of water until smooth; let stand for 2 minutes.

3. In a medium saucepan, combine 2 cups of the heavy cream with the sugar and vanilla seeds and bring to a simmer, whisking to dissolve the sugar. Add the softened gelatin and cook over moderately low heat, stirring, until the gelatin is dissolved. Remove the pan from the heat and stir in the remaining 2 cups of heavy cream. Pour the panna cotta into eight 6-ounce ramekins, then cover and refrigerate until set, at least 6 hours or overnight.

4. Make the caramel sauce In a large skillet, melt the sugar over low heat, swirling the skillet occasionally, until an amber caramel forms, 7 to 8 minutes. Add the cream and butter (the caramel will seize) and cook, stirring occasionally, until the caramel is smooth, about 5 minutes. Scrape into a heatproof bowl, stir in a pinch of salt and let cool to room temperature.

5. Make the milk crumble Preheat the oven to 350°. Line a baking sheet with parchment paper. In a medium bowl, combine all of the ingredients, using your fingertips to blend in the butter until clumps form. Transfer to the baking sheet and bake for about 15 minutes, until golden and crisp. Transfer to a rack to cool.

6. To serve, invert the panna cotta onto plates. Spoon some of the caramel sauce over each panna cotta and top with some of the granita. Garnish with some of the milk crumble and serve. —*Jeremiah Stone and Fabián von Hauske*

MAKE AHEAD The granita can be frozen for up to 1 week. The milk crumble can be stored in an airtight container for 3 days. The panna cotta and caramel sauce can be refrigerated separately for 2 days; reheat the caramel slightly before serving.

Candied Lady Apples

⏱ Total **40 min**; Makes **12**

Pomegranate juice adds a pretty rose color and lovely flavor to these cute little candied apples.

Twelve 6-inch lollipop sticks

12 **Lady apples**

1½ **cups sugar**

¾ **cup pomegranate juice**

¾ **cup light corn syrup**

1. Line a baking sheet with parchment paper. Firmly insert the lollipop sticks in the apples.

2. In a heavy 3-quart saucepan, combine the sugar with the pomegranate juice and corn syrup. Cook over moderately high heat, swirling occasionally, until the mixture reaches 305° on a candy thermometer, about 20 minutes. Remove from the heat. Working quickly and carefully, turn each apple in the candy until it's coated, letting the excess drip back into the pan; transfer to the prepared baking sheet to set for at least 20 minutes before serving. —*Justin Chapple*

MAKE AHEAD The candied apples can be stored on the kitchen counter at room temperature overnight.

Fruit Salad with Grappa Syrup

Active **20 min**; Total **50 min**; Serves **6**

Grappa, a spirit made from grape must, originated in Italy's Friuli region in the 15th century, and it's still very popular there. Here it adds a boozy punch to fruit salad. You can use any mix of fruit and any sorbet, though a tart citrus one works especially well.

2 **Tbsp. sugar**

One 3-inch strip of lemon zest

¼ **cup grappa**

¾ **lb. strawberries, hulled and halved or quartered if large (2½ cups)**

6 **oz. raspberries (1½ cups)**

2 **peaches, cut into thin wedges**

Blood orange sorbet, for serving

1. In a small heatproof bowl, combine the sugar, lemon zest and 2 tablespoons of boiling water and stir to dissolve the sugar. Let cool. Discard the zest; stir in the grappa.

2. In a medium bowl, combine the strawberries, raspberries, peaches and ¼ cup of the grappa syrup; add more syrup to taste or reserve for another use. Let macerate for 15 minutes, then serve with sorbet. —*Giampaolo Venica*

Charred Mangoes with Ricotta, Honey and Caramelized Lime

⏱ Total **30 min**; Serves **4**

A simple spiced honey syrup, fresh ricotta and grilled lime showcase these mangoes beautifully. In the summer, you can use firm but ripe peaches in place of mangoes.

2 **large, ripe mangoes, peeled and cut into 2 halves each (2 lbs. total)**

1 **tsp. extra-virgin olive oil**

¼ **cup honey**

1 **large cinnamon stick**

½ **vanilla bean, split lengthwise, seeds scraped**

2 **medium limes, halved crosswise**

1 **Tbsp. sugar**

1 **cup fresh ricotta cheese**

1. Heat a grill pan over moderately high heat until hot. In a medium bowl, toss the mango halves with the olive oil. Grill the mangoes until nicely charred on all sides, about 12 minutes. Transfer to a cutting board and cut each half into 6 wedges.

2. Meanwhile, in a small saucepan, combine the honey, cinnamon stick, vanilla bean and seeds and ¼ cup of water. Cook over moderate heat, stirring occasionally, until the syrup coats the back of a spoon, about 7 minutes. Discard the vanilla bean and cinnamon stick.

3. Sprinkle the lime halves with the sugar. Grill, cut side down, until the sugar caramelizes, about 4 minutes.

4. Arrange the charred mangoes on plates. Dollop the ricotta alongside and drizzle with the honey syrup. Serve with the caramelized lime halves. —*Three Blue Ducks*

MAKE AHEAD The honey syrup can be refrigerated for up to 3 days. Rewarm gently before serving.

Goat Ricotta with Peaches

Active **35 min**; Total **1 hr 15 min**; Serves **6**

Making homemade ricotta is far easier than it seems. Aaron Silverman of Rose's Luxury in Washington, DC, uses fresh goat milk to give his cheese a pleasant tang and mixes in a bit of olive oil for extra lushness.

2 **cups whole milk**

2 **cups goat milk (see Note)**

2 **cups buttermilk**

2 **cups heavy cream**

¼ **cup extra-virgin olive oil, plus more for drizzling**

Kosher salt and pepper

3 **peaches—halved, pitted and cut into thin wedges**

Honey, for drizzling

Mint and shiso, for garnish

1. In a large saucepan, combine the whole milk with the goat milk, buttermilk and heavy cream and bring to a boil over high heat. Boil over moderately high heat for 1 minute, then remove from the heat and let stand until curds form and rise to the surface, about 5 minutes.

2. Line a colander with a double layer of moistened cheesecloth and set it over a large bowl. Using a fine sieve, scoop the milk mixture into the colander. Drain the ricotta until thick, about 30 minutes. Transfer to a medium bowl. Stir in the ¼ cup of olive oil; season with salt.

3. Spoon the ricotta onto plates. Top with the peaches and season with salt and pepper. Drizzle with olive oil and honey, garnish with mint and shiso and serve. —*Aaron Silverman*

NOTE Fresh goat milk is available at specialty food markets.

MAKE AHEAD The ricotta can be refrigerated in an airtight container for 5 days.

CANDIED
LADY APPLES

CAKES, COOKIES AND MORE

Ellen Bennett, founder of Hedley & Bennett aprons, savors a slice of coconut cake (p. 329). OPPOSITE Banana and Chocolate Cream Pie Parfaits (p. 346).

Vanilla Sponge Cake with Blackberry-Tarragon Jam

📷 PAGE 407

Active **40 min**; Total **1 hr 45 min**
Serves **8**

French and British baking traditions unite in pastry genius Dominique Ansel's homey creation: It's an airy sponge, the foundation of France's intricate layer cakes, baked in a loaf pan like an English quick bread.

CAKE

- **2 Tbsp. unsalted butter, melted, plus more for brushing**
- **½ cup all-purpose flour**
- **¼ cup cake flour**
- **¾ tsp. baking powder**
- **½ tsp. fine salt**
- **1 Tbsp. plus 1 tsp. honey**
- **1 vanilla bean, split lengthwise and seeds scraped, or ½ tsp. pure vanilla extract**
- **3 large egg yolks**
- **1 cup granulated sugar**
- **7 large egg whites**
- **Confectioners' sugar, for dusting**

JAM

- **8 oz. blackberries**
- **½ cup granulated sugar**
- **1 Tbsp. tarragon leaves, chopped**
- **1 tsp. gin**
- **1 tsp. fresh lemon juice**
- **¼ tsp. black pepper**

1. Make the cake Preheat the oven to 375°. Brush a 9-by-4-inch loaf pan with butter. In a medium bowl, whisk both flours with the baking powder and salt. In a small bowl, mix the 2 tablespoons of melted butter with the honey and vanilla seeds.

2. In a stand mixer fitted with the whisk, beat the egg yolks with ½ cup of the granulated sugar at high speed until thick and pale, about 5 minutes. Scrape into a medium bowl. Clean the mixer bowl and whisk.

3. In the stand mixer fitted with the whisk, beat the egg whites at high speed until soft peaks form, about 2 minutes. With the machine on high, gradually add the remaining ½ cup of granulated sugar and beat until stiff, about 3 minutes more. Using a rubber spatula, fold a large scoop of the beaten egg whites into the egg yolk mixture to lighten it. Gently fold the egg yolk mixture into the egg whites until no streaks remain.

4. Sift the dry ingredients over the eggs, then gently fold them in. Fold in the butter mixture. Scrape the batter into the prepared pan and smooth the top. Bake for about 25 minutes, until springy and browned. Let cool completely, then unmold onto a platter and dust with confectioners' sugar.

5. Meanwhile, make the jam In a large mortar, using a pestle, lightly crush the blackberries with the granulated sugar, tarragon, gin, lemon juice and pepper until a coarse jam forms. Transfer to a serving bowl. Cut the cake into slices and serve with the jam. —*Dominique Ansel*

MAKE AHEAD The cake can be stored in an airtight container for up to 3 days. The jam can be refrigerated for up to 3 days.

Pumpkin Layer Cake with Mascarpone Frosting

Active **50 min**; Total **3 hr**
Serves **10 to 12**

The tangy mascarpone frosting on this delicately spiced pumpkin cake beats plain old buttercream hands down.

CAKE

- **Unsalted butter, for greasing**
- **3 cups all-purpose flour, plus more for dusting**
- **2 Tbsp. ground cinnamon**
- **1½ Tbsp. ground ginger**
- **1½ tsp. baking soda**
- **1 tsp. baking powder**
- **1½ tsp. kosher salt**
- **4 large eggs**
- **1½ cups packed light brown sugar**
- **One 15-oz. can pure pumpkin puree**
- **1 cup canola oil**

FROSTING

- **1½ sticks unsalted butter, softened**
- **3 cups confectioners' sugar**
- **1½ tsp. pure vanilla extract**
- **Kosher salt**
- **1½ cups mascarpone cheese**

1. Make the cake Preheat the oven to 350°. Butter two 9-inch round cake pans and line the bottoms with parchment paper. Butter the paper and dust with flour, tapping out the excess.

2. In a medium bowl, whisk the 3 cups of flour with the cinnamon, ginger, baking soda, baking powder and salt. In a large bowl, using a hand mixer, beat the eggs with the brown sugar, pumpkin and oil at medium-high speed until blended. At low speed, beat in the dry ingredients.

3. Scrape the batter into the prepared pans and bake in the middle of the oven until a toothpick inserted in the centers of the cakes comes out clean, about 40 minutes. Let the cakes cool in the pans for about 30 minutes, then invert onto a rack to cool completely. Peel off the parchment paper.

4. Meanwhile, make the frosting In a large bowl, using a hand mixer, beat the butter with the confectioners' sugar, vanilla and a pinch of salt at medium speed until smooth. Add the mascarpone and beat at high speed just until smooth; do not over-beat. Refrigerate the frosting until just set, about 30 minutes.

5. Set 1 cake layer on a platter. Spread ¾ cup of the frosting on top and cover with the second cake layer. Spread a thin layer of frosting all over the cake and refrigerate until set, about 15 minutes. Spread the remaining frosting over the top and side of the cake. Refrigerate until firm, at least 30 minutes, before serving. —*Justin Chapple*

MAKE AHEAD The cake can be refrigerated for up to 3 days.

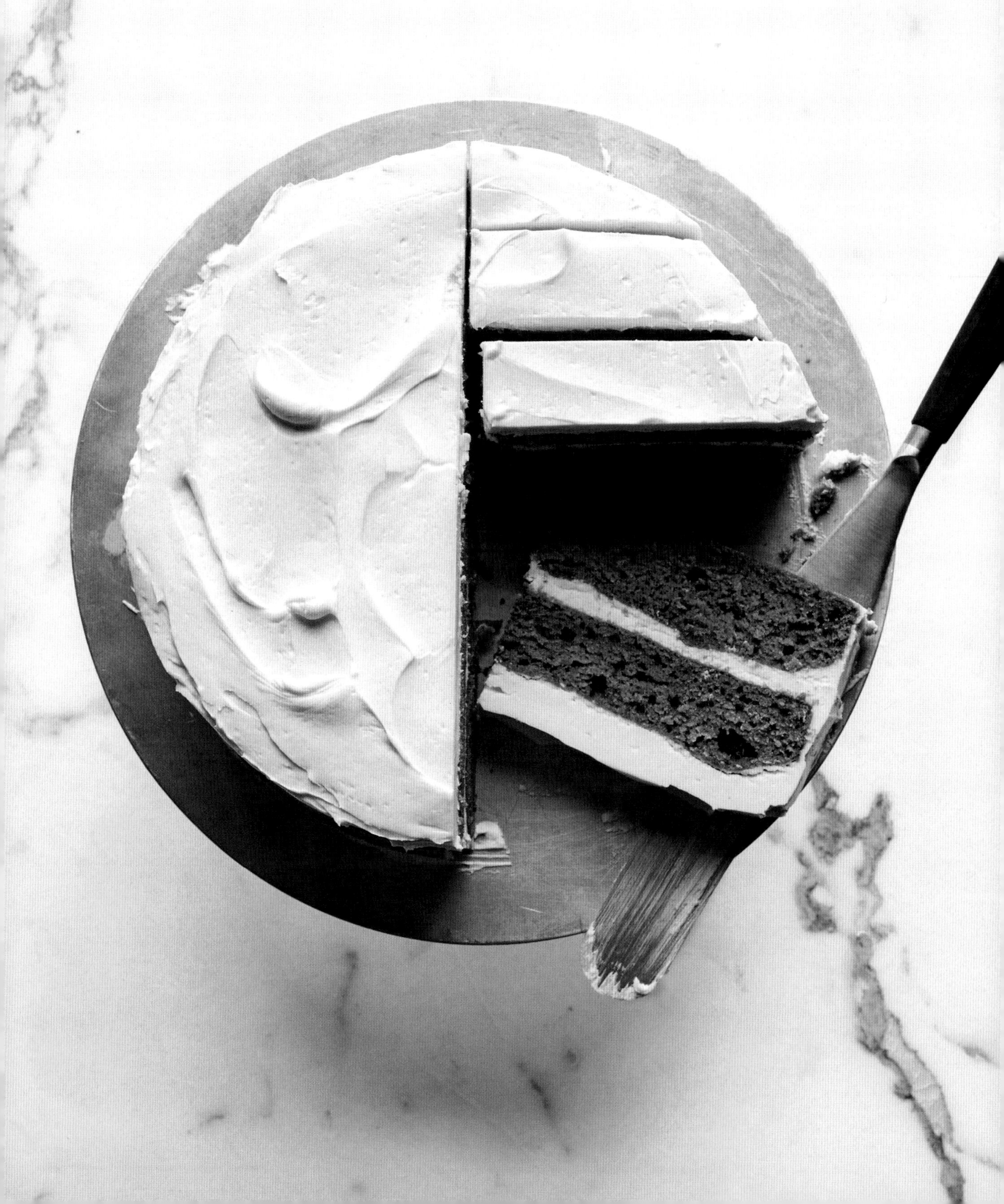

PUMPKIN LAYER CAKE WITH MASCARPONE FROSTING

Raspberry Whole-Wheat Butter Cake

Active **30 min**; Total **2 hr 40 min**
Makes **one 10-inch cake**

- 2 sticks unsalted butter, at room temperature, plus more for greasing
- 1¼ cups almond flour
- ¾ cup whole-wheat flour
- ½ cup all-purpose flour
- ¼ cup wheat germ
- 2¼ tsp. baking powder
- 2 cups plus 2 Tbsp. sugar
- 2¼ tsp. kosher salt
- 2 Tbsp. pure vanilla extract
- 7 large eggs
- 2 cups fresh raspberries, plus more for serving
  Whipped cream, for serving

1. Preheat the oven to 350°. Butter a 10-inch round cake pan and line the bottom with parchment paper. Butter the paper.

2. In a medium bowl, whisk all of the flours with the wheat germ and baking powder until well blended. In the bowl of a stand mixer fitted with the paddle (or using a hand mixer), combine the 2 sticks of butter with 2 cups of the sugar and the salt and beat at medium speed until pale yellow and fluffy, about 3 minutes. Beat in the vanilla, then beat in the eggs 1 at a time, scraping down the side and bottom of the bowl (the mixture will look broken). Add the dry ingredients and beat at low speed just until they are incorporated and the batter is smooth. Scrape the batter into the prepared pan and smooth the top. Arrange the 2 cups of raspberries in a single layer on top, then sprinkle with the remaining 2 tablespoons of sugar. Bake until the cake is golden and a cake tester inserted in the center comes out clean, about 50 minutes. Transfer to a rack to cool for 15 minutes.

3. Run a thin, sharp knife around the edge of the cake. Invert the cake onto a large plate; peel off the parchment paper. Turn the cake right side up on a serving plate and let cool until warm, about 1 hour. Serve with whipped cream and fresh raspberries. —*Zoe Nathan and Laurel Almerinda*

MAKE AHEAD The cake can be stored at room temperature overnight.

Lemon-Blueberry Yogurt Loaf Cake

Active **30 min**; Total **3 hr**
Makes **one 9-by-4-inch loaf**

- ¾ cup refined coconut oil, melted and cooled slightly, plus more for greasing
- 2 cups all-purpose flour
- 1¼ tsp. baking powder
- ½ tsp. baking soda
  Kosher salt
- 1 cup granulated sugar
- 3 large eggs
- 1¼ cups whole-milk Greek yogurt
- 2 Tbsp. finely grated lemon zest
- ¾ tsp. pure vanilla extract
- ¼ cup plus 2 Tbsp. fresh lemon juice
- 1 cup blueberries
- ¾ cup confectioners' sugar

1. Preheat the oven to 350°. Grease a 9-by-4-inch metal loaf pan and line with parchment paper, allowing at least 2 inches of overhang on the 2 long sides.

2. In a medium bowl, whisk the flour with the baking powder, baking soda and ¾ teaspoon of salt. In a large bowl, using a hand mixer, beat the ¾ cup of coconut oil with the granulated sugar at medium speed until very smooth, about 1 minute. Beat in the eggs 1 at a time, then beat in the yogurt, lemon zest, vanilla and ¼ cup of the lemon juice. Scrape down the side and bottom of the bowl, then beat in the dry ingredients in 3 additions until just incorporated. Using a rubber spatula, fold in the blueberries.

3. Scrape the batter into the prepared pan and spread in an even layer. Bake for about 1 hour and 15 minutes, until a cake tester inserted in the center of the cake comes out clean. Transfer the pan to a rack and let the cake cool completely, about 1 hour.

4. In a small bowl, whisk the confectioners' sugar with the remaining 2 tablespoons of lemon juice and a pinch of salt. Using the overhanging parchment paper, lift the cake out of the pan. Drizzle the glaze over the top and let stand until set, about 15 minutes. Cut into slices and serve. —*Justin Chapple*

MAKE AHEAD The cake can be kept in an airtight container for up to 3 days.

Babette Friedman's Apple Cake

Active **45 min**; Total **2 hr 40 min plus cooling**; Serves **8 to 10**

Babette Friedman didn't know she was helping to shape a chef's palate when she baked this pound cake–like dessert for her grandson Daniel Rose, chef at Le Coucou in New York City and Spring in Paris. He stirs Calvados-spiked apples into the batter, then tops the cake with more of the boozy fruit.

CAKE

- 3 Fuji or Gala apples (1½ lbs.)—peeled, cored and sliced ½ inch thick
- 1 Tbsp. Calvados
- 1 tsp. finely grated peeled fresh ginger
- ½ tsp. ground cinnamon
- 2¼ cups plus 2 Tbsp. sugar
- 3 sticks unsalted butter, at room temperature, plus more for brushing
- ¼ tsp. kosher salt
- 3 large eggs
- 3 cups all-purpose flour
- 1 Tbsp. baking powder

GLAZE

- ¼ cup sugar
- 2 Tbsp. heavy cream
- 2 Tbsp. unsalted butter

1. Make the cake In a large bowl, toss the apples with the Calvados, ginger, cinnamon and 2 tablespoons of the sugar. Let stand for 30 minutes.

2. Preheat the oven to 350°. Brush a 9-inch springform pan with butter.

3. In a large bowl, using a hand mixer, beat the 3 sticks of butter with the remaining 2¼ cups of sugar and the salt until pale yellow and fluffy, about 3 minutes. Beat in the eggs 1 at a time until smooth. Using a wooden spoon, stir in the flour and baking powder until a thick, smooth batter forms. Fold in 8 of the apple slices. Spread the batter in the prepared pan.

4. Arrange the remaining apples in slightly overlapping concentric circles on the batter and drizzle on the apple juices. Bake for about 1 hour and 40 minutes, until a cake tester inserted in the center comes out clean.

5. Meanwhile, make the glaze In a small saucepan, combine the sugar with 2 tablespoons of water and bring to a simmer without stirring. Cook over moderate heat, swirling the pan, until an amber caramel forms, about 4 minutes. Carefully add the cream and butter (the mixture will sputter) and cook, whisking, until the caramel is smooth, 2 minutes.

6. Transfer the cake to a rack and let stand for 10 minutes. Unmold the cake and brush the top with the glaze. Let cool slightly and serve warm or at room temperature. —*Daniel Rose*

MAKE AHEAD The cake can be stored in an airtight container for up to 2 days.

Apple Cake with Cranberries

Active **20 min**; Total **1 hr 25 min**
Makes **one 9-inch cake**

- 1 Granny Smith apple—peeled, halved, cored and sliced ½ inch thick
- ½ cup fresh or frozen cranberries
- ½ cup packed light brown sugar
- 2 large eggs
- ¾ cup granulated sugar
- ¾ cup sour cream
- 1 tsp. pure vanilla extract
- 1½ cups all-purpose flour
- 1 stick unsalted butter, melted and cooled slightly
- 1 tsp. baking powder
- ½ tsp. kosher salt

1. Preheat the oven to 350°. Line a 9-inch round cake pan with parchment paper. Arrange the apple slices in the cake pan in 2 slightly overlapping concentric circles and scatter the cranberries around the edge. Sprinkle the brown sugar on top.

2. In a large bowl, using a hand mixer, beat the eggs with the granulated sugar, sour cream and vanilla until smooth. Beat in the flour, butter, baking powder and salt. Scrape the batter into the cake pan and smooth the surface with a spatula.

3. Bake the cake for about 50 minutes, until a toothpick inserted in the center comes out clean. Let cool for 15 minutes, then invert onto a platter. Cut into wedges and serve warm. —*Justin Chapple*

MAKE AHEAD The cake can be stored in an airtight container for up to 2 days.

Chocolate-Buttermilk Snack Cakes

Active **1 hr**; Total **2 hr 30 min**; Makes **18**

"I would love to say that I celebrate Valentine's Day by baking for my husband, but he's not into sweets," says pastry chef Mindy Segal of Mindy's HotChocolate in Chicago. Instead, she makes cookies and cakes and gives them to her friends in vintage tins. These chocolate-buttermilk cakes with sweet mascarpone filling, a nod to Hostess cupcakes, are a favorite.

CAKES

- 1 cup buttermilk
- 1 cup brewed coffee, cooled
- 1 tsp. pure vanilla extract
- 2 cups all-purpose flour
- ⅔ cup unsweetened cocoa powder
- 1 Tbsp. baking soda
- 1 tsp. kosher salt
- 1⅓ cups granulated sugar
- ¾ cup canola oil
- 1 large egg

FILLING AND FROSTING

- ¾ cup mascarpone cheese
- ¾ cup heavy cream
- ½ cup confectioners' sugar
- ¾ tsp. pure vanilla extract
- ½ tsp. instant espresso powder
  Pinch of kosher salt
- 12 oz. chopped bittersweet chocolate, melted and cooled slightly
  Assorted sprinkles, for coating

1. Make the cakes Preheat the oven to 350°. Generously coat the cups of three 12-cup muffin tins with nonstick spray. In a small bowl, whisk the buttermilk with the coffee and vanilla. In a medium bowl, sift the flour with the cocoa powder, baking soda and salt.

2. In a large bowl, using a hand mixer, beat the granulated sugar with the oil at medium-high speed until blended; beat in the egg. At low speed, beat in the dry ingredients and the buttermilk mixture in 3 alternating batches. Spoon about 2 tablespoons of batter into each muffin cup.

3. Bake the cakes for about 12 minutes, until risen and a toothpick inserted in the centers comes out clean. Let cool in the pans for 3 to 5 minutes. Carefully invert the cakes onto a parchment paper–lined

baking sheet (this will help them flatten slightly). Let cool completely, about 30 minutes.

4. Make the filling and frosting In a large bowl, beat the mascarpone, cream, confectioners' sugar, vanilla, espresso and salt at medium speed until smooth and thick.

5. Spread the mascarpone filling onto the flat sides of half the cakes. Top with the remaining 18 cakes, pressing down to spread the filling. Dip one half of each cake in the melted chocolate and coat with sprinkles. Refrigerate until set, at least 1 hour or up to 3 days. Serve the cakes cold. —*Mindy Segal*

Fallen Olive Oil Soufflé Cake

⏱ Active **20 min**; Total **40 min**; Serves **4**

This unconventional Portuguese cake called *pão de ló*—a cross between a fallen soufflé and an olive oil cake with a creamy center—is from chef Nuno Mendes of Taberna do Mercado in London. Instead of serving individual portions, Mendes likes guests to dig into the cake with their spoons, straight from the platter.

- 9 large egg yolks
- 2 large eggs
- ½ cup sugar
- 3 Tbsp. extra-virgin olive oil, plus more for drizzling
- 1 Tbsp. all-purpose flour
  Flaky sea salt, for garnish

1. Preheat the oven to 350°. Line an 8-inch round cake pan with parchment paper, allowing a 3-inch overhang all around. In a bowl, beat the egg yolks, eggs and sugar at medium-high speed until fluffy and doubled in volume, about 6 minutes. With the mixer at low speed, drizzle in the 3 tablespoons of olive oil, then beat in the flour just until incorporated. Scrape into the prepared pan. Bake until puffed and set around the edge and golden on top but slightly wobbly in the center, 18 to 20 minutes. Transfer the pan to a rack and let the soufflé cool for 10 minutes.

2. Using the parchment, carefully transfer the soufflé to a platter. Drizzle with olive oil, sprinkle with sea salt and serve hot or at room temperature. —*Nuno Mendes*

DIY Concord Cake

GADI PELEG of Breads Bakery in New York City shows how to make this lost Franco-American classic—a deeply chocolaty, crispy, creamy, chewy meringue-and-mousse confection covered with crunchy chocolate meringue sticks.

Concord Cake

Active **1 hr 30 min**; Total **2 hr 30 min plus 6 hr chilling**; Makes **one 8-inch cake**

CHOCOLATE MOUSSE

- **10 oz. semisweet chocolate (64%), finely chopped**
- **5 Tbsp. unsalted butter, cut into small pieces**
- **½ cup plus 3 Tbsp. sugar**
- **¼ cup water**
- **2 large egg whites**
- **½ vanilla bean, split**
- **2 cups heavy cream, chilled**

CHOCOLATE MERINGUE

- **2 cups confectioners' sugar, plus more for dusting**
- **1 cup unsweetened cocoa powder**
- **9 large egg whites**
- **1⅓ cups granulated sugar**

MAKE THE MOUSSE

1. In a heatproof medium bowl set over a pot of simmering water, melt the chocolate with the butter, stirring occasionally, until smooth. Remove from the heat and keep warm.

2. In a small saucepan, combine the sugar and water and boil over moderately high heat, without stirring, until the sugar syrup reaches 240° on a candy thermometer, about 7 minutes.

3. Meanwhile, in the bowl of a stand mixer fitted with the whisk, beat the egg whites at medium-high speed until soft peaks form, about 3 minutes.

4. Gradually pour the hot syrup into the egg whites in a steady stream and beat at medium-high speed until the whites are stiff and glossy, about 5 minutes (Italian meringue). Using a large rubber spatula, fold in the melted chocolate until no streaks of white remain. Scrape the chocolate mixture into a large bowl. Wash and dry the mixing bowl and whisk.

5. In the stand mixer fitted with the whisk, scrape the vanilla bean seeds into the heavy cream. Beat the cream at medium speed until firm. Using a rubber spatula, fold the whipped cream into the chocolate mixture until no streaks remain. Cover the mousse with plastic wrap and refrigerate until firm, at least 2 hours or overnight.

MAKE THE CHOCOLATE MERINGUE

6. Meanwhile, in a medium bowl, sift the 2 cups of confectioners' sugar with the cocoa powder. Line 4 rimmed baking sheets with parchment paper. Trace an 8-inch circle on 2 of the sheets.

7. In the stand mixer fitted with the whisk, beat the egg whites at low speed until foamy. Increase the speed to medium-high and beat until soft peaks form. Beat in the granulated sugar 3 tablespoons at a time, beating well after each addition. Once all of the sugar has been added, beat the whites until stiff and glossy, about 3 minutes longer (French meringue). Transfer the meringue to a large bowl and, using a large rubber spatula, gradually fold in the cocoa powder and confectioners' sugar until just a few streaks remain.

8. Scrape the meringue into a piping bag fitted with a ½-inch tip. Pipe the meringue into the traced circles in a spiral, beginning at the center; there should be no space between the spirals. On the other 2 prepared sheets, pipe the remaining meringue in long sticks, leaving about 1 inch between them. Let the meringue rounds and sticks stand at room temperature for 30 minutes.

STEP-BY-STEP CONCORD CAKE LESSON

MAKE THE MOUSSE Fold melted chocolate and butter into Italian meringue, then blend in firmly whipped cream and chill.

PREP THE CHOCOLATE MERINGUE Make French meringue and fold in confectioners' sugar and unsweetened cocoa powder.

SHAPE THE CAKE LAYERS Pipe a chocolate meringue spiral onto each of two parchment paper–lined baking sheets.

FORM THE CRUNCHY TOPPING Pipe the remaining meringue onto parchment-lined sheets in long sticks, about an inch apart.

9. Preheat the oven to 350°. Bake the meringue rounds for about 25 minutes, until they are firm and can be lifted off the parchment with an offset spatula. Transfer to racks to cool completely.

10. Bake the meringue sticks for 12 to 14 minutes, until firm enough to be lifted off the parchment. Cut them into 6-inch lengths and transfer to a rack to cool completely. Using a sharp knife, cut the sticks into 1½- to 2-inch lengths.

ASSEMBLE THE CAKE

11. Transfer a meringue round to a cake stand or platter. Spoon half of the chilled chocolate mousse onto the meringue and spread it in an even layer with a large offset spatula. Cover with the second meringue round and spread the remaining mousse on top, mounding it slightly in the center. Cover the cake entirely with the meringue sticks. Refrigerate until the mousse is firm, at least 6 hours or overnight. Dust the cake with confectioners' sugar just before serving.

MAKE AHEAD The cake can be refrigerated for 1 day.

Assembling this rich chocolate dessert is easy and forgiving: Any imperfections can be hidden by the whimsical meringue sticks that cover the cake.

CUT THE MERINGUE STICKS
Use a sharp knife to create 1½- to 2-inch pieces for decorating the cake.

FILL THE CAKE Using an offset spatula, spread half of the chilled chocolate mousse over one of the meringue spirals.

ADD ANOTHER LAYER Place the second round of meringue on top and cover with the remaining chocolate mousse.

FINISH THE DESSERT Arrange the meringue sticks over the top and side and chill. Dust with confectioners' sugar.

Bibi's Coconut Cake

Active **1 hr 30 min**; Total **3 hr 45 min**
Serves **12**

Food blogger Julie Tanous uses coconut in every part of this festive dessert inspired by her grandmother Bibi.

FILLING

- 1¾ cups whole milk
- ¾ cup granulated sugar
- 1 Tbsp. plus ½ tsp. pure coconut extract
- Kosher salt
- 3 large egg yolks
- 2 Tbsp. cornstarch
- 1 cup sweetened shredded coconut
- 2 Tbsp. unsalted butter
- ¼ cup heavy cream

CAKE

- 2 sticks unsalted butter, at room temperature, plus more for greasing
- 3 cups cake flour, plus more for dusting
- 1 Tbsp. plus 1½ tsp. baking powder
- ½ tsp. kosher salt
- 1 cup unsweetened coconut milk
- ½ cup whole milk
- 1 Tbsp. pure coconut extract
- 2⅓ cups granulated sugar
- 5 large egg whites

FROSTING

- 8 oz. cream cheese, at room temperature
- 1 stick unsalted butter, at room temperature
- 4 cups confectioners' sugar
- 1 to 2 Tbsp. whole milk
- 1 tsp. pure coconut extract
- 3 cups unsweetened coconut flakes, toasted

1. Make the filling In a medium saucepan, simmer the milk with the granulated sugar, coconut extract and a pinch of salt over moderate heat, stirring, until the sugar is dissolved, about 3 minutes.

2. In a small bowl, beat the egg yolks with the cornstarch. Gradually whisk ½ cup of the hot milk into the yolks. Scrape this mixture into the saucepan and cook over moderately high heat, whisking, until thickened, about 5 minutes. Remove from the heat.

Whisk in the shredded coconut and butter. Scrape into a medium bowl; let cool.

3. In another medium bowl, whisk the cream until stiff. Fold the whipped cream into the cooled coconut filling. Press a piece of plastic directly on the surface and refrigerate until well chilled, about 1 hour.

4. Meanwhile, make the cake Preheat the oven to 350°. Butter two 8-inch round cake pans and line them with parchment paper. Butter the paper and dust the pans with cake flour.

5. In a medium bowl, whisk the cake flour, baking powder and salt. In another medium bowl, whisk the coconut milk with the whole milk and coconut extract. In a stand mixer fitted with the paddle, beat the 2 sticks of butter with the granulated sugar at medium speed until fluffy, about 2 minutes. At medium-high speed, beat in the egg whites in 3 additions. At low speed, beat in half of the dry ingredients until they are nearly incorporated. Beat in the wet ingredients, then beat in the remaining dry ingredients until just incorporated; scrape down the side of the bowl as needed.

6. Pour the batter into the prepared pans and bake for 40 to 45 minutes, until the cakes are golden and springy. Transfer the cakes to a rack to cool for 15 minutes, then turn them out onto the rack, peel off the parchment and let cool completely, about 45 minutes.

7. Make the frosting In a stand mixer fitted with the paddle, beat the cream cheese with the butter until smooth. At low speed, beat in the confectioners' sugar, 1 tablespoon of the milk and the coconut extract until just incorporated, then beat at medium speed until light and smooth, 1 to 2 minutes; add another tablespoon of milk if the frosting is too thick.

8. Using a serrated knife, cut each cake in half horizontally to create 4 layers. Set 1 cake layer cut side up on a cake plate. Spread one-third of the filling on top. Repeat with 2 more cake layers and the remaining filling. Cover with the last cake layer. Freeze until well chilled, 15 minutes. Frost the cake with a thin layer of frosting and freeze until set, about another 15 minutes. Frost the cake with the remaining frosting and coat the side with the coconut flakes. Refrigerate until the frosting is set, about 1 hour, before serving. —*Julie Tanous*

Chocolate–Olive Oil Cake with Walnuts

Active **30 min**; Total **1 hr 30 min plus cooling**; Makes **one 9-inch cake**

- 1 cup walnut halves
- ¾ cup unsweetened cocoa powder, plus more for dusting
- 3½ cups all-purpose flour
- 4½ tsp. baking powder
- 2 tsp. kosher salt
- 2 cups superfine sugar
- 1 cup plus 3 Tbsp. water
- 1 cup plus 3 Tbsp. extra-virgin olive oil
- 4 large eggs, separated
- Confectioners' sugar, for sifting

1. Preheat the oven to 350°. Spread the walnuts in a cake pan and bake until fragrant and lightly toasted, about 8 minutes. Transfer the walnuts to a work surface and let cool, then coarsely chop.

2. Spray a 9-inch springform pan with nonstick spray and dust with cocoa powder. In a large bowl, whisk the flour with the baking powder and salt. In a medium saucepan, stir all but 2 tablespoons of the superfine sugar with the ¾ cup of cocoa powder. Whisk in the water in a steady stream until incorporated. Bring the cocoa mixture to a boil over moderate heat, whisking occasionally. Remove from the heat and whisk in the olive oil.

3. In a medium bowl, beat the egg yolks lightly with a fork to break them up. Beat a large spoonful of the cocoa mixture into the egg yolks, then scrape the yolk mixture into the saucepan and whisk until no streaks remain. Using a rubber spatula, stir the chocolate mixture into the dry ingredients, then fold in the chopped walnuts.

4. In a medium bowl, using a hand mixer, beat the egg whites until soft peaks form. Gradually add the remaining 2 tablespoons of superfine sugar and beat until the egg whites are thick and glossy, about 5 minutes. Fold the beaten whites into the batter in 3 additions.

5. Spread the batter in the prepared pan and bake for about 1 hour, until a skewer inserted in the center comes out with a few moist crumbs attached. Transfer the cake to a rack and let cool completely before unmolding. Sift confectioners' sugar over the top before serving. —*Skye McAlpine*

Cranberry Gingerbread

Active **20 min**; Total **1 hr 20 min plus cooling**; Serves **8**

Fresh ginger gives this cranberry-flecked gingerbread loaf great zing. The bread is excellent on its own or spread with butter and served alongside a cup of hot tea.

- ½ **cup canola oil, plus more for greasing**
- ¾ **cup unsulfured molasses**
- ¾ **cup packed light brown sugar**
- 2 **large eggs**
- 1 **Tbsp. finely grated peeled fresh ginger**
- 1½ **cups fresh cranberries (6 oz.), coarsely chopped**
- 2 **cups all-purpose flour**
- 2 **tsp. baking powder**
- ½ **tsp. baking soda**
- ½ **tsp. ground cinnamon**
- ½ **tsp. ground cloves**
- ½ **tsp. kosher salt**

1. Preheat the oven to 350°. Grease an 8-by-4-inch loaf pan. In a large bowl, whisk the ½ cup of oil with the molasses, brown sugar, eggs, ginger and cranberries. In a medium bowl, sift the flour with the baking powder, baking soda, cinnamon, cloves and salt. Whisk the flour mixture into the molasses mixture until well blended.

2. Scrape the batter into the prepared pan and bake for about 50 minutes, until a cake tester inserted in the center comes out clean with a few moist crumbs attached. Transfer to a rack and let cool for 10 minutes, then unmold the gingerbread and let cool to room temperature before slicing and serving. —*Kay Chun*

MAKE AHEAD The gingerbread can be stored in an airtight container at room temperature for up to 3 days.

Swirled Meringue Roulade with Praline Whipped Cream

Total **1 hr 15 min plus 3 hr chilling**; Serves **8**

To ensure that her cocoa-laced meringue emerges crisp, cookbook author Malika Ameen preheats the oven to a high temperature, then reduces it for baking.

MERINGUE

- **Baking spray**
- 1 **Tbsp. confectioners' sugar**
- 4 **large egg whites, at room temperature**
- **Pinch of cream of tartar**
- 1 **cup plus 2 Tbsp. granulated sugar**
- 2 **tsp. ground cinnamon**
- 1 **tsp. cornstarch**
- ¾ **tsp. freshly grated nutmeg**
- **Scant ¼ tsp. kosher salt**
- ¾ **tsp. finely grated orange zest**

COCOA SWIRL

- 2 **tsp. espresso powder or instant coffee**
- 2 **tsp. unsweetened cocoa powder**
- 1½ **tsp. pure vanilla extract**

WALNUT PRALINE

- ½ **cup walnuts**
- ¼ **cup granulated sugar**
- 1 **tsp. corn syrup**

WHIPPED CREAM

- 1 **cup heavy cream**
- 1 **tsp. pure vanilla extract**
- 2 **Tbsp. grated bittersweet chocolate**
- **Blackberries and pomegranate seeds, for garnish (optional)**

1. Make the meringue Preheat the oven to 400°. Grease a 9-by-13-inch metal baking pan with baking spray. Line the pan with parchment paper, leaving 1 inch of overhang on the short sides. Grease the parchment with baking spray and dust with the confectioners' sugar.

2. In the bowl of a stand mixer fitted with the whisk, beat the egg whites with the cream of tartar at medium speed until frothy, about 2 minutes. With the machine on, slowly beat in the granulated sugar, 1 tablespoon at a time. Increase the speed to medium-high and beat until the meringue is shiny and tripled in volume and stiff peaks form, about 10 minutes. In a small

bowl, mix the cinnamon with the cornstarch, nutmeg and salt. Sift the cinnamon mixture over the meringue, then add the orange zest. Fold until well combined. Spread the meringue evenly in the prepared baking pan.

3. Make the cocoa swirl In a small bowl, combine the espresso powder, cocoa and vanilla with 2 teaspoons of water and mix well. Spoon small dots of the cocoa mixture all over the top of the meringue. Using a skewer or a bread knife, swirl the dots decoratively. Reduce the oven temperature to 350° and bake the meringue for about 25 minutes, until puffed and cooked through. Transfer to a rack to cool completely.

4. Meanwhile, make the walnut praline Line a baking sheet with parchment paper. Spread the walnuts in a pie plate and toast in the oven for about 10 minutes, until golden. Let cool, then chop into ½-inch pieces.

5. In a small saucepan, combine the granulated sugar, corn syrup and 2 tablespoons of water and bring to a simmer, brushing down the side of the pan with a wet pastry brush. Cook over moderately low heat, swirling the pan, until an amber caramel forms, about 10 minutes. Stir in the walnuts, then scrape the praline onto the prepared baking sheet and spread in an even layer. Let cool completely, then chop into ½-inch pieces.

6. Make the whipped cream In a medium bowl, using a hand mixer, beat the cream with the vanilla at medium speed until medium peaks form.

7. Assemble the roulade Gently invert the meringue onto a parchment paper–lined work surface with a long side facing you and peel the parchment off the meringue. Spread the whipped cream all over the meringue, leaving a 1-inch border. Sprinkle the walnut praline over the whipped cream, then scatter the grated chocolate on top. Starting at a long side, roll up the meringue to form a log. Transfer to a platter and refrigerate until chilled, at least 3 hours or up to 1 day. Serve garnished with blackberries and pomegranate seeds, if desired. —*Malika Ameen*

MAKE AHEAD The baked meringue and walnut praline can be stored separately at room temperature overnight.

Sticky Toffee Whole-Wheat Date Cake

Active **45 min**; Total **3 hr 45 min**
Makes **one 8-inch-square cake**

Chef Jessica Koslow of Sqirl in L.A. reinvents classic sticky toffee pudding as a cake. She tones down the sugar but adds a big boost of flavor with plump Medjool dates and hearty whole-wheat flour.

CAKE

- 1 stick plus 6 Tbsp. unsalted butter, softened, plus more for greasing
- ½ lb. pitted Medjool dates, chopped
- 1 Tbsp. fresh lemon juice
- ½ cup dried currants
- 1 cup whole-wheat flour
- ½ cup plus 2 Tbsp. all-purpose flour
- 1 tsp. baking soda
- 1 tsp. ground cinnamon
- ¾ tsp. fine sea salt
- ½ tsp. ground cardamom
- ¼ tsp. ground ginger
- ¾ cup packed light brown sugar
- 2 large eggs
- ½ tsp. pure vanilla extract

TOFFEE

- ½ cup agave nectar
- ½ cup packed light brown sugar
- ¼ tsp. fine sea salt
- 2 Tbsp. unsalted butter
  Fleur de sel, for sprinkling

1. Make the cake Preheat the oven to 325°. Butter an 8-inch-square baking pan. In a small saucepan, combine the dates with the lemon juice and ¾ cup of water; cook over moderately low heat, stirring, until the dates are very soft, about 6 minutes. Stir in the currants and let cool.

2. In a medium bowl, whisk both flours with the baking soda, cinnamon, fine sea salt, cardamom and ginger. In a stand mixer fitted with the paddle, beat the 1 stick plus 6 tablespoons of butter with the brown sugar at medium-high speed until light and fluffy, about 3 minutes. Beat in the eggs 1 at a time, then beat in the cooled date mixture and the vanilla. At low speed, beat in the dry ingredients until incorporated, scraping down the side and bottom of the bowl as needed.

3. Scrape the batter into the prepared pan and bake for about 55 minutes, until a toothpick inserted in the center of the cake comes out clean. Transfer the pan to a rack set over a baking sheet.

4. Meanwhile, make the toffee In a small saucepan, whisk the agave with the brown sugar and fine sea salt and bring just to a boil, stirring to dissolve the sugar. Remove from the heat and stir in the butter.

5. Gradually spoon half of the warm sticky toffee over the cake, allowing it to be absorbed slightly before adding more. Let cool completely, about 2 hours.

6. Rewarm the remaining toffee topping if necessary and spread it evenly over the cake. Sprinkle with fleur de sel. Cut the cake into squares and serve.
—*Jessica Koslow*

Praline Brownies

Active **45 min**; Total **1 hr 30 min plus cooling**; Makes **one 9-by-13-inch pan**

It's hard to improve on perfectly fudgy brownies, but pastry chef Kelly Fields of Willa Jean in New Orleans does it by studding them with crunchy bites of pecan praline—the quintessential NOLA candy.

PRALINE

- 1½ cups pecans (5 oz.)
- 1½ cups packed light brown sugar
- ¾ cup granulated sugar
- 6 Tbsp. unsalted butter
- ¾ cup heavy cream
- ¾ tsp. kosher salt
- ¾ tsp. pure vanilla extract

BROWNIES

- Baking spray
- 2 cups all-purpose flour
- ½ cup unsweetened cocoa powder (not Dutch-process)
- 1 cup granulated sugar
- 1½ sticks unsalted butter
- 2 cups finely chopped dark chocolate (70%), preferably Valrhona (7 oz.)
- 6 large eggs
- 1½ cups packed light brown sugar
- 1 tsp. kosher salt

1. Make the praline Preheat the oven to 350°. Spread the pecans on a baking sheet and toast for about 10 minutes, until golden. Leave the oven on.

2. In a medium saucepan, combine both sugars with the butter and cream and cook over moderate heat, stirring occasionally, until the mixture registers 230° on a candy thermometer, about 8 minutes. Stir in the toasted pecans and salt. Cook, stirring occasionally, until the mixture reaches 240°, about 2 minutes longer. Remove the pan from the heat and stir in the vanilla. Let the mixture cool down to 210°, then stir with a wooden spoon until it stiffens and looks cloudy. Scrape the praline onto a parchment paper–lined baking sheet. Spread in an even layer and let cool. Transfer the praline to a work surface and coarsely chop.

3. Meanwhile, make the brownies Coat a 9-by-13-inch baking pan with baking spray. In a medium bowl, sift the flour with the cocoa powder and granulated sugar. In a medium saucepan set over another saucepan of gently simmering water, melt the butter with the chocolate, stirring until smooth, about 5 minutes. Let cool slightly.

4. In a large bowl, using a hand mixer, beat the eggs with the light brown sugar and salt at medium speed for 2 minutes. Beat in the dry ingredients in 4 additions, scraping down the side and bottom of the bowl. With the mixer on, drizzle in the chocolate mixture and beat at low speed until well combined. Fold in the chopped praline.

5. Scrape the brownie batter into the prepared pan and bake for about 40 minutes, until a cake tester inserted in the center comes out clean with just a few moist crumbs attached. Transfer to a rack to cool completely before cutting into bars. —*Kelly Fields*

MAKE AHEAD The brownies can be refrigerated for up to 5 days.

Hazelnut Chocolate Bars

Active **25 min**; Total **1 hr 15 min**; Makes **12**

To make these supersimple chocolate bars, blogger Molly Yeh grinds up hazelnuts into "a chewy marzipan situation." (She warns not to overblend, though, or you could end up with nut butter.) Yeh dunks the nut candies in melted chocolate and tops them with colored sprinkles. To make them look like store-bought candy bars, wrap the sweets individually in foil, then paper.

- 2 cups peeled toasted hazelnuts (see Note)
- 1 cup confectioners' sugar
- 1 tsp. pure vanilla extract
- ½ tsp. pure almond extract
- ¼ tsp. kosher salt
- ½ cup light corn syrup
- 8 oz. dark chocolate, finely chopped
  Sprinkles, for garnish

1. In a food processor, pulse the hazelnuts just until finely ground. Add the sugar, vanilla extract, almond extract and salt and pulse to combine. With the machine on, drizzle in the corn syrup and blend until the mixture comes together. Turn the mixture out onto a parchment paper–lined baking sheet and form into a 12-by-2-inch bar. Cut the bar crosswise into 12 equal pieces and freeze until firm, at least 15 minutes.

2. In a microwave-safe medium bowl, melt the chocolate in 30-second intervals, stirring, until smooth. Let cool to room temperature.

3. Using a fork, dip the hazelnut candy into the chocolate to evenly coat, letting the excess drip off. Arrange the bars on the baking sheet and top with sprinkles. Refrigerate until firm, at least 30 minutes. Serve cold. —*Molly Yeh*

NOTE The recipe also works well with unsalted pistachios or almonds.

MAKE AHEAD The bars can be refrigerated for up to 5 days.

Chocolate Chunk Cookie for One

Total **30 min**; Makes **1**

If you're looking to avoid gorging on sweets, bake this chewy-crisp cookie for one in the toaster oven. Note: The photo opposite is not to scale!

- 1 Tbsp. unsalted butter
- 1 Tbsp. packed light brown sugar
- 1 tsp. granulated sugar
- ⅛ tsp. pure vanilla extract
  Maldon salt
- 2 Tbsp. all-purpose flour
- 1½ Tbsp. dark chocolate chunks or chips

Preheat a toaster oven to 350°. In a small microwave-safe bowl, microwave the butter until just softened, about 10 seconds. Using a fork, blend in both sugars, the vanilla and a pinch of salt. Blend in the flour, then stir in the chocolate chunks. Scoop the batter onto a parchment paper–lined toaster tray and sprinkle with salt. Bake for 13 to 15 minutes, until lightly browned. Let cool slightly before eating. —*Justin Chapple*

Buttery Diamond Cookies

Active **20 min**; Total **3 hr 30 min plus cooling**; Makes **4 dozen**

- 1¼ cups all-purpose flour
- 12 Tbsp. unsalted butter, cubed and chilled
- ¼ tsp. kosher salt
- 1 cup confectioners' sugar
- ½ large egg yolk
- 1 tsp. pure vanilla extract
- ½ cup turbinado sugar
- 1 large egg white, lightly beaten

1. In a food processor, pulse the flour, butter and salt until small pea-size pieces form. Transfer to a medium bowl and add the confectioners' sugar, egg yolk and vanilla. Using your hands, knead and press the mixture just until a dough forms; divide in half. On a lightly floured surface, roll each dough half into a 12-inch log. Wrap the logs in plastic and refrigerate until firm, about 2 hours.

2. Line 2 baking sheets with parchment paper. Spread the turbinado sugar on a large plate. Brush the logs with the egg white and roll in the turbinado sugar. Slice crosswise ½ inch thick and arrange

the slices on the prepared sheets, spacing them 2 inches apart. Freeze for 1 hour.

3. Preheat the oven to 375°. Bake the cookies for 12 to 14 minutes, shifting the pans from top to bottom and front to back halfway through, until the bottoms are golden. Transfer to racks to cool completely. —*Daniel Rose*

MAKE AHEAD The cookies can be stored in an airtight container at room temperature for up to 1 week.

Almond Shortbread Cookies

Total **45 min plus cooling**
Makes **about 2 dozen**

Almonds in three forms—sliced, butter and meal—along with coconut oil give these cookies a deeply nutty flavor.

- ½ cup sliced almonds
- 1¼ cups all-purpose flour
- ½ cup almond meal
- ½ tsp. kosher salt
- ½ cup smooth unsalted roasted almond butter
- ½ cup refined coconut oil, melted
- ½ cup granulated sugar
- ¼ cup turbinado sugar
- 1 tsp. pure vanilla extract

1. Preheat the oven to 350°. Line a baking sheet with parchment paper.

2. Spread the sliced almonds in a pie plate and bake for about 8 minutes, until golden. Let cool, then coarsely chop.

3. In a medium bowl, whisk the flour with the almond meal and salt. In a large bowl, using a hand mixer at medium speed, beat the almond butter with the coconut oil, both sugars and the vanilla until well blended, about 1 minute. Beat in the flour mixture and chopped almonds just until combined.

4. Scoop 2-tablespoon-size mounds of dough onto the prepared baking sheet 1 inch apart and flatten to a ¼-inch thickness. Bake the cookies for 15 to 18 minutes, until golden. Transfer to a rack and let cool completely. —*Kay Chun*

MAKE AHEAD The cookies can be refrigerated in an airtight container for up to 1 week.

CHOCOLATE CHUNK
COOKIE FOR ONE

FINNISH STICKS AND
SLIGHTLY CHEWY
GINGER COOKIES

Finnish Sticks

Active **30 min**; Total **1 hr 45 min plus cooling**; Makes **24 cookies**

Although they're called Finnish Sticks, says Magnus Nilsson, the chef at Fäviken in Järpen, Sweden, these pearl-sugar-topped almond cookies are beloved in his home country. They're one of the most popular snacks for fika, or coffee breaks.

- **1¼ cups cake flour, plus more for dusting**
- **7 Tbsp. unsalted butter, at room temperature**
- **¼ cup granulated sugar**
- **½ tsp. pure almond extract**
- **3 Tbsp. whole milk**
- **1 large egg, beaten**
- **1 Tbsp. finely chopped roasted almonds**
- **1 Tbsp. pearl sugar (see Note)**

1. In a food processor, combine the 1¼ cups of flour with the butter, granulated sugar and almond extract and pulse until a dough forms. Shape into a ball and flatten into a 1-inch-thick disk. Cover with plastic wrap and refrigerate for 1 hour.

2. Preheat the oven to 350°. In a small bowl, beat the milk with the egg.

3. Divide the cookie dough in half. On a lightly floured work surface, roll each piece of dough into a ¾-inch-thick log. Brush the logs with the milk-egg wash and sprinkle with the almonds and pearl sugar. Cut the logs into 2-inch pieces and arrange on a parchment paper–lined baking sheet. Bake the cookies for 12 to 14 minutes, until barely golden. Transfer to a rack to cool before serving. —*Magnus Nilsson*

NOTE Pearl sugar is available at specialty food stores and from kingarthurflour.com.

MAKE AHEAD The cookies can be stored in an airtight container for up to 3 days.

Almond Linzer Heart Cookies

Active **1 hr 15 min**; Total **2 hr 40 min** Makes **16 sandwich cookies**

- **2 sticks plus 2 Tbsp. unsalted butter, at room temperature**
- **¾ cup confectioners' sugar, plus more for dusting**
- **1¾ cups all-purpose flour**
- **½ cup potato starch**
- **Pinch of sea salt**
- **½ cup granulated sugar**
- **½ cup roasted almonds, very finely chopped**
- **One 12-oz. jar raspberry jam**

1. In the bowl of a stand mixer fitted with the paddle, beat the butter and the ¾ cup of confectioners' sugar at low speed until well blended, then beat at medium-high speed until smooth and lightened, scraping down the side of the bowl, about 5 minutes. At low speed, add the flour, potato starch and salt and beat just until the dough comes together; it will be quite soft. Scrape the dough onto a sheet of parchment paper and pat 1 inch thick. Top with another sheet of parchment paper and roll out ¼ inch thick. Transfer the dough to a baking sheet and refrigerate until firm, about 1 hour.

2. Meanwhile, line a baking sheet with parchment paper. In a small saucepan, combine the granulated sugar with ½ cup of water and bring to a boil. Add the almonds and cook over moderately low heat, stirring occasionally, until the syrup is thick and reduced by half, about 15 minutes. Drain the almonds in a sieve. Spread on the prepared sheet in a single layer and let cool completely.

3. Preheat the oven to 350°. Line 2 more baking sheets with parchment paper. Using a 2-inch heart-shaped cookie cutter, stamp out cookies and arrange them 1 inch apart on the prepared sheets. Using a smaller heart-shaped cookie cutter, stamp out the centers of half of the cookies. Transfer the whole cookies to 1 prepared baking sheet and the cutout cookies to another. Gather all of the scraps and reroll them between 2 sheets of parchment to stamp out more cookies. Scatter the candied almonds on top of the cookies with the centers cut out and press gently to help them adhere.

4. Bake the cookies for about 18 minutes, rotating and shifting the pans halfway through, until golden around the edges. Transfer to racks to cool completely.

5. Spoon a scant tablespoon of raspberry jam onto the whole cookies. Dust the cutout cookies with confectioners' sugar and assemble the sandwiches; press gently to adhere. —*Laurent Tourondel*

MAKE AHEAD The sandwich cookies can be stored at room temperature for up to 3 days.

Slightly Chewy Ginger Cookies

Total **30 min**; Makes **24**

Unlike most shortbread cookies, these are made with whole-wheat flour, which gives them a nice toasty flavor.

- **1¼ cups whole-wheat flour**
- **1 tsp. ground ginger**
- **½ tsp. baking soda**
- **Pinch of kosher salt**
- **1 stick plus 2 Tbsp. unsalted butter, at room temperature**
- **⅓ cup plus 1 Tbsp. sugar**
- **2 Tbsp. Lyle's Golden Syrup (treacle; see Note)**

1. Preheat the oven to 350°. Sift the whole-wheat flour with the ginger, baking soda and salt into a small bowl. In a medium bowl, using a hand mixer, beat the butter with the sugar and syrup at medium speed until pale yellow and fluffy, about 3 minutes. Beat in the flour mixture just until incorporated. Knead the dough a few times in the bowl and divide in half.

2. On a parchment paper–lined baking sheet, roll each piece of dough into a 12-inch log, about 1 inch wide. Arrange the logs on the prepared baking sheet 6 inches apart and bake for about 15 minutes, until golden; they will spread a lot. Transfer to a rack to cool until warm. On a work surface, cut the logs crosswise into 1¼-inch slices. Transfer the cookies to a rack to cool before serving. —*Magnus Nilsson*

NOTE Golden syrup is widely available at Whole Foods and specialty food stores.

MAKE AHEAD The cookies can be stored in an airtight container for up to 3 days.

Almond Crescents

Active **30 min**; Total **1 hr 15 min plus cooling**; Makes **about 36**

These butter cookies from Dorie Greenspan's book *Dorie's Cookies* are rich and crumbly crowd-pleasers. They're dusted with confectioners' sugar here, but for a festive pop, sprinkle them with colorful granulated sugar instead.

- **2 sticks unsalted butter, softened**
- **½ cup granulated sugar**
- **½ tsp. fine sea salt**
- **1½ tsp. pure vanilla extract**
- **¼ tsp. pure almond extract**
- **1¾ cups all-purpose flour**
- **1⅓ cups almond flour**
- **1½ cups confectioners' sugar, plus more for dusting**

1. Preheat the oven to 350° and line a large rimmed baking sheet with parchment paper. In a large bowl, using a hand mixer, beat the butter with the granulated sugar and salt at medium speed until light and fluffy, about 3 minutes. Beat in both extracts. Reduce the speed to low and add both flours, mixing until just combined. Refrigerate the dough until firm, about 30 minutes.

2. Scoop 12 rounded tablespoonfuls of the dough onto the prepared baking sheet. Using your hands, roll each ball into a 4-inch rope, then shape into a crescent; return to the baking sheet. If the dough gets too soft, refrigerate until firm. Bake the cookies, rotating the sheet halfway through, until lightly browned around the edges, 13 to 15 minutes. Transfer to a wire rack and let cool for 5 minutes.

3. Sift the 1½ cups of confectioners' sugar into a shallow bowl. Dredge the warm cookies in the confectioners' sugar; return to the rack and let cool completely. Repeat the baking and dredging with the remaining dough. Dust the cookies with more confectioners' sugar before serving. —*Dorie Greenspan*

Swedish Sugared Sweet Pretzels

Active **40 min**; Total **2 hr 20 min plus cooling**; Makes **12**

According to chef Magnus Nilsson, cardamom-flavored sweets are everybody's favorite in his native Sweden. When he makes these tender, sugared pretzels for his kids, he adds a little extra spice.

- **½ cup warm milk (105°–115°)**
- **1 Tbsp. active dry yeast**
- **1½ cups plus 1 tsp. sugar**
- **2 large eggs**
- **3¾ cups all-purpose flour**
- **1 Tbsp. baking powder**
- **¼ tsp. kosher salt**
- **¾ tsp. ground cardamom**
- **1 stick plus 2 Tbsp. unsalted butter, at room temperature, cubed**
- **6 Tbsp. melted butter, for brushing**

1. In the bowl of a stand mixer fitted with the paddle, mix the warm milk with the yeast and 1 teaspoon of the sugar. Let stand until foamy, 5 minutes. Add the eggs, flour, baking powder, salt, cardamom and ¼ cup of the sugar and mix at medium speed, scraping down the bowl, until a shaggy dough forms, about 2 minutes. Add the stick of butter and mix until the dough comes together and is smooth and shiny, about 5 minutes. Shape the dough into a loose ball and cover the bowl with plastic wrap. Let stand at room temperature until doubled in bulk, about 1 hour.

2. On a lightly floured surface, using a lightly floured rolling pin, roll out the dough to an 8-by-12-inch rectangle, with a long side facing you. Spread the remaining 2 tablespoons of butter over the bottom half of the dough. Fold the buttered half over the top half and press down gently; you should have a 4-by-12-inch rectangle. Cut the dough crosswise into twelve 1-inch-wide strips.

3. Twist each piece of dough into a 12-inch-long rope. To form pretzels, shape each rope into a U; cross the 2 sides of the U over each other, twist and press the ends down to form a pretzel shape. Arrange the pretzels about 1 inch apart on 2 parchment paper–lined baking sheets. Cover with a clean kitchen towel and let rest for 30 minutes.

4. Preheat the oven to 425°. Bake the pretzels for 12 to 15 minutes, shifting the pans once, until pale golden. Let cool slightly.

5. Place the remaining 1¼ cups of sugar in a bowl. Put the melted butter in another bowl. While the pretzels are still warm, brush them all over with the melted butter and roll them in sugar to coat. Transfer to a rack to cool before serving. —*Magnus Nilsson*

MAKE AHEAD The pretzels can be frozen in an airtight container for up to 1 month.

Almond-Meringue Cookies

Active **15 min**; Total **2 hr 15 min plus cooling**; Makes **30**

Skye McAlpine, the Venice-based author of the blog From My Dining Table, bakes these cookies at a low temperature so the outsides get crisp while the middles stay chewy. You can swap another nut for the almonds if you prefer.

- **¾ cup whole raw almonds**
- **4 cold large egg whites**
- **1 cup superfine sugar**

1. Preheat the oven to 350°. Spread the almonds in a cake pan and bake until lightly toasted, about 8 minutes. Let cool slightly, then coarsely chop. Reduce the oven temperature to 225°.

2. Line 2 rimmed baking sheets with parchment paper and coat lightly with nonstick cooking spray. In a medium bowl, using a hand mixer, beat the egg whites at low speed until foamy. At moderately high speed, beat in the sugar 1 tablespoon at a time; continue beating until glossy, firm peaks form, about 10 minutes. Fold in the almonds.

3. Scoop fifteen 2-tablespoon-size mounds of the meringue onto each of the prepared baking sheets. Bake for 1 hour, until the meringues are firm. Turn the oven off; leave the cookies in for 30 minutes, then transfer to a rack to cool. —*Skye McAlpine*

SWEDISH SUGARED
SWEET PRETZELS

Bakewell Biscotti

Active **1 hr**; Total **2 hr plus cooling**
Makes **about 30 biscotti sandwiches**

For the opening of his London bakery, New York City pastry chef Dominique Ansel dreamed up riffs on time-honored British classics. The inspiration for these cherry-filled biscotti sandwiches was the 19th-century Bakewell tart, pie pastry layered with jam and frangipane (almond cream).

BISCOTTI

- 2½ **cups bread flour, plus more for dusting**
- ½ **tsp. baking soda**
- ¼ **tsp. fine salt**
- 1⅓ **cups granulated sugar**
- 4 **Tbsp. unsalted butter, softened**
- 1 **tsp. finely grated lemon zest**
- 3 **large eggs**
- ¾ **cup dried sour cherries, chopped**

FILLING

- 1 **stick unsalted butter, softened**
- ¾ **cup confectioners' sugar**
- 2 **large eggs**
- 1½ **cups almond flour**
- 2 **Tbsp. cornstarch**
- 1 **Tbsp. dark rum**
  Cherry jam, for spreading

1. Make the biscotti Preheat the oven to 350°. Line a large baking sheet with parchment paper. In a medium bowl, whisk the 2½ cups of bread flour with the baking soda and salt.

2. In a stand mixer fitted with the paddle, beat the granulated sugar with the butter and lemon zest at medium speed until pale and creamy, about 2 minutes. Beat in the eggs 1 at a time until incorporated. At low speed, beat in the dry ingredients until the dough just comes together, then beat in the dried cherries.

3. Scrape the dough onto the prepared baking sheet; using lightly floured hands, shape it into a 15-by-5-inch log. Bake for about 35 minutes, until golden and just firm, then let cool completely on the baking sheet.

4. Meanwhile, make the filling In a stand mixer fitted with the paddle, beat the butter with the confectioners' sugar at medium speed until smooth. Beat in the eggs 1 at a time until incorporated; scrape down the side and bottom of the bowl as needed. Beat in the almond flour and cornstarch until combined, then beat in the rum. Transfer the almond cream to a medium bowl and refrigerate until just set, about 20 minutes.

5. Transfer the baked log to a cutting board. Using a serrated knife, cut it crosswise into ¼-inch-thick slices. Spread a scant tablespoon of the almond cream on half of the slices and arrange them on 2 large parchment paper–lined baking sheets. Spread a teaspoon of cherry jam on the almond cream. Close the sandwiches with the remaining slices.

6. Bake the biscotti sandwiches for about 15 minutes, until lightly browned and nearly crisp. Let cool completely before serving. —*Dominique Ansel*

MAKE AHEAD The biscotti sandwiches can be stored in an airtight container for up to 5 days.

Peanut Butter and Jelly Sandwich Cookies

Active **40 min**; Total **1 hr 30 min**
Makes **12 sandwich cookies**

Tiffany MacIsaac of Buttercream Bakeshop in Washington, DC, gives her PB&J sandwich cookies extra nutty crunch by sprinkling honey-roasted peanuts on the dough before baking.

COOKIE DOUGH

- 1½ **cups all-purpose flour**
- 1½ **tsp. baking soda**
- ¼ **tsp. kosher salt**
- 1 **stick unsalted butter, at room temperature**
- ½ **cup lightly packed light brown sugar**
- ½ **cup granulated sugar**
- 1 **large egg**
- ½ **tsp. pure vanilla extract**
- ½ **cup creamy natural peanut butter**
- ¼ **cup chopped honey-roasted peanuts**

FILLING

- ⅓ **cup creamy natural peanut butter**
- 5 **Tbsp. unsalted butter, softened**
- ¼ **cup confectioners' sugar**
- ¼ **tsp. pure vanilla extract**
- ⅛ **tsp. kosher salt**
- ¼ **cup seedless jam, such as Concord grape, raspberry or strawberry**

1. Make the dough Preheat the oven to 350°. Line 2 large baking sheets with parchment paper. In a medium bowl, whisk the flour, baking soda and salt. In another medium bowl, using a hand mixer, beat the butter with both sugars at medium speed until light and fluffy, about 3 minutes. Beat in the egg and vanilla, then beat in the dry ingredients in 3 batches, mixing well between additions. Fold in the peanut butter until fully incorporated.

2. Scoop 24 one-inch balls of dough onto the baking sheets at least 2 inches apart. Press the balls down slightly; they should be about 1½ inches in diameter. Sprinkle the tops with the chopped peanuts. Bake the cookies for 10 to 12 minutes, until the edges are light golden brown and the tops are slightly cracked; rotate the baking sheets halfway through. Let the cookies cool for 10 minutes on the baking sheet, then transfer to a rack to cool completely.

3. Meanwhile, make the filling In a bowl, using a hand mixer, whip the peanut butter with the butter, confectioners' sugar, vanilla and salt at medium speed until fluffy, about 5 minutes. Refrigerate for about 45 minutes, until chilled.

4. Spoon 1½ tablespoons of the filling on the underside of 12 cookies. Spread 1 teaspoon of jam on the underside of the remaining cookies. Sandwich the halves together and serve. —*Tiffany MacIsaac*

Macadamia and Milk Chocolate–Peppermint Cream Sandwich Cookies

Active **1 hr**; Total **3 hr 15 min**
Makes **about 30 sandwich cookies**

COOKIES

- **2 cups finely chopped macadamia nuts (10 oz.)**
- **2 sticks unsalted butter, softened**
- **½ cup packed light brown sugar**
- **½ cup granulated sugar**
- **1½ tsp. pure vanilla extract**
- **2 cups all-purpose flour**
- **1 tsp. kosher salt**

FILLING

- **5 oz. milk chocolate, finely chopped**
- **2 oz. bittersweet chocolate, finely chopped**
- **½ cup heavy cream**
- **½ tsp. peppermint extract**
- **Pinch of kosher salt**

1. Make the cookies Preheat the oven to 350°. Spread the nuts on a baking sheet and toast for about 8 minutes, until light golden. Let cool.

2. In a medium bowl, using a hand mixer, beat the butter with both sugars at medium speed until light and fluffy, about 3 minutes. Beat in the vanilla, then add the flour and salt and mix just until a dough forms. Stir in the nuts. On a sheet of parchment paper, roll out the dough ¼ inch thick. Transfer the parchment and dough to a baking sheet and refrigerate for 1 hour.

3. Line 2 baking sheets with parchment paper. Using a 1½-inch cookie cutter, stamp out rounds from the dough and arrange them 1 inch apart on the prepared sheets. Gather the scraps and stamp out more rounds. Refrigerate the cookies for 1 hour.

4. Bake the cookies for about 12 minutes, rotating the baking sheets halfway through, until golden. Transfer to a rack to cool.

5. Meanwhile, make the filling In a heatproof medium bowl, combine the chocolates. In a small saucepan, bring the cream to a simmer. Pour the cream over the chocolate and let stand for 2 minutes; stir until smooth. Stir in the peppermint extract and salt and refrigerate for about 1 hour, until thick.

6. Spread 1½ teaspoons of the filling on the underside of half of the cookies and sandwich with the remaining cookies. —*Jonathan Waxman*

MAKE AHEAD The sandwich cookies can be kept in an airtight container for up to 3 days.

Seaweed Shortbread

Active **25 min**; Total **2 hr plus cooling**
Makes **about 30 cookies**

These sweet and savory shortbreads get a pleasant brininess from an unexpected ingredient: seasoned roasted seaweed, which is commonly used in Asian desserts, like Korean junbyung cookies.

- **2 sticks unsalted butter, softened, plus more for greasing**
- **2 cups plus 2 Tbsp. all-purpose flour**
- **½ cup rice flour**
- **½ tsp. kosher salt**
- **½ cup plus 3 Tbsp. seasoned roasted seaweed (kimjaban; see Note)**
- **½ cup superfine sugar, plus more for sprinkling**
- **1 large egg beaten with 1 tsp. water**
- **Flaky sea salt, for sprinkling**

1. Preheat the oven to 300°. Grease a 9-inch-square baking pan and line with parchment paper, leaving a few inches of overhang at 2 ends. Line a rimmed baking sheet with parchment paper.

2. In a medium bowl, whisk both flours with the kosher salt. Place the seaweed in a small resealable plastic bag and lightly crush with a rolling pin. Whisk ½ cup of the crushed seaweed into the dry ingredients.

3. In a large bowl, using a hand mixer, beat the 2 sticks of butter at moderately high speed until light and fluffy, about 2 minutes. Add the ½ cup of sugar and beat until the mixture is smooth and pale yellow, scraping down the side of the bowl as needed, about 2 minutes more. Beat in the dry ingredients; the mixture will resemble wet sand and hold together when pressed. Transfer the dough to the prepared pan and pat into an even layer. Bake for about 1 hour and 20 minutes, or until the shortbread is a light golden brown. Let cool on a rack for 5 minutes.

4. Using the parchment overhang, transfer the shortbread to a work surface. Brush the top with the egg wash and sprinkle with sugar, flaky sea salt and the remaining 3 tablespoons of crushed seaweed. Cut the shortbread square into thirds, then slice crosswise into ¾-inch-wide cookies. Transfer to the prepared baking sheet and bake until golden brown on top, about 10 minutes. Transfer the cookies to a rack and let cool completely before serving. —*Judy Joo*

NOTE Kimjaban, a crumbled seaweed snack seasoned with sesame oil, salt and sugar, is available at Asian grocery stores and on amazon.com. You can also use sheets of seasoned roasted seaweed.

MAKE AHEAD The cookies can be stored in an airtight container for up to 1 week.

Chocolate Chip Espresso Meringues

Active **20 min**; Total **1 hr 20 min plus cooling**; Makes **8**

- **3 large egg whites, at room temperature**
- **½ tsp. cream of tartar**
- **1 cup superfine sugar**
- **2 oz. bittersweet chocolate, finely chopped (scant ½ cup)**
- **Kosher salt**
- **1 Tbsp. unsweetened cocoa powder**
- **2 tsp. espresso powder**

1. Preheat the oven to 225°. Line a large rimmed baking sheet with parchment paper. In a medium bowl, using a hand mixer, beat the egg whites with the cream of tartar at low speed until foamy, about 30 seconds. Increase the speed to medium and beat in the sugar, 1 tablespoon at a time; beat until the whites are stiff and glossy, about 1 minute. Fold in the chopped chocolate and a pinch of salt. Sift the cocoa powder and espresso powder over the meringue and fold 2 or 3 times to incorporate; the meringue should look marbled.

2. Spoon eight ½-cup mounds of meringue onto the prepared baking sheet. Using the back of a spoon, gently spread the meringues into 3-inch rounds. Bake until the meringues are firm on the outside but still chewy in the center, about 1 hour. Let cool completely. —*Abigail Quinn*

MAKE AHEAD The meringues can be stored in an airtight container for up to 1 week.

Caramel "Falafel"

Active **2 hr**; Total **3 hr 30 min plus overnight freezing**; Makes **about 20**

Although these golden nuggets look like falafel balls, they are in fact exquisite cream puffs fried with a genius coating of chocolaty panko.

CHOUX

- ¼ **cup whole milk**
- 5½ **Tbsp. unsalted butter, cubed and softened**
- 1 **tsp. granulated sugar**
- 1 **tsp. kosher salt**
- ⅔ **cup all-purpose flour**
- 3 **large eggs**
- 1 **large egg beaten with 1 large egg yolk**

FILLING

- 1½ **cups heavy cream**
- ⅔ **cup light corn syrup**
- ¼ **cup packed dark brown sugar**
- ½ **cup granulated sugar**
- ½ **tsp. fleur de sel**

COATING

- 1 **cup panko**
- 1 **Tbsp. unsweetened cocoa powder**
- 1 **large egg beaten with 1 large egg yolk**

  Grapeseed or canola oil, for frying

  Confectioners' sugar, for dusting

1. Make the choux Preheat the oven to 375°. Line a large baking sheet with parchment paper.

2. In a medium saucepan, combine ⅓ cup of water with the milk, butter, granulated sugar and kosher salt and bring to a boil over moderate heat. When the butter melts, add the flour all at once and beat with a wooden spoon until a tight dough pulls away from the side of the pan, about 2 minutes.

3. Scrape the dough into a medium bowl. Using a wooden spoon, beat in the eggs 1 at a time until smooth. The dough should be glossy and fall slowly from the spoon in thick ribbons. Scoop the dough into a pastry bag fitted with a ½-inch plain tip. Pipe 1½-inch mounds onto the prepared baking sheet, spacing them 1 inch apart. Brush the mounds with the beaten egg and bake for about 30 minutes, until browned and puffed; rotate the sheet halfway through baking. Let the choux cool completely.

4. Meanwhile, make the filling In a medium saucepan, combine the cream, corn syrup and brown sugar and bring just to a boil, stirring. Keep warm over very low heat.

5. In another medium saucepan, cook ¼ cup of the granulated sugar over high heat, without stirring, until it starts to caramelize, about 3 minutes. Gradually whisk in the remaining ¼ cup of sugar, letting it start to caramelize before adding more. Cook, swirling the pan occasionally, until a deep amber caramel forms, about 3 minutes. Remove from the heat and carefully whisk in the warm cream mixture.

6. Bring the caramel to a boil over high heat and cook, whisking occasionally, until it reaches 228° on a candy thermometer, about 12 minutes. Remove from the heat and stir in the fleur de sel. Let cool completely. Transfer to a pastry bag fitted with a ¼-inch plain tip. Refrigerate until just chilled, about 45 minutes.

7. Insert the piping tip in the bottom of each choux and pipe in the caramel filling.

8. Make the coating In a medium bowl, whisk the panko with the cocoa powder. Brush each choux with some of the beaten egg, then dredge in the panko and return to the baking sheet. Freeze overnight.

9. In a large saucepan, heat 3 inches of oil to 350°. In batches, fry the choux over moderate heat, turning, until browned and crisp, about 4 minutes per batch. Using a slotted spoon, transfer the falafel to paper towels to drain. Let stand for 10 minutes, then dust with confectioners' sugar and serve. —*Dominique Ansel*

Rice Pudding with Apricot Preserves

Active **15 min**; Total **2 hr 15 min**
Serves **6 to 8**

British pastry chef James Parker borrows his grandmother's trick of swirling sweetened condensed milk into rice pudding to make it extra rich and glossy.

- 1 **cup arborio rice (½ lb.)**
- 2 **cups whole milk**
- 1 **cup heavy cream**
- 1¼ **cups sugar**
- ¼ **cup sweetened condensed milk**

  Demerara sugar, apricot preserves and sliced dried Blenheim apricots, for serving

1. Preheat the oven to 325°. Bring a medium saucepan of water to a boil. Stir in the rice and simmer for 5 minutes. Remove from the heat and let stand for 5 minutes. Drain the rice and rinse under cold water, then drain again.

2. In a 2-quart ovenproof baking dish, mix the rice with the milk, cream and sugar. Bake, stirring every 30 minutes, until the rice is tender and the pudding has thickened, 1 hour and 45 minutes. Let the pudding cool on a rack for 10 minutes, then fold in the condensed milk. Serve the rice pudding with demerara sugar, apricot preserves and dried apricots. —*James Parker*

DIY Doughnuts

ALEX TALBOT and **AKI KAMOZAWA** of Curiosity Doughnuts in Stockton, New Jersey, tinkered with the recipe for apple cider doughnuts until they deemed them perfect. Top them with a luscious glaze or roll them in cinnamon-cardamom sugar.

Apple Cider Doughnuts

Active **1 hr 45 min**; Total **7 hr 15 min**
Makes **about 13 doughnuts and doughnut holes, plus scraps**

DOUGHNUTS

- 1¼ cups plus 2 Tbsp. fresh apple cider
- 3 Tbsp. unsalted butter
- 4½ cups plus 1 Tbsp. all-purpose flour, plus more for dusting
- 1 cup heavy cream
- 1 cup granulated sugar
- 2 large eggs
- 2 tsp. vanilla bean paste
- 1 Tbsp. baking powder
- 2 tsp. fine salt
- 1 tsp. baking soda
  Canola or rice bran oil, for frying

CIDER GLAZE

- ¼ cup granulated sugar
- ¼ cup heavy cream
- ¼ cup boiled cider (see Note)
- 3 Tbsp. unsalted butter
- 1 tsp. fine salt
- ¼ cup plus 2 Tbsp. buttermilk
- 2¼ cups confectioners' sugar

CINNAMON-CARDAMOM SUGAR

- 1 cup granulated sugar
- 1½ Tbsp. ground cinnamon
- 2 tsp. ground cardamom

MAKE THE DOUGH

1. In a small saucepan, combine ¼ cup plus 2 tablespoons of the apple cider and the butter and bring to a boil over moderate heat. Stir in ¼ cup plus 1 tablespoon of the flour and cook, stirring constantly, until a paste forms and pulls away from the pan, 1 to 2 minutes. Scrape the paste into a small bowl and let cool, then refrigerate until well chilled, about 2 hours.

2. In a blender, combine the cider paste with the cream, granulated sugar, eggs, vanilla bean paste and the remaining 1 cup of cider and puree until smooth. In a large bowl, whisk the remaining 4¼ cups of flour with the baking powder, salt and baking soda. Add the wet ingredients and, using a rubber spatula, stir until a sticky dough forms.

3. Scrape the dough out onto a plastic-lined large baking sheet. Cover with a large sheet of plastic wrap and pat the dough 1 inch thick. Refrigerate until well chilled, at least 4 hours.

MAKE THE TOPPINGS

4. Make the glaze In a small saucepan, combine the granulated sugar with 1 tablespoon of water and cook over moderately high heat, swirling occasionally, until an amber caramel forms, 5 to 7 minutes. Remove from the heat and carefully add the cream and boiled cider; the caramel will seize. Cook over moderate heat, stirring with a wooden spoon, until the caramel dissolves, about 2 minutes. Gradually add the butter and cook until thickened slightly, about 2 minutes. Stir in the salt. Scrape the mixture into a medium bowl and let cool completely. Whisk in the buttermilk and confectioners' sugar until the glaze is smooth.

5. Make the cinnamon sugar In a medium bowl, whisk the granulated sugar with the ground cinnamon and cardamom.

MAKE THE DOUGHNUTS

6. Remove the top sheet of plastic wrap and invert the dough onto a floured work surface. Peel off the plastic and dust the dough with flour. Roll out the dough ½ inch thick. Using a 3-inch round biscuit cutter, stamp out 13 rounds. Using a 1-inch round cutter, stamp out the center from each round. Cut the scraps into 2-inch pieces. Transfer the doughnuts,

---

STEP-BY-STEP DOUGHNUT LESSON

MAKE A CIDER PASTE Boil fresh apple cider with butter, then add flour and cook until a thick paste forms. Let cool, then chill.

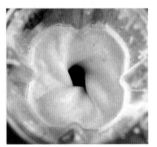

GET OUT YOUR BLENDER Add the chilled cider paste, cream, sugar, eggs, vanilla and cider and blend until smooth.

MAKE THE DOUGH Mix the wet ingredients into the dry until a tacky dough forms. Pat out on a baking sheet and chill.

ROLL IT OUT Unwrap the chilled dough on a floured work surface and roll it out about ½ inch thick.

The dough, glaze and spiced sugar can all be prepared ahead. Then, you only need to spend a half hour at the stove for the ultimate luxury: warm doughnuts.

holes and scraps to 2 baking sheets and refrigerate until chilled, about 30 minutes.

7. In a large saucepan, heat 3 inches of canola oil to 375° and top 2 baking sheets with racks. Keep the doughnuts chilled. Add one-third of the scraps at a time to the hot oil and fry, turning once, until browned, about 2 minutes per batch. Using a slotted spoon, transfer the scraps to a rack.

8. Return the oil to 375°. Add the doughnut holes and fry until browned all over, 1 to 2 minutes. Using a slotted spoon, transfer to a rack. Toss the doughnut scraps and holes in the cinnamon-cardamom sugar until coated and transfer to a platter.

9. Return the oil to 375°. In batches, fry the doughnuts, turning once, until browned, about 3 minutes per batch. Using a slotted spoon, transfer the doughnuts to a rack to cool for 10 minutes.

10. Stir the glaze. Dip one side of each doughnut in the glaze and let stand until set before serving.

NOTE Boiled cider is available online from kingarthurflour.com.

MAKE AHEAD The recipe can be prepared ahead through Step 5; refrigerate the doughnut dough and glaze overnight.

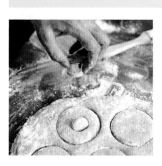

GO AROUND IN CIRCLES Using 3-inch and 1-inch round cutters, stamp out doughnuts and holes. Cut scraps into 2-inch pieces.

FRY AND TOSS Fry the scraps and holes in separate batches and toss to coat in cinnamon-cardamom sugar while warm.

KEEP ON FRYING Cook the doughnuts in batches, turning once, until browned. Let cool on a rack for 10 minutes.

GET YOUR GLAZE ON Hold each doughnut and dip it in cider glaze to coat; transfer to a rack and let stand until set.

FLAN DE CARAMELO

Flan de Caramelo

Active **30 min**; Total **1 hr 30 min plus 2 hr chilling**; Serves **8**

"For the home cook, nothing is more comforting than a custard—nothing," says *Bizarre Foods* host Andrew Zimmern. "And this one is phenomenally delicious, thanks to the simple addition of orange, a Spanish signature."

CARAMEL

- **1 cup sugar**
- **2 Tbsp. light corn syrup**
- **2 Tbsp. fresh orange juice plus 1 Tbsp. finely grated orange zest**

CUSTARD

1½ cups milk

1½ cups heavy cream

3 large eggs

2 large egg yolks

⅔ cup sugar

1 Tbsp. finely grated orange zest

1½ tsp. pure vanilla extract

Kosher salt

1. Make the caramel In a small saucepan, gently stir the sugar with the corn syrup, orange juice and 2 tablespoons of water. Bring to a boil over moderate heat. Cook, without stirring, until an amber caramel forms, 6 to 8 minutes. Brush down the side of the pan with a wet pastry brush if crystals form. Remove the pan from the heat and swirl in the orange zest. Working quickly, pour the caramel into eight 6-ounce ramekins, tilting to coat the bottoms.

2. Make the custard Preheat the oven to 350°. In a medium saucepan, combine the milk and cream and cook over moderate heat until the temperature reaches 160° on a candy thermometer, 5 to 7 minutes. Meanwhile, in a large heatproof bowl, whisk the eggs with the egg yolks, sugar, orange zest, vanilla and a pinch of salt. While whisking constantly, slowly add the hot milk mixture to the eggs. Strain the custard through a fine-mesh sieve set over a large heatproof measuring cup.

3. Line a roasting pan with a kitchen towel and set the ramekins on the towel. Pour the custard into the ramekins. Add enough boiling water to the roasting pan to reach halfway up the sides of the ramekins.

4. Loosely tent the pan with foil and bake the flans for 35 to 40 minutes, until just set but still jiggly in the center. Using tongs, carefully transfer the ramekins to a rack and let the flans cool to room temperature. Cover with plastic wrap and refrigerate for at least 2 hours or, preferably, overnight.

5. Run a thin knife around each flan. Invert a plate over each ramekin, then turn the flan out onto the plate, shaking the ramekin gently if necessary. Serve immediately. —*Andrew Zimmern*

MAKE AHEAD The flans can be wrapped in plastic and refrigerated for up to 4 days.

WINE Young tawny port: Quinta do Noval 10 Year Old.

Chocolate Pot de Crème with Candied Brioche Whipped Cream

Active **1 hr 15 min**; Total **2 hr plus cooling** Serves **8**

Chef Gavin Kaysen of Minneapolis's Spoon and Stable created this dessert in honor of his grandmother Dorothy. "She used to make a big bowl of chocolate pudding and then set it in the middle of the table with a handful of spoons," he recalls.

PUDDING

- **2 cups heavy cream**
- **1½ Tbsp. instant espresso powder**
- **5 oz. dark chocolate (60% cocoa), finely chopped**
- **2 large eggs**
- **2 large egg yolks**
- **½ cup sugar**
- **¼ tsp. kosher salt**

CROUTONS

- **3 oz. brioche, cut into ½-inch dice**
- **¾ cup sugar**
- **Ground cinnamon, for sprinkling**

WHIPPED CREAM

- **¼ cup warm heavy cream, plus ½ cup chilled heavy cream**
- **1 Tbsp. sugar**

1. Make the pudding Preheat the oven to 325°. Set an 8-inch round soufflé dish in a small roasting pan. In a medium saucepan, whisk the cream with the espresso powder and bring just to a simmer over moderately high heat. Remove from the heat, add the chocolate and let stand for 2 minutes; whisk until smooth.

2. In a large bowl, whisk the eggs and yolks with the sugar and salt. Gradually whisk in one-fourth of the hot chocolate cream until smooth; gradually whisk in the remaining cream. Strain the pudding through a fine sieve into the soufflé dish. Add enough hot water to the roasting pan to reach halfway up the side of the soufflé dish. Bake the pudding for about 50 minutes, until just set. Let cool slightly, then remove from the water bath and let cool completely.

3. Meanwhile, make the croutons Spread the brioche on a baking sheet and toast in the oven until golden, about 12 minutes. Transfer the croutons to a bowl and let cool completely. Wipe off the baking sheet and line it with a sheet of parchment paper.

4. In a medium saucepan, combine the sugar with ¼ cup of water and cook over moderately high heat, stirring occasionally, until the temperature reaches 240° on a candy thermometer, about 7 minutes. Stir in the brioche and cook, stirring, until the croutons are coated in an amber caramel, 3 to 5 minutes. Spread on the prepared baking sheet and sprinkle with cinnamon. Let cool completely, then coarsely crush the candied croutons.

5. Make the whipped cream In a blender, combine the ¼ cup of warm heavy cream with the sugar and one-fourth of the candied croutons; puree until smooth. Let cool.

6. In a large bowl, using a hand mixer, beat the ½ cup of cold heavy cream at high speed until soft peaks form. Fold in the candied brioche cream and beat at high speed until stiff peaks form. Spoon the chocolate pot de crème into glasses and top with the candied brioche whipped cream and the remaining candied croutons. —*Gavin Kaysen*

MAKE AHEAD The pudding can be refrigerated overnight; bring to room temperature before serving. The croutons can be stored in an airtight container at room temperature overnight.

Chocolate-Cookie Crunch Trifle

Active **50 min**; Total **4 hr 15 min**; Serves **8**

PUDDING

- 2 **cups heavy cream**
- 2 **cups whole milk**
- 1 **cup granulated sugar**
- ¼ **cup cornstarch**
- ¼ **cup unsweetened cocoa powder**
- 2 **large eggs**
- 6 **oz. bittersweet chocolate, coarsely chopped (1½ cups)**
- 1 **Tbsp. unsalted butter**
- ¼ **tsp. kosher salt**

WHIPPED CREAM

- 2 **cups heavy cream, chilled**
- ½ **cup confectioners' sugar**
- 1 **tsp. pure vanilla extract**
  Pinch of kosher salt
- 4 **cups coarsely chopped crunchy cookies, such as Oreos, Thin Mints, shortbread, biscotti, Nutter Butters or Samoas**

1. Make the pudding In a medium saucepan, combine 1¾ cups of the heavy cream with the milk and granulated sugar and bring to a bare simmer over moderately low heat, stirring occasionally, about 12 minutes. Meanwhile, sift the cornstarch and cocoa powder into a medium bowl, then whisk in the eggs and the remaining ¼ cup of heavy cream to form a smooth paste. Gradually whisk 1 cup of the hot milk into the cornstarch mixture, then scrape the mixture into the saucepan and cook over moderately low heat, stirring constantly, until the pudding is thick enough to coat the back of a spoon, about 30 minutes.

2. Put the chopped chocolate in a heatproof medium bowl and set a fine sieve over it. Strain the pudding over the chocolate and let stand for 3 minutes. Whisk until smooth, then whisk in the butter and salt. Press a sheet of plastic wrap directly on the surface of the pudding and refrigerate until chilled, about 3 hours.

3. Make the whipped cream In a medium bowl, using a hand mixer, beat the heavy cream with the confectioners' sugar, vanilla and salt until firm, about 5 minutes.

4. In a 3-quart trifle bowl, make 4 layers each of the pudding, whipped cream and crushed cookies. Serve. —*Tiffany MacIsaac*

MAKE AHEAD The recipe can be prepared through Step 2 and refrigerated for up to 4 days.

Banana and Chocolate Cream Pie Parfaits

📷 PAGE 320

Active **45 min**; Total **1 hr 45 min**; Serves **6**

PUDDING

- ¼ **cup plus 1 Tbsp. cornstarch**
- ½ **cup sugar**
- 1 **Tbsp. light corn syrup**
- ¼ **tsp. kosher salt**
- ¼ **cup plus 2 Tbsp. unsweetened cocoa powder**
- 1½ **oz. bittersweet chocolate, finely chopped**
- 1 **Tbsp. unsalted butter**

CRUMBS

- 9 **whole graham crackers, coarsely crushed**
- 2 **Tbsp. unsalted butter, melted**
- 2 **tsp. honey**
- ½ **tsp. ground cinnamon**
  Pinch of kosher salt

BANANA CREAM

- 1 **cup heavy cream**
- ⅓ **cup sugar**
- ¼ **cup mashed banana**
- ½ **vanilla bean, split lengthwise and seeds scraped**
- 2 **bananas, peeled and sliced, for serving**
- 1 **pint banana or vanilla ice cream, for serving**

1. Make the pudding In a small bowl, whisk the cornstarch with ½ cup of water. In a medium saucepan, combine the sugar, corn syrup and salt with 1½ cups of water and bring to a boil. Whisk in the cocoa powder, then whisk in the cornstarch slurry and cook over moderate heat until thick, about 1 minute. Remove from the heat and whisk in the chocolate and butter until smooth. Scrape the pudding into a bowl and press a piece of plastic wrap directly on the surface. Let cool, then refrigerate until chilled, about 1 hour.

2. Meanwhile, make the crumbs In a medium bowl, toss the crushed graham crackers with the butter, honey, cinnamon and salt until evenly moistened.

3. Make the banana cream In a large bowl, using a hand mixer, beat the cream with the sugar, mashed banana and vanilla seeds to stiff peaks.

4. Spoon the pudding into six 8-ounce jars or cups. Top with a sprinkling of the graham cracker crumbs, a layer of sliced bananas and a scoop of ice cream. Garnish the parfaits with a dollop of the banana cream and more graham cracker crumbs and serve. —*Michelle Karr-Ueoka*

MAKE AHEAD The pudding can be refrigerated for up to 3 days. The crumbs can be stored in an airtight container for up to 3 days.

COOKBOOK WISDOM

Sweet Inspiration

Great cookbooks not only offer stellar recipes, they dispense expert, why-didn't-I-think-of-that? advice. Here, dessert pointers from a few of our favorite titles.

VEGAN WHIPPED CREAM Spoon the firm layer of coconut cream off the top of a can of chilled unsweetened coconut milk—it can be whipped and used just like heavy cream.
—The Kitchn Cookbook, *Sara Kate Gillingham and Faith Durand*

CHEESECAKE ESSENTIAL When making cheesecake, use a commercial brand of cream cheese, rather than a natural or specialty kind, for the best and most consistent flavor and texture.
—The Baking Bible, *Rose Levy Beranbaum*

HEAT-RETAINING VESSELS Cook caramel or chocolate frosting in a copper pot or Dutch oven to keep it warm and spreadable for longer.
—Sweet & Southern, *Ben Mims*

CHOCOLATE-COOKIE
CRUNCH TRIFLE

PEACH-BUTTERMILK
ICE CREAM

Vanilla-Almond Ice Cream with Cherries and Pistachios

Active **45 min**; Total **6 hr 45 min plus overnight freezing**; Makes **about 1 quart**

Justin Chapple, star of F&W's Mad Genius Tips videos, makes his fabulous "cheater's ice cream" without an ice cream machine. He freezes homemade custard overnight in a resealable bag, then pulses it in a food processor until it's light and creamy.

- **6 large egg yolks**
- **1½ cups heavy cream**
- **1½ cups whole milk**
- **¾ cup sugar**
- **¾ tsp. kosher salt**
- **1 vanilla bean, split lengthwise and seeds scraped**
- **½ tsp. pure almond extract**
- **¾ cup fresh cherries, pitted and halved**
- **¼ cup shelled pistachios, coarsely chopped**

1. Set a medium bowl in a large bowl of ice water. In another medium bowl, beat the egg yolks until pale, 1 to 2 minutes.

2. In a medium saucepan, whisk the cream with the milk, sugar, salt and the vanilla bean and seeds. Bring to a simmer, whisking, until the sugar is completely dissolved. Very gradually whisk half of the hot cream mixture into the beaten egg yolks in a thin stream, then whisk this mixture into the saucepan. Cook over moderately low heat, stirring constantly with a wooden spoon, until the custard is thick enough to lightly coat the back of the spoon, about 12 minutes; don't let it boil.

3. Strain the custard through a medium-mesh strainer into the bowl set in the ice water; discard the vanilla bean. Let the custard cool completely, stirring occasionally. Stir in the almond extract. Pour into a large resealable freezer bag and seal, pressing out the air. Lay the bag flat in the freezer and freeze until firm, at least 8 hours or overnight.

4. Working quickly, in batches if necessary, transfer the frozen custard to the bowl of a food processor. Pulse at 5-second intervals until smooth. Transfer the custard to a chilled 9-by-4-inch metal loaf pan and fold in the cherries and pistachios. Cover with plastic wrap and freeze until firm, about 6 hours or overnight. —*Justin Chapple*

MAKE AHEAD The ice cream can be frozen for up to 1 week.

VARIATIONS Instead of cherries and pistachios, fold in 1 cup of chopped chocolate-covered pretzels or chopped halvah.

Peach-Buttermilk Ice Cream

Active **40 min**; Total **1 hr 30 min plus 7 hr chilling and freezing**; Makes **1½ quarts**

Be sure to use the best buttermilk you can get for this recipe: The ice cream is just as much about the rich, tangy buttermilk as it is about the fragrant peaches.

- **1½ lbs. peaches (about 6 small), plus sliced peaches for serving**
- **1 cup farm-fresh buttermilk**
- **1 tsp. grated lemon zest plus 2 Tbsp. fresh lemon juice**
- **6 large egg yolks**
- **2 cups heavy cream**
- **1 cup sugar**
- **⅛ tsp. kosher salt**
- **1 vanilla bean, split lengthwise, seeds scraped**

1. Bring a medium saucepan of water to a boil. Fill a large bowl with ice water. Using a sharp paring knife, mark an X on the bottom of each whole peach. Add the peaches to the saucepan and blanch until the skins start to peel away, 1 to 2 minutes. Transfer the peaches to the ice bath and let cool completely. Wipe out the saucepan.

2. Peel and chop the peaches. Transfer to a food processor and puree until smooth. Scrape into a large bowl and whisk in the buttermilk, lemon zest and lemon juice. Cover and refrigerate until cold.

3. In a heatproof medium bowl, whisk the egg yolks. In the medium saucepan, simmer the cream with the sugar, salt and the vanilla bean and seeds over moderate heat, whisking occasionally, until the sugar has dissolved, about 5 minutes. While whisking constantly, slowly stream half of the hot cream mixture into the egg yolks.

Pour the mixture back into the saucepan and cook over moderately low heat, whisking constantly, until the custard is thick enough to coat the back of a spoon, 8 to 10 minutes. Strain the custard through a fine sieve set over a heatproof bowl and let cool to room temperature. Whisk in the chilled buttermilk-peach mixture. Press a sheet of plastic wrap directly onto the surface of the custard and refrigerate until very cold, at least 3 hours.

4. Working in 2 batches, freeze the ice cream base in an ice cream machine according to the manufacturer's instructions. Pack the ice cream into plastic containers and freeze until firm, at least 4 hours or overnight. Serve the ice cream topped with sliced peaches. —*Lisa Donovan*

MAKE AHEAD The ice cream can be frozen for up to 2 weeks.

Apple-Caramel Ice Cream Sundaes

Total **15 min**; Serves **4**

When apples are in abundance, chop them up and mix them into a buttery brown sugar caramel for an exceptional ice cream topping.

- **6 Tbsp. unsalted butter**
- **2 Honeycrisp or Pink Lady apples— peeled, halved, cored and cut into ½-inch pieces**
- **⅓ cup heavy cream**
- **½ cup packed light brown sugar**
- **½ tsp. kosher salt**
- **Vanilla ice cream, whipped cream and julienned fresh apples, for serving**

In a large nonstick skillet, melt the butter. Add the apples and cook over moderate heat, stirring occasionally, until lightly browned and tender, about 5 minutes. Add the heavy cream, sugar and salt and simmer until thickened, about 3 minutes. Let cool slightly before serving with vanilla ice cream, whipped cream and julienned apples. —*Justin Chapple*

MAKE AHEAD The sauce can be refrigerated for up to 2 days. Rewarm gently in the microwave at 15-second intervals.

DIY Ice Cream Cake

At Launderette in Austin, Texas, pastry chef **LAURA SAWICKI** creates a layered ice cream cake that's a nostalgic nod to the Carvel and Baskin-Robbins cakes she loved as a kid. Read on to learn how to build this ultimate frozen dessert.

Ice Cream Birthday Cake

Active **1 hr 30 min**; Total **5 hr plus overnight freezing**; Serves **16**

DEVIL'S FOOD CAKE

- 1 cup all-purpose flour
- ½ tsp. baking powder
- ½ tsp. baking soda
- ½ tsp. kosher salt
- ½ cup plus 1 Tbsp. unsweetened cocoa powder
- ½ cup hot water
- 4 Tbsp. unsalted butter, at room temperature
- 1¾ cups dark brown sugar
- 1 large egg plus 1 large egg yolk
- ½ cup buttermilk
- ½ tsp. pure vanilla extract

HOT FUDGE

- 1 cup heavy cream
- 6 Tbsp. dark brown sugar
- 4½ Tbsp. unsweetened cocoa powder
- ¼ cup plus 2 Tbsp. light corn syrup
- 9 oz. bittersweet chocolate, coarsely chopped
- 1½ Tbsp. unsalted butter
- ½ tsp. kosher salt

CAKE ASSEMBLY

- 2 pints each chocolate chip and strawberry ice cream, softened slightly
- 2½ cups heavy cream, chilled
- 3 Tbsp. granulated sugar
- 8 oz. bittersweet chocolate, coarsely chopped
- Maraschino cherries and rainbow sprinkles, for decorating (optional)

MAKE THE DEVIL'S FOOD CAKE

1. Preheat the oven to 350°. Spray an 8-inch springform pan with nonstick cooking spray. In a medium bowl, whisk the flour with the baking powder, baking soda and salt. In a small bowl, whisk the cocoa powder with the water until a smooth paste forms. In the bowl of a stand mixer fitted with the paddle, beat the butter with the brown sugar at moderate speed for 3 minutes. Beat in the egg, egg yolk, buttermilk and vanilla. At low speed, beat in the dry ingredients and cocoa paste in 2 alternating batches.

2. Scrape the batter into the prepared pan and bake for 30 to 35 minutes, until a toothpick inserted in the center comes out with a few moist crumbs attached. Let the cake cool for 15 minutes, then remove the ring and let the cake cool completely on a rack. Leave the oven on.

3. Using a serrated knife, cut a ¼-inch-thick layer off the top of the cake. In a food processor, pulse the cake top until fine crumbs form. Spread the crumbs on a small rimmed baking sheet and bake for 10 to 12 minutes, turning the pan halfway through, until the crumbs are crisp. Let the crunchies cool completely.

MAKE THE HOT FUDGE

4. In a small saucepan, combine the cream with the brown sugar, cocoa powder and corn syrup and bring to a boil over moderate heat, whisking constantly. Reduce the heat to low and simmer for 1 minute. Remove from the heat and add the chocolate, butter and salt; whisk until smooth. Scrape the hot fudge into a bowl and let cool to room temperature.

ASSEMBLE THE CAKE

5. Using scissors, trim a sheet of clear acetate to 6-by-24 inches. Wrap the acetate around the cake and secure it with tape. Secure the springform pan ring around the acetate-wrapped cake.

6. Using an offset spatula, spread half of the hot fudge evenly over the cake and top with half of the cake crunchies. Freeze until the fudge is firm, about 20 minutes.

STEP-BY-STEP ICE CREAM CAKE LESSON

SLICE OFF THE TOP After you've baked the cake, shave a ¼-inch slice off the top to level the surface.

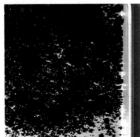

MAKE CRUNCHIES Break up the cake top and pulse in a food processor to create fine crumbs. Bake until crisp, then let cool.

SET UP THE MOLD Wrap a sheet of acetate around the cake to form a support collar, then reattach and secure the ring.

START LAYERING Spread cooled hot fudge sauce over the cake. Top with chocolate crunchies and freeze the cake until firm.

7. Using the spatula, spread the chocolate chip ice cream over the fudge layer and top with the remaining cake crunchies; press down to help them adhere. Freeze the cake for 20 minutes, until firm.

8. Remove the cake from the freezer and spread the remaining fudge over the crunchies. Freeze for 20 minutes. Spread the strawberry ice cream over the fudge and freeze for another 20 minutes.

9. In a stand mixer fitted with the whisk, beat 1½ cups of the heavy cream with the granulated sugar until it holds soft peaks. Spread 2 cups of the whipped cream over the strawberry ice cream layer; refrigerate the rest of the whipped cream for decorating. Freeze the cake overnight.

10. Place the chocolate in a heatproof medium bowl. In a small saucepan, bring the remaining 1 cup of heavy cream to a boil. Pour the hot cream over the chocolate and let stand until melted, about 5 minutes. Stir until smooth, then tap the bowl on the counter to pop any air bubbles. Let the ganache cool down to 80°, about 30 minutes.

11. Remove the springform ring and acetate from the cake. Transfer the cake to a rack set over a rimmed baking sheet. Working quickly, pour the ganache onto the center of the cake in one fluid motion, allowing the excess to drip over. Freeze the cake until the ganache is firm, 30 minutes.

12. Meanwhile, whisk the reserved whipped cream until stiff peaks form. Transfer to a pastry bag fitted with a star tip. Pipe whipped cream around the edge of the cake and garnish with maraschino cherries and rainbow sprinkles, if desired. Freeze the cake for 30 minutes before serving.

This recipe, with a devil's food base, chocolate crunchies, cold hot fudge and a seriously thick chocolate ganache glaze, is for true chocolate lovers.

ADD ICE CREAM Spread ice cream on the cake, followed by more chocolate crunchies, fudge, ice cream and whipped cream.

MAKE GANACHE Combine chopped chocolate with hot cream. Let stand until the chocolate is melted, then stir.

UNMOLD THE CAKE Remove the springform ring and transfer the cake to a rack set over a baking sheet. Peel off the acetate.

DECORATE AND SERVE Pour the ganache onto the cake and freeze until set. Decorate, then cut the cake with a hot knife.

Marbled Smoothie Pops

Active **15 min**; Total **4 hr 15 min**
Makes **ten 3-oz. ice pops**

This recipe proves that smoothies have so much potential beyond breakfast. Layer two simple flavors in ice pop molds before swirling and freezing to create an impressive frozen treat.

- 3 **medium bananas, chopped**
- 2 **cups full-fat Greek yogurt**
- ¼ **cup honey**
- 1 **tsp. pure vanilla extract**
- 1 **cup fresh or frozen berries (see Note)**

In a blender, puree the bananas with the yogurt, 2 tablespoons of the honey and the vanilla. Transfer 1½ cups of the banana smoothie to a medium bowl. Add the berries and the remaining 2 tablespoons of honey to the blender and puree with the remaining banana smoothie. Spoon 2 tablespoons of the banana smoothie into each of ten 3-ounce ice pop molds. Top each with 2 tablespoons of the berry smoothie, then add the remaining banana smoothie. Using a skewer, lightly swirl the layers for a marbled effect. Insert popsicle sticks and freeze until very firm, about 4 hours.
—*David Frenkiel and Luise Vindahl*

NOTE To give these marbled pops a tropical twist, substitute 1½ cups of chopped ripe mango for the berries.

Coffee-Cardamom Granita

Active **20 min**; Total **3 hr**; Serves **8**

- 4 **tsp. instant coffee**
- ½ **tsp. ground cinnamon**
- ¼ **tsp. ground cardamom**
- ½ **cup sugar**
- 3 **cups hot water**

Combine all of the ingredients in a medium bowl and whisk until the sugar is dissolved. Pour the mixture into a 9-by-13-inch metal baking pan and freeze for 1 hour. Scrape the frozen granita around the edges into the center and freeze for about 2 hours longer, scraping every 30 minutes, until the granita is icy and flaky throughout.
—*Eli and Max Sussman*

MAKE AHEAD The granita can be frozen for up to 3 days. Scrape it once more before serving.

Coconut Mochi Ice Cream Sandwiches

Active **30 min**; Total **2 hr 30 min**
Makes **twelve 2-inch ice cream sandwiches**

  Cornstarch, for dusting
- 1½ **cups sweet glutinous rice flour (mochiko flour; available at Asian markets)**
- ¾ **cup sugar**
- ¼ **cup unsweetened coconut milk**
- ¼ **tsp. kosher salt**
- 1½ **pints (3 cups) coconut ice cream, softened slightly**

1. Using a damp cloth, wipe down a large work surface. Stretch a 14-inch sheet of plastic wrap over the surface and use the damp cloth to smooth it out. Sift a generous layer of cornstarch over the plastic wrap. Dust a large rimmed baking sheet with cornstarch.

2. In a large microwave-safe bowl, mix the rice flour with 1 cup of water, the sugar, coconut milk and salt. Cover the bowl tightly with plastic wrap. Microwave the mochi mixture at high power for 2 minutes, until the batter starts to thicken at the edge. Remove the plastic wrap and, using a rubber spatula, stir the mixture until it is mostly smooth; a few small lumps are OK. Cover the bowl with the plastic wrap and microwave at high power for another 2 minutes; the dough should be stiff and sticky. Using a rubber spatula, stir the dough quickly and vigorously until smooth, about 30 seconds.

3. Working quickly, scrape the mochi dough out onto the prepared work surface and sift a fine layer of cornstarch over it. Pat the dough into a 9-inch round. Using a rolling pin lightly dusted with cornstarch, roll out the dough ¼ inch thick.

4. Dip a 2-inch round cutter in cornstarch and stamp out 24 rounds, rerolling the scraps as needed. Transfer the mochi to the prepared baking sheet. Cover with plastic wrap and freeze until firm, about 1 hour.

5. Meanwhile, scrape the softened ice cream into a gallon-size resealable freezer bag. Using a small spatula, spread the ice cream evenly so it's about ¾ inch thick in the bag, then squeeze out any excess air and seal. Freeze until firm, about 1 hour.

6. Line a 12-cup muffin tin with paper or foil liners. Using a pastry brush, dust the excess cornstarch off the mochi rounds. Place 1 mochi round in each cup. Lay the bag of ice cream flat on the counter and snip around the top of the bag, then peel it off. Using a 2-inch round cutter, stamp out 12 rounds of ice cream. Working quickly, lightly brush the 12 mochi in the muffin cups with water and top with the ice cream rounds. Brush each of the remaining 12 mochi rounds with water and set them damp side down on the ice cream. Press lightly to help the mochi and ice cream stick together. Freeze until firm, about 1 hour. Let the mochi sandwiches soften for about 10 minutes before serving. —*Jen Yee*

Sesame-Matcha Bark

Active **15 min**; Total **2 hr 15 min**
Makes **one 9-by-13-inch sheet**

- 1½ **tsp. vegetable oil, plus more for greasing**
  One 12-oz. bag bittersweet chocolate chips (2 cups)
- 1 **Tbsp. matcha powder**
  Two 12-oz. bags white chocolate chips (4 cups)
- 1 **tsp. black sesame seeds**

1. Lightly grease a 9-by-13-inch baking pan and line it with parchment paper, leaving a 1-inch overhang. In a medium bowl, microwave 1½ cups of the bittersweet chocolate chips in 30-second bursts until just melted; stir until smooth. Stir in the remaining ½ cup of bittersweet chocolate until melted. Spread in an even layer in the prepared baking pan.

2. In a small bowl, whisk the matcha with the 1½ teaspoons of oil. In a large bowl, microwave 3½ cups of the white chocolate chips in 30-second bursts until just melted; stir until smooth. Stir in the remaining ½ cup of white chocolate until melted.

3. Mix ½ cup of the melted white chocolate with the matcha until no streaks remain. Scatter large spoonfuls of the matcha chocolate and the white chocolate over the dark chocolate layer and, working quickly, use a small spatula to decoratively swirl the matcha chocolate with the white chocolate. Sprinkle with the sesame seeds. Let stand at room temperature until firm, 2 hours. Remove the bark from the pan, cut into pieces and serve. —*Anna Painter*

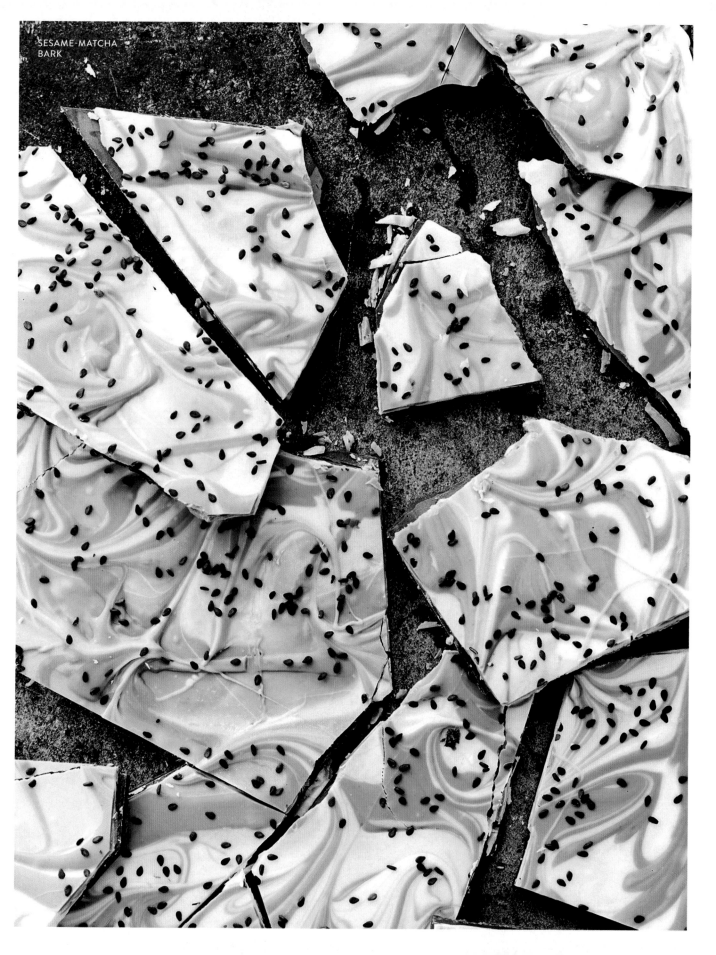

SESAME-MATCHA
BARK

ARMAGNAC
CHOCOLATE
TRUFFLES

Armagnac Chocolate Truffles

Active **1 hr 15 min**; Total **6 hr 30 min plus 2 hr cooling**; Makes **about 50**

Dipped in melted dark chocolate and rolled in cocoa powder, these Armagnac-spiked beauties are exquisite after a meal, with an espresso or creamy milk tea.

GANACHE

- 1 **cup heavy cream**
- ½ **cup sugar**
- 9 **oz. dark chocolate (66% cacao), preferably Valrhona Caraïbe, finely chopped**
- 2 **tsp. Armagnac or Cognac**

COATING

- 12 **oz. dark chocolate (66% cacao), preferably Valrhona Caraïbe, finely chopped**
- ½ **cup unsweetened cocoa powder**

1. Make the ganache In a small saucepan, bring the heavy cream and sugar just to a boil, stirring to dissolve the sugar. In a heatproof medium bowl, pour the hot cream over the chopped chocolate. Let stand for 2 minutes, then add the Armagnac and whisk until smooth. Press a piece of plastic directly onto the surface of the ganache and refrigerate until firm, at least 4 hours.

2. Scoop 2-teaspoon-size mounds of the ganache onto a parchment paper–lined baking sheet. Refrigerate the mounds until firm, about 30 minutes.

3. Using your hands, roll each mound of ganache into a ball. Refrigerate the balls until very firm, about 1 hour.

4. Make the coating In a microwave-safe medium bowl, heat the chocolate at high power in 20-second intervals until nearly melted; stir between intervals. Let stand for 1 minute, then stir until smooth. Let cool slightly.

5. Put the cocoa powder in a medium bowl. Using a fork, dip each ganache ball in the melted chocolate, letting the excess drip back into the bowl, then coat in the cocoa powder and return to the baking sheet. Refrigerate the truffles for 2 hours before serving. —*Dominique Ansel*

MAKE AHEAD The coated truffles can be refrigerated in an airtight container for up to 3 days.

Chai Caramels with Salted Pepitas

Total **1 hr plus overnight setting**
Makes **about 115**

- 300 g. **(2 sticks plus 5 Tbsp.) room-temperature unsalted butter, cut into 1-inch pieces, plus more for greasing**
- 235 g. **(1 cup) heavy cream**
- 3 **chai tea bags (8 g.)**
- 18 g. **(1 Tbsp. plus 1½ tsp.) pure vanilla extract**
- 9 g. **(1 Tbsp.) kosher salt**
- 438 g. **(1¼ cups plus 1 Tbsp.) light corn syrup**
- 800 g. **(4 cups) sugar**
- 100 g. **(¾ cup) roasted salted pepitas (hulled pumpkin seeds)**
- **5-inch squares of cellophane or wax paper, for wrapping**

1. Lightly butter a 9-by-13-inch metal baking pan and line with parchment paper, leaving a 1-inch overhang on all 4 sides.

2. In a small saucepan, bring the cream to a boil; remove from the heat. Add the tea bags, cover and let stand for 12 minutes. Gently squeeze the tea bags to release any cream, then discard. Stir in the vanilla and salt; keep warm.

3. In a medium, heavy-bottomed saucepan, cook the corn syrup over moderately high heat, swirling the pan occasionally, until it begins to bubble, 2 minutes. Sprinkle one-third of the sugar over the corn syrup and, using a small heatproof spatula, poke the sugar into the hot syrup until incorporated. Do not stir. Repeat with the remaining sugar in 2 batches, using a wet pastry brush to wash down any crystals on the side of the pan. Continue cooking over moderately high heat, swirling the pan occasionally, until a dark amber caramel forms and the temperature reaches 330° on a candy thermometer, about 15 minutes.

4. Remove the saucepan from the heat and gradually add the warm cream, whisking constantly, until incorporated. Add the 300 grams of butter in 2 batches, whisking until melted before adding more. Continue whisking the caramel vigorously until it is glossy and registers 190° on a candy thermometer, about 5 minutes. Fold in the pepitas.

5. Scrape the caramel into the prepared pan, then gently tap it on a work surface to release any air bubbles. Let stand at room temperature for at least 3 hours, cover loosely with foil and let stand overnight.

6. Invert the caramel onto a work surface, peel off the parchment paper and cut into 1-inch squares. Wrap each caramel in a square of cellophane and twist the ends to seal. —*Jami Curl*

MAKE AHEAD The wrapped caramels can be stored in an airtight container at room temperature for up to 6 months.

Chocolate-Tahini Fudge

Total **30 min plus 2 hr chilling**
Makes **about 80 pieces**

- ¾ **cup whole milk**
- 6 **Tbsp. unsalted butter**
- 3 **cups sugar**
- 12 **oz. dark chocolate (70%), finely chopped**
- ¼ **cup tahini**
- 2 **Tbsp. toasted sesame oil**
- 1 **Tbsp. hot water (optional)**
- 2 **cups Marshmallow Fluff (8 oz.)**
- 1½ **tsp. pure vanilla extract**
- 2 **Tbsp. lightly toasted sesame seeds**
- **Flaky sea salt**

1. Line a 9-inch-square baking pan with parchment paper. In a medium saucepan, combine the milk and butter and cook over moderate heat until the milk is hot and the butter is melted. Whisk in the sugar and cook, stirring occasionally, until the mixture reaches 240°, about 5 minutes.

2. Remove the saucepan from the heat. Add the chocolate, tahini and sesame oil and stir until the chocolate is completely melted. If the mixture separates, whisk in the hot water until it is smooth again. Add the Fluff and vanilla extract and stir vigorously until the Fluff is completely incorporated.

3. Scrape the fudge into the prepared pan and smooth the surface. Sprinkle with the toasted sesame seeds and let cool, then refrigerate until cold, about 2 hours.

4. Cut the fudge into 1-inch squares and sprinkle with sea salt. —*John daSilva*

MAKE AHEAD The fudge can be stored in an airtight container for up to 1 week.

Citrus Lollipops

Active **40 min**; Total **1 hr 30 min**; Makes **30**

At Quin candy shop in Portland, Oregon, Jami Curl upgrades classic favorites by using all-natural ingredients. To make these these bright citrus lollipops, look for a natural food dye that is high-heat stable so that it maintains its color when added to the hot sugar. For the best results, do as Curl does and use a scale to weigh ingredients in grams.

	Canola oil
	Thirty 4-inch lollipop sticks
134 g.	(⅓ cup plus 1 Tbsp.) light corn syrup
200 g.	(1 cup) sugar
75 g.	(¼ cup plus 4 tsp.) water
7 g.	(1 Tbsp. plus 1 tsp.) finely grated lemon, lime, tangerine or grapefruit zest
2 g.	(½ tsp.) citric acid
2	to 3 drops of natural food coloring, plus more as needed
	Thirty 5-inch squares of cellophane and twist ties, for wrapping

1. Lightly grease thirty 1½-inch plastic or silicone lollipop molds with canola oil. Place a lollipop stick in each indentation, with ¾ inch of the stick inside the round mold. Alternatively, line a large baking sheet with a silicone baking mat.

2. In a small saucepan, bring the corn syrup, sugar and water to a boil. Do not stir. Continue to cook without stirring until the syrup reaches 300° on a candy thermometer, 7 minutes. Remove from the heat and stir in the citrus zest, citric acid and food coloring. Spoon some of the syrup onto a white plate to check the color. Add more food coloring if needed.

3. Working quickly, spoon 1 teaspoon of the syrup into each mold. Alternatively, spoon teaspoonfuls of the syrup onto the prepared baking sheet, 2 inches apart, and place a stick in each lollipop, turning it to cover with syrup. Let the lollipops harden at room temperature for 30 minutes. Wrap in cellophane and secure with a twist tie. —*Jami Curl*

Vanilla-Mint Marshmallows

Total **1 hr plus 3 hr setting**; Makes **about 50**

	Canola oil
98 g.	**(¼ cup plus 1 Tbsp.) light corn syrup**
12 g.	**(1 Tbsp.) pure peppermint extract**
1	**vanilla bean, split lengthwise and seeds scraped**
57 g.	**(20 sheets) silver leaf gelatin (see Note)**
108 g.	**(⅓ cup plus 2 Tbsp.) ice water**
600 g.	**(3 cups) granulated sugar**
255 g.	**(1 cup plus 1 Tbsp.) water**
15	**drops natural red food coloring**
114 g.	**(1 cup plus 1 Tbsp.) confectioners' sugar**
114 g.	**(1 cup) cornstarch**

1. Lightly grease a 9-by-13-inch metal baking pan with canola oil. In a stand mixer fitted with the whisk attachment, beat the corn syrup with the peppermint extract and vanilla seeds at low speed until combined. Reserve the vanilla bean pod for another use.

2. In a heatproof medium bowl, cover the gelatin sheets with the ice water and let stand, stirring occasionally, until the gelatin is evenly moistened and all of the water is absorbed, about 5 minutes. In a medium saucepan, bring 2 inches of water to a simmer. Set the bowl with the gelatin over the simmering water and cook, stirring once or twice, until melted, about 5 minutes. Do not let the bowl touch the water. Carefully remove the saucepan from the heat.

3. In a small, heavy-bottomed saucepan, bring the granulated sugar and water to a boil. Cook, without stirring, until the sugar syrup registers 225° on a candy thermometer, 8 to 10 minutes. Use a wet pastry brush to wash down the side of the pan.

4. With the stand mixer at low speed, slowly stream the hot sugar syrup into the corn syrup. Add the warm gelatin and continue beating until slightly thickened and opaque, about 2 minutes. Increase the speed to moderately high and beat until the marshmallow is thick and glossy and registers 105°, about 12 minutes.

5. Lightly grease a rubber spatula. Scatter the food coloring over the marshmallow, then, using the spatula, quickly scrape the marshmallow into the prepared pan, swirling the food coloring as you go. Let stand at room temperature until set, at least 3 hours or overnight.

6. Sift the confectioners' sugar and cornstarch into a shallow bowl. Invert the marshmallow onto a work surface and cut into 2-inch squares. Toss in the sugar mixture, shaking off any excess, then serve. —*Jami Curl*

NOTE Silver leaf gelatin is available at most baking supply shops and on amazon.com.

MAKE AHEAD The vanilla-mint marshmallows can be stored in an airtight container at room temperature for up to 1 month.

Coconut Whipped Cream

Total **10 min plus overnight chilling** Makes **3 cups**

This sweetened coconut whipped cream from vegan chef Tal Ronnen's cookbook *Crossroads* can be used in all sorts of desserts. Layer it in parfaits, fold it into pumpkin puree for a quick mousse or use it as a topping for chocolate desserts and ice cream sundaes.

	Two 15-oz. cans unsweetened coconut milk, refrigerated overnight
½	**cup confectioners' sugar**
1	**vanilla bean, split lengthwise and seeds scraped**

1. Open the chilled cans of coconut milk and carefully spoon the thick coconut cream into a medium bowl (you should have about 1½ cups total). Reserve the remaining coconut milk for another use. Add the confectioners' sugar and vanilla bean seeds to the coconut cream.

2. Using a hand mixer, beat the cream at moderately high speed until soft peaks form and the cream has nearly doubled in volume, about 5 minutes. Refrigerate or serve immediately. —*Tal Ronnen*

MAKE AHEAD The coconut cream can be refrigerated for up to 2 days. Rewhip as needed before serving.

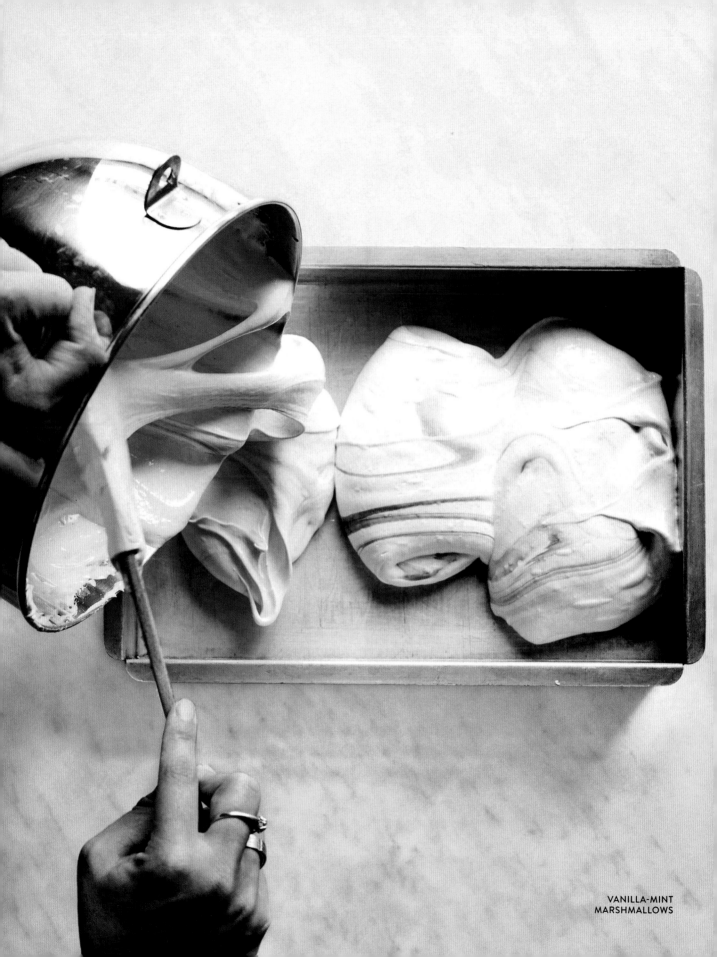

VANILLA-MINT
MARSHMALLOWS

SNACKS, CONDIMENTS AND SAUCES

Nestling onions and shallots in hot coals caramelizes them beautifully (p. 363). OPPOSITE Sardines topped with Two-Chile Harissa (p. 364).

Curried Cashews

Total **20 min plus cooling; Makes 2 cups**

A combo of Thai red curry paste and honey gives these nuts a wonderfully complex sweet-spiciness. Their flavor intensifies as they keep in the refrigerator.

- **2 Tbsp. vegetable oil**
- **2 Tbsp. light brown sugar**
- **4 tsp. Thai red curry paste**
- **1 Tbsp. honey**
- **2 cups raw cashews**
- **1½ tsp. Maldon sea salt**

1. Preheat the oven to 350°. Line a rimmed baking sheet with parchment paper. In a medium skillet, combine the vegetable oil with the sugar, curry paste and honey. Cook over moderate heat, stirring constantly, until the sugar dissolves, about 1 minute. Add the cashews and stir to coat.

2. Spread the nuts on the prepared baking sheet and bake, stirring every 4 minutes, until golden brown, about 12 minutes total. Sprinkle with the salt and let cool completely before serving. —*David Lebovitz*

MAKE AHEAD The cashews can be refrigerated in an airtight container for up to 2 weeks. Serve at room temperature.

Fried Spiced Red Lentils

Total **10 min plus 1 hr soaking**
Makes **1½ cups**

To make this addictive snack, simply pan-fry lentils and toss them with salt, pepper and smoked paprika.

- **2 cups red lentils, soaked for 1 hour and drained**
- **Canola oil, for frying**
- **¼ tsp. smoked paprika**
- **Kosher salt and pepper**

Pat the lentils dry with paper towels. In a large cast-iron skillet, heat ¼ inch of oil until shimmering. Fry the lentils in batches, stirring, until yellow and crisp, about 2 minutes. Transfer to a paper towel–lined plate to drain. In a small bowl, toss the fried lentils with the paprika, season with salt and pepper and serve. —*Kay Chun*

Sweet and Spicy Black Sesame Seed and Nut Mix

Active **15 min;** Total **45 min plus cooling**
Makes **12 cups**

This mix was inspired by the sesame candy that Los Angeles chef Jessica Koslow always ate as a kid. She likes it on its own but says it also makes a killer sprinkle for salad or ice cream.

- **1½ cups raw sunflower seeds**
- **1½ cups raw pumpkin seeds**
- **1½ cups raw almonds**
- **1½ cups puffed millet**
- **½ cup black sesame seeds**
- **½ cup light agave nectar**
- **¼ cup light brown sugar**
- **3 Tbsp. extra-virgin olive oil**
- **1½ tsp. chipotle powder**
- **¾ tsp. fine sea salt**

Preheat the oven to 350°. In a large bowl, combine all of the ingredients; toss well to coat. Spread the mix in an even layer on a large rimmed baking sheet lined with parchment paper. Bake for about 30 minutes, until very lightly browned, stirring halfway through. Let cool completely, then break the mix up into bite-size pieces. —*Jessica Koslow*

MAKE AHEAD The mix can be stored in an airtight container for up to 1 week.

Nori Chips

Active **10 min;** Total **30 min plus cooling**
Makes **32**

These sheets of nori are baked until they become supercrunchy. A healthier alternative to potato chips, they satisfy any cravings for a crisp, salty snack.

- **12 sheets of unseasoned roasted nori (8-inch squares)**
- **Extra-virgin olive oil, for brushing**
- **Kosher salt**

1. Preheat the oven to 300°. Line a baking sheet with parchment paper.

2. Arrange 1 nori sheet, smooth side up, on a work surface. Using a pastry brush, lightly brush all over with water. Top with another nori sheet, smooth side up, and press firmly to help it adhere. Repeat this process with 4 more nori sheets; brush the top sheet with olive oil and season with salt. Using scissors, cut the stack in quarters, then cut each square into 4 triangles. Repeat with the remaining 6 nori sheets. Arrange the triangles on the prepared baking sheet and bake for 18 to 20 minutes, until crisp and shriveled. Transfer to a rack to cool completely; the chips will continue to crisp as they cool. —*Kay Chun*

MAKE AHEAD The chips can be stored in an airtight container for up to 3 days.

Honey-Butter Potato Chips

⟳ Total **25 min;** Serves **4**

Packaged honey-butter potato chips are a sensation in Seoul, where people stand in line to buy them. Chef Tory Miller makes a DIY version at his restaurant Sujeo in Madison, Wisconsin, glazing the just-fried chips with butter and clover honey.

- **Vegetable oil, for frying**
- **2 baking potatoes (1 lb.), peeled and sliced crosswise ¹⁄₁₆ inch thick on a mandoline**
- **6 Tbsp. unsalted butter**
- **¼ cup clover honey**
- **Fine sea salt and gochugaru (red pepper flakes), for seasoning**

1. In a large enameled cast-iron casserole, heat 3 inches of oil to 325°. Line a baking sheet with paper towels.

2. Fry the potatoes in batches, stirring, until light golden and crisp, 3 to 4 minutes. Using a slotted spoon, transfer the potato chips to the paper towels to drain.

3. In a large nonstick skillet, melt 3 tablespoons of the butter with 2 tablespoons of the honey and bring to a boil. Add half of the potato chips and remove the pan from the heat. Gently toss the potato chips until evenly coated and transfer to a serving bowl; season with sea salt and gochugaru. Repeat with the remaining butter, honey and potato chips and more sea salt and gochugaru. —*Tory Miller*

FRIED SPICED
RED LENTILS

BLOODY MARY–PICKLED
GREEN BEANS

Whole-Wheat Rosemary Crisps

Active **30 min**; Total **2 hr**
Makes **two 12-inch rounds**

F&W's Justin Chapple adds a secret ingredient to his crispy homemade crackers: chicken bouillon cubes. He uses the seasoning in the dough and also grates some of it over the crackers for an additional hit of flavor.

- **2 chicken bouillon cubes (about ½ oz. each)**
- **⅓ cup hot water**
- **¾ cup all-purpose flour, plus more for dusting**
- **½ cup whole-wheat flour**
- **1½ tsp. sugar**
- **½ tsp. kosher salt**
- **4 Tbsp. cold unsalted butter**
- **Milk, for brushing**
- **Crushed dried rosemary leaves, for sprinkling**

1. In a small bowl, dissolve 1 of the bouillon cubes in the hot water. Let the broth cool completely, then refrigerate until chilled, about 15 minutes.

2. In a food processor, pulse both flours with the sugar and salt. Scatter the butter on top and pulse until a coarse meal forms. Add the broth and pulse until the dough comes together. Transfer to a work surface and gather into a ball. Cut in half and pat into disks; wrap in plastic and refrigerate for 1 hour.

3. Preheat the oven to 400°. Line 2 baking sheets with parchment paper. On a lightly floured work surface, roll out each disk of dough to a 12-inch round and transfer to a prepared baking sheet. Brush the rounds with milk and sprinkle with rosemary. Finely grate the second bouillon cube on top.

4. Bake the crackers for about 18 minutes, until crisp. Let cool completely, then break into large shards and serve.
—*Justin Chapple*

Bloody Mary–Pickled Green Beans

Active **20 min**; Total **3 hr**; Makes **1 quart**

These green beans are quick-pickled in a fantastic Bloody Mary "brine" made with tomato juice, vinegar, horseradish, peppercorns and garlic. They're amazing eaten on their own, but also the perfect garnish for an actual Bloody Mary.

- **10 oz. haricots verts or other thin green beans**
- **1 cup water**
- **½ cup tomato juice**
- **⅓ cup rice vinegar**
- **2 Tbsp. prepared horseradish**
- **2 Tbsp. kosher salt**
- **1 tsp. black peppercorns**
- **2 garlic cloves, crushed**

Pack the green beans in a heatproof 1-quart glass jar. In a medium saucepan, combine all of the remaining ingredients and bring to a boil. Pour the brine over the beans and let cool completely, then seal the jar and refrigerate for at least 2 hours before serving. —*Justin Chapple*

MAKE AHEAD The pickled green beans can be refrigerated for up to 5 days.

Apricot-Walnut-Date Power Bars

Active **15 min**; Total **30 min plus chilling**
Makes **12**

There is no added sugar in these naturally sweet, chewy bars. For the best flavor, be sure to use the California Blenheim apricots called for below rather than other imported varieties.

- **1½ cups extra-thick rolled oats**
- **1½ cups walnuts**
- **1 cup dried California Blenheim apricots, coarsely chopped (5 oz.)**
- **1 cup pitted Medjool dates (8 oz.)**
- **1 cup toasted unsweetened flaked coconut**
- **¼ cup flax seeds**
- **½ tsp. kosher salt**

1. Preheat the oven to 375°. Line a 9-by-9-inch metal pan with plastic wrap.

2. Spread the oats and walnuts on 2 separate baking sheets; toast until golden, about 8 minutes for the walnuts and 15 minutes for the oats. Let cool, then finely chop the walnuts.

3. In a food processor, puree the apricots and dates to a paste. Scrape into a medium bowl and stir in the oats, walnuts, coconut, flax seeds and salt. Press the mixture into the prepared pan and chill until firm, about 1 hour. Cut into 12 bars and serve.
—*Kay Chun*

MAKE AHEAD The bars can be refrigerated for 1 week or frozen for 1 month.

Whole Smoked Onions

📷 PAGE 359

Total **3 hr plus cooling**; Makes **½ cup**

George Mendes of Lupulo in New York City gets the most out of his coals when grilling. He tucks whole vegetables like onions in the spent coals, which gives them an ultra-tender, deep-golden interior. The smoky onions are incredibly versatile and can be folded into dips, smeared on steaks or whisked into vinaigrettes.

- **4 medium unpeeled yellow onions or large shallots**

When the embers in your grill are beginning to die down, carefully tuck in the onions at the edge. Cook until charred and tender throughout, at least 3 hours, depending on the volume and heat of your embers. Let cool completely, then scoop the smoky flesh into a bowl.
—*George Mendes*

Smoked Onion Dressing

Active **10 min**; Total **3 hr 10 min plus cooling**; Makes **1 cup**

Here, silky smoked onions are mixed into a sweet-tart dressing that's delicious on grilled vegetables and meats.

- **½ cup Smoked Onions (recipe above)**
- **2 Tbsp. distilled white vinegar**
- **2 tsp. grainy mustard**
- **Pinch of sugar**
- **½ cup canola oil**
- **Kosher salt and pepper**

Finely chop the smoked onion flesh and transfer to a medium bowl. Whisk in the vinegar, mustard and sugar. While whisking constantly, slowly drizzle in the oil until emulsified. Season with salt and pepper.
—*Anna Painter*

Smoked Onion Dip

Active **10 min;** Total **3 hr 10 min plus cooling;** Makes **1½ cups**

Greek yogurt lightens the flavor of this toasty dip and adds a pleasant tang.

- ½ cup **Smoked Onions (p. 363)**
- 1 cup **Greek yogurt**
- ¼ cup **mayonnaise**
- 1 Tbsp. **chopped parsley**
  - **Kosher salt and pepper**

In a food processor, pulse the smoked onions until coarsely chopped. Add the yogurt and mayonnaise and puree until smooth. Stir in the parsley and season with salt and pepper. —*Anna Painter*

SERVE WITH Potato chips or pretzels.

Cultured Butter

Active **20 min;** Total **3 days;** Makes **1¼ cups**

You'll need a stand mixer, some cheese-cloth, a sieve and a jar (plus a few days) to make this outstanding homemade butter, but the process is actually quite simple and incredibly rewarding. Chef Iliana Regan of Chicago's Elizabeth restaurant serves the butter with fresh bread and berry preserves (p. 366) for the ultimate snack.

- 3¼ cups **heavy cream**
- ⅓ cup **buttermilk**
- 1½ tsp. **kosher salt**

1. In a medium bowl, whisk all of the ingredients together until well blended. Cover with plastic wrap and let stand at room temperature for 48 hours, then refrigerate for 24 hours.

2. In a stand mixer fitted with the whisk, beat the cultured cream mixture at low speed until the butter forms and the buttermilk separates out, 8 to 10 minutes. Drain the butter in a cheesecloth-lined sieve; save the whey for another use. Wrap the cheesecloth around the butter and squeeze out all of the excess buttermilk. Transfer the butter to a medium bowl or a jar, cover and refrigerate. —*Iliana Regan*

MAKE AHEAD The butter can be refrigerated for up to 2 weeks.

Two-Chile Harissa

📷 PAGE 358

Total **45 min plus overnight soaking** Makes **3 cups**

You may never want to buy harissa again once you've tried the amazing version from Seattle chef Renee Erickson. She loves it on toast with grilled or canned sardines and with roast chicken; we loved it with grilled eggplant and zucchini, on eggs and slathered on sandwiches.

- 3 oz. **dried guajillo chiles (about 15)**
- 1½ oz. **dried ají amarillo chiles (about 5)**
- 3 Tbsp. **caraway seeds**
- 2 Tbsp. **cumin seeds**
- 1 Tbsp. **coriander seeds**
- 1½ tsp. **fennel seeds**
- 3 **garlic cloves**
- 1 tsp. **dried organic rose petals (available at amazon.com)**
- ⅓ cup **fresh lime juice**
- ½ tsp. **rosewater**
  - **Extra-virgin olive oil**
  - **Kosher salt**

1. In a large saucepan, cover the chiles with water and bring to a boil. Remove from the heat. Top with a bowl to keep the chiles submerged and let stand overnight.

2. Stem and seed the chiles and transfer to a large bowl. Reserve the soaking liquid.

3. In a medium skillet, toast the caraway, cumin, coriander and fennel seeds over moderate heat until fragrant. Transfer to a bowl and let cool completely. In a mortar or a spice grinder, lightly crush the seeds.

4. In a food processor, combine the crushed seeds with the garlic and rose petals and pulse until a coarse paste forms. Add the seeded chiles and ½ cup of the reserved soaking liquid along with the lime juice and rosewater. Process until the chiles are very finely chopped, scraping down the side of the bowl as needed. Add ¼ cup of olive oil and 1½ tablespoons of kosher salt and pulse to combine. Season with additional salt if necessary. Scrape the harissa into jars, cover with a thin layer of olive oil and a lid and refrigerate for up to 2 months. —*Renee Erickson*

Miso-Honey Mustard

⋯ Total **10 min;** Makes **1 cup**

Chef Ravi Kapur of San Francisco's Liholiho Yacht Club combines white miso with honey and Dijon mustard to give this familiar staple a terrific, umami-rich flavor. Serve it with grilled chicken or pork as well as vegetables like cabbage and turnips.

- ½ cup **Dijon mustard**
- 3 Tbsp. **white miso (see Note)**
- ½ cup **honey**

In a medium bowl, mix the mustard and miso until smooth. Gradually whisk in the honey until incorporated. —*Ravi Kapur*

NOTE White miso (also called shiro miso) is made from fermented soy beans and rice. It's not fermented for long, so the flavor is quite mild. It's the most versatile of misos. Look for it at large supermarkets.

MAKE AHEAD The miso-honey mustard can be refrigerated for up to 1 week. Bring to room temperature before using.

Misoyaki Sauce

Total **15 min plus cooling;** Makes **1¾ cups**

This sweet-savory condiment doubles as a sauce for creamy avocado and a marinade for tuna belly. Just a little dab goes a long way.

- 3 Tbsp. **mirin**
- ¼ cup **sake**
- ½ cup **white miso**
- ¼ cup **sugar**
  - **Sliced avocado, for serving**

In a small saucepan, combine the mirin and sake and boil for 1 to 2 minutes. Add the miso and sugar and simmer, stirring to dissolve the sugar, until slightly thickened. Transfer to a small bowl and let cool completely. Serve drizzled over sliced avocado. —*Ravi Kapur*

NOTE The sauce can be used as a marinade for tuna steaks; cover the fish with it and refrigerate for 1 hour before cooking to your liking.

MAKE AHEAD The misoyaki sauce can be refrigerated for up to 2 weeks.

Creamy Sesame-Garlic Tofu Dressing

Total **10 min**; Makes **1¼ cups**

This versatile, dairy-free dressing gets its creaminess from silken tofu. It's fantastic on anything from salad and roasted vegetables to grilled meats and fish.

- **8** oz. silken tofu, drained
- **¼** cup toasted sesame seeds
- **¼** cup canola oil
- **1** Tbsp. fresh lemon juice
- **3** garlic cloves
- **½** tsp. toasted sesame oil
- Kosher salt

In a blender, combine the tofu, sesame seeds, canola oil, lemon juice, garlic and sesame oil and puree until smooth. Season the dressing with salt. —*Kay Chun*

Snipped-Herb Salsa Verde

Total **10 min**; Makes **¾ cup**

F&W's Justin Chapple, who loves a good shortcut, has an easy, no-mess alternative to chopping the herbs for his salsa verde with a knife on a cutting board: Snip them with scissors or kitchen shears directly into a bowl. His green sauce features fresh parsley and mint, plus a little bit of ground fennel for a floral aroma.

- **2** oz. bunch of parsley
- **2** oz. bunch of mint
- **½** cup extra-virgin olive oil
- **¼** cup fresh lemon juice
- **¾** tsp. ground fennel
- Kosher salt and pepper

Hold the herb bunches in one hand. Using scissors, finely snip the herbs over a bowl until you reach the thick stems. Stir in the olive oil, lemon juice and fennel. Season with salt and pepper. —*Justin Chapple*

SERVE WITH Grilled lamb or chicken.

Sauce Verte

📷 PAGE 358

Active **20 min**; Total **1 hr**; Makes **¾ cup**

This vibrant herb sauce is wonderful on so many things, like canned sardines, grilled or poached fish, roast chicken and smashed and fried potatoes.

- **4** salt-packed anchovy fillets, rinsed
- **2** Tbsp. salt-packed capers, rinsed
- **3** cups lightly packed parsley leaves
- **1½** cups lightly packed mint leaves
- **½** cup lightly packed tarragon leaves
- **½** cup minced chives
- **1** medium shallot, coarsely chopped
- **1** large garlic clove, crushed
- **2** tsp. finely grated lemon zest plus 1 tsp. fresh lemon juice
- **⅛** tsp. crushed red pepper
- **½** cup extra-virgin olive oil
- Kosher salt

1. In a bowl, cover the anchovies and capers with cold water and let stand for 45 minutes. Drain and pat dry.

2. In a food processor, combine the anchovies and capers with all of the remaining ingredients except the olive oil and salt and pulse until finely chopped. Drizzle in the olive oil and process until a smooth sauce forms. Season with salt. —*Renee Erickson*

MAKE AHEAD The sauce can be refrigerated overnight with plastic wrap pressed directly on the surface. Let come to room temperature before using.

WINE Citrus- and herb-inflected Spanish white: 2014 Rafael Palacios Louro do Bolo Valdeorras Godello.

Vegan Basil Pesto

Total **5 min**; Makes **¾ cup**

We love this cheese-free pesto from chef Tal Ronnen of L.A.'s buzzy vegan Crossroads restaurant. He uses nutritional yeast to mimic the savory notes of an aged cheese. His cookbook *Crossroads* has loads of similar substitutes.

- **2** cups basil leaves
- **½** cup parsley leaves
- **¼** cup nutritional yeast
- **¼** cup pine nuts, toasted
- **4** garlic cloves
- **¼** tsp. crushed red pepper
- **½** cup extra-virgin olive oil
- Kosher salt and black pepper

In a food processor, pulse the basil, parsley, nutritional yeast, pine nuts, garlic and crushed red pepper until a coarse paste forms. With the machine running, slowly stream in the olive oil; season the pesto with salt and black pepper. —*Tal Ronnen*

Cashew Cream

Total **5 min plus overnight soaking** Makes **4½ cups**

This supereasy cashew cream from L.A. chef Tal Ronnen is the ultimate vegan swap for milk or heavy cream. Use it to enrich a soup or as the base for a béchamel—the natural fats in cashews cause it to thicken like cream.

- **2** cups whole raw cashews, rinsed
- **3** cups filtered water, plus more for soaking

1. In a medium bowl, cover the rinsed cashews with filtered water. Wrap with plastic and refrigerate overnight.

2. Drain the cashews and rinse well. In a blender, combine the drained cashews with the 3 cups of filtered water; blend until very smooth and creamy, 3 to 5 minutes. —*Tal Ronnen*

MAKE AHEAD The cashew cream can be refrigerated for up to 4 days. Whisk or blend to re-emulsify.

Nectarine and Bay Leaf Jam

Active **1 hr**; Total **4 hr plus overnight macerating**; Makes **3 pints**

At General Porpoise in Seattle, chef Renee Erickson offers five kinds of doughnuts; one is always stuffed with seasonal jam, like nectarine and bay leaf. This recipe makes a big batch of jam, which keeps for months and is fabulous spread on toast and croissants, with pound cake or spooned over ice cream.

- **5 lbs. firm, ripe nectarines—halved, pitted and sliced ½ inch thick**
- **2½ cups sugar**
- **3 Tbsp. fresh lemon juice**
- **3 fresh bay leaves**
- **½ tsp. kosher salt**

1. In an enameled medium cast-iron casserole, toss the nectarines with the sugar, lemon juice, bay leaves and salt. Cover and bring the nectarines to a simmer over moderate heat. Remove from the heat.

2. Uncover the casserole. Carefully press a round of parchment paper directly on top of the hot nectarine mixture and let cool to room temperature, about 2 hours. Refrigerate overnight.

3. Place a small plate in the freezer. Discard the parchment paper round. Bring the jam to a simmer over moderate heat, skimming off any foam with a ladle. Cook, stirring occasionally, until the nectarines begin to break down and the juices fall off the side of a spoon in thick, heavy drops, about 1 hour and 40 minutes. Spoon 1 tablespoon of the jam onto the chilled plate and refrigerate until it comes to room temperature, 3 minutes; the jam is ready when it thickens like jelly and a spoon leaves a trail when it's pulled through. If necessary, continue simmering and testing. Discard the bay leaves.

4. Spoon the jam into three 1-pint canning jars, leaving ¼ inch of space at the top of each. Seal the jars and let the jam cool to room temperature. —*Renee Erickson*

MAKE AHEAD The jam can be refrigerated for up to 3 months.

Fresh Raspberry Preserves

Total **1 hr**; Makes **1½ cups**

Chicago chef Iliana Regan uses many kinds of berries to make her signature preserves. Here she uses juicy raspberries, which she balances with a bit of acidic red wine vinegar to temper the sweetness.

- **24 oz. raspberries (6 cups)**
- **1 tsp. kosher salt**
- **1½ Tbsp. red wine vinegar**
- **½ cup sugar**

In a medium saucepan, cook the raspberries with the salt over moderate heat until they start to break down and release their juices, about 5 minutes. Add the vinegar and sugar and cook over moderately low heat, stirring occasionally and crushing the berries with the back of a spoon, until very thick, about 45 minutes. Transfer the preserves to a small bowl and let cool to room temperature, then refrigerate. —*Iliana Regan*

MAKE AHEAD The preserves can be refrigerated for up to 2 weeks.

Cranberry-Apricot Relish

Total **30 min**; Makes **3 cups**

This sweet and tangy relish has a surprise twist of capers and dried fruit. It's a terrific acompaniment to turkey and pork.

- **4 cups fresh cranberries (1 lb.)**
- **¾ cup sugar**
- **1 cup chopped celery**
- **3 oz. dried apricots, chopped (½ cup)**
- **6 Medjool dates, pitted and chopped (½ cup)**
- **¼ cup capers**

In a small saucepan, combine the cranberries with the sugar and cook over moderate heat, stirring, until the sugar dissolves and the cranberries release their juices, 10 minutes. Let cool, then stir in the remaining ingredients and serve. —*Kay Chun*

MAKE AHEAD The relish can be refrigerated for up to 3 days.

Blueberry Jam

Total **1 hr**; Makes **2 cups**

- **4 cups blueberries**
- **1½ cups sugar**
- **2 tsp. fresh lemon juice**

1. Place a small plate in the freezer. In a nonreactive medium saucepan, combine the blueberries with ½ cup of water and bring to a boil over moderately high heat. Stir in the sugar and lemon juice and cook over moderately low heat, skimming off any foam as necessary, until the liquid has thickened and most of the blueberries have burst, about 40 minutes.

2. Spoon 1 tablespoon of the jam onto the chilled plate and refrigerate until it comes to room temperature, 3 minutes; the jam is ready when it thickens like jelly and a spoon leaves a trail when it's pulled through. If necessary, continue simmering and testing.

3. Spoon the jam into a 1-pint jar, leaving ¼ inch of space at the top. Seal the jar and let cool to room temperature. —*Renee Erickson*

MAKE AHEAD The jam can be refrigerated for up to 3 months.

SUPEREASY CHEF HACK

Canned Cranberry

"I'm not afraid to admit it: I'm a sucker for canned cranberry sauce–the jelly kind with the ridges. But, if you get the 'other' kind (whole cranberry sauce), dress it up with some citrus, vanilla and even a touch of mulled wine." —*Chef Kelly Fields, Willa Jean, New Orleans*

DOUGHNUTS
FILLED WITH
BLUEBERRY
JAM AND
NECTARINE
AND BAY
LEAF JAM

DRINKS

New Orleans's Pontchartrain Hotel is renowned for its cocktails, including a killer Sazerac (p. 374). OPPOSITE Tangy Hibiscus-Tangerine Iced Tea (p. 378).

Tangled Up

⏱ Total **5 min**; Makes **1 drink**

"In southern Spain, they love rebujitos," says Washington, DC, bartender Derek Brown of Mockingbird Hill about the sherry–lemon soda spritzer. He gives his version a pleasantly bitter boost with Suze, a French aperitif. "It's very refreshing," he says, "but you get a little more than just sweet and easy."

- 2 oz. oloroso or cream sherry
- ¼ oz. Suze
     Ice
- 4 oz. bitter lemon soda or San Pellegrino Limonata
- 1 spiral-cut lemon twist, for garnish

In a chilled highball glass, mix the sherry and Suze. Add ice and stir well. Stir in the lemon soda and garnish with the lemon twist. —*Derek Brown*

Normandie Club Spritz

⏱ Total **10 min**; Makes **1 drink**

Devon Tarby features this lovely, light spritz at The Normandie Club in L.A. "It's like the best grapefruit soda you can imagine," she says, "and tame enough that you can chug a few."

- 1 oz. dry vermouth, preferably Dolin
- 1 oz. St-Germain elderflower liqueur
- 1 oz. fresh grapefruit juice
- ½ oz. fresh lemon juice
- ¼ oz. grapefruit liqueur
- ¼ oz. blanco tequila
- ¼ oz. pisco, preferably Campo de Encanto
     Ice
- 2½ oz. chilled club soda
- ½ grapefruit wheel, for garnish

In a cocktail shaker, combine the vermouth, St-Germain, grapefruit juice, lemon juice, grapefruit liqueur, tequila and pisco. Fill the shaker with ice and shake for 5 seconds. Strain into a chilled, ice-filled collins glass. Stir in the club soda and garnish with the grapefruit wheel half. —*Devon Tarby*

Skyliner

📷 PAGE 375

⏱ Total **10 min**; Makes **1 drink**

A little heat can have a cooling effect. The subtle habanero spice on the finish brings complexity to this grapefruit-tinged vodka collins.

- 1½ oz. vodka, preferably Cathead Honeysuckle
- 1 oz. fresh grapefruit juice
- ½ oz. fresh lime juice
- ½ oz. Campari
- ½ oz. Simple Syrup (p. 373)
- 8 drops of habanero bitters, preferably Bittermens
     Ice
- 1 oz. chilled club soda
- 1 lime wheel, for garnish

In a cocktail shaker, combine the vodka, grapefruit juice, lime juice, Campari, Simple Syrup and bitters. Fill the shaker with ice and shake well. Strain into a chilled, ice-filled collins glass and top with the club soda. Garnish with the lime wheel and serve immediately. —*Benton Bourgeois*

The Rabbit Gin Sour

⏱ Total **5 min**; Makes **1 drink**

This tangy, thirst-quenching cocktail gets a frothy head from shaken egg whites.

- 1½ oz. London dry gin
- 2 tsp. superfine sugar
- 2 large egg whites
- 2 Tbsp. fresh lemon juice
     Ice cubes, plus crushed ice for serving
- 1 lemon zest strip, for garnish

In a cocktail shaker, combine the gin, sugar, egg whites and lemon juice. Fill the shaker with ice and shake vigorously. Strain into a chilled, crushed ice–filled rocks glass and garnish with a strip of lemon zest. —*Tim Allen*

Civic Treasure

⏱ Total **5 min**; Makes **1 drink**

"Bitter flavors are a love-or-hate thing; I've always been in the love camp," says chef Renee Erickson. At Barnacle in Seattle, she offers about 70 different amaros (bittersweet digestivos), such as the rhubarb-based Zucca in the drink here. "When you turn amaros into a cocktail, they become richly flavored and textured in a way that doesn't happen with other spirits."

- 1 oz. dry gin
- 1 oz. Cappelletti (wine-based aperitivo)
- 1 oz. Zucca (rhubarb-flavored amaro)
- 2 dashes of rhubarb bitters
     Ice
- 1 orange twist
     Chilled club soda

In a mixing glass, combine the gin with the Cappelletti, Zucca and bitters. Fill the mixing glass with ice and stir well. Strain into a chilled, ice-filled collins glass. Add the orange twist and top with club soda. —*Renee Erickson*

Rosemary's Baby

⏱ Total **10 min**; Makes **1 drink**

This perfectly balanced gin cocktail gets a nice bitterness from Cocchi Americano and a wonderful fragrance from fresh rosemary leaves muddled into the drink.

- 1 tsp. rosemary leaves, plus 1 small rosemary sprig for garnish
- ¾ oz. Cocchi Americano (fortified, slightly bitter aperitif wine)
- 1½ oz. London dry gin
     Ice
- 1 oz. chilled Prosecco

In a mixing glass, gently muddle the rosemary leaves with the Cocchi Americano. Add the gin, fill the glass with ice and stir for 30 seconds. Strain into a chilled coupe and top with the Prosecco. Garnish with the rosemary sprig. —*Jeremy Fox*

FROZEN HONEYDEW-
BASIL MARGARITAS

Frozen Honeydew-Basil Margaritas

Total **20 min plus freezing and chilling**
Makes **4 drinks**

This margarita riff combines blanco tequila and lime juice with chunks of frozen honeydew melon and a brightly flavored sweet basil puree. While you can make the basil puree ahead of time, it's always best to squeeze the lime juice right before blending the drink so it retains its fresh flavor.

- ½ **cup sugar**
- ½ **cup basil leaves, plus 4 sprigs for garnish**
- 4 **cups chopped honeydew melon, frozen**
- ½ **cup plus 2 Tbsp. blanco tequila**
- 1 **cup fresh lime juice**

1. In a small saucepan, combine the sugar and ½ cup of water and bring to a boil, stirring to dissolve the sugar. Add the basil leaves and blanch just until wilted, about 20 seconds. Pour the basil syrup into a blender and let cool slightly, then puree until smooth. Refrigerate until cold.

2. In the blender, combine the frozen melon with the tequila, lime juice and 6 tablespoons of the basil puree; puree until smooth. Pour into chilled glasses and garnish with basil sprigs. —*Kay Chun*

MAKE AHEAD The sweet basil puree can be refrigerated overnight.

ESSENTIAL SWEETENER

Simple Syrup

This clear syrup is indispensable for sweetening many of the cocktails in this book.

In a small saucepan, simmer 1 cup **sugar** with 1 cup **water** over moderate heat, stirring, until the sugar is completely dissolved. Let the syrup cool completely, then refrigerate for up to 1 month. Makes about 12 oz.

Beet It

Total **10 min**; Makes **1 drink**

"I've always felt tequila had a natural affinity for earthy ingredients," says San Diego bartender Lindsay Nader, who makes this invigorating cocktail with beets. "Try not to spill, because the stain can be more perilous than red wine!"

- 2 **oz. blanco tequila**
- 1 **oz. fresh beet juice**
- ¾ **oz. Simple Syrup (below left)**
- ½ **oz. fresh cucumber juice**
- ½ **oz. fresh lime juice**
  Ice
- 1 **cucumber ribbon, for garnish**

In a cocktail shaker, combine all of the ingredients except the ice and cucumber ribbon. Fill with ice and shake well. Strain into a chilled, ice-filled rocks glass and add the garnish. —*Lindsay Nader*

Tequila-Watermelon Aguas Frescas with Prosecco

Total **30 min**; Makes **12 drinks**

Prosecco adds a lively spritz to this light, watermelon-forward margarita. If you happen to have a juicer on hand, you can certainly use it here.

- ½ **cup sugar**
- 1 **chilled seedless watermelon (15 lbs.), rind discarded and watermelon cubed (20 cups)**
- ¾ **cup blanco tequila**
- 6 **limes, thinly sliced**
- 3 **mint sprigs, plus mint leaves for garnish**
  Ice
- 1 **chilled 750-ml bottle Prosecco**

1. In a small saucepan, combine the sugar and ½ cup of water and bring just to a boil, stirring until the sugar is completely dissolved. Transfer the simple syrup to a heatproof bowl and let cool.

2. In a food processor or blender, puree the watermelon in batches until smooth. Strain the puree into a large bowl or pitcher. Stir in the simple syrup, tequila, lime slices, mint sprigs and ½ cup of cold water.

3. To serve, pour the watermelon agua fresca into chilled, ice-filled glasses, leaving 1 inch at the top. Top off the drinks with Prosecco and garnish with mint leaves. —*Eli and Max Sussman*

MAKE AHEAD The strained watermelon juice can be refrigerated overnight.

Fresh Tomato Bloody Mary

Total **15 min**; Makes **4 drinks**

To get the richest flavor for your Bloody Mary mix, use very ripe tomatoes. If you can't find adequate vine-ripened tomatoes, use red cherry tomatoes in their place.

- 1½ **lbs. ripe red tomatoes**
  One 9-inch English cucumber, peeled and chopped (2 cups)
- 2 **Tbsp. chopped dill**
- 1 **Tbsp. finely grated fresh horseradish**
- 1 **Tbsp. fresh lemon juice**
- ¼ **oz. dried shiitake mushrooms, crumbled**
  Kosher salt and pepper
  Ice
- 1 **cup aquavit or vodka (optional)**
  Dill sprigs, cucumber slices and lemon wedges, for garnish

1. In a blender, puree the tomatoes with the cucumber, dill, horseradish, lemon juice and dried mushrooms and season with salt and pepper. Strain the mix through a fine-mesh sieve set over a pitcher, pressing on the solids. You should have 3 cups of Bloody Mary mix.

2. For each drink, fill a cocktail shaker with ice and shake with ¾ cup of Bloody Mary mix and ¼ cup of aquavit or vodka, if using. Strain into a chilled, ice-filled highball glass. Garnish with a dill sprig, cucumber slice and lemon wedge and serve immediately. —*Spoon and Stable, Minneapolis*

MAKE AHEAD The Bloody Mary mix can be refrigerated overnight.

PDT/Crif Frozen Piña Colada

Total **10 min plus 4 hr freezing**
Makes **4 drinks**

Jeff Bell of PDT in New York City says a piña colada is his guilty pleasure. In place of the typical overly sweetened cream of coconut, he makes this superfresh, pineapple-y version with coconut water and coconut puree (available frozen at specialty markets).

- 5 oz. fresh pineapple juice
- 5 oz. fresh lime juice
- 3 oz. coconut water
- 15 oz. chilled white rum
- 6 oz. frozen coconut puree
- 3 oz. cane syrup
- 4 pineapple wedges, for garnish

Mix the pineapple juice, lime juice and coconut water and pour into an ice cube tray. Freeze until solid, about 4 hours; transfer to a blender. Add the rum, coconut puree and cane syrup and blend until smooth. Pour into 4 chilled double rocks glasses and garnish with the pineapple wedges. —*Jeff Bell*

Papaya Caliente

Total **10 min; Makes 2 drinks**

For this fruity rum cocktail, Julio Cabrera, co-owner of The Regent Cocktail Club in Miami Beach, re-creates the flavors of *jugo de papaya con anis*, a popular weight-loss drink in the Dominican Republic and Puerto Rico. His version here has no purported slimming effects.

- 4 oz. white rum
- 2 oz. Simple Syrup (p. 373)
- 1 oz. fresh lime juice
- 1½ tsp. pastis, preferably Pernod
  Six 1-inch chunks of ripe papaya
- 2 cups ice cubes
- 2 tarragon sprigs, for garnish

In a blender, combine the rum, Simple Syrup, lime juice, pastis, papaya chunks and ice and blend until smooth. Pour into 2 large chilled martini glasses and garnish each drink with a tarragon sprig. —*Julio Cabrera*

Daiq on a Hot Tin Roof

Total **10 min; Makes 1 drink**

Passion fruit adds a tiki twist to the classic daiquiri. Smith & Cross rum is highly recommended, as it adds a spiced tropical note to the drink.

- 1½ oz. Papa's Pilar blonde rum
- 1 oz. fresh lime juice
- 1 oz. passion fruit nectar
- ½ oz. Jamaican rum, preferably Smith & Cross
- ½ oz. Simple Syrup (p. 373)
  Ice
- 1 lime wheel, for garnish

In a cocktail shaker, combine the blonde rum, lime juice, passion fruit nectar, Jamaican rum and Simple Syrup. Fill the shaker with ice and shake well. Strain into a chilled coupe and garnish with the lime wheel. —*Benton Bourgeois*

Palmer Park Swizzle

Total **10 min plus 2 hr steeping**
Makes **1 drink**

- 2 cups bourbon
- 1 black tea bag, preferably Luzianne
- 1 oz. fresh lime juice
- ¾ oz. Simple Syrup (p. 373)
- 8 mint leaves, plus 1 mint sprig for garnish
  Ice cubes, plus crushed ice for serving

In a 1-quart jar, steep the bourbon with the tea bag for 2 hours; discard the tea bag. In a cocktail shaker, combine the lime juice, Simple Syrup, mint leaves and 2 ounces of the tea-infused bourbon. Fill the shaker with ice cubes and shake well. Strain into a chilled, crushed ice–filled collins glass and garnish with the mint sprig; serve right away. —*Bayou Bar, New Orleans*

Morrison Mule

Total **10 min; Makes 1 drink**

- Ice
- 4 oz. ginger beer
- 1½ oz. bourbon
- ½ oz. Peychaud's Aperitivo or Aperol
- ½ oz. fresh lime juice
  One 3-inch strip of orange zest, for garnish

Fill a copper mug with ice, then add the ginger beer, bourbon, Peychaud's Aperitivo and lime juice; stir well. Garnish with the strip of orange zest and serve immediately. —*Benton Bourgeois*

Amaretto Sour

Total **5 min; Makes 1 drink**

Jeffrey Morgenthaler, bar manager of Pepe Le Moko in Portland, Oregon, proves with this balanced drink that amaretto sours don't have to be cloyingly sweet. If you have Simple Syrup (recipe, p. 373), you can substitute it for the dissolved superfine sugar.

- 1 oz. fresh lemon juice
- ¾ oz. overproof bourbon
- ½ oz. amaretto
- ½ oz. beaten egg white
- 1 tsp. superfine sugar dissolved in ½ tsp. water
  Ice
- 1 lemon zest strip and 1 brandied cherry, for garnish

In a cocktail shaker, combine the lemon juice, bourbon, amaretto, egg white and sugar mixture and shake vigorously. Fill the shaker with ice and shake again. Strain into a chilled, ice-filled rocks glass. Garnish with the lemon zest strip and brandied cherry. —*Jeffrey Morgenthaler*

Brandy Sazerac

Total **10 min; Makes 1 drink**

- Ice
- ¼ oz. Legendre Herbsaint (anise-flavored liqueur)
- 2 oz. Rémy Martin 1738 Accord Royal Cognac
- ¼ to ½ oz. Simple Syrup (p. 373)
- 4 to 5 dashes of Peychaud's bitters
- 1 lemon twist, for garnish

Fill a chilled rocks glass with ice and add the Herbsaint. In a mixing glass, combine the Cognac, Simple Syrup and bitters. Fill the mixing glass with ice and stir well. Discard the ice and the Herbsaint from the rocks glass, then strain the drink into it. Garnish with the lemon twist and serve immediately. —*Yon Davis*

CLOCKWISE FROM TOP RIGHT:
DAIQ ON A HOT TIN ROOF,
SKYLINER (P. 370), BRANDY
SAZERAC, PALMER PARK
SWIZZLE, MORRISON MULE

CHAI BOURBON
MILK PUNCH

Granny's Brandy

Total **10 min; Makes 1 drink**

San Diego bartender Lindsay Nader adds pisco, the South American grape brandy, to this tart, slightly herbal juice. Omit the pisco for a mocktail with surprising flavor and complexity.

- **2 oz. pisco**
- **2 oz. fresh Granny Smith apple juice**
- **½ oz. fresh celery juice**
- **¼ oz. honey mixed with ¼ oz. water**
- **¼ oz. fresh fennel juice**
-    **Ice**
- **2 oz. chilled club soda**
- **1 celery stalk, for garnish**

In a cocktail shaker, combine the pisco, apple and celery juices, honey and fennel juice. Fill the shaker with ice; shake well. Strain into a chilled, ice-filled collins glass, stir in the club soda and garnish with the celery stalk. —*Lindsay Nader*

Chai Bourbon Milk Punch

Total **10 min plus 1 hr steeping**
Makes **1 drink**

Kenta Goto, owner and head bartender of New York City's Bar Goto, infuses bourbon with chai tea, then shakes the drink with cream and maple syrup. The result reminds us of a boozy chai latte.

- **2 oz. Chai Bourbon (below)**
- **¾ oz. heavy cream**
- **½ oz. pure maple syrup**
- **¼ oz. Simple Syrup (p. 373)**
-    **Ice**

In a cocktail shaker, combine the Chai Bourbon, cream, maple syrup and Simple Syrup; shake well. Fill the shaker with ice and shake again. Strain into a chilled coupe. —*Kenta Goto*

CHAI BOURBON

In a jar, steep 1 Tbsp. **loose chai tea** in 8 oz. **bourbon** for 1 hour. Strain and keep at room temperature for up to 1 month. *Makes 8 oz.* —*KG*

Rosé Sangria with a Mixed-Berry Ice Ring

Active **30 min;** Total **1 hr 15 min plus 8 hr freezing;** Serves **6**

Adding ice cubes to a big batch of sangria will dilute the drink. Instead, F&W's Justin Chapple freezes an oversize ice ring filled with fruit in a Bundt pan. It keeps the punch chilled while also looking festive in the bowl.

- **1 cup blueberries**
- **1 cup raspberries**
- **1 cup sliced strawberries**
- **1 cup blackberries**
- **½ cup fresh currants (optional)**
-    **Distilled water**
-    **Two 750-ml bottles rosé**
- **8 oz. white rum**
- **8 oz. Simple Syrup (p. 373)**
- **4 oz. Campari**
- **2 oz. fresh lemon juice**
-    **Ice cubes, for serving (optional)**

1. Layer the berries and currants in a Bundt pan. Gradually add just enough distilled water to cover. Freeze until solid, at least 8 hours or up to 3 days.

2. In a large punch bowl, stir the wine with the rum, Simple Syrup, Campari and lemon juice. Refrigerate the sangria until chilled, about 45 minutes.

3. Fill a large bowl with very hot water. Dip the bottom of the Bundt pan in the water to loosen the ice ring and invert it onto a plate. Gently add the ice ring to the sangria. Serve in chilled wineglasses, with or without ice cubes. —*Justin Chapple*

MAKE AHEAD The mixed-berry ice ring can be frozen for up to 3 days. The sangria can be refrigerated overnight.

Grilled Strawberry-Rhubarb Sangria

Total **30 min plus 45 min chilling**
Serves **6 to 8**

This white wine sangria gets a subtly smoky kick from fruit that's grilled until caramelized. Feel free to use this recipe as a template: Pair grilled peaches with fresh basil or grilled watermelon with sliced cucumber and mint.

- **½ cup light brown sugar**
- **½ cup dry white wine, such as Sauvignon Blanc**
- **2 pints strawberries, hulled**
- **1¼ cups coarsely chopped rhubarb (2 large stalks), plus 4-inch grilled stalks for garnish (optional)**
-    **One 2-inch piece of vanilla bean, split lengthwise**
- **1 sprig lemon verbena or lemon thyme, plus more for garnish**
- **6 wooden skewers, soaked in water**
- **1 chilled 750-ml bottle Prosecco Brut**
-    **Ice**

1. In a small pot, combine the brown sugar and white wine with ½ cup of water and bring to a simmer, stirring, until the sugar dissolves. Dice 4 of the strawberries and add them to the syrup along with the chopped rhubarb and the vanilla bean. Simmer until the rhubarb is tender, about 4 minutes. Transfer the syrup to a heatproof bowl and add the sprig of lemon verbena. Let cool, then refrigerate until cooled completely, about 45 minutes. Strain the rhubarb syrup through a fine sieve set over a bowl, pressing on the solids.

2. Light a grill. Thread the remaining strawberries on the skewers and grill over moderately high heat until lightly charred, about 5 minutes. Let cool completely, then cut the strawberries in half lengthwise.

3. In a pitcher, combine the rhubarb syrup with half of the grilled strawberries and the Prosecco. Serve the sangria over ice, garnished with the remaining grilled strawberries, lemon verbena sprigs and grilled rhubarb stalks, if using. —*Albert Di Meglio*

Vinho Verde Sangria with a Mint-and-Cucumber Ice Ring

Active **30 min**; Total **1 hr 15 min plus 8 hr freezing**; Serves **6**

The green ice ring in this white sangria is not only pretty, it keeps the drink chilled without diluting it too much.

- **3** Persian cucumbers, thinly sliced lengthwise
- **8** mint sprigs
- **2** limes, thinly sliced
  - Distilled water
  - Two 750-ml bottles Vinho Verde
  - Two 12-oz. bottles ginger beer
- **6** oz. gin
- **1½** oz. fresh lime juice
  - Ice cubes (optional)

1. Layer the cucumbers, mint sprigs and limes in a Bundt pan. Gradually add just enough distilled water to cover. Freeze until solid, at least 8 hours or up to 3 days.

2. In a large punch bowl, stir the wine with the ginger beer, gin and lime juice. Refrigerate the sangria until chilled, about 45 minutes.

3. Fill a large bowl with very hot water. Dip the bottom of the Bundt pan in the water to loosen the ice ring and invert it onto a plate. Gently add the ice ring to the sangria. Serve in chilled wineglasses, with or without ice. —*Justin Chapple*

MAKE AHEAD The mint-and-cucumber ice ring can be frozen for up to 3 days. The sangria can be refrigerated overnight.

PRO PARTY TIP

Drink Calculator

"I count two per woman and three for men, but it's important they're not made to kill. I really like a signature drink that's well balanced and goes with the food, made beforehand in big batches. I print the recipe on coasters."
—*Marcy Blum, event planner and owner of Marcy Blum Associates in New York City*

Cucumber-and-Mint "Fauxjito"

Total **5 min**; Makes **1 drink**

Packed with fresh mint and topped with club soda, this virgin riff on a classic mojito has a cooling quality from cucumber and a hint of sweetness from agave.

- **6** thin slices of English cucumber, plus 1 long, thin slice for garnish
- **6** large mint leaves, plus 1 sprig for garnish
- **2** oz. fresh lime juice
- **½** oz. agave nectar
  - Ice
- **4** oz. chilled club soda

In a cocktail shaker, muddle the 6 cucumber slices with the mint leaves. Add the lime juice and agave and fill with ice; shake well. Strain into a chilled, ice-filled collins glass. Add the club soda; stir once. Garnish with the long cucumber slice and the mint sprig. —*Justin Chapple*

Apple Cider–Ginger Shrub Mocktail

Total **15 min**; Makes **4 drinks**

When combined with sparkling water, this zingy shrub (a vinegar-based syrup) makes for an easy, complex-tasting mocktail. It's as good for a party as it is for a hangover.

- **3** Pink Lady apples, chopped into 1-inch pieces, plus thin slices for garnish
- **⅓** cup finely chopped peeled fresh ginger
- **4½** tsp. unpasteurized apple cider vinegar
  - Ice
  - Chilled seltzer, for topping

1. In a blender, combine the chopped apples, ginger, vinegar and 1 tablespoon of water and puree until smooth. Strain through a fine sieve, pressing on the solids.

2. Fill a cocktail shaker with ice. Add half of the apple-ginger juice and shake well. Strain into 2 coupes and top each with a splash of seltzer. Repeat with the remaining juice and more seltzer. Garnish with apple slices and serve. —*Kay Chun*

Hibiscus-Tangerine Iced Tea

PAGE 368

Active **10 min**; Total **30 min**; Serves **4**

Mixing fresh tangerine juice with tart hibiscus tea results in a not-too-sweet, fruity-floral drink.

- **12** hibiscus tea bags
- **4** cups boiling water
- **2** cups fresh tangerine juice, plus 1 thinly sliced tangerine
  - Ice

1. In a heatproof bowl, cover the tea bags with the boiling water. Let steep for 20 minutes. Strain the tea through a fine sieve into another heatproof bowl. Let cool to room temperature, then stir in the juice.

2. Divide the tea and all but 4 tangerine slices among 4 chilled, ice-filled glasses. Garnish with the reserved tangerine slices. —*Kay Chun*

MAKE AHEAD The strained hibiscus tea can be refrigerated for up to 2 days.

Cardamom Rosewater Iced Tea

Active **10 min**; Total **25 min plus chilling** Serves **8**

This recipe will definitely up your iced tea game. Toasted cardamom and rosewater add warm, exotic notes to this creamy, honey-sweetened iced summer drink.

- **½** cup green cardamom pods (2 oz.)
- **12** black tea bags
- **½** cup honey
  - Ice
- **¾** cup heavy cream
- **8** drops of rosewater

1. In a small skillet, toast the cardamom pods over moderate heat, stirring, until very fragrant and deep golden, about 5 minutes. Transfer to a heatproof bowl. Add the tea bags and 8 cups of hot water and let steep for 15 minutes. Strain the tea into another bowl and stir in the honey. Cover and refrigerate until cold.

2. Pour the tea into 8 chilled, ice-filled glasses. Top each drink with 1½ tablespoons of cream and 1 drop of rosewater. —*Eli and Max Sussman*

MAKE AHEAD The strained cardamom tea can be refrigerated for up to 3 days.

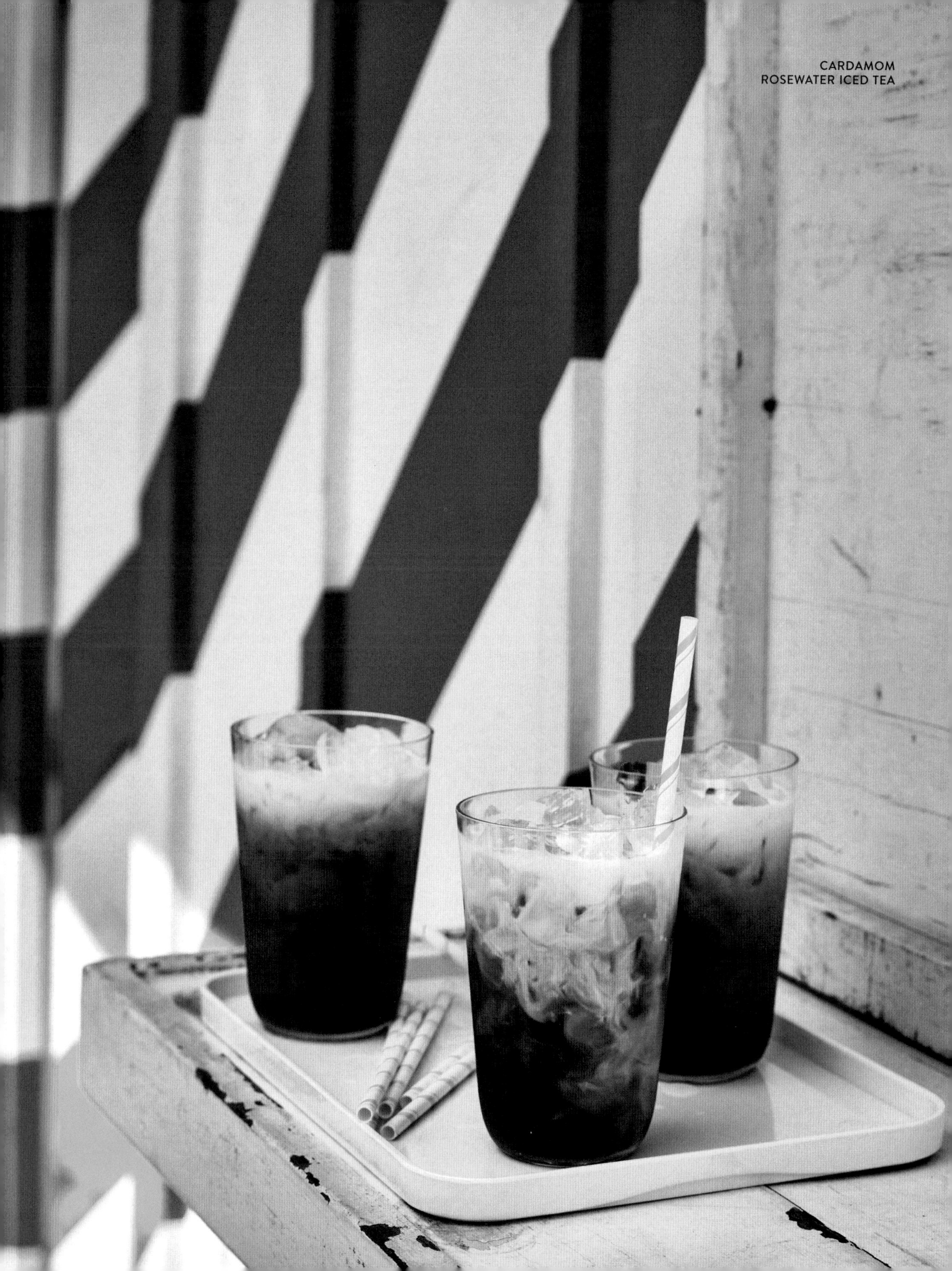

CARDAMOM
ROSEWATER ICED TEA

Health Juice

⏱ Total **10 min**; Makes **two 12-oz. drinks**

F&W editor in chief Nilou Motamed is obsessed with the signature green juice at the Hotel Bel-Air in Los Angeles. It's the perfect balance of tart and sweet. If time permits, chill the drink in the fridge for one to two hours before serving.

- **3** Granny Smith apples, quartered
- **2** lemons, peeled
- **4** cups chopped Tuscan kale leaves
- **1** cup packed parsley sprigs
- **1** celery rib
- **1½ tsp.** ground turmeric

In an electric juicer, juice the apples, lemons, kale, parsley and celery. Stir in the turmeric and serve. —*Hugo Bolanos*

Purple Haze

⏱ Active **10 min**; Total **25 min**
Makes **two 8-oz. drinks**

Star chef Paul Kahan helped create the drinks menu at Chicago's Left Coast Food + Juice, where they serve this sweet, vibrant drink that gets a savory kick from sea salt. It's best served chilled or on ice.

- **1** medium beet, peeled and quartered
- **1** large Granny Smith apple, quartered
- **1** medium carrot, chopped
- **1** medium orange, peeled
  One 4-inch piece of fresh ginger
- **⅛ tsp.** fine Himalayan pink salt

Using an electric juicer, juice the beet, apple, carrot, orange and ginger. Stir in the salt and chill for at least 15 minutes before serving. —*Brad Alexander*

Cantaloupe Juice with Ginger and Lime

⏱ Active **10 min**; Total **40 min**
Makes **two 8-oz. drinks**

Use the ripest cantaloupe you can find for this tropical juice. Freezing the fruit before juicing it adds body to the drink.

- **2** cups chopped cantaloupe
- **2** cups chopped pineapple
  One 2-inch piece of fresh ginger
- **½** lime

1. On a rimmed baking sheet lined with parchment paper, spread the cantaloupe and pineapple in an even layer and freeze until just frozen, about 30 minutes.

2. In an electric juicer, juice the frozen fruit with the ginger and lime half. Serve immediately. —*Emily Tylman*

Turmeric Elixir

Active **15 min**; Total **1 hr**
Makes **two 12-oz. drinks**

If the weekend was particularly hard on your liver, this invigorating drink is an ideal detox. It's spiked with "it" ingredient turmeric, which is known for its anti-inflammatory properties.

- **¼** cup honey
  One 4-inch cinnamon stick
- **2** green cardamom pods
- **2** large mint leaves
- **2** pinches of cayenne
- **¼ tsp.** fine sea salt
- **4 oz.** fresh turmeric
  One 4-inch piece of fresh ginger
- **1½ tsp.** fresh lemon juice

1. In a small saucepan, bring 2½ cups of water to a boil with the honey, cinnamon stick and cardamom over moderate heat. Remove from the heat and whisk in the mint, cayenne and salt. Let cool to room temperature, then refrigerate until chilled. Discard the cinnamon stick, cardamom and mint.

2. In an electric juicer, juice the turmeric and ginger. Whisk the juice with the spiced honey syrup and the lemon juice. Serve chilled. —*Anna Painter*

Electro Shot

⏱ Total **5 min**; Makes **four 2-oz. shots**

This vitamin C–packed juice, flavored with fresh fennel and green apple, is an immunity booster. It's beloved at the New York City outposts of Joe & the Juice, a Copenhagen cult favorite juice bar.

  Ice
- **1** large fennel bulb— trimmed, cored and quartered
- **1** medium Granny Smith apple, quartered

Fill a large glass measuring cup with ice and place it underneath the spout of an electric juicer. Juice the fennel and apple over the ice. Strain the juice into four 2-ounce glasses and serve immediately. —*Joe & the Juice*

Cilantro-Celery Punch

⏱ Total **10 min**; Makes **two 15-oz. juices**

- **10** celery stalks with leaves
- **3** small Granny Smith apples
- **1½** cups packed cilantro leaves
  One 1-inch piece of peeled ginger
- **1 Tbsp.** fresh lemon juice
  Ice

In an electric juicer, juice the celery with the apples, cilantro and ginger. Stir in the lemon juice. Serve the punch over ice. —*Amanda Chantal Bacon*

MAKE AHEAD The punch can be refrigerated for up to 2 days.

Petal-and-Berry Beauty Tonic

Active **10 min**; Total **2 hr 10 min**
Makes **4 drinks**

The goji berries, hibiscus flowers and Schisandra berries used in this recipe are available from amazon.com.

- ½ cup goji berries
- ¼ cup dried hibiscus flowers
- 1 tsp. ground Schisandra berries
- 1 Tbsp. honey
- 2 tsp. rosewater
  Ice and sparkling water or wine, for serving (optional)

In a small saucepan, bring 4 cups of water to a boil. Remove from the heat and add the goji berries, hibiscus flowers and Schisandra berries. Let stand at room temperature for 1 hour. Strain the tonic through a fine-mesh sieve set over a large jar. Whisk in the honey and rosewater, cover and refrigerate until chilled, about 1 hour. Serve warm or, if desired, over ice topped with sparkling water or wine. —*Amanda Chantal Bacon*

MAKE AHEAD The tonic can be refrigerated for up to 1 week.

RECIPE IMPROV

3 Great Shakes

There's nothing we love more than a creamy, frosty milk shake. Get your straws (and spoons) ready for this rich, thick base recipe, plus two flavor variations.

VANILLA In a blender, combine 1 pint softened vanilla ice cream, ¼ cup milk and ¼ tsp. pure vanilla extract and blend until smooth. Stir and pour into 2 tall glasses.

CHOCOLATE Add ¼ cup chocolate syrup to the vanilla shake above.

STRAWBERRY Puree 10 oz. thawed frozen strawberries in light syrup with 2 Tbsp. superfine sugar, then strain. Blend ½ cup of the strawberry puree into the vanilla shake above.
—*Grace Parisi, cookbook author*

The Giant Peach

Active **15 min**; Total **1 hr 15 min plus chilling**
Makes **6 drinks**

Homemade peach syrup sweetens a refreshing coffee soda. Tonic syrup adds a beautiful herbal note, but tonic water is a good stand-in.

- 6 medium peaches (about 2 lbs.), pitted and chopped, plus peach slices for garnish
- 2 cups pomegranate juice
- 2 Tbsp. fresh lemon juice
- 1½ cups sparkling water
- 1 cup plus 2 Tbsp. cold-brew coffee
- 1 cup plus 2 Tbsp. Jack Rudy Small Batch Tonic Syrup (see Note)
  A few dashes of Angostura bitters
  Ice

1. In a medium saucepan, bring the chopped peaches, pomegranate juice, lemon juice and 4 cups of water to a boil. Cook over moderate heat, stirring occasionally, until thickened and reduced to 2 cups, 45 to 50 minutes. Strain through a fine sieve set over a medium bowl, pressing on the solids; discard the solids. Let the peach syrup cool completely, then refrigerate until chilled.

2. In a pitcher, mix the peach syrup with the sparkling water, coffee, tonic syrup and bitters. Pour the coffee soda into chilled, ice-filled glasses and garnish with peach slices. —*Andy Mumma*

NOTE The tonic syrup is available from jackrudycocktailco.com. Alternatively, use 3 cups of tonic water and omit the sparkling water.

It's a Date! Shake

Total **5 min**; Serves **2**

Any dairy-free ice cream, such as coconut or almond, can be used for this vegan milk shake. Medjool dates are a rich natural sweetener, while the cinnamon crumb topping adds great texture.

- 1 pint dairy-free vanilla ice cream
- ½ cup unsweetened almond milk
- 8 Medjool dates, pitted and coarsely chopped
- 1 cup ice
  Ground cinnamon and Cinnamon Crumb Topping (recipe follows), for serving

In a blender, combine the ice cream with the almond milk and half of the dates. Blend until smooth, 1 to 2 minutes. Add the ice and the remaining dates and blend until smooth, about 1 minute. Pour the shake into 2 chilled glasses, top with cinnamon and the Cinnamon Crumb Topping and serve. —*Chloe Coscarelli*

CINNAMON CRUMB TOPPING
Active **5 min**; Total **25 min plus cooling**
Makes **1 cup**

This supercrunchy spiced crumble makes an excellent vegan topping for ice cream, banana pudding or roasted fruit. It's also great on coffee cake muffins or banana bread; simply sprinkle the unbaked crumbs on top of the batter before baking.

- ½ cup plus 2 Tbsp. all-purpose flour
- 1 tsp. ground cinnamon
  Pinch of sea salt
- 2½ Tbsp. granulated sugar
- 2½ Tbsp. light brown sugar
- ¼ cup vegan margarine, melted

Preheat the oven to 325° and line a rimmed baking sheet with parchment paper. In a medium bowl, whisk the flour with the cinnamon, salt and both sugars. Add the melted margarine and mix until pea-size clumps form. Spread the crumb topping on the prepared baking sheet and bake until brown and crisp, about 20 minutes. Let cool. —*CC*

DIY Rosé Vermouth

JACKSON CANNON, bar director of The Hawthorne, Eastern Standard and Island Creek Oyster Bar in Boston, makes his own aromatic fortified wine with rosé. No commercial vermouth can match its freshness and balanced flavor.

Rosé Vermouth

Total **3 hr plus 2 days infusing**
Makes **3 quarts**

- 1 lb. strawberries, hulled and sliced
- 2¼ cups unaged (clear) brandy, preferably French
- 2¾ cups sugar
- 4 small rosemary leaves
- 7 small sage leaves
- 2 tsp. oregano leaves
- 1 tsp. thyme leaves
- 1 Tbsp. bitter orange peel
- 2 tsp. wormwood root
- ½ tsp. gentian root
- ¼ tsp. ground ginger
- One 1½-inch piece of vanilla bean
- Three 750-ml bottles (9½ cups) rosé, preferably Spanish Garnacha
- 1 cup ruby port
- ½ tsp. finely grated orange zest

1. In a glass jar or pitcher, cover the strawberries with the brandy and let macerate for 2 days at room temperature; the strawberries should be completely submerged.

2. Strain the strawberry-infused brandy through a cheesecloth-lined sieve; discard the strawberries.

3. In a large nonreactive saucepan, combine the sugar with ¼ cup of water and cook over moderately low heat, swirling the pan occasionally, until the sugar is dissolved and a medium-amber caramel forms, about 10 minutes. Remove the saucepan from the heat and carefully add the strawberry-infused brandy; the caramel will harden. Cook over low heat, stirring, until the caramel is dissolved. Remove from the heat.

4. In a medium nonreactive saucepan, combine the rosemary, sage, oregano, thyme, bitter orange peel, wormwood, gentian, ginger, vanilla bean and 3 cups of the rosé. Bring to a boil, then remove from the heat and let stand for 10 minutes. Stir in the port.

5. Add the infused port and the remaining 6½ cups of rosé to the strawberry-brandy caramel syrup. Stir in the orange zest and refrigerate until cold, about 2 hours.

6. Strain the vermouth through a cheese-cloth-lined sieve. Pour into bottles and refrigerate. Serve the vermouth as an aperitif or over ice, or use it in a cocktail, like the Fifty-Fifty martini or Cannon's Frobisher (recipe above right).

MAKE AHEAD The vermouth can be refrigerated for up to 4 months.

Frobisher

Total **5 min**; Makes **1 drink**

- 2 oz. Plymouth gin
- ¾ oz. rosé vermouth (left)
- ¼ oz. Luxardo maraschino liqueur
  Ice
- 1 orange peel
- 1 maraschino cherry, for garnish

In a mixing glass, stir the gin with the rosé vermouth and maraschino liqueur. Add ice and stir again until well chilled. Strain into a chilled cocktail glass and twist an orange peel over the drink; discard the orange peel. Garnish the cocktail with a maraschino cherry.

VERMOUTH-MAKING TUTORIAL

INFUSE THE BRANDY Soak hulled and sliced fresh strawberries in unaged brandy for two days, then strain.

MAKE BRANDY CARAMEL SYRUP Make caramel, then stir in the strawberry-infused brandy.

STEEP THE PORT Add rosé, herbs, bitter orange peel, ginger, gentian, wormwood and vanilla.

STRAIN OUT AROMATICS Mix the infused port and more rosé with the brandy caramel syrup and chill. Strain the vermouth.

Mix rosé vermouth with gin or vodka for a Fifty-Fifty martini (pictured), or serve it in a rocks glass over a large ice cube for an ultra-refreshing aperitif.

GRILLED WATERMELON
WITH AVOCADO, CUCUMBER
AND SALSA (P. 31)

Recipe Index

Page numbers in **bold** indicate photographs.

Contributors

RECIPES

GRANT ACHATZ, a Food & Wine Chef-in-Residence and F&W Best New Chef 2002, is the chef and co-owner of Alinea, Next and The Aviary cocktail bar, all in Chicago. He is a co-author of *Alinea* and *Life, On the Line*.

MAIA ACQUAVIVA is the chef at Oda House in New York City.

VICTOR ALBISU is the chef and owner of Del Campo in Washington, DC, and Taco Bamba in Falls Church, Springfield and Vienna, Virginia.

BRAD ALEXANDER is the chef at Left Coast Food + Juice in Chicago.

EVAN ALGORRI is the owner of Condimento, a condiments purveyor in Los Angeles.

TIM ALLEN is the chef at The Wild Rabbit in Kingham, Oxfordshire, England.

LAUREL ALMERINDA is the pastry chef at Huckleberry Bakery & Café in Los Angeles.

MALIKA AMEEN is a pastry chef and the author of *Sweet Sugar, Sultry Spice*.

GIUSEPPE ANGELINI is the chef at Masseria Le Carrube near the town of Ostuni in the Puglia region of Italy.

DOMINIQUE ANSEL is a pastry chef and the owner of Dominique Ansel Bakery in New York City, Tokyo and London and Dominique Ansel Kitchen in New York City. He is the author of *Dominique Ansel: The Secret Recipes*.

NATE APPLEMAN, an F&W Best New Chef 2009, is the culinary director at Chipotle Mexican Grill nationwide.

CATHAL ARMSTRONG, an F&W Best New Chef 2006, is the chef and owner of Restaurant Eve, Eamonn's and The Majestic, all in Alexandria, Virginia. He is the author of the cookbook *My Irish Table*.

AMANDA CHANTAL BACON is the founder of Moon Juice in Los Angeles and author of *The Moon Juice Cookbook*.

JIMMY BANNOS, JR., is the chef and co-owner of The Purple Pig in Chicago.

DAVID BARZELAY, an F&W Best New Chef 2016, is the chef at Lazy Bear in San Francisco.

CHRISTOPHER BATES is a master sommelier and the chef and co-owner of FLX Wienery in Dundee and FLX Table in Geneva, both in the Finger Lakes region of New York.

BAYOU BAR is in the Pontchartrain Hotel in New Orleans.

FRANKLIN BECKER is the chef and co-owner of The Little Beet and The Little Beet Table, with locations in New York City, Chicago and Washington, DC. He is the author of several cookbooks, including *Good Fat Cooking*.

JEFF BELL is the general manager of PDT, a cocktail bar in New York City.

ELLEN BENNETT is the founder of Hedley & Bennett, an apron and chef wear company in Los Angeles.

JOHN BESH, an F&W Best New Chef 1999, is the chef and owner of the Besh Restaurant Group, which includes August and Domenica in New Orleans and Lüke in San Antonio. He is the author of four cookbooks, including *Besh Big Easy*.

JAMIE BISSONNETTE is a co-chef and co-owner of Coppa and Little Donkey in Boston and Toro in Boston and New York City.

APRIL BLOOMFIELD, an F&W Chef-in-Residence and Best New Chef 2007, is the chef and co-owner of The Spotted Pig, The Breslin, The John Dory Oyster Bar, Salvation Burger, Salvation Taco and White Gold, all in New York City, and Tosca Cafe in San Francisco. She is the author of *A Girl and Her Pig* and *A Girl and Her Greens*.

THOMAS BOEMER is the chef and co-owner of Corner Table and Revival in Minneapolis.

HUGO BOLANOS is the chef at Hotel Bel-Air in Los Angeles.

MATT BOLUS is the chef at 404 Kitchen in Nashville.

STEPHANE BOMBET is a restaurateur and the founder and owner of Bombet Hospitality Group in Los Angeles.

GABRIELE BONCI is the chef at Pizzarium in Rome.

DANIEL BOULUD is the chef and owner of dozens of restaurants, including Daniel and DB Bistro Moderne in New York City, Café Boulud in Toronto and Maison Boulud in Beijing. He is the author of *Letters to a Young Chef* and co-author of *Daniel Boulud's Café Boulud Cookbook* and *Braise*.

BENTON BOURGEOIS is the bar chef at the Hot Tin bar in the Pontchartrain Hotel in New Orleans.

TESS BOUSKA was formerly the pastry chef at Revival in Minneapolis.

SEAN BROCK is the chef and co-owner of McCrady's and Minero in Charleston, South Carolina, and Husk in Charleston and Nashville. He is the author of *Heritage*.

DEREK BROWN is the president of Drink Company and the owner of four bars and restaurants in Washington, DC, including Mockingbird Hill.

JULIO CABRERA is a co-owner and bartender at The Regent Cocktail Club in Miami Beach.

STEFANO CALLEGARI is the chef at Sbanco in Rome.

JACKSON CANNON is a co-owner and bar director of The Hawthorne and bar director of Eastern Standard and Island Creek Oyster Bar, all in Boston.

ANDREW CARMELLINI, an F&W Best New Chef 2000, is the chef and co-owner of The Dutch Miami in Miami Beach and several restaurants in New York City, including Locanda Verde, Lafayette and Leuca. He is a co-author of *Urban Italian* and *American Flavor*.

JENNIFER CARROLL is the chef and co-owner of Requin in Fairfax, Virginia.

TIM CASPARE is a co-chef at Pasquale Jones in New York City.

JUSTIN CHAPPLE is an F&W Test Kitchen senior editor, the talent behind the Mad Genius Tips videos on foodandwine.com and the author of *Mad Genius Tips*.

MANEET CHAUHAN is the chef and co-owner of Chauhan Ale & Masala House in Nashville and a judge on Food Network's *Chopped*.

CYRILLE CHAUSSADE is the chef at La Villa du Cap, the restaurant at La Villa Fabulite in Cap d'Antibes, France.

KAY CHUN is a former F&W Test Kitchen senior editor.

JOSIAH CITRIN, an F&W Best New Chef 1997, is the chef and owner of Melisse and Charcoal Venice in Los Angeles. He is also the author of *In Pursuit of Excellence*.

MELISSA CLARK is a staff food writer for the *New York Times* and the author of dozens of cookbooks, including *Dinner* and *In the Kitchen with a Good Appetite*.

BRIAN CLEVENGER is the chef and owner of Vendemmia, East Anchor Seafood and Raccolto, all in Seattle.

ADAM COATES is a co-owner of The Roadhouse in Byron Bay, New South Wales, Australia.

ENZO COLAIACOMO is the chef at Eremito, a monastery-inspired hotel near Orvieto, Italy.

ABRAHAM CONLON is the chef and co-owner of Fat Rice in Chicago and a co-author of *The Adventures of Fat Rice*.

CHLOE COSCARELLI is the chef and co-owner of Sweets by Chloe and By Chloe vegan fast-casual restaurants in New York City and Los Angeles. She is a former champion of Food Network's *Cupcake Wars* and the author of several cookbooks, including *Chloe's Kitchen*.

JUSTIN CROXALL is the chef at Stems & Skins in Charleston, South Carolina.

JAMI CURL is the founder of Quin, a candy company in Portland, Oregon. She is the author of *Candy is Magic*.

NICK CURTOLA is the chef at The Four Horsemen in Brooklyn.

TIM CUSHMAN, an F&W Best New Chef 2008, is the chef and co-owner of O Ya in Boston and New York City and Covina and Roof at Park South in New York City.

BEN DAILEY is the chef and owner of Cebo in the Finger Lakes town of Geneva, New York.

ARCANGELO DANDINI is the chef at Ristorante L'Arcangelo in Rome.

JOHN DASILVA is the chef at Spoke in Somerville, Massachusetts.

YON DAVIS was formerly the bar manager for the Pontchartrain Hotel in New Orleans.

GUILLAUME DELAUNE is the chef at Commanderie de Peyrassol wine estate in Flassans-sur-Issole, Provence, France.

GREG DENTON and **GABRIELLE QUIÑÓNEZ DENTON,** F&W Best New Chefs 2014, are the chefs and owners of Ox Restaurant in Portland, Oregon.

BEN DEVLIN is the chef at Paper Daisy at Halcyon House, a boutique hotel in Cabarita Beach, New South Wales, Australia.

ANGELA DIMAYUGA is the chef at Mission Chinese Food in New York City.

ALBERT DI MEGLIO is the chef at Barano in Brooklyn.

KRISTIN DONNELLY is a food writer and recipe developer. She is the author of *Modern Potluck*.

LISA DONOVAN is the creator of Bakeshop at Buttermilk Road, an online bakery, and the CSA-style BakeShare in Nashville.

CHARLOTTE DRUCKMAN, a writer and editor in New York City, is the author of *Stir, Sizzle, Bake*.

NAOMI DUGUID is a food writer and cookbook author in Toronto. Her latest cookbook is *Taste of Persia*.

VICTORIA ELÍASDÓTTIR is the chef at Dóttir in Berlin.

RENEE ERICKSON is the chef and owner of six restaurants in Seattle, including The Whale Wins, The Walrus and the Carpenter, Barnacle and General Porpoise. She is the author of *A Boat, a Whale and a Walrus*.

PAUL EVERETT is a cook at Sqirl in L.A.

JESSE TYLER FERGUSON is an actor on ABC's *Modern Family*, an avid home cook and a co-author of the blog Julie and Jesse's Recipes.

ANYA FERNALD is the co-founder and CEO of Belcampo, an artisanal food and agritourism company based in Northern California. She is a judge on Food Network's *Iron Chef America* and *The Next Iron Chef* and the author of *Home Cooked*.

KELLY FIELDS is the pastry chef at Willa Jean in New Orleans.

KEVIN FINK, an F&W Best New Chef 2016, is the chef and owner of Emmer & Rye in Austin, Texas.

BEN FORD is the chef and owner of the Los Angeles restaurant Ford's Filling Station. His latest cookbook is *Taming the Feast*.

JEREMY FORD is the winner of *Top Chef* Season 13 and the chef at Matador Room in Miami Beach.

MARC FORGIONE, winner of Food Network's *The Next Iron Chef* Season 3, is the chef and co-owner of American Cut and the chef and owner of Marc Forgione, both in New York City. He is the author of the cookbook *Marc Forgione*.

JEREMY FOX, an F&W Best New Chef 2008, is the chef at Rustic Canyon in Santa Monica, California.

DAVID FRENKIEL is a co-creator of the Stockholm-based blog Green Kitchen Stories and a co-author *The Green Kitchen, Green Kitchen Travels* and *Vegetarian Everyday*.

JOSE GARCES is the chef and owner of a food truck and numerous restaurants, including Distrito and Tinto in Philadelphia; Amada in Philadelphia and New York City; Mercat in Chicago; and El Jefe in Palm Springs, California. His latest cookbook is *The Latin Road Home*.

MEGAN GARRELTS is the pastry chef and co-owner of Bluestem in Kansas City, Missouri, and Rye in Leawood, Kansas. She is a co-author of *Bluestem: The Cookbook*.

INA GARTEN is the host of Food Network's *Barefoot Contessa*. She has written ten *Barefoot Contessa* cookbooks.

SHAWN GAWLE, an F&W Best New Pastry Chef 2012, is the pastry chef at Quince and Cotogna, both in San Francisco.

KEVIN GILLESPIE is the chef and owner of Gunshow in Atlanta and Revival in Decatur, Georgia. He is the author of *Fire in My Belly* and *Pure Pork Awesomeness*.

SUZANNE GOIN, an F&W Best New Chef 1999, is the chef and co-owner of several restaurants in Los Angeles, including Lucques and A.O.C. She is the author of *Sunday Suppers at Lucques* and *The A.O.C. Cookbook*.

KENTA GOTO is the owner and head bartender of Bar Goto in New York City.

DORIE GREENSPAN has authored and co-authored numerous cookbooks, including *Around My French Table* and *Dorie's Cookies*.

SARAH GRUENEBERG is the chef and owner of Monteverde in Chicago.

ALEX GUARNASCHELLI, a judge on Food Network's *Chopped* and winner of *The Next Iron Chef* Season 5, is the chef at Butter in New York City. She is the author of *Old-School Comfort Food*.

MICHAEL GULOTTA, an F&W Best New Chef 2016, is the chef and owner of MoPho and Tana in New Orleans.

KATHY GUNST is a Maine-based food writer and the author and co-author of numerous cookbooks, including *Notes from a Maine Kitchen* and *Soup Swap*.

RYAN HARDY is the chef and co-owner of Charlie Bird and a co-chef and co-owner of Pasquale Jones, both in New York City.

NABIL HASSED is the chef at Salumeria Roscioli in Rome.

KAREN HATFIELD is the pastry chef and co-owner of Hatfield's and The Sycamore Kitchen in Los Angeles.

CONTRIBUTORS

JASMINE HEMSLEY and her sister **MELISSA HEMSLEY** are London-based nutritional consultants who created the wellness blog Hemsley + Hemsley. They co-authored *The Art of Eating Well*.

MARGOT HENDERSON is the chef at Rochelle Canteen and a co-owner of Arnold & Henderson catering in London.

OLIA HERCULES, a former chef at Ottolenghi in London, is a food stylist and writer. She is the author of *Mamushka: Recipes from Ukraine and Eastern Europe*.

HH & CO. is the Italian-inflected restaurant at the Lime Wood Hotel, a 13th-century hunting lodge turned Regency residence in Lyndhurst, Hampshire, England.

DEUKI HONG is the chef at a forthcoming New York City restaurant focused on fermentation. He is a co-author of *Koreatown*.

VIVIAN HOWARD is the chef and co-owner of Chef & the Farmer and Boiler Room in Kinston, North Carolina. She is the host of the TV documentary and cooking series *A Chef's Life* and the author of *Deep Run Roots*.

SARAH HYMANSON is a co-chef and co-owner of Madcapra falafel stand in Los Angeles's Grand Central Market and the forthcoming L.A. restaurant Kismet.

JOE & THE JUICE is a Copenhagen-based chain of juice and coffee bars with locations in northern Europe and New York City.

JOSEPH "JJ" JOHNSON is the chef at The Cecil and Minton's in New York City's Harlem neighborhood.

ANNA JONES is the London-based author of *A Modern Way to Cook*.

JUDY JOO, the first female winner of *Iron Chef UK*, is the chef and owner of Jinjuu in London and Hong Kong. She hosts the Cooking Channel's *Korean Food Made Simple* and is the author of a cookbook of the same name.

EDOUARDO JORDAN, an F&W Best New Chef 2016, is the chef and owner of Salare in Seattle.

CHRIS KAJIOKA is a co-chef and co-owner of Senia in Honolulu.

AKI KAMOZAWA is a co-owner of Curiosity Doughnuts in Stockton, New Jersey, and a co-author of the website Ideas in Food and several cookbooks, including *Maximum Flavor*.

RAVI KAPUR, an F&W Best New Chef 2016, is the chef at Liholiho Yacht Club in San Francisco.

MICHELLE KARR-UEOKA is the pastry chef and co-owner of MW Restaurant in Honolulu.

GAVIN KAYSEN, an F&W Best New Chef 2007, is the chef and owner of Spoon and Stable in Minneapolis.

THOMAS KELLER is the chef and co-owner of The French Laundry and Ad Hoc in Napa Valley, Per Se in New York City and multiple locations of Bouchon bakeries and bistros. He is the author of several cookbooks, including *The French Laundry Cookbook*.

ED KENNEY is the chef and owner of Town, Mud Hen Water, Kaimuki Superette and Mahina & Sun's in Honolulu.

BRAD KILGORE, an F&W Best New Chef 2016, is the chef at Alter in Miami.

MAURA KILPATRICK is the pastry chef and co-owner of Sofra in Boston and a co-author of the cookbook *Soframiz*.

SOHUI KIM is the chef and co-owner of The Good Fork and Insa in Brooklyn and author of *The Good Fork Cookbook*.

BRANDON KIRKSEY is the chef de cuisine at The Slanted Door in San Francisco.

DAN KLUGER, an F&W Best New Chef 2012, is the chef and co-owner of Loring Place in New York City.

ALEX KNEZEVIC is the chef at Vertical Detroit, a wine bar in Detroit.

TYLER KORD is the chef and co-owner of the No. 7 restaurant and sub shops in New York City and the author of *A Super Upsetting Cookbook About Sandwiches*.

JESSICA KOSLOW is the chef and owner of Sqirl in Los Angeles and an active member of Edible School Yard, Bakers Will Bake, Farm on Wheels and Sustainable Kitchen, all initiatives that aim to promote healthful eating habits. She is the author of *Everything I Want to Eat: Sqirl and the New California Cooking*.

SARA KRAMER is a co-chef and co-owner of Madcapra falafel stand in Los Angeles's Grand Central Market and the forthcoming L.A. restaurant Kismet.

ELLIE KRIEGER is a nutritionist, the host of Food Network's *Healthy Appetite* and the author of several cookbooks, including *You Have It Made*.

TREVOR KUNK is the chef at The Breslin in New York City.

SIMON LAMB is the director of operations at The Lunatic, The Lover & The Poet in Chicago.

JESSICA LARGEY is the chef and co-owner of Simone in Los Angeles.

JOSH LAURANO is the chef at La Sirena in New York City.

ANDREW LE is the chef and owner of The Pig & the Lady in Honolulu.

DAVID LEBOVITZ is a Paris-based pastry chef and creator of an eponymous blog. He is the author of seven books, including the cookbooks *The Perfect Scoop* and *My Paris Kitchen* and the memoir *The Sweet Life in Paris*.

BONJWING LEE is a photographer and author of the blog The Ulterior Epicure.

LES ARCADES is a restaurant that serves quintessential southern French food in Biot, a town outside Nice.

L'ESTAGNOL is a seafood restaurant in Bormes-Les-Mimosas in the south of France.

TRAVIS LETT is the chef and co-owner of Gjelina, Gjelina Take Away and Gjusta, all in Los Angeles, and the author of the cookbook *Gjelina*.

ROB LEVITT is the butcher and owner of The Butcher & Larder in Chicago.

JOSH LEWIS is the chef and co-owner of Fleet restaurant in Byron Bay, New South Wales, Australia.

L'ORANGERIE is a bistro at La Bastide de Gordes, a chateau-turned-hotel in Provence, France.

MATT LOUIS is the chef and owner of Moxy and The Franklin Oyster House in Portsmouth, New Hampshire.

JAMES LOWE is the chef at Lyle's in London.

CHRIS LUSK is the chef at the Pontchartrain Hotel's Caribbean Room in New Orleans.

TIFFANY MACISAAC is the pastry chef and co-owner of Buttercream Bakeshop and the pastry chef at All-Purpose, both in Washington, DC.

FRANCIS MALLMANN is the chef and owner of Patagonia Sur in Buenos Aires; 1884 Restaurante and Siete Fuegos in Mendoza, Argentina; El Garzón in Uruguay; and Los Fuegos at the Faena Hotel in Miami. He is the author of the cookbook *Seven Fires*.

MARCO MATTANA is the chef at Trattoria Epiro in Rome.

ANDREA MATTEI is the chef at Borgo Santo Pietro near Siena, Italy.

IGNACIO MATTOS is the chef and co-owner of Estela, Café Altro Paradiso and Flora Bar in New York City.

SKYE MCALPINE is the Venice-based author of the blog From My Dining Table.

ISAAC MCHALE is the chef at The Clove Club in London.

CHRISTINA MCKEOUGH is the chef and co-owner of Graft Wine + Cider Bar in the Finger Lakes town of Watkins Glen, New York.

GEORGE MENDES, an F&W Best New Chef 2011, is the chef and owner of Aldea, Lupulo and Bica in New York City and the author of *My Portugal: Recipes and Stories*.

NUNO MENDES is the chef at Chiltern Firehouse and the owner of Taberna do Mercado, both in London.

KATY MILLARD is the chef and co-owner of Coquine in Portland, Oregon.

TORY MILLER is the chef at L'Etoile, Graze, Sujeo and Estrellón, all in Madison, Wisconsin.

RICK MOONEN is the chef and owner of RM Seafood and RX Boiler Room in Las Vegas.

BONNIE MORALES is the chef and co-owner of Kachka in Portland, Oregon.

JEFFREY MORGENTHALER is the bar manager of Clyde Common and Pepe Le Moko in Portland, Oregon, and a co-author of *The Bar Book*.

KRIS MORNINGSTAR is the chef and co-owner of Terrine in Los Angeles.

SEAMUS MULLEN is the chef and owner of Tertulia and El Colmado, both in New York City, and the author of *Hero Food*.

ANDY MUMMA is the owner of Barista Parlor in Nashville.

LINDSAY NADER co-founded Elysium Craft Cocktail Services in Los Angeles.

ZOE NATHAN is the chef and co-owner of Huckleberry Bakery & Café, Milo & Olive and Sweet Rose Creamery and co-owner of Rustic Canyon, Cassia and Esters, all in Santa Monica, California. She is a co-author of *Huckleberry*.

BRYANT NG, an F&W Best New Chef 2012, is the chef and co-owner of Cassia in Santa Monica, California.

MAGNUS NILSSON is the chef at Fäviken in Järpen, Sweden, and the author of *The Nordic Cookbook* and *Fäviken*.

PETTER NILSSON is the chef at the Spritmuseum in Stockholm.

KEN ORINGER is a co-chef and co-owner of Coppa and Little Donkey in Boston and Toro in Boston and New York City.

KAMIL OSEKA is the chef at The Pig Near Bath in Somerset, England.

ANNA PAINTER is the Food & Wine Test Kitchen associate editor.

PAUL PANSERA is the chef at Sorpasso in Rome.

JAMES PARKER is a development chef for Rich's U.K.

GADI PELEG is a co-owner of Breads Bakery in New York City.

NATASHA PHAN is head of business development and marketing at Kogi in Los Angeles and a co-author of *L.A. Son*.

JOSHUA PINSKY is the chef at Nishi in New York City.

NAOMI POMEROY, an F&W Best New Chef 2009, is the chef and owner of Beast and the chef and co-owner of Expatriate, both in Portland, Oregon. She is the author of *Taste & Technique*.

CARMEN QUAGLIATA is the chef at Union Square Cafe in New York City.

ABIGAIL QUINN is a baker, formerly of Proof Bakeshop in Atlanta.

ILIANA REGAN, an F&W Best New Chef 2016, is the chef and owner of Elizabeth in Chicago.

ERIC RIPERT is the chef and co-owner of Le Bernardin and Aldo Sohm Wine Bar in New York City and chef-adviser for Blue by Eric Ripert in Grand Cayman. He is the host of the Cooking Channel's *Avec Eric* and the author of several books, including *Avec Eric* and the memoir *32 Yolks*.

MISSY ROBBINS, an F&W Best New Chef 2010, is the chef and co-owner of Lilia in Brooklyn.

TAL RONNEN is the chef and owner of Crossroads, a vegan restaurant in Los Angeles, and the author of *Crossroads* and *The Conscious Cook*.

DANIEL ROSE is the chef and co-owner of Le Coucou in New York City and Spring in Paris.

ALBA ESTEVE RUIZ is the chef at Marzapane in Rome.

SADELLE'S is a Jewish bakery and restaurant in New York City.

MARCUS SAMUELSSON is the chef and co-owner of Red Rooster and American Table in New York City and American Table Brasserie and Bar in Stockholm. He is also the author of *Yes, Chef: A Memoir* and *The Red Rooster Cookbook*.

LAURA SAWICKI is the pastry chef at Launderette in Austin, Texas.

MICHAEL SCELFO is the chef and owner of Alden & Harlow and Waypoint, both in Cambridge, Massachusetts.

MINDY SEGAL is the pastry chef and owner of Mindy's HotChocolate in Chicago and the author of *Cookie Love*.

MICHAEL SERPA is the chef and co-owner of Select Oyster Bar in Boston.

ANEKA SIDOTI is the owner of Corner Kitchen in Bangalow, near Australia's Byron Bay.

RAMON SIEWERT is the chef at Union Larder in San Francisco.

JANE SIGAL is the France correspondent for *Food & Wine* and the author of several cookbooks, including *Bistronomy: Recipes from the Best New Paris Bistros*.

AARON SILVERMAN, an F&W Best New Chef 2016, is the chef and owner of Rose's Luxury and Pineapple and Pearls in Washington, DC.

SHELDON SIMEON, an F&W Best New Chef 2014, is the chef and co-owner of Tin Roof in Kahului, Maui.

SOHO FARMHOUSE is a retreat in Chipping Norton, a town in the Oxfordshire countryside of England.

ANA SORTUN is the chef and owner of Oleana and chef and co-owner of Sofra, both in Boston. She is the author of *Spice* and a co-author of *Soframiz*.

ARTURO SPICOCCHI is the chef at the San Luis Hotel in Avelengo, in the Alto Adige region of Italy.

SPOON AND STABLE is a restaurant serving seasonally inspired cuisine in Minneapolis.

SUSAN SPUNGEN is a food writer, stylist and cookbook author based in New York City. She is the author of *What's a Hostess to Do?* and *Recipes: A Collection for the Modern Cook*.

JEREMIAH STONE, an F&W Best New Chef 2016, is a co-chef and co-owner of Contra and Wildair, both in New York City.

ERIC STONESTREET is an Emmy award–winning actor on ABC's *Modern Family* and an avid home cook based in Los Angeles.

ELI SUSSMAN and his brother, **MAX SUSSMAN,** are the chefs and co-owners of Samesa and Ed & Bev's, both in Brooklyn. Their latest cookbook is *Classic Recipes for Modern People*.

MICHAEL SYMON, a Food & Wine Best New Chef 1998 and winner of Food Network's *The Next Iron Chef* Season 1, is the chef and co-owner of Lola, Lolita and Mabel's BBQ in Cleveland; Roast in Detroit; B Spot in Detroit, Cleveland and Columbus, Ohio; and Symon's Burger Joint in Austin, Texas. He is a co-host of ABC's *The Chew* and the author and co-author of several books, including *Michael Symon's Carnivore*.

CONTRIBUTORS

ALEX TALBOT is a co-owner of Curiosity Doughnuts in Stockton, New Jersey, and a co-author of the website Ideas in Food and the cookbook *Maximum Flavor*.

JULIE TANOUS, a writer and recipe developer based in Los Angeles, co-creates the blog Julie & Jesse's Recipes.

DEVON TARBY is a co-owner of The Walker Inn and The Normandie Club in Los Angeles.

THREE BLUE DUCKS is a café that helped spearhead the local and sustainable food scene in Australia, with locations in Sydney and Byron Bay.

LAURENT TOURONDEL, an F&W Best New Chef 1998, is the chef and owner of several restaurants globally, including L'Amico in New York City and BLT Steak, with locations in New York City, Washington, DC, and San Juan, Puerto Rico. He is the author of *Bistro Laurent Tourondel: American Bistro Cooking*.

FABIO TRABOCCHI, an F&W Best New Chef 2002, is the chef and co-owner of Fiola, Casa Luca, Fiola Mare and Sfoglina, all in Washington, DC. He is a co-author of *Cucina of Le Marche*.

TRATTORIA AL CACCIATORE DELLA SUBIDA is an avant-garde restaurant in Cormòns, in Italy's Friuli region.

TRATTORIA AL GROP is a restaurant serving rustic cuisine in Tavagnacco, Friuli, Italy.

ANGELO TROIANI is the chef and co-owner of Il Convivio Troiani in Rome.

JIMMY TU is the chef and owner of Bunker in Queens, New York.

JULIA TURSHEN is a food writer and cookbook author based in upstate New York. Her latest cookbook is *Small Victories*.

EMILY TYLMAN is an assistant food stylist at NBC's *Today Show*.

WADE UEOKA is the chef and co-owner of MW Restaurant in Honolulu.

GIAMPAOLO VENICA is the owner of Venica & Venica winery in Gorizia, Friuli, Italy.

LUISE VINDAHL is a co-creator of the Stockholm-based blog Green Kitchen Stories and a co-author of *The Green Kitchen, Green Kitchen Travels* and *Vegetarian Everyday*.

FABIÁN VON HAUSKE, an F&W Best New Chef 2016, is a co-chef and co-owner of Contra and Wildair, both in New York City.

JONATHAN WAXMAN is the chef and owner of Barbuto and Jams in New York City and Adele's in Nashville. He is a co-author of *A Great American Cook* and *Italian, My Way*.

RAVINDA WEERAVARDANA is the chef at Litro, a wine bar in Rome.

MELISSA WELLER is the master baker and co-owner of Sadelle's in New York City and a consulting baker for Rebelle in New York City and its forthcoming offshoot in Philadelphia.

TIM WIECHMANN is the chef and co-owner of T.W. Food in Cambridge and Bronwyn in Somerville, Massachusetts.

TANDY WILSON is the chef and owner of City House in Nashville.

LEE ANNE WONG is the chef and owner of Koko Head Cafe in Honolulu.

RACHEL YANG is a co-chef and co-owner of Joule, Revel and Trove in Seattle and Revelry in Portland, Oregon.

JEN YEE, an F&W Best New Pastry Chef 2014, is a pastry chef based in New York City and author of the blog Jen Yee Pastry.

MOLLY YEH is the author of the blog My Name is Yeh and the cookbook *Molly on the Range*.

KRIS YENBAMROONG, an F&W Best New Chef 2016, is the chef and owner of Night + Market Song and Night + Market Weho, both in Los Angeles.

JUSTIN YU, an F&W Best New Chef 2014, is the chef and owner of Oxheart and a co-owner of Public Services, both in Houston.

GEOFFREY ZAKARIAN is the chef and owner of The National and The Lambs Club, both in New York City, and the culinary director of The Plaza Hotel in New York City and The Water Club at Borgata in Atlantic City, New Jersey. He is a judge on Food Network's *Chopped* and a co-host of *The Kitchen*. He is also the author of *My Perfect Pantry*.

ANDREW ZIMMERN, an F&W Chef-in-Residence, is the writer of the Kitchen Adventures column on foodandwine.com, the host and creator of Travel Channel's *Bizarre Foods* and the chef behind the AZ Canteen food truck in the Minneapolis area. He is also the author of three cookbooks, including *The Bizarre Truth*.

PHOTOS

ROLAND BELLO 9, 168

PAUL COSTELLO 83

ADRIAN GAUT 379

ALANNA HALE 211

CHRISTINA HOLMES 76, 102, 103, 240, 347, 353

ELIESA JOHNSON 235

JOHN KERNICK 17, 38, 39, 45, 51, 71, 72, 97, 123, 127, 128, 140, 141, 145, 146, 149, 153, 164, 167, 171, 174, 180, 186, 195, 203, 209, 215, 219, 229, 237, 252, 267, 281, 287, 294, 299, 300, 304, 310, 311, 319, 334, 337, 342, 343, 348

EVA KOLENKO 6, 14, 113, 139, 173, 185, 189, 210, 216, 264, 268, 271, 280, 297, 321, 328, 358, 359, 361, 362, 367, 369, 375, back cover (cake)

DAVID MALOSH 33, 48, 61, 78, 79, 124, 184, 250, 251, 263, 302, 303, 326, 327, 350, 351, 357, 371, 376, 382, 383

MARTIN MURRELL 8

MAGNUS NILSSON 67

MARCUS NILSSON, 290, 338, 354, 407

TARA PEARCE 160, 196, 222

PEDEN + MUNK 36, 154

CON POULOS front cover, 4, 5, 13, 18, 23, 24, 27, 30, 41, 42, 52, 55, 56, 62, 66, 74, 75, 82, 85, 86, 89, 92, 98, 101, 104, 107, 108, 112, 115, 118, 131, 132, 135, 136, 150, 157, 163, 170, 177, 183, 190, 200, 206, 225, 226, 230, 234, 245, 248, 256, 259, 272, 277, 278, 284, 292, 293, 296, 308, 312, 315, 316, 320, 323, 333, 344, 368, 372, 384, back cover (veal chop & fattoush)

MOLLY YEH 68, 257, 260

VANILLA SPONGE CAKE
WITH BLACKBERRY-
TARRAGON JAM (P. 322)

Measurement Guide

BASIC MEASUREMENTS

GALLON	QUART	PINT	CUP	OUNCE	TBSP	TSP	DROPS
1 gal	4 qt	8 pt	16 c	128 fl oz			
½ gal	2 qt	4 pt	8 c	64 fl oz			
¼ gal	1 qt	2 pt	4 c	32 fl oz			
	½ qt	1 pt	2 c	16 fl oz			
	¼ qt	½ pt	1 c	8 fl oz	16 Tbsp		
			⅞ c	7 fl oz	14 Tbsp		
			¾ c	6 fl oz	12 Tbsp		
			⅔ c	5⅓ fl oz	10⅔ Tbsp		
			⅝ c	5 fl oz	10 Tbsp		
			½ c	4 fl oz	8 Tbsp		
			⅜ c	3 fl oz	6 Tbsp		
			⅓ c	2⅔ fl oz	5⅓ Tbsp	16 tsp	
			¼ c	2 fl oz	4 Tbsp	12 tsp	
			⅛ c	1 fl oz	2 Tbsp	6 tsp	
				½ fl oz	1 Tbsp	3 tsp	
					½ Tbsp	1½ tsp	
						1 tsp	60 drops
						½ tsp	30 drops

US TO METRIC CONVERSIONS

The conversions shown here are approximations. For more precise conversions, use the formulas to the right.

VOLUME		WEIGHT		TEMPERATURE		CONVERSION FORMULAS
1 tsp	= 5 mL	1 oz	= 28 g	475°F	= 246°C	tsp × 4.929 = mL
1 Tbsp	= 15 mL	¼ lb (4 oz)	= 113 g	450°F	= 232°C	Tbsp × 14.787 = mL
1 fl oz	= 30 mL	½ lb (8 oz)	= 227 g	425°F	= 218°C	fl oz × 29.574 = mL
¼ c	= 59 mL	¾ lb (12 oz)	= 340 g	400°F	= 204°C	c × 236.588 = mL
½ c	= 118 mL	1 lb (16 oz)	= ½ kg	375°F	= 191°C	pt × 0.473 = L
¾ c	= 177 mL			350°F	= 177°C	qt × 0.946 = L
1 c	= 237 mL	**LENGTH**		325°F	= 163°C	oz × 28.35 = g
1 pt	= ½ L	1 in	= 2.5 cm	300°F	= 149°C	lb × 0.453 = kg
1 qt	= 1 L	5 in	= 12.7 cm	275°F	= 135°C	in × 2.54 = cm
1 gal	= 4.4 L	9 in	= 23 cm	250°F	= 121°C	(°F − 32) × 0.556 = °C